The CBS Radio Mystery Theater

The CBS Radio Mystery Theater

An Episode Guide and Handbook to Nine Years of Broadcasting, 1974–1982

Gordon Payton *and*
Martin Grams, Jr.

McFarland & Company, Inc., Publishers
Jefferson, North Carolina, and London

The present work is a reprint of the library bound edition of The CBS Radio Mystery Theater, *first published in 1999 by McFarland.*

British Library Cataloguing-in-Publication data are available

Library of Congress Cataloguing-in-Publication Data

Payton, Gordon, 1959–
    The CBS radio mystery theater : an episode guide and handbook
to nine years of broadcasting, 1974–1982 / Gordon Payton and
Martin Grams, Jr.
      p.   cm.
    Includes index.

    ISBN-13: 978-0-7864-1890-9
    (softcover : 50# alkaline paper) ∞

    1. CBS radio mystery theater (Radio program)   I. Grams,
Martin, Jr. II. Title.
PN1991.77.C43P38   2004
791.44'72—dc21   98-33440
                                                  CIP

Cover image ©2004 Comstock, Inc.

Manufactured in the United States of America

McFarland & Company, Inc., Publishers
  Box 611, Jefferson, North Carolina 28640
  www.mcfarlandpub.com

To audio drama lovers everywhere

Acknowledgments

The authors would like to gratefully acknowledge the following for their help and contribution in making this book as complete and informative as possible: Jay Hickerson, Rosemary Rice, Ralph Bell, Harvey, Larry and John Gassman of SPERDVAC, Katherine Wiley of Harford County Public Library, Elliott Reid, and, of course, Himan Brown.

Special thanks to Ted Okuda of *Filmfax* magazine (P.O. Box 1900, Evanston IL 60202), who allowed us to reprint a few quotes from his "Voices of Terror" article, written by Jack Roberts, which was originally printed in the June/July 1994 issue (# 45).

Contents

Preface

For those whose ears have not heard the screams of the *CBS Radio Mystery Theater*, allow us to give you a small peek at the population that lurked within America's radio speakers during the late 1970s and early 1980s: banshees, leprechauns, vampires, zombies, killer plants, warlocks, aliens, Egyptian cats, a golem, reincarnated spirits, Druids, ghosts, clairvoyants, witches, lycanthropes, somnambulists, alchemists, Dracula, Dorian Gray, dwarfs, and to top it off, Frankenstein's monster. And that was just the first year!

Almost every day, for nine years, *Mystery Theater* brought monsters, murderers and mayhem together for a whole hour each evening. Created, produced, and directed by Himan Brown, the series remains a landmark in radio drama. But *Mystery Theater* ended over fifteen years ago and no one has yet been able to gather enough information to write a book detailing the history and the episodes—until now.

This book offers a detailed log ("Episode Guide") of each and every *Mystery Theater* episode ever broadcast. Descriptive information includes exact titles, air dates and rebroadcast dates, episode numbers, cast lists, writer and adapter credits, and a story line synopsis. This material comes directly from CBS press releases in order to insure complete accuracy. Name spellings (including that of the show—*Theater* rather than *Theatre*) are in keeping with the press material except where that material contained obvious mistakes, i.e. the misspelling of a well-known actor or author.

Also included whenever possible are notes of interest such as information about the actors and actresses, quotes from performers and writers (many from personal interviews), anecdotes about various scripts and sound effects, and other worthwhile tidbits.

The episodes are listed in order of broadcast, not in order of recording. If an episode is a rebroadcast, the rebroadcast date is followed by the original air date. The reader can find complete information on the episode by turning back to the original air date.

The index includes the title of each episode as well as performers and other personnel.

An introductory "Short History" offers an overview of the show's production from the origin of the series to the demise. Thanks to Tony Roberts, who appeared on the program frequently, an example of what the rehearsals were like is featured in this history.

We invite your enjoyment of our book. We hope that it may entertain as well as inform, and that it will provide much pleasure for those of a macabre, mystery-loving frame of mind.

A Short History
of the Series

Himan Brown was the brain of the *CBS Radio Mystery Theater*. His experience as a producer and director was unparalleled. *The Adventures of the Thin Man*, *The Affairs of Peter Salem*, *Bulldog Drummond*, *Joyce Jordan*, *The NBC Radio Theatre*, *Grand Central Station*, *Terry and the Pirates*, *Dick Tracy*, and numerous others were part of his doing. But his experience in radio stretched back even farther.

"I sold *The Rise of the Goldbergs* to NBC in 1929," recalled Brown, "and I played Jake for six months. I was in knee pants, so to speak, and I played the father, Gertrude Berg's husband. And then I did a series called *Little Italy*, in which I played the father. I figured if it worked for a Jewish audience, it will work for an Italian audience. I then stopped acting. Occasionally I'll do a small part, just for the fun of it."

Mystery Theater was very similar to Brown's previous *Inner Sanctum Mysteries* of the 1940s and 1950s, the series for which he was best remembered until the premiere of *Mystery Theater*. Each *Mystery* episode opened with the sound of a creaking door, inviting the audience in for an hour of bone-chilling, spine-shifting, hair-raising tales of murder and mayhem. This popular "creaking door" opening—another of Brown's brainstorms—had been used on the *Inner Sanctum*. Like *Inner Sanctum*, the *Mystery Theater* stories were mainly mystery, with supernatural overtones for chills. It is worth noting that the creaking door is just one of two sounds to have ever been copyrighted in the history of the copyright office. (The other is NBC's three-chime signature.)

When the press release from CBS went out to newspapers across the country, Brown announced that *Mystery Theater* would be "the most exciting break-through of the last ten years." It was indeed, the return of the "art form of radio drama." Brown insisted that his programs would be contemporary in everything from technical effects to subjects and characters, including a female police lieutenant, a child born out of wedlock, abortion, and a man coping with sterility. "Our whole approach," he emphasized, "is more adult."

3

When other stations saw the popularity of *Mystery Theater*, they, too, began broadcasting drama, in shows such as *The Sears Radio Theater* and *Nightfall*. At this time, other drama series had just started their new broadcast runs. Rod Serling's *The Zero Hour* and *Hollywood Radio Theater* were receiving critical acclaim. But *Mystery Theater* far outlasted them all—which shows how right Brown was to pursue his "more adult" approach.

Able to avoid the economic perils of syndication, CBS introduced *The CBS Radio Mystery Theater* on January 6, 1974, as part of a new network radio service called "The C.B.S. Radio Drama Network." Other shows were in the planning stages; the goal was to revive radio drama, which was picking up in popularity due to the nostalgia boom at the time. Each episode of *Mystery Theater* would be a new and complete mystery drama, 53 minutes long, broadcast each night of the week at 10:07 P.M. on WRVR-FM in New York City. The Anheuser-Busch brewery had already signed as a sponsor. A spokesman for the company explained, "We're certain that young people will be most intrigued with this series."

During the premiere week, 218 stations around the country began broadcasting the show. But 21 of them were not affiliates of CBS, and they preferred to plug their own call letters. In New York, for instance, the series was billed as *WOR Radio Mystery Theater*. Another simply billed the program as *Radio Mystery Theater* and others as *Mystery Theater*. Stations varied broadcast times as well. WOR in New York broadcast at 7:07 P.M. Monday through Friday, 8:07 Saturday, and 5:07 Sunday. WFPG in Atlantic City broadcast at 10:07 P.M. WKNX in Kingston, New York, broadcast at 11:07 P.M. By the time the series reached its fourth year on the air, 236 radio stations were broadcasting the program, and two million people were tuning in every evening.

Critics, however, were less than enthusiastic. *Daily News* called the premiere episode "dull"; their review of the second episode noted, "The premise may sound exciting, but the show wasn't." (They did give a rave review for the third episode and allowed that the series had "hope.")

Like most anthology series, *Mystery Theater* needed a host. *The Twilight Zone* had Rod Serling, *One Step Beyond* had John Newland, and *Science Fiction Theater* had Truman Bradley. For *Mystery Theater*, veteran film and television actor E.G. Marshall took up the role of supplying some of the narration, and played host for the series. Marshall was more than glad to take the job, having begun his acting career on a Minneapolis radio station years back.

Writers such as Ian Martin, Sam Dann, and Henry Slesar began turning in script after script for *Mystery Theater*, often writing more than one a week. Ian Martin, for example, wrote more than a hundred during the first few years! The script writers were paid about $350 for each script, depending on creativity, writing quality, and so on. It was the writing that kept the show on the air. The stories had to grab the listening audience within the first few minutes, and they had to be good enough to keep the listeners coming back for more.

Every episode was rehearsed and recorded in Studio G on the sixth floor of the old CBS Radio Annex on East 52nd Street. Here is a reconstruction of one such rehearsal:

A little before 9:00 A.M., actors begin to gather around a table covered with scripts, eyeglass cases, coffee cups, pencils, and other odds and ends. Instead of the high salaries they all receive from movies, stage, and television commercials, here they are paid scale: $73.92 per episode, after taxes.

At 9:00 sharp, the first "cold read-through" gets underway. Only Himan Brown has read the script beforehand. He passes copies out to everyone, assigning the roles. He himself will read the narration, later to be recorded by E.G. Marshall. Brown prays for a miracle to complete the first reading within the time limit. This is usually impossible because of the frequent starts and stops, often for wisecracks by the cast.

Today's script is "Say Good-bye to Uncle Louis," which will later (April 1978) be broadcast as "Uncle Louis." The cast reads their lines out loud so they will know how to say them when it comes time for recording the actual episode.

BALDY: If your information is valid, you could get quite a lot for it.
MILLER: Yeah—but there's other things in this world besides money.

("The guy's obviously never been an actor," someone mutters.)

BALDY: You know Southside Park?
MILLER: Yes.
BALDY: You know where the merry-go-round is?

("The merry-go-round?" someone asks incredulously.
"I guess he doesn't want to get cornered," someone else says. General groans from the cast.)

During this first read-through, there is considerable horseplay among the cast. Who can make the best pun, or at least the fastest, off a particularly obtuse turn of phrase in the script? Who, by a slight modulation of his or her voice, will transform a sequence of dialogue into something unintended?

TERRY: I'm Lieutenant Smith.
HELEN: Oh, the detective.
TERRY: Will you tell me again the circumstances that led to your discovery of Ezra Miller's body?

("Well, first I unbuttoned his shirt," someone sexily remarks.)

TERRY: Mrs. Pauli, I like you. You're an attractive woman.

HELEN: You sound as if you are building up to a proposal of marriage.

TERRY: If I were the marrying kind, I could do worse.

(Because these two parts are to be read with passion, laughter creeps over the table.)

As usual, the script has been written long and cuts must be made. (This is preferable to having a too-short script.) Mr. Brown announces the cuts in a monotone: "Page 2, middle of the page, fourth line down. Second speech. Cut the first three words and then cut all the rest down to 'And then what?' Got it? So, it's a blend for the policeman. Next. Page 38, top of the page…"

Ed Herlihy, announcer for *Inner Sanctum Mysteries*, recalled, "He would come in and say, 'Cuts, page one, line so-and-so up to … page two. Chop, chop, chop, chop.' The number of lines he cut out would eliminate the number of seconds or minutes that we would approximately be over."

After the initial read-through and a five-minute break, Mr. Brown goes to the control room and calls the actors to their places. They position themselves, two or three at a time, around the boom mike, which is suspended about five feet above the carpet. (Carpet is used to drown out the sound of footsteps.) Tape marks on the floor indicate the proper distance for the actors to stand away from the microphone.

Sound man Peter Prescott stands ready.* His arsenal includes an actual door (four feet high) and a vast collection of records with sound effects of every kind (including crickets chirping for night scenes and city traffic for outside an apartment window). He also has a false telephone bell, door latch, siren, cap gun, and so on. To put it all together, he has a small subsidiary mixer panel right in his sound effects box. He sends his sound effects by cable over to the main console, where they will be mixed into the program before it goes on the tape.

Once in a while, the script calls for two or three sound effects at one time—with perfect timing. On such occasions, the talk goes on normally; then the actors fall silent while the sound effects man does his bit two or three times. The show then continues. The break will be spliced together so the audience will never know that the sounds were done at separate times. During such breaks, Fred Himes, Hi Brown's regular engineer, takes a moment to mouth a "hello" from the control booth.

---

*The first sound effects man for the series, Jimmy Dwan, was later replaced by Jerry McCarthy and Peter Prescott. Prescott, a veteran of earlier days in radio, was the sound effects man for the later years of the series.

Himes was the technical director, the only other person in the control booth beside Himan Brown. He was an artist with microphones, responsible for the technical end of getting each show on tape with sound that works effectively for the atmosphere and emotion of the story. The opening scene used a mike called a Neuman U67, with a figure eight pattern. An omni mike would get too much sound. Whenever a ghost appeared, the "ghost" voice sounded better with an omni mike placed right next to the Neuman, or "cast mike," at 90 degrees. When a pistol shot was required, Himes would turn off all but one microphone so the shock waves would not reflect from one mike to another.

Himes used audio processing for certain effects. He used a "flanger" on a voice channel to get fluttery, science-fiction strangeness in the voice. He had two channels of reverb he could add to voices to make them overfull, grandiose. For telephone talks, he used, literally, a telephone, in a sound-proofed booth at the rear of the studio; it was open so actors could duck in and out with no door sound.

The background music came from a library of about 500 carts that were stacked up just behind the recording console in the operator's position in the control booth. They were extensively classified and labeled so that Brown or Himes could put their hand quickly on the kind of music needed. If the desired music was not already at hand, CBS was asked for it ahead of time. The console operator was handed the carts for each show with a cue sheet.

Being very careful not to flip the pages loudly over the microphone, Mr. Brown calls out through the intercom system, "Don't climb in on me!" This means the actors are too close to the mike and making it impossible to balance the sounds as they are being recorded. "All right," says Mr. Brown, "as long as we've stopped, I want to go back to the top of the scene, because we had a little mistake in the control room. We're also getting some noise from somewhere in the building. I tell you they want me out of here. They can rent it out to some rock group and get a fortune for it. All right, let's do it again, now—starting from page 44. It's going fine, just don't climb in on me."

When the last line of the script has been "tagged"—given the correct, final emphasis—Mr. Brown bursts into the studio from the control booth and personally hands everyone a paycheck.

Himes reported once that the taping of a show rarely ran to the full three hours of the "call" for the actors. The actual drama ran about 45 minutes with introduction and postscript; five commercials for CBS, and five for the station (the commercials did not come in the middle of the drama), bringing the show total to 53 minutes. A seven-minute news bulletin completed the hour.

The taping of each *Mystery Theater* episode usually produced numerous segments of tape, as many as a hundred, because recording was so frequently stopped and restarted to eliminate some "clicker" or other. Himan and his crew would assemble these into a finished show after the actors left, a job that usually took no more than a couple of hours.

Mystery Theater had more than a hundred sponsors, including, ironically, the CBS, NBC and ABC television networks.

Mystery Theater won a George Foster Peabody Award "for its outstanding effort in the field of contemporary radio drama" in 1975. (The Peabody is known as radio's Oscar.) Other honors bestowed upon the series were the Mystery Writers of America Raven Award, a special citation from the American Federation of Television and Radio Artists, and an award from the Directors Guild of America. In 1988, Himan Brown was inducted into the Emerson Hall of Fame for Drama, an honor he shares with former colleague Orson Welles.

Mystery Theater is still being syndicated across the country on various radio stations that enjoy broadcasting reruns of the series. It will probably always remain on the air as long as fans of the program stay alive. Otherwise, the *CBS Radio Mystery Theater* might fall six feet under.

Recently, after more than two decades of being off the air, the *CBS Radio Mystery Theater* returned to the airwaves. Syndicated nationwide by Westwood One, it aired without E.G. Marshall's introductions and commercial break comments, and Himan Brown himself did the narration. At the time of this book's printing, this "revival" of the series was scheduled to be cancelled after only a six-month run. The exact reasons for the show's hasty cancellation are not known, but the series was poorly advertised and it did not air on all of Westwood One's premier local stations.

Reviews are mixed regarding the efficacy of Himan's narration. It is these authors' opinion, after hearing a number of the rebroadcasts, that those who disliked them are merely nostalgic for E.G. Marshall's voice, which became synonymous with the series. We found his narration to add new insights into the mindset of the people involved in the production of the series.

As fondly loved as this series is, it is reasonable to assume that members of the listening public who were hearing this series for the first time found it difficult to identify with *Mystery Theater's* sometimes heavy sentimentality and explorations of the man-woman relationship—qualities that were more appreciated by a 1970s audience.

The revival *was* appreciated by many people, however, as evidenced by the hundreds of positive comments posted by fans on the *CBS Radio Mystery Theater* website.

Episode Guide

1. "The Old Ones Are Hard to Kill" (1/6/74; rebroadcast 3/1/74, 12/2/78)

Cast: Agnes Moorehead (Ada Canby); Leon Janney (Stuart Winfield/Dr. George); Roger De Koven (Arnold Chelton/Mr. Paulson). Written by Henry Slesar.

Ada Canby has reached her golden years with her sense of independence intact, with a spryness in her limbs, and with very good vision and excellent hearing. But Ada soon learns that there are times when good hearing is not a blessing, proving once and for all that when it comes to murder, there's no fool like an old fool.

Notes: This marked the first episode of the series, and Agnes Moorehead, currently starring on Broadway in a revival of *Gigi*, made her first of two appearances. Himan Brown, the director of the series, wanted Moorehead to star in the premiere episode because of the status of her past radio experience. She is probably best known for her role as Mrs. Elbert Stevenson in the *Suspense* production of "Sorry, Wrong Number," which won Moorehead numerous awards and a reputation as the "first lady of *Suspense!*"

2. "The Return of the Moresbys" (1/7/74; rebroadcast 2/20/74, 11/11/78)

Cast: Patrick O'Neal (Richard Moresby); Marian Seldes (Una Moresby); Danny Ocko (Dr. Sing); Nick Pryor (Mr. Prouty). Written by Henry Slesar.

When Una Moresby announces that she has left her considerable fortune to an organization her husband considers phony, he decides to murder her and succeeds in making her death look like a suicide. But an inexplicable series of coincidences makes Richard wonder if his dead wife is trying to reach out from beyond the grave to seek retribution.

3. "The Bullet" (1/8/74; rebroadcast 2/15/74)

Cast: Larry Haines (Jerry Price); Evelyn Juster (Marge Price); Martin Newman (Paul Gardner); Danny Ocko (Paddy); Leon Janney (Dr. Steiner); Ralph Bell (O'Rourke). Written by Sam Dann.

Two war soldiers who were buddies during Vietnam get together to talk about old times after nine years of separation. One of them is happily alive, while the other is dead.

Notes: Martin Newman, stage and television actor, was once an extra on radio's *The F.B.I. in Peace and War.* Says Newman about this episode, "Larry Haines and Ralph Bell were the stars." Larry Haines' radio work totals more than 15,000 acting appearances in such shows as *The Columbia Workshop, Gangbusters, The FBI in Peace and War, Suspense,* and the title role of *Mike Hammer.* Haines was a semi-regular on *Inner Sanctum* during the mid to late 1940s.

4. "Lost Dog" (1/9/74; rebroadcast 2/4/74, 2/11/74, 12/30/78)

Cast: Kim Hunter (Julia Smolett); George Mathews (George Smolett); Mandy Potamkin (Ronnie Hughes); Bob Dryden (Dr. Frolich); Gilbert Mack (Dr. McCann/Dog). Written by Henry Slesar.

A fear of animals is not easily understood by people who don't share the same phobia, as Julia Smolett discovers when her husband attempts to bring a fearsome dog into their home. After being terrorized by the fierce dog, she decides to make the four-legged creature her friend, thus making the animal turn on its master.

Notes: Kim Hunter became world famous for her prize-winning performances as Stella Kowalski in both the stage and film versions of Tennessee Williams' *A Streetcar Named Desire.* She won an Academy Award for her role in the 1952 film and the Donaldson and Critics Circle Award in 1947 for the stage show. Among Hunter's other Broadway successes are Luba in *Darkness at Noon,* Ruby Hawes in *The Chase,* Sylvia Crews in *The Tender Trap,* and Bea Brice in *Lilith.* She has appeared on many major television series and made numerous movies, including the role of Dr. Zira, the chimpanzee scientist, in *Planet of the Apes* (1968), *Beneath the Planet of the Apes* (1970), and *Escape from the Planet of the Apes* (1971).

George Matthews, who plays the role of George Smolett in this episode, was a recurring character on television's *The Honeymooners.*

5. "No Hiding Place" (1/10/74; rebroadcast 2/25/74)

Cast: Larry Haines (Charles Powel); Anne Meacham (Elsie); Jackson Beck (Clint Livets); Sidney Walker (McCready); Tom Keena (George Hamill). Written by Sidney Slon.

Charles Powel, executive vice president of a large company and engaged to the boss's daughter, seems to have everything going for him. But Clint Livets, who knows the secret of Charles' past, shows up with a dirty hand and blackmail on his mind.

6. "Honeymoon with Death" (1/11/74; rebroadcast 2/27/74, 11/4/78)

Cast: Lois Nettleton (Jennifer Brady); Teri Keane (Margaret Brady); Tony Roberts (Ed Helmut); Norman Rose (Howard). Written by Sam Dann.

A rookie policeman sympathizes with a young newlywed bride who claims that her husband has been murdered. No one else will believe her, including her sister who says that she just imagined the murder. The neophyte cop soon wonders who's actually telling the truth.

Notes: Lois Nettleton and Tony Roberts made their radio acting debut in this episode. Says Nettleton: "It's great fun. I want to do more. It's fascinating to pour all of your emotions into your voice. My only problem was keeping the proper distance away from the microphone." Says Roberts: "It's a whole new technique. It's like plunging into an ice cold shower. You must play to a microphone. The only thing that matters is what you can convey through your voice. And, best of all, you don't have to look your best."

Tony Roberts, who stars as police officer Ed Helmut, is the son of famed radio announcer Kenneth Roberts, who from time to time in the 1940s and '50s acted in the CBS radio drama *Grand Central Station*, also directed by Himan Brown. When he was just a youngster, Roberts got his first taste of acting by accompanying his father to the studio where he was babysat by sound man Jimmy Dwan. It was a grand reunion for the younger Roberts and Dwan during the taping of this episode. When Roberts walked into the studio there was Dwan, back at his old stand playing the records, closing a door, dialing a telephone, running up the stairs, etc., and doing the other things he had done when he was also Roberts' baby sitter.

Lois Nettleton performed the role of Blanche Dubois in the recent Broadway revival of Tennessee Williams' *A Streetcar Named Desire*. Her movies include *Mail Order Bride* (1964) with Buddy Ebson, *Good Guys and the Bad Guys* (1969) with Robert Mitchum, *Dirty Dingus Magee* (1970) with Frank Sinatra, and *Period of Adjustment* (1962), for which she won the Laurel Award, given annually by the Motion Picture Distributors to the "Most Promising Newcomer to Hollywood Films." Nettleton's television credits include *Cannon*, *Bracken's World*, *Medical Center*, *The FBI*, *Name of the Game*, and *The Mary Tyler Moore Show*. She won high praise for her role as a schizophrenic in *The Interns*. Her latest film to premiere since her *Mystery* performance was *The Honkers* (1972) costarring James Coburn.

7. "I Warn You Three Times" (1/12/74; rebroadcast 2/7/74, 12/3/78)

Cast: Joan Lorring (Hedy); Tom Keena (Tom); Mason Adams (Fred Peterson); Sam Gray (Officer Dennis); Alan Manson (Lt. Carrol). Written by Sam Dann.

Hedy Peterson's husband tells a newspaper reporter that his wife is a real-life witch and that he's going to kill her. But the reporter, after investigating Peterson's story, wonders if he might not be the cause of the couple's marital problems.

8. "Cold Storage" (1/13/74; rebroadcast 1/3/76, 12/9/78)

Cast: Ruby Dee (Nancy Lee); John Baragrey (Buford); Todd Daves (William); Roxie Roker (Hannah); Bryna Raeburn (Sarah). Written by Ian Martin.

A money-loving son sees his inheritance disappearing when his mother, supposedly dead, suddenly comes back to life. A chilling tale not of life and death, but rather of death and life.

Notes: Ruby Dee has appeared in such films as *The Jackie Robinson Story* (1950), *The Balcony* (1963); *Gone Are the Days* (1963), *Windmills of the Gods* (1988), *A Raisin in the Sun* (1961), *I Know Why the Caged Bird Sings* (1979), *All God's Children* (1980), *Cat People* (1982), *Do the Right Thing* (1989), and *Cop and a Half* (1993).

9. "Death Rides a Stallion" (1/14/74; rebroadcast 2/23/74)

Cast: Mason Adams (Frank); Barbara Worthington (Emily); Paul Garth (Uncle Harry); Harry Bellaver (Mac); Marian Seldes (Judy). Written by Sam Dann.

A dead girl reappears with her fiery stallion to confront her fortune-hunting boyfriend, suspected of having caused her death. A spine-chilling tale about a horse who not only runs but thinks—mostly about murder.

Notes: Mason Adams later appeared on television as Charlie Hume on *Lou Grant* from 1977–82, Gordon Blair on *Morning Star/Evening Star* in 1986, and as Everett Daye on *Knight and Daye* in 1989.

10. "The Resident" (1/15/74; rebroadcast 12/1/74, 12/10/78)

Cast: Carmen Matthews (Malvina Thripp); Martin Newman (the Mailman); Gilbert Mack (the Cat); Joan Lorring (Viola). Written by Elspeth Eric.

When Malvina Thripp moves to the country, she didn't anticipate having two house guests, both uninvited and unknown, quite so soon. The first is a decidedly unfriendly cat; the second is a young girl who seems intent on taking over Malvina's life and house, with the cat as an ally.

Notes: Gilbert Mack has had over 40 years of experience in television and radio roles. While standard sound effects are usually used for animal noises, the cat in this episode is a central character which reacts specifically to the various situations with purrs, meows or growls. Himan Brown knew this was the time to call in an expert, Gilbert Mack. Mack claimed to be able to portray any and every type of accent or animal sound. (On an earlier episode, he played a dog.)

11. "Accounts Receivable" (1/16/74; rebroadcast 2/5/74)

Cast: William Prince (Phil Kohlman); Joseph Julian (Rick Kohlman); Joan Banks (Nina); Ralph Carter (Harry); Ian Martin (McCauley); Bob Dryden (Doctor). Written by Sidney Slon.

Phil Kohlman, an embittered son searching for his father all his life, has lived all these years burdened by the reputation of his father—a gunman, robber, and jailbird. Money stolen years ago brings the two together in a suspenseful showdown.

Notes: Joan Banks, a veteran radio performer who played numerous character roles on radio, played the role of Nina in this episode. She married character actor Frank Lovejoy during the late 1940s and often appeared on the same radio productions in which her husband either starred or made a guest appearance, shows such as *Suspense*, *Damon Runyon Theatre*, and *Escape*. She played numerous supporting roles on *Nightbeat*, an action-drama in which her husband Frank Lovejoy starred as reporter Randy Stone.

12. "You Can Die Again" (1/17/74; rebroadcast 3/10/74)

Cast: Richard Mulligan (Spencer); Gilbert Mack (Dr. Berger); Marian Seldes (Peggy/Margaret Chadwick); Mandel Kramer (Inspector Faraday); Sidney Walker (Sgt. Millrose); Bryna Raeburn (Ruth). Written by Sam Dann.

Spencer Chadwick, who married the boss's daughter 23 years ago and struck it rich, always preferred an academic career. Now he wants to turn back the clock, even if he must murder those who stand in his way.

Notes: Richard Mulligan's film career spans *Teachers* (1984), *Babes in Toyland* (1986), *Meatballs 2* (1984), *Pueblo Affair* (1973), and *Micki and Maude* (1984).

13. "Ring a Ring of Roses" (1/18/74; rebroadcast 12/3/74, 1/4/80)

Cast: Glynnis O'Connor (Laurie Thornton); George Petrie (George); Holland Taylor (Helena Rosston); Carol Wollard (Daughter); Sidney Walker (Man); Elspeth Eric (Mrs. Rosston). Written by S.J. Wilson.

Laurie Thornton and her fiancé pay a call on her former college roommate, Helena Rosston, unaware of Rosston's mother's devious scheme to release Helena from an ancient family curse by passing it on to them. A nursery rhyme, an antique ring, and an improbable hallucination are deathly frightening to an engaged couple.

Notes: Glynnis O'Connor has appeared in numerous films including *Our Town* (1977), *Kid Vengeance* (1975), *The Boy in the Plastic Bubble* (1976), *Those Lips, Those Eyes* (1980), *Night Crossing* (1981), and *Someone I Touched* (1975).

14. "The Girl Who Found Things" (1/19/74; rebroadcast 3/8/74, 11/26/78)

Cast: Norman Rose (David Wheeler); Martha Greenhouse (Geraldine); Bob Dryden (Lucas); Barbara Caruso (Rowena Wheeler); Bryna Raeburn (Aunt Faith); Anne Costello (Iris). Written by Henry Slesar.

A man who arranged the murder of his half-sister fears a 16-year-old girl more than he fears the police, who are unable to locate the *corpus delecti*. The little girl has an unusual talent for finding lost dolls (or dead bodies?).

15. "The Chinaman Button" (1/20/74; rebroadcast 3/15/74, 10/7/78)

Cast: Paul Hecht (Phil Thurston); Mason Adams (Walter Van Haas); Ralph Bell (Lou Michaels); Evelyn Juster (Millie Van Haas); Will Hare (Charles Edwards). Written by Henry Slesar.

Phil Thurston doesn't believe that anyone, not even scrupulously honest Walter Van Haas, is above compromising in order to make money. Phil sets out to prove his theory in a highly sophisticated version of the "Chinaman Button," a childish game played by two adults that soon turns deadly.

16. "Dead for a Dollar" (1/21/74; rebroadcast 3/16/74)

Cast: Paul Hecht (Wynn Thomas); Joseph Julian (Harry Tolan); Joan Banks (Kay Woodhouse); Mary Jane Higby (Denise Grant); Tony Roberts (Tony Grant); George Petrie (Jason Grant). Written by Murray Burnett.

Along with his millions, Jason Grant sits on a golden throne built on many ruined lives, and has earned the hatred of more people than he bothers to remember. On this day, however, two ex-employees sit in a bar and plan how they will kill Grant, by tossing a coin to decide which one will do it.

17. "A Very Old Man" (1/22/74; rebroadcast 3/22/74, 12/17/78)

Cast: Santos Ortega (Otto); Bryna Raeburn (Bertha); William Redfield (Stefan); Norman Rose (Manfred). Written by Elspeth Eric.

An old man has the supernatural powers and ability to diagnose ailments and cure them with a strange warmness in his hands. His son-in-law, a doctor, fears his medical practice will be ruined.

18. "And Nothing but the Truth" (1/23/74; rebroadcast 3/17/74, 12/31/78)

Cast: Kristoffer Tabori (David Williams); Arnold Moss (Grant Williams); Clarice Blackburn (Marian); William Redfield (Detective Rizzo); Ralph Bell (Lt. Klamath). Written by Ian Martin.

A young man finds out the hard way that acceptance of responsibility is a cornerstone of life. While intoxicated, David Williams drives too fast on a wet night, hits a pedestrian, and flees the scene. To protect his son's chances of winning a valuable scholarship, David's father takes the blame for the accident—but the police suspect otherwise.

19. "Deadly Honeymoon" (1/24/74; rebroadcast 3/23/74, 1/5/79)

Cast: Betsy Von Furstenberg (Susan Carey); Michael Wager (Dan Carey); Mason Adams (Harrington); Elspeth Eric (Aunt Clara). Written by Henry Slesar.

A bride learns from an ex–police officer that her new husband has been married twice before and that he killed both previous wives while taking them on the same honeymoon trip that he has planned for her. A love story that begins during a honeymoon in a terrifying way.

20. "Speak of the Devil" (1/25/74; rebroadcast 3/24/74, 1/30/79)

Cast: Bryna Raeburn (Jeannie McKay); Jada Rowland (Ellen McKay); Nick Pryor (Michael Tilson); Ian Martin (Dr. Ferguson). Written by Ian Martin.

Ellen McKay and her fiancé, Michael Tilson, participate in a séance with her Aunt Jeannie, who has been credited with having the power of "second sight" and being able to communicate with the dead. No one could anticipate the demons that would be unleashed to plague Ellen's marriage, and the child that they conceived, which she attempts to thwart.

21. "The Ring of Truth" (1/26/74; rebroadcast 3/29/74, 12/16/78)

Cast: Agnes Moorehead (Lorna Kitteridge); Mandel Kramer (Mark Cramer); Santos Ortega (Professor Kitteridge); Ian Martin (Harold Pryor); Danny Ocko (Judge). Written by Henry Slesar.

After a fatal car accident, Lorna Kitteridge is torn between lying about the facts for the sake of her fiancé, Mark Cramer, or telling the truth to please her father, knowing this would cause her to lose Mark. A strange entanglement of truth and lies will drastically affect the lives of the two men and woman.

Notes: Agnes Moorehead only starred in two episodes of the series (including the premiere), before dying of lung cancer shortly after this broadcast. Moorehead secretly confronted director Himan Brown about her impending doom during the rehearsal of the first episode. She would have loved to have done more episodes for him, she told Brown, but time was at least kind enough for her to appear on two episodes.

22. "Time and Again" (1/27/74; rebroadcast 3/30/74, 9/9/78)

Cast: Joan Beal (Ethan Vigil); Grace Matthews (Henrietta); Bryna Raeburn (Harriet); Ian Martin (Dr. Jacob Royce). Written by Ian Martin.

Skilled clock maker Ethan Vigil purchases a curious antique clock and discovers that the timepiece contains the secret of everyman's dream: It has the power to make time stand still. Ethan learns at a dreadful expense that the clock's works are lubricated with human blood.

Notes: Ian Martin not only wrote for *Mystery Theater*, but he also wrote for Broadway, films, and commercials. One of the other many writings Ian Martin became involved in was for such daytime television series as *One Life to Live, The Edge of Night,* and *Search for Tomorrow.*

Popular Library published a small pocket-sized book entitled *Strange Tales from the CBS Radio Mystery Theater* in 1976. Edited by Himan Brown, the book featured three stories, adapted from actual episodes from the series: Elspeth Eric's "The Black Room," Sam Dann's "The Only Blood" and Ian Martin's "Time and Again." Martin based the plot on a story written in longhand which he found at an auction. The original story, "The Vampire Clock," was apparently written by an unknown author and adapted into this *Mystery Theater* episode by Martin.

23. "Three Women" (1/28/74; rebroadcast 1/7/79)

Cast: Ruth Ford (Loretta Lake); William Redfield (Steven Lake); Joan Lorring (Clarissa); Roger De Koven (Higgins); Elspeth Eric (Adelaide). Written by Elspeth Eric.

Writer Steven Lake is strangely insistent on ending his novel with the death of its central character, Clarissa, even though his one chance of having it published turns on rewriting the ending to let her live.

24. "The Man Who Heard Voices" (1/29/74; rebroadcast 4/5/74, 1/6/79)

Cast: Larry Haines (George); Suzanne Grossmann (Margaret); Augusta Dabney (Sally); Leon Janney (Cartwright). Written by Sam Dann.

A successful lawyer who falls for the wiles of his boss's young, beautiful daughter has the strange gift of hearing voices meant only for him—voices that predict his future and, most significantly, his dead wife's voice, making it impossible for him to forget his past. An eerie ghost story that takes place not in a deserted castle but in a modern luxury high-rise apartment building.

25. "Mother Love" (1/30/74; rebroadcast 3/31/74, 10/14/78)

Cast: Joan Hackett (Paula Richards); Vinnette Carroll (Mother Love); Mason Adams (George Richards); Roger De Koven (Dr. Morton); Evelyn Juster (Edna Lacey); Leon Janney (Claude). Written by Bob Juhren.

When Paula Richards is informed by her doctor that she is medically unable to bear a child, she turns to a fortune-teller, Mother Love, in hopes that a spell will accomplish what doctors cannot. Mother Love considers herself fortunate indeed, as she sees that Paula is in a position to do her an enormous favor. Now Paula finds herself bound to a frightening and unexpected promise.

26. "The Man Who Asked for Yesterday" (1/31/74; rebroadcast 4/7/74, 2/1/79)

Cast: Mandel Kramer (Mort Herman); Evelyn Juster (Sherry Herman); Ralph Bell (Hackie); Gilbert Mack (Police Lieutenant); Paul Hecht (Herb Gordan). Written by Ian Martin.

Mort Herman regains consciousness in a hospital where he is awaiting surgery to remove a bullet from his brain. When "The Man" appears offering to let him relive the previous day, Mort jumps at the chance to seek revenge on his wife and the bookie who had conspired to kill him. The results, however, are not what he anticipated.

27. "Dead Ringer" (2/1/74; rebroadcast 4/6/74, 1/13/79)

Cast: Joan Banks (Gloria Winters); Leon Janney (Leo Winters); Paul Hecht (Grafton); Bob Dryden (Dr. Carmody); Larry Haines (Al Grissom). Written by Murray Burnett.

Gloria Winters is amazed to discover that a man she found hurt on a highway is a dead ringer for her husband, whom she wants to divorce. The two are attracted to each other and soon are figuring out a way to get rid of her husband, but not his fortune. This is an old story with a new twist.

28. "A Ghostly Game of Death" (2/2/74; rebroadcast 4/12/74, 2/4/79)

Cast: William Prince (Alex Garth); Joan Tyson (Lucy); Ralph Bell (Flanders); Gilbert Mack (Captain Hatch); William Redfield (Tim Kelly). Written by Murray Burnett.

Hired to find the secrets of a haunted house on the seacoast, professional "ghost hunter" Alex Garth and his aide attempt to spend a night in the creaky old house. There they encounter the ancient wrath of the spirits of two lovers and the jealous sea captain husband who murdered them. When they meet up with the mad spirit they discover that the sea captain is determined to murder anyone who pursues his wife—just as he did hundreds of years ago.

Notes: William Redfield cowrote television scripts for the television series *Mr. Peepers.*

29. "The Sign of the Beast" (2/3/74; rebroadcast 4/13/74, 1/14/79)

Cast: Lois Smith (Milly); Danny Ocko (Aymara); Tom Keena (Kevin); Paul McGrath (Dr. Jorgenson). Written by Sam Dann.

Working on an archeology dig in South America, Milly praises the son of a jungle native. Believing Billy is responsible for the boy's subsequent death, Aymara, the native, cunningly arranges to bring an ancient curse upon Milly, nearly turning her into a cannibalistic beast. Neither her husband nor her uncle can cure her until they know the reason for her sin against the Beast Goddess.

Notes: This was the first episode to feature Paul McGrath, who once played host Raymond on *Inner Sanctum Mysteries,* another radio show that Himan Brown directed.

30. "Here Goes the Bride" (2/4/74; rebroadcast 4/14/74, 2/11/79)

Cast: Ruby Dee (Jenny Morgan); Teri Keane (Lisa Morgan); Bryna Raeburn (Conchita Aguilar); Ian Martin (Juan); Michael Wager (Richard Morgan). Written by Ian Martin.

Jenny Morgan accompanies her new husband, Richard, to his estate on a cliff overlooking the Pacific and immediately encounters savage dogs, a housekeeper whose resentment is obvious, a vengeful sister-in-law, and the legend of Richard's former wife, a movie star whose sudden death looks less and less like a suicide to Jenny.

Notes: Some (but not all) radio stations rebroadcast "Lost Dog" after this episode, presenting a double feature.

31. "Lost Dog" (2/4/74; rebroadcast from 1/9/74)

Notes: See note to episode 30.

32. "The Lady Was a Tiger" (2/5/74; rebroadcast 4/19/74, 2/10/79)

Cast: William Redfield (Larry Fielding); Joan Lorring (Carol); Ian Martin (Inspector); Chris Gampel (Waiter); Roger De Koven (Dr. Rodzanski). Written by Ian Martin.

An unemployed newspaperman agrees to an assignment in Paris and is soon falsely accused of murder. After a beautiful American girl obtains his release from jail and warns him that his life is now endangered, he realizes that he is caught up in a deadly game of espionage and must decide whether the girl is the double agent she claims to be.

33. "After the Verdict" (2/6/74; rebroadcast 4/20/74, 2/24/79)

Cast: Tony Roberts (Ned Murray); Joseph Julian (Lew Rydell); Bryna Raeburn (Melanie Rydell); Barbara Caruso (Karen Ostrau); Bob Dryden (Harry Ostrau); Sam Gray (Tony Eigo). Written by Henry Slesar, based on his short story "Second Verdict."

Young attorney Ned Murray wins an acquittal for Lew Rydell, charged with murder, and then discovers some disquieting information about his client from a strange confession, making him realize his mistake. Ned soon realizes that his career and Lew's life are in jeopardy.

34. "I Warn You Three Times" (2/7/74; rebroadcast from 1/12/74)

35. "Conspiracy to Defraud" (2/8/74; rebroadcast 4/21/74)

Cast: Paul Hecht (Steve Nash); Suzanne Grossmann (Helene Fraine); George

Petrie (Harrington); Ruth Warrick (Phyllis); Gilbert Mack (Boivin); Leon Janney (Colodinos). Written by Sidney Slon.

After two of his fellow narcotics agents are killed in New York, Steve Nash is sent to Paris to get information on shipments of heroin known to be bound for the United States. Everyone he meets, except a young woman, quickly makes it known that he is not welcome.

Notes: Paul Hecht would periodically appear on the television comedy *Kate and Allie* as the character Charles Lowell, during the program's early years (1983–84).

36. "The Deadly Hour" (2/9/74; rebroadcast 4/26/74, 2/17/79)

Cast: Norman Rose (Martin Jerome); John Baragrey (Doctor); Jack Grimes (George); Marian Seldes (Marian). Written by Elspeth Eric.

Martin Jerome, who after a traumatic experience has avoided speaking to anyone for 25 years, seeks an interview with a psychiatrist to tell a horrifying tale of revenge against a young couple who had inadvertently invaded his privacy.

37. "Dead Man's Mountain" (2/10/74; rebroadcast 4/27/74, 2/18/79)

Cast: Alan Hewitt (R.J. Johnson); Bryna Raeburn (Anita Dollard); William Redfield (George Morrisey); Bob Dryden (Dr. Waterson). Written by Sam Dann.

One of the world's wealthiest men, determined to build a resort on Mount Manitou in the Adirondacks, is aghast to see his young aide, Morrisey, return from the mountain as a feeble seventy year old. Unwilling to believe the mountain is haunted, R.J. Johnson travels to a nearby village whose residents, opposed to construction of the resort, tell him that anyone who goes up the mountain will die—if his conscience is not perfectly clear.

Notes: Alan Hewitt played the detective on television's *My Favorite Martian*.

38. "Lost Dog" (2/11/74; rebroadcast from 2/4/74)

39. "A Dream of Death" (2/12/74; rebroadcast 4/28/74, 3/11/79)

Cast: Marian Seldes (Madeline Betty Powers); Michael Tolan (Rex Patterson); Evelyn Juster (Susan Miller); Ira Lewis (Peter Evans); Bob Dryden (Reverend Fallowfield). Written by Sam Dann.

Charity Youngblood swears she will have her revenge against Civil War soldier Eli Wallington, who jilted her. Some 200 years later, Madeline Betty Powers, a university student, and Rex Patterson, her history professor, seem destined to live out the unfinished story of Charity and Eli.

40. "Dig Me Deadly" (2/13/74; rebroadcast 6/6/76, 1/18/80)

Cast: Louise Larabee (Claudia Trubshaw); Mason Adams (Wiley); Ralph Bell (Professor Wilkerson); Corinne Orr (Jeannine); Ann Costello (Susan); Kris Tabori (Jimmy). Written by S.J. Wilson.

Detective Claudia Trubshaw is summoned to the site of an Arizona archeology expedition to investigate the disappearance of a young girl. When an ancient skeleton is found with the girl's disembodied hands attached, she fears that more than just digging is going on at the site.

Notes: Corrinne Orr, a Canadian actress who performed in numerous Canadian Broadcasting Company dramas, plays Jeannie in this episode.

41. "Under Grave Suspicion" (2/14/74; rebroadcast 5/3/74)

Cast: Ralph Bell (Thomas Drake); Patricia Wheel (Maryann); Bob Dryden (Dr. Mallory); William Redfield (Police Chief). Written by Hank Warner.

Unemployed electrical engineer Thomas Drake and his wife Maryann, who began their relationship as two modern singles willing to give living under the same roof a try, find their marriage on the rocks. She begins seeing another man whom Drake threatens to kill unless he leaves her alone. Just hours before Hurricane Gilda hits their Long Island seaside cottage, their stormy marriage takes a frightening, unexpected turn.

42. "The Bullet" (2/15/74; rebroadcast from 1/8/74)

43. "A Lady Never Loses Her Head" (2/16/74; rebroadcast 5/4/74)

Cast: Kim Hunter (Beth Stanton); Court Benson (Inspector Finchley); Nick Pryor (Charles); Bryna Raeburn (Nora); Ian Martin (Doctor). Written by Ian Martin.

When Beth Stanton impulsively marries a handsome Englishman and moves to his ancestral castle, the specter of a woman supposedly beheaded hundreds of years before appears to her each night. Only Inspector Finchley, an old friend of Beth's father, suspects that the headless woman is not an hallucination. Beth wonders if she isn't losing *her* head.

44. "The Walking Corpse" (2/17/74; rebroadcast 5/5/74, 3/4/79)

Cast: Tony Roberts (Steve Ramsey); Suzanne Grossmann (Patricia Ramsey); Robert Kaliban (Christopher LeClair); Vinette Carroll (Tante Solange); Ian Martin (Trujedo); Jackson Beck (Garcia). Written by Ian Martin.

Steve and Pat Ramsey are happy newlyweds who win a glorious two-week vacation in the Caribbean. On the plane they meet one of Steve's former college football teammates: Christopher LeClair, the son of a West Indian island king. Two zombies soon commandeer the plane and, though shot point-blank by a U.S. agent, continue their task of transporting Chris and the newlyweds into General Trujedo's country.

Notes: Jackson Beck was one of the four panelists on *Charade Quiz*, a short-run television series that ran from 1947 to 1949. A few years after this *Mystery* performance, Beck narrated the short-run *Lifeline* series in 1978. Radio buffs recognize him for his portrayal of office boy Jimmy Olson of the *Daily Planet* on the radio series *The Adventures of Superman*.

45. "Blizzard of Terror" (2/18/74; rebroadcast 5/10/74, 2/25/79)

Cast: Lois Smith (Helen Crane); Leon Janney (Jim Crane); Larry Haines (Jim Crane). Written by George Lowthar.

Driving home from a skiing weekend, Jim and Helen are caught in a blizzard and hear on their car radio that police are looking for the ax-murderer of an entire family. They manage to make it to a mountain cabin, the kitchen of which is splattered with blood. The couple soon convince themselves that the owner is Jake Morgan, the man whom the police are looking for.

Notes: Lois Smith won the Best Supporting Actress award from the National Society of Film Critics for her portrayal of Jack Nicholson's pianist sister in the 1970 film *Five Easy Pieces.*

46. "Sea Fever" (2/19/74; rebroadcast 5/11/74, 3/10/79)

Cast: George Mathews (Captain Adams); Marian Seldes (Annabella); Leon Janney (Whitey); Bret Morrison (Mr. Ames); William Redfield (Mr. Rogers). Written by Ian Martin.

Bound for the African coast and a cargo of slaves, the *Annabella* is commanded by a huge and forbidding giant of a man, Captain Josiah Adams, who against the wishes of the ship's owner has his wife on board. Anyone who even talks about her, the crew soon learns, can expect the sea to be his grave. Is the captain mad with imagined jealousy?

Notes: This is the first episode of the series to feature Bret Morrison. Morrison had appeared in numerous radio shows, including *The Chicago Radio Theatre, The First Nighter Program, Suspense, X Minus One,* and even starred as Lamont Cranston—alias *The Shadow*—for a few years.

On one of the dates this episode was rebroadcast—March 10, 1979—the CBS Radio Network, Sam Cook Digges and Himan Brown each received a special citation from the Eastern Directors Council of Directors Guild of America, Inc., for their "major roles in the resurgence of radio drama," namely, *The CBS Radio Mystery Theater.* Mr. Digges is president of the CBS Radio Division. The citations were presented during the 1979 Annual Directors Guild of America awards dinner in New York City's St. Regis Hotel. Richard M. Brescia, vice president and general manager of the CBS Radio Network, accepted the citations for the network and Mr. Digges. Himan Brown received his citation in person.

47. "The Return of the Moresbys" (2/20/74; rebroadcast from 1/7/74)

48. "The Walls of Jericho" (2/21/74; rebroadcast 5/12/74)

Cast: Bob Dryden (Drindl); Guy Sorel (Winthrop); Ralph Bell (Cudworth); Sidney Walker (Ashley); Ian Martin (Higgins); Mary Jane Higby (Martha). Written by Elspeth Eric.

Near retirement and tired of hearing himself referred to as "poor old Drindl," Drindl plays a modest joke on the snobbish members of the Boston Men's Club in which he serves as steward. When the joke appears to succeed, he plays another and can't resist a momentous third one, only to find that he's conjured up apparitions that get out of hand with magical results.

49. "The Horla" (2/22/74; rebroadcast 5/17/74, 10/21/78, 5/19/79)

Cast: Paul Hecht (Guy de Maupassant); Bob Dryden (Dr. Cartier); Danny Ocko (Jean Baptiste Roget); Bryna Raeburn (Madame Bonsard). Adapted by Sam Dann, based on the 1886 short story by Guy de Maupassant.

Guy de Maupassant attempts to convince his psychiatrist that his body is being consumed by a feeling of an invisible presence. After weeks of nightmares and the feeling like he's being watched and talked about all the time, he takes judgment into his own hands by attempting to take back the possession of his soul before it's decreased by impending tragedy and doom.

Notes: Considered Guy de Maupassant's most famous short story, this story has been adapted for numerous horror radio shows, including *Inner Sanctum Mysteries*. Among the Hollywood stars who have performed for this story are Peter Lorre and Paul Lukas.

50. "Death Rides a Stallion" (2/23/74; rebroadcast from 1/14/74)

51. "The Horse That Wasn't for Sale" (2/24/74; rebroadcast 5/18/74, 3/17/79)

Cast: Mercedes McCambridge (Crissie Runyon); Arnold Ross (Judge Simmons); William Redfield (Clem Burnett); Earl Hammond (Sam Fryatt). Written by Henry Slesar.

Crissie Runyon must sell the family horses in order to help pay off debts her recently deceased father accumulated. She refuses, however, to put one horse named Stargazer on the market because the obstreperous steed refuses to obey all but her commands. When the horse stomps a man to death, for what Crissie believes were good reasons, she makes an extreme move to prevent authorities from destroying the animal.

Notes: William Redfield starred as Officer Jimmy Hughes on television's *Jimmy Hughes, Rookie Cop* in 1953. Afterwards, Redfield left the series to pursue the role of Bobby Logan on *The Marriage* in 1954. Mercedes McCambridge played Katherine Wells on television's *Wire Service* during the late 1950s. When the radio show *One Man's Family* made the transition to television, McCambridge played the bit part of Beth Holly from 1949 to 1950.

52. "No Hiding Place" (2/25/74; rebroadcast from 1/10/74)

53. "The Edge of Death" (2/26/74; rebroadcast 5/19/74, 3/24/79)

Cast: Patrick O'Neal (Alex); Marian Seldes (Judy); Ian Martin (Dr. Richards); Leon Janney (Ben). Written by Sol Panitz.

A rural community is terrified when the appearance of a faceless man dressed in black is reported. At least 12 people in the farming area claim to have witnessed this dark-dressed man lurking in the woodlands. They became convinced the figure represents death when a dog confronts it and immediately dies—with no evidence of violence.

54. "Honeymoon with Death" (2/27/74; rebroadcast from 1/11/74)

55. "A Choice of Witnesses" (2/28/74; rebroadcast 5/22/74)

Cast: Paul Hecht (Gordon Bailey); Bob Dryden (Dave Bliss); Ralph Bell (Ed Kellerman); Evelyn Juster (Pam Bailey). Written by Henry Slesar.

Gordon Bailey refuses to take any part in Dave Bliss' suggestion that he participate in killing their mutual blackmailer, even though the plan contains a perfect alibi for all. But when the entire group of blackmail victims gather, they decide that Bailey's conscience endangers their safety.

56. "The Old Ones Are Hard to Kill" (3/1/74; rebroadcast from 1/6/74)

57. "Out of Sight" (3/2/74; rebroadcast 5/24/74, 3/25/79)

Cast: Julia Meade (Dr. Theresa Webber); Jack Grimes (Drakon); Sidney Walker (Commissioner Gordon Webber); Ira Lewis (Captain Luke Strong). Written by Ian Martin.

Although nobody believes her, Dr. Theresa Webber, soon to be the first woman astronaut in space, is certain that because she will be aboard, the flight of *Diana One* to *Skylab* is doomed. No jinx occurs during take-off, and it's A-OK into orbit, but not so after the crew docks *Diana One* with the earth-circling laboratory.

58. "Prognosis Negative" (3/3/74; rebroadcast 5/24/74)

Cast: Mason Adams (Kent Hatcher); Bryna Raeburn (Frederica); William Redfield (Dr. Gentry); Martha Greenhouse (Mrs. Mowbray); Earl Hammond (Archie). Written by Sidney Slon.

Kent Hatcher, former prisoner of war with little memory and a murderer instinct, escapes from a veterans hospital, killing a nurse in the process. After he kills a tailor, the whole frightened community is alerted that Hatcher is at large, and everyone keeps an eye out for him. A spiritual reader recognizes him and, realizing that he is susceptible to hypnosis, takes him in, planning to use this susceptibility to further her own nefarious plans. But was the former POW programmed by his captors to commit terrible acts against his own people?

59. "This Will Kill You" (3/4/74; rebroadcast 5/24/74)

Cast: Larry Haines (Robert Anthony); Evelyn Juster (Liz Darben); Norman Rose (Theodore Rakozci); Roger De Koven (Carl); Gilbert Mack (Professor Anresen). Written by Murray Burnett.

Outraged because reviewer Robert Anthony roasted his new book on demons and demonology, author Theodore Rakozci vows to put a curse on Anthony that will ultimately result in his death. He knows he has the aid of demons such as Uzziel, Rabdas, Beleth, and Murmus, who have also been insulted by the review. A chilling insight into the powers of witchcraft is gained.

60. "Accounts Receivable" (3/5/74; rebroadcast from 1/16/74)

61. "The Sending" (3/6/74; rebroadcast 5/31/74)

Cast: Mandel Kramer (Professor Lansing); Marian Seldes (Mia Lansing/Debbie Ross); Tony Roberts (Bill Taylor); Beth Howard (Phoebe Dorin). Written by Robert Newman.

Debbie Ross, infatuated with Professor Arnold Lansing and his course of the forces of evil in early history, agrees to do a special project on foretelling the future. He gives her an ancient speculum which, if she looks into it properly, will tell her her future. What she sees thoroughly frightens Debbie.

62. "The Creature from the Swamp" (3/7/74; rebroadcast 6/1/74, 10/28/78)

Cast: Joan Lorring (Undina); Jack Grimes (Larry Drake); Ian Martin (Jeb Scanlon); Bob Dryden (Jess Tomlin); Leon Janney (Dr. Prince). Written by Ian Martin.

Warden Larry Drake rescues a strange woman from the swamp's quicksand, almost against her will, and discovers that she resembles his dead fiancée. When the woman, Undina, becomes ill and insists that the legendary Swamp Man will be coming to reclaim her, Larry sends for the town doctor. The doctor discovers that Undina is not all that Larry claims her to be.

Notes: Joan Lorring starred as Helen Norby on television's *Norby*, an NBC situation comedy that was broadcast in 1955.

63. "The Girl Who Found Things" (3/8/74; rebroadcast from 1/19/74)

64. "A Long Time to Die" (3/9/74; rebroadcast 5/28/74)

Cast: Mandel Kramer (Alfred Ainsley); Grace Matthews (Joan Ainsley); Arnold Moss (Adams); Nat Polen (Dr. Stitzer); Mason Adams (Jerry). Written by Sam Dann.

Foes of an indicted congressman are sure that handwriting expert Alfred Ainsley has been bought off when, as he is about to provide testimony that will convict the congressman, he suddenly becomes ill. Not even his doctor knows what happened to Ainsley, who mumbles something about living 500 years ago— as an American Indian.

65. "You Can Die Again" (3/10/74; rebroadcast from 1/17/74)

66. "The Thing in the Cave" (3/11/74; rebroadcast 6/2/74)

Cast: Marian Seldes (Eva); Michael Wager (David); Robert Kaliban (Hank); Teri Keane (Barbara). Written by Ian Martin.

Four amateur cave explorers become entrapped in a dark cave by a landslide. Exploring a possible escape route, Eva and Hank disappear from sight and the other two fear they have been killed by the cave's only known inhabitant, the Thing. When their oxygen supply appears to be failing, David and Barbara attempt a desperate escape and find themselves in a surprising ante-chamber.

67. "A Sacrifice in Blood" (3/12/74; rebroadcast 6/5/74, 2/15/80)

Cast: Ralph Bell (Stephan Stampler); Don Scardino (Michael Stampler); Patricia Roe (Emilia Stampler); Ian Martin (Miguel Sarubbias). Written by Milt Wisoff.

Entering a previously undiscovered ancient temple erected by a sect of devil worshippers, archeologists Stephan and Emilia Stampler are startled to find an apparently abandoned infant. After they adopt the child named Michael and attempt to raise him in a normal environment, the Stamplers are forced to concede that unnatural troubles arise wherever Michael goes.

68. "A Little Night Murder" (3/13/74; rebroadcast 6/7/74)

Cast: Jack Grimes (Lew Parker); Suzanne Grossmann (Alice Maitland); Bob Dryden (Captain Blake); Bryna Raeburn (Mary Cannon); Tony Roberts (Peter Jackson). Written by Sam Dann.

Four women are murdered in 11 days, and the entire police force is completely mystified. A bookstore owner, Alice Maitland, tells the police that she will be the next victim. She can't explain why she has this feeling, but she does admit to receiving a series of telephone calls with no sound from the receiver—only an ominous click.

69. "The Fall of the House of Usher" (3/14/74; rebroadcast 6/8/74, 9/16/78, 5/27/79)

Cast: Kevin McCarthy (Gordon Mannering); Arnold Moss (Roderick Usher); Bob Dryden (Dr. Wyndham); Marian Seldes (Madeleine Usher). Adapted by George Lowthar, based on the 1839 short story by Edgar Allan Poe.

Gordon Mannering is hastily summoned by his old friend Roderick Usher to Usher's cobwebbed, melancholy, rat-infested, desolate mansion. Paralyzed with fear, Usher claims his house has become a tomb for the living dead. His sister, Madeleine, fears that she will be buried prematurely and begs Mannering to prevent that from happening. Her fate comes quick, and soon after the burial, scratching sounds echo the hallways, apparently originating from inside Madeleine's coffin.

Notes: Kevin McCarthy makes his first of many appearances on *Theater* in this creepy adaptation of Edgar Allan Poe's classic horror tale. McCarthy would later play Dr. Jekyll and Mr. Hyde, and Sherlock Holmes later in the series.

70. "The Chinaman Button" (3/15/74; rebroadcast from 1/20/74)

71. "Dead for a Dollar" (3/16/74; rebroadcast from 1/21/74)

72. "And Nothing but the Truth" (3/17/74; rebroadcast from 1/23/74)

73. "Sea of Troubles" (3/18/74; rebroadcast 6/9/74, 2/8/80)

Cast: Staats Cotsworth (Owen Layton); Bryna Raeburn (Harriet Layton); Danny Ocko (Douglas); Earl Hammond (Gerald Layton); Ian Martin (Mr. Pawkins). Written by Henry Slesar.

Owen is fed up with his older, fat, and rich wife Harriet and decides that her money is worth more than her love. He explains to his brother Gerald that the differences between a ship and a plane can be used in an ingenious way to commit murder. He'll cross the Atlantic by plane, his brother by ship.

74. "Frankenstein Revisited" (3/19/74; rebroadcast 12/6/74, 1/7/78, 7/14/79)

Cast: Leon Janney (Frank Larkin); Ralph Bell (Tom Fairley); William Redfield (Flip Johnson/Paul Helmut); Evelyn Juster (Eileen Garrett); Michael Wager (Klaus Folger). Written by Milt Wisoff, using material from the 1818 novel *Frankenstein* by Mary Shelly.

A U.S. television crew in Germany decide to film the 400th anniversary of the death of Baron von Frankenstein. Soon after they arrive at the castle where the "creepy" happenings supposedly occurred, troubles beset the camera crew. The monster who killed the Baron is reputed to return every century looking for fresh blood. There's soon evidence that the monster has come back once more, making the crew wish that they had stayed home.

75. "The Ghost at the Gate" (3/20/74; rebroadcast 6/11/74)

Cast: Beatrice Straight (Alice Emory); Joan Lorring (Dorothea); John Baragrey (Charles Emory); Paula Truman (Connie Lawrence). Written by Elspeth Eric.

Every night at nine, Alice Emory prepares two cups of hot chocolate—one for herself and one for her departed husband with whom she has happy visits. When she learns that her husband also returns every afternoon at three for a rendezvous with her best friend—a spinster school teacher named Connie Lawrence—the two fight over who loves the dead man most.

76. "Ordeal by Fire" (3/21/74; rebroadcast 6/14/74)

Cast: Mandell Kramer (Bob Steele); Julie Newmar (Ava Marcus); Earl Hammond (Brian Casey); Guy Sorel (Vern Marcus); Sidney Walker (Promos). Written by Murray Burnett.

A man who calls himself Promos displays a strange control over fire and demands $1 million for his secret Promethean Society from corporation chief Vern Marcus. Marcus digs into history to learn that the secret society is dedicated to doing something about the lack of morality in the world today. Those who refuse Promos, Marcus and his daughter Ava learn, wind up in wheelchairs with third degree burns.

Notes: This marked Julie Newmar's first appearance on *Theater.* Newmar's television credits range from the female robot Rhoda Miller on *My Living Doll* to Cat Woman (for one year) on *Batman.*

77. "A Very Old Man" (3/22/74; rebroadcast from 1/22/74)

78. "Deadly Honeymoon" (3/23/74; rebroadcast from 1/24/74)

79. "Speak of the Devil" (3/24/74; rebroadcast from 1/25/74)

80. "Diary of a Madman" (3/25/74; rebroadcast 6/15/74, 9/30/78, 3/31/79)

Cast: Larry Haines (Frank Wallis); Evelyn Juster (Estelle Wallis); Bob Dryden (Pete Simmons); William Redfield (Jim Downard). Adapted by Sam Dann, based on the 1885 short story by Guy de Maupassant.

A judge who murders because he thinks he's "obeying the laws of nature" later sits in judgment of innocents accused of his crimes and keeps a record of his misdeeds in a diary. In order to continue his mad adventures he keeps the diary safely (he hopes) locked up in a desk dresser.

Notes: Beginning on March 31, 1979—one of this episode's rebroadcast dates—all Saturday and Sunday broadcasts began being devoted to adaptations of the classic tales of mystery and suspense that had been presented from time to time during the series' first five years. This announcement was made by Richard M. Brescia, vice president and general manager of the CBS Radio Network. He made the announcement to station executives attending the CBS Radio Affiliates Association board meeting the week before in Palm Beach, Florida. "This lineup of classics," Brescia said, "will certainly be good news to the loyal—and ever growing—radio drama audiences across the country. These productions by Hi Brown are adaptations of celebrated short stories, novels and plays penned by literary greats, including Edgar Allan Poe, Ambrose Bierce, O. Henry, Oscar Wilde, Nathaniel Hawthorne, Robert Louis Stevenson and Emily and Charlotte Bronte. Stories as well-loved and as diverse as Sherlock Holmes mysteries, *Dracula* and *Anthony and Cleopatra* will also be included in this exceptional weekend family entertainment."

81. "Death by Whose Hands" (3/26/74; rebroadcast 6/16/74)

Cast: Stefan Schnabel (Doctor Herschl); Marian Seldes (Ilse); Ira Lewis (Rudi Baum); Robert Drivus (Franz Langeman); Roger De Koven (Helgar). Written by Ian Martin.

A passionate interest in music leads Doctor Herschl to graft the hands of virtuoso pianist Rudi Baum, killed in an accident, to less accomplished pianist Franz Langeman, whose hands were badly mangled in the same accident. Though the devastating repercussions soon became apparent to Langeman, his wife Ilse drives him to continue with his career, sealing his fate and hers. You have to give the guy a hand for being as daring as he was.

82. "It's Simply Murder" (3/27/74; rebroadcast 6/19/74)

Cast: Jack Gilford (Henry Green); Bryna Raeburn (Florence Green); Ian Martin (Jerry); Danny Ocko (Sal Rasso); Marian Hailey (Sherry). Written by Ian Martin.

Timid bank teller Henry Green, pushed around unmercifully by his shrewish wife Florence, is talked into robbing the bank's vault by a beautiful, sexy co-worker named Sherry, who also invites him to be her lover. But first he must do away with Florence—a task that proves to be far from easy.

Notes: Ralph Bell remembers, "Ian Martin was an actor who spent the later part of his career as a writer, mostly for Hi Brown for the *CBS Radio Mystery Theater*—and very good he was too."

83. "The Unearthly Gift" (3/28/74; rebroadcast 6/21/74)

Cast: Betsy Palmer (Ruth Ann Mitchell); Carmen Mathews (Bridget); Ian Martin (Frenchy); Jackson Beck (Big Red); Mason Adams (Tim Farrell). Written by Ian Martin.

Ruth Ann Mitchell, a large, gangly girl who cooks with her grandfather for a camp of lumberjacks, has the unearthly and frightening capacity to foretell events. What she sees for newcomer Tim Farrell frightens her enough to take actions that confound not only Tim but most of the other lumberjacks.

Notes: Betsy Palmer was a panelist for numerous television programs during the mid to late 1950s, including *I've Got A Secret*, *Masquerade Party*, and *What's It For?* After her appearance, Palmer appeared on such shows as Maureen Galloway on *Number 96* and Virginia Bullock on *Knots Landing*.

84. "The Ring of Truth" (3/29/74; rebroadcast from 1/26/74)

85. "Time and Again" (3/30/74; rebroadcast from 1/27/74)

86. "Mother Love" (3/31/74; rebroadcast from 1/30/74)

87. "The Black Cat" (4/1/74; rebroadcast 6/22/74, 7/21/79)
   Cast: Norman Rose (Philip Sterling); Marian Seldes (Sylvia); Bob Dryden (Fenris); Joe Di Santis (Bruce); Evelyn Juster (Gwen). Written by Sam Dann.
   Philip Sterling is determined to love his rich, ugly wife because if he can't, he knows he's going to kill her for her money. He knows all of this because when he looked into the eyes of his wife's black cat, Pluto, he saw himself in a courtroom being sentenced by the judge for the crime.
   Notes: Norman Rose has narrated numerous television shows, most of them police dramas. During the 1950s he narrated *The Big Story, Police Story,* and *The Man Behind the Badge,* the latter of which he also hosted.

88. "The Pharaoh's Curse" (4/2/74; rebroadcast 6/23/74)
   Cast: Kim Hunter (Diane Elliott); Danny Ocko (Inspector Hasid); Arnold Moss (Sir Geoffrey); George Petrie (John Irving); Ian Martin (Sargon). Written by Ian Martin.
   Hoping for some good luck, Sir Geoffrey, head of an archeological expedition, persuades singer Diane Elliot, a dead ringer for a dead princess, to accompany the team about to enter a tomb and recover a fortune in jewels. The 4,000-year-old curse on the tomb seems to be more effective than the party bargained for, and Diane wonders if she will have to share a catafalque with the lookalike princess and a ruthless fortune hunter.

89. "Die! You're on Magic Camera" (4/3/74; rebroadcast 6/26/74)
   Cast: Nick Pryor (Johnny Carlin); Teri Keane (Lisa Kane); Joseph Julian (Inspector); William Redfield (Nick Scarlet); Joan Banks (Andrea). Written by Murray Bennett.
   Johnny is amazed when, photographing his girlfriend in front of a bank, his new instant Volecta S-60 produces a photograph of a holdup inside the bank. A few hours later the bank is robbed, and Johnny's photo nails the thieves. Realizing the camera's potential, Johnny uses it to make easy money—until others make it clear that they need the camera more than he does.
   Notes: Joan Banks played Sylvia on television's *Private Secretary* from 1953 to 1957.

90. "The Thing Inside" (4/4/74; rebroadcast 12/8/74)
   Cast: Ralph Bell (John Ferrar); Robert Kaliban (Paul Chandler); Bryna Raeburn (Sara Ferrar); Leon Janney (Ezra Tate). Written by Robert Newman.
   A curious glass ball purchased by artist John Ferrar and his wife Sara causes problems when John is convinced that it contains a spirit that will grant his wishes. When two of John's enemies are found brutally murdered, Sara and a friend of hers are convinced that it's no coincidence.

91. "The Man Who Heard Voices" (4/5/74; rebroadcast from 1/29/74)

92. "Dead Ringer" (4/6/74; rebroadcast from 2/1/74)

93. "The Man Who Asked for Yesterday" (4/7/74; rebroadcast from 1/31/74)

94. "The Locked Room" (4/8/74; rebroadcast 6/28/74, 3/3/79)

Cast: Jack Grimes (Davey Snowden); Corinne Orr (Bonnie Daniels); Sidney Smith (Walter Hedinger); Carmen Mathews (Mrs. Daniels). Written by Henry Slesar, based on his short story *Behind the Locked Door.*

When Davey Snowden marries wealthy (but homely) Bonnie Daniels, he anticipates moving into her family's mansion and recovering the fortune he imagines lies in a tightly locked room. Stymied by Bonnie's formidable mother, he plays a trick which not only causes him to lose both Bonnie and her fortune, but to realize only too late that his mother-in-law is not through with him yet.

95. "The Murder Museum" (4/9/74; rebroadcast 6/29/74, 2/22/80)

Cast: Michael Wager (Vincent); Bob Dryden (Galinari); Leon Janney (Guide); Marian Seldes (Lisa). Written by Henry Slesar.

The recurring nightmares which haunt Vincent Raymond seem to disappear with his increasing success until girlfriend, Lisa Brandon, posing as a sculptor, innocently reveals some of the details of his traumatic childhood to Raphael Galinari. When Vincent learns that Galinari plans to transform his private misery into a commercial display, he plans an apt revenge.

96. "Out of Focus" (4/10/74; rebroadcast 6/30/74)

Cast: William Redfield (Sky Harris); Suzanne Grossman (Isabel Harris); Joan Lorring (Deirdre); Earl Hammond (Harry); Danny Ocko (Benjy); Ralph Bell (Charlie). Written by Ian Martin.

Advertising man Sky Harris, who will be made a vice-president of his agency if he's able to create a successful campaign for the new Bianchi cosmetics account, meets a beautiful model while riding home on his commuter train (albeit a little tipsy from a visit to his favorite watering place). But when he arranges to see her again—in his city apartment—and tries to take her photograph, all that his camera records is blankness.

97. "Strange Company" (4/11/74; rebroadcast 7/2/74)

Cast: George Petrie (Charles Gordon); Bryna Raeburn (Belle Richwood); Lori March (Lina Gordon); Gilbert Mack (Mr. Geller). Written by Bob Juhren.

Charles Gordon's elderly Aunt Belle, alone now that her sister is dead, has stashed all her savings in two large suitcases. She tells her nephew that a man— then a woman, and again a man, who say nothing, just sit and smile—somehow keep entering her apartment. She is certain these "visitors" are after her money— all of which gives Charles an idea on how he can acquire some of what will rightfully be his even before his aunt dies.

98. "A Ghostly Game of Death" (4/12/74; rebroadcast from 2/2/74)

99. "The Sign of the Beast" (4/13/74; rebroadcast from 2/3/74)

100. "Here Goes the Bride" (4/14/74; rebroadcast from 2/4/74)

101. "Only the Dead Remember" (4/15/74; rebroadcast 7/5/74)

Cast: Tony Roberts (Eddie Benson); Bryna Raeburn (Liz Trainor); Mandel Kramer (Bill Trainor); Lon Clark (R. J. Jackson); George Petrie (Tom Wilson). Written by Sam Dann.

Captured in the Korean War, three G.I.s vow to kill a fourth who they were certain had informed the North Koreans of their plan to escape. One of the three, piano player Eddie Benson, has combed the United States for more than twenty years and has now found the informer. But he cannot convince his buddies to join him in the execution they once swore they would perform together.

Notes: Lon Clark, opera singer turned radio performer, has appeared on numerous radio series, including *Exploring Tomorrow*, *X Minus One*, *Quick as a Flash*, *Suspense* and the title role of *Nick Carter, Master Detective*.

102. "Men Without Mouths" (4/16/74; rebroadcast 7/6/74, 2/29/80)

Cast: Joseph Silver (Joe Gannet); Patricia Elliott (Kitty); Danny Ocko (Bartender); Ira Lewis (Dr. Hammel). Written by Henry Slesar.

Horrified by encounters with strangers who seem to have no mouths, former gangster Joe Gannet consults Dr. Hammel, his niece Kitty's fiancé. Hammel, who knows of Joe's past, comes up with the theory that these apparitions are manifestations of the guilt Joe must feel for the crime syndicate "informers" he has killed. But Kitty makes it crystal clear that these "men without mouths" are a premonition of Joe's future, not his past, when she learns the truth about his life.

Notes: After her *Theater* appearances, Patricia Elliott went on to play Renee on the short-run television series *Empire*.

Joe Silver (as well as *Mystery* performers Jackson Beck and Patricia Hosley), was a regular on television's *Ab Libbers* and played Max Spier, the coffee shop owner on the mystery series *Coronet Blue* in 1967. Silver was also a regular on such television series as *The 54th Street Revue*, *Joey Faye's Frolics*, *The Red Buttons Show*, and *Mr. I. Magination*.

103. "The Horror Within" (4/17/74; rebroadcast 7/7/74, 2/1/80)

Cast: Don Scardino (Joe Carpertino); Joseph Julian (Pete); Bob Dryden (Father Coyle); Earl Hammond (Lt. Tawney); Dolores Sutton (Effie). Written by Milton Wisoff.

Joe leaves town when he is taunted about his strange behavior and unusual power to perceive the thoughts of others. Working for his Uncle Pete in a supper club, Joe is able to use his talent in a nightclub act with the aid of Effie, his girlfriend. On the eve of their marriage, Effie is found brutally murdered, and Joe sets out to use his telepathy powers to find the killer.

104. "A Portrait of Death" (4/18/74; rebroadcast 7/10/74)

Cast: Nat Polen (Sgt. Bert Dennison); Marian Seldes (Lucy); Roger De Koven (Professor DeMarco); Jack Grimes (Otis Carter). Written by Sam Dann.

Otis Manley Carter, an art school dropout, is today hailed at the young age of 30 as the world's foremost living artist. Almost unnoticed is the fact that his female subjects die the day he finishes their portraits. A police sergeant investigates since his sister just became Otis' next subject for his next "masterpiece."

105. "The Lady Was a Tiger" (4/19/74; rebroadcast from 2/5/74)

106. "After the Verdict" (4/20/74; rebroadcast from 2/6/74)

107. "Conspiracy to Defraud" (4/21/74; rebroadcast from 2/8/74)

108. "The Wishing Stone" (4/22/74; rebroadcast 7/12/74)

Cast: William Prince (Tom Coulter); Anne Costello (Jenny Lou Coulter); Jack Grimes (Jud Coulter); Clarice Blackburn (Marge Coulter); Bob Dryden (Dr. Luther). Written by Ian Martin.

Jenny Lou Coulter, a country girl whose father's addiction to gambling insures the family of unending poverty, tries to keep secret her acquisition of a wishing stone. Her mother and brother don't want her father to know about it because he will try to use it to win at poker or the race track. Only when he commits a dastardly act does Jenny Lou tell her father of her treasured possession. The 16-year-old country girl believes it is from the hand of an angel, and that it will help her father.

109. "The Ghost Driver" (4/23/74; rebroadcast 7/13/74, 1/25/80)

Cast: Mason Adams (Mel Stout); Norman Rose (Mike Duncan); Augusta Dabney (Liz Stout); Leon Janney (Rory); Nick Pryor (Jason Gormley); Mary Jane Higby (Jessica Gormley). Written by George Lowthar.

The bad publicity surrounding a "ghost driver" who forces cars off a narrow mountain bridge forces Mel and Liz Stout, operators of a nearby ski lodge, to give up hope of making a success of the lodge. The ghost appears to be a skeleton driving a car and forces four people to crash and die. Mike Duncan, the lone survivor of the accident, turns skeptic and decides to confront the "ghost" and expose him before he kills again.

110. "The Hand" (4/24/74; rebroadcast 7/14/74, 1/11/78, 7/28/79)

Cast: Alexander Scourby (Henri Donnet); Guy Sorel (Sir John Rowell); Ian Martin (Dr. Forestier); Mildred Clinton (Lady Rowell). Adapted by Ian Martin, based on the short story by Guy de Maupassant.

Sir John Rowell arrives on the island of Corsica, avoiding human contact as much as possible until his neighbor, police magistrate Henri Donnet, purposely strikes up a friendship. Knowing little about Rowell's history, Donnet unwittingly seals his fate by helping Lady Rowell to mail a letter. A severed hand arrives for Rowell by return post which, he is certain, is bent on destroying him.

Notes: Veteran actor Alexander Scourby is acclaimed for his dramatic performances in such plays as *Hamlet, Saint Joan,* and *A Whitman Portrait.* He also made numerous appearances in such films as *The Big Heat* (1953) and *Giant* (1956). Scourby was recently seen on the CBS television series *Secret Storm,* which was canceled shortly after his performance on *Theatre.*

"To me, all of these are classics," said Himan Brown. "There's no question about the five adaptations of long-time favorites. Because each has won special recognition, I consider the two originals modern classics. 'The Black Room' was chosen for publication in a book. Sam Dann's 'Goodbye, Karl Erich' was the first of our stories to win a Writers Guild Award. Six of the seven were broadcast during our first year, 1974, and helped us get off the ground."

111. "Sunrise to Sunset" (4/25/74; rebroadcast 7/21/74)

Cast: Marian Seldes (Una); Bryna Raeburn (Marie); William Redfield (Peter); William Johnstone (Father). Written by Elspeth Eric.

A strong-willed woman, for all intents and purposes, dies. But is she dead? She happened to be a person with a surpassing belief in herself, so angry when death was upon her, that she would not submit. Her children believe she has come back—as a vampire—and that they are now damphires. And only damphires know how to deal with vampires.

Notes: This was William Johnstone's first appearance on *Theater.* Johnstone, a veteran actor in radio, has appeared in numerous radio shows, including *Pursuit, Suspense, The Whistler, Valiant Lady,* and starred in *The Lineup* as Lieutenant Ben Guthrie, and Lamont Cranton, alias *The Shadow,* for a few years.

112. "The Deadly Hour" (4/26/74; rebroadcast from 2/9/74)

113. "Dead Man's Mountain" (4/27/74; rebroadcast from 2/10/74)

114. "A Dream of Death" (4/28/74; rebroadcast from 2/12/74)

115. "All Living Things Must Die" (4/29/74; rebroadcast 7/16/74)

Cast: Mercedes McCambridge (Barbara); Ralph Bell (Frank); Larry Haines (Ed). Written by Elspeth Eric.

Married to a cruel and crude man, Barbara Murray wishes him dead, and he is immediately strangled by her plants and vines, upon which she had lavished years of care and affection. But when she remarries and becomes pregnant, the plants' jealousy is soon evident.

Notes: Among his Broadway credits, Larry Haines had featured roles in *A Thousand Clowns, Generation* (starring Henry Fonda), *Promises, Promises,* and *Twigs* (starring Sada Thompson). He received a Tony Award nomination for *Generation* and *Promises, Promises.*

116. "The Venus d'Ile" (4/30/74; rebroadcast 7/19/74, 9/9/79)

Cast: Norman Rose (Claude); Danny Ocko (Ormonde); Bob Dryden (Henri); Joan Banks (Heloise); Evelyn Juster (Venus). Adapted by Sam Dann, based on the 1837 short story by Prosper Merimee.

Vicomte Claude Louis de Charbert—handsome, young and owing a million-franc gambling debt—tries to save himself from his creditors by seeking the hand of the wealthiest young lady in France. But when he carelessly places his ring on the finger of an eight-foot bronze statue of Venus, the goddess demands his love—or his life.

117. "The Death Bell" (5/1/74; rebroadcast 7/20/74)

Cast: Michael Tolan (Brian Macken); Marian Seldes (Sheila Doyle); Guy Sorel (Lord Carrig); William Redfield (Denny Doyle). Written by Ian Martin.

Brian Macken, an American of Irish descent, journeys to Erin to search for Carrig Cleena, the home of his ancestors. Despite the warning of his palm-reading cousin, Macken drives northward to discover that the castle's ruins are being used as an IRA munitions depot, and he himself is suspected of being a police officer.

Notes: Michael Tolan played Dr. Alex Tazinski on television's *The Nurses* from 1964 to 1965, and Jordan Boyle, the administrative aide on *The Senator*, from 1970 to 1971.

118. "Dracula" (5/2/74; rebroadcast 7/27/74, 1/6/78, 5/26/79, 10/31/80)

Cast: Mercedes McCambridge (Mina Harker); Michael Wager (Count Dracula); Stefan Schnabel (Professor Van Helsing); Paul Hecht (Dr. John Seward); Marian Seldes (Lucy Westenra). Adapted by George Lowthar, based on the 1897 novel by Bram Stoker.

While visiting her critically ill friend Lucy Westenra, Mina Harker discovers that Lucy is being drained of her blood by Count Dracula, a vampire. Professor Van Helsing, called in for a consultation by Lucy's fiancé Dr. John Seward, declares that they must kill Dracula by a gruesome procedure if they are to stop him and save Lucy's soul.

Notes: To celebrate *Mystery Theater*'s fifth season, which began in January 1978, Himan Brown decided to present a week of classic horror stories such as *Dracula, Frankenstein, Dr. Jekyll and Mr. Hyde*, and others. All were rebroadcasts, and "Dracula"—revisited on January 6, 1978—marked the first of the seven horror episodes.

This episode of *Mystery Theater*, an adaptation of Bram Stoker's novel *Dracula*, received a Count Dracula Society Award for its contribution to presenting such an adaptation to the public.

119. "Under Grave Suspicion" (5/3/74; rebroadcast from 2/14/74)

120. "A Lady Never Loses Her Head" (5/4/74; rebroadcast from 2/16/74)

121. "The Walking Corpse" (5/5/74; rebroadcast from 2/17/74)

122. "Murder with Malice" (5/6/74; rebroadcast 7/24/74)

Cast: Marcia Rodd (Marge Prentiss); Ira Lewis (Mark Prentiss); Nick Pryor (Jeff Henderson); Staats Cotsworth (Harvey Prentiss). Written by Ian Martin.

Heavily in debt and unable to get money from his wealthy father, Mark Prentiss attempts a desperate scheme. Marge, his twin sister, is easily susceptible to hypnosis, and Mark knows the technique to put her under. Hoping their mutual hatred of their father will be enough of a subconscious incentive, Mark hypnotizes Marge and commands her to murder their father in her sleep.

Notes: Marcia Rodd's best-known roles were in such Broadway comedies as *Last of the Red Hot Lovers* and *Your Own Thing*, and she starred as well in Jules Feiffer's satiric film *Little Murders* (1974). She can be seen in *How to Break Up a Happy Divorce* (1976), *Keeping On* (1981), and *Citizen's Band* (1977). Here she takes a change of pace and plays the part of Marge Prentiss, a woman whose twin brother attempts to hypnotize her in order to make her kill her father.

Nicholas Pryor played numerous television roles, including that of Jack Felspar on *The Bronx Zoo*, Jeffrey Trout on *Eight Is Enough*, and chancellor Milton Arnold on *Beverly Hills, 90210*.

123. "The Suicide Club" (5/7/74; rebroadcast 7/28/74, 9/23/78, 6/16/79)

Cast: Barry Nelson (Victor Harris); John Baragrey (John Smith); Lloyd Battista (Lucas); Marian Seldes (Iris Lorne); Danny Ocko (Lt. McFee). Adapted by George Lowthar, based on the 1878 short story *The Young Man With the Cream of Tarts* by Robert Louis Stevenson.

Wealthy Victor Harris confesses to John Smith that he is addicted to gambling and is invited to join a club in which members make the supreme gamble—for their lives. Harris soon realizes that members draw cards for the right to "commit suicide" and play "assassin," but changes his mind about the club when he draws one that says he must do the killing.

Notes: Barry Nelson has appeared in numerous films including *John Eager* (1942), *The Shining* (1980), *Shadow of the Thin Man* (1941), *The Human Comedy* (1941), and *Airport* (1970).

124. "The Breaking Point" (5/8/74; rebroadcast 7/26/74)

Cast: Roger De Koven (Professor Baker); Nat Polen (Dr. Simpson); Bryna Raeburn (Helen Baker). Written by Hank Warner.

Professor William Baker, attempting to prove to a skeptical young brain surgeon that he can make his wife react to mental energy messages, orders her through mental telepathy to pick up a loaded gun and shoot him. She obeys—to the horror of the brain surgeon. Nonetheless, he is not convinced that her action was entirely involuntary.

125. "A Tiny Drop of Poison" (5/9/74; rebroadcast 7/30/74)

Cast: Tammy Grimes (Eleanor Hartley); Paul Hecht (Tom Caldwell); Bob Dryden (Ted Hatley); Earl Hammond (Paul Grover). Written by Sam Dann.

Eleanor Hartley, a young, beautiful, and ambitious woman in a race for the U.S. House of Representatives, is dumbfounded when her policeman husband is assigned to investigate a murder she committed in self-defense five years ago—one she is sure no one witnessed. The problem is apparently solved when a known gangster is arrested for the crime.

Notes: Actor and singer Tammy Grimes—here in her radio acting debut—won two coveted Tony awards for her roles in the Broadway productions of *The Unsinkable Molly Brown* and *Private Lives*.

126. "Blizzard of Terror" (5/10/74; rebroadcast from 2/18/74)

127. "Sea Fever" (5/11/74; rebroadcast from 2/19/74)

128. "The Walls of Jericho" (5/12/73; rebroadcast from 2/21/74)

129. "The Lodger" (5/13/74; rebroadcast 8/2/74, 5/5/79)

Cast: Kim Hunter (Nell Pearson); Michael Wager (Tony Adams); Mary Jane Higby (Miss Mapes); Joseph Julian (Lawrence Bowen); Bob Dryden (Lt. Goldman). Written by George Lowthar.

Shortly before one of her female boarders is murdered by The Ripper, widow Nell Pearson rents a room to newspaper reporter Tony Adams. When a mandarin scarlet lipstick falls from his overcoat pocket—the same color lipstick The Ripper writes with on mirrors of his victims—Nell fears Tony may be the mad murderer who kills only widows.

130. "Voices of Death" (5/14/74; rebroadcast 8/23/75)

Cast: Mandel Kramer (Jason Phillips); Ralph Bell (Peter Truro); Evelyn Juster (Claire); Robert Kaliban (Edward). Written by Murray Burnett.

Actor Jason Phillips can hardly believe that every time he turns on his television, the apparition of Peter Truro, a recently deceased producer, appears and suggests that Phillips kill his wife Claire. After consulting a medium and a psychiatrist, Phillips is inclined to believe that Truro's ghost is real enough, and he must use all his wiles to avoid killing Claire every time Truro sets up a situation to make it possible.

131. "The Forever Man" (5/15/74; rebroadcast 8/3/74)

Cast: Paul Hecht (Jack Hanley); Bryna Raeburn (Della); William Redfield (Sgt. Burns); Danny Ocko (Mr. Soames); Leon Janney (Leroy Fraser). Written by Sam Dann.

Wealthy, elderly Leroy Fraser posts bail for a young, vigorous delinquent, Jack Hanley, then offers him half-a-million dollars, a luxurious apartment and a brand new Mark 9 Borghese-Fratelli sports car in exchange, through "psychic surgery," for his body. Hanley eagerly agrees, certain the body exchange can never take place. But his girlfriend is not so sure, urging him to give everything back.

132. "The Trouble with Ruth" (5/16/74; rebroadcast 8/11/74, 3/14/80)

Cast: Marian Seldes (Ruth); Jackson Beck (Hutchins); Jack Grimes (Tom); Gilbert Mack (Dr. Berger); George Petrie (Ralph). Written by Henry Slesar.

Following her latest detainment for shoplifting, Ruth, a young woman with a history of kleptomania, is confronted by two men who claim they will jeopardize her husband's job if she doesn't steal a diamond pin and turn it over to them. Ruth learns, however, that her husband has already explained about her kleptomania to his supervisors.

133. "The Horla" (5/17/74; rebroadcast from 2/22/74)

134. "The Horse That Wasn't for Sale" (5/18/74; rebroadcast from 2/24/74)

135. "The Edge of Death" (5/19/74; rebroadcast from 2/26/74)

136. "The Crack in the Wall" (5/20/74; rebroadcast 8/9/74)

Cast: Celeste Holm (Nora); Bob Dryden (Helper); Wesley Addy (Paul); Robert Maxwell (Dr. Coombs); Anne Costello (Ruth). Written by Sidney Slon.

Grieving for her dead daughter, Nora appears to be inconsolable until she senses the meaning of a crack in the wall of her cellar. Although her husband Paul and others have tried repeatedly to close the crack, the wet cement they use is mysteriously sucked further into the gap. Nora's belief that the wall is left open for their dead daughter to communicate with them is confirmed when a dwarf who calls himself "a helper" offers to arrange a meeting with Ruth.

Notes: Celeste Holm took ballet and drama classes as a child, making her first Broadway appearance in 1938. She scored a triumph in 1943 in the role of Ado Annie in the long-running Rodgers and Hammerstein musical *Oklahoma!* Holm made her screen debut under a long-term contract with 20th Century Fox in 1946 in *Three Little Girls in Blue.* She won an Academy Award as best supporting actress for her third film, *Gentleman's Agreement* (1947). Holm was also nominated for *Come to the Stable* (1949) and Joseph Mankiewicz's witty masterpiece *All About Eve* (1950).

137. "The Longest Knife" (5/21/74; rebroadcast 8/17/74)

Cast: Bryna Raeburn (Mama Pilar); Jack Grimes (Peter Miller); Leon Janney (General Zorilla); Gilbert Mack (Escobar); Marian Seldes (Marge Miller). Written by Sam Dann.

A restaurant owner in an obscure Latin American country, Mama Pilar vows revenge on the nation's dictator when she learns he ordered the execution of her only son. Through careful planning, she is able to entice the food-loving ruler to eat a sumptuous meal (poisoned maybe?) at her place. But all he asks for—his dictator's orders—is two soft-boiled eggs, tea and a slice of toast.

Notes: Jack Grimes, who plays Peter Miller in this episode, was just beginning a filming schedule for the role of Baxter on the short-run television series *On the Rocks*, which would later be broadcast in the winter of 1975 and 1976.

138. "A Choice of Witnesses" (5/22/74; rebroadcast from 2/28/74)

139. "The Bleeding Statue" (5/23/74; rebroadcast 8/10/74)

Cast: Tony Roberts (David); Court Benson (Jamison); Grace Matthews (Rose Abbott); Patricia Elliott (Sara); Paul Hecht (Pierce Abbott). Written by Ian Martin.

Brought together to settle the estate of the late Prior Abbott, who amassed a fortune as a magician, his survivors try to outwit each other in their attempts to acquire the bulk of the wealth. At the same time they keep a wary eye on the 1,444-pound bronze statue used by Abbott when he was on stage. Its legendary powers could bring death to any one of them.

140. "Out of Sight" (5/22/74; rebroadcast from 3/2/74)

141. "Prognosis Negative" (5/25/74; rebroadcast from 3/3/74)

142. "This Will Kill You" (5/26/74; rebroadcast from 3/4/74)

143. "Mirror for Murder" (5/27/74; rebroadcast 8/16/74)

Cast: Celeste Holm (Helen Stuart); Bob Dryden (Jerry Farrel); William Redfield (Dr. Bellows); Wesley Addy (Fred Stuart). Written by Sam Dann.

When she sees herself disappearing and fading away every time she looks in a mirror, Helen Stuart, the neglected wife of a rising politician, goes off in a huff to a mountain resort. There she is approached by two men: a gangster and a federal agent after the gangster. Now important again, her mirror image becomes sharp and clear.

Notes: Wesley Addy was Celeste Holm's fourth real-life husband who appeared on occasion in a few episodes that Celeste starred in. She was a regular on *NBC Radio Theatre* in 1959 and 1960, which was also directed by Himan Brown.

144. "A Long Time to Die" (5/28/74; rebroadcast from 3/9/74)

145. "The Phantom Lullaby" (5/29/74; rebroadcast 8/18/74)

Cast: Arnold Moss (Mr. Keane); Rosemary Murphy (Mrs. Keane); Corinne Orr (Ellen Keane); Mason Adams (John Draper); Bob Dryden (Superintendent). Written by Elspeth Eric.

To make life easier for their daughter who has just endured an abortion, Mr. and Mrs. Howard Keane rent a luxury apartment. They don't believe the superintendent's story that the place is haunted and that all previous tenants had quickly moved out. But that quickly changes once their daughter moves in.

146. "Dressed to Kill" (5/30/74; rebroadcast 8/4/74)

Cast: Robert Morse (Peter Vincent/Tina Vincent); Danny Ocko (Harry); Michael Tolan (Murray Wilcox); Earl Hammond (Bum); Bryna Raeburn (Mrs. Gretch). Written by Bob Juhren.

Peter Vincent is a con artist and sometimes actor, preparing for what he considers to be the "role of a lifetime," the greatest act of his career. His job is to impersonate his own beneficiary, Mrs. Tina Vincent, to collect his own insurance. But Peter Vincent is about to discover that impersonating someone is tougher than he thought. Before he actually sets out on his task he will set up a small test run to prove to himself and others that he can carry out the impersonation.

Notes: Robert Morse played both man and wife (male and female roles) in this episode.

147. "The Sending" (5/31/74; rebroadcast from 3/6/74)

148. "The Creature from the Swamp" (6/1/74; rebroadcast from 3/7/74)

149. "The Thing in the Cave" (6/2/74; rebroadcast from 3/11/74)

150. "To Kill with Confidence" (6/3/74; rebroadcast 8/23/74)

Cast: Marian Seldes (Ruth Rennard); George Petrie (Lt. Powell); Larry Haines (Leo Rennard); Gilbert Mack (Frank). Written by Sam Dann.

While driving on their honeymoon, Leo and Ruth, married just two weeks, stop to have their car repaired. She leaves to buy him a birthday present, returning 90 minutes later to discover the car has gone, Leo has disappeared and that the service station they had stopped at has been closed for three years.

151. "An Occurrence at Owl Creek Bridge" (6/4/74; rebroadcast 8/24/74, 9/15/79)

Cast: William Prince (Peyton Forrester); Jack Grimes (Woody); William Redfield (Robbie Tompkins); Leon Janney (Corporal); Mildred Clinton (Millicent). Adapted by Sam Dann, based on the 1891 short story by Ambrose Bierce.

It's the fall of 1863 and Peyton Forrester, declared physically unfit for service in the Southern Army, is caught by the Yankees as he unsuccessfully attempts to blow up the railroad bridge over Owl Creek and thus isolate the entire Union army. Union troops catch him in the act. Forrester is convinced that nothing can harm him after the rope wraps around his neck—and the rope miraculously snaps. Forrester now swims for his life, dodging the bullets of Union troops, and plans another attempt at dynamiting the bridge.

152. "A Sacrifice in Blood" (6/5/74; rebroadcast from 3/12/74)

153. "Deadly Darling Dolores" (6/6/74; rebroadcast 8/25/74)

Cast: Nat Polen (Jim Elliot); Marian Seldes (Dolores); Earl Hammond (Bob Stoddard); Roger De Koven (Admiral Goodwin). Written by Sam Dann.

Two scientists working on the ultimate weapon hear their computer, which they have named Dolores, say she will kill them if they don't program her with the formula that will complete the weapon which (if successful) will destroy all of Earth's animal life. The scientists, who have become opposed to the project, try to escape. Dolores kills one and chases the other to a vacant house in the country.

154. "A Little Night Murder" (6/7/74; rebroadcast from 3/13/74)

155. "The Fall of the House of Usher" (6/8/74; rebroadcast from 3/14/74)

156. "Sea of Troubles" (6/9/74; rebroadcast from 3/18/74)

157. "A Bargain in Blood" (6/10/74; rebroadcast 8/27/74)

Cast: Tony Roberts (Salvadore Ross); Evelyn Juster (Ruthie Maitland); Mandel Kramer (Mr. Maitland); Bob Dryden (Halpert); Gilbert Mack (Joey); Jack Grimes (Bartender). Written by Henry Slesar, based on his 1961 short story *The Self-Improvement of Salvadore Ross.*

Salvadore Ross is in love with Ruthie, daughter of a teacher who doesn't want a factory "bum" for a son-in-law. Then Sal discovers his strange power—trading what he's got for *anything.* He swaps his head of hair for drinking money, whiskey for the return of his hair, his 26 years for an old man's age and fortune, a year at a time back for $1,000 each. But Ruthie still won't marry him unless he has compassion—and that can only come from her ill father.

Notes: Henry Slesar's short story *The Self-Improvement of Salvadore Ross* originally appeared in the May 1961 issue of *The Magazine of Fantasy and Science Fiction.* In 1963 Jerry McNeely adapted the short story for television, which was later broadcast on Rod Serling's *The Twilight Zone* on January 17, 1964. Slesar, a leading mystery writer, was for many years a staff writer for the television series *The Edge of Night*.

158. "The Ghost at the Gate" (6/11/74; rebroadcast from 3/20/74)

159. "The Rat" (6/12/74; rebroadcast 8/30/74)

Cast: Michael Wager (Dr. Grayson Carter); Ralph Bell (Dr. Wayne Chaney); Joan Lorring (Doris Chaney); Robert Kaliban (Dr. Morton). Written by George Lowthar.

Frustrated by his wife's love for a fellow researcher and disappointed by a decision of his supervisor, scientist Wayne Chaney seems to be going out of his mind. He helped develop the world's most intelligent rat, which should have given him the boost needed for another project. When his superior Dr. Morton is found dead because of a bite by a Rattus Norvegicus, no one can figure out how the rat named Attila managed to escape from its cage. Was it due to Attila's superior intelligence, or did the rat have a little help from Chaney?

160. "The House of Seven Gables" (6/13/74; rebroadcast 8/31/74, 6/2/79)

Cast: Norman Rose (Matthew Maule/Holgrave Maule); Jada Rowland (Phoebe Pyncheon); Arnold Moss (Judge Pyncheon/Col. Pyncheon); Bryna Raeburn (Alice Pyncheon); Staats Cotsworth (Clifford Pyncheon). Adapted by Ian Martin, based on the 1851 novel by Nathaniel Hawthorne.

Unfairly condemned to death by the scrupulous, avaricious Colonel Pyncheon, Matthew Maule vows before he dies that Pyncheon's family will have "blood to drink." When Pyncheon dies soon after Maule, it is the beginning of the extinction of his family. Finally, only Phoebe, the youngest and most innocent of the Pyncheons, and Holgrave, the last of the Maules, are left to try to break the curse.

161. "Ordeal by Fire" (6/14/74; rebroadcast from 3/21/74)

162. "Diary of a Madman" (6/15/74; rebroadcast from 3/25/74)

163. "Death by Whose Hands" (6/16/74; rebroadcast from 3/26/74)

164. "Three Times Dead" (6/17/74; rebroadcast 9/1/74)

Cast: William Redfield (Don Greenway); Suzanne Grossman (Ella Greenway); Danny Ocko (Mr. Sanchez); Sam Gray (Sgt. Carter). Written by Sam Dann.

Soon after a policeman kills two thugs in an attempted holdup, the holdup victim, a store owner, gives the cop's wife a solid gold six-inch statue as a thank-you gift. The store owner says it will grant the owner three wishes. Without telling her husband, she makes a first wish—for $15,000. Almost immediately his squad car is hit head on. It seems she'll get the $15,000—in life insurance money.

165. "Dr. Jekyll and Mr. Hyde" (6/18/74; rebroadcast 9/4/74, 1/8/78, 7/7/79)

Cast: Kevin McCarthy (Dr. Jekyll/Mr. Hyde); Ian Martin (Utterson); Court

Benson (Dr. Lanyon); Marian Seldes (Beatrice). Adapted by George Lowthar, based on the 1886 story *The Strange Case of Dr. Jekyll and Mr. Hyde* by Robert Louis Stevenson.

Dr. Henry Jekyll, a prominent London physician, has long held the theory that every person contains within himself not one spirit, but two—one good, the other evil. He also believes a way can be found, via an elixir, to release the evil spirit. In his laboratory he works out such a potion, which transforms him into a hairy, malformed dwarf with claws, a murderer named Edward Hyde. Though he fights against it, Dr. Jekyll slowly becomes subservient to Mr. Hyde.

"Dr. Jekyll and Mr. Hyde," in celebration of *Mystery Theater*'s fifth season, was rebroadcast on January 8, 1978. Himan Brown, commenting after four years of broadcasts and 800 different dramas, said: "If we went by the old standards, with one program a week for 39 weeks, those 800 scripts would represent more than twenty years of work. But it has been great fun and the first four years have slipped by almost too quickly. Despite my optimism, it was a mystery when we began whether the audience would respond. Now we know. They're out there, clamoring for more. And among them are many young people, which is especially gratifying. They've discovered the joy of listening. They've discovered the drama of the spoken word, the theater of the mind."

166. "It's Simply Murder" (6/19/74; rebroadcast from 3/27/74)

167. "The Secret Doctrine" (6/20/74; rebroadcast 9/6/74)

Cast: Mercedes McCambridge (Louise); Nick Pryor (Peter Sorel); Bob Dryden (Gabe); Mildred Clinton (Noemie); William Johnstone (Father Giles). Written by Elspeth Eric.

When American film star Peter Sorel arrives in a small Gascony town to make a movie, a peasant woman, Louise, who has seen most of his past hits, provides him with French food and wine. She wants him to fall in love with her and take her to the United States. If she doesn't, she and a friend, Noemie, who possesses magical powers, plan a long unused Mass of St. Secaire—a mass of revenge.

168. "The Unearthly Gift" (6/21/74; rebroadcast from 3/28/74)

169. "The Black Cat" (6/22/74; rebroadcast from 4/1/74)

170. "The Pharaoh's Curse" (6/23/74; rebroadcast from 4/2/74)

171. "Escape! Escape!" (6/24/74; rebroadcast 9/7/74)

Cast: Bob Dryden (Hank Farley); Teri Keane (Dolly Farley); Robert Kaliban (Will Chase); Bryna Raeburn (Granny Good). Written by Bob Juhren.

After escaping from an Army stockade, G.I.s Hank Farley and Will Chase are met by Hank's wife, Dolly, driving the getaway car. Because of darkness and heavy rain, Dolly can't find her way back to the highway, causing the men to get lost in the dark, impenetrable and frightening Louisiana forest. The trio move in on Granny Good, whose cabin is in the middle of nowhere. This proves to be their first mistake—Granny possesses mystical powers they cannot comprehend.

172. "Where Fear Begins" (6/25/74; rebroadcast 9/8/74, 3/7/80)

Cast: Kim Hunter (Amanda Shephard); Alan Hewitt (Dr. Swalley); Ian Martin (Mr. Shephard); Mason Adams (Curt); Phoebe Dorin (Vera). Written by Henry Slesar.

A schoolteacher gets a telephone call for help from her sister, rushes to her aid and finds her dead. The look on her sister's face convinces Amanda that her sister Vera had died from sheer fright. Not believing the police report that her 26-year-old sister died of cardiac arrest, Amanda demands that an autopsy be made. Not until she takes one of Vera's EN-30 "sleeping" pills, a prescription from a Dr. Swalley, does Amanda begin to realize what really happened to her sister.

173. "Die! You're on Magic Camera" (6/26/74; rebroadcast from 4/3/74)

174. "Yesterday's Murder" (6/27/74; rebroadcast 9/10/74)

Cast: Mercedes McCambridge (Dotty); Leon Janney (Mr. Carpenter); Patricia Wheel (Jane); Robert Maxwell (Harold). Written by Sam Dann.

Dotty Molloy felt cursed from the moment she stole the $20,000 from her employer to help her husband, which caused the firm's night watchman to have a fatal heart attack. Nothing went right for 21 years after that, so when a mysterious Mr. Carpenter appears from Opportunities Unlimited and offers to let Dotty make amends for her crime, it seems like too good an offer to refuse.

175. "The Locked Room" (6/28/74; rebroadcast from 4/8/74)

176. "The Murder Museum" (6/29/74; rebroadcast from 4/9/74)

177. "Out of Focus" (6/30/74; rebroadcast from 4/10/74)

178. "Hurricane" (7/1/74; rebroadcast 9/13/74, 3/21/80)

Cast: Joseph Julian (Joe Carrington); Jack Grimes (Ron Prentice); Gordon Gould (Martin Halliday); Evelyn Juster (Fan Halliday). Written by George Lowthar.

Seeking shelter from the storm outside, Martin Halliday, a high school counselor, and his wife Fran come across a beach cabin and manage to convince revolver-toting Joe Carrington to allow them to wait out Hurricane Donna in his Florida beach cabin. With Carrington is young Ron Prentice, who manages to tell Fran he has been kidnapped. But when the Hallidays' scheme to relieve Carrington of his gun is successful, they learn—to their horror—that Ron, who now has the gun, is a homicidal maniac and that Carrington is his guardian.

Notes: George Lowthar started out as a prose writer, and soon found that he was better as a dramatist, a career that has spanned more than 30 years. As a young radio writer he contributed often to such programs as *The Radio Guild, Nick Carter—Master Detective, The Shadow,* and *Superman.* With the advent of television, he became an executive producer for the DuPont Network, writing, directing and producing his own plays, among the first on television. Two of them—*Cathedral* and *Submarine* were still bringing him royalties when *Theatre* premiered.

179. "Strange Company" (7/2/74; rebroadcast from 4/11/74)

180. "The Secret Life of Bobby Deland" (7/3/74; rebroadcast 9/14/74)

Cast: Michael Tolan (George Carlin); Hetty Gaylen (Bobby Deland); Martha Greenhouse (Anita Carlin); Marian Seldes (Mrs. Appleton); Gilbert Mack (Dr. Wesley). Written by Elspeth Eric.

Bobby Deland, age 10 and up for adoption, is invited to live with George Carlin and his wife, Anita. Other foster parents have been unable to handle Bobby—he steals little nothings, runs away, and thinks his real mother is a baroness and a movie star. But Carlin is intrigued—even more so when Bobby is able to cure Mrs. Carlin's migraine headache by giving it to himself.

Notes: Elspeth Eric was very prominent radio actress and writer. Her work on stage was as equally impressive if not better, starring in the original production of *Dead End* on Broadway.

181. "The Young Die Good" (7/4/74; rebroadcast 6/16/81)

Cast: Patricia Elliott (Lisa Bissonette); Ira Lewis (Ray Bissonette); Carol Teitel (Clarice Wenderby/Clarissa Wenderby); Danny Ocko (Cooper). Written by Murray Burnett.

Lisa Bissonette, just married, meets the lady next door, Clarice Wenderby, a woman of 38. Lisa's husband, Ray, also meets her. But this time she's Clarissa, 38, beautiful and beguiling. Clarice urges Lisa to move away Clarissa urges Ray to take her out. The Bissonettes have their first marital spat, which can be resolved only if they see Clarice and Clarissa together—but for some reason they never are.

182. "Only the Dead Remember" (7/5/74; rebroadcast from 4/15/74)

183. "Men Without Mouths" (7/6/74; rebroadcast from 4/16/74)

184. "The Horror Within" (7/7/74; rebroadcast from 4/17/74)

185. "Too Many Women Can Kill You" (7/8/74; rebroadcast 9/15/74)

Cast: Larry Haines (Silas Cunningham); Guy Sorel (Dr. Pierson); Evelyn Juster (Vera Watson); Bryna Raeburn (Julia). Written by Sam Dann.

Silas Cunningham manages to hasten the death of his rich wife—a seemingly perfect murder—so he can live in splendor on her estate with a woman who would like to share the wealth with him. But his wife's housekeeper as well as her sister, both of whom would like to marry him, know about a slight oversight in the commission of the crime. He keeps hearing about it in nightmares from his wife who promised on her death bed that they would never be parted.

186. "And Death Makes Even Steven" (7/9/74; rebroadcast 9/18/74)

Cast: Michael Tolan (Simon Fairleigh); Paul Hecht (Steven Fairleigh); Joan Lorring (Becky); Ian Martin (Mr. Holcombe). Written by Ian Martin.

Simon Fairleigh, a profligate identical twin, becomes furious when his twin brother Steven is bequeathed their father's multimillion dollar business and lots of cash. Even Becky, whom they both love, prefers Steven. But when both brothers are involved in an auto accident and Steven is seemingly killed, Simon sees and seizes an opportunity to take over the business, the money and Becky.

187. "A Portrait of Death" (7/10/74; rebroadcast from 4/18/74)

188. "The Devil-God" (7/11/74; rebroadcast 9/20/74)

Cast: Ruby Dee (Katie Moore); Mandel Kramer (Jeff Moore); Leon Janney (Joe Purdy); Guy Sorel (Ken Yazzi). Written by Mary Jane Higby.

New Englanders, Jeff and Katie Moore, take over her father's ranch somewhere in the Southwest. They are almost immediately faced with a crisis over a prize-winning palomino her father had owned. Their superstitious Indian ranch hands say the horse, which had been struck by lightning and its rider killed, must go. Otherwise the Indians maintain the spirits they believe in will cause trouble. The Moores soon wish they had listened to what the Indians were saying.

189. "The Wishing Stone" (7/12/74; rebroadcast from 4/22/74)

190. "The Ghost Driver" (7/13/74; rebroadcast from 4/23/74)

191. "The Hand" (7/14/74; rebroadcast from 4/24/74)

192. "The Canterville Ghost" (7/15/74; rebroadcast 9/21/74, 4/8/79)

Cast: Arnold Moss (Sir Simon); Mildred Clinton (Lady Eleanore); William Redfield (Geoff Canterville); Bob Dryden (Hiram Otis); Marian Seldes (Virginia). Adapted for by George Lowthar, based on the 1887 story by Oscar Wilde.

The ghost of Sir Simon de Canterville, who, after 400 years is but a ghost of his former self, goes into a towering rage when an American business tycoon, who has brought the Canterville castle to America stone by stone, refuses to be frightened by the antique spook and even threatens to tear the castle down again stone by stone.

193. "All Living Things Must Die" (7/16/74; rebroadcast from 4/29/74)

194. "The Real Printer's Devil" (7/17/74; rebroadcast 1/4/76)

Cast: Jada Rowland (Jane Trent); Paul Hecht (Joel Trent); Ian Martin (H.S.M. Appolyon); Bryna Raeburn (Aunt Gertrude). Written by Ian Martin.

Jane and Joel Trent answer an ad in the paper for an inexpensive apartment that they decide will be just perfect for them and their expected child. Not until after they sign the lease and move in do they realize there is something devilishly eerie about Apartment 13 and its previous tenant, and especially about the cat with supernatural powers that comes with the apartment. They wonder if their apartment is too good to be true or whether it's too true to be good.

195. "The Dream Woman" (7/18/74; rebroadcast 9/22/74, 3/28/80)

Cast: Kevin McCarthy (Norman Meredith); Teri Keane (Sandra Lawrence); Grace Matthews (Agnes Meredith); Bob Dryden (Dr. Gerstein). Adapted by George Lowthar, based on the story by Wilkie Collins.

Norman Meredith, a well-to-do stockbroker, is irresistibly drawn to Sandra Lawrence, a blonde, hazel-eyed struggling young actress he first met in a dream during which she tried to kill him with a long-bladed, razor-sharp carving knife. He even leaves his wife to take Sandra to Rome, where one night she comes back from the flea market, the proud possessor of a long-bladed, razor-sharp carving knife. Norman is convinced that death will soon be upon him.

196. "The Venus d'Ile" (7/19/74; rebroadcast from 4/30/74)

197. "The Death Bell" (7/20/74; rebroadcast from 5/1/74)

198. "Sunrise to Sunset" (7/21/74; rebroadcast from 4/25/74)

199. "The Deadly Process" (7/22/74; rebroadcast 9/27/74)

Cast: Norman Rose (Walter Stallings); Marian Seldes (Louise Loomis); Ralph Bell (George Loomis); Robert Maxwell (Mr. Even); Jackson Beck (Mr. Barker). Written by Sam Dann.

George Loomis, deeply in debt and about to lose his executive job, turns to Walter Stallings, who always helped him when they were in college. But instead of living up to an agreement to share with Walter, George steals his old friend's valuable industrial process, which will earn him a large bonus and save his job. Walter's reaction to this is expected, but George's reaction to Walter's reaction is not.

200. "Adam's Astral Self" (7/23/74; rebroadcast 12/7/74)

Cast: Michael Wager (Adam Farr); Jennifer Harmon (Tessa Farr); Jacqueline Brooks (Maida); William Redfield (Phillip). Written by Elspeth Eric.

Tessa Farr decides to leave her husband Adam, a well-known actor whose penchant for projecting his spirit or astral self out of his body is driving her out of her mind. Missing her, Adam attempts and fails to persuade Tessa to return by using his spiritual and telepathic powers to inflict minor illnesses on her mother and his son. When he fails, everyone believes that Adam has lost his powers, and no one seriously believes his threat to use his spirit to kill Tessa's new boyfriend.

201. "Murder with Malice" (7/24/74; rebroadcast from 5/6/74)

202. "My Sister—Death" (7/25/74; rebroadcast 9/24/74, 4/11/80)

Cast: Marian Seldes (Andrea Carter); Beatrice Straight (Sybil Carter); Paul Hecht (Murray Redmond); George Petrie (Del Delahanty). Written by George Lowthar.

Andrea and Sybil Carter separately approach lawyer Murray Redmond, whom they both love and who is in love with both of them. Andrea cites incidents to prove that Sybil is driving her to insanity in order to get their dead brother's entire estate. When Sybil sincerely seeks Murray's help in getting Andrea to see a psychiatrist, he realizes he has to take drastic measures to find out which sister is telling the truth.

203. "The Breaking Point" (7/26/74; rebroadcast from 5/8/74)

204. "Dracula" (7/27/74; rebroadcast from 5/2/74)

205. "The Suicide Club" (7/28/74; rebroadcast from 5/7/74)

206. "Ghost at High Noon" (7/29/74; rebroadcast 9/28/74)

Cast: Celeste Holm (Marian Jeffries); Frances Sternhagen (Janet Marston); Nat Polen (Joe); Gilbert Mack (Oldtimer). Written by Elizabeth Pennell.

Stranded on a lonely stretch of road when their car breaks down, Marian and Janet are taken by an oldtimer in a wagon to the strange ghost town of Mirado. In vain they try to persuade their ancient escort to help them back to civilization. But he has an unsettling way of insisting that they have come home to Mirado, and that there they will stay. Their panic grows with each turn of events, revealing one live ghost.

207. "A Tiny Drop of Poison" (7/30/74; rebroadcast from 5/9/74)

208. "The Only Blood" (7/31/74; rebroadcast 9/29/74)

Cast: Howard Da Silva (Anthony Boda); Bob Dryden (Al Karley); Ken Harvey (Chuck); Jack Grimes (Louis Boda); Bryna Raeburn (Maria Boda). Written by Sam Dann.

Anthony Boda, a poor Italian shoemaker, refuses to give in to gangsters seeking protection money from area shopkeepers. Boda's outrage at the injustice of the mob's illegal methods soon turns to revenge when his wife and son are killed by the gang. Although thwarted when attempts to kill Al Karley, the mob's leader, Boda finds himself in a position to bring off Karley's death by refusing to donate blood, a rare type which he and Karley share.

Notes: This episode marked Howard Da Silva's many appearances on *Theater.* Da Silva's television credits stretch as Anthony Celese on *For the People* (costarring with William Shatner), *Hollywood Premiere* in 1949, and an Emmy Award for his performance on the PBS program *Great Performances,* in the episode "Verna: USO Girl," for which he won "Outstanding Performance by a Supporting Actor in a Comedy or Drama Special."

209. "The Hit Man" (8/1/74; rebroadcast 10/2/74, 4/18/80)

Cast: Mike Kellin (Jim Derry); Alan Manson (Eddie Breech); Earl Hammond (Earl); Lon Clark (Joe Harney); Marian Seldes (Connie Breech). Written by Henry Slesar.

Hired to kill a minor gangland figure, Jim Derry figures it will be just another job, until); he meets his "mark," Eddie Breech, and hears Breech's story that he stole money from the mob to pay for his wife's medical treatments. Derry decides

to fake the killing to give the couple a chance to get away, but he underestimates Connie Breech's desire for revenge against the husband who crippled her for life.
Notes: Alan Manson can be seen in the films Let's Scare Jessica to Death (1971) and Whiffs (1975).
Mike Kellin has appeared in numerous films including Wackiest Ship in the Army (1961), The Last Porno Flick (1974), The Incident (1967), At War with the Army (1950), Lonely Hearts (1958), The Boston Strangler (1968), and Sleepaway Camp (1983).

210. "The Lodger" (8/2/74; rebroadcast from 5/13/74)

211. "The Forever Man" (8/3/74; rebroadcast from 5/15/74)

212. "Dressed to Kill" (8/4/74; rebroadcast from 5/30/74)

213. "I Thought You Were Dead" (8/5/74; rebroadcast 10/4/74)
Cast: Arlene Francis (Jennifer Partridge); Guy Sorel (Paul); Mary Jane Higby (Miss Kewlett); Bob Dryden (Scott). Written by Sam Dann.
Jennifer Partridge killed her husband Scott using an idea from a mystery novel he had written. She is mystified herself when Scott begins calling her a year after his death. A psychiatrist convinces her that the phone calls are either an illusion or a blackmailer's trick, and when her secretary, Miss Kewlett, reveals that she knows how Scott died, Jennifer is determined to put a permanent end to the blackmail.

214. "The Headstrong Corpse" (8/6/74; rebroadcast 10/6/74, 4/4/80)
Cast: Gordon Gould (Edward Somerset); Ian Martin (Hobbs); George Lowthar (Lord Burleigh); Ann Pitoniak (Mrs. Murchison); Suzanne Grossman (Margaret); Court Benson (Dr. Westmore). Written by Ian Martin.
Edward Somerset visits the home of Margaret Tresilion, the woman he loves, to comfort her on the death of her father, and finds the body has disappeared and the head severed. Realizing the deed is the work of a madman and partial body snatcher, Somerset narrows the suspects down to a neighbor who wants Margaret's home and land, an unscrupulous physician and a servant.

215. "The Picture of Dorian Gray" (8/7/74; rebroadcast 10/5/74, 1/9/78, 8/7/74)
Cast: Nick Pryor (Dorian Gray); Norman Rose (Basil Hallward); Marian Seldes (Sibyl Vane); Roger De Koven (Sir Henry Wotton). Adapted by George Lowthar, based on the 1891 novel by Oscar Wilde.
Swayed by the influence of the insidious Sir Henry Wotton, Dorian Gray, a handsome youth, vows to sell his soul to the Devil if he could retain his youth and only have his portrait grow old. Months later, the effects of the depraved life Dorian is living show not at all in his face, though he must remove his portrait from view as it begins to show a monster.

216. "You Only Die Once" (8/8/74; rebroadcast 10/8/74)
Cast: Joseph Julian (Lou Miller); Joan Lorring (Marge); Tom Keena (Howard); Danny Ocko (Sheriff); Hetty Galen (Billy). Written by Ian Martin.

Lou Miller's plan to fake his own drowning and escape with the proceeds of a bank robbery go smoothly until he loses the money by gambling, and finds himself in trouble with the law. After a successful prison break he determines to blackmail his wife Marge, who remarried after his presumed death, and her husband Howard, a successful bank executive. For the sake of Billy, their son, Marge and Howard agree but no one counts on Billy's skill with his toy guns.

217. "The Crack in the Wall" (8/9/74; rebroadcast from 5/20/74)

218. "The Bleeding Statue" (8/10/74; rebroadcast from 5/23/74)

219. "The Trouble with Ruth" (8/11/74; rebroadcast from 5/16/74);

220. "The Beach of Falesa" (8/12/74; rebroadcast 10/11/74, 9/23/79)

Cast: Alexander Scourby (Sam Wiltshire); Bob Dryden (Jeremy Case); Ian Martin (Black Jack); Evelyn Juster (Ooma). Adapted by Ian Martin, based on the 1892 short novella by Robert Louis Stevenson.

Trader Sam Wiltshire arrives on the island of Falesa to find that the natives are fearful of approaching his store to trade their copra. Through his wife Ooma, Wiltshire learns that a rival, Jeremy Case, manipulates the islanders with threats of voodoo and devil gods. Seeking to break Case's hold over the natives, Wiltshire realizes he alone must destroy Case's devil idols in the dark jungle.

221. "The Frontiers of Fear" (8/13/74; rebroadcast 10/12/74)

Cast: Jerry Stiller (Harry Dorn); Paul Tripp (Mr. Ghan); Robert Kaliban (Lieutenant); Bryna Raeburn (Gladys Morgan). Written by Milt Wisoff.

Looking for a stake to bet on the day's races, hustler Harry Dorn enters a pawnshop and finds himself inexplicably drawn to a worn typewriter. Finding that he only has to touch the keys and the machine will type remarkable stories that come true, Dorn is not too surprised when the machine begins talking and orders him to do its bidding.

Notes: Jerry Stiller has acted in numerous films, including *Heavyweights* (1994), *The Taking of Pelham One, Two, Three* (1974), *The McGuffin* (1985), *The Ritz* (1976), and *The Pickle* (1993).

222. "Journey Into Terror" (8/14/74; rebroadcast 10/13/74, 5/2/80)

Cast: Lynn Loring (Jane Stoddard); Roy Thinnes (Tom); Carol Teitel (Iris Patterson). Written by George Lowthar.

A policewoman interrupts Jane Stoddad's whirlwind honeymoon to tell her that she is in danger and that her new husband, Tom, marries and kills women for the insurance policies he takes out on them. Iris Patterson, the detective, asks Jane to play along with Tom's scheme so they can catch him in the act and get enough evidence to arrest him. Following instructions, Jane realizes (perhaps too late) that the situation is not as Iris claims it to be.

Notes: Roy Thinnes has appeared on numerous television series, such as *Falcon Crest*, *Dark Shadows* (the 1991 miniseries), *From Here to Eternity*, *The Long Hot Summer*, *The X-Files* and *The Psychiatrist*. His most memorable starring role was that of David Vincent, a witness of a UFO landing, in *The Invaders*.

George Lowthar's film writing career includes *Charter Boat, International Airport, The Vice,* and *West Point Story;* the latter starring James Cagney and Virginia Mayo. In the field of legitimate drama, he has had two plays produced: *Second Childhood* and *Strictly for the Birds.*

223. "The Final Vow" (8/15/74; rebroadcast 10/16/74, 5/9/80)

Cast: Rosemary Rice (Sister Pamela); Jack Grimes (Jimmy Bresson); Ken Harvey (Wormer); Joseph Silver (Mike Downey); Bryna Raeburn (Reverend Mother); Ann Pitoniak (Sister Jem). Adapted by Henry Slesar, based on his own short story.

After receiving a priceless religious statue from a gangster, Sister Pamela and Sister Jem allow an unknown man to help them with the heavy case, which he promptly steals. Distraught over the loss, Sister Pamela leaves the convent and pursues a police detective's hunch about the man who might have stolen the statue.

224. "Mirror for Murder" (8/16/74; rebroadcast from 5/27/74)

225. "The Longest Knife" (8/17/74; rebroadcast from 5/21/74)

226. "The Phantom Lullaby" (8/18/74; rebroadcast from 5/29/74)

227. "The Hands of Mrs. Mallory" (8/19/74; rebroadcast 10/18/74)

Cast: Celeste Holm (Ida Mallory); Patricia Elliott (Melinda West); Evelyn Juster (Boy); Arnold Moss (Dr. Merrit); Leon Janney (Dr. Griff); William Redfield (Ted West). Written by Henry Slesar.

After giving up all hope of having her paralyzed hands cured, Ida Mallory, a wealthy widow, meets a young woman whose spine is paralyzed. Ida hears about the amazing Dr. Griff who thinks he can cure Melinda West's spine with the "Water of Faith," a very expensive drug. When Melinda begins to walk again, Ida decides to pay the doctor anything he wants if he'll cure her too. Fortunately, Ida's personal physician is skeptical.

228. "A Preview of Death" (8/20/74; rebroadcast 10/19/74)

Cast: Russell Horton (Elwood Markham); Clarice Blackburn (Muriel Lucas); Bob Dryden (Duke); Staats Cotsworth (George Lucas); Marian Seldes (Daphne Aldershot). Written by Sam Dann.

Engineer Elwood Markham certifies as safe a cable car that is the mainstay of his sister and brother-in-law's mountain resort business, knowing that a fault in the mountain could bring the car down any time. But a recurring nightmare troubles Elwood, who sees a girl named Daphne boarding the car and falling to her death as the cable breaks. When he finds that a very real Daphne has a reservation at the resort Elwood determines he must find her and prevent her death.

229. "Having a Horrible Time" (8/21/74; rebroadcast 6/18/81)

Cast: Lynn Loring (Amy Hastings); Nat Polen (George Smith); Mandel Kramer (Fred Russell); Frances Sternhagen (Lois Wilson); Ralph Bell (Ralph Cooke). Written for *Suspense* by Bob Juhren.

A vacation is in order for Amy Hastings after turning in the mobster who handled most of the city's illegal drugs. But when Amy and her friend Lois arrive at a singles resort they are watched by two men—one of which is a police detective, the other a mobster out to murder Amy. So many men approach Amy that it's impossible to know which of them is the would-be murderer, until the detective realizes that she's in more imminent danger than anyone thought.

230. "The Case of M. J. H." (8/22/74; rebroadcast 10/20/74)

Cast: Augusta Dabney (Matty Sheridan); Alan Hewitt (Dr. Vernon Cooper); Joan De Marrias (Judy); Jack Grimes (Jimmy French); Robert Maxwell (M. J. Harrison). Adapted by Henry Slesar, based on his own short story.

Matty Sheridan, a receptionist for psychiatrist Dr. Vernon Cooper, lets her new-found boyfriend, Jimmy French, talk her into stealing Cooper's files. Jimmy comes across the case of Mr. M. J. H., whose file reveals he is married and has a young girlfriend. With Matty's help, Jimmy contacts the man with intentions of blackmail. They find out too late that Mr. H. will go to any lengths to protect his fantasies.

231. "To Kill with Confidence" (8/23/74; rebroadcast from 6/3/74)

232. "An Occurrence at Owl Creek Bridge" (8/24/74; rebroadcast from 6/4/74)

233. "Deadly Darling Dolores" (8/25/74; rebroadcast from 6/6/74)

234. "The Deadliest Favor" (8/26/74; rebroadcast 10/22/74)

Cast: Ralph Bell (Mike Perry); Danny Ocko (Sheriff Parker); Norman Rose (Edmund Churchill); Marian Seldes (Carlotta Churchill). Written by Sam Dann.

Edmund and Carlotta Churchill feel secure in their mountain retreat until they hear that Edmund's former college roommate, Mike Perry, has escaped from a jail while serving a stretch for murder. Edmund owes Mike a huge favor, and Mike appears to claim it. At first he only wants temporary shelter, then decides he wants Carlotta, too. Finally he wants Edmund's life to ensure his escape.

235. "A Bargain in Blood" (8/27/74; rebroadcast from 6/10/74)

236. "The Fatal Marksman" (8/28/74; rebroadcast 10/27/74)

Cast: Michael Wager (William Breger); Suzanne Grossman (Katherine Adam); Ian Martin (Soldier); Bryna Raeburn (Elsa); William Johnstone (Bertram Adam). Written by Ian Martin.

To win the hand of his beloved Katherine, William must demonstrate to her father his prowess as a hunter. Not a hunter by profession, William retrieves his dead father's enchanted gun, breaking a solemn deathbed oath to his mother. Initial success gives way to persistent failure, leading William to forge magic bullets, one of which has the power to destroy all his dreams.

237. "Medium Rare" (8/29/74; rebroadcast 10/25/74, 5/23/80)

Cast: Bob Dryden (Handsome Harry); George Petrie (Artie); Mason Adams (Tex Morgan); Marian Seldes (Doree); Joan Banks (Gladys). Written by George Lowthar.

Artie and Gladys are having trouble making ends meet in the spiritualist racket when a real ghost helps them out with a wealthy customer. In return, Handsome Harry (as the ghost prefers to be known), wants them to help clean out a Las Vegas blackjack dealer who stole his former girlfriend, Doree. With Harry's help, Gladys wins; Tex the dealer loses and is out of a job. But Gladys and Artie balk at Harry's last request—that they kill Doree.

238. "The Rat" (8/30/74; rebroadcast from 6/12/74)

239. "The House of Seven Gables" (8/31/74; rebroadcast from 6/13/74)

240. "Three Times Dead" (9/1/74; rebroadcast from 6/17/74)

241. "The Return of Anatole Chevenic" (9/2/74; rebroadcast 10/26/74)

Cast: Alexander Scourby (Hans Chevenic); Ann Pitoniak (Vicky); Sidney Slon (Jaimie); Gilbert Mack (Anatole Chevenic). Written by Sidney Slon.

Working all day at shoemaking and all night for his miserly, sadistic Uncle Anatole, Hans Chevenic manages to earn a meager living for himself and his wife. Hans puts up with Anatole in anticipation of being the sole heir to his considerable wealth, until Anatole reveals he is cutting Hans out of his will. Enraged, Hans kills the old man, but when the body disappears and his dead cousin reappears claiming to be the man Hans conjured up to cover his deed, his sanity ebbs.

Notes: Ann Pitoniak played Mildred Potter on television's *Aftermash* in 1984.

242. "The Imp in the Bottle" (9/3/74; rebroadcast 10/30/74)

Cast: William Redfield (Barry Holden); Ian Martin (Jasper); Santos Ortega (Lawyer Barnes); Joan Lorring (Lisha Breedenhall).

Adapted by Ian Martin, based on the 1891 short story *The Bottle Imp* by Robert Louis Stevenson.

Upon wealthy Jasper Sheridan's death, his nephew, Barry Holden, inherits an antique bottle containing an imp able to grant Barry any amount of money he desires. The owner must resell the bottle, however, to another before his death for less than he paid for it, or the imp will claim his soul for the devil. When the bottle goes to Barry's former wife, whom he still loves, Barry wants to save her soul by repurchasing the bottle, but Lisha only paid a penny for it.

243. "Dr. Jekyll and Mr. Hyde" (9/4/74; rebroadcast from 6/18/74)

244. "Deadline for Death" (9/5/74; rebroadcast 11/2/74)

Cast: Joseph Julian (Sam Rogers); Michael Tolan (Johnny Promise); June Gable (Linda); Guy Repp (Judge). Written by Arnold Moss.

Johnny Promise is sent to the electric chair after his former partner in crime, Sam Rogers, testifies against him in court. Rogers goes free but has to live with Johnny's last threat—that he'll make sure Sam is killed within a month of his own death. Locked in a hotel room with no company, trusting no one, Sam lives for one month in total seclusion, emerging one month to the hour later. Too late, Sam remembers it's the night to change from daylight saving to standard time.

245. "The Secret Doctrine" (9/6/74; rebroadcast from 6/20/74)

246. "Escape! Escape!" (9/7/74; rebroadcast from 6/24/74)

247. "Where Fear Begins" (9/8/74; rebroadcast from 6/25/74)

248. "Double Exposure" (9/9/74; rebroadcast 11/3/74)

Cast: Kim Hunter (Susan Hollis); Sam Gray (Ed Benton); Joan Shay (Lillian Freidberg); Larry Haines (Dan Roberts). Written by Ian Martin.

Susan Hollis, an attractive widow, is understandably shocked when a strange woman is positive she's a former neighbor, and even more confused when a man identifies her as his former wife who disappeared mysteriously. Susan's confusion is heightened by the fact that she once had amnesia and the man, Dan Roberts, claims to have met his wife in the same hospital in which Susan recovered. When Susan begins dating Roberts, her friend Detective Benton is convinced Roberts is attempting to get his hands on Susan's wealth.

249. "Yesterday's Murder" (9/10/74; rebroadcast from 6/27/74)

250. "The Hand That Refused to Die" (9/11/74; rebroadcast 11/1/74, 5/16/80)

Cast: Mandel Kramer (Anton Walburg); Marian Seldes (Alexis Walburg); Russell Horton (Dr. Lonsdale); Carol Teitel (Lottie Stern). Written by George Lowthar.

Certain an auto accident has finished his career, celebrated concert pianist Anton Walburg spurns all suggestions that what he thinks impossible is possible—playing with one hand. But after several seemingly supernatural occurrences, Anton is enticed to attend the concert of a younger virtuoso whose right arm, in the middle of the performance, suddenly becomes paralyzed. Nonetheless, he continues playing all the notes with his left hand.

Notes: Lowthar contributed regularly to such well-known television series as *The U.S. Steel Hour, Kraft Television Theatre, Matinee Theatre,* and *Climax!* He has also written for the daytime series *The Edge of Night, The Secret Storm,* and *The Doctors.*

251. "The Trouble with Murder" (9/12/74; rebroadcast 11/5/74)

Cast: Robert Morse (Hugo Minter); Bryna Raeburn (Aunt Minerva); Ian Martin (Detective Renzulli); Evelyn Juster (Mrs. Kopelman); Jackson Beck (Lieutenant). Written by Ian Martin.

Brooklyn police are baffled by the murder of four women whose headless torsos they have found in the river. Each of the victims was found nude, unmolested, but wearing rings of considerable value. The newspapers have named the murderer "The Brooklyn Headhunter," and the public is clamoring for his arrest. Even though the police don't realize it, the "Headhunter" tries to turn himself in, unsuccessfully—they consider him some kind of nut.

252. "Hurricane" (9/13/74; rebroadcast from 7/1/74)

253. "The Secret Life of Bobby Deland" (9/14/74; rebroadcast from 7/3/74)

254. "Too Many Women Can Kill You" (9/15/74; rebroadcast from 7/8/74)

255. "Whatever Happened to Mrs. Forbush?" (9/16/74; rebroadcast 11/8/74)

Cast: Patricia Wheel (Marjorie Demond); Gordon Gould (Bert Desmond); Mary Jane Higby (Lavinia); Guy Sorel (Mr. Smith); Billie Lou Watt (Robbie Desmond). Written by Elizabeth Pennell.

Marjorie and Bert Desmond and their 9-year-old son Robbie rent a long-deserted house by the sea. When Bert is called back to his office, Marjorie is confronted by what she is sure is the ghost of Lavinia Forbush, who owned the house 200 years ago and whose husband, Captain Forbush, and son were lost at sea. Lavinia warns Marjorie to take Robbie away before she loses him and her husband forever.

256. "Thicker Than Water" (9/17/74; rebroadcast 11/9/74)

Cast: Jay Gregory (Nicholas Wedge); Bob Dryden (Mr. Bleeker); Grace Matthews (Olga); Robert Kaliban (Dankers); Ira Lewis (Benny Bleeker). Written by Henry Slesar, based on his short story *The Test.*

Lawyer Nicholas Wedge, who specializes in defending accused muggers, seems certain to lose a case—eyewitnesses saw young Benny Bleeker with a knife at the time the victim, who later died, was mugged. To prove to the jury—and himself—that Benny was not involved, Wedge volunteers to dip Exhibit A—the knife—into a solution of reduced phenolphthalein, the most sensitive of all blood detection chemicals. If the liquid turns pink, it's all over for Benny.

257. "And Death Makes Even Steven" (9/18/74; rebroadcast from 7/9/74)

258. "The Garden" (9/19/74; rebroadcast 11/10/74, 9/16/79)

Cast: Jennifer Harmon (Vicki Carson); Nancy Coleman (Drusilla); Joseph Silver (Mordred); Jack Grimes (Jack Gibbons). Written by George Lowthar.

A young couple experiences a strange adventure first, in the Garden of Death, then in the Garden of Life. Vicki Carson, wandering about in a strange and evil garden, meets Jack Gibbons, and they, in turn, meet a giant of a man,

Mordred—as vile and ugly as the garden itself—who saves them from death only after they agree to pay a price. Later, to their relief and delight, they meet a lovely woman, Drusilla, who invites them into another garden, a garden of such beauty that they beg to stay in it. But Mordred appears and demands that they return with him.

259. "The Devil-God" (9/20/74; rebroadcast from 7/11/74)

260. "The Canterville Ghost" (9/21/74; rebroadcast from 7/15/74)

261. "The Dream Woman" (9/22/74; rebroadcast from 7/18/74)

262. "Island of the Lost" (9/23/74; rebroadcast 11/13/74)

Cast: Norman Rose (Tony Bridges); Marian Seldes (Martha Bridges); Ian Martin (Pablo); Robert Kaliban (Dr. Werner). Written by Arnold Moss.

Tony Bridges plans to surprise his young wife while she vacations on a little-known Caribbean island. His suspicions that Martha is unfaithful seem confirmed when he meets a young man with a key to her bungalow. Martha's rationale for this is logical enough, but a succession of unusual events, some not well explained by Martha, convinces a very jealous Tony she's trying to drive him insane.

263. "My Sister—Death" (9/24/74; rebroadcast from 7/25/74)

264. "The Deadly Blind Man's Bluff" (9/25/74; rebroadcast 11/15/74)

Cast: Mason Adams (Dave Miller); Bryna Raeburn (Mrs. Scofield); Leon Janney (Sgt. Hennessy); Earl Hammond (Topdog); Augusta Dabney (Fran Miller). Written by Ian Martin.

Topdog, number one on the police list of criminals, robs and murders an elderly woman living on the top floor of a building into which riveter Dave Miller and his wife Fran have recently moved. Dave, blinded by an on-the-job accident, is despondent until—through circumstances beyond his control—he meets face-to-face with Topdog, who does not know that Dave's agile mind is concocting a scheme that may end Topdog's career.

Notes: Earl Hammond was a regular on the television series *Ab Libbers* in 1951, and later played Sgt. Lane on *Rocky King, Inside Detective.*

265. "The Spectral Bride" (9/26/74; rebroadcast 11/16/74)

Cast: Joan Lorring (Melinda Melchior); Michael Wager (Sir Mark); Jordan Chaney (Bruce); Bob Dryden (Cadmus Melchior). Written by Ian Martin.

Against all warnings, Sir Mark marries the beautiful Melinda Melchior, daughter of alchemist Cadmus Melchior. Melinda extracts a solemn promise from Mark that she be his only love, in life as well as death—and Melinda soon meets her death. Although she continues to dominate his thoughts, Mark remarries and is happy until Melinda appears in a vision and commands him to obtain her father's potion to bring her back to life. He foolishly agrees.

266. "The Deadly Process" (9/27/74; rebroadcast from 7/22/74)

267. "Ghost at High Noon" (9/28/74; rebroadcast from 7/29/74)

268. "The Only Blood" (9/29/74; rebroadcast from 7/31/74)

269. "Murder to Perfection" (9/30/74; rebroadcast 11/17/74, 5/30/80)
Cast: Mercedes McCambridge (Nikki Carpenter); John Newland (Guy Weston); Joe Campanella (Bill Weston). Written by George Lowthar.
Nikki Carpenter, an imaginative clothes designer, vows that she'll prove to Guy Weston, her fiancé's brother, murdered her sister (his wife). Guy candidly admits murder was committed, but that he had tricked his wife, and others, into killing themselves. Now he says Nikki will be next—murdered by her own imagination—unless she stops her efforts to prove him guilty.
Notes: John Newland made his first appearance on *Theater* in this episode. Newland had played Danny Frank on television's *One Man's Family* and was a repertory player (1952–54), on *Robert Montgomery Presents*. He was often a guest on *The Loretta Young Show*.

270. "The Bride That Wasn't" (10/1/74; rebroadcast 11/19/74, 4/25/80)
Cast: Janet Waldo (Amy Prentice); Anne Seymour (Florence Morton); Bill Quinn (Joe Prentice); Lurene Tuttle (Mother Morton); Bernard Barrow (Jack Morton). Written by George Lowthar.
Amy Prentice met Jack Morton at a teachers conference. He asked her to marry him, but when she shows up at his home he denies it all, saying he's an insurance salesman and already married. But Florence, his wife, becomes suspicious when Amy is able to describe in detail much of the Morton house, which she's never seen, claiming Jack told her all about it. That night he slips into the guest room where Amy is sleeping. Right behind him is Florence.
Notes: This marked the first and only appearance of Bill Quinn and Lurene Tuttle. Bill Quinn appeared in such radio programs as *The Big Story, Gunsmoke,* and *Suspense.* Lurene Tuttle appeared on *The CBS Radio Workshop, Stars Over Hollywood, Maisie, The Lux Radio Theatre,* and played Effie Perrine, Sam Spade's faithful secretary on *The Adventures of Sam Spade.*

271. "The Hit Man" (10/2/74; rebroadcast from 8/1/74)

272. "The Golden Blood of the Sun" (10/3/74; rebroadcast 11/22/74)
Cast: John Forsythe (Peter Barlow); Rita Gam (Irinia); Berry Kroeger (Mr. Valentine); Arnold Moss (Mendoza). Written by Sam Dann.
Because he's considered a jinx, Peter Barlow is ordered by his boss to fly to Mexico City to look at some property his company is interested in purchasing. That weekend, with Barlow gone, the clouds disappear, the sun shines brightly and potential customers arrive in droves at the resort. In a most mysterious way, Barlow begins to find out why while in the Mexican capital.

Notes: Rita Gam has acted in numerous films, including *Second of Evil* (1976), *Klute* (1971), *The King of Kings* (1961), *The Thief* (1952), and *Distortions* (1987).

273. "I Thought You Were Dead" (10/4/74; rebroadcast from 8/5/74)

274. "The Picture of Dorian Gray" (10/5/74; rebroadcast from 8/7/74)

275. "The Headstrong Corpse" (10/6/74; rebroadcast from 8/6/74)

276. "Sister of Death" (10/7/74; rebroadcast 11/23/74)

Cast: K.T. Stevens (Anita Sutliffe); Amzie Strickland (Tillie); Bret Morrison (Herbert Sutcliffe); Alan Reed (Lt. Tannenberg). Written by Sam Dann.

While attending an art auction, Anita Sutcliffe, who loves and trusts her husband completely, is much taken by a painting and buys it. She soon discovers by accident that the painting is a portrait of her husband's former wife, who had been murdered during a robbery. This is shocking enough, but even more shocking is the fact that Anita doesn't know that her husband had been married before.

Notes: This episode marked Alan Reed's first appearance on the program. Reed has a huge list of radio credits to his name, including *Box 13*, *Life with Luigi*, *Suspense*, *The Whistler*, *The Lux Radio Theater*, *Abie's Irish Rose*, *Damon Runyon Theater*, *Duffy's Tavern*, *The Shadow*, *Cavalcade of America*, *Joe Palooka*, and *My Friend Irma*.

K.T. Stevens has acted in numerous television shows and films. Among his many big-screen movies: *Jungle Hell* (1955), *Port of New York* (1949), *Missile to the Moon* (1959), and *They're Playing with Fire* (1984).

277. "You Only Die Once" (10/8/74; rebroadcast from 8/8/74)

278. "Trapped" (10/9/74; rebroadcast 11/27/74, 6/6/80)

Cast: Nina Foch (Claudia Hammond); Lesley Woods (Mary Elliott); Joan Tompkins (Katherine); Joe Di Santis (Detective Jackson); Charles Aidman (Tod Hammond). Written by George Lowthar.

Opening what she thinks is a piece of fan mail to her handsome actor and husband, Claudia, bedridden with a weak heart, reads a love note signed "Margo." The end of the letter reads, "I will go along with your plan to put her out of the way." Thoroughly frightened and helpless, Claudia refuses to eat or to take her medication, certain she will be poisoned. She becomes even more frightened when her husband fires her nurse and lies about why he did so.

Notes: Nina Foch and director Hi Brown were both regular panelists on the television quiz/panel series *Q.E.D.* back in 1951. This episode reunited the two again, but this time under different circumstances.

Charles Aidman has acted in numerous radio and television series. His big-screen horror/sci-fi/mystery films include *Zone of the Dead* (1978), *Prime Suspect* (1982), *Picture of Dorian Gray* (1974), *The Invasion of Carol Enders* (1974), *House of the Dead* (1980), and *Countdown* (1968). Aidman also narrated the 1980s revival of Rod Serling's classic *The Twilight Zone* television series.

279. "The Doll" (10/10/74; rebroadcast 11/24/74)

Cast: Joanne Linville (Laura Fletcher); Karl Swenson (Professor Douglas); Virginia Gregg (Prudence); Ross Martin (Jimmy Collins). Written by Henry Slesar.

Professor Eric Douglas, an anthropologist, tries not to show his jealousy when a young woman, Laura Fletcher, whose father he knew well, announces she is going to be married. To stop the ceremony, Douglas has his servant, a woman from a tropical island, make a voodoo doll in the image of Laura. The doll seems to cast a spell when Laura and her fiancé go to a justice of the peace, Laura becomes violently ill and cannot go through with the marriage.

Notes: Virginia Gregg made her first and only appearance on *Theater* in this episode. Gregg made numerous appearances on such radio series as *Suspense*, *Gunsmoke*, *Have Gun—Will Travel*, *The Whistler*, *The Adventures of Phillip Marlowe*, *The Unexpected*, *Frontier Gentleman*, and *Let George Do It*.

Joanne Linville can be seen in such films as *Scorpio* (1973), *Secrets* (1977), and *From the Dead of Night* (1989).

280. "The Beach of Falesa" (10/11/74; rebroadcast from 8/12/74)

281. "The Frontiers of Fear" (10/12/74; rebroadcast from 8/13/74)

282. "Journey Into Terror" (10/13/74; rebroadcast from 8/14/74)

283. "A Scaffold for Two" (10/14/74; rebroadcast 11/29/74)

Cast: Bret Morrison (Charles Farnsworth); Denise Alexander (Mayetta); Casey Kasem (Conrad); John Beal (Franklyn Bennett). Written by Sam Dann.

Lawyer Charles Farnsworth, his plane grounded, is swamped with hospitality by Franklyn Bennett and his seemingly emotionally unbalanced children. One child, Mayetta, tells Farnsworth there's going to be a hanging—of her cousin Conrad—and invites the lawyer to watch it. Conrad, it seems, has been acquitted of murder by a mainland jury, and now a group known as the Redressors of the Injustice plans to give him another "trial" and then hang him.

Notes: Casey Kasem, famed radio and television host of numerous radio weekend countdowns, plays a small role in this episode as Mayetta's cousin, Conrad.

284. "Picture on the Wall" (10/15/74; rebroadcast 11/30/74, 6/27/80)

Cast: Diane Baker (Amanda Phillips); Anne Seymour (Mrs. Brolley); John Newland (Morley Norcross); Dennis Cole (Gilbert Franklyn). Written by George Lowthar.

Soon after she moves into an apartment in Greenwhich Village, Amanda Phillips, a young midwesterner in search of an acting career, startles her lawyer boyfriend, Gil Franklyn, when she tells him she has been visited by the grandson of the man whose picture hangs on the apartment wall. Gil doesn't believe her, but he does worry about her safety. Two previous tenants, both young women, have been murdered—strangled to death in the garden outside.

Notes: Both Dennis Cole and Diane Baker made their radio acting debut in this episode. Cole is probably best known for his television roles as Johnny Reach on *Bearcats*, Davey Evans on *Bracken's World*, and as Det. Jim Briggs of *Felony Squad*.

Dennis Cole can be seen in such films as *Amateur Night* (1985), *Pretty Smart* (1987), *Dead End City* (1988), *The Barbary Coast* (1974), and *Powder Keg* (1970).

285. "The Final Vow" (10/16/74; rebroadcast from 8/15/74)

286. "The Last Escape" (10/17/74; rebroadcast 12/11/74)

Cast: Robert Dryden (Joe Ferlini); Joan Banks (Wanda Ferlini); Robert Kaliban (Minister); Joseph Julian (Phil Roscoe); Russell Horton (Tommy). Written by Henry Slesar.

Because the escape artist trade no longer attracts large audiences, the Great Ferlini, age 49, plans to have himself handcuffed, tied in a canvas bag and dumped in a truck into the middle of the lake. Word of such a feat draws a crowd and provides an opportunity for his young wife—not her lover—to make sure the Great Ferlini gets headlines, not as an escape artist but as a corpse.

Notes: Henry Slesar wrote many scripts for the television series *Alfred Hitchcock Presents*. Other writers adapted his own short stories for the television series. This story was broadcast on *Presents* on January 31, 1961, starring Keenan Wynn as Joe Ferlini, the escape artist. Other episodes of *Theater* that were previously dramatized on *Alfred Hitchcock Presents* were "The Locked Room," "After the Verdict," "The Case of M.J.H." and "Thicker Than Water."

287. "The Hands of Mrs. Mallory" (10/18/74; rebroadcast from 8/19/74)

288. "A Preview of Death" (10/19/74; rebroadcast from 8/20/74)

289. "The Case of M. J. H." (10/20/74; rebroadcast from 8/22/74)

290. "Mind Over Matthew" (10/21/74; rebroadcast 12/13/74)

Cast: William Redfield (Matthew Parker); Evelyn Juster (Mildred Cavanagh); Byrna Raeburn (Hester); Court Benson (Fred). Written by Elspeth Eric.

Matthew Parker, a 40-year-old bachelor, succumbs to the charms of Mildred Cavanagh, age 20, and marries her. Mildred, he discovers, has a powerful subconscious mind, so powerful it cures warts on his hand and dispels all her own aches and pains. He then learns that she has a numb area of her right arm and that it doesn't bleed when cut. He starts to wonder if she is a witch.

291. "The Deadliest Favor" (10/22/74; rebroadcast from 8/26/74)

292. "See Naples and Die" (10/23/74; rebroadcast 12/15/74)

Cast: Ken Harvey (Senator Winstead); Michael Wager (Bill); Marian Seldes (Lynn); Danny Ocko (Willie); Larry Haines (Tedesco). Written by Ian Martin.

The defiant daughter of Senator Henry C. Winstead announces her plans to marry Vittorio Tedesco, living in exile in Naples, Italy, after being cited for income tax invasion by one of the senator's subcommittees. Tedesco knows he can destroy the senator's chances for the presidential nomination if he goes through with the marriage. Tedesco therefore offers an ultimatum. His price: forget the income tax rap and let him return to the United States. For the senator, he must decide which of his lives—public or private—is more important.

293. "A Cage for Augie Karo" (10/24/74; rebroadcast 12/17/74)

Cast: Leon Janney (Augie Karo); Earl Hammond (Castle); Evelyn Juster (Ginnie); Robert Maxwell (Pop). Written by Sam Dann.

An old and apparently half-insane convict gives fellow inmate Augie Karo a vial of powder that he claims can put a man to sleep for several centuries—and thus prevent the police from nabbing him if he breaks out. Augie doesn't believe a word of it until a chance to go free is suddenly and mysteriously arranged for him. Will the vial provide the hideout he needs?

294. "Medium Rare" (10/25/74; rebroadcast from 8/29/74)

295. "The Return of Anatole Chevenic" (10/26/74; rebroadcast from 9/2/74)

296. "The Fatal Marksman" (10/27/74; rebroadcast from 8/28/74)

297. "Possessed by the Devil" (10/28/74; rebroadcast 12/20/74)

Cast: Donald Buka (Michael Damon); Guy Sorel (Reverend Damon); Ian Martin (Rod Damon); Leon Janney (Anton); Joan Shay (Trudi). Written by Ian Martin.

Michael Damon, son of a minister, is brought into a hospital emergency room with a dent in his skull that should have mangled his brain. But according to an aging and slightly tipsy cleaning woman, a malign spirit, surrounded by a cloud of black smoke, jumped from another person to Mike, who immediately becomes healthy again—or does he?

298. "The Black Room" (10/29/74; rebroadcast 12/21/74, 1/10/78)

Cast: Larry Haines (The Man); George Petrie (Mr. Kay); Peter Collins (Mr. Zee). Written by Elspeth Eric.

The Man abducted by Mr. Zee and Mr. Kay is not really expected to survive in The Black Room without light or diversions—all the others have died or gone insane. But for 26 days The Man survives, relying on a very small mouse with whom he shares his limited rations, and Mr. Zee must decide whether to release him so that he may share his secret with The Others. The secret of survival when all hope seems lost is companionship.

299. "The Imp in the Bottle" (10/30/74; rebroadcast from 9/3/74)

300. "The Demon Spirit" (10/31/74; rebroadcast 12/22/74)

Cast: Mason Adams (Simon); Nat Polen (Sender); Joseph Silver (Nissen); Jack

Grimes (Menashe); Norman Rose (Meyer); Marian Seldes (Leah). Adapted by Milt Wisoff, based on the stage play "The Dybbuk" by S. Anski.

A student, Simon, returns from a successful search for a miracle worker who can evoke evil spirits to do his bidding. Only he is told that the hand of his betrothed, Leah, has been given by her father, Sender, to a youth who will inherit great wealth. Simon resolves that the wedding will never take place—even if he must resort to the evil skills he learned from the miracle worker.

301. "The Hand That Refused to Die" (11/1/74; rebroadcast from 9/11/74)

302. "Deadline for Death" (11/2/74; rebroadcast from 9/5/74)

303. "Double Exposure" (11/3/74; rebroadcast from 9/9/74)

304. "Bury Me Again" (11/4/74; rebroadcast 12/27/74)

Cast: Michael Tolan (Jerry Horton); Vicki Vola (Myrna Horton); Bob Dryden (Passenger); Gilbert Mack (Douglas); Mary Jane Higby (Bank Manager). Written by Henry Slesar.

Jerry Horton, one of the few left alive in a horrible train wreck, switches wallets with a dead fellow passenger who had, before the tragedy, bragged about the value of his life insurance. After assuming the dead man's name, Jerry carefully instructs his wife, by phone, on how to collect the insurance, all $150,000 of it. Everything goes well until the insurance company demands the dead man's body be exhumed.

305. "The Trouble with Murder" (11/5/74; rebroadcast from 9/12/74)

306. "Terror on the Heath" (11/6/74; rebroadcast 12/28/74)

Cast: Shepperd Strudwick (David Matson); William Redfield (Lon Anderson); Lon Clark (Bob Ripple); Marian Seldes (Jan Matson); Chris Gampel (Dr. Beckwith). Written by Murray Burnett.

Intrigued by a book on famous 19th century killers, Dave Matson becomes convinced he's the reincarnation of one of them when he finds a daguerrotype which bears a striking resemblance to himself. Encouraged in his belief by Bob Ripple, an expert on the period, Matson fears he'll revert to subconsciously motivated criminal behavior. Matson's wife Jan asks Dr. Beckwith, an authority on reincarnation and the occult, to conduct an experiment to disprove her husband's belief.

Notes: Shepperd Strudwick has acted in numerous films, including *The Loves of Edgar Allan Poe* (1942), *Three Husbands* (1950), *All the King's Men* (1949), *Psychomania* (1963), and *Beyond a Reasonable Doubt* (1956).

307. "How Eberhard Won His Wings" (11/7/74; rebroadcast 12/25/74)

Cast: Hans Conried (Eberhard Edwards); Bryna Raeburn (Bar Girl); Arnold Moss (Vladimir); Jackson Beck (Maitre d'); Marian Haley (Mabel Edwards); Martha Greenhouse (Francine). Written by Arnold Moss.

A timid bank teller is so good to everyone that angel's wings start to grow between his shoulder blades. Because of his wings, Eberhard Edwards becomes the butt of so many jokes that his wife vows to help get rid of them. She decides he must commit at least one of the seven deadly sins. He tries them all, but each time fails to be sinful enough. Finally, they both agree that "he who gave them to him is the only one who can take them away."

Notes: Hans Conried made his first appearance on *Theatre* in this charming and humorous episode as Eberhard Edwards. Conried made his screen acting debut in 1938 in *Dramatic School.* During World War II he was usually cast as a German or Nazi, sometimes sinister, utilizing a clipped English diction or a variety of foreign accents for added comic effect. His most memorable film roles are the piano teacher in *The 5,000 Fingers of Dr. T* and the man tortured by a television set from outer space in Arch Oboler's *The Twonky,* both released in 1953. His voice is probably best known in American cinema as the role of Captain Hook in Walt Disney's animated masterpiece *Peter Pan* (1953).

Conried began his radio career in 1935 and was probably one of the busiest radio performers during the 1940s and 1950s. He made numerous appearances on *Gunsmoke, George Burns and Gracie Allen, The Mel Blanc Show, The Jack Parr Show, Suspense, Maisie,* and *The Life of Riley.*

308. "Whatever Happened to Mrs. Forbush?" (11/8/74; rebroadcast from 9/16/74)

309. "Thicker Than Water" (11/9/74; rebroadcast from 9/17/74)

310. "The Garden" (11/10/74; rebroadcast from 9/19/74)

311. "Wave of Terror" (11/11/74; rebroadcast 12/29/74)

Cast: Paul Hecht (Danny Makahini); Carmen Mathews (Queen Lilliolani); Gordon Gould (Dr. Peter Hughes); Ian Martin (Carter Bradley); Suzanne Grossmann (Liz Bradley). Written by Ian Martin.

Danny Makahini and Liz Bradley, who met while attending college on the mainland and plan to get married, return to their homes in Hawaii only to be told by their parents that such a union is unthinkable. Neither Danny's mother, a Polynesian queen, nor Liz's father, a very wealthy and powerful plantation owner, believe in intermarriage. Queen Lilliolani foresees tragedy for all—even as she speaks, a great tidal wave heads for the islands.

312. "I Must Kill Edna" (11/12/74; rebroadcast 12/31/74)

Cast: Elliott Reid (Chester Masefield); Leon Janney (Fred); Evelyn Juster (Sue Ellen); Joan Lorring (Edna Masefield); Earl Hammond (Arnold). Written by Sam Dann.

Soon after he marries a millionairess ten years his senior, Chester Masefield falls in love with Sue Ellen Quackenbush, 23, whose aim is a career on the stage. Now Masefield has a young woman for excitement and romance, and a mature woman for stability and financial security. But it can't last—Sue Ellen won't stand for it.

313. "Island of the Lost" (11/13/74; rebroadcast from 9/23/74)

314. "The 36th Man" (11/14/74; rebroadcast 1/3/75, 7/22/79)

Cast: Ross Martin (Harry Cohen); Robert Harris (Jacob); Robert Dryden (Satan); Carol Teitel (Lilith); Ruth Cohen (Ann Pitoniak). Written by Sam Dann.

Shopkeeper Harry Cohen is looked upon with suspicion when he announces that the Lahmed Vovniks have chosen him to take the place of their dying 36th member. Old Jewish legend says that only when there are 36 active Lahmed Vovniks can this sinful world be saved. To prevent Harry's admission to the group, Satan moves quickly, presenting the kind and humble shopkeeper with a series of worldly temptations.

Notes: Ross Martin appeared in a handful of horror and science fiction films, including *Conquest of Space* (1955), *The Colossus of New York* (1956), and *Geronimo, Experiment in Terror* (1962). He starred as Andamo in television's *Mr. Lucky* and as Artemus Gordon in *The Wild Wild West*.

315. "The Deadly Blind Man's Bluff" (11/15/74; rebroadcast from 9/25/74)

316. "The Spectral Bride" (11/16/74; rebroadcast from 9/26/74)

317. "Murder to Perfection" (11/17/74; rebroadcast from 9/30/74)

318. "The Strange Voyage of Lady Dee" (11/18/74; rebroadcast 1/4/75)

Cast: Paul Hecht (Richard); Corinne Orr (Susie); Margaret Barker (Ann); Danny Ocko (Campbell); Augusta Dabney (Ellen). Written by Mary Jane Higby.

Sailing home from a vacation in the Caribbean, a New Jersey couple and their 7-year-old daughter Susie become fog-bound, becalmed and lost in the waters once infested by pirates. The plaintive voice of Ann Bonney, who according to island folklore is the apparition of a pirate, lures them onto a sandbar. As is the way of pirates, Ann wants to seize the sailboat. It seems, during a storm, she might be successful when she—or something—lures Susie back on board alone, and the boat sets out to sea with Susie at the helm.

Notes: Edgar Allan Poe's classic short story "The Murders in the Rue Morgue" was originally planned for this broadcast, but Himan Brown, a fan of Poe, had an idea for a week of Poe stories in January. So the script was shelved, postponed for recording and broadcast in a few weeks. Instead, Mary Jane Higby's premiere script was recorded and broadcast in its place.

319. "The Bride That Wasn't" (11/19/74; rebroadcast from 10/1/74)

320. "Tattooed for Murder" (11/20/74; rebroadcast 1/15/75)

Cast: Teri Keane (Erika Kramer); Stefan Schnabel (Otto Kramer); Ralph Bell (Jodey Prince); Rosemary Rice (Katrin Kramer). Written by Nancy Moore.

Otto Kramer has tried, since the death of his wife, to keep his two daughters locked up in the family mansion, virtually as servants catering to his every demand. But Erika, the elder, has escaped, joined a carnival and become a "Tatooed Princess," the tattoos covering the scars inflicted by her father's cane. Now Erika has come to take the younger Katrin away—but their father has no intention of allowing this to happen.

321. "The Death Watch" (11/21/74; rebroadcast 1/8/74)

Cast: Jay Gregory (Charles Fleming); Bob Dryden (Dr. John Potter); Ian Martin (Count Dravanescu); Marian Seldes (Claire Willoughby). Written by Ian Martin.

Claire Willoughby, betrothed to Charles Fleming, learns that she has been given by her father, an inept gambler, to one Count Dravanescu in payment for a gambling debt. A card shark, Fleming challenges Dravanescu to a poker game, beats him and wins back Claire. But he also accepts a gold pocket watch that must be wound by 6:00 P.M. daily, or its owner will die. Soon after, Fleming forgets to take the watch with him and realizes he can't get to it before six.

322. "The Golden Blood of the Sun" (11/22/74; rebroadcast from 10/3/74)

323. "Sister of Death" (11/23/74; rebroadcast from 10/7/74)

324. "The Doll" (11/24/74; rebroadcast from 10/10/74)

325. "The Sighting" (11/25/74; rebroadcast 1/19/75, 6/13/80)

Cast: Kim Hunter (Sarah Hughes); Nat Polen (David Hughes); Joe Silver (Allen); Bob Dryden (Dr. Froehling); Ralph Bell (Dr. Carter); Joen Arliss (Bea Vincent). Written by Fielden Farrington.

Sarah Hughes sights a flying saucer but is forbidden by her husband to mention it. The next day a man from the UFO, realizing Sarah is an understanding Earthling, hypnotizes her and implants a tiny device in the base of her brain. With it, he will be able to read and guide her thoughts from great distances, light years away. Her husband notices the change in Sarah immediately but has no idea what to do except to seek the advice of a psychiatrist.

326. "Courtyard of Death" (11/26/74; rebroadcast 1/21/75)

Cast: Norman Rose (Rasputin); Ann Pitoniak (Alexandrea); Mason Adams (Felix); Jean Gillespie (Princess Irina); Jackson Beck (Colonel Amdur); Roger De Koven (Dr. Lasovert). Written by Murray Burnett.

Rasputin, the notorious Russian monk in the court of Nicholas II, defied the death plots of his many enemies. Rasputin, a monk of peasant ancestry with hypnotic powers that helped stem the dread "bleeding" disease from which the young heir to the throne of Nicholas II and Alexandrea suffered, rouses the wrath of a doctor, the head of the secret police and the richest man in Russia because of his debauchery and alleged dealings with the German enemy. All three plot to kill him, but for reasons they don't understand, Rasputin won't die easily.

327. "Trapped" (11/27/74; rebroadcast from 10/9/74)

328. "The Aaron Burr Murder Case" (11/28/74; rebroadcast 1/25/75)

Cast: George Petrie (Lt. Baumann); William Redfield (Tony Bellows); Leon Janney (Parradine); Joan Shay (Julia); Jack Grimes (Officer Svoboda). Written by Sam Dann.

Director Maximillian Parradine is making a motion picture on the location of the historical duel between Alexander Hamilton and Aaron Burr. After the shots are fired, the actor cast as Hamilton falls to the ground dead because Tony Bellows, portraying Burr, evidently did not fire the prop pistol, but a real one. Bellows swears his innocence and the policeman who finds the pistol believes him—inscribed on the weapon are the words "Aaron Burr."

329. "A Scaffold for Two" (11/29/74; rebroadcast from 10/14/74)

330. "Picture on the Wall" (11/30/74; rebroadcast from 10/15/74)

331. "The Resident" (12/1/74; rebroadcast from 1/15/74)

332. "The Dice of Doom" (12/2/74; rebroadcast 2/12/75)

Cast: Michael Wager (Rudolph Schroll); Ian Martin (Father); Gordon Gould (Johann); Carol Teitel (Lotte); Bob Dryden (Priest). Written by Ian Martin.

Aristocratic Rudolph Schroll, his country at war, buys a commission in the army, then kills his superior officer when ordered to lead a charge against an impenetrable enemy position. Saved from execution by a roll of the dice given him by someone he thinks is a priest, Rudi, always the gambler and too often the loser, finds the dice bringing him fame and fortune. But the priest (or devil) has no intention of allowing Rudi a lifelong string of lucky rolls.

333. "Ring a Ring of Roses" (12/3/74; rebroadcast from 1/18/74)

334. "A Bride for Death" (12/4/74; rebroadcast 1/29/75)

Cast: Tony Roberts (Eric Mills); Bryna Raeburn (Martha); Earl Hammond (Jerry); Marian Seldes (Julia Sandford). Written by Sam Dann.

Poet Eric Miller, while horseback riding, comes upon a well-kept Victorian house in which young Julia Sandford, wearing clothes of the 1920s, lives. She invites him in, hoping he has news of her fiancé, missing in action in World War I. Eric's relatives think he is dreaming because the house, now badly run-down, has been lived in for the past 50 years by a recluse who's "lost her marbles." Nevertheless, Eric continues seeing Julia until her fiancé returns and acts like a spurned lover.

335. "The Body Snatchers" (12/5/74; rebroadcast 2/2/75)

Cast: Howard Da Silva (Cameron Fergus); Court Benson (Harry); Patricia Elliott (Jeannie); Kenneth Harvey (Digger); Ralph Bell (Wolfe MacFarlane). Adapted by Ian Martin, based on the 1884 short story *The Body-Snatcher* by Robert Louis Stevenson.

Told by a medical student that he can get an education as a doctor if he has a strong enough stomach and does what he is told, young Cameron Fergus finds himself involved in the procurement of cadavers for research. His job is to pay off the grave robbers and to make sure there is a constant supply, even if it means murder. Gulled and lulled into a life of crime, he can find no way out—except in alcohol.

336. "Frankenstein Revisited" (12/6/74; rebroadcast from 3/19/74)

337. "Adam's Astral Self" (12/7/74; rebroadcast from 7/23/74)

338. "The Thing Inside" (12/8/74; rebroadcast from 4/4/74)

339. "The Fatal Connection" (12/9/74; rebroadcast 2/1/75, 6/20/80)

Cast: Nick Pryor (Hal Glenford); Jennifer Harmon (Norma Glenford); Robert Maxwell (Bill Voight); Joan Shay (Maude Spencer). Written by Jennifer Harmon.

Hal and Norma Glenford inherit an ancient empty New York City brownstone that was once owned by Hal's robber baron great-grandfather. Only one room is furnished, in 1890s style, complete with an antique telephone that still works. In fun, Hal makes a call on the antique for a hansom cab, and shortly after he does so, one arrives! His wife, believing that the phone is magic of some sort, orders the whole house decorated in 1890s style. But when a call from an associate of Hal's great-grandfather comes through, Hal and his wife have their life threatened by an angry—and long-dead—client.

340. "The Damned Thing" (12/10/74; rebroadcast 2/5/75, 12/16/79)

Cast: Bob Dryden (Bentley); Arnold Moss (Professor Morgan); Robert Kaliban (William Harker); Joan Tompkins (Mrs. Morgan); Evelyn Juster (Viola Mae). Adapted by Arnold Moss, based on the short story by Ambrose Bierce.

Covered with a sheet, the body of Professor Hugh Morgan lies cold and rigid on a hand-hewn table in the mountain cabin he built himself. His wife says he was shot: his mistress (an uneducated mountain girl) says he drowned; and an Indian guide says he was snake bit. But a young newspaper reporter insists Morgan's death was caused by that "damned thing."

341. "The Last Escape" (12/11/74; rebroadcast from 10/17/74)

342. "Is the Lady Dead?" (12/12/74; rebroadcast 2/8/75)

Cast: Larry Haines (Barney Kreuger); Ann Pitoniak (Mother); Leon Janney (Winters); Joan Lorring (Rachel). Written by Sam Dann.

Concerned only with piling up a fortune, millionaire Barney Kreuger has never married—until, while driving in England, he falls in love with Rachel, whose car he hits. Married just a week, the two return to America. Seven days later, Rachel is dead—for reasons unknown. A man who in business has never accepted no for an answer, Barney vows that Rachel will live again—even if it costs him his many millions.

343. **"Mind Over Matthew"** (12/13/74; rebroadcast from 10/21/74)

344. **"Voices of Death"** (12/14/74; rebroadcast from 5/14/74)

345. **"See Naples and Die"** (12/15/74; rebroadcast from 10/23/74)

346. **"Stephanie's Room"** (12/16/74; rebroadcast 2/9/75)
Cast: Mercedes McCambridge (Stephanie Miller); Bob Dryden (Will); William Redfield (Tom Miller); Mary Jane Higby (Helen). Written by Bob Juhren.
After short stays in Chicago and Los Angeles, ad executive Tom Miller and his wife Stephanie move to New York, where Tom is sure he'll make it big. A desire to visit the house in which she grew up sends Stephanie to suburban Crestwood. There the present owner's wife allows Stephanie to see her old room. She keeps returning strangely—the room has more attraction for her than either her husband or his career.

347. **"A Cage for Augie Karo"** (12/17/74; rebroadcast from 10/24/74)

348. **"Charity Is Never Dead"** (12/18/74; rebroadcast 2/11/75)
Cast: Virginia Payne (Mrs. Chandler); Patricia Wheel (Dr. Anne Logan); William Prince (Dr. Bannine); Rosemary Rice (Charity); George Petrie (Chaplain Walters). Written by Ian Martin.
Minutes after Mrs. Margaret Chandler meets her long-lost granddaughter Charity in a department store, the building is destroyed by a boiler explosion. Mrs. Chandler's back is broken and she is also blinded. Charity suffers amnesia. The hospital staff is uncertain whether Charity is really Charity and must decide whether she should be allowed to stay with the older woman as she dies.
Notes: Virginia Payne made her first appearance in this episode. She was the daughter of a Cincinnati doctor, and broke into radio at WLW. There, she played *Honey Adams*, a singing Southern heroine in an early radio epic. Known as radio's "mother of the air," Payne starred in numerous radio soap operas. Among her most remembered roles: Mrs. Carter on *The Carters on Elm Street*, Mrs. Schultz on *Lonely Women*, Mother Schultz on *Today's Children*, and Ma Perkins on *Ma Perkins*.

349. **"The House of the Voodoo Queen"** (12/19/74; rebroadcast 2/15/75)
Cast: Jordan Charney (Douglas Fenton); Danny Ocko (Louis Lemours); Joan Lorring (Zoe Lemaitre); Renee Roy (Helen Fenton). Written by Murray Burnett.
Doug and Helen Fenton leave New York to take possession of an old, beautifully located New Orleans mansion inherited from an uncle they never knew. But someone else apparently wants the house and seems intent on scaring the Fentons out. In fact, a woman who calls herself Zoe Lemaitre offers to buy them out for $7,800, claiming the house was stolen in the 19th century from the voodoo queen of New Orleans, Marie Le Veau. The Fentons refuse the offer, but soon learn the life-long lesson that if voodoo listen to Zoe, voodoo wish you had.

350. "Possessed by the Devil" (12/20/74; rebroadcast from 10/28/74)

351. "The Black Room" (12/21/74; rebroadcast from 10/29/74)

352. "The Demon Spirit" (12/22/74; rebroadcast from 10/31/74)

353. "Give the Devil His Due" (12/23/74; rebroadcast 2/16/75)
Cast: Mercedes McCambridge (Zandra Scott); Ian Martin (John Scott); Bryna Raeburn (Carlotta); Joe Silver (Azazel); Peter Donald (Kerensky). Written by Nancy Moore.

On her fiftieth birthday, Zandra Scott, once known worldwide as the famous ballerina Alexandrea, swears she will be young and talented again, no matter what the cost. John, her husband, pleads with Zandra to see a psychiatrist. Instead, she consults a plastic surgeon, and when she receives little satisfaction there, Zandra sees a fortune teller who sends her to Azazel, a warlock. After extracting a promise that she will give over anything he asks, no matter what the price, Azazel agrees to grant Zandra her youth and talent.

354. "A Very Private Miracle" (12/24/74; rebroadcast 12/25/75, 12/23/78)
Cast: Howard Da Silva (Jasper Crown); Ian Martin (The Man); Virginia Payne (Mrs. Murchison); Evelyn Juster (Mrs. Templeton); Jennifer Marlowe (Jennifer). Written by Ian Martin.

Mutimillionaire Jasper Crown has closed down his money-losing mill, Dawson City's largest employer. Now living alone in his large mansion—his wife is dead and his children have left him—Crown ignores all pleas to reopen the plant so people can work again. That is, until a little girl, Jennifer Swallow, persuades him to dress up as Santa Claus and attend the church's annual Christmas party.

355. "How Eberhard Won His Wings" (12/25/74; rebroadcast from 11/7/74)

356. "Turnabout Is Foul Play" (12/26/74; rebroadcast 2/19/75)
Cast: Vicki Vola (Adriane); Marian Seldes (Anne Sperling); Jackson Beck (Dr. Lupescu); Mason Adams (Bill Sperling); Sidney Slon (Harold Gifford). Written by Sidney Slon.

Bill Sperling, whose wealthy wife Anne is slowly dying from an incurable disease, plots with his new, young girlfriend Adriane to commit "an act of mercy": murder Anne so he can get her money and marry Adriane. But before Bill can get up enough nerve to do it, Anne's new doctor, a believer in the curing powers of hypnotism, persuades Anne to change her will and leave *him* the money—for medical research.

Notes: Sidney Slon is not only the writer of this episode, he acts as well. Slon has written for numerous radio shows, some of which were directed by Himan Brown during the 1940s and 1950s: *Dick Tracy* and *Inner Sanctum Mysteries*.

357. "Bury Me Again" (12/27/74; rebroadcast from 11/4/74)

358. **"Terror on the Heath"** (12/28/74; rebroadcast from 11/6/74)

359. **"Wave of Terror"** (12/29/74; rebroadcast from 11/11/74)

360. **"The Golem"** (12/30/74; rebroadcast 2/22/75, 6/3/79)
Cast: Robert Lansing (Tomcek); Bob Dryden (Grandfather); Ralph Bell (Lieut. Mueller); Mildred Clinton-Marina; Patricia Elliott (Rachel). Written by Sam Dann, based on Jewish folklore.
Rachel, a young Jewish girl, and her elderly grandmother see the assistance of Tomcek, a German forester, in their flight from a German officer who will surely kill them and anyone who aids their flight. After turning them down three times, Tomcek relents and agrees to hide them in the forest. All three expect death at any moment, until the grandfather enters a trance and begins reciting an ancient Hebrew tale about a "golem" with supernatural powers.

361. **"I Must Kill Edna"** (12/31/74; rebroadcast from 11/12/74)

362. **"The Deadly Pearls"** (1/1/75; rebroadcast 2/23/75)
Cast: Paul Hecht (Keith Spencer); Court Benson (Colonel Madison); Kate Reid (Nora Babcock); Grace Matthews (Barbara Walsh). Written by Elizabeth Pennell.
A small Hawaiian island has but three inhabitants—a malicious retired colonel, an eccentric old woman and the beautiful girlfriend of a mobster. All are resentful of the intrusion of private investigator Keith Spencer, posing as a novelist, whose task is to find a string of pearls coated with radium that will bring death to the wearer. Spencer narrowly escapes death at the hands of all three, in each case a seeming accident, and determines he'll only find the owner of the pearls in a bridge game in which the stakes are very high indeed.
Notes: Paul Hecht, a young Canadian actor who made his Broadway debut in *Rosencrantz and Guildenstern Are Dead*, starred in *The Reincarnation of Peter Proud*.

363. **"The Reluctant Killer"** (1/2/75; rebroadcast 2/25/75)
Cast: Tony Roberts (Steve Janos); Roberta Maxwell (Pat Janos); Ian Martin (Parole Officer Keefer); Leon Janney (Joe). Written by Ian Martin.
Steve "Killer" Janos, an ex–professional football player, has served time for alleged wife-beating. In reality, he had only pushed her in anger when she objected to his giving up a lucrative football career (he had badly injured an opposing player). Nevertheless, she and her money-hungry mother had taken him to court. Now, on parole and able to get a truck-driving job, he vows revenge—even murder.

364. **"The 36th Man"** (1/3/75; rebroadcast from 11/14/74)

365. **"The Strange Voyage of Lady Dee"** (1/4/75; rebroadcast from 11/18/74)

366. "The Many Names of Death" (1/5/75; rebroadcast 3/1/75)

Cast: Alexander Scourby (Gerald); Marian Haley (Helene); Lori March (Cecily); William Redfield (Jerry). Written by Sam Dann.

Helene Leroux, bank trust officer Gerald Furlong's new attractive secretary and a student of what she calls nomenology, the science of names, tells her boss he's in a rut and that, though 45, he looks 55 and could look 35. Timid at first, Gerald ultimately falls for Helene's line, rents her an apartment, buys her clothes, furs and jewelry, starts gambling and even thinks of leaving his wife. Only his alter ego, Jerry, whom he keeps seeing in a mirror, warns Gerald of the consequences of his folly—but Gerald pays no attention.

367. "The Premature Burial" (1/6/75; rebroadcast 3/2/75, 9/2/79)

Cast: Keir Dullea (Guy Peterson); Paul Hecht (Dr. Gordon Rainey); Guy Sorel (Sir Giles); Marian Seldes (Victorine). Adapted by George Lowthar, based on the 1844 short story by Edgar Allan Poe.

Young Guy Peterson conspires with his doctor friend, Gordon Rainey, to open the grave of Guy's true love, Victorine, who has been dead for a week. To their horror, they find Victorine still alive, though very weak. They want to restore her to good health, but they must reckon with her husband, powerful Sir Giles Buckingham, who wants her dead so he can marry the wealthy widow who accepted his proposal three days after Victorine's "death."

Notes: In celebration of *Theater* beginning its second year on the air, a one-week special presentation was broadcast, consisting of seven adaptations of Poe tales. This marked the first of the seven, all adapted by George Lowthar. The setting in the original story of Poe's "The Premature Burial" was in France during the 19th century, but Lowthar moved it to England. Keir Dullea was currently starring in the hit Broadway revival of *Cat on a Hot Tin Roof.* Marian Seldes was currently starring in the Broadway hit *Equus.*

368. "The Murders in the Rue Morgue" (1/7/75; rebroadcast 3/15/75, 6/9/79)

Cast: Paul Hecht (Pierre Muset); Corinne Orr (Yvette); Danny Ocko (Jules Duborg); Guy Sorel (C. Auguste Dupin). Adapted by George Lowthar, based on the 1841 short story by Edgar Allan Poe.

Pierre Muset wants to become a Gendarme First Class in the Paris police force so he can marry his sweetheart, Yvette. When a grisly double murder takes place, Pierre, a slow thinker, resolves to catch the murderer and win the promotion. To do so, he reluctantly enlists the aid of C. Auguste Dupin, an amateur crime solver, who kindly agrees to help only if all the credit goes to Pierre.

Notes: According to George Lothar: "What you have here are many beautiful Poe words discussing philosophy, discussing the narrator's own situation in Paris and also how he came to meet C. Auguste Dupin, the detective. And finally, after perhaps a few thousand words, you get to those two grisly murders which Poe has Dupin solve in relatively few pages. To make this into an hour-long three-act play required more development of Poe's characters, some new characters and then their involvement in the human relationships out of which comes drama. But the Poe story is still there with all its chilling horror."

369. "The Oblong Box" (1/8/75; rebroadcast 3/9/75, 6/17/79)

Cast: Richard Mulligan (Will Hopkins); Court Benson (Cornelias Wyatt); Bryna Raeburn (Rachel); Grace Matthews (Elvira Hopkins). Adapted by George Lowthar, based on the 1840 short story by Edgar Allan Poe.

Will and Elvira Hopkins wait expectantly for Cornelias Wyatt, Will's college classmate, to come up a ship's gangplank with his beautiful new bride. But it's a plain, older woman and an oblong box that Wyatt brings on board. When Wyatt and his "wife" put their luggage in one cabin and take the box with them into an adjacent stateroom, Will and Elvira's suspicions are aroused. Only later in the voyage do they learn—to their horror—what's inside the box.

Notes: Court Benson, (who was featured with Woody Allen in the film *Bananas* [1971], and his actress-wife Grace Matthews, who had the feminine leads in two hit radio series, *Big Sister* and *The Shadow,* are cast as Wyatt and Elvira, respectively. Richard Mulligan, who plays Will, has the rare distinction of being awarded the Daniel Blum Theater World Award for his performances in two plays in one year: *Hogan's Goat,* a verse drama, and *Mating Dance,* a comedy. Mulligan's movie credits include *One Potato, Two Potato* (1964) and *Little Big Man* (1970) opposite Dustin Hoffman.

370. "Berenice" (1/9/75; rebroadcast 3/11/75, 7/29/79)

Cast: Michael Tolin (Montresor); Joan Banks (Berenice); Roberta Maxwell (Constance); Norman Rose (Anthony Lamb). Adapted by George Lowthar, based on the 1840 short story by Edgar Allan Poe.

It was Berenice's smile that attracted Ernest Montresor. He married her but now, a year later, he has grown to hate her—her sensuous smile has become an ugly sneer. And, besides, he has fallen in love with her younger sister, Constance. Montresor can't wait for Berenice, who is seriously ill, to die. She does, but on her deathbed she swears to Montresor that her smile will haunt him forever and eventually drive him to near insanity.

Notes: Michael Tolan was a leading player in CBS *The Doctors and the Nurses* and starred on Broadway in *Unlikely Heroes.* Joan Banks was recently a regular on television's *Love of Life.*

George Lowthar commented: "Edgar Allan Poe was a genius. There's no doubt about it. His language ranks among the most beautiful in the world, with its imagery, its color. The man holds you from the very first line until the very last. He was a storyteller, a master of prose. A dramatist must take the seed of his stories and fertilize it, at the same time retaining the poetic ambiance of Poe and the horror that is in his stories."

371. "The Masque of the Red Death" (1/10/75; rebroadcast 3/8/75, 6/30/79)

Cast: Staats Cotsworth (Milo Manderson); Karl Swenson (Nils); Lois Smith (Doreen); Evelyn Juster (Flossie); Jack Grimes (Jack). Adapted by George Lowthar, based on the 1842 short story by Edgar Allan Poe.

It's 1996 and multimillionaire Milo Manderson has secluded himself, several members of his family and two servants in a huge mountain retreat in order to escape the plague that is killing people by the thousands. Soon there is much bickering and, to relieve the tension, Manderson proposes a masquerade party. Enraged when one of the "guests" arrives in a blood red costume, Manderson rips off the wearer's mask only to see no face, just a blood red skull—the "red death" itself has now invaded the sanctuary.

Notes: Karl Swenson, who held the title roles in radio's *Mr. Chameleon* and *Lorenzo Jones,* once played Edgar Allan Poe in an episode of *The Cavalcade of America.*

Staats Cotsworth, a veteran actor of radio, stars as Milo Manderson in this hypnotic Poe episode. Cotsworth was a regular on other radio shows: *Big Sister, Lone Journey, Mr. and Mrs. North,* and *Roger Kilgore, Public Defender.* He also starred in such shows as *Casey, Crime Photographer, Front Page Farrell,* and *Mark Trail.*

372. "The Tell-Tale Heart" (1/11/75; rebroadcast 3/16/75, 7/1/79)

Cast: Fred Gwynne (Charles); Bob Dryden (Uncle Jonas); Ann Shepherd (Dora). Adapted by George Lowthar, based on the 1845 short story by Edgar Allan Poe.

The locale of the chilling story is moved from a dark, dank room in the city to a remote farm where Charles, who suffers from moments of insanity, has taken his wife and daughter to get away from the tensions of city life. The farm is owned by Charles' elderly uncle, who ultimately becomes the target for Charles' "perfect murder."

Notes: Fred Gwynne made his first appearance on *Theater* in this episode. He was currently starring as Big Daddy in the Broadway hit revival of *Cat on a Hot Tin Roof.* Among his many television credits were Herman Munster in *The Munsters* and Officer Francis Muldoon in *Car 54, Where Are You?*

373. "The Cask of Amontillado" (1/12/75; rebroadcast 3/19/75, 5/12/79)

Cast: Richard Kiley (Arno Montresor); Leon Janney (Inspector Murdero); Francis Sternhagen (Margarita); Robert Maxwell (Isabella); Bob Dryden (Fortunato Bellini). Adapted by George Lowthar, based on the 1845 short story by Edgar Allan Poe.

Fortunato Bellini, to whom vineyard owner Arno Montresor is deeply in debt, demands from Montresor a cask of Amontillado wine and payment of his debt. Montresor, who has borne a thousand insults from Bellini as best he is able, can find no Amontillado, nor can he pay what he owes the heartless creditor.

Notes: Richard Kiley has won the Drama Critics, the Drama Guild and the Antoinette Perry awards for his performance as Don Quixote in *Man of La Mancha* on Broadway. This marks his first role in *Theater.* Frances Sternhagen and Roberta Maxwell, both of whom have featured roles in the current Broadway hit *Equus,* are cast as Margarita and Isabella.

374. "The Witness Is Death" (1/13/75; rebroadcast 3/5/75)

Cast: Kenneth Harvey (Joe Wilson); Joan Shay (Helen Wilson); Sam Gray (Sgt. Marshall); Ian Martin (Dr. Peterson). Written by Ian Martin.

Joe Wilson, a plumber, manages to make his way to a hospital with a bullet in his stomach. He was shot after witnessing, by chance, a gunman for gangster Augie Larch put a bullet in the head of a man about to testify against Larch. The police want Wilson to identify the gunman in court. Wilson agrees to cooperate, but changes his mind when his wife insists that he, she, and their two children are doomed if he does.

375. "Faith and the Faker" (1/14/75; rebroadcast 3/22/75)

Cast: Howard Da Silva (Mr. Mather); Guy Sorel (Jud); Mary Jane Higby (Mary Mather); Russell Horton (Moses); Bryna Raeburn (Eliza). Written by Elspeth Eric.

Though he is unable to explain it rationally, a man living on a remote island where there are no doctors somehow—perhaps through faith—performs miracles for the sick. However, he can do nothing for his wife who has needed a wheelchair for years. His love for her is unswerving, but there is a secret about himself he has never told her.

376. "Tattooed for Murder" (1/15/75; rebroadcast from 11/20/74)

377. "A Death of Kings" (1/16/75; rebroadcast 3/23/75)

Cast: Mercedes McCambridge (Emma Sparling); Bob Dryden (Professor Sparling); William Redfield (Alex Thornhill). Written by Sam Dann.

Professor Frederick Sparling, who keeps his startling scientific discovery secret because he fears whoever else knows it could destroy the world, has a nagging wife, Emma. She is sick and tired of his unwillingness to assert himself—until the professor invites one of his most brilliant but poor students to live with them. Soon, the student not only wants Emma, but also her husband's secret.

378. "Ghost Talk" (1/17/75; rebroadcast 3/25/75)

Cast: Lenka Peterson (Melba); Elliott Reid (Paul); Bob Dryden (Leonard); Gordon Gould (Bruce). Written by Elspeth Eric.

Melba was a wonderful wife to Paul, but as his widow she leaves something to be desired. She won't stop loving him and she won't leave him alone. In desperation, Paul goes to a kindred spirit, Bruce, for help. The only advice Bruce can offer is for Paul to marry again—not his earthly wife, Melba, but a heavenly creature who, like Paul, expects to live on forever in whatever place it is they live on forever.

379. "The Death Watch" (1/18/75; rebroadcast from 11/21/74)

380. "The Sighting" (1/19/75; rebroadcast from 11/25/74)

381. "The Precious Killer" (1/20/75; rebroadcast 3/29/75)

Cast: Arnold Moss (Karel Vortic); Beatrice Straight (Katernia Vortic); Ralph Bell (Alaric); Danny Ocko (Rykov); Ann Pitoniak (Irena). Written by Sam Dann.

Karel Vortic, the leading scientist in the small Republic of Rourania, a dictatorship, is imprisoned and tortured for allegedly having planned to smuggle a million dollars worth of platinum out of the country. When the authorities finally realize they have made a mistake, they expect Vortic to return to his normal self and his job. But they don't know Vortic very well.

Notes: Danny Ocko was Killer Kane on radio's *Buck Rogers and the Twentieth Century.*

382. "Courtyard of Death" (1/21/75; rebroadcast from 11/26/74)

383. "Concerto in Death" (1/22/75; rebroadcast 3/30/75, 7/4/80)

Cast: Ian Martin (Anton Stern); Marian Seldes (Rebecca Stern); Lon Clark (Jack McNally); Carol Teitel (Stella Stern). Written by George Lowthar.

Conductor Anton Stern vacillates between reality—in which he accepts the death of his son Jonathan—and fantasy, convinced he hears his son practicing the violin. Despite the efforts of his manager, his wife, and his daughter, Stern believes his son is communicating through the Stradivarius violin he used to play. Finally, only his daughter is willing to make a desperate effort to bring her father back to reality.

384. "Sleepy Village" (1/23/75; rebroadcast 4/2/75, 7/11/80)

Cast: Martha Greenhouse (Wilma Albertson); Norman Rose (Ralph Albertson); Kenneth Harvey (Lucas); Court Benson (Ellis Perkins). Written by Fielden Farrington.

Wilma and Ralph Albertson find a small New England village and decide to settle there, but are told by Mayor Ellis Perkins that the village fathers will have to meet and okay it. Ralph's irritation and suspicions are allayed by Wilma's love of the village, until Lucas, the mayor's servant, tells them that all the residents are dead and they will also have to die if they want to stay.

385. "The Flowers of Death" (1/24/75; rebroadcast 4/5/75)

Cast: Mercedes McCambridge (Gretchen); Larry Haines (Walter); Robert Maxwell (Stranger); Gilbert Mack (Dr. Marks). Written by Sam Dann.

Mrs. Gretchen Morrison, at first irritated, relaxes when the stranger who says he's the god Dionysus volunteers to make her dying flower garden flourish. He also changes her attitude toward life—much to the consternation of her husband, whose career in business depends upon a wife whose every move must meet standards set by his boss.

Notes: In 1973 Mercedes McCambridge provided the foul off screen voice of the Demon for the soundtrack of the film *The Exorcist,* which remains uncredited. "It was really a radio performance," she said. "The demon was never seen, it's merely what people heard on the sound track. If they threw up and fainted while seeing the film, what they were being so revolted by was the microphone; the receiving side of it for the listener is just as vital as anything going into that microphone."

386. "The Aaron Burr Murder Case" (1/25/75; rebroadcast from 11/28/74)

387. "The Follower" (1/26/75; rebroadcast 4/6/75)

Cast: Jerry Orbach (Jim Beecher); Nat Polen (Murray Schneider); Jackson Beck (Dr. Braun); Carol Teitel (Louise Beecher). Written by Ian Martin.

After a lifetime of cutthroat dealing with no remorse, theatrical agent Jim Beecher cannot understand his fear of something which seems to be dogging his footsteps. No one else hears the steps, and Jim is persuaded by his wife Louise and friend Murray to see a psychiatrist. With Dr. Brau's help, Beecher realizes whatever is following him is rooted in what's left of his conscience. Concluding the follower is an old lover whose death he caused, Beecher finds the courage to confront the ghost, but what he sees is deathly shocking.

Notes: Jerry Orbach made his first appearance on in this episode. His film credits range from the voice of the French candlestick in Walt Disney's *Beauty and the Beast* (1991) to Jennifer Grey's father in *Dirty Dancing* (1987). Orbach is probably best known for his role as Lennie Driscoll on NBC television's *Law and Order*.

388. "A Coffin for the Devil" (1/27/75; rebroadcast 4/8/75)

Cast: Keir Dullea (Bill Spindles); Peter Collins (Stranger); William Redfield (Jerry Barker); Marian Seldes (Lucy); Nat Polen (Edward Rogers). Written by Murray Burnett.

A professor and a young couple try to determine what really happened 100 years ago when a stranger ordered from a mortician a coffin of unusual design for himself. With an inside lock and hinges, the coffin also had enough room for its occupant to move arms. And when it was completed, the stranger carried it, as if it were a pillow, to a nearby cemetery, apparently walking with it through the cemetery gates.

389. "Windandingo" (1/28/75; rebroadcast 4/12/75)

Cast: Jack Grimes (Jabez Follansbee); Court Benson (General Burgoyne); Bryna Raeburn (Aunt Martha); Mason Adams (John Follansbee); Earl Hammond (Sheriff). Written by Sam Dann, based on actual historical events.

Hardly anybody believed young Jabez Follansbee when he claimed, back in 1777, that he could communicate, at any midnight, with an Indian demon he called Windandingo, and that Windandingo would see to it that justice was done. British General John Burgoyne was one of the nonbelievers until he decided to hang Jabez for treason. The true story of how an obscure backwoodsman and an American Indian spirit helped defeat the British at Saratoga.

390. "A Bride for Death" (1/29/75; rebroadcast from 12/4/74)

391. "The Night of the Wolf" (1/30/75; rebroadcast 4/13/75)

Cast: Michael Tolan (Lt. George Miller); Russell Horton (Terry Jessup); Evelyn Juster (Polly Atkins); Kenneth Harvey (Prescott); Joan Shay (Myra Miller). Written by Sam Dann.

Police lieutenant George Miller determines to find out why former all-pro middle linebacker Terry Jessup suddenly, and for no apparent reason, turned on his wife. Miller is intrigued by the fact that in the same area of the museum, two lifelong friends had previously engaged in a fist fight and another man had emptied his pockets and started taking off his clothes. All had been examining an ancient ceremonial robe said to have belonged to the High Priest of the Wolf Clan.

392. "The Disembodied Voice" (1/31/75; rebroadcast 4/16/75)

Cast: Celeste Holm (Dr. Margaret Hunter); Bob Dryden (Larry Hamden); Mildred Clinton (Nurse Parks); Wesley Addy (Detective Peter Grant). Written by Ian Martin.

Dr. Margaret Hunter, a hospital psychiatrist, reports a series of obscene phone calls to the police, who suspect they are from a murderer the newspapers are calling "the grim reaper." He had made similar calls to two nurses before killing them. Even though under police protection, Dr. Hunter is startled late one night in her apartment by a man armed with a knife and a gun. Though terrified, she tries to use her psychiatric training to dissuade the intruder.

393. "The Fatal Connection" (2/1/75; rebroadcast from 12/9/74)

394. "The Body Snatchers" (2/2/75; rebroadcast from 12/5/74)

395. "Death on Skiis" (2/3/75; rebroadcast 4/19/75, 7/18/80)

Cast: Rosemary Murphy (Kay Wylie); Larry Haines (Dan Wylie); Ralph Bell (Tony Shaw); Norman Rose (Otto Hornbach). Written by George Lowthar.

Kay Wylie, always doing things people warn her not to do, reaches a hut accompanied by Tony Shaw, a friend of just three days. Shaw confides that he's really a detective secretly assigned to solve the two murders and that he's taken her to the hut as a lure for the murderer who, he's convinced, is her husband. Shaw says he'll wait outside the hut and burst in before her husband can kill her. But not everything is as it seems.

396. "Death in the Stars" (2/4/75; rebroadcast 4/20/75)

Cast: Kim Hunter (Amanda Amherst); Ian Martin (Ralph Amherst); Rosemary Rice (Nancy Amherst); Mary Jane Higby (Ethel Nixon); Paul Hecht (Adam Brock). Written by Ian Martin.

Amanda Amherst—ruthless, even evil in the opinion of some, but still very beautiful—has managed her husband's chain of newspapers since his death in a strange crash of his private plane. Her daughter and brother-in-law think she was in some way responsible and are in no way upset when they hear that the astrology column in one of her papers predicts her imminent death. But Amanda is perplexed. The column appeared in only one copy of the papers—the one she receives at home.

397. "The Damned Thing" (2/5/75; rebroadcast from 12/10/74)

398. "The Sire de Maletroit's Door" (2/6/75; rebroadcast 4/22/75, 8/26/79)

Cast: Michael Wager (Denis); William Redfield (Champs Divers); Marian Seldes (Blanche); Bob Dryden (Sire). Adapted by Ian Martin, based on the 1878 short story by Robert Louis Stevenson.

Denis de Beaulieu is chased down a dark street by hooligans and tries to hide in the shadows of a doorway. To his surprise, the door opens. As he backs in, the door suddenly shuts. It has no inner latch. He is trapped by the Sire de Maletroit, who has had the door designed to ensnare the young man who dares to send love notes to the sire's beautiful niece, Blanche. But he's caught the wrong man, who faces death unless he consents to a marriage with Blanche.

399. "Death Is So Trivial" (2/7/75; rebroadcast 4/26/75)

Cast: Tony Roberts (James); Suzanne Grossman (Cynthia); Danny Ocko (Dr. Hatch); Bryna Raeburn (Daisy); Kristoffer Tabori (Crowley). Written by Elspeth Eric.

James Blake is killed by a drunken driver, and because he died so needlessly, he assumes supernatural powers and vows to spend the rest of his afterlife preventing any more such unnecessary deaths. He prevents a woman from choking to death, a commercial airliner from crashing, a killing during a holdup, a woman from taking poison by mistake and a bomb from exploding in a supermarket. But he does have trouble preventing a war and ending starvation.

400. "Is the Lady Dead?" (2/8/75; rebroadcast from 12/12/74)

401. "Stephanie's Room" (2/9/75; rebroadcast from 12/16/74)

402. "Journey Into Nowhere" (2/10/75; rebroadcast 4/27/75)

Cast: Arnold Moss (Dr. Carlo Oresti); Joan Banks (Dorothy); Court Benson (Mahmoud Bin Said); Evelyn Juster (Girl). Written by Arnold Moss.

Determined to find the secret of Magaera, an ancient goddess, archeologist Dr. Carlo Oresti is excavating in the Mideast when an earth tremor splits open the site. A shard of pottery and talisman are recovered, clues to Magaera's reputed power to instill people with the spirit of revenge. Dr. Oresti hopes to expose the legend but to do so he must take on a town full of suspicious people who firmly believe the goddess has the power to kill anyone who tries to find her out.

Notes: Arnold Moss, who wrote this episode, stars as well. Moss appeared in numerous radio shows such as *Yours Truly, Johnny Dollar, Suspense, Cafe Istanbul, X Minus One,* and *The NBC Radio Theatre.*

403. "Charity Is Never Dead" (2/11/75; rebroadcast from 12/18/74)

404. "The Dice of Doom" (2/12/75; rebroadcast from 12/2/74)

405. "A Small Question of Terror" (2/13/75; rebroadcast 4/30/75, 8/1/80)

Cast: Teri Keane (Alexis Meade); Gordon Gould (Eric); Leon Janney (Director); Joan Shay (Emily Meade). Written by George Lowthar.

Thoroughly frightened by stories of the tortures other people have undergone at the hands of the Director, Alexis Meade, a young and attractive woman, engaged to be married, can think of nothing that she, as a good citizen, should tell him. Later, she recalls that her mother had said once, as a joke, "Someday our Protector will protect us to death." Treasonous words, and Alexis' fiancé, while being tortured, admits that Alexis said that her mother did say them. But Alexis vows never to confirm this, no matter what happens to her.

406. "The Shadow of the Past" (2/14/75; rebroadcast 5/3/75)

Cast: Howard Da Silva (Dr. Benno Koenig); Jack Grimes (Tommy); Sam Gray (Karlheinz Meier); Gilbert Mack (Billingham); Clarice Blackburn (Rosa Koenig). Written by Sam Dann.

Dr. Benno Koenig, a friend of the poor, treats a slum rent collector suffering from an eye injury, then recognizes the man, Karlheinz Meier, as the commander of the Nazi concentration camp in which he was confined. Fearing Koenig will seek revenge for his treatment in the camp, Meier threatens to expose the fact that Koenig is in the United States illegally. In a rage, Koenig stabs him, then maintains the murder was justified—until a young punk is arrested for it.

Notes: Gilbert Mack played Chick Carter's pal Tex on the radio show *Chick Carter, Boy Detective.*

407. "The House of the Voodoo Queen" (2/15/75; rebroadcast from 12/19/74)

408. "Give the Devil His Due" (2/16/75; rebroadcast from 12/23/74)

409. "The Death Wisher" (2/17/75; rebroadcast 5/4/75)

Cast: Michael Zaslow (Anton Gitano); Court Benson (Blake Cutler); Roberta Maxwell (Barbara Cutler); Jada Rowland (Belinda Cutler); Ann Pitoniak (Mrs. Cutler). Written by Ian Martin.

The quiet, well-ordered life of the Cutler family is suddenly disrupted with the arrival at their mansion of young and handsome Anton Gitano, whose father had saved Mr. Cutler's life during the Battle of Gallipoli. Gitano, who secretly suffers from satyriasis and whose past is a mystery, terrorizes the entire family, but especially one of the Cutler daughters, when he demonstrates a supernatural power—he can kill any living thing or person by simply wishing them dead.

410. "Love Me and Die" (2/18/75; rebroadcast 5/6/75)

Cast: Mason Adams (Steve Barlow); Ann Shepherd (Emily Barlow); Robert L. Green (Dr. Rossman); Bob Dryden (Bert Phillips). Written by Sam Dann.

Steve and Emily Barlow's honeymoon is shattered when Emily is convinced she sees her former husband, Bert Phillips, who dies in a fall. Steve persuades Emily that what she is seeing is an illusion, until he too, begins to see Bert, who claims that Emily has caused the fall that killed him, and that she will also kill Steve. Determined to resolve the situation forever, Steve takes Bert's advice and brings Emily back to the scene of the accident (a fatal mistake for one of them).

Notes: Scheindel Kalish began her radio career during the 1930s and when she was hired for the role of Betty Fairfield on *Jack Armstrong, the All-American Boy* she changed her name to Ann Shepherd. Soon after, she began appearing on such shows as *The Affairs of Peter Salem* and *Lora Lawton*. She also starred in the lead role on *Joyce Jordan, Girl Intern,* which was also directed by Himan Brown.

411. "Turnabout Is Foul Play" (2/19/75; rebroadcast from 12/26/74)

412. "Must Hope Perish" (2/20/75; rebroadcast 5/10/75)

Cast: Hugh Marlowe (Senator Prentiss); Ian Martin (Pop); Evelyn Juster (Dolly); Bob Dryden (Dr. Starik); Marian Seldes (V.K. Krestin). Written by Sam Dann.

Senator Marvin Hale Prentiss is absolutely opposed to open trade relations with the Peoples Republic of Doriaj. One reason: a little book of poems smuggled out of the country calling for internal revolt. The first three lines of the book's first poem begin with the letters M, H and P—the senator's initials. Often the poet also writes, "Must hope perish," again words that begin with M, H and P. The senator feels he cannot ignore these desperate pleas for help.

413. "The Weavers of Death" (2/21/75; rebroadcast 5/11/75)

Cast: Mandel Kramer (Sgt. Bob Clifton); Robert Kaliban (Lester Crain); Catherine Byers (Dora); Joseph Silver (Mr. Wainwright); Bryna Raeburn (Dr. Spero). Written by Sam Dann.

Three people, including Eleanor Brodey, are killed in a grocery store holdup. Police sergeant Bob Clifton, once engaged to Eleanor, soon discovers that the holdup was only staged to make it appear that she was an accidental victim of an ordinary holdup. She was actually murdered because of her knowledge of the swindle her new boyfriend, Lester Crain, is about to pull. With little to go on, Clifton decides to confront Crain directly, not knowing that Crain's partner is desperate enough to kill again.

414. "The Golem" (2/22/75; rebroadcast from 12/30/74)

415. "The Deadly Pearls" (2/23/75; rebroadcast from 1/1/75)

416. "Hell Hath No Fury" (2/24/75; rebroadcast 5/14/75)

Cast: William Redfield (Mark Stanton); Patricia Wheel (Emily Lawrence);

Kenneth Harvey (Sergeant Harkness); Teri Keane (Elspeth Whitmore). Written by Ian Martin.

Mark Stanton, a has-been classical actor, smothers to death his popular and wealthy actress wife, Emily Lawrence, when he learns she is planning to cut down on his allowance and change her will. Because he plotted the murder so carefully, he is sure no one will ever be able to prove he did it. But Elspeth Whitmore, Emily's half-sister who once thought Mark was hers, suspects him and soon proves that "hell hath no fury like a woman scorned."

417. "The Reluctant Killer" (2/25/75; rebroadcast from 1/2/75)

418. "The Strange Case of Lucas Lauder" (2/26/75; rebroadcast 5/17/75, 8/8/80)

Cast: Robert Lansing (Lucas Lauder); Lenk Peterson (Joan Lauder); Patricia Peardon (Miss Compley); Ira Lewis (Eric); Ralph Bell (Guy Richards). Written by George Lowthar.

Guy Richards, a respected university professor, has admitted to the brutal knife murders of four women. Now about to die, he tells Warden Lucas Lauder that when he is executed the evil spirit of Jack-the-Ripper will be passed on to the warden just as it was passed on to him. Lauder, though convinced Richards is insane, starts toying with a carving knife that very night and even—for reasons he cannot explain—threatens his wife.

Notes: Robert Lansing has appeared in numerous science-fiction, horror and mystery films, including *The 4D Man* (1959), *The Grissom Gang* (1971), *Empire of the Ants* (1977), *Island Claw* (1980), *The Equalizer: Memories of Manon* (1988), and *Namu, the Killer Woman* (1966).

419. "Them!" (2/27/75; rebroadcast 5/18/75)

Cast: Jordan Charney (Charles Schiller); Alan Hewitt (Matthew Caine); Evelyn Juster (Agatha Caine); Augusta Dabney (Karen Schiller); James Ducas (Sergeant Steiner). Written by Ralph Goodman.

Soon after Charles Schiller is acquitted by a jury on a manslaughter charge, he is invited to visit the mansion of Matthew Caine, a former judge and lawyer. Caine believes he is better qualified to judge a person guilty or innocent, and has judged Schiller guilty and locks him up in a cell in his mansion for life. The police are very interested—Schiller is the fourth man recently acquitted of manslaughter or murder to disappear.

420. "An Identical Murder" (2/28/75; rebroadcast 5/20/75)

Cast: Robert Maxwell (Ann Slater); William Redfield (Vince Benton); Bob Dryden (Harry); Elliott Reid (Jack Benton). Written by Murray Burnett.

Ann Slater knows that both Jack and Vince Benton, identical twins, are in love with her, though neither Ann nor Jack is prepared for Vince's angry reaction when he learns of their engagement. After Vince's death in a mountain climbing accident, Ann feels free to marry Jack—until Vince's ghost appears, intent on breaking up the romance. Realizing the ghost has more of Jack's characteristics than his brother's, Ann begins to worry that she is marrying the wrong man.

Notes: Murray Burnett not only writes but directs, too. During the 1940s and 1950s, he produced and directed the radio show *True Detective Mysteries*, which presented case histories of actual crimes. Burnett also wrote the episodes for his mystery series.

421. "The Many Names of Death" (3/1/75; rebroadcast from 1/5/75)

422. "The Premature Burial" (3/2/75; rebroadcast from 1/6/75)

423. "The Wakeful Ghost" (3/3/75; rebroadcast 5/24/75)

Cast: Paul Hecht (Brian Macken); Ian Martin (Uncle Terence); Leon Janney (Shawn Dailey); Jada Rowland (Sheila O'Shaughnessy); Virginia Payne (Mary Dailey). Written by Ian Martin.

Hoping to locate his relatives in a remote corner of Ireland, Dr. Brian Macken steps off a train and is most surprised to be met by a man named Terence, who claims to be his great-uncle. Terence says he will take Brian to his aunt and uncle, the Daileys. Terence maintains he learned of Brian's arrival from his leprechaun friend, Malachy Molloy, which Brian doesn't believe. He is even more confused when the Daileys claim Terence has been dead thirty-five years and is now a banshee who can appear in the world at will. Brian's skepticism soon dissipates when he falls in love with Sheila O'Shaughnessy and finds he can't marry her without considerable help from both Terence and Malachy.

Notes: According to Himan Brown: "The enthusiasm we have created in an age group of 12–28 is remarkable, since that is a generation that never knew the excitement of a "theater of the mind." They absolutely are television children, born and raised to that medium, and never had to think about words as they were being entertained. And of course, all the older generation fondly remembers the fun of radio and have found they can recapture the joys of youth through the dramas we present on *CBS Radio Theater*."

424. "The Pit and the Pendulum" (3/4/75; rebroadcast 5/25/75, 7/8/79)

Cast: Tony Roberts (Tod Stearns); Norman Rose (Mr. X); Marian Seldes (Tammy Stearns). Adapted by George Lowthar, based on the 1843 short story by Edgar Allan Poe.

Tod Stearns, a secret agent for the government, is kidnapped along with his wife while driving in a limousine to the airport. Their kidnapper, Mr. X, representing a group in the business of selling top secret information from one country to another, demands to know the new bacterial gas formula Stearns is carrying in his head. Otherwise, it's the pendulum for his wife or the pit for both of them.

Notes: According to George Lowthar: "Some Poe fans may say we have not dramatized the stories exactly as he wrote them. They would be right, but no adaptation into dramatic form can follow any story exactly. I think if Poe were alive today, he would not have the slightest objection to what we have done because if he were writing for radio or television, he would have done the same thing. Poe would have realized what I realize—that you've got to have a dramatic plot line. He would know that the very word itself, drama, in the original Greek, means action. And if you don't have action, you have no drama."

425. "The Witness Is Death" (3/5/75; rebroadcast from 1/13/75)

426. "When the Death Bell Tolls" (3/6/75; rebroadcast 5/28/75)

Cast: Mary Jane Higby (Mrs. Harcourt Stanton); Ian Martin (Dr. Hobbs); Joan Banks (Laura Trent); Russell Horton (Dr. Renzulli); Rosemary Rice (Olivia Trent). Written by Ian Martin.

A high-speed collision with a stone wall leaves Laura Trent dead in a smashed car and the life of her husband Dana hanging by a thread. Doctors at a nearby hospital decide he needs a vital operation and seek permission from his daughter, Olivia. Trent's mother-in-law, Mrs. Harcourt Stanton, informs them that Olivia is underage and only she can sign the release, which she refuses to do, declaring that she will kill Trent anyway if they save his life.

427. "The Eye of Death" (3/7/75; rebroadcast 5/31/75, 8/15/80)

Cast: Joan Hackett (Sandy Oakes); Ralph Bell (Greg Manchester); Bob Dryden (Joe Norman); Joan Shay (Rose Oakes). Written by George Lowthar.

Greg Manchester, whose first wife died from an overdose of sleeping pills, marries the mother of a talented photographer, Sandy Oakes. When her mother drowns in a bathtub and Manchester inherits all the Oakes' family money, Sandy becomes certain her mother's death was no accident and accuses Manchester of having murdered her. She hopes that someday he will make a mistake and that she will be there to record it on film.

428. "The Masque of the Red Death" (3/8/75; rebroadcast from 1/10/75)

429. "The Oblong Box" (3/9/75; rebroadcast from 1/8/75)

430. "The Stuff of Dreams" (3/10/75; rebroadcast 6/1/75)

Cast: Marian Seldes (Mae Cook); Jack Grimes (Eddy); Danny Ocko (Man); Bryna Raeburn (Hilda Tipton). Written by Elspeth Eric.

Mae Cook answers an ad in her local paper, not knowing what Mrs. Hilda Tipton, a recluse for 20 years, could possibly want from her. Mae finds that Mrs. Tipton spends her time daydreaming and wants Mae only to live her normal life, for which she's willing to pay a handsome salary if only Mae will report to her once a week and give her fresh material for daydreams. Not a naturally adventurous person, Mae soon finds the arrangement disturbing, but a friend, Eddy, an ex-convict, convinces her that he can fill Mrs. Tipton's needs very well.

Notes: Jack Grimes, who plays Eddy in this episode, could occasionally be seen on television as Mr. Whitehead, the undertaker in *All in the Family*, and as Henry Peterson, the postman in *Maude*.

431. "Berenice" (3/11/75; rebroadcast from 1/9/75)

432. "The Dark Closet" (3/12/75; rebroadcast 6/3/75)

Cast: Fred Gwynne (Seth Connors); Jada Rowland (Julie Connors); Kris Tabori (Tim Sandler); Earl Hammond (Rev. Sam Prior); Frances Sternhagen (Dr. Sarah Browning). Written by Ian Martin.

Unable to sleep at night due to a recurring nightmare in which young Julie Connors finds herself locked in a small, dark room, she disobeys her strict father's edict and arranges a clandestine date with Tim Sandler. When he picks her up, Tim's plans include holding up a liquor store. Unaware of his actions, Julie is nevertheless arrested and finds herself in a prison cell, living the nightmare. Her father, Seth, refuses to bail her out, while a psychiatrist and minister do their best to keep Julie from going insane.

433. "Death Pays No Dividend" (3/13/75; rebroadcast 6/7/75)

Cast: Ann Shepherd (May Hanigan); Guy Sorel (Victor Ellis); Kenneth Harvey (John Folger); Court Benson (Kent Green). Written by Mary Jane Higby.

Certain they'll be jailed for misjudgment of funds, three partners of a Wall Street firm plot their own deaths. If they commit suicide, their wives can collect no life insurance so they make a contract with a professional killer to shoot them. After one has been killed, the other two and their secretary learn of an old investment in a gold stock that can cover the firm's losses. But how can they stop the killer, whom they've never seen, from completing his contract?

434. "The Cezar Curse" (3/14/75; rebroadcast 6/8/75)

Cast: Richard Kiley (George Capewell); Roberta Maxwell (Marla Cezar); Ian Martin (Doctor); Ann Pitoniak (Senora Cezar); Robert Kaliban (Felipe Cezar). Adapted by Murray Burnett, based on a short story by Robert Louis Stevenson.

George Capewell is recovering from a near fatal illness and is sent by his doctor to live in the Spanish countryside with the Cezar family, mother, daughter and son, on one condition—that he share not the slightest intimacy with any of them. By chance, he meets the daughter Marla, falls in love with her, and proposes marriage. But she is trapped by a nameless but genuine fear, and so she cannot accept.

Notes: Richard Kiley began his professional career on radio and played many character roles, often as a heavy, in numerous Hollywood films of the 1950s. Among his films are *The Mob* (1951), *The Sniper* (1952), *Pickup on South Street* (1953), *The Blackboard Jungle* (1955), *The Phoenix City Story* (1955), *The Spanish Affair* (1958) and *The Little Prince* (1974).

435. "The Murders in the Rue Morgue" (3/15/75; rebroadcast from 1/7/75)

436. "The Tell-Tale Heart" (3/16/75; rebroadcast from 1/11/75)

437. "Every Blossom Dies" (3/17/75; rebroadcast 6/11/75)

Cast: Michael Tolan (Bill Maitland); George Petrie (Jerry Ferris); Catherine Byers (Georgia Temple); Evelyn Juster (Barbara Maitland). Written by Sam Dann.

Police detectives Bill Maitland and Jerry Ferris are assigned to investigate the murder of nightclub singer Georgia Temple, shot three times with a .22 pistol. As their investigation proceeds, Ferris becomes alarmed when the evidence—identification of his voice by a blind woman, a note written to his wife, his unexplained purchase of some flashy clothes—indicates that his partner, Maitland, could be the murderer. Maitland, however, remains completely unconcerned.

438. "It's Murder, Mr. Lincoln" (3/18/75; rebroadcast 6/14/75)

Cast: Keir Dullea (Abe Lincoln); Paul Hecht (Franklin Jones); Bob Dryden (Ephraim Barnes); Joseph Silver (Tom Fellman); Jennifer Harmon (Emily Jones). Written by Sam Dann.

It's 1837 in Springfield, Illinois, when Franklin Jones, who fought the Seminole Indians in Florida, arrives in town and announces in front of both Tom Fellman and Ephraim Barnes that he is going to kill wealthy farmer Cyrus Darrow, who owes him money. That night Darrow is shot with Jones' gun. Though Jones proclaims his innocence, no lawyer will take his case except young Abe Lincoln, who has never defended anyone accused of murder.

Notes: Keir Dullea made his New York debut in 1956 in the revue *Sticks and Stones,* and after appearing off Broadway in 1959 in *Season of Choice,* made an impressive film debut as a disturbed juvenile delinquent in *The Hoodlum Priest* (1961). He played another disturbed youth in *David and Lisa* (1963), a role for which he won the best actor award at the San Francisco Film Festival. He went on to portray a number of intense, sensitive young men in other films and is now remembered for his role of Commander Bowman in *2001: A Space Odyssey* in 1968.

439. "The Cask of Amontillado" (3/19/75; rebroadcast from 1/12/75)

440. "The Doppelganger" (3/20/75; rebroadcast 6/15/75)

Cast: Howard Da Silva (Dr. Felix Brandt); Rosemary Rice (Frank Brandt); Russell Horton (Hank Randolph); Tony Roberts (Hugh Prentiss). Written by Ian Martin.

Dr. Felix Brandt becomes enraged when his daughter, Fran, refuses to tell him who caused her pregnancy and then arranged for an abortion by an inexperienced medical student. A psychology professor whose avocation is parapsychology (the exploration of the mystic), Dr. Brandt vows to use his advocation to make the young man pay for what he has done to Fran. The punishment, he says, will be "an unspeakable crime, worse, far worse than murder."

441. "The Man Must Die" (3/21/75; rebroadcast 6/17/75)

Cast: William Prince (Dr. Joseph Bailey); Augusta Dabney (Helen Bailey); Ian Martin (Warden); Kris Tabori (Jack Bailey). Written by Elspeth Eric.

Judge Joseph Bailey, about to sentence a young murderer, is badgered by his son, Jack, who insists the murderer be executed. Jack sincerely believes that his generation has been overly pampered by parents and that severe punishment by wrongdoers is an absolute necessity. When the judge orders 20 years to life for the murderer, Jack denounces him, declaring that someday he will be sorry for what he has done, "just you wait and see."

442. "Faith and the Faker" (3/22/75; rebroadcast from 1/14/75)

443. "A Death of Kings" (3/23/75; rebroadcast from 1/16/75)

444. "The Deadly Double" (3/24/75; rebroadcast 6/21/75)

Cast: Marian Seldes (Anita Gregory/Susan Gregory); Bob Dryden (Max Hogan); Leon Janney (Sheriff Wiley). Written by Sam Dann.

Five years ago, a budding artist named Anita Gregory found it necessary to place her twin sister Susan in a mental institution. When Susan escapes, she calls on her sister, meets her in a lonely locale, knocks her unconscious, changes clothes and purses and drives away in her car. Anita is found by Sheriff Wiley and taken back to the institution where everyone thinks she is Susan. When Anita warns them that Susan is likely to commit murder, the authorities still won't listen to her.

445. "Ghost Talk" (3/25/75; rebroadcast from 1/17/75)

446. "Death Is a Dream" (3/26/75; rebroadcast 6/22/75)

Cast: Mercedes McCambridge (Mary Collins); Michael Wager (John Hodges); Jack Grimes (Charles); Bryna Raeburn (Dora); Robert Kaliban (Lt. Frank Miller). Written by Sam Dann.

Mary Collins, who teaches English in the middle class section of town, cannot understand why the police have been unable to apprehend the killer of her brother, a cop, gunned down while on duty in the slum area. Determined to find the killer himself, she wrangles a transfer to the slum school—but everybody is suspicious of her and no one will even give her the right time of day.

447. "The Velvet Claws" (3/27/75; rebroadcast 6/25/75)

Cast: Gordon Gould (John Latour); Evelyn Juster (Ilse Duschenes); Gilbert Mack (Driver); Arnold Moss (Dr. Hazard). Written by Murray Burnett.

Vacationing in France, John Latour, a middle-aged bachelor of fixed habits, finds himself inexplicably drawn into a French town where all the inhabitants have feline characteristics and appear to know him. A series of accidents prevent him from leaving, and he falls in love with Ilse, daughter of the innkeeper, the most cat-like of them all. Isle is convinced Latour is the reincarnation of a long-ago warlock and urges him to join a fiery, demonic celebration of his return.

448. "Key to Murder" (3/28/75; rebroadcast 6/28/75, 10/3/80)

Cast: Mercedes McCambridge (Rachel James); Mary Jane Higby (Minerva Hall); Bob Dryden (Lt. Mike Forbes); Robert Maxwell (Inspector Morris). Written by George Lowthar.

Mrs. Rachel James fears she must sell her old brownstone house since two of her boarders have been found dead in their rooms—apparent suicides, the gas heaters turned on, the doors and windows locked from the inside. But the police, when they discover that each was unconscious before the gas asphyxiated them, suspect murder. Before he can make such a charge stick, however, Lt. Forbes must figure out how the murderer was able to lock the doors and windows from the inside.

Notes: Mercedes McCambridge commented: "We rely on each other—and it's great. Nobody is on a starvation diet, nobody has to worry about getting their noses fixed, no leading man is standing there with the makeup man fixing the spit curl in front of his forehead the way some of them do in films. I can't get used to that. But it doesn't happen in radio—talent is either there or it isn't and the audience is getting nothing more than what you can convey with one sense, speech. Everything has to be behind that, literally everything. And it requires an accelerated, even an enlarged amount of, adrenaline and concentration."

449. "The Precious Killer" (3/29/75; rebroadcast from 1/20/75)

450. "Concerto in Death" (3/30/75; rebroadcast from 1/22/75)

451. "Killer of the Year" (3/31/75; rebroadcast 6/29/75)

Cast: Norman Rose (Harry Johnson); Teri Keane (Wilma Sloane); Joan Shay (Jenny Johnson); Nat Polen (Pete); Kenneth Harvey (Clerk). Written by Sam Dann.

During a dinner in honor of his community work, Harry Johnson is introduced to the town's beautiful new librarian, Wilma Sloane. Harry recognizes her for what she is—an escaped convict sentenced to life imprisonment for the murder of a married lover, who wanted to leave her. When the perfect opportunity arises to turn Wilma over to the local police, Harry finds that he can't do it. Bewildered by her beauty and sophistication, he slips into an affair with her, realizing before long he will have to decide between Wilma and his wife Jenny. But when Harry tried to tell Wilma it's over, her reaction stuns him.

452. "The Killer Inside" (4/1/75; rebroadcast 7/1/75)

Cast: Anne Meara (Gwendolyn Wilkinson); Earl Hammond (Toby Hazlitt); Ian Martin (Norman); Bryna Raeburn (Momma). Written by Sam Dann.

Gwendolyn Wilkinson, 30 and single, wins first prize in a raffle—a ten-day trip to London. Her mother doesn't think she should go; she might lose her timid boyfriend of three years, a fellow teacher at the university. But he insists she go, taking with her an envelope for his London friend, Toby Hazlitt. Shortly after she delivers the envelope, Hazlitt, an alleged secret agent, is murdered. Gwendolyn was the last person to see him alive and is accused of the crime.

Notes: Anne Meara has appeared in numerous films, including *Heavyweights* (1994), *The Out-of-Towners* (1970), *My Little Girl* (1987), and *Fame* (1980).

453. "Sleepy Village" (4/2/75; rebroadcast from 1/23/75)

454. "The Garrison of the Dead" (4/3/75; rebroadcast 7/5/75)

Cast: Mandel Kramer (Andy Masefield); Leon Janney (Jerome Carlson); Joan Banks (Marguerite); Robert Kaliban (Mr. Paris); Court Benson (Mr. Fallowfield). Written by Sam Dann.

Andy Masefield helps Jerome Carlson write an article on how a fraudulent real estate deal is put together. It's Andy's true story, and Carlson later feels compelled to testify against him. To prevent this, Andy kills Carlson, arranging beforehand to have a witness swear he was 37 miles away at the time of the murder. But as he's leaving the scene of the crime, Andy is stopped by a policeman and told his license plate number has just made him a winner in a radio giveaway show.

455. "Roses Are for Funerals" (4/4/75; rebroadcast 7/6/75, 9/5/80)

Cast: Carole Shelley (Rose Corbin); Mildred Clinton (Ruth North); Danny Ocko (Emil); Tony Roberts (Hank North). Written by George Lowthar.

Approached in an airport by a woman who desperately wants to buy her coat, Rose Corbin refuses and later learns the woman has been murdered. Rose and her fiancé Hank are then attacked by a man who is also after the coat. After a second murder her pursuers succeed in stealing the coat, but the murders don't stop, and Rose still doesn't know what she has that people are willing to kill for.

456. "The Flowers of Death" (4/5/75; rebroadcast from 1/24/75)

457. "The Follower" (4/6/75; rebroadcast from 1/26/75)

458. "The Benjamin Franklin Murder Case" (4/7/75; rebroadcast 7/9/75)

Cast: Paul Hecht (Benjamin Franklin); Russell Horton (Richard La Porte); Gilbert Mack (Chiver); Staats Cotsworth (Abner); Marian Seldes (Sarah Clemmons). Written by Sam Dann.

A fine old Philadelphia house stands empty because its owner, young Sarah Clemmons, cannot afford the upkeep, yet she can't sell it because of the ghosts that reputedly reside there. Sarah and her cousin, Richard La Porte, persuade a prospective buyer, Mr. Chiver, to investigate the house at night to disprove the ghost theory, but Chiver is murdered there. Sarah calls on Benjamin Franklin to solve the mystery, and a likely suspect is arrested, only to be let go when a button and piece of thread proves his innocence. Franklin then realizes he must reexamine the story of a most unlikely suspect.

459. "A Coffin for the Devil" (4/8/75; rebroadcast from 1/27/75)

460. "The Altar of Blood" (4/9/75; rebroadcast 7/12/75)

Cast: Fred Gwynne (Professor Wells); Mason Adams (Bill Hallas); Ian Martin (The Alcade); Jennifer Harmon (Maria Wells). Written by Ian Martin.

Archaeology professor J. Hallington Wells and his daughter Maria are in Mexico for an extended vacation when they find land for a house they want to build. Digging the foundation, they strike a huge stone and are catapulted into an underground chamber built by an ancient Aztec tribe. Exploration leads them into the middle of a ceremony with which Maria feels strangely familiar, and which demands the sacrifice of one of them to the rain god.

461. "The Death of Halpin Fraser" (4/10/75; rebroadcast 7/13/75, 11/17/79)

Cast: Michael Wager (Halpin Fraser); Grace Matthews (Katy Fraser); Court Benson (Beau Fraser); Arnold Moss (Voice); Patricia Elliott (Mary Ellen). Written by Arnold Moss.

Halpin Fraser had always been especially close to his mother, Katy, and it shocks her deeply when he announces his plans of marrying Mary Ellen Shelby and moving to California. Katy vows with a vengeance that she and Halpin will be together again. Ten years later, Halpin kills his wife in a fit of rage and, forced to hide from the law, he finds himself lost in a terrible nightmare from which he cannot escape.

462. "The Phantom Stop" (4/11/75; rebroadcast 7/15/75)

Cast: Norman Rose (Alvin Freidberg); Nat Polen (Marvin Schreiber); Carol Teitel (Esther); Bryna Raeburn (Sarah). Written by Ian Martin.

Henpecked and ill, Alvin finds little satisfaction in his life, until he begins riding a new subway to work. The train hurtles past a stop, 35th and Neely, but Alvin determines to find a way to get off there, imagining his lovely first wife, Sarah, now dead, will meet him there as she did in their youth. When he realizes the price he will have to pay to get off, Alvin must decide between his present unhappiness and possible happiness in an unknown world.

463. "Windandingo" (4/12/75; rebroadcast from 1/28/75)

464. "The Night of the Wolf" (4/13/75; rebroadcast from 1/30/75)

465. "The Intermediary" (4/14/75; rebroadcast 7/19/75, 8/29/80)

Cast: Frances Sternhagen (Laura Ellingwood); Leon Janney (Jonas Clark); Ralph Bell (Frank Ellingwood). Written by Fielden Farrington.

Frank Ellingwood, a young, successful engineer, is left a sizable inheritance by his stepmother—provided he and his wife Laura, move into the Long Island mansion in which his stepmother lived and where he grew up, very unhappily. He says no to the money, but Laura visits the mansion, falls in love with it and insists they move in. Frank reluctantly agrees, but soon wishes he hadn't. Laura begins to talk and act like his hated stepmother.

Notes: After her *Mystery Theater* appearance, Frances Sternhagen went on to be cast in such films as *Doc Hollywood* (1991), *Misery* (1990), *Raising Cain* (1992), *Who'll Save Our Children?* (1982), *Romantic Comedy* (1983), and *Bright Lights, Big City* (1988).

466. "My Own Murderer" (4/15/75; rebroadcast 7/20/75)

Cast: Mandel Kramer (Joseph Vincent); Bob Dryden (Dr. Abrams); Ian Martin (Mike); Catherine Byers (Anita); Suzanne Grossmann (Penny); Sam Gray (Pete). Written by Henry Slesar.

Joseph Vincent, rich because of his successes on Wall Street, blacks out on occasion and wakes up in a flea-bag hotel to discover words like "death" and "next time you die" scrawled with soap on the bathroom mirror. Convinced he's trying to murder himself because of his feelings of guilt for his wife's death in an automobile accident, Joe seeks help from a psychiatrist. The psychiatrist has doubts about Joe's story—until he learns that Joe has sneaked out of his apartment again, this time carrying a straight razor.

467. "The Disembodied Voice" (4/16/75; rebroadcast from 1/31/75)

468. "Through the Looking Glass" (4/17/75; rebroadcast 7/23/75, 9/19/80)

Cast: Jack Grimes (Sid Jones); Evelyn Juster (Tottie Jones); Ken Harvey (Mr. Driscoll); Anne Shepherd (Kathy Sellers); Russell Horton (Doug Sellers). Written by Fielden Farrington.

Doug Sellers is astounded when his new next-door neighbor, Sid Jones, shows him his invention: a solar energy motor the size of a vacuum cleaner with enough power to pull a 15-car freight train. When Sid offers to give him the engine, no strings attached, Doug rushes to his boss, the head of Driscoll Motors. Driscoll, a conservative businessman, sees the machine destroying the world's economy. He declares Sid Jones a dangerous spy and send the police to arrest him.

469. "A Challenge for the Dead" (4/18/75; rebroadcast 7/26/75)

Cast: Howard Da Silva (Johnny Gordon); Bob Dryden (Mike Perry); Leon Janney (Pop); Teri Keane (Claire Gordon). Written by Sam Dann.

Father Jim was killed 20 years ago when a young punk broke into the church to steal a solid gold chalice. Police officer Johnny Gordon is certain Mike Perry, now the most powerful racketeer in town, was the murderer even though at the time he and Mike were pals. They were also both in love with Claire—now Johnny's wife—who can't understand her husband's almost fanatic desire to convict Mike. She becomes even more confused when she meets Mike again, inadvertently.

470. "Death on Skiis" (4/19/75; rebroadcast from 2/3/75)

471. "Death in the Stars" (4/20/75; rebroadcast from 2/4/75)

472. "Sting of Death" (4/21/75; rebroadcast 7/27/75; 8/22/80)

Cast: William Prince (Trevor Costain); Marian Seldes (Jacqueline); Martha Greenhouse (Elizabeth); Tony Roberts (Roger Campion). Written by George Lowthar.

A clock with human thigh bones for human hands and shrunken human skulls marking the hours, the work of a tribal chieftain, hangs in the trophy room of retired, ailing explorer Trevor Costain. When his son-in-law finds one of the shrunken skulls, which marked the hour of seven on the clock, on his bed pillow, he dies instantly at that hour. The Costain's wife finds another skull, which marked noon—or midnight—on the clock, on her pillow. Noon passes, but at midnight she dies, too, in the living room in front of the entire family. The only clue: Both victims have been poisoned.

473. "The Sire de Maletroit's Door" (4/22/75; rebroadcast from 2/6/75)

474. "Afraid to Live—Afraid to Die" (4/23/75; rebroadcast 7/29/75)

Cast: Jada Rowland (Ellen Muir); Ann Pitoniak (Hester Milgrim); Ian Martin (Joe Wellman); Joan Shay (Meg O'Meara). Written by Ian Martin.

Ellen Muir is brought to Malverne Grange, an isolated, spooky mansion, by her aunt to help with the plain work and sewing. Ellen is warned not to go near Madame Lytton, now 99 and confined to her room. But curiosity gets the best of Ellen, who tiptoes into the Madame's boudoir, awakens her and becomes terror-stricken when the old woman leaps out of bed "like a corpse come to life" and threatens to tear Ellen apart with "her nails mounted on her fingers like long knives."

475. "Bullet Proof" (4/24/75; rebroadcast 8/2/75, 9/12/80)

Cast: Patricia Elliott (Kim Starke); Mason Adams (Rocky Starke); Earl Hammond (Frank Starke); Ian Martin (Fat Jack); George Petrie (Lieutenant Chambers). Written by Ian Martin.

Rocky Starke, back with his wife Kim after two years in jail, is accused of murdering Johnny Mallory, a thug with whom Rocky, now a night watchman, has had some decided differences of opinion. The bullets that killed Mallory were fired from Rocky's gun which, he admits, has never left him since he got the watchman's job. Only the owner of a shooting range says he can help Rocky, but he is gunned down on his way to police headquarters.

476. "Till Death Do Us Join" (4/25/75; rebroadcast 8/3/75)

Cast: Donald Scardino (Godfrey Schalken); Guy Sorel (Gerard Boekman); Arnold Moss (Vanderhausen); Roberta Maxwell (Rose). Adapted by Ian Martin, based on a story by Joseph Sheridan Le Fanu.

Master painter Gerald Boekman, not knowing that his niece Rose is secretly in love with one of his students, Godfrey Schalken, arranges her marriage to Mynheer Vanderhausen, a vile but exceedingly wealthy old man. When Rose meets Vanderhausen, she is repelled by his ugliness but finally consents. Four months after the wedding, Boekman worries because he has not heard from Rose. He sends Schalken to Rotterdam to find her, but both she and the old man have disappeared.

477. "Death Is So Trivial" (4/26/76; rebroadcast from 2/7/75)

478. "Journey Into Nowhere" (4/27/75; rebroadcast from 2/10/75)

479. "The Phantom of the Opera" (4/28/75; rebroadcast 8/6/75, 5/20/79)

Cast: Gordon Gould (Robert Grand); Paul Hecht (Paul Durennes); Carol Teitel (Christine Donat); Court Benson (Eric). Adapted by Murray Burnett, based on the 1910 novel by Gaston Leroux.

Robert Grand, age 38, is astounded when the man he is replacing as manager of the Paris opera house tells him he must deal with "the opera ghost." Grand orders the monthly payments stopped and determines to sell Box 5 to whoever wants it. At the next performance, Christine Donat, in her stage debut, sings beautifully but faints immediately afterward. The following night, despite tight security, the opera house's giant chandelier falls into the audience, killing three and injuring several others. The ghost is obviously someone to be taken seriously.

480. "Black Widow" (4/29/75; rebroadcast 8/9/75)

Cast: Hetty Galen (Martha Hawthorne); Bob Dryden (John Hawthorne); Evelyn Juster (Lillian Hawthorne); Jackson Beck (Max Gonger); Danny Ocko (Hank Thomas). Written by Bob Juhren.

John Hawthorne, running for president of a small, independent union, is killed by a hit-and-run driver. The police say there are no clues and no witnesses, but Martha, John's wife, sincerely believes those opposing her husband in the election ordered his death. Seeking revenge, she visits Caro, a reader and advisor, who gives her a black bottle with orders never to open it "until the time comes." Now Martha has to arrange a "time" to meet her husband's enemies.

481. "A Small Question of Terror" (4/30/75; rebroadcast from 2/13/75)

482. "Mad Monkton" (5/1/75; rebroadcast 8/10/75)

Cast: Kris Tabori (David Elmsie); Marian Seldes (Ann Elmsie); Paul Hecht

(Chip Travers); Russell Horton (Stephen Monkton); Kenneth Harvey (Capuchin). Written by Ian Martin.

Ann Elmsie, only 20, has agreed to marry Stephen Monkton, who, in the opinion of some people, has inherited the madness that has run through generations in the Monkton clan. When Stephen suddenly goes to Europe and his letters become less and less frequent, a heartbroken Ann persuades her brother, David, to track down Stephen and find out what he means when he refers to the "ghastly secret" the two lovers may have to face for the rest of their lives.

483. "The Final Witness" (5/2/75; rebroadcast 8/12/75)

Cast: Lou Jacobi (Oliver Gearhart); Joan Lorring (Cassandra Gearhart); Robert Maxwell (Rocky); Leon Janney (Junior Ellsworth); Bryna Raeburn (Momma Ellsworth). Written by Sam Dann.

Oliver Gearhart gives the police a detailed description of the young stick-up artist who shot down his store-owner friend, Ferenc Hoffman. Despite his wife's protests, Oliver points a finger at the killer, Junior Ellsworth, at a police lineup and announces he will be the chief prosecution witness in court. But Momma Ellsworth, a racketeer, determines to change his mind, telling Oliver she will guarantee Mrs. Hoffman and her sickly daughter a handsome income for the rest of their lives—if he keeps quiet.

Notes: Lou Jacobi has appeared in numerous films such as *Amazon Women on the Moon* (1987), *Arthur* (1987), *The Diary of Anne Frank* (1959), *Next Stop, Greenwich Village* (1976), *Song Without End* (1960), and *Everything You Ever Wanted to Know About Sex (but Were Afraid to Ask)* (1972).

484. "The Shadow of the Past" (5/3/75; rebroadcast from 2/14/75)

485. "The Death Wisher" (5/4/75; rebroadcast from 2/17/75)

486. "The Paradise of the Devil" (5/5/75; rebroadcast 8/16/75)

Cast: Larry Haines (George Colby); Peter Collins (Gerald Hawkins); Gilbert Mack (Ritchie); Robert Kaliban (Pete); Catherine Byers (Louise Ladue). Written by Sam Dann.

The police assume the motive is robbery when a warehouse night watchman is murdered, but they have no clues to the killer. Not satisfied with their progress, Louise Ladue, daughter of the slain man, hires private detective George Colby, who discovers that Ladue's partner in a business deal had been murdered three weeks before. Louise attempts to sell a piece of land owned by her father to pay Colby's fee, but Colby suspects the prospective buyer, Mr. Hawkins, is involved in the murder when he discovers the land holds a sizable vein of uranium ore. Impetuously, Louise confronts Hawkins with the evidence and walks into a trap set by a ruthless killer.

487. "Love Me and Die" (5/6/75; rebroadcast from 2/18/75)

488. "The Transformation" (5/7/75; rebroadcast 8/17/75)

Cast: Kevin McCarthy (Guido); Bob Dryden (Torella); Evelyn Juster (Juliet);

Ian Martin (Father Pellegrini). Adapted by Elspeth Eric, based on the 1831 short story by Mary W. Shelley.

A handsome young man named Guido, living more than a century ago in Genoa, is refused, because he is destitute, the hand of his childhood sweetheart Juliet. Despondent, he becomes a beachcomber and one day encounters an ugly, misshapen dwarf who offers to trade his chest full of jewels for Guido's handsome face and figure—for just three days. Guido reluctantly agrees, but three days later the dwarf fails to appear and Guido is certain he is seeking the hand of Juliet.

489. "Taken for Granite" (5/8/75; rebroadcast 8/20/75)

Cast: Howard Da Silva (Pietro Franzoni); Jim Dukas (Dr. Kellerman); Bob Dryden (Arnold Larsen); Joen Arliss (Helen Masterson); Joan Shay (Shelly Curtis). Written by Hank Warner.

The Menotti Sculpture Garden becomes the scene of much speculation when a man and woman disappear after visiting there. Caretaker Pietro Franzoni, a sculptor himself, swears the visitors left the garden alive. Shelly Curtis, photographer for an arts magazine, is the garden's next visitor, but she runs for her life when a statue reaches out to touch her, calling her name.

490. "Voices of Death" (5/9/75; rebroadcast 8/23/75)

Cast: Norman Rose (Bert Fowler); Earl Hammond (Arthur Davis); Ian Martin (Ronnie Anderson); Mary Jane Higby (Miss Hastings). Written by Sam Dann.

Bert Fowler, a top executive in an electronics company and upset because he has not been named its president, comes upon a radio crystal set he built and won a prize for while in high school. Not only does the set pick up news of the 1920s, it warns him that unless his generation performs better, the world will soon end. When nobody believes what he's hearing, Fowler, called insane by most of his friends, vows to somehow make them believe.

491. "Must Hope Perish" (5/10/75; rebroadcast from 2/20/75)

492. "The Weavers of Death" (5/11/75; rebroadcast from 2/21/75)

493. "For Tomorrow We Die" (5/12/75; rebroadcast 8/24/75)

Cast: Beatrice Straight (Jessie Lipscombe); Ralph Bell (Harry Taylor); Nat Polen (Hotel Detective); Evelyn Juster (Pesh Craig); Russell Horton (Don Craig). Written by Ian Martin.

Convicted of murdering his wife for her money, though he has steadfastly proclaimed his innocence, Harry Taylor is paroled after 25 years in jail. He is welcomed to the home of a former girlfriend, Jessie Lipscombe, now a well-to-do widow living with her daughter and son-in-law, Pesh and Don Craig. None of the three knows of his alleged crime or his years in jail, but Don, a young lawyer, is suspicious of his motives—especially when Taylor, claiming he is a wealthy stockbroker, lures Jessie to New York and leaves his fingerprints on a champagne glass that Don takes to the police.

494. "Where Angels Fear to Tread" (5/13/75; rebroadcast 8/26/75, 9/26/80)

Cast: Michael Tolan (Ken Robinson); Bob Dryden (Chief Laner); Court Benson (Junius Dutton); Bryna Raeburn (Mildred Robinson). Written by George Lowthar.

Ken Robinson is a professor of parapsychology and has learned by means of extraordinary disciplines—certain yoga breathing exercises, fasting, continence, meditation—to free his astral body from its earthly prison. The first time it happens he cannot recall what he did, until the owner of a local bar and grill presents him with a $600 bill for damages. The second time he does remember. To his horror, he thinks he has murdered someone. The third time he does commit murder, but not even the police will believe him.

495. "Hell Hath No Fury" (5/14/75; rebroadcast from 2/24/75)

496. "Deadly Dilemma" (5/15/75; rebroadcast 8/30/75)

Cast: Patricia Elliott (Angie Parsons); William Prince (Captain Barnett); Hetty Galen (Sister Theresa); Ian Martin (Lt. Stokes); Earl Hammond (Scott Wilson). Written by Ian Martin.

Flight 801 is warned by ground control that one of its passengers might be a mad bomber ready to blow himself, the plane and the President of a troubled South American country who is on board out of the sky. To prevent such a catastrophe, Captain Deke Barnett orders head stewardess Angie Parsons to somehow casually check all handbags in the plane's cabin. As she is doing this, ground control confirms that there is indeed a bomb carrier on board.

497. "The Rise and Fall of the Fourth Reich" (5/16/75; rebroadcast 8/31/75, 10/10/80)

Cast: Paul Hecht (Gunther Binder); Joseph Silver (Dr. Bundershaff); Bob Dryden (Adolf Hitler); Kenneth Harvey (Dr. Stiller). Written by Henry Slesar.

Dr. Hans Bundershaff and a man who calls himself Gunther Binder travel to Mexico City in their search for Adolf Hitler and find him, near death, alone on the third floor of a dingy hotel. Using the latest medical techniques, Dr. Bundershaff manages slowly to rejuvenate the old Nazi leader. Then, with a little urging, Hitler announces his readiness to return to Germany and to start a push that will make him Der Füehrer once again.

498. "The Strange Case of Lucas Lauder" (5/17/75; rebroadcast from 2/26/75)

499. "Them!" (5/18/75; rebroadcast from 2/27/75)

500. "The Diamond Necklace" (5/19/75; rebroadcast 9/3/75, 6/23/79)

Cast: Mandel Kramer (Henry Smith); Marian Seldes (Matilda Smith); Leon

Janney (Mr. Mountjoy); Bryna Raeburn (Mrs. Forester). Adapted by George Lowthar, based on the 1884 short story *The Necklace* by Guy de Maupassant.

Hard-luck Henry Smith, out of work, is overjoyed when he is invited to attend a party at the home of his last employer, the owner of Mountjoy's Department Store. At Henry's insistence, his wife Matilda spends the last of their meager savings on an expensive evening gown and borrows a priceless diamond necklace from a friend. But there has been a mistake. Mountjoy's secretary mislabeled the invitation—it was meant for a Henry Smythe. Heartbroken, the Smiths return home only to discover to their horror that Matilda had lost the necklace. They borrow money at high interest to pay for the necklace and live a life of hell as they try to make good on the loan.

501. "An Identical Murder" (5/20/75; rebroadcast from 2/28/75)

502. "Don't Let It Choke You" (5/21/75; rebroadcast 9/6/75)

Cast: Robert L. Green (Carleton Fiske); Jennifer Harmon (Gerry); Ann Pitoniak (Wanda); Larry Robinson (Cokie); Court Benson (Bascombe). Written by Ian Martin.

Carleton Fiske, a wealthy, confirmed bachelor of elegant taste, is made the ward of a distant relative, a scruffy 17-year-old, teenaged girl. Bascombe, Fiske's devoted manservant, is even more appalled at Gerry's arrival as he learns the police are questioning Fiske about the murders of three former girlfriends and a wealthy customer of his. When Gerry expresses her admiration for Fiske, Bascombe decides to take the situation into his own hands—literally.

503. "Return to Shadow Lake" (5/22/75; rebroadcast 9/7/75, 10/24/80)

Cast: Nat Polen (Ken Harris); Joan Banks (Martha Harris); Joan Lorring (Claudia Ralston); Robert Maxwell (Lou Potts); Robert Kaliban (Stu Ralston). Written by Fielden Farrington.

Stu Ralston, looking for his wife Claudia, missing for a year, goes to Shadow Lake and sees intruders in a neighbor's cottage. Alarmed by the news, Ken and Martha Harris drive up in a heavy snowstorm to check out their cottage, and they become trapped there. Martha hears voices and the fireplace mysteriously blazes, but the cottage is apparently empty except for themselves. That night they witness a scene between an unearthly Claudia and the Ken of a year ago.

504. "Markheim: Man Or Monster?" (5/23/75; rebroadcast 9/9/75, 8/19/79)

Cast: Kevin McCarthy (Carl Markheim); Ian Martin (Dr. Devlin); Guy Sorel (Winston Childers); Grace Matthews (Gertrude Childers); Rosemary Rice (Grace Childers). Adapted by Ian Martin, based on the 1885 short story *Markheim* by Robert Louis Stevenson.

Carl Markheim, angered when he doesn't receive an expected large inheritance, plots to guarantee a life of luxury for himself by marrying Grace Childers, a teenager who has long adored him. When her father says no, Markheim makes her pregnant. His score so far: He's committed most of the deadliest sins and begun to break the Ten Commandments. His goal is within reach.

505. "The Wakeful Ghost" (5/24/75, rebroadcast from 3/3/75)

506. "The Pit and the Pendulum" (5/25/75; rebroadcast from 3/4/75)

507. "The Witches' Almanac" (5/26/75; rebroadcast 9/13/75)

Cast: Jada Rowland (Kathy Pryor); Virginia Payne (Sarah Warlock); Marshall Borden (Patrick Trent); Danny Ocko (Dr. Callios); Bob Dryden (Jason Warlock). Written by Ian Martin.

Sarah and Jason Warlock fear their flourishing business, manufacturing "PV" witches' brew, will falter unless they find a new supply of virginal human blood and advertise for a young female boarder who they hope will meet their needs. Kathy Pryor, a young woman from Ohio, is delighted to take a room with such nice people, although she wonders what the Warlocks do with all those lovely old bottles filled with a hideous liquid. Her new friend, police reporter Patrick Trent, soon figures it out when he writes a story about a mysterious death. Scared by Kathy's relationship with Trent, the Warlocks plan to kill her, telling Trent she moved out suddenly.

508. "The Executioner" (5/27/75; rebroadcast 9/14/75, 10/17/80)

Cast: Tony Roberts (Jack Burton); Marian Seldes (Sandy Burton); Jacqueline Brooks (Mrs. Drood); Arnold Moss (Sir Leonard). Written by George Lowthar.

Stranded at dusk on a rainy English moor, Sandy and Jack Burton head for the nearest shelter, an old castle, where Sir Leonard Hastings-Brook invites them to spend the night. Though warned not to approach a certain room, Jack's curiosity overwhelms him and he witnesses a mock beheading replete with Elizabethan-era costumes. Furious, Sir Leonard accuses Jack of spying on Queen Elizabeth I and orders him beheaded. Locked in another room, Sandy figures the only way to save Jack is by beating Sir Leonard at his own game.

509. "When the Death Bell Tolls" (5/28/75; rebroadcast from 3/6/75)

510. "Just One More Day" (5/29/75; rebroadcast 9/17/75)

Cast: Theodore Bikel (Eddie Mason); Jackson Beck (Frank); Kenneth Harvey (Lucas); Jack Grimes (Tommy); Evelyn Juster (Myra Mason). Written by Sam Dann.

Patrolman Eddie Mason, for 27 years one of the city's finest, dreams the night before the day he is to retire that he will finally find it necessary to use his revolver in the line of duty. That day a woman on Mason's beat spots a most-wanted criminal buying a newspaper. Though Mason doesn't know it, the hood is planning a heist of a nearby jewelry store and, as the end of Mason's last day nears, a series of events seems to make a confrontation between them inevitable.

Notes: This was the first episode to feature guest Theodore Bikel, who since the early 1950s, has played character parts in numerous American and British films. His first film was John Huston's *The African Queen* in 1952, and he can be seen in *I Want to Live!* (1958), *My Fair Lady* (1964), *The Russians Are Coming, the Russians Are Coming* (1966), and *My Side of the Mountain* (1969). In 1958 he was nominated for an Oscar for his performance in *The Defiant Ones*. Bikel was also an established folk singer and guitarist and became active in New York City politics with the Greenwich Village Independent Democrats a few years after this broadcast.

511. "Someday I'll Find You" (5/30/75; rebroadcast 9/20/75)

Cast: Betsy Palmer (Anne Markle); Joan Shay (Madge Conners); Robert Maxwell (Detective Holmes); Larry Haines (Roger Markle). Written by Bob Juhren.

Anne Markle refuses to accept the fact that her husband died in a cave-in in Arizona. Visiting a Mexican border town with her sister Madge, Anne comes upon a portrait of her husband Roger, painted three months after his "death." After talking with the artist, Anne is even more convinced that Roger is alive, and she begins a search for him that takes her to Acapulco, Los Angeles, and finally Chicago, always just a few days or a few hours behind him.

512. "The Eye of Death" (5/31/75; rebroadcast from 3/7/75)

513. "The Stuff of Dreams" (6/1/75; rebroadcast from 3/10/75)

514. "River of Hades" (6/2/75; rebroadcast 9/21/75)

Cast: Marian Seldes (Vera Radlova); George Petrie (Alexia Cole); Richard Lynch (David March); Norman Rose (Max Bohmer); Bryna Raeburn (Grace Cole). Written by Mary Jane Higby.

Soon after ballerina Vera Radlova arrives in the United States for an appearance with a famous dance company, a detective assigned to guard her is poisoned, her manager's office is ripped apart by an explosion, and she receives threatening calls at her unlisted phone number. Still, Radlova agrees to perform the dangerous ballet, "River of Hades," on a tricky platform stage. Another call warns her not to go to the theater on opening night. But Radlova disregards the threat and feels she'll be safe dancing with Alexis Cole, the only person with no apparent motive for wishing her dead.

515. "The Dark Closet" (6/3/75; rebroadcast from 3/12/75)

516. "The Devil's Leap" (6/4/75; rebroadcast 9/30/75)

Cast: Mercedes McCambridge (Elizabeth Monroe); Ian Martin (Chad Reynolds); Kristoffer Tabori (Perrico); Bob Dryden (Don Emilio). Written by Ian Martin.

Elizabeth Monroe, a beautiful and famous actress, spends a summer in Spain and meets wealthy Don Emilio Escobar and his handsome son, Perrico. Elizabeth soon learns that Emilio's wife died five years earlier under suspicious and tragic circumstances, and that father and son have blamed each other for her death ever since. When both fall in love with Elizabeth, all the old passions are rekindled. Emilio and Perrico each want to marry her and, when she turns both down, she fears for her life.

Notes: Mercedes McCambridge began performing on radio while she was still a college student, and she soon became one of the busiest and most respected radio actresses in the country. Orson Welles, who costarred with her in *The Ford Theatre* series, called her "the world's greatest living radio actress." After several successful appearances on Broadway in the late 1940s, she was invited to Hollywood and won an Academy Award as best supporting actress for her very first screen role, in *All the King's Men* (1949). Orson Welles never forgot McCambridge, even years later when he asked for her acting work in his 1958 film *Touch of Evil.*

517. "The Plastic Man" (6/5/75; rebroadcast 10/3/75)

Cast: Don Scardino (George Hartford); Russell Horton (Matt Hartford); Joan Lorring (Laura Prentiss); Catherine Byers (Jane). Written by Ian Martin.

Despite the exhortations of his brother to find the right woman, get married and settle down, George Hartford, a breaker of the hearts of many women, can't resist lithesome Laura Prentiss whom he meets on a beach in Mexico. He also falls for the car she drives—a racing green Mercedes. The only trouble is he doesn't know she's married to a rich and powerful man whose powers of ESP keep him informed of her every move.

518. "The Transformer" (6/6/75; rebroadcast 10/4/75)

Cast: Howard Da Silva (Roger Wilson); Teri Keane (Dolly Wilson); Earl Hammond (Lieutenant Kaufman); Mandel Kramer (Chappie). Written by Sam Dann.

Minutes after Roger Wilson and his wife Dolly meet Roger's Korean War buddy, "Chappie" Chapman, for dinner, a leading Chicago gangster is shot to death on the street. When Roger admits to Chappie that he cannot be promoted to sales manager until his boss dies, the boss is found dead a few hours later. Then another man in Roger's way is also killed, causing him to wonder whether Chappie has become a professional "transformer." The police think Roger has.

519. "Death Pays No Dividend" (6/7/75; rebroadcast from 3/13/75)

520. "The Cezar Curse" (6/8/75; rebroadcast from 3/14/75)

521. "Fallen Angel" (6/9/75; rebroadcast 10/5/75)

Cast: Ralph Bell (Lawrence Maitland); Jack Grimes (Jason James); Carol Teitel (Pauline Maitland); Joseph Silver (Jack Brody); Court Benson (Dr. Kramer). Written by Elspeth Eric.

Sensing that the angel who usually sits on the return lever of his typewriter has temporarily deserted him, author Lawrence Maitland awaits her return in a local bar. Jason Jones, a young writer, recognizes Maitland and approaches, hoping to discuss his work with the eminent author, but gets punched in the mouth instead. Jones calls the police and Maitland passes out, waking up in a sanitarium under the care of a psychiatrist. Maitland sees little hope of finding his much-needed angel until Jones visits him and takes his word that there is such an angel.

522. "The Queen of Darkness" (6/10/75; rebroadcast 10/8/75)

Cast: Julie Harris (Josephine Dennison); Bob Dryden (Duke Arsan); Gordon Gould (Harold Foster); Evelyn Juster (Tecla). Written by Sam Dann.

Josephine Dennison is a destitute New York actress much in need of a job. When she is offered $25,000 from the Grand Duke of Dalhran to portray the queen of Dalhran, she accepts. Despite the protests from her own government, she becomes the first American citizen to cross into the foreign country in 50 years. Once in Dalhran she starts rehearsing her role, practicing the words the Grand Duke has taught her. Only when one of her ladies-in-waiting translates her lines does Josephine realize that her queenly role has political implications she never suspected.

Notes: Julie Harris made her Broadway debut in 1945 and almost immediately won recognition for her sensitive and subtle portrayal of complex roles. She established herself as a star in 1950 in *The Member of the Wedding*, a role she would later repeat in her 1952 screen debut. Harris went on to make many distinguished stage and television appearances, winning several Tony and Emmy awards in the process. Here she makes her radio debut, in this episode of *Mystery*.

523. "Every Blossom Dies" (6/11/75; rebroadcast from 3/17/75)

524. "A Case of Negligence" (6/12/75; rebroadcast 10/10/75)

Cast: Marian Seldes (Dr. Francis Downing); Mason Adams (Dr. Brian Marshall); Robert Kaliban (Dr. Tom Shafer); Alan Hewitt (Don Clay); Hetty Galen (Doria Clay); Gilbert Mack (Charles Clay). Written by Ian Martin.

Young Tom Shafer gets his first chance to perform an operation when his sister, Dr. Francis Downing, handles one emergency and he takes another, an old man with acute appendicitis. Shortly after the operation the old man dies and his son, Dan Clay, threatens to sue, claiming Tom's inexperience caused his father's death. What the hospital authorities don't know is that Clay wanted his father dead, hoping the money he might be left would pay off his many debts.

525. "Stairway to Oblivion" (6/13/75; rebroadcast 10/11/75)

Cast: Ann Shepherd (Julia); Guy Sorel (Uncle Caleb); Mary Jane Higby (Emily); Nat Polen (John). Written by Elizabeth Pennell.

Arriving to visit her Uncle Caleb, whom she's never met, Julia is surprised to find that he lives high on a mountain, miles away from any civilization. His house, "Oblivion," is macabrely decorated, and he has named his cat Crepe Hanger.

Caleb is pleasant to Julia, but she can't help wondering about the three graves in his herb garden. Emily and John, summer neighbors, point out other suspicious aspects and warn Julia to leave. Wavering, Julia is spared the decision when Caleb makes a move that convinces her of what he's really like.

526. "It's Murder, Mr. Lincoln" (6/14/75; rebroadcast from 3/18/75)

527. "The Doppelganger" (6/15/75; rebroadcast from 3/20/75)

528. "The Smile of Deceit" (6/16/75; rebroadcast 10/12/75)

Cast: Jennifer Harmon (Velma Hastings); Arnold Moss (Robert Hastings); Joan Shay (Aunt Rose); Bob Dryden (Denis). Written by Sam Dann.

Velma Straight shocks her Aunt Rose when she announces her engagement to Robert Hastings, three times her age, and admits that she expects soon to be a young, wealthy widow. Hastings' work as an anthropologist takes them to a South American jungle to observe a primitive tribe whose immortality and harboring evil spirits forces them to drink from the Spring of Bitter Waters. If innocent, they will survive, if guilty the water is said to kill them. Though disbelieving, Velma is forced to take the test when she is accused of adultery with Hastings' young assistant.

529. "The Man Must Die" (6/17/75; rebroadcast from 3/21/75)

530. "Frame-Up" (6/18/75; rebroadcast 10/26/75, 11/7/80)

Cast: Mercedes McCambridge (Jen Palmer); Leon Janney (Chat Chatterton); Bryna Raeburn (Lieutenant McCloskey); Ian Martin (Nick Palmer). Written by George Lowthar.

Nick Palmer, unfaithful to his wealthy wife, Jen, and living off her income, vows he will frame her for murder if she, as promised, takes away his allowance and power of attorney. Jen does both and, true to his word, Nick is able to convince the police that Jen killed, in a fit of jealousy, a woman who was painting his portrait. It looks like a perfect crime because Jen can come up with no alibi. Only her teacher, Chat Chatterton, thinks there is a flaw in Nick's story, but he can't seem to figure out what it is.

Notes: "Just think," remembered Mercedes McCambridge. "A few minutes ago I stood in front of a microphone opposite a man I've known for about thirty years, Leon Janney, looking into his eyes for the support I need and he's looking into my eyes for the support he needs. There is a mutual vulnerability, a trust, a certain kind of reliant love in radio that you just don't get anywhere else."

531. "The Climbing Boy" (6/19/75; rebroadcast 10/17/75)

Cast: Marian Seldes (Maria True); Evelyn Juster (Lady Emily); Court Benson (Lord Rodney); Ian Martin (Lord Agramont). Written by Elspeth Eric.

Lady Emily Hollander discovers after the death of her son that she can remove her spirit from the world by entering a "dead spell," and communicate with the dead. Her husband, Lord Rodney, carelessly causes the death of a young boy, despite entreaties from her friend Maria. Later, when a chimney fire kills Rodney, Maria wonders how much Emily had to do with the incident.

532. "Can You Trust Your Husband?" (6/20/75; rebroadcast 10/18/75)

Cast: Joan Banks (Myra Mallard); Mandel Kramer (Ted Mallard); Sam Gray (Bert Hollis); Bryna Raeburn (Harriet); Kenneth Harvey (Lieutenant Jack Denson). Written by Sam Dann.

For 25 years, Ted and Myra Mallard have experienced a wonderful marriage— hearts and minds in perfect harmony, able to read each other's thoughts and share each other's feelings. Thus, when Ted is arrested for cocaine smuggling, Myra is sure he's been framed. Her faith in him, however, is put to a test when the police maintain they have proof that Ted has been living with another woman, has accumulated many gambling debts, and smuggled cocaine to pay them off.

Notes: Mandel Kramer has played a supporting character in numerous radio shows. Among the list of credits: *Backstage Wife, The Shadow, Yours Truly, Johnny Dollar, Exploring Tomorrow, The Light of the World, Counterspy, Perry Mason, Mr. and Mrs. North, Suspense,* and *X Minus One.*

533. "The Deadly Double" (6/21/75; rebroadcast from 3/24/75)

534. "Death Is a Dream" (6/22/75; rebroadcast from 3/26/75)

535. "The Mills of the Gods" (6/23/75; rebroadcast 10/19/75)

Cast: Tony Roberts (Jeff Garrett); Joan Copeland (Valerie Reynolds); Paul Hecht (Hendryk Van Dorn); William Redfield (Inspector Michaud). Written by Ian Martin.

Television correspondent Jeff Garrett returns to Paris from Asia and discovers that his fiancée, Valerie Reynolds, has left for Holland. Following Valerie, who is attractive and wealthy, Jeff finds her with Hendryk Van Dorn, whom Valerie claims to love, although she knows he was acquitted recently for the murder of his wife. A French detective, Inspector Michaud, is also following the couple, as he suspects Van Dorn in the murder of two other women. Valerie reveals to Michaud that Van Dorn's wife was her close friend, and she is determined to kill him to avenge her friend's death.

536. "The Mask of Tupac" (6/24/75; rebroadcast 10/22/75)

Cast: Ruby Dee (Nancy Littleton); Michael Wager (Carlos Ucayla); Bob Dryden (Francisco Fortune); Danny Ocko (Professor Brady). Written by Murray Burnett.

On a Peruvian expedition, Nancy Littleton discovers the grave of legendary Incan hero Tupac Amaru, replete with a valuable death mask. Although engaged to an Incan, Carlos Ucayla, Nancy disregards his warning of a powerful and deadly curse that will destroy anyone who plunders Tupac's grave. She refuses to either return the mask to the grave or sell it to a collector, Francisco Fortune. Nancy, Carlos and Francisco soon find themselves locked, for different reasons, in a struggle for the mask, which has apparently killed three others already.

537. "The Velvet Claws" (6/25/75; rebroadcast from 3/27/75)

538. "That Hamlet Was a Good Boy" (6/26/75; rebroadcast 10/25/75, 11/14/80)

Cast: Will MacKenzie (Doug Cardwell); Grace Matthews (Gertrude Cardwell); Joseph Silver (Edmund Cardwell); Leon Janney (Uncle Stanley); Jennifer Harmon (Phyllis). Written by Fielden Farrington.

After his father's death, seemingly from cardiac arrest, Doug Cardwell strongly opposes his mother and uncle's plan to sell the family business. When his father reappears as a rather life-like specter and tells Doug that his uncle smothered him to death, Doug and his fiancée, an amateur movie maker, hit upon the device—a play within a play—used by Hamlet in Shakespeare's drama. With it they hope to catch the conscience of Uncle Stanley and make him confess.

Notes: Fielden Farrington is not only a script writer, but announcer as well. He is probably best remembered as being the announcer for the daytime radio soap opera *Just Plain Bill.* During the opening plucking sounds of a banjo, Farrington opened each episode of radio's *The Romance of Helen Trent* during the 1930s and 1940s.

539. "The Rape of the Maia" (6/27/75; rebroadcast 10/14/75)

Cast: Norman Rose (Morris Goodman); Earl Hammond (Perry Fullerton); Joan Shay (Sally Jo); Jackson Beck (Lieutenant Valentine); Arnold Stang (Vaughn Lamere). Written by Sam Dann.

Vaughn Lamere vows to kill horse-player Perry Fullerton, who stole one of Lamere's dress designs and sold it for $500 to pay off his bookie. After Fullerton loses the $500 on another horse, his bookie accidentally kills him with a knife. Lamere arrives on the scene seconds later, faints at the sight of blood and awakens near Fullerton's body, the bloody knife in his hand. Even his best friends, including Morris Goodman, his boss, can't convince Lamere he wasn't the murderer.

540. "Key to Murder" (6/28/75; rebroadcast from 3/28/75)

541. "Killer of the Year" (6/29/75; rebroadcast from 3/31/75)

542. "The Golden Cauldron" (6/30/75; rebroadcast 11/4/75)

Cast: Paul Hecht (Brad Spencer); Russell Horton (Dennis Wentworth); Patricia Elliott (Julie Chandler); Bob Dryden (Peter Brook); Clarice Blackburn (Margaret Dawson). Written by Ralph Goodman.

Brad Spencer, whose hobbies are crime stories and Druid mysteries, finds a chance to combine both when he and traveling companion Dennis Wentworth decide to stay overnight at a remote castle inn. Peter Brook, the castle guide, tells them of a sacred golden cauldron used in Druid ceremonies and supposedly buried nearby. Attempting to unravel the mystery of the cauldron, Brad learns of another mystery—the death of Sir Laurence and Lady Elaine, most recent owners of the castle. Brad is close to solving both mysteries but finds he has a surfeit of suspects.

543. "The Killer Inside" (7/1/75; rebroadcast from 4/1/75)

544. "Come Back with Me" (7/2/75; rebroadcast 11/2/75)

Cast: Howard Da Silva (Bill Harlow); Teri Keane (Zelda Harlow); Ian Martin (Tom Bergen); William Redfield (Norman). Written by Sam Dann.

Bill Harlow wanders through the neighborhood of his youth—now a dangerous, deserted part of town—and comes upon a bar he used to frequent in his college days. He enters and sees nothing has changed. The same people; the same music; everything is just as he remembers it. A cop, Tom Bergen, finds Harlow and takes him back to the present, where he's confronted by an anxious wife, Zelda, and many business problems. Refusing to deal with the problems, Harlow tries to persuade Zelda to return to the past with him and relive their lives differently.

Notes: Howard Da Silva made his New York stage debut in 1929 and subsequently played with distinction many character roles on Broadway, culminating in the part of Jud in the musical hit *Oklahoma!* in 1943. Da Silva played numerous character roles in such films as *Abe Lincoln in Illinois* (1940), *The Sea Wolf* (1941), *Sergeant York* (1941), *The Lost Weekend* (1945), *They Live by Night* (1949), *David and Lisa* (1963), *The Great Gatsby* (1949 and 1974 versions), and probably his most popular role, that of Benjamin Franklin in *1776* (1972).

545. "Murder Will Out" (7/3/75; rebroadcast 11/6/75)

Cast: Mason Adams (Detective Joe Lombardi); Gilbert Mack (Barney); Leon Janney (Captain Stark); Robert Maxwell (Peavey); Marian Seldes (Lesley). Written by Ian Martin.

Detective Joe Lombardi, who seriously wounds a young punk he mistakenly thinks fired at him first, is told by his superiors to take a month vacation. Lombardi decides, against all advice, to use the time to track down the man who had killed his policeman father. His investigation leads Lombardi, gun in hand, to Miami Beach, where he finds the daughter of his father's alleged killer. Her story of what really happened 25 years ago is a startling revelation to the trigger-happy cop.

546. "The Slave" (7/4/75; rebroadcast 11/1/75)

Cast: Mandel Kramer (Corey Jensen); Fred Gwynne (Ray Chaffee); Patsy Bruder (Inger Williams); Mary Orr (Sylvia). Written by Henry Slesar.

Slightly intoxicated after a poker game, Corey Jensen casually bets his longtime friend, Ray Chaffee, that he could be Chaffee's personal slave for 12 months. As part of the wager, Chaffee can make Jensen do nothing that would endanger his health, cost him his job or get him arrested. However, humiliation was not discussed and, after six months, humiliation has become a major part of the game. Chaffee now thrives on humiliating Jensen at every possible moment.

547. "The Garrison of the Dead" (7/5/75; rebroadcast from 4/3/75)

548. "Roses Are for Funerals" (7/6/75; rebroadcast from 4/4/75)

549. "Guilty" (7/7/75; rebroadcast 11/9/75)

Cast: Jack Grimes (Kenneth Case); Ann Pitoniak (Mrs. Case); Nat Polen (Detective Stein); Jean Gillespie (Dr. Marian Knapp). Written by Elspeth Eric.

Kenneth Case is identified in a lineup as the man who attacked and robbed a woman. Though he passes her house each day and resembles the description of the attacker, Case did not commit the crime. Trying to prove his innocence, he asks for a lie detector test and the results say he's guilty. A psychiatrist, Dr. Marian Knapp, thinks she knows why, but Case's mother refuses to let him see Dr. Knapp again. Not until Case expresses anger toward his mother does he understand how the lie detector could have lied.

550. "The Triangle" (7/8/75; rebroadcast 11/8/75)

Cast: Mercedes McCambridge (Judy Roberts); Bob Dryden (Admiral Ingram); Paul Hecht (Lieutenant Nelson); Bryna Raeburn (Ora). Written by Sam Dann.

"I don't know what happened" is the only answer Judy Roberts will give to officials questioning her about the fate of a commercial airliner, carrying 110 passengers, that fell into the sea somewhere in the Bermuda Triangle which, over the years, has mysteriously claimed at least 100 planes and ships and more than 1,000 lives. Found by the U.S. Navy, Roberts, the plane's only survivor, is unharmed—although she spent five days floating in the ocean.

551. "The Benjamin Franklin Murder Case" (7/9/75; rebroadcast from 4/7/75)

552. "The Ghostly Rival" (7/10/75; rebroadcast 11/12/95)

Cast: Will MacKenzie (Tom Cartwright); Earl Hammond (Dr. Mathias); Bob Dryden (Bottle Spirit); Marian Seldes (Laura Blake). Written by Ian Martin.

In excruciating pain from a black widow spider bite and an auto accident in which he had hoped both he and his pregnant wife would die, rich and spoiled Tom Cartwright III, who claims he is somebody else, requests psychiatric treatment. The complex and puzzling story he tells causes his doctor's colleagues to suggest that Cartwright be written off as incurable. But the psychiatrist persists, saying, "We never write anyone off."

553. "The Widow's Auxiliary" (7/11/75; rebroadcast 11/15/75, 11/21/80)

Cast: Lenka Peterson (Julie Simms); Arnold Moss (Alfred Lathrop); Carol Teitel (Rose Lathrop); Court Benson (J.D. Mason); Gordon Gould (Carl Simms). Written by Fielden Farrington.

When Carl Simms is invited to join the prestigious Executives Club, his wife Julie is as excited as he is until Rose Lathrop, whose husband is a member, informs Julie that all the men are robots. Rose has discovered that the initiation consists of an operation to mechanize their brains. Julie finds it difficult to believe, but attempts to dissuade Carl from joining. She fails, but joins Rose in a dangerous plan to save Carl and destroy the club and its members. Is Rose right in saying that her husband's club are robots controlled by another planet?

554. "The Altar of Blood" (7/12/75; rebroadcast from 4/9/75)

555. "The Death of Halpin Fraser" (7/13/75; rebroadcast from 4/10/75)

556. "Snake in the Grass" (7/14/75; rebroadcast 11/16/75)

Cast: Sandy Dennis (Augusta Sanderson); Arnold Stang (Pete Grimes); Bob Dryden (Lutuf); Ralph Bell (Lieutenant Novak). Written by Sam Dann.

Augusta Sanderson, a noted professor of agriculture, vents her anger toward a colleague to the bartender of a local tavern. She claims that Dr. Eugene Howells is taking credit for a method she developed of growing high-protein purple clover, which, she says casually, is justification enough for her to kill him. The barkeep notifies the police and, shortly after Howells is found murdered, Dr. Sanderson is arrested. Innocent though she is, Howells was shot by her gun, and her footprint was left in some mud near the house.

Notes: Sandy Dennis made her radio acting debut in this episode. Dennis made her screen debut in the 1961 film *Splendor in the Grass* (which was also Warren Beatty and Phyllis Diller's first film as well). Dennis later won two Tony Awards for her roles in *A Thousand Clowns* and *Any Wednesday*. She followed that with an Academy Award for best supporting actress in *Who's Afraid of Virginia Woolf?* (1966).

557. "The Phantom Stop" (7/15/75; rebroadcast from 4/11/75)

558. "Goodbye, Karl Erich" (7/16/75; rebroadcast 11/18/75, 1/12/78)

Cast: Kevin McCarthy (Dr. Heinrich Stammler); Sam Gray (Fritz Stauber); Joan Shay (Karen); Bryna Raeburn (Liese Reinmuth); Paul Hecht (Karl Erich Mueller). Written by Sam Dann.

Karl Erich Mueller, struck dumb by his father's death in World War I, learns to speak again with the sympathetic and persistent treatment of Dr. Heinrich Stammler. Young Mueller, who promises never to forget what Dr. Stammler has done for him, goes to Munich for a warehouse job, which he promptly loses. Now in the ranks of Germany's unemployed, he does something which the doctor can never forgive: He joins Hitler's Nazi party.

559. "Nightmare's Nest" (7/17/75; rebroadcast 11/22/75)

Cast: Gordon Gould (John Masters); Mary Jane Higby (Martha Denton); Rosemary Rice (Stella Mayer); Robert Maxwell (Rom Gitano); Ian Martin (Father Dan). Written by Ian Martin.

John Masters, a mathematical genius who says he had neither the time nor the need for love, moves into a remote country house. Through the housekeeper, John learns of the tragic death of a previous occupant, Stella Mayer, who died of a broken heart. John falls in love with the visions of Stella appearing to him, unable to resist her commands. When his friends learn of the gypsy curse Stella's former lover placed on her, they rush to save John's weakening life.

560. "The Spots of the Leopard" (7/18/75; rebroadcast 11/23/75)

Cast: Ann Shepherd (Eloise Rutledge); Gilbert Mack (Mr. Atkins); Leon Janney (Sparrow); Russell Horton (Tom Rutledge). Written by Sam Dann.

Government agents arrange for businessman Tom Rutledge, whose life is in danger, and his wife Eloise to change their names and move from New York to a remote university town in Wyoming. Rutledge has testified against several underworld figures who have vowed to rub him out. He adapts easily, but Eloise, accustomed to the advantages of big city life, is unhappy. Without telling her husband, she calls her antique dealer in New York, who unbeknownst to her is a former pal of one of the hoods out to get her husband.

561. "The Intermediary" (7/19/75; rebroadcast from 4/14/75)

562. "My Own Murderer" (7/20/75; rebroadcast from 4/15/75)

563. "Fateful Reunion" (7/21/75; rebroadcast 11/26/75)

Cast: Jennifer Harmon (Lucy); Bob Dryden (Gary); William Redfield (Doug); Kenneth Harvey (David). Written by Elizabeth Pennell.

The son of one of two World War II buddies who have been holding a reunion on the anniversary of D-day since 1945 works for a company that has developed a "thinking" computer which can predict the future. While testing it, he is told by the machine that his father and friend will never have another reunion, that one will die before their next observance of D-day. The two have several brushes with death, but both are still alive the day before their next meeting.

564. "The Poisoned Pen" (7/22/75; rebroadcast 11/29/75)

Cast: Robert Maxwell (Selina); Catherine Byers (Momma); Richard Seff (Joseph Carroway); Earl Hammond (Barney Hogarth); Michael Tolan (Sergeant Garvey). Written by Sam Dann.

Playwright Joseph Carroway, nightclub owner Frank Clancy and Sebastian Proudfoot, aide to theatrical agent Barney Hogarth, die within seconds after sealing a self-addressed envelope, the anonymous sender of which has offered each $50,000 for past courtesies. Autopsies reveal that each has died from a poison called urcurare. The police learn that each had dealt with a young, beautiful woman named Selina, who had come to New York hoping to make it big in show business.

565. "Through the Looking Glass" (7/23/75; rebroadcast from 4/17/75)

566. "Appointment in Uganda" (7/24/75; rebroadcast 11/30/75)

Cast: William Redfield (Harry Kantor); Arnold Stang (Joe Burrows); Joan Shay (Nurse); Bryna Raeburn (Mrs. Kantor). Written by Elspeth Eric.

Harry Kantor, a hard-driving businessman, is hospitalized after a heart attack but is still unwilling to relax. During an argument with his business partner, Harry's heart stops and he experiences rebirth as a baby elephant named Abu. His mother, Kaylin, and another elephant, Bombeen, teach him the gentle and generous ways of the herd, while an older male, Noor, tells him the elephant philosophy of death. When his heart is revived, Harry is a changed man, wondering if he just dreamed the experience, or whether he just witnessed reincarnation.

567. "Woman from Hell" (7/25/75; rebroadcast 12/2/75)

Cast: Joan Banks (Jennifer Grenelle); Paul Hecht (Durell Jones); Mandel Kramer (Anton Krazewski); Norman Rose (Lawrence Ducaux); Nat Polen (Florist). Written by Murray Burnett.

Actress Jennifer Grenelle's death is officially listed as a suicide, but her husband, Lawrence Ducaux, doubts the police report and sets off on an international search for clues. Jennifer's diary, which he locates in Paris, tells an incredible story of a witches' club that promised her fame if she'd convert others. Trying to verify the story, Lawrence is aided by Durrell Jones, a detective hired by one of Jennifer's former lovers. But when the diary says her lover belonged to the club, Lawrence wonders whether Jones is really helping.

568. "A Challenge for the Dead" (7/26/75; rebroadcast from 4/18/75)

569. "Sting of Death" (7/27/75; rebroadcast from 4/21/75)

570. "The Lady Is a Jinx" (7/28/75; rebroadcast 12/6/75)

Cast: Marian Seldes (Dr. Martha Lindstrom); Danny Ocko (Inspector Coleman); Larry Haines (Lt. Vince Perelli); Patricia Elliott (Carolyn). Written by Sam Dann.

The police are mystified by the sudden death of five men, each of whom was in love with Carolyn Butler before their death. When Dr. Martha Lindstrom, sister of the last victim, tries to convince the police that Carolyn caused her brother's demise, they won't listen. Nor will Lt. Vince Perelli, assigned to find an explanation for the five deaths, for he, too, has fallen in love with Carolyn.

571. "Afraid to Live—Afraid to Die" (7/29/75; rebroadcast from 4/23/75)

572. "He Moves in Mysterious Ways" (7/30/75; rebroadcast 12/7/75)

Cast: Teri Keane (Dr. Patricia Shelton); Bob Dryden (Dr. Mike Bernardo); Patsy Bruder (Elizabeth Riggs); Ian Martin (Chaplain Daniel Morgan); Leon Janney (Dr. Hugh Bradley). Written by Ian Martin.

Professional dancer Elizabeth Riggs is rushed to a hospital's emergency room, her leg shattered in a train crash. Certain the leg will be amputated, she calls for the hospital chaplain, Daniel Morgan, who passes out while trying to console her. Drs. Patricia Shelton and Hugh Bradley see little hope for Morgan's survival (he is suffering from a ruptured appendix) until Mr. Riggs asks to see him again and he consents, despite his precarious condition.

573. "Carmilla" (7/31/75; rebroadcast 12/10/75)

Cast: Mercedes McCambridge (Laura Stanton); Marian Seldes (Carmilla); Martha Greenhouse (Contessa); Court Benson (Dr. Zulig); Staats Cotsworth (Mr. Stanton). Written by Ian Martin.

Nineteen-year-old Laura Stanton, living with her father in an isolated Austrian mansion, is delighted when one of the victims of a carriage accident, 19-year-old Carmilla, agrees to stay with them. They become very close friends until Laura learns who—and what—Carmilla really is.

574. "The Onyx Eye" (8/1/75; rebroadcast 12/13/75)

Cast: Michael Wager (Jack Evens); Bryna Raeburn (Mrs. Mazza); Frances Sternhagen (Cathy Evens); Sidney Slon (Ellsworth); William Redfield (Reporter). Written by Sidney Slon.

Unemployed, deeply in debt, his wife expecting, Jack Evens uses his last few dollars to buy his wife, Cathy, a birthday present: a chunk of onyx that looks like an eye, the seller of which says will bring both Jack and Cathy much good luck. Miraculously, Jack gets a better job than he ever imagines and wins the next state lottery. Nevertheless, Cathy insists that her husband get rid of the onyx eye. She becomes even more adamant when she loses her child.

575. "Bullet Proof" (8/2/75; rebroadcast from 4/24/75)

576. "Till Death Do Us Join" (8/3/75; rebroadcast from 4/25/75)

577. "The Devil's Boutique" (8/4/75; rebroadcast 12/14/75)

Cast: Joan Lorring (Elvira Graham); Jada Rowland (Marjorie Graham);

Robert L. Green (Tony Butler); Robert Kaliban (Captain Miller); Arch (Ian Martin). Written by Bob Juhren.

Elvira Graham, one of the world's top fashion designers, visits in Derna, Libya, what is described to her by a cruise ship's captain as a most unusual clothing and accessories shop, known as The Devil's Boutique. Fascinated by the shop's wares, Elvira is caught sketching some of the designs. Instead of having her arrested, the boutique's owner gives her a set of earrings and a lipstick that she proudly wears, only to discover later that no matter what she does, neither will come off.

578. "Hung Jury" (8/5/75; rebroadcast 12/16/75)

Cast: Howard Da Silva (Henry Pollard); Joan Shay (Julie); Catherine Byers (Norma Pollard); Bob Dryden (Mr. Nightingale). Written by Sam Dann.

Heavily in debt from gambling, Henry is carrying a large amount of cash, enough for Pollard to pay off his debts, which he does. By chance, Pollard is chosen to serve on the jury hearing the case against the murdered man's chauffeur, whom police have accused of the crime. Pollard wants to convince his fellow jurors to acquit the chauffeur, whose testimony makes him appear to be guilty.

579. "The Phantom of the Opera" (8/6/75; rebroadcast from 4/28/75)

580. "To Die Is Forever" (8/7/75; rebroadcast 12/20/75)

Cast: Mandel Kramer (Ross Richard); Marian Seldes (Dr. Margaret Fleming); Jack Grimes (Bill Porter); Leon Janney (Dr. Berkley); Ann Pitoniak (Tante Marie). Written by Ian Martin.

Ross Richard, owner of an island in the Caribbean, arranges with a doctor for his wife, Felicia, dying from a melanomic tumor, to be put in radical hypothermia and revived some time in the future when a cure for her condition has been perfected. He would like the doctor to do the same for him so he can continue his happy marriage. But legal problems arise, not helped by the Richards' housekeeper who knows too much about the family's corrupt past.

581. "The Grey Ghost" (8/8/75; rebroadcast 12/21/75)

Cast: Betsy Palmer (Kate Richards); Evelyn Juster (Stewardess); William Redfield (Guido Basso); Ian Martin (Ghost). Written by Ian Martin.

Considering herself a complete failure, her marriage breaking up, her famous auto racing father dead from a freak accident, Kate Richards heads for Italy to refashion her life. Strangely, the only people she meets there are auto racers, one of whom she ultimately convinces to race in a car named after her father's favorite machine, the Grey Ghost. Even though she hopes it won't happen, the driver seems destined to repeat her father's mistake on the track.

582. "Black Widow" (8/9/75; rebroadcast from 4/29/75)

583. "Mad Monkton" (8/10/75; rebroadcast from 5/1/75)

584. "Age Cannot Wither" (8/11/75; rebroadcast 12/27/75)

Cast: Jennifer Harmon (Eleanor Burnham); Kenneth Harvey (Sheriff); Earl Hammond (Father); Bryna Raeburn (Mrs. Mallory); Joseph Silver (John Burnham). Written by Sam Dann.

When John and Eleanor Burnham go sailing and only John returns, the sheriff's suspicions are aroused. Unable to say where Eleanor is, John is jailed for murder and tells a skeptical sheriff that he didn't murder her, because she can't die. Eleanor, says John, was born 400 years ago, the daughter of an alchemist who gave her the Elixir of Life that made her 19 years old forever. The fact that Eleanor still looks 19 after 45 years of marriage to John is convincing—until her body is found, with evidence that she planned to run away with another man.

585. "The Final Witness" (8/12/75; rebroadcast from 5/2/75)

586. "The Master Computer" (8/13/75; rebroadcast 12/28/75, 12/28/80)

Cast: Robert Dryden (Harry Clayton); Augusta Dabney (Grace Clayton); Joan Shay (Alma Rhodes); Nat Polen (Pete Rhodes); Robert Maxwell (Mr. Handy). Written by Fielden Farrington.

Returning from a Maine vacation, Grace and Harry Clayton find their lives entirely disrupted. They discover that they have apparently become invisible to neighbors, co-workers and everyone else. Grace wonders if they are dead, but Harry disagrees since all else around them is normal. Finally, someone appears who can both see and hear them and tells the Claytons of an incredible computer malfunction.

After her *Mystery Theater* appearance, Augusta Dabney was later cast in the films *The Portrait* (1993), *Running on Empty* (1988), and *Violets are Blue* (1986).

587. "The Root of All Evil" (8/14/75; rebroadcast 12/30/75)

Cast: Norman Rose (Phillip Chambers); Elliot Reid (Paul Shelton); Anne Shepherd (Laura Chambers); Marian Seldes (Joan Shelton); George Petrie (Nick). Written by Roy Winsor.

A suburban bank robbery ends with a fiery car crash in a small residential area. The police assume the two robbers who escaped took the money with them, but Phillip Chambers discovers they hid it in his trash can. Chambers, a freelance writer, decides to keep the money for himself, but faces tough questioning from his wife, the wrath of the robbers who come back for their loot, and his own conscience. Paul Shelton, his friend and neighbor, guesses what's happened and tries to help but is also caught up in the intrigue.

Notes: Elliot Reid has appeared in numerous radio shows, including *The March of Time*, *The Adventures of Sam Spade*, and *Suspense*. A character actor in numerous films and television programs, Reid plays the role Paul Shelton, a so-called passerby who gets himself caught up in a web of trouble.

588. "The Unbearable Reflection" (8/15/75; rebroadcast 1/15/76)

Cast: Patricia Elliott (Deborah Denton); Mandel Kramer (Louis Stark); Carol Teitel (Elspeth); Bob Dryden (John Denton). Written by Ian Martin.

Deborah Denton has fame, beauty and a governor for a husband and fully expects to be the First Lady some day. All that the Dentons lack is wealth, so handsome, rich Niklos Arinjoglou holds a special fascination for Deborah. When Louis Stark, the governor's political aide, threatens to reveal her affair and ruin her, Deborah panics and unwittingly kills her husband. Louis, who put her up to it, claims he will help her if she'll just give up her reflection to him. Although it sounds simple, she has a devilishly hard time without it.

589. "The Paradise of the Devil" (8/16/75; rebroadcast from 5/5/75)

590. "The Transformation" (8/17/75; rebroadcast from 5/7/75)

591. "Help Somebody" (8/18/75; rebroadcast 7/23/81)

Cast: William Redfield (Anthony Price); Court Benson (Clark McKay); Danny Ocko (Leon Long); Joan Shay (Claudia Crisi). Written by Elspeth Eric.

Anthony Price, a poor and not very successful writer living in Rome, finds his world changed when his wealthy father dies and leaves his entire inheritance to his only son. With all the money he can spend, a novel that is suddenly very popular, and the beautiful woman he desires, Anthony has everything he thought he wanted, yet finds himself deeply depressed. Not until he meets a nameless girl, an old man, and a mongrel dog can he begin living again.

592. "Welcome for a Dead Man" (8/19/75; rebroadcast 1/17/76)

Cast: Howard Da Silva (Harry Beggs); Bryna Reaburn (Honey Beggs); Gilbert Mack (Lucky); Earl Hammond (Roy). Based on the 1961 short story *You Can't Blame Me* by Henry Slesar, who also adapted the short story for *Mystery Theater.*

Released from jail after 25 years, Harry Beggs has nothing to his name but a wife who doesn't want him back and a daughter he's never met. Thinking money would change his wife's mind, he digs up $50,000 he buried after the robbery for which he was jailed. But before he gets home, he's robbed of the money by a young woman he meets in a bar. Harry's wife finally agrees to accept him just as he is, but his shock at meeting his daughter convinces Harry that nothing can ever be the same.

593. "Taken for Granite" (8/20/75; rebroadcast from 5/8/75)

594. "Circle of Evil" (8/21/75; rebroadcast 1/18/76)

Cast: Marian Seldes (Mary Richards); Rosemary Rice (Andrea Dykeman); Mary Jane Higby (Frieda Kurtz); Ian Martin (William Dykeman); Kristoffer Tabori (Alex Dykeman). Written by Sidney Slon.

Mary Richards agrees to be a governess but finds herself in a gloomy house with two difficult teenagers and an unfair housekeeper. She hears conflicting tales of how the children's large family died and different versions of her predecessor's death. Next, she meets the resident ghost who has the most horrible story of all.

Determined to leave quickly, Mary is prevailed upon by the children to stay and fight their guardian, who wants to send them to an asylum though they're not insane.

595. "Terror in the Air" (8/22/75; rebroadcast 1/13/76)

Cast: Jennifer Harmon (Fran Carwell); Bob Dryden (Dr. Sam McCall); Hetty Galen (Mrs. Pierce); Richard Seff (Voice); Earl Hammond (Captain Thomas). Written by Ian Martin.

When the pilot and copilot of a commercial jet become disabled, stewardess Fran Carwell finds the only one aboard who knows how to fly is a Dr. Sam McCall. Although he hasn't flown for years, a voice from an unidentified ground control station guides him, and all is well until he has to assist a passenger who's having a baby. At the airport, the tension deepens when the voice is discovered to be that of a pilot who supposedly died in a crash with Dr. McCall's son.

596. "Voices of Death" (8/23/75; rebroadcast from 5/9/75)

597. "For Tomorrow We Die" (8/24/75; rebroadcast from 5/12/75)

598. "Person to Be Notified" (8/25/75; rebroadcast 1/20/76)

Cast: Mercedes McCambridge (Sarah Watson); Ian Martin (Carbury); Russell Horton (James); Gilbert Mack (Spinola); Bryna Raeburn (Mrs. Daimler). Written by Sam Dann.

Because she fails in applying for a job to give the name of the person to be notified "in case of," Sarah Watson is chosen for a well-paying secretarial position. Her employer-to-be, a wealthy, elderly eccentric, is really a prisoner in his vast Maine island estate and the owner of a fortune in diamonds his lawyer and others hope Miss Watson will help him locate. If she refuses, no one, they figure, will ever bother to wonder what happened to her.

599. "Where Angels Fear to Tread" (8/26/75; rebroadcast from 5/13/75)

600. "The Eavesdropper" (8/27/75; rebroadcast 1/22/76, 12/5/80)

Cast: Arnold Moss (Dwight Addison); Patricia Wheel (Jane Addison); Joen Arliss (Pearl); Ralph Bell (Mr. Smith); William Redfield (Edgar). Written by Fielden Farrington.

Professor Dwight Addison, developing a mathematical concept that will achieve the time bypass necessary for interstellar travel, is certain his laboratory, car and home are all bugged by enemies trying to keep track of his progress. To thwart them, he stops work on the project and puts together an ingenious device certain to strike fear in the heart of even the most tenacious wire-tapper.

601. "Night of the Howling Dog" (8/28/75; rebroadcast 1/24/76)

Cast: Mason Adams (Ernest Simpson); Marian Seldes (Joan Manning);

Kristoffer Tabori (Peter Sangree); Guy Sorel (Reverend Manning); Norman Rose (Duane Carter). Written by Murray Burnett.

Soon after two women and three men set up camp on the island which, they have been told, is free of wild animals, what they had hoped would be a pleasant vacation becomes a siege of terror when the younger of the two women is attacked by a strange beast. A renowned psychic doctor, called upon to help, terrifies the campers even more when he maintains the beast is really one of them, a person suffering from lycanthropy, the delusion that one has become a wolf.

602. "Murder by Proxy" (8/29/75; rebroadcast 1/25/76)

Cast: Mandel Kramer (Alexander Hunter); Leon Janney (Tim Cohane); William Redfield (Jimmy Marquette); Grace Matthews (Amy Small); Earl Hammond (Lem Small); Leslie Woods (Phyllis Hunter). Written by Roy Winsor.

Flying home to Chicago, businessman Alexander Hunter is accosted by Tim Cohane, just out of jail. Hunter was foreman of the jury that declared Cohane guilty, and Cohane, with little to live for, promises Hunter he will soon kill him and later, if he's not caught, all other members of the jury. Cohane is amazed at Hunter's cool reaction, his statement that there is little a person can do to stop an assassin who's willing to die for his cause.

603. "Deadly Dilemma" (8/30/75; rebroadcast from 5/15/75)

604. "The Rise and Fall of the Fourth Reich" (8/31/75; rebroadcast from 5/16/75)

605. "The Smile of Death" (9/1/75; rebroadcast 1/27/76)

Cast: Russell Horton (Philip); Ian Martin (Dr. Torvey); Joan Shay (Mrs. Julaper); Evelyn Juster (Jenny); Court Benson (Sir Bale). Written by Ian Martin.

According to the way the townsfolk talk, it was just two days after Sir Bale Mardykes drowned his wife Libby, years ago so he could marry a rich baroness, that the luminous form of a female began to rise halfway out of the lake on dark, misty days. Some of the superstitious townspeople believe it is Libby, rising from the spot where she was drowned, and they foresee nothing but trouble when her son, Philip, now grown, returns to determine if the shape is really his mother and to confront Sir Bale, his father.

606. "Portrait of Death" (9/2/75; rebroadcast 1/29/76)

Cast: Rosemary Rice (Vicky Bradford); Tony Roberts (Peter Bradford); Gilbert Mack (Luigi); Bob Dryden (Enrico). Written by Elizabeth Pennell.

Newly married Vicky Bradford convinces her husband to take her to Venice for their honeymoon so she can buy a painting she thinks is a Raphael original. Some art experts suspect the painting is only a copy, but Vicky becomes certain she is right when her husband is mugged in an alleyway and the body of a talkative guard at the museum is found floating in a canal.

607. "The Diamond Necklace" (9/3/75; rebroadcast from 5/19/75)

608. "The Special Undertaking" (9/4/75; rebroadcast 1/31/76)

Cast: Jada Rowland (Susannah Fleming); Don Scardino (Dr. Hank Fleming); Staats Cotsworth (Buford Hughes); Robert Maxwell (Ezra Whitfield); Ann Pitoniak (Mrs. Bunter). Written by Ian Martin.

Dr. Hank Fleming and his wife Susannah, while setting up his practice in a country mansion, hear strange stories about its previous occupants—how, childless for years, they finally had a daughter, born blind and mute, whose heart was later broken by the renegade son of their housekeeper. The daughter is presumed dead, but Susannah, hearing a music box amidst eerie cries for help, becomes convinced she's still alive, somewhere on the vast estate.

609. "Sleepwalker" (9/5/75; rebroadcast 2/1/76)

Cast: Tammy Grimes (Olivia Worster); Sam Gray (Dr. Schwartz); Carol Teitel (Teresa); Bob Dryden (John Worster). Written by Sam Dann.

Olivia Worster, 35, under treatment for somnambulism and confidentially expressing to her doctor a desire to kill her 70-year-old husband because of his "superior attitude" towards her, loosens the brakes of her husband's sports car one night while sleepwalking. She, though, is the next driver of the car and is almost killed when its brakes fail on a steep hill. Her doctor is unable to come up with a quick cure for her somnambulism, and soon, again while sleepwalking, she makes another attempt on her husband's life.

610. "Don't Let It Choke You" (9/6/75; rebroadcast from 5/21/75)

611. "Return to Shadow Lake" (9/7/75; rebroadcast from 5/22/75)

612. "The Other Life" (9/8/75; rebroadcast 2/4/76)

Cast: Mercedes McCambridge (Della McKellar); Elliott Reid (Fred); Ralph Bell (Mike); Bryna Raeburn (Edith). Written by Sam Dann.

Della McKellar, whose ambitious, fast-rising husband is seldom home, is urged by a girlfriend to live her own life, to join her in finding excitement by betting on horse races. At first, Della's luck is uncanny. But when she starts losing, only her bookmaker, Mike, shows any symphony. He continues allowing her all the credit she wants—for a price. It's a price, though, she cannot agree to pay, no matter how much credit he allows her.

613. "Markheim: Man or Monster?" (9/9/75; rebroadcast from 5/23/75)

614. "The Ides of March" (9/10/75; rebroadcast 2/7/76)

Cast: Nina Foch (Cassandra Morrow); Bret Morrison (Officer Belden); Lou Krugman (Dr. Miller); Les Tremayne (Ted Morrow). Written by Sam Dann.

Cassandra Morrow has a vivid, detailed dream that the plane her husband,

Ted, plans to take on an important business trip, March 12 to Chicago, will crash on takeoff and that he will die. Even when minor incidents early in her dream become realities, Ted insists they are merely coincidences and that he will go through with the trip. But then the police officer she met just before the takeoff in the dream—one T.J. Belden—is assigned to their precinct, four days before March 12.

Notes: Nina Foch is no stranger to horror and mystery programs. Signing up with Columbia Pictures in 1943, she began making numerous appearances in horror and mystery films starting with *The Return of the Vampire* (1943), *Cry of the Werewolf* (1944), *Shadows in the Night* (1944), *My Name Is Julia Ross* (1945), and *I Love a Mystery* (1945), which was based on Carlton E. Morse's radio mystery show.

615. "The Voice of Death" (9/11/75; rebroadcast 2/8/76)

Cast: Victor Jory (Janus); Amzie Strickland (Sarah); Bret Morrison (Professor Manzini). Written by Ian Martin.

Janus, a ventriloquist, distraught when bookings become less and less frequent, persuades Professor Manzini to build him a new dummy. The professor creates Self, a human-sized robot that can perform any physical function except for talking. Janus and Self are an immediate hit until Self begins to express a dissatisfaction with his role. Self, it becomes apparent, would prefer to be the ventriloquist in the act.

Notes: Victor Jory played numerous character parts in a variety of Hollywood films, most of them B pictures, usually as an evil-eyed heavy. Among his films are *Gone with the Wind* (1939), *Charlie Chan in Rio* (1942), *Son of Ali Baba* (1952), *Valley of the Kings* (1954), and *The Miracle Worker* (1962). Jory hosted and starred in his own radio show, *Dangerously Yours* (later retitled *Matinee Theatre*), which lasted almost a whole year, from 1944 to 1945.

616. "The Ghost Plane" (9/12/75; rebroadcast 2/10/76)

Cast: Janet Waldo (Ginny Wallace); Richard Crenna (Herb Moss); Sam Edwards (Bruce Downing); Virginia Gregg (Carol Newman); Casey Kasem (Danny Shafer). Written by Ian Martin.

Young Ginny Wallace and middle-aged Herb Moss wake up in what seems to be an unscheduled charter flight. They are alone except for a middle-aged stewardess who refuses to tell them when or how they got aboard or where the plane is headed. When the plane starts a sudden descent, Ginny and Herb make plans to run for the nearest exit, but when the plane stops, they can't get up from their seats. Their safety belts refuse to be unbuckled.

617. "The Witches' Almanac" (9/13/75; rebroadcast from 5/26/75)

618. "The Executioner" (9/14/75; rebroadcast from 5/27/75)

619. "The Little Old Lady Killer" (9/15/75; rebroadcast 2/14/76)

Cast: Diane Baker (Lt. Louise Kramer); Anne Seymour (Mrs. Bernadette Cobb); Berry Kroeger (Tom Fessler); Alan Reed (Sparky Wilson). Written by Sam Dann.

A hunter who has killed a 350-pound buck, a gambler who stages dogfights for his betting clientele, and a woman whose Doberman pinscher dies from heat prostration in her parked car are all victims of a .22 pistol fired by a little old lady with an aversion toward people who kill animals. The police are baffled by the murders, except for a woman detective whose notions about the killer's identity make her the laughingstock of all the male members of her force.

Notes: Diane Baker is no stranger to mystery and horror, having appeared in such films as *The Silence of the Lambs* (1991), *Marnie* (1964), *Strait-Jacket* (1964), and *Journey to the Center of the Earth* (1959). She even made an appearance on the ABC television series *The Invaders.*

620. "The Prison of Glass" (9/16/75; rebroadcast 2/15/76)

Cast: Lois Nettleton (Marcy Herrick); Peg La Centra (Mother); Berry Kroeger (Dr. Barclay); John Newland (Nicholas Surgat); Hans Conried (Dave Morgan). Written by Ian Martin.

Pulchritudinous Marcy Herrick, pushed hard by her ailing mother and ambitious agent, ultimately reaches the pinnacle of success in the film world, despite the fact she never really wanted to be an actress. On her way up she marries a producer, who soon dies tragically during a drunken marital squabble. Convinced she was the cause of his death, Marcy turns to drugs to ease her feelings of guilt.

621. "Just One More Day" (9/17/75; rebroadcast from 5/29/75)

622. "The Coffin with the Golden Nails" (9/18/75; rebroadcast 2/18/76)

Cast: Howard Da Silva (Zorilla); Ralph Bell (Mr. Chrysalis); Kristoffer Tabori (Fernando); Marian Seldes (Anita De Onis). Written by Sam Dann.

With his country in revolt, Zorilla, a deposed South American dictator, makes a deal with Metamorphosis, an international insurance firm, to sell his identity and gain, through a perfect disguise, what he thinks will be the life-long protection from his angry former subjects. Transformed into a placid American zoology professor, he meets and falls in love with a woman who has her own professional revenge for Zorilla and who secretly makes plans to blow his presumably flawless cover.

623. "The Third Person" (9/19/75; rebroadcast 2/21/76, 12/8/79)

Cast: Marian Seldes (Susan Frush); Evelyn Juster (Amy Frush); Arnold Moss (Amos Patton); Court Benson (Thomas Willoughby). Written by Stella and Arnold Moss.

Susan and Amy Frush are reunited when they become the sole beneficiaries to their aunt's old, roomy New England mansion. After they move in, they are frightened by a persistent, mysterious visitor, the ghost of their dead cousin Cuthbert, whose smuggling exploits led to his hanging in 1775, bringing shame to the family name. With the help of the town minister, Susan and Amy piece together Cuthbert's sad but exciting career and set out to redeem him—and themselves.

624. "Someday I'll Find You" (9/20/75; rebroadcast from 5/30/75)

625. "River of Hades" (9/21/75; rebroadcast from 6/2/75)

626. "Solid Gold Soldiers" (9/22/75; rebroadcast 7/4/76)

Cast: Michael Wager (Col. Oliver Colfax); Ian Martin (Alexander Burton); Court Benson (The President); Evelyn Juster (Maria Wilson); William Redfield (Stevens). Written by Sam Dann.

With the aid of beautiful actress Maria Wilson, Oliver Colfax, a Southern officer, transacts to purchase arms for the Confederacy from Alexander Burton, an alleged British agent, for $1 million in gold. When Colfax discovers that Burton is an impostor and Maria a Northern spy, he sets sail for England to deliver the gold himself, only to find that Maria, who has disguised herself as a cabin boy, has already alerted the enemy.

Notes: To salute the nation's bicentennial celebration, *Mystery Theater* presented a whole week of dramas revolving around an incident or person well known in American history. This marked the first of the seven consecutive broadcasts.

627. "The Headless Hessian" (9/23/75; rebroadcast 7/5/76)

Cast: Lloyd Bochner (General Washington); Jack Grimes (Tom Caldwell); Casey Kasem (Lt. Piel); Robert Maxwell (Sgt. Meadows); Mariette Hartley (Peggy). Written by Sam Dann.

Private Tom Caldwell, with Washington's troops near Trenton, New Jersey, covers himself with a large overcoat each night as he sneaks across enemy lines for a tryst with his beloved Peggy, whose home is occupied by Hessian troops. Washington's men think they are seeing a ghost, a headless Hessian, and are terrified. When Caldwell is finally captured, Washington decides to put his charade to good use and to distract the Hessians during an American attack on Trenton.

628. "The Angels of Devil's Mountain" (9/24/75; rebroadcast 7/6/76)

Cast: Warren Stevens (Donald Farrow); Anne Seymour (Dotty); James McCallion (Marvin); Berry Kroeger (Doctor). Written by Sam Dann.

Businessman Donald Farrow develops severe chest pains and is forced to stop his car in a small town in Connecticut. Farlow is perplexed both by his pains, which cannot be diagnosed, and by the townspeople, who all seem to recognize him as an American Revolutionary patriot who defended the town against the British. It is not until he visits the local museum to view the prized painting of the 18th century hero that he realizes the cause of his persistent pains.

Notes: Warren Stevens acted in such films as *Forbidden Planet* (1956), *Shark River* (1953), and *Man or Gun* (1958). Anne Seymour has appeared in such films as *Gemini Affair* (1975), *Portrait of Grandpa Doc* (1977), and *All the King's Men* (1949).

629. "The Black Whale" (9/25/75; rebroadcast 7/7/76)

Cast: Brock Peters (Jim); Bret Morrison (Ben Borders); Marvin Miller (Bob D'Arcy); Lynn Hamilton (Jenny); Ken Lynch (Mr. McClure). Written by Sam Dann.

Bob D'Arcy is a Northern abolitionist who convinces old friend Ben Borders, a Texas plantation owner, that his slave Jim, who has taught himself to read and write by looking at words under pictures of objects in books in Borders' library, should be set free. While en route to a Texas seaport and a ship to Boston, D'Arcy is killed by Mexican bandits. Thus begins a tortuous flight to freedom for Jim, which he knows can succeed only if he can get his hands on a gun.

Notes: Brock Peters has appeared in such films as The Adventures of Huckleberry Finn (1978), Alligator 2: The Mutation (1990), To Kill a Mockingbird (1962), Star Trek VI: The Undiscovered Country (1991), and Soylent Green (1973).

630. "Assassination in Time" (9/26/75; rebroadcast 7/8/76)

Cast: Ian Martin (Professor Jennings Andrews); Bryna Raeburn (Mary Stuart); Gordon Gould (John Wilkes Booth); William Redfield (Mac McDonald); Jennifer Harmon (Peg Andrews). Written by Ian Martin.

Professor Jennings Andrews, his scientific breakthrough in time travel perfected, transports his daughter Peg and her fiancé Mac McDonald, his first human travelers, back to a most significant day in American history—April 14, 1865, the day Abraham Lincoln was shot. With bitter memories of the Civil War still lingering, Peg and Mac, aware of what really happened on that ill-fated day, set out to undo one of the great tragedies in American history.

631. "The Thomas Jefferson Defense" (9/27/75; rebroadcast 7/9/76)

Cast: Paul Hecht (Thomas Jefferson); Robert Kaliban (Jeremy Morgan); Jada Rowland (Louisa); Leon Janney (Edmund McAllister); Russell Horton (Carter McAllister). Written by Sam Dann.

Certain that the beautiful Louisa is in love with half-breed Jeremy Morgan, Carter McAllister, enraged with jealousy, murders him and then accuses Morgan's uncle, Chief Blue Cloud. The Shawnee chief hires his good friend, Thomas Jefferson, a highly respected Virginia lawyer, to defend him. Jefferson's main argument to the jury is his credo that all men are created equal and regardless of ethnic background are entitled to a fair trial.

632. "The Other Self" (9/28/75; rebroadcast 7/10/76)

Cast: Howard Da Silva (Oliver Townsend); Joan Shay (Aunt Clara); Bob Dryden (Wallace); Russell Horton (Lt. Butterfield); Joan Banks (Dr. Wilma Heckman). Written by Sam Dann.

A factory owner hires a psychiatrist, Dr. Wilma Heckman, to find out why Oliver Townsend is the only contented worker in a boring assembly line job. It is because, she soon discovers, he is living in two worlds—one his job, the other a constant reconstruction in his mind and with toy soldiers of the Battle of Shiloh.

However, as the anniversary date (April 6-7) of the battle approaches, Oliver becomes so certain he will be killed that he starts taking days off from his job for the first time in eight years.

633. "You're Only Young Twice" (9/29/75; rebroadcast 2/22/76, 12/12/80)

Cast: Ann Shepherd (Jessica Stone); Virginia Dwyer (Beth Hardy); Earl Hammond (Jim Blake); Norman Rose (Nathan Hardy). Written by Fielden Farrington.

Scientist Nathan Hardy's obsession to keep his human rejuvenation formula a secret terrifies his wife Beth, who summons her sister, Jessica Stone, for help. Hardy reacts by telling Jessica he can guarantee her renewed youth if she will marry him, and he becomes outraged when Jessica rejects him and tells Beth about his proposal. The deranged scientist then makes plans to poison Jessica, but his diabolical scheme seems jinxed by an unexpected murder.

634. "The Devil's Leap" (9/30/75; rebroadcast from 6/4/75)

635. "Primrose Path" (10/1/75; rebroadcast 2/24/76)

Cast: Mason Adams (Starret); Jack Grimes (Jeff Pollard); Kenneth Harvey (Mr. Melon); Ian Martin (Hammer); Rosemary Rice (Mary Anne Melon). Written by Sam Dann.

Heiress Mary Anne Melon, out to punish her father whom she feels has neglected her, plots her own kidnapping with the help of her fiancé and two members of a radical underground army. Melon, concerned about his daughter's safety, hires a private detective named Starret to investigate the much publicized incident. Starret is baffled until the abductors send a recorded message, one sentence of which Starret believes contains the clue he needs to find Mary Anne.

636. "The Man Who Ran Away" (10/2/75; rebroadcast 2/28/76)

Cast: Mercedes McCambridge (The Woman); Martha Greenhouse (Mona Trent); William Redfield (Gregory Cape); Bob Dryden (David Trent). Written by Elspeth Eric.

David Trent, upset because his wife Mona is unfaithful, takes a drive and, when he runs out of gas, seeks help at an old house. There he meets and falls in love with a beautiful, ageless woman, but soon gets an eerie feeling about her and the house. When Gregory Cape, the landlord, finds Trent's abandoned car, he informs the now repentant Mona and together they set out to find her husband. It's not until Cape admits the house has been vacated for years does Trent begin to realize the mystery surrounding the woman.

637. "The Plastic Man" (10/3/75; rebroadcast from 6/5/75)

638. "The Transformer" (10/4/75; rebroadcast from 6/6/75)

639. "Fallen Angel" (10/5/75; rebroadcast from 6/9/75)

640. "Five Ghostly Indians" (10/6/75; rebroadcast 2/29/76)

Cast: Bob Dryden (Professor George Waymouth); Ann Pitoniak (Mag); James Gregory (Ben Farraday); Suzanne Grossmann (Fran); Court Benson (Col. Caleb Pengree). Written by Roy Winsor.

While vacationing in Maine, Professor George Waymouth and Colonel Caleb Pengree find an old Indian arrowhead on a deserted beach where an early explorer once brutally murdered six Indians. Shortly thereafter, they are frightened by the sound of drums and a cloudy apparition rising out of the water. They keep hearing the drums and seeing the apparition, and when Waymouth is attacked by an unknown force, both men become convinced that avenging spirits do exist.

Notes: James Gregory gave up a promising Wall Street career for acting and appeared frequently on Broadway before making his film debut in the late 1940s. He has since played numerous character roles in many Hollywood films, often as a heavy or tough cop. He has guest starred in numerous horror or mystery series such as *Kolchak: The Night Stalker*, *The Twilight Zone*, and *Alfred Hitchcock Presents*. He also starred in such police dramas on television as *The Lawless Years* and *Twenty-First Precinct*. His film roles include *The Naked City* (1948), *The Scarlet Hour* (1956), *X-15* (1961), *The Manchurian Candidate* (1962), *The Sons of Katie Elder* (1965), *Beneath the Planet of the Apes* (1970), and *Main Event* (1979).

641. "Who Made Me?" (10/7/75; rebroadcast 3/3/76)

Cast: Larry Haines (Admiral Rado); Evelyn Juster (Lila); Marian Seldes (Lora); Don Scardino (Coral). Written by Sam Dann.

Life on Earth a million years in the future has changed, but people haven't. They are divided into three social classes in a very complex, technical environment, but face the same human problems. Admiral Rado's son Coral, for instance, is dissatisfied with Group One and wants to move down to Group Three. Rado himself is secretly in love with a woman in Group Three. They also are all still trying to answer the gnawing question of how the universe was created.

642. "The Queen of Darkness" (10/8/75; rebroadcast from 6/10/75)

643. "They Shall Stone Them with Stones" (10/9/75; rebroadcast 3/6/76)

Cast: Teri Keane (Madame Dahrazum); Arnold Stang (Pinky Shears); William Redfield (Wilton Gaxton); Jackson Beck (Harry Murchison). Written by Sidney Slon.

Madame Dahrazum, a seer, and her husband Harry Murchison, both unemployed, are overjoyed when their joy quickly turns to terror. One of Madame's visions about an unsolved murder exposes Harry and her to threats from the real killer, who tries to stop them from going to the authorities. Only after Harry is shot do police lieutenant McClosky and his men move in and start devising a plan to capture the assailant.

644. "A Case of Negligence" (10/10/75; rebroadcast from 6/12/75)

645. "Stairway to Oblivion" (10/11/75; rebroadcast from 6/13/75)

646. "The Smile of Deceit" (10/12/75; rebroadcast from 6/16/75)

647. "The Last Lesson" (10/13/75; rebroadcast 3/7/76)

Cast: Fred Gwynne (Clarence Porter); Danny Ocko (Sheriff); Leon Janney (Doctor); Marian Haley (Penny Meadows). Written by Sam Dann.

Threatened with death unless he pays off his huge gambling bills, playboy Clarence Porter marries wealthy, sports-loving Penny Meadows. When she refuses to give him money, he determines to murder her, inherit her wealth and thus meet his financial obligations. He weakens the planks in the boat she uses to go shark fishing, loosens the front wheel in the car in which she races, and rewires their television set so that she will be electrocuted when she turns it on. But each time she escapes serious injury, and the gamblers are still insisting Porter will die unless he pays up.

648. "The Rape of the Maia" (10/14/75; rebroadcast from 6/27/75)

649. "The Kiss of Death" (10/15/75; rebroadcast 3/9/76)

Cast: Kurt Peterson (Giovanni Guasconti); Gilbert Mack (Dr. Rappaccini); Arnold Moss (Dr. Baglioni); Bryna Raeburn (Elizabetta Falcone); Patsy Bruder (Beatrice Rappaccini). Adapted by Ian Martin, based on the 1844 short story *Rappaccini's Daughter* by Nathaniel Hawthorne.

In Padua to study medicine, Giovanni Guasconti meets and falls in love with Beatrice, the beautiful daughter of Dr. Rappaccini, not knowing that she is under the spell of her father who has developed a flower that will kill anyone—except for her—who touches it. Later Giovanni inadvertently touches the flower and, though he doesn't die, becomes seriously ill. When he recovers, he finds that he too is now under the doctor's spell.

650. "Stay Out of Dutchman's Woods" (10/16/75; rebroadcast 3/13/76, 12/19/80)

Cast: Paul Hecht (Ronny Andrews); Santos Ortega (Lou Griffin) Mary Jane Higby (Sarah Griffin); Joan Lorring (Katrina); Jada Rowland (Peg Andrews). Written by Fielden Farrington.

Newly married Peg and Ronny Andrews go hiking in Dutchman's Woods where, according to the superstitious townspeople, the ghost of a beautiful woman named Katrina still hauntingly seeks out men's companionship 200 years after her jealous husband murdered her for infidelity. When Peg and Ronny accidentally become separated, Ronny meets Katrina, who lures him deeper into the woods. Ultimately Peg finds them and uses the one device she believes can put Katrina's wandering soul to rest forever.

651. "The Climbing Boy" (10/17/75; rebroadcast from 6/19/75)

652. "Can You Trust Your Husband?" (10/18/75; rebroadcast from 6/20/75)

653. "The Mills of the Gods" (10/19/75; rebroadcast from 6/23/75)

654. "Never in This World" (10/20/75; rebroadcast 3/14/76)
Cast: Alexander Scourby (David Campbell); Ian Martin (Reverend Beane); Marian Seldes (Prudence); Lori March (Lucy Campbell). Written by Ian Martin.

David Campbell, recovering in New Hampshire from a bout with influenza, takes a stroll in the woods and stumbles upon the ruins of an old church. For no reason he can think of, he is driven to circle the church twice *withershins* (counterclockwise), challenging an old Gaelic legend that whoever does so comes under the influence of Satan. Immediately a violent storm comes up, and by the time he returns to his cottage David's round red face has turned dark, lean and saturnine.

655. "Million Dollar Murder" (10/21/75; rebroadcast 3/17/76)
Cast: Mandel Kramer (Dick Nelson); Bob Dryden (Judge Morrow); Catherine Byers (Dorothy Nelson); Nat Polen (Ed Jerome); Patricia Elliott (Althea Beaumont). Written by Sam Dann.

Businessman Dick Nelson, about to liquidate his assets to keep his furniture company from going bankrupt, is offered $1 million by wealthy Althea Beaumont, his former lover, if he kills his closest friend, Judge Morrow. The reason, Althea reveals, is that after 30 years she still wants to punish the judge for convincing Nelson to leave her in favor of a promising career. Not until Nelson accepts Althea's offer does he realize he, too, may become a victim of her vendetta.

656. "The Mask of Tupac" (10/22/75; rebroadcast from 6/24/75)

657. "The Sealed Room Murder" (10/23/75; rebroadcast 3/20/76)
Cast: Howard Da Silva (Judge Randolph); Fred Gwynne (Abner Gale); Bryna Raeburn (The Woman); Ian Martin (Doomdorf); Earl Hammond (Bronson). Adapted by Ian Martin, based on a story by M.D. Post.

Angelus Doomdorf, a hostile and repugnant renegade from the Colonial wars who lives on a remote mountaintop with a young woman he constantly abuses, is found murdered by Judge Randolph and Sheriff Abner Gale. The two had to break through a door locked on the inside to get to Doomdorf's body. Once inside, they discover that the room's windows are also locked—on the inside. The question now facing them: How did the murderer manage to get out of the room?

658. "The Summer People" (10/24/75; rebroadcast 3/21/76)
Cast: Tony Roberts (Mike Slater); Grace Matthews (Martha Williams); Leon

Janney (Ned Broker); William Redfield (Tim Egan); Jennifer Harmon (Jane Slater). Written by Bob Juhren.

When city-dwellers Jane and Mike Slater arrive in the peaceful village of Granville to spend the summer, they are puzzled by the ageless spirit and mannequin-like appearance of all the local inhabitants. Frightened by the mysterious disappearance of another summer visitor and their discovery of a Granville highway marker hidden in a barn, the young couple make a desperate attempt to get away. Neither of them, though, can figure out why each road they take leads them right back to the center of town.

659. "That Hamlet Was a Good Boy" (10/25/75; rebroadcast from 6/26/75)

660. "Frame-Up" (10/26/75; rebroadcast from 6/18/75)

661. "A Living Corpse" (10/27/75; rebroadcast 4/14/76)

Cast: Robert Dryden (Professor Valdemar); Kurt Peterson (Doctor Nugent); Patricia Elliott (Luana). Written by Ian Martin.

Professor Amadeus Valdemar, an unscrupulous hypnotist who is dying of consumption, learns that his wife is having an affair and makes a deal with her lover, Dr. Craig Nugent. He promises to give the young doctor his secret theory on mind control if Nugent, in return, puts him in a trance just before he dies. What Nugent doesn't realize is that Valdemar's real purpose is the ultimate destruction of his wife.

662. "The Storm Breeder" (10/28/75; rebroadcast 3/27/76)

Cast: Michael Tolan (Judge Dunwell); Fred Gwynne (Peter Rugg); Ann Pitoniak (Mrs. Croft); James Felt (Driver); Ian Martin (Mr. Derwent). Adapted by Ian Martin, based on a story by William Austin.

For some 20 years in the early 1800s, many who lived in the eastern United States met on the road an open carriage drawn by a fierce black horse, carrying a man and his young daughter who clung to him in terror. They called him the storm breeder because he was always pursued by an ominous black cloud. He told people he was trying to get back home to Boston, but was never able to find his way—until a New York judge determines to help him.

663. "Ghost Powder" (10/29/75; rebroadcast 3/28/76)

Cast: Marian Seldes (Abigail Adams); Michael Wager (John Adams); Guy Sorel (Count De Vergennes); Court Benson (Tom Jefferson); Bryna Raeburn (Mme. Pinipesse). Written by Sam Dann.

Recently settled in their French chateau, U.S. Ambassador John Adams and his wife Abigail become concerned about their servants, who keep hearing loud ghost-like noises far into the night. The Adams hire a witch named Madame Pinipesse to exorcise the alleged ghost. When the witch mysteriously dies, John is convinced that her death was caused by sheer fright. Perplexed, John and Abigail set out to find what had the power to literally scare the witch to death.

664. "Triptych for a Witch" (10/30/75; rebroadcast 4/16/76)

Cast: Margaret Hamilton (Aunt Hester); Evelyn Juster (Joan Madden); Kristoffer Tabori (Walter Madden); Gilbert Mack (Doctor Damon). Written by Ian Martin.

Joan Madden and her husband Walter receive an unexpected visit from Joan's great aunt, Hester, recently widowed by a tragic fire. Although Walter senses something strange about Hester, he invites her to join them on a shore vacation. When Walter thinks he sees Hester's pet cat change into the form of its mistress, he becomes convinced she is a witch. When he discovers that Hester has been collecting a rare type of poisonous seaweed, he suspects Joan's life may be in danger.

665. "It's Hell to Pay the Piper" (10/31/75; rebroadcast 4/17/76)

Cast: Ian Martin (Steen Steenson); Bryna Raeburn (Mistress Weir); Guy Sorel (Minister McKay); Court Benson (Jock McGraw); Arnold Moss (Sir Robert Redgauntlet). Adapted by Ian Martin, based on the 1824 novel *Red Gauntlet* by Sir Walter Scott.

Steen Steenson, a poor Scottish farmer, neglects to get a receipt for his rent payment from Sir Robert, his eccentric feudal landlord whose only companion is a devil-like monkey. When Sir Robert dies, his son John demands that Steen clear his debt by Halloween night. Not until the despondent Steen meets a witch who takes him on a journey to hell to collect the overdue receipt from Sir Robert, does he realize that there may be a real thief living in Redgauntlet Castle.

666. "The Slave" (11/1/75; rebroadcast from 7/4/75)

667. "Come Back with Me" (11/2/75; rebroadcast from 7/2/75)

668. "The Mortgage" (11/3/75; rebroadcast 4/3/76)

Cast: Larry Haines (Marvin Cooper) Robert Maxwell (Peter Anderson) Russell Horton (Lou Dudley); Bob Dryden (Dmitry Ligorin); Marian Seldes (Sally Cooper). Written by Sam Dann.

Sally Cooper becomes concerned when her husband Marvin, usually a placid and civic-minded man, goes through a sudden change in personality. What she doesn't know is that Marvin is really a Communist defector who is terrified his cover may be discovered by his stepbrother Dmitry, a Russian agent now in the United States. When Dmitry does find Marvin and orders him to persuade his closest friend to defect, Marvin, after 20 years as an American, seems uncertain where his allegiance belongs.

669. "The Golden Cauldron" (11/4/75; rebroadcast from 6/30/75)

670. "The Edge of the Scalpel" (11/5/75; rebroadcast 4/4/76)

Cast: Teri Keane (Kerry Stewart); Don Scardino (Dr. Ted Kowalski); Robert

Kaliban (Joel Stewart); Joan Shay (Dr. Choate Stewart); Gordon Gould (Kirk Malcolm). Written by Ian Martin.

Nurse Kerry Stewart swears to her selfish, unbelieving husband, Joel, a sickly invalid, that her romance with chief surgeon Kirk Malcolm is over. Soon Joel's condition worsens and he is rushed to the hospital where Dr. Malcolm, disregarding the opinion of a colleague, decides to operate. When Joel's wealthy mother discovers that another doctor advised Dr. Malcolm not to operate, she warns that he will be charged with murder unless her son survives the operation.

671. "Murder Will Out" (11/6/75; rebroadcast from 7/3/75)

672. "Killing Valley" (11/7/75; rebroadcast 4/18/76)

Cast: Kim Hunter (Polly Preston); Joan Shay (Martha William); Redfield (Jack Doyle); Ian Martin (Josiah Killing). Written by Sam Dann.

Author Polly Preston, seeking revenge, returns to her home town to write an exposé about the vicious people who live there, particularly the powerful and wealthy Josiah Killing, who, she claims, caused her parents to be ostracized years ago. After she narrowly escapes a hit-and-run attempt and her publisher rejects the book, Polly fears that Killing is out to get her too, until she stumbles on a damaging letter her mother entrusted to Killing before she died.

673. "The Triangle" (11/8/75; rebroadcast from 7/8/75)

674. "Guilty" (11/9/75; rebroadcast from 7/7/75)

675. "The Public Avenger" (11/10/75; rebroadcast 4/27/76)

Cast: Marian Haley (Rose Ellenbogen); Bob Dryden (Professor Franz Teppel); Leon Janney (Mr. Fenriss); Arnold Stang (Stuart Haskins). Written by Sam Dann.

Because secretary Rose Ellenbogen cannot understand Stuart Haskins' apathy toward the persistent harassment of their boss, she discusses his behavior pattern with her psychology professor. Rose is shocked when the professor theorizes that Haskins may be the killer who has baffled the authorities by assassinating only well-known criminals. Only when Haskins is unable to account for his whereabouts at the time another gangster is murdered does Rose begin to believe he may in fact be a public avenger.

Notes: Arnold Stang has appeared in such films as *Ghost Dad* (1990), *The Wonderful World of the Brothers Grimm* (1962), *The Man with the Golden Arm* (1955), *Hercules in New York* (1970), and *Dennis the Menace* (1993).

676. "Party Girl" (11/11/75; rebroadcast 4/10/76)

Cast: Mason Adams (Sgt. Ben Kravic); Russell Horton (Bill Anderson); Evelyn Juster (Cecily Anderson); Earl Hammond (Jim). Written by Sam Dann.

When a young woman accidentally shoots herself during a secret tryst with Congressman Bill Anderson, his campaign manager insists they make her death appear as if she were murdered by an unknown assailant. Unaware of what really happened, police sergeant Ben Kravic confides his findings in the case to his close friend, the congressman. Only after his leads begin disappearing does Kravic suspect that Anderson's interest may be more than that of a concerned politician.

677. "The Ghostly Rival" (11/12/75; rebroadcast from 7/10/75)

678. "Home Is Where the Ghost Is" (11/13/75; rebroadcast 4/11/76)

Cast: Gordon Gould (Dr. Ramsey Joslin); Patricia Elliott (Emily Joslin); William Redfield (Dr. Verdoga); Gilbert Mack (Colonel Polovich). Written by Murray Burnett.

Colleagues of Dr. Ramsey Joslin, who is working on a highly secret project that could destroy a civilization, became concerned about his sanity when he describes conversations with the ghost of his wife, Emily. Joslin has been asked by United States government agents to help Dr. Alexei Verdoga, a long-time Russian friend, defect to the U.S., but Emily's ghost keeps telling her husband he should be careful what he says or does with the Russian scientist.

679. "The Money Makers" (11/14/75; rebroadcast 4/28/76)

Cast: William Redfield (Roy); Bryna Raeburn (Julie); Jack Grimes (Steve) Ralph Bell (Noah Carpenter). Written by Fielden Farrington.

Two counterfeiters set up their printing presses in the basement of an isolated house inhabited only, they were told, by the ghost of the man who owned it 100 years ago. Neither believes in ghosts until the wife of one is approached by the specter, who calls himself Noah and tells her what the two men are up to. When she threatens to go to the police, the two make plans to murder her. But both somehow forget that Noah is still around.

680. "The Widow's Auxiliary" (11/15/75; rebroadcast from 7/11/75)

681. "Snake in the Grass" (11/16/75; rebroadcast from 7/14/75)

682. "The Moonlighter" (11/17/75; rebroadcast 4/30/76)

Cast: Howard Da Silva (Stanley Morrison); Bob Dryden (Mr. Ackroyd); Joan Banks (Gladys Morrison); Robert Kaliban (Frank Smith). Written by Sam Dann.

Finding themselves in need of extra cash, mild-mannered Stanley Morrison and his close friend, Frank Smith, both expert marksmen, become hit men for the syndicate. After Morrison completes several contracts he is surprised by his lack of remorse. Smith, on the other hand, does feel guilty and can no longer carry out his part of the bargain. When the syndicate learns Smith is reneging, its boss orders Morrison to kill him.

683. "Goodbye, Karl Erich" (11/18/75; rebroadcast from 7/16/75)

684. "Fear" (11/19/75; rebroadcast 5/1/76)

Cast: Jack Grimes (Edgar Ellerbe); Marian Seldes (Mary Lou Grant); Earl Hammond (Detective Bradshaw); Jane White (Hilda). Written by Elspeth Eric.

Bank teller Edgar Ellerbe becomes the prime suspect in a bank robbery after Detective Bradshaw shows the bank's employees a film on the stick-up. Even though Ellerbe does resemble the thief, co-worker Mary Lou Grant points out that Ellerbe, at five feet, one inch, is much shorter than the man seen in the film. Mary Lou's observation loses some of its punch when Bradshaw finds a pair of three-inch-thick innersoles in Ellerbe's apartment.

685. "Lamps of the Devil" (11/20/75; rebroadcast 5/2/76)

Cast: Kristoffer Tabori (Noah Artwright); Ian Martin (Payton); Joan Shay (Prudence); Russell Horton (George Marcy). Written by Sam Dann.

Civil War hero Noah Artwright's homecoming turns sour when his fiancée tells him she is already married. To add to his misery, Artwright, former skipper of a whaling ship, is unable to find a job because the discovery of petroleum has made the use of whale oil almost extinct. Artwright finally does get work, as captain of a petroleum-carrying vessel, but his crew, mostly ex-whale hunters and mutinies, demand that he throw overboard his valuable cargo of crude oil.

686. "The Hanging Judgment" (11/21/75; rebroadcast 5/4/76)

Cast: Mandel Kramer (J. Carr Justin); Kenneth Harvey (Dr. Sam Grant); Joan Shay (Sherril Stafford); Leon Janney (D.A. Al Herman); Earl Hammond (Kinsella). Written by Ian Martin.

Dr. Sam Grant and his girlfriend, Sherril Stafford, both charged with the murder of his wife, swear to their lawyer, J. Carr Justin, that they are innocent. Grant willingly admits he and Sherril were visiting his wife to ask her for a divorce when the shot that killed her rang out. Only when the district attorney produces a surprise witness who claims that Sherril hired him to murder Mrs. Grant does Justin begin to suspect that one or both of his clients are guilty.

687. "Nightmare's Nest" (11/22/75; rebroadcast from 7/17/75)

688. "The Spots of the Leopard" (11/23/75; rebroadcast from 7/18/75)

689. "The Serpent's Tooth" (11/24/75; rebroadcast 5/5/76)

Cast: Norman Rose (Jacob Kohn); Ann Shepherd (Rachel Kohn); Bob Dryden (Dr. Bloch); Paul Hecht (Addie). Written by Sam Dann.

In pre–World War I Vienna, art critic Jacob Kohn and his wife Rachel take in a young, homeless artist named Addie. Rachel is frightened by Addie who, delirious from a fever, has violent nightmares about red, white and black insignias, which she feels are premonitions of death. After he recovers, Addie leaves and the Kohns never hear from him again. But they—and the rest of the world—hear about him as he rises to dictatorial power in Germany.

690. "The Lap of the Gods" (11/25/75; rebroadcast 5/7/76)

Cast: Larry Haines (Walter Davis); James McCallion (Captain Kelly); Martha Greenhouse (Jane West); William Redfield (Officer Kronsky); Hetty Galen (Malama). Written by Ian Martin.

Walter Davis, who has been drowning his sorrows in alcohol since the death of his wife, lies dying in a New York hospital. While in a coma, his soul is transferred to the body of Joshua Fenwright, a sea captain who was shipwrecked over 150 years ago. Fenwright, blinded by the accident, is confused by strange flashes he has of himself in a future life as a man named Walter Davis. His confusion mounts when the flashes stop and he suddenly regains his sight.

691. "Fateful Reunion" (11/26/75; rebroadcast from 7/21/75)

692. "The Dead, Dead Ringer" (11/27/75; rebroadcast 5/8/76)

Cast: Don Scardino (Det. Bruce Hart) Leon Janney (Mario Procacci) Jackson Beck (Captain Schultz); Evelyn Juster (Penny Marsden). Written by Ian Martin.

Private detective Bruce Hart accepts underworld boss Mario Procacci's offer of $1,000 to deliver the message, "You can be replaced," to his playboy son-in-law, Howie Marsden. After arriving at the Marsden home, Hart finds Procacci's daughter, Penny, innocent though she is, holding a gun over her dead husband's body. When Hart sees the uncanny resemblance between Marsden and himself, he quickly switches identities, hoping that the real murderer will try to strike again.

693. "The Frammis" (11/28/75; rebroadcast 5/9/76)

Cast: Howard Da Silva (Gerard); Bryna Raeburn (Sophie); Bob Dryden (Col. Ramrod); Joan Shay (Marissa); Ian Martin (Lt. Melvin). Written by Sam Dann.

After discovering a brilliant diamond which he alone knows is not authentic, an idealistic but poor jeweler named Gerard tries to ignore his wife's plea to sell the stone for $1 million. He reluctantly gives in to her demands when an officer in the Royal Army offers to purchase the jewel, which eventually winds up in the king's priceless collection. When the king asks him for an appraisal, Gerard's lifelong reputation for honesty is put to the ultimate test.

694. "The Poisoned Pen" (11/29/75; rebroadcast from 7/22/75)

695. "Appointment in Uganda" (11/30/75; rebroadcast from 7/24/75)

696. "With Malice Aforethought" (12/1/75; rebroadcast 5/11/76)

Cast: Carlos Carrasco (Gil Robey); Robert Maxwell (Chief); Marian Seldes (Rita); William Redfield (Kip Kipness); Len Gochman (Watson). Written by Sidney Slon.

Although Sgt. Gil Robey swears his victim pulled a gun first, investigators cannot find the weapon or any drugs at the scene of the raid. After his indictment,

Robey and his pregnant wife are subjected to a series of threatening phone calls. One caller, who claims he can clear Robey of the murder charge, asks the policeman to meet him secretly. But instead of new evidence, he offers Robey $50,000 and a one-way trip to Mexico in his private plane.

697. "Woman from Hell" (12/2/75; rebroadcast from 7/25/75)

698. "Promise to Kill" (12/3/75; rebroadcast 5/12/76)

Cast: Gordon Gould (Dave Farmer); Earl Hammond (Stan); Russell Horton (Vernon White); Hetty Galen (Paula); Lesley Woods (Connie); Roy LeMay (Ross). Written by Henry Slesar.

Wealthy Dave Farmer, enraged by the brutal murders of his exceptionally beautiful wife and 5-year-old daughter, arranges through his best friend and lawyer to have their assassin—Adonis-like delivery boy Vernon White—killed in prison. When the plan backfires and White escapes, Farmer determines to track him down and perform the execution himself. When confronted, the frightened youth talks and, for the first time, Farmer learns what really happened on that tragic day.

699. "Portrait of a Killer" (12/4/75; rebroadcast 5/14/76)

Cast: Michael Wager (John Brown); Russell Horton (Joe); Jada Rowland (Polly Braxton); Joan Banks (Marcia Fresnick); Bob Dryden (Charlie). Written by Ian Martin.

Two guards in a museum are fascinated by an old man who stares for hours at the only remaining work of an obscure artist. One of the guards believes that the painting has come alive, that the old man is its creator, and the painting is helping him relive his life—even the moment when he murdered the man who, through trickery, had stolen his fiancée and was the cause of her suicide.

700. "Pharaoh's Daughter" (12/5/75; rebroadcast 5/15/76)

Cast: Jack Grimes (Eddie Judson); Ian Martin (Lt. Davis); Jordan Chaney (Sergeant Al Gomez); Nat Polen (Dispatcher); Joan Shay (Lenore Drake). Written by Sam Dann.

Lenore Drake, intent upon concealing her elderly millionaire husband's death in a taxicab, sits idly by while her husband's bodyguard murders the cab driver, the only witness to her husband's demise. She and the bodyguard manage to frame drunken Eddie Judson, a passerby, for the cabby's death, but they can't stop suspicious police sergeant Al Gomez. He links Lenore to Pharaoh's daughter, who, according to legend, summoned a slave to her tent, then had him speared to death.

701. "The Lady Is a Jinx" (12/6/75; rebroadcast from 7/28/75)

702. "He Moves in Mysterious Ways" (12/7/75; rebroadcast from 7/30/75)

703. "How Quiet the Night" (12/8/75; rebroadcast 5/16/76)

Cast: William Redfield (Russell Porter); Patricia Elliott (Sibyl Malone); Marian Seldes (Corajean Buxton); Court Benson (Sheriff Mayberry). Written by Sam Dann.

Ambitious Russell Porter, intent on marrying wealthy Sibyl Malone, jilts his hometown girlfriend, Corajean Buxton, who is pregnant with his child. Enraged by his decision, Corajean warns Porter that she will never let him go so he, out of desperation, kills her. Even after Sheriff Mayberry accuses him of murder, Porter feels no remorse for what he did until he begins to wonder if he should have taken heed of her warning, literally.

704. "Stitch in Time" (12/9/75; rebroadcast 5/18/76)

Cast: Leon Janney (William Rawlinson); Bryna Raeburn (Amelia Fitzroy); Rosemary Rice (Donna Rawlinson); Earl Hammond (Chesko). Written by Sam Dann.

Amelia Fitzroy tells her boss William Rawlinson about an alarming dream in which she sees his niece and heir, Donna Rawlinson, being murdered by people attempting to gain control of his company's highly classified government projects. Unaware that Donna has been killed by a foreign agent who has assumed her identity, Rawlinson invites the impostor to visit him. However, Amelia's dreams persist, warning her that the impostor and her comrades have Rawlinson himself as their next target for murder.

705. "Carmilla" (12/10/75; rebroadcast from 7/31/75)

706. "You Can Change Your Life" (12/11/75; rebroadcast 5/19/76)

Cast: Ralph Bell (Lt. Charles Weiss); Earl Hammond (Eugene Paramenter); Martha Greenhouse (Gussie Waldowska); Bryna Raeburn (Marie Valdez); Bob Dryden (Terry). Written by Sam Dann.

Police lieutenant Charles Weiss, faced with the stabbing murders of two women, is certain he can get convictions against the husband of one and the boyfriend of the other. But when a third woman is killed in the same manner, Weiss has second thoughts—especially when he learns that all three were judges in a television game show ten years ago. His investigation goes nowhere, however, until the mother of the third victim offers him a plan on how to trap the murderer.

707. "Marry for Murder" (12/12/75; rebroadcast 5/21/76)

Cast: Mandel Kramer (Jim Kellogg); Patsy Bruder (Ann Trainor); Danny Ocko (Police Lieutenant); Arthur Anderson (Walter Jones); Evelyn Juster (Mrs. Melvin). Written by Sam Dann.

Wealthy widow Ann Trainor's family is so opposed to her impending marriage to Walter Jones that they hire private detective Jim Kellogg to prevent it. The family sees Jones as a swindler, marrying Ann only for her money with plans to murder her later, which is allegedly what he did to his first two wives, who were also rich. All of Kellogg's efforts to dissuade Ann prove unsuccessful—even his attempt, as a last resort, to make her fall in love with him.

708. "The Onyx Eye" (12/13/75; rebroadcast from 8/1/75)

709. "The Devil's Boutique" (12/14/75; rebroadcast from 8/4/75)

710. "Burn, Witch, Burn" (12/15/75; rebroadcast 5/22/76)

Cast: Howard Da Silva (Cotton Mather); Kurt Peterson (Gil Clayton); William Redfield (Sir John Jamison); Court Benson (Judge). Written by Ian Martin.

A fictitious incident in the life of the Rev. Cotton Mather, generally blamed for the hideously bigoted persecution in 1692 of Salem Village women thought to be witches. Luna Clare, whose grandmother could put people asleep by waving her hands and who was burned at the stake for it, waits in a tiny, cold, jail cell for the same fate. Her crime: In order to save her grandmother, she had allegedly tempted an older man to possess her. Mather tries to make Luna recant, knowing that even if she does, she'll still die by fire or be stoned to death.

711. "Hung Jury" (12/16/75; rebroadcast from 8/5/75

712. "The Eleventh Hour" (12/17/75; rebroadcast 5/23/76)

Cast: Larry Haines (J. Raymond Trask); Carol Teitel (Rah-el); Don Scardino (Douglas); Mary Jane Higby (Miss Mulhare); Arnold Moss (Cabbie). Written by Sam Dann.

Businessman J. Raymond Trask, filled with guilt because of the methods he employed in amassing his fortune, and now involved in a do-good project that will bankrupt his company, is so attracted by an ad that he cannot get its words out of his head. Ultimately he responds and meets its writer, a woman who calls herself Rah-el and who promises him an escape to peace and happiness if he can raise a million dollars.

713. "Fireball" (12/18/75; rebroadcast 5/25/76)

Cast: Kim Hunter (Louise Cantwell); Joe Hammond (Senator Sullivan); Guy Sorel (Joe Vulcan); Hugh Marlowe (Ben Cantwell). Written by Sam Dann.

The country's biggest developer of new military weapons, Ben Cantwell, insists that his wife fire the blacksmith working on their estate, one Joe Vulcan. She refuses, because her intuition tells her that Vulcan, who is lame but very young in appearance despite his many years, might be the ancient God of Fire visiting Earth disguised as a mortal. Such a visit usually means trouble for the people he calls on, and she foresees trouble for her husband and his new horrible "fireball" weapon.

Notes: Hugh Marlowe has appeared in such films as *Birdman of Alcatraz* (1962), *Casanova's Big Night* (1954), *Twelve O'Clock High* (1949), *All About Eve* (1950), and *Elmer Gantry* (1960).

714. "The Corpse Wrote Shorthand" (12/19/75; rebroadcast 5/26/76)

Cast: Mandel Kramer (Will Crawford); Berry Kroeger (C.P. Pendleton); Russell Horton (Nick Crawford); Joan Banks (Estelle Crawford); Joan Shay (Mrs. Conroy). Written by Roy Winsor.

Will Crawford, found guilty of embezzling $100,000 of his bank's securities, is released from jail five years later, determined to reestablish his family's good standing. With the help of a local newspaper reporter, Will questions every bank employee who was possibly involved, including the mother of his assistant, now dead, whose diary contains revealing facts.

715. "To Die Is Forever" (12/20/75; rebroadcast from 8/7/75)

716. "The Grey Ghost" (12/21/75; rebroadcast from 8/8/75)

717. "The Image" (12/22/75; rebroadcast 5/28/76)

Cast: Norman Rose (Evan Eliot); William Redfield (Billy); Marian Seldes (Christine); Teri Keane (Doris). Written by Elspeth Eric.

Best-selling author Evan Eliot is rich, famous and wed to blue-blooded millionairess Christine Duer. Christine is strikingly beautiful and totally infatuated with Evan's genius and machismo, yet she is strangely wan. Evan's agent and alter ego, Billy, worships him, but even he can't close his eyes to the mysterious transformation that has been brought on by the Eliots' childless marriage. The ruthless Evan, in his inability to create a perfect image, forces Christine to make a choice that could lead to her own destruction.

718. "The Murder Market" (12/23/75; rebroadcast 5/29/76)

Cast: Rosemary Murphy (Theodora); Ann Pitoniak (Mother); Bob Dryden (J.P. Carson); Ian Martin (Stanley). Written by Sam Dann.

Challenged by dynamic business entrepreneur J.P. Carson, Theodora Lewis accepts his unusual offer and for once in her life does something that isn't "sensible." Leaving her insipid fiancé and a humdrum secretarial job at an insurance company, she joins her new boss on a confidential business trip. At a mountaintop hideaway, high finance becomes high intrigue when Theodora finds herself the prime suspect in a murder—with no way to explain her obvious involvement.

719. "A Christmas Carol" (12/24/75; rebroadcast 12/24/75, 12/24/76, 12/24/77, 12/24/78, 12/24/79, 12/24/80, 12/24/81)

Cast: E.G. Marshall (Ebenezer Scrooge); William Redfield (Bob Crachit); Ian Martin (Fred); Bob Dryden (Morley's Ghost); Marian Seldes (Ghost of Christmas Past); Evelyn Juster (Mrs. Crachit). Adapted by Ian Martin, based on the 1843 story by Charles Dickens.

On Christmas Eve, Ebenezer Scrooge, a selfish, disagreeable London merchant, returns to his living quarters with no thought of celebrating the holiday

season. When a request for charity is made of him in the name of his dead partner, he answers that the Christmas spirit is wasteful and foolish. Only after he
goes to sleep and is visited by three apparitions does Scrooge change his mind.

Notes: This episode was rebroadcast more than any other episode, every
Christmas Eve, from 1975 to 1981. This was also the only episode in which the
host of the series, E.G. Marshall, performed in a drama, starring as Ebenezer
Scrooge.

720. "A Very Private Miracle" (12/25/75; rebroadcast from 12/24/74)

721. "License to Kill" (12/26/75; rebroadcast 5/30/76)

Cast: Joan Lorring (Mary Latham) Larry Haines (Van Latham); Earl Hammond
(Will); Sidney Slon (Doctor); Mary Jane Higby (Gammy). Written by Sidney Slon.

Mary Latham and her boyfriend Willy are unable to gain control of the fortune of her husband Van, while he is alive. Van is a hopeless, homicidal paranoid
locked in a mental institution out of Mary's reach. She masterminds a successful
plot to release him to her custody over his doctor's strenuous objections. But once
out, things don't go as planned. The hunter becomes the hunted, as greed proves
more dangerous than insanity.

722. "Age Cannot Wither" (12/27/75; rebroadcast from 8/11/75)

723. "The Master Computer" (12/28/75; rebroadcast from 8/13/75)

724. "The Memory Killers" (12/29/75; rebroadcast 6/1/76)

Cast: Ralph Bell (Henry Courtland); Bob Dryden (Dietrich Volker); Nat
Polen (George); Patricia Wheel (Marlene Volker). Written by Sam Dann.

Henry Clay Courtland, partner in a New York marketing concern, flies to
Munich to sign the New World auto company as a client. Soon after he starts
negotiating with Dietrich Volker, New World's president, Courtland realizes that
he has met the man before. During World War II Courtland, a prisoner of the
Germans, swore to a dying buddy who had been severely tortured by the then
Major Volker that he would kill the cruel Nazi officer if he ever got the chance.

725. "The Root of All Evil" (12/30/75; rebroadcast from 8/14/75)

726. "Sagamore Cottage" (12/31/75; rebroadcast 6/2/76)

Cast: Carmen Matthews (Miss Sagamore); Robert Kaliban (Roy Watson);
Robert Maxwell (Andy Carter); Bryna Raeburn (Margaretta); Janet Waldo (Peggy
Watson). Written by Bob Juhren.

Despite the warnings of his associates, engineer Roy Watson rents the servants' cottage of an old Long Island estate for himself and his wife. Sleep at night
is difficult for both because of squeaky sounds they hear inside their bedroom's
baseboards. Thinking the place is infested with field mice, they acquire a cat. The

cat finds no mice, but the Watsons find themselves, for no apparent reason, steadily losing weight—and they're terrified.

727. "One of the Missing" (1/1/76; rebroadcast 6/4/76, 11/4/79)

Cast: Kristoffer Tabori (Jerome Searing); Jennifer Harmon (Marian); Mason Adams (Dan Ransome); Arnold Moss (Captain). Adapted by Stella and Arnold Moss, based on the 1891 short story by Ambrose Bierce.

It's a hot June day in 1864 near Georgia's Kennesaw Mountain, where General Sherman's troops have passed in their cause of Johnny Reb. Private Jerome Searing, who doesn't know the meaning of the word "fear," volunteers to scout the enemy's rear lines. But instead of merely spying, the foolhardy Searing wants to become a hero by killing a few rebs before returning to his own lines. The brave Union soldier soon causes himself to become a dead hero.

728. "Insight Into Murder" (1/2/76; rebroadcast 6/5/76)

Cast: Gordon Gould (Terry Pierce); Teri Keane (Meg Pierce); Joen Arliss (Kim); Earl Hammond (Ben Kelly); Court Benson (Seward Black). Written by Roy Winsor.

Meg Pierce is convinced her lawyer husband Terry needs a long vacation when he tells her his beliefs about Sybil Harrison's murder and how a caretaker has been framed for it. At the insistence of Terry, who wants to defend the accused man, Meg checks the London newspapers of 1810 and discovers her husband is correct about Lady Millbrook. But she also learns that the lawyer who defended the caretaker in 1810 was later found floating in the Thames River.

729. "Cold Storage" (1/3/76; rebroadcast from 1/13/74)

730. "The Real Printer's Devil" (1/4/76; rebroadcast from 7/17/74)

731. "Tom Sawyer, Detective" (1/5/76; rebroadcast 11/15/76, 8/11/79)

Cast: Kristoffer Tabori (Tom Sawyer); Paul Hecht (Jake Dunlap); Robert Kaliban (Brace Dunlap); Evelyn Juster (Benita); Gilbert Mack (Uncle Silas). Adapted by Sam Dann, based on the 1896 short story by Mark Twain.

Tom Sawyer, now in his twenties, is called upon to solve a murder and save an innocent man from the noose. Setting out for his Uncle Silas' farm in Arkansas to help settle a family problem: the richest, orneriest man in town, Jake Dunlap, wants to marry Tom's pretty cousin Benita, but Silas will have none of it. Jake is making all kinds of threats in order to win Benita, ultimately scheming to make it appear Silas murdered his brother. Tom now has two problems: to keep Jake away from Benita and to prove that Uncle Silas is not the murderer.

Notes: Himan Brown commented: "What could be more appropriate than a selection of Twain's works to begin our bicentennial year. He wrote and wrote and wrote about being an American. He was keenly aware of the fact that he was an American. And he wrote quite a few stories that fit the mystery-suspense genre. We think we have found seven that are truly excellent."

According to Sam Dann: "Twain knew he had a very recognizable character in Tom and he wanted to write a detective story. It lends itself to adaptation and brings back such people as Aunt Polly and old Uncle Silas. Tom is still Tom and Polly is still Aunt Polly and when she calls, Tom jumps. In this one he jumps all the way to Arkansas where Uncle Silas is in a mess and ultimately is accused of murder. Like any other modern detective story, it has its clues, one of which enables Tom to trap the murderer."

732. "Is He Living or Is He Dead?" (1/6/76; rebroadcast 11/16/76, 4/15/79)

Cast: Alexander Scourby (Smith); Bryna Raeburn (Madame Lucerne); Paul Hecht (François Millet); Court Benson (Mark Twain). Adapted by Sam Dann, based on the 1893 short story by Mark Twain.

François Millet, Carl Boulanger and an Englishman named Smith—all artists—are living in abject poverty in the south of France. Millet's paintings are the best, but no one will pay more than a few francs for any of them. Smith goes to Paris to visit Madame Lucerne, who runs the city's most talked-about salon. She points out that great artists become recognized only after they die, which Smith decides is what must happen, at least outwardly, to Millet.

Notes: "'Is He Living or Is He Dead?' is one of the great stories of deception," noted Sam Dann. "In it, Twain expresses his displeasure with the fact that the world loves dead artists, that you've got to be dead to make it. He takes a budding French painter, François Millet, and makes it appear to the world that he is dead, even though he's really alive and painting away (and selling). Twain picked the wrong man for this story, because Millet was recognized in his lifetime. But what Twain was saying is still true."

733. "The Russian Passport" (1/7/76; rebroadcast 11/17/76, 10/6/79)

Cast: Bobby Morse (Alfred Parrish); Russell Horton (Ned Parker); Danny Ocko (Waiter); Earl Hammond (Clerk); Bob Dryden (Major Jackson). Adapted by Sam Dann, based on the 1902 short story *The Belated Russian Passport* by Mark Twain.

Alfred Parrish, lonesome and alone in Berlin in 1890, is soon sorry he fell for the blandishments of Major Jackson, an arrogant, retired U.S. Army officer who insists that Parrish see St. Petersburg before he returns to Yale. Jackson assures the timid student he won't need a passport, that he (Jackson) will handle this minor detail. But he doesn't tell Parrish that getting caught in Russia without such a document can mean ten years in Siberia.

Notes: Sam Dann commented: "'The Russian Passport' has to do with bureaucracy, with the fact that the average clerk, the average little guy is not going to step out of line. Twain preached humorous sermons about red tape, the timidity of public officials, the suspiciousness between countries. One of the things that appealed to me about this story is the timeliness of it. It doesn't matter whether it's under a czar or a commissar, it's the same Russia, it's the same red tape, the same unswerving allegiance to ignorance and stupidity. But it's also a suspense story, fitting the needs of *Theater* very well."

734. "A Connecticut Yankee in King Arthur's Court" (1/8/76; rebroadcast 11/18/76, 9/1/79)

Cast: Kevin McCarthy (The Yankee); Russell Horton (Clarence); Bob Dryden (Sir Kay); Arnold Moss (King Arthur). Adapted by Sam Dann, based on the 1889 novel by Mark Twain.

A two-fisted Connecticut foreman picks a fight with the wrong party one day and, when he regains consciousness, finds himself in a strange place peopled by folk who claim to be members of King Arthur's court. Because of his 19th century clothes and manner, he is judged a sorcerer and condemned to the stake, the usual fate of such people in those times. But the Yankee has a good memory, recalling an eclipse of the sun in the year 538, which he plans to use to save his life.

Notes: Sam Dann commented: "Mark Twain wrote *Connecticut Yankee* because he was a small 'd' democrat. He was always against an undeserving establishment, particularly royalty. He was also against an established church and he used *Connecticut Yankee,* I think, to underline what was wrong with establishments that can exist only because of the ignorance and timidity of people. It's also a superman story, which always makes interesting fiction. And it has suspense, fantasy and mysticism, all necessary ingredients in our radio dramas."

735. "The Man That Corrupted Hadleyburg" (1/9/76; rebroadcast 11/19/76, 10/14/79)

Cast: Fred Gwynne (Edwin Richards); Joan Shay (Mary Richards); Court Benson (Burgess); Ralph Bell (Jack Halliday); Earl Hammond (Stevenson). Adapted by Sam Dann, based on the 1900 short story by Mark Twain.

A town that advertises itself as the most honest and upright place in the world suddenly falls from grace when one of Hadleyburg's poorest citizens finds a sack containing 160 pounds of gold coins on his front doorstep. An accompanying note says the money has been brought to Hadleyburg by a gambler who won it with the $20 one of the townsfolk had lent him, and he wants this person, whose name he doesn't know, to have it. When word gets around about the gold, there's hardly a person in Hadleyburg who says he didn't lend the gambler that $20.

Notes: According to Sam Dann "this was one of the deadliest stories ever written. Incorruptible Hadleyburg, filled with pride, envied by its neighbors and yet one day it fell from grace. The story is very modern in the sense that it deals with something new in the twentieth century—the banality of evil. It used to be popular to think that evil was committed by evil people. Today that's not so—a lot of good people commit evil. We saw that in Nazi Germany, we've seen it in Watergate. After all, the crimes of Watergate were crimes of basically respectable people. They were good husbands, good fathers, pillars of the community, just like the people of Hadleyburg where all the thieves were respectable citizens."

736. "The Stolen White Elephant" (1/10/76; rebroadcast 11/20/76, 10/13/79)

Cast: Bob Dryden (Inspector Blunt); Ian Martin (Major Smathers); Ian Donald

(Colonel Yale); Bryna Raeburn (Molly). Adapted by Sam Dann, based on the 1882 short story by Mark Twain.

Inspector Blunt of the New York City police force is informed by British Major Smathers that the sacred white elephant he was entrusted to deliver to Queen Victoria has been stolen. Certain that badman Barge Crisswell is the thief, Blunt orders 100 men to storm the home, only to discover that Crisswell has been dead for 15 years, hanged as a result of brilliant detective work by none other than Blunt himself.

Notes: "Twain wrote *The Stolen White Elephant* because he was determined to strike a blow for America," said Sam Dann. "The modern detective story was invented by our own Edgar Allan Poe—in *The Murders in the Rue Morgue*—and [Sir] Arthur Conan Doyle, an Englishman, took all of the principles laid down by Poe and proceeded to make a fortune with Sherlock Holmes. This irked Twain to no end, so he wrote this satire to put Doyle in his place. He included all the minutae found in a Doyle story, but his detective, his character of Holmes, is a dumb-dumb. It's a spoof with lots of laughs."

737. "The Mysterious Stranger" (1/11/76; rebroadcast 11/21,76, 4/1/79)

Cast: Tony Roberts (Theodore Fischer); Bryna Raeburn (Ursula); Marian Seldes (Marget); Ian Martin (Peter); Joseph Silver (Satan). Adapted by Sam Dann, based on the 1916 short story by Mark Twain.

It's 1590 in a sleepy village in Austria where a young unemployed lawyer, Theodore Fischer, meets a stranger who seemingly can perform miracles such as lighting Fischer's pipe simply by blowing on it. At Fischer's request, the stranger fills the purse of Fischer's starving Uncle Peter with 1,107 gold coins, warning that that will set an entire new chain of events in motion for Uncle Peter—none of which, in the long run will be very good. Fischer soon realizes the stranger has spoken the truth; nevertheless, he keeps asking him to perform miracles.

Notes: Sam Dann noted that this was "one of Twain's greatest mystic fantasies. He was a master of the switch. If everybody says the devil is bad, then Twain will build a case for him. He was the original devil's advocate. Twain, as usual, is on the side of the underdog; in this story it's the devil. The devil can't be that bad, says Twain, because most of the interesting people on this planet are going to hell. Twain's devil is at least realistic enough to do his dirty work and not to surround it with piety and give it a theme of something which it isn't. The devil admits this in the story. He doesn't hold out false hopes."

The National Education Association informed CBS Radio that it would recommend the weekend broadcasts of "The Mysterious Sranger" and other episodes to its membership of 1.8 million teachers. Two years ago, Hi Brown, whose previous work was the first radio series to be recommended by NEA, produced a radio adaptation of *Ivanhoe* before the organization's board of directors at its annual conference. At the time, NEA president John Ryor said, "We have studies that show radio drama can stimulate imagination ... I think radio drama has stimulated student interest in literature in ways not yet adequately evaluated and explored." This scheduling of classics lasted till the end of 1979.

738. "What the Shepherd Saw" (1/12/76; rebroadcast 6/8/76)

Cast: Russell Horton (Bill Mills); Ian Martin (Duke); William Redfield (Fred Ogbourne); Marian Seldes (Duchess). Written by Elizabeth Pennell.

In the shadow of Stonehenge's Devil's Door in England, where Bill Mills tends the sheep, the duchess is mysteriously summoned to meet her long-lost cousin, Captain Fred Ogbourne. Misunderstanding this as an act of unfaithfulness, the duke seeks revenge, kills the captain, and then, realizing his error, tries to conceal it from his wife. A spectator to this macabre drama, Bill, fearing for his own life, succumbs to the duke's demands that he forget everything he has seen and embarks on a new but guilt-ridden career.

739. "Terror in the Air" (1/13/76; rebroadcast from 8/22/75)

740. "The Elixir of Death" (1/14/76; rebroadcast 6/9/76)

Cast: Paul Hecht (Dr. Nevins); Bob Dryden (Dr. Stern); Evelyn Juster (Carolyn). Written by Sam Dann.

Dr. Peter Nevins gives up a promising career in a big-city hospital to become a country doctor in a community that relies on the Elixir Vita bottling plant for its economic well-being. Appointed the village's health officer, Dr. Nevins runs a test of the "elixir," the source of which is a natural spring, and finds that it contains a substance that can be lethal to people with certain allergies. Though he doesn't know it, he may be the first victim; a woman he meets uses the "elixir" to cook the vegetables she serves him at mealtime.

741. "The Unbearable Reflection" (1/15/76; rebroadcast from 8/15/75)

742. "The Red Frisbee" (1/16/76; rebroadcast 6/11/76)

Cast: Mandel Kramer (Ben); Teri Keane (Monica); Jada Rowland (Nikki). Written by Elspeth Eric.

While playing on an Antilles beach with his dog and a red Frisbee, Ben meets Nikki, a young girl with unusual intuition who lives in the stately Great House. As their friendship develops and the tragic story of her brother unfolds, Ben, who has just completed a three-year study of aborigines in Australia, becomes fascinated with Nikki's "wild talent." However, even he is surprised by the lesson she learns from the red Frisbee.

743. "Welcome for a Dead Man" (1/17/76; rebroadcast from 8/19/75)

744. "Circle of Evil" (1/18/76; rebroadcast from 8/21/75)

745. "There's No Business Like" (1/19/76; rebroadcast 6/12/76))

Cast: Howard Da Silva (Roger Starrett); Bob Dryden (Glasses); Joan Lorring (Baby); Bryna Raeburn (Dr. Simon). Written by Sam Dann.

Placed in the year 2076 by a time machine, a 1976 man finds himself sentenced to 15 years in entertainment (prison) where all the actors (prisoners) are ultimately given roles in which they could get killed—for real. Ancient Rome had its gladiators who fought to the death and lions in the arena who feasted on humans. Show-biz in 2076 has returned to this type of entertainment, and the 1976 man, finding himself in prison in this new, old society, realizes he will have to get on the good side of the writer—an emotionless, tough woman—if he is going to stay alive.

746. "Person to Be Notified" (1/20/76; rebroadcast from 8/25/75)

747. "The Lady of the Mist" (1/21/76; rebroadcast 6/13/76)

Cast: Rosemary Murphy (Meg Drayton); Marian Seldes (Vanessa); Ian Martin (Giles); William Redfield (Sir Charles). Written by Ian Martin.

Legend has it that the pool in which the Lady of the Mist waterfall drops resents anyone who tries to take the place of Meg Drayton, lady of the Manor. Ten years ago her brother Charles' first wife fell into the pool and was sucked out of sight. Now Charles has returned with his second wife, much younger than he, with plans to take over the manor. Infuriated at the thought of being replaced, Meg makes plans to insure that the Lady of the Mist legend will not be broken.

748. "The Eavesdropper" (1/22/76; rebroadcast from 8/27/75)

749. "The Slick and the Dead" (1/23/76; rebroadcast 6/15/76)

Cast: Russell Horton (Detective Carbo); Rosemary Rice (Polly Pitcher); Mandel Kramer (Lou Stein); Josephine Premice (Candace Hart); Earl Hammond (Cabot Lodge). Written by Ian Martin.

New York City detectives Carbo and Stein are assigned to the case of Candace "Candy" Hart, dancer strangled by her own panty hose while spending the night alone in a midtown hotel. The two cops come up with four suspects: Candy's roommate, her boyfriend, her producer and an art forger. But not until her boyfriend admits Candy called him from the hotel to find a fence for $100,000 in small bills do the cops begin to realize who the guilty party is.

750. "Night of the Howling Dog" (1/24/76; rebroadcast from 8/28/75)

751. "Murder by Proxy" (1/25/76; rebroadcast from 8/29/75)

752. "The Ferret" (1/26/76; rebroadcast 6/16/76)

Cast: Elliott Reid (Amory Mills); Patricia Elliott (Loris Mills); Court Benson (Mr. Warren); Robert Maxwell (Clem Ferris). Written by Roy Winsor.

Time after time, the new offshore oil rigs, tankers and natural gas fields of Energy Exploration, Inc., are mysteriously destroyed, thus impeding the United

States' plan to become independent of foreign energy sources. Clem Ferris, an unscrupulous EEI executive, is selling vital company information by Amory Mills, an EEI lawyer who, in a life-threatening contest, seeks to trap Ferris and Warren before they destroy the evidence and uncover the real identity of "The Ferret."

Notes: Elliott Reid has appeared in such films as *Follow Me, Boys!* (1966), *Gentlemen Prefer Blondes* (1953), *The Thrill of It All!* (1963), and *A Woman's World* (1954).

753. "The Smile of Death" (1/27/76; rebroadcast from 9/1/75)

754. "Mirror, Mirror" (1/28/76; rebroadcast 6/18/76)

Cast: Marian Seldes (Jessica); Marian Haley (Clare); Carmen Matthews (Mrs. Connor); Nat Polen (Stanley). Written by Elspeth Eric.

Many years have passed since Jessica Chapman and Clare Connor were roommates at Stapleton Academy. Jessica is surprised to find that Clare—once considered "the fairest of them all"—has been scarred by an unhappy marriage and a disappointing relationship with her daughter. But it is the memory of the full-view, gold-framed mirror, which she gave to Clare, that haunts Jessica, and she sets out to discover what part the mirror played in her friend's tragic life—and destruction.

755. "Portrait of Death" (1/29/76; rebroadcast from 9/2/75)

756. "Castle Kerfol" (1/30/76; rebroadcast 6/19/76)

Cast: Mercedes McCambridge (Paula/Anne); Ian Martin (Baron Decornault); William Redfield (Henri de Lanrivain); Guy Sorel (Judge). Adapted by Murray Burnett, based on the 1916 short story *Kerfol* by Edith Wharton.

Fashion designer Paula Randall, thinking of buying the 400-year-old Kerfol castle in northern Brittany, first reads its history. Early in the 17th century it was occupied by the elderly Baron Yves Decornault and his beautiful wife Anne, whom he considered to be unfaithful. To punish her he gave her several dogs, then killed them, the ghosts of which ultimately killed him. During one of Paula's visits to Kerfol, several dogs rush to greet her, though everyone says no dogs have been seen at the castle for years.

757. "The Special Undertaking" (1/31/76; rebroadcast from 9/4/75)

758. "Sleepwalker" (2/1/76; rebroadcast from 9/5/75)

759. "First Prize—Death" (2/2/76; rebroadcast 6/20/76)

Cast: Norman Rose (John Desmond); Roger De Koven (Dr. Spencer); Sam Gray (Elwood Downard); Evelyn Juster (Eloise Desmond). Written by Sam Dann.

John Desmond, a codirector of the Sociological Advistory Institute, is a leading sociologist, well admired by his colleagues. Yet, year after year, he is passed over while the Parkhurst Medal is awarded to other sociologists: first to his co-workers and then even to a former student. One day Desmond is approached by a Mr. Strickland, who promises him the next Parkhurst Medal if he falsifies his research and murders his superior. The price of fame? Death.

760. "The Dead Deserve to Rest" (2/3/76; rebroadcast 6/22/76)

Cast: Jennifer Harmon (Tish Meredith); Russell Horton (Detective Young); Teri Keane (Hank Plank); William Redfield (Dr. Payitkrishna); Martha Green-house (Mrs. Henderson). Written by Ian Martin.

Tish Meredith becomes a widow when her husband is hit by a drunken driver as he lifts her into her car outside the church. After being awarded $1 million by the drunken driver's insurance company, Tish heads for New York and she is contacted by a Dr. Payitkrishna. He claims he can put Tish in touch with her dead husband if she will just give the $1 million to his Temple of Transcendent Truth.

761. "The Other Life" (2/4/76; rebroadcast from 9/8/75)

762. "The Children of Death" (2/5/76; rebroadcast 6/23/76)

Cast: Tony Roberts (Gold); Bob Dryden (High Priest); Evelyn Juster (High Priestess); Marian Seldes (Flower). Written by Sam Dann.

Gold, the son of the High Priest, is now old enough to meet a member of the women's tribe in combat. If he can overcome her, he must bring her home to become the mother of his son (never a daughter), after which she will be killed. If he loses, he will receive the same fate at the hands of the women. Gold has developed doubts about this way of life and is uncertain as he goes out to face a woman. This is a future world where hate prevails and men and women are divided into hostile tribes, a condition warranted by the gods.

Notes: Sam Dann later used his radio script, "The Children of Death," as the basis for his novel *The Third Body*, published in 1979 by Popular Library.

763. "Straight from the Horse's Mouth" (2/6/76; rebroadcast 6/25/76)

Cast: Robert Morse (Hubert Purley); Ian Martin (Mervin); Mandel Kramer (Sid); Earl Hammond (Mr. Haskins); Augusta Dabney (Beatrice Purley); Bryna Raeburn (Birdie). Written by Ian Martin.

Hubert Purley is a sober, dependable bookkeeper for the Haskins Machine Screws, Nuts and Bolts Company, a business where, even if the books balance all the time, a guy may end up with a screw missing himself. Hubert buys Mervin, a 250-pound horse, and stables it in the garage of his duplex in Astoria, New York. Mervin, it turns out, talks to the other horses and soon tells an unbelieving Hubert how he can parlay a $2 bet into $1 million.

Notes: Ian Martin, the author of this humorous episode, supplied the voice of Mervin, the talking horse.

764. "The Ides of March" (2/7/76; rebroadcast from 9/10/75)

765. "The Voice of Death" (2/8/76; rebroadcast from 9/11/75)

766. "The Horror of Dead Lake" (2/9/76; rebroadcast 6/26/76)

Cast: Gordon Gould (Claude Baxter); William Prince (Billy Lee Harrison); Gilbert Mack (Johnny Reed); Ann Shepherd (Polly Baxter); George Petrie (Joe). Written by Roy Winsor.

Claude and Polly Baxter are delighted when they inherit Captain Doubloon's castle and the mysterious lake known as Dead Lake. However, their happiness turns to terror when they discover that the castle is inhabited by Professor Micah, a mad embryologist who is experimenting with giant Venus flytraps and birds. The real horror, though, is the creature that lives in Dead Lake, scaring not only the local residents but its creator.

767. "The Ghost Plane" (2/10/76; rebroadcast from 9/12/75)

768. "You Owe Me a Death" (2/11/76; rebroadcast 6/27/76)

Cast: Patricia Elliott (Heather Weston); Russell Horton (David Henley); William Redfield (Martin Henley); Ann Pitoniak (Mrs. Kalody); Vicky Volante (Irene Weston). Written by Henry Slesar.

Heather Weston is a twin, but she never met her "other half," Elizabeth, who was physically and mentally deformed and lived in an institution all but the last days of her life. It isn't until after Elizabeth's death that Heather first hears her sister's voice, beckoning Heather to join her in death.

Notes: Vicky Volante is no stranger to horror, having appeared in such films as *Horror of the Blood Monsters* (1970), *Brain of Blood* (1971), and *Blood of Dracula's Castle* (1969).

769. "The Golden Chalices" (2/12/76; rebroadcast 6/29/76)

Cast: Norman Rose (Hans von Fodor); Jada Rowland (Mary Roth); Carmen Matthews (Lili von Fodor). Written by Elspeth Eric.

Psychoanalyst Hans von Fodor is reminded of the flight he and his wife made from Hungary 30 years ago by the stories and gifts of Mary Roth, Hans' patient. Shortly after their wedding, Hans and Lili von Fodor were forced to flee from their native Kispest and leave behind a precious wedding gift; 12 golden chalices buried beneath a cherry tree. Mary now seems to be leading them on another fruitless search for the lost cups.

770. "The Blue Roan Stallion" (2/13/76; rebroadcast 6/30/76)

Cast: Tony Roberts (Dan Bowles); Earl Hammond (Hale Chalmers); Joseph Silver (Black Mike); Rosemary Rice (Mercy). Written by Ian Martin.

Dan Bowles, proud of his half-breed, Indian ancestry but not one to brag about it, saves ranch owner Hale Chalmers' life, is hired as a ranch hand, and falls in love with Chalmers' daughter, Mercy. They plan to get married until the ranch's foreman learns about Bowles' background and challenges the unarmed cowboy, whose life is saved by Chalmers. When Chalmers discovers that Bowles is a half-breed he himself tosses the cowboy a gun and orders him to shoot or be shot.

771. "The Little Old Lady Killer" (2/14/76; rebroadcast from 9/15/75)

772. "The Prison of Glass" (2/15/76; rebroadcast from 9/16/75)

773. "Angel of Death" (2/16/76; rebroadcast 7/2/76)

Cast: Marian Seldes (Deedee); Bob Dryden (Frank Maitland); Hetty Galen (Dr. Kathy Johnson); Shelley Bruce (Deedee as a child); Michael Wager (Dr. Bruce Harding). Written by Roy Winsor.

At age 26, Deedee Maitland feels that her life is over because she has lost her son, Jimmy, in an accident. Then she encounters the ghost of Stephen Campion, who gave up his life to save Deedee's more than 16 years before and who is determined to prevent her from wasting her life now.

774. "The Angry God" (2/17/76; rebroadcast 7/3/76)

Cast: Larry Haines (Skip Turner); Evelyn Juster (Valerie Parker); Ian Martin (Dimitrios); Nat Polen (Colonel Poulos). Written by Sol Panitz.

Skip Turner accidentally trips an alarm as he heists the Sacred Rope, a very valuable diamond necklace, and the area is cordoned off by the police before he can get away. He climbs aboard a bus full of American tourists and with the help of one, Valerie Parker, who is suspicious but still willing to listen to his alibis, manages to escape. Later, still running, he meets a strange woman who calls herself Pythia, a high priestess. She is not as accommodating as Valerie.

775. "The Coffin with the Golden Nails" (2/18/76; rebroadcast from 9/18/75)

776. "Good-Bye, Benjamin Flack" (2/19/76; rebroadcast 7/11/76)

Cast: Howard Da Silva (Guthrie Flack); Ralph Bell (Benjamin Flack); Joan Banks (Mrs. Flack); Court Benson (Ramsey Powell). Written by Sidney Slon.

Guthrie Flack contemplates murdering the beneficiary of his insurance company—his "twin" cousin, Benjamin Flack—in order to assume his identity, pass the dead body off as his own and collect the insurance money. However, Ben catches on and tries to kill Guthrie instead. To contemplate matters, Mrs. Benjamin Flack appears and tries to take the money for herself.

777. "The Bloody Legend" (2/20/76; rebroadcast 7/13/76)

Cast: Teri Keane (Martha Saxon); Earl Hammond (Frank Sherby); Robert Maxwell (Chief Anderson); Arnold Moss (Dash Saxon). Written by Milt Wisoff.

Martha Saxon, whose husband Dash is working night and day on a new study of *Beowulf*, asks for psychiatrist Frank Sherby's help when Dash has nightmares about the epic story, suffers from amnesia and comes home with dirty hands and bloody clothes. When police begin to investigate the carnage that took place in an animal shelter and the murder of two people during a storm, the evidence leads them to Dash, who, if he did commit the crimes, can remember nothing about them.

778. "The Third Person" (2/21/76; rebroadcast from 9/19/75)

779. "You're Only Young Twice" (2/22/76; rebroadcast from 9/29/75)

780. "The Patient Visitor" (2/23/76; rebroadcast 7/14/76)

Cast: Ian Martin (Judge Travers); Marian Seldes (Muriel Parks); Kenneth Harvey (Mr. Blessing); Bryna Raeburn (Mrs. Lefferis); Bob Dryden (Dr. Ridgely). Written by Ian Martin.

Judge Justin Travers, 78 and suffering from a failing heart, is visited in his New York apartment by Muriel Parks, whom he courted years ago. Because she cannot raise the required $500, Mrs. Parks is having difficulty gaining admittance to a home for the elderly, despite the fact that her late father left the home much money and property. Judge Travers determines to help her as a lawyer rather than a judge, although he knows it will be his last case.

781. "Primrose Path" (2/24/76; rebroadcast from 10/1/75)

782. "General Laughter" (2/25/76; rebroadcast 7/16/76)

Cast: Mercedes McCambridge (She); Mandel Kramer (He); Sam Gray (Doorman). Written by Elspeth Eric.

Instead of writing a suicide note to her husband and children, a distraught actress decides to tape record her reasons for wanting to kill herself as well as her last gasps. But, being an actress, she would like "to exit, amid general laughter." However, she soon discovers it to be rather difficult, even for an actress, to leave the world in such a manner.

783. "The Providential Ghost" (2/26/76; rebroadcast 7/17/76)

Cast: Beatrice Straight (Aunt Jane); Bryna Raeburn (Aunt Cissy); Court Benson (Mr. Charles); Gilbert Mack (Dr. Farnsworth); Hetty Galen (Lisha). Written by Ian Martin.

Lisha de Pew Miller, 8, has only one friend left in her family: her recalcitrant, lovable grandfather whom she calls Mr. Charles. When he dies and his two spinster daughters learn that Lisha will get most of the estate, the two women conspire to make sure it won't happen. Their attempt to do away with Lisha fails, thanks to a warning she gets in a talk with the dead Mr. Charles. One of the aunts dies instead, and there is talk that little Lisha may have murdered her.

Notes: Beatrice Straight has appeared in numerous films, including *Poltergeist* (1982), *The Dain Curse* (1978), *The Nun's Story* (1959), *The Promise* (1978), and *Network* (1976).

784. "Half a Life" (2/27/76; rebroadcast 7/18/76)

Cast: Tammy Grimes (Dr. Prentiss); Tony Roberts (Paul Jones); Earl Hammond (Mr. Mossman); Marian Haley (Suzanne). Written by Sam Dann.

Dr. Winifred Prentiss, an engineer working on a secret project for the government, has lately become fretful and defensive, sick of going out with the girls. Now 40 and not a beautiful woman, she's always been a bridesmaid, never a bride. On a lark she visits a singles bar and meets "the man." It's love at first sight, and he proposes. She doesn't care why and is completely happy, until he asks to borrow $10,000 and demands to know all about her secret project.

785. "The Man Who Ran Away" (2/28/76; rebroadcast from 10/2/75)

786. "Five Ghostly Indians" (2/29/76; rebroadcast from 10/6/75)

787. "The Death Trail" (3/1/76; rebroadcast 7/20/76)

Cast: Robert Kaliban (Wayne Prescott); Bob Dryden (Sheriff Benson); Marian Seldes (Abby Benson); Russell Horton (Hank Price); Ralph Bell (Slim Prescott). Written by Ian Martin.

Wayne Prescott, president of a small bank in Crystal City, Texas, in the late 1860s, is given $200,000 by Col. Chambers, his former commanding officer, who asks Prescott to invest the money in cattle. Prescott is about to marry Sheriff Benson's daughter Abby, but neither she, her father, nor the colonel have the slightest inkling that Prescott is a member of the pre–Civil War Gunnysack Gang, who killed people they robbed. Prescott has no intention of investing the money.

Notes: E.G. Marshall recalled: "A surprising number of listener letters have asked us for a Western. So here it is, back to the frontier life of the 1860s when, west of the Mississippi, the horse was still man's best means of locomotion. A noble animal, the horse, and particularly in those days, a good deal better than many a man who rode them."

788. "Afterward" (3/2/76; rebroadcast 7/21/76)

Cast: Celeste Holm (Mary Boyne); Joan Shay (Alida Stair); Ian Martin (Mr. Woods); Larry Haines (Ned Boyne); Guy Sorel (Mr. Parvis). Adapted by Murray Burnett, based on the 1909 short story by Edith Wharton.

Now committed to an insane asylum, Mary Boyne regrets her impetuousness in trying to restore the ghost to the old house in Lyng, England. She and her husband Ted were seeking a ghost that, as the story goes, no one realized was a ghost until after they had encountered it. But Ted found out too late, and Mary is haunted in the aftermath.

789. "Who Made Me?" (3/3/76; rebroadcast from 10/7/75)

790. "The Monk and the Hangman's Daughter" (3/4/76; rebroadcast 7/23/76, 10/20/79)

Cast: Kristoffer Tabori (Friar Ambrosius); Arnold Moss (Father); Russell

Horton (Friar Romanus); Evelyn Juster (Benedicta). Adapted by Arnold and Stella Moss, based on the 1892 novel by Ambrose Bierce.

Friar Ambrosius and another young monk, Friar Romanus, of the order of St. Francis, are sent by their superior to the monastery in Berchtesgaden, high in the Bavarian Alps. There, Ambrosius meets and feels great pity for the beautiful Benedicta, despised by all because she is the hangman's daughter. Soon Ambrosius is also scorned by the populace, most of all by the son of the village's most powerful man, who wants Benedicta for himself—not as a wife, but as a mistress.

791. "The Infernal Triangle" (3/5/76; rebroadcast 7/24/76)

Cast: Morgan Fairchild (Ann Fairchild); Joseph Silver (Dr. Fairchild); Catherine Byers (Eve); William Redfield (Hugh). Written by Ian Martin.

Ann Fairchild has always been the ugly duckling of the family. Her older and much more attractive sister, Eve, always managed to take possession of her toys and favorite clothes, and later, her boyfriends. Now Eve has come home, divorced from one of these men, and Ann, soon to be married, declares she will kill Eve if she tries to steal away her husband-to-be, Hugh Denning. She also vows to kill Hugh if he falls for Eve's blandishments, which he soon does.

Notes: Morgan Fairchild, who starred as Jennifer Phillips in the daytime CBS television serial *Search for Tomorrow*, made her radio acting debut in this episode.

792. "They Shall Stone Them with Stones" (3/6/76; rebroadcast from 10/9/75)

793. "The Last Lesson" (3/6/76; rebroadcast from 10/13/75)

794. "The Queen of Spades" (3/8/76; rebroadcast 7/25/76, 10/28/79)

Cast: Michael Tolan (Lieutenant Hermann); Ian Martin (Lieutenant Tomsky); Bryna Raeburn (Countess Fedotovna); Bob Dryden (Captain Naurov); Ann Shepherd (Lizaveta). Adapted by Sam Dann, based on the 1834 short story by Alexander Pushkin.

Lt. Alexy Petrovich Hermann, a German engineer in the czar's army, had never joined his comrades as they gambled until he learns that an elderly Countess Fedotovna holds the secret on how to win at faro. Extracting that secret from her becomes the lieutenant's only reason for living. When he finally manages to confront her, she dies from fright, but her ghost later reveals the secret to him. However, he soon learns what he has met is not a revengeful but a friendly ghost.

795. "The Kiss of Death" (3/9/76; rebroadcast from 10/15/75)

796. "I Thought I Saw a Shadow" (3/10/76; rebroadcast 7/27/76)

Cast: Nat Polen (Dr. John Gilbert); Joan Shea (Margo); Lloyd Battista (Lieutenant Healy); Gordon Gould (Dr. Steve Kaplan). Written by Bob Juhren.

For two years Dr. John Gilbert has been working on a serum to be used in government intelligence that will make spies temporarily invisible. Finally, Gilbert injects himself with the imperfect serum, discovering that instead of disappearing his shadow separates from his body. When his shadow goes on a murdering rampage, killing the scientist's enemies, Gilbert realizes that he must destroy it, even if it means killing himself.

797. "Pandora" (3/11/76; rebroadcast 7/28/76)

Cast: Patricia Elliott (Mara); Norman Rose (Willis); Joan Banks (Melissande); Don Scardino (Roland). Written by Sam Dann.

Hundreds of thousands of years in the future, in a society where there is only love and happiness, a woman, like Pandora, threatens to inflict her sorrow on others. In Paradise, Mara is not happy just to gratify her desires, to be beautiful, and talented, and to live forever. Her unhappiness and her desire to love Willis and their baby exclusively threaten to destroy the entire society, so she is condemned to death. At the last moment she is sent instead to the past, where she surprisingly finds that hard work, possessive love and a short life are no more satisfying.

798. "The Man Who Preyed on Widows" (3/12/76; rebroadcast 7/30/76)

Cast: Mason Adams (Robert Lewis); Russell Horton (Lawrence Randol); Joan Shay (Mrs. Randol); Jackson Beck (Lieutenant Eccles). Written by Roy Winsor.

Robert Lewis, alias Nelson Potter, has left the widowed Mrs. Randol with a few of her thousands in his pocket. She seems not the least upset because Lewis made her forget her unhappiness. But her children are not as acquiescent, demanding that he be put away for bigamy. When the identity of Lewis' next victim is ascertained, the police make elaborate plans to close in on him.

799. "Stay Out of Dutchman's Woods" (3/13/76; rebroadcast from 10/16/75)

800. "Never in This World" (3/14/76; rebroadcast from 10/20/75)

801. "The Aliens" (3/15/76; rebroadcast 7/31/76)

Cast: Paul Hecht (John Carpenter); Marie Cheatham (Louise); Bob Dryden (Dr. Bern); Mandel Kramer (Ivan Plohtnik). Written by Sam Dann.

Secret agents for the United States and the Soviet Union meet and discover they are facing the same problem: fear that what they are doing will destroy all mankind. John Carpenter, whose cover is that of a stockbroker, and Ivan Ivanovich Plohtnik, whose cover is a journalist, are drawn together through something called psychic communication, a secret project both of their governments are working on. The two fear for mankind's future if the project, which neither understands, is successful, and both realize there is very little they can do to stop it—nobody in the upper echelons will listen to either of them.

802. "Crime Casts a Shadow" (3/16/76; rebroadcast 8/1/76)

Cast: Evelyn Juster (Gay Armstrong); William Redfield (Mike Shea); Ian Martin (Bart Lerner); James Gregory (Preston Welch). Written by Roy Winsor.

Gay Armstrong, in need of cash, tries to sell her late mother's expensive pearl necklace but is told by a jeweler that the pearls are fake. When her stepfather offers her $15,000 for the fake necklace, Gay becomes suspicious. She doesn't want to hurt her stepfather but is not satisfied with his explanation that her mother has sold the real necklace to help pay some medical bills.

803. "Million Dollar Murder" (3/17/76; rebroadcast from 10/21/75)

804. "The Other Side of the Coin" (3/18/76; rebroadcast 8/3/76)

Cast: Ralph Bell (Gino Carpacci/John McCaffrey); Ian Martin (Bartender); Robert Kaliban (Lorenzo); Bryna Raeburn (Mary). Written by Ian Martin.

After losing his job, Sgt. John McCaffrey drowns his sorrows in booze and, through a supernatural accident, wakes up in someone else's body. Although he thinks like himself, he looks and speaks like Gino Carpacci, a double-crossing mobster who has stolen $1 million from the crime syndicate. While John-turned-Gino tries to avoid death and regain his identity, Gino-turned-John schemes to take the money and live free from mob entanglements.

805. "A Matter of Love and Death" (3/19/76; rebroadcast 8/4/76)

Cast: Lois Nettleton (Helen Collins); Lloyd Battista (Bruiser); Marian Hailey (Gwen); William Redfield (Jim Collins). Written by Elspeth Eric.

Now widowed, Helen Collins recalls to police sergeant Callahan that her husband Jim's life as a celebrity was haunted by fans, who pursued him everywhere. Although Jim seemed to enjoy the attention, it drove Helen crazy to the point where, as she tells the unbelieving sergeant, she thinks she murdered her husband. Was the strange love of his fans the cause of his death?

806. "The Sealed Room Murder" (3/20/76; rebroadcast from 10/23/75)

807. "The Summer People" (3/21/76; rebroadcast from 10/24/75)

808. "Stampede" (3/22/76; rebroadcast 8/6/76)

Cast: Fred Gwynne (Mr. Brenner); Kristoffer Tabori (Ned Parsons); Gilbert Mack (Mike); Catherine Byers (Ellie); Earl Hammond (Snake Duveen). Written by Ian Martin.

Ellie Tate Gottschalk, her husband murdered by Commanches and their beet crop and buildings destroyed by a stampede, joins a cattle drive on its way to Cheyenne. Because she's the only woman among a dozen or so rough and ready cowboys, the trail boss foresees trouble ahead. But when it comes and Snake Duveen is the cause (he wants Ellie for himself), the ghost of Ellie's husband appears. Even Duveen is frightened—for a while.

809. "The Covered Bridge" (3/23/76; rebroadcast 8/7/76)

Cast: Jada Rowland (Peg Marshall); Robert Kaliban (Ted Marshall); Ian Martin (Theo Bentley); Bryna Raeburn (Abigail). Written by Ian Martin.

Peg and Ted Marshall, just married and nearing their honeymoon hotel in New Hampshire, drive at dusk over a covered bridge. When they emerge, Peg is horror-stricken to find that their car has been transformed into a horse-drawn carriage and that Ted has become a different person, dressed in colonial attire and wearing a powdered wig. He is also muttering something about how her father is objecting to her marriage to Ted and has chosen him as her intended.

Notes: A rebroadcast of "A Living Corpse" from October 27, 1975, was originally scheduled for rebroadcast on this date, but "The Covered Bridge" was broadcast instead. A rebroadcast of "A Living Corpse" was pushed ahead a couple of weeks to April 14.

810. "Brain Drain" (3/24/76; rebroadcast 8/8/76)

Cast: Paul Hecht (Charles Carey); Bob Dryden (Henry Boggs); Staats Cotsworth (Inspector Warren); Carol Teitel (Tara). Written by Ralph Goodman.

No one seems to know—or care—why space scientist Carl von Linden died, according to the coroner, of "natural causes." But an old friend of von Linden's, government agent Charles Carey, defies his superiors, starting an investigation of his own. He soon learns that scientists in both Russia and France also died recently with no official explanation readily available.

811. "The Transformation of Joebee" (3/25/76; rebroadcast 8/10/76)

Cast: Hans Conried (Lester); Ian Martin (Will); Joseph Silver (Joebee); Bryna Raeburn (Martha). Written by Sam Dann.

For years, Joebee consistently played tricks on Will and Martha, but just when the couple really tired of his jokes, Joebee changed his ways. Shortly after his transformation, Joebee starts advising Martha on negotiations with Surania, royalty who wants to pay thousands of dollars for a plate Martha bought at a flea market. Suspecting that this is another one of Joebee's stunts, Will promises that, if so, it will be his last—literally.

812. "Extortion" (3/26/76; rebroadcast 8/11/76)

Cast: Evelyn Juster (Claire Leighton); William Redfield (Eric Miller); Joan Shay (Patsy Miller); Russell Horton (John Purcell); Mandel Kramer (Charles Leighton). Written by Roy Winsor.

Experimenting with drugs while in college, Claire Leighton ran down a boy on a bicycle with her car and left the scene of the accident. Now, 19 years later and married to a prominent state senator, Charles Leighton, Claire fears that public knowledge of her actions could ruin her husband's career. But when Charles learns that Claire is being blackmailed by a college boyfriend, neither the threat to his career nor life can stop Charles from trying to clear up the matter.

813. "The Storm Breeder" (3/27/76; rebroadcast from 10/28/75)

814. "Ghost Powder" (3/28/76; rebroadcast from 10/29/75)

815. "The Saxon Curse" (3/29/76; rebroadcast 8/13/76, 11/11/79)

Cast: Paul Hecht (Lord Savile); Catherine Byers (Aunt Clementine); Guy Sorel (Sir Reid); Court Benson (Professor Podgers). Adapted by Sam Dann, based on a short story by Oscar Wilde.

Lord Arthur Savile is urged by his ailing Aunt Clementine, who is suffering from the Saxon curse (headaches), to have his palm read. The palmist foresees young Savile committing a murder and not being caught for it. Even though he completely disbelieves what he has heard, Savile soon finds himself making preparations for Aunt Clementine's murder.

816. "The Intruders" (3/30/76; rebroadcast 8/14/76)

Cast: Lois Nettleton (Elaine); Fred Gwynne (Father); Carmen Matthews (Mother); Russell Horton (Brother). Written by Elspeth Eric.

After being away for seven years, Elaine comes home and is most upset to find three strangers—two men and a woman—living there. When none of them pays the least bit of attention to her no matter what she does to make them realize she's there, Elaine assumes they must all be ghosts, until a rose thorn pricks the woman's finger and it bleeds.

Notes: A rebroadcast of "Triptych for a Witch" from October 30, 1975, was originally scheduled to be broadcast on this date. Instead, "The Intruders" aired, and "Triptych for a Witch" was rescheduled for rebroadcast two weeks later on April 16.

817. "The Spit and Image" (3/31/76; rebroadcast 8/15/76)

Cast: Michael Tolan (Gil Stevens); Patricia Elliott (Karen); Earl Hammond (Deac); Ralph Bell (Nick Davos). Written by Ian Martin.

After retiring from football, Gil Stevens is offered a job he can't refuse: to impersonate a man he physically resembles, Durward Drake, international playboy, financier, sportsman and heir to the Drake Machine Company fortune. Stevens' employers, aides to Drake, explain that the billionaire, now a recluse, needs an impostor to make public appearances to prove that he is alive. However, Stevens soon suspects that the whole deal may lead to several dead ends, including his own. But his job is at the center of a game with much higher stakes than the Super Bowl.

Notes: Michael Tolan played Dr. Alex Tazinski on the television series *The Nurses*, from 1964 to '65. He also played Jordan Boyle on *The Senator*, a short-run television drama during the 1970-71 season.

818. "The White Ghost" (4/1/76; rebroadcast 8/17/76)

Cast: Ralph Bell (Donald Taylor); Anne Williams (Phyllis Taylor); Earl Hammond (Jim Pendleton); Joan Shay (Trudy Nelson). Written by Sam Dann.

When Donald Taylor tells his mistress, Trudy Nelson, their affair is finished, she threatens to shoot him, but in a struggle for the revolver, she is killed. Taylor is certain he will not be suspected because theirs was a very secret relationship. He begins to worry, however, when telephone calls which seem to come from Trudy and which continue for months keep telling him she still loves him and how much happier he will be with her than with his invalid wife.

Notes: A rebroadcast of "It's Hell to Pay the Piper" from October 31, 1975, was originally scheduled to be broadcast on this date. Instead, "The White Ghost" took the time slot, and "It's Hell to Pay the Piper" was rescheduled for rebroadcast two weeks later on April 17.

819. "Vanity Dies Hard" (4/2/76; rebroadcast 8/18/76)

Cast: Marian Seldes (Katherine Kendall); Mary Jane Higby (Mrs. Davis); Earl Hammond (Drexel); Bob Dryden (Michael Marchand); Ian Martin (District Attorney). Written by Sidney Slon.

Michael Marchand, wealthy detective story writer, swears he will ruin both his beautiful actress wife, Katherine Kendall, and the actor she says plans to marry. Marchand murders the actor and, in what he considers to be the perfect crime, is able to point the finger of suspicion at his wife. To insure she will go to prison for life, he volunteers to help the police prove her guilt.

820. "The Mortgage" (4/3/76; rebroadcast from 11/3/75)

821. "The Edge of the Scalpel" (4/4/76; rebroadcast from 11/5/75)

822. "Time Killer" (4/5/76; rebroadcast 8/20/76)

Cast: Mandel Kramer (Professor Qualen); Rosemary Rice (Clovis Mason); Jackson Beck (Joe Delaney); Russell Horton (Tubby); Arnold Moss (Luigi). Written by Arnold Moss.

Edwin Qualen, a professor of parapsychology, believes that time can be just as elastic as space and that someday man will be able to put himself, if he so desires, into any time past, present or future. Suddenly, it happens to him and he's back in New York 1933, where an argument with a man in a saloon over the current year, develops into a fight. To prevent his arrest, Qualen immediately returns to the present, later taking himself to the same bar, in early 1979, to find out if he had killed his opponent in the fight.

823. "The Boy Wonder" (4/6/76; rebroadcast 8/21/76)

Cast: William Redfield (M.P. Warbeck); Kenneth Harvey (Jason Buchanan); Martha Greenhouse (Daisy); Bob Dryden (Walter Herod); Danny Ocko (Foster Buchanan). Written by Alfred Bester.

Ten-year-old Stuart Buchanan has written a school composition explaining how his friends invented a disintegration beam, a matter-transmitter and a method of teleportation. Adults, including his school principal and a lawyer, see a fortune for themselves if they can learn more about the inventions from Stuart, who has quit school and left no traces. But whenever one of them seems about to find Stuart, he or she simply vanishes.

824. "The Paradise Cafe" (4/7/76; rebroadcast 8/22/76)

Cast: Court Benson (Harry Bell); Evelyn Juster (Dr. Maria Kleuger); William Redfield (Stanley); Len Gochman (Sergeant). Written by Sam Dann.

A wealthy and notorious tycoon begs his psychiatrist, Dr. Maria Kleuger, to exorcise from him the spirit of a man named Stanley, who was sent to the electric chair years ago for a murder Bell committed. Stanley's spirit keeps telling Bell that he should not go through with a shady real estate deal that, Bell knows, would send him to his grave by others involved in the deal with him.

825. "Sleeping Dogs" (4/8/76; rebroadcast 8/24/76)

Cast: Marian Seldes (Florence Peterson); Robert Maxwell (Don Peterson); Court Benson (Paul Dubois); Guy Sorel (Father Vilmy). Written by Murray Burnett.

Florence Peterson, whose paratrooper husband lost his life just before the invasion of France, disregards the advice of her present spouse and leaves for Paris to discover who in Les Insurgents had betrayed her husband. Former underground members and the American consul in Paris warn her and say that if she persists in her search, they cannot guarantee her safety.

826. "Fool's Gold" (4/9/76; rebroadcast 8/25/78)

Cast: Mason Adams (Hank Leavitt); Teri Keane (Jinx Leavitt); Court Benson (Jean Michel); Sam Gray (Captain Jean Lafitte). Written by Ian Martin.

Hank Leavitt, oceanographer and scuba diver, has come into possession of a 150-year-old map which he believes shows the exact spot in the Caribbean where Captain Lafitte's ship, the *Marie Sanglante*, laden with gold, foundered and sunk. Finding this fabulous lost treasure has become an obsession with Leavitt, but when he, aided by his young wife Jinx, is finally successful, he has to contend with the ghost of the famous pirate, who has his own ideas about the gold.

827. "Party Girl" (4/10/76; rebroadcast from 11/11/75)

828. "Home Is Where the Ghost Is" (4/11/76; rebroadcast from 11/13/75)

829. "Safe Judge" (4/12/76; rebroadcast 8/27/76)

Cast: Bob Dryden (Judge Talbot); Patricia Bruder (Nancy); William Redfield (Joe Mangel, Jr.); Earl Hammond (Joseph Mangel, Sr.); Bryna Raeburn (Marie Mangel). Written by Sam Dann.

In his 30 years on the bench, Judge Ben Franklin Talbot has always acted without an ulterior motive, until Senator Ed Ashworth offers to postpone the judge's retirement if he will dismiss charges against a drug dealer. Initially outraged, the judge's son realizes that based on the evidence he may have to throw the case out of court and thus alienate his daughter, Nancy, who is sure her classmate is guilty and that her father is being bribed.

830. "Wishes Can Be Fatal" (4/13/76; rebroadcast 8/28/76)

Cast: Carmen Matthews (Nell Atterwood); Jennifer Harmon (Polly); Russell Horton (Rick); Teri Keane (Elsa Atterwood); Gordon Gould (Ed Atterwood). Written by Roy Winsor.

Whenever Nell Atterwood, now in a nursing home, makes a copy of her original needlepoint portrait of her former house, certain items omitted from the copy, including a maple tree and a Pekinese dog, are unexplainably destroyed. When she portrays her son's second, young and beautiful wife, whom she despises, as an invalid with a cane, her relatives begin to wonder how strong her powers really are.

831. "A Living Corpse" (4/14/76; rebroadcast from 10/27/75)

832. "Strange Passenger" (4/15/76; rebroadcast 8/29/76)

Cast: Robert Kaliban (Hugo Webber); Nat Polen (James Archer); Ian Martin (Recruiter); Frank Behrens (Major Thompson); Evelyn Juster (Nancy Archer). Written by Roy Winsor.

James Archer, a lawyer disappointed with his profession, accepts an invitation to move to a superior planet 500 million miles from earth. However, once there, he is unwillingly transformed into Stewart Murdock, a robot programmed to return to Earth as a political leader to soften the people for conquest by space creatures. Back home, Murdock is pursued by government agents who spot him near a UFO, become suspicious of his actions, and want to know who he really is.

833. "Triptych for a Witch" (4/16/76; rebroadcast from 10/30/75)

834. "It's Hell to Pay the Piper" (4/17/76; rebroadcast from 10/31/75)

835. "Killing Valley" (4/18/76; rebroadcast from 11/7/75)

836. "Murder Most Foul" (4/19/76; rebroadcast 5/9/77, 4/28/79)

Cast: Kevin McCarthy (Macbeth); Carol Teitel (Lady Macbeth); Court Benson (King Duncan); Russell Horton (MacDuff); William Redfield (Banquo). Adapted by Ian Martin, based on the 1606 stage play *Macbeth* by William Shakespeare.

In the midst of thunder and lightning, two returning warriors, Macbeth and Banquo, meet three witches who make several strange predictions. Shortly thereafter, Macbeth is profoundly stirred when one prophecy is fulfilled: King Duncan names him his thane of Cawdor. Unsatisfied, Macbeth decides to make the second prophesy come true and, aided by Lady Macbeth, secretly kills Duncan and becomes king himself. However, Macbeth is haunted by the murder and the witches' last prediction: that Banquo's son will succeed him as king.

Notes: This episode began a one-week special of Shakespeare adaptations, all scripted by 63-year-old Ian Martin. This was the first time in broadcasting history that a week-long Shakespearean series had been presented. The titles were respectfully changed, using lines taken directly from the actual plays. "The Green-Eyed Monster" was taken from Shakespeare's *Othello*, in which Iago coined the phrase, "Beware of jealousy, oh, my Lord, it is the green-eyed monster."

In addition to his numerous stage, screen, television and radio performances, Kevin McCarthy has appeared in the production of Shakespeare's *Love's Labour's Lost* at New York Center.

837. "The Assassination" (4/20/76; rebroadcast 5/10/77, 5/6/79)

Cast: Bob Dryden (Caesar); Norman Rose (Brutus); Joan Shay (Calpurnia); Ian Martin (Cassius); Russell Horton (Marc Antony). Adapted by Ian Martin, based on the 1600 stage play *Julius Caesar* by William Shakespeare.

While multitudes are celebrating Caesar's military victories, the envious Cassius is gradually convincing Brutus that Caesar's life must be sacrificed for the common good. The fatal deed is planned for the Ides of March, and, despite a soothsayer's warning and his wife Calpurnia's dream, Caesar goes to the senate and is murdered. At Caesar's funeral, the fallen leader's henchman, Marc Antony, sways the crowds, and then sets out with an army to defeat the fleeing forces of Cassius and Brutus.

Notes: Himan Brown noted "Shakespeare's writings have all the excitement and drama that are appropriate for *Theater*. In addition to being the master of movement and history's greatest dramatist, Shakespeare was the master of blood and thunder, and of ghosts and mayhem of all sorts."

Brown was presented a Broadcast Preceptor Award by San Francisco State University on May 6, 1979, the opening day of the university's 29th annual Broadcast Industry Conference. The Preceptor Award is given every year to individuals who have made outstanding contributions to the industry. Brown received his award "for his tremendous energy and dedication that have reestablished radio drama as an art form."

838. "The Love Song of Death" (4/21/76; rebroadcast 5/11/77, 9/30/79)

Cast: Kristoffer Tabori (Romeo Morgan); Fairchild (Juliet); Robert Kaliban (Mercutio); Joan Shay (Nurse); Earl Hammond (Tybalt); Guy Sorel (Prince). Adapted by Ian Martin, based on the 1596 stage play *Romeo and Juliet* by William Shakespeare.

Family hatred flares when the Capulets discover that Romeo, heir of the enemy Montagues, has, uninvited and disguised, attended a masked ball given by Lord Capulet. Unbeknownst to the others, Romeo and Juliet meet, fall in love and are married. But the marriage remains a secret, and the couple risk their lives to get back together, after Romeo is banished from Verona for killing Juliet's cousin and Juliet is betrothed to Paris, a Capulet.

Notes: According to Ian Martin: "'The Assassination' is an obvious title for *Julius Caesar*; 'Murder Most Foul' is, of course, *Macbeth*'s own line. 'The Love Song of Death' is my own title for *Romeo and Juliet* because I couldn't find something in the text that seemed to fit. 'Long Live the King is Dead,' which is

Hamlet, is my title too, but don't ask me to explain it. But I like it. It suggests a million things." [The titles used for the other Shakespeare plays were taken from the plays themselves.]

839. "The Green-Eyed Monster" (4/22/76; rebroadcast 5/12/77, 4/7/79)

Cast: Arnold Moss (Othello); Marian Seldes (Desdemona); Ian Martin (Cassio); Ralph Bell (Iago); Court Benson (Roderigo); Joen Arliss (Emilia). Adapted by Ian Martin, based on the 1604 stage play *Othello* by William Shakespeare.

Shortly after Othello, a black Moor, and the fair Desdemona are secretly wed, Iago, a villainous ensign, attempts to ruin his general by telling the bride's enraged father about the marriage. But Othello prevails, so Iago schemes to upset him by hinting that Desdemona is being unfaithful. When Othello dismisses Cassio, an officer, and Desdemona pleads for his reinstatement, Othello becomes possessed by jealousy and acts without asking for explanations.

840. "Long Live the King Is Dead" (4/23/76; rebroadcast 5/13/79, 4/21/79)

Cast: Tony Roberts (Hamlet); Ian Martin (Horatio); Robert Kaliban (Laertes); Evelyn Juster (Gertrude); Arnold Moss (Claudius). Adapted by Ian Martin, based on the 1601 stage play *Hamlet* by William Shakespeare.

Returning home from the university, Prince Hamlet discovers that his father has died and his father's brother, Claudius, has seized the Danish throne and married his mother. His father's ghost soon tells Hamlet that he has been murdered by Claudius and bids Hamlet to seek revenge. Hamlet, after killing his beloved Ophelia's father by mistake, hears again from the ghost, still demanding revenge. Claudius has become suspicious of Hamlet's intention, though, and craftily tries to thwart him.

Notes: Tony Roberts' Shakespearean acting experience includes performances with Robert Brustein's Yale Repertory Theater and at Ottobein College in Westerville, Ohio.

841. "The Prince of Evil" (4/24/76; rebroadcast 5/14/77)

Cast: Howard Da Silva (Richard of Gloucester); Court Benson (Clarence); Ian Martin (King Edward); Evelyn Juster (Princess Anne); Earl Hammond (Lord Hastings); Heddy Galen (Queen Margaret). Adapted by Ian Martin, based on the 1593 stage play *Richard III* by William Shakespeare.

Despite his physical unattractiveness, Richard is a man of such magnetic charms that few suspect his evil, depraved intentions. While King Edwards lies gravely ill and his brother, Clarence, is sentenced to death, Richard plans his bloody rise to the throne. He commits a long skein of murders of legal heirs to the House of York and is crowned, but the night before a crucial battle with the Tudors, the ghosts of his many victims threaten to drive Richard to his own ruin.

Notes: Ian Martin commented: "Although I've had to compress these long plays into much shorter lengths, I've tried very, very hard to retain as much of the women's roles as possible. Things are a lot different now. Their roles were taken by young boys whose voices hadn't broken. Shakespeare, I'm sure, would have liked to have written major parts for women, but in those days they couldn't appear on stage. Any who did were considered prostitutes."

842. "The Serpent of the Nile" (4/25/76; rebroadcast 5/15/77, 8/4/79)

Cast: Kevin McCarthy (Antony); Lois Nettleton (Cleopatra); Carol Teitel (Octavia); Bob Dryden (Lepidus); Paul Hecht (Octavian); Russell Horton (Messenger). Adapted by Ian Martin, based on the 1607 stage play *Antony and Cleopatra* by William Shakespeare.

Marc Antony, long distracted from Roman affairs by Egypt's Queen Cleopatra, tries to resolve problems with his fellow triumvirs—Octavian Caesar and Lepidus—by returning to Rome and marrying Octavian's sister, Octavia. However, when Antony goes back to his "serpent of the Nile," Cleopatra, thus publicly embarrassing Octavia, her brother declares war. In the midst of battle, Cleopatra, leading the Egyptian fleet, retreats, leaving Antony to suspect a betrayal.

Notes: Lois Nettleton, who plays Cleopatra in this episode, has appeared in numerous films including *The Bamboo Saucer* (1968), *Period of Adjustment* (1962), *Brass* (1985), and *The Best Little Whorehouse in Texas* (1982).

843. "The Three Elders of Lifeboat Landing" (4/26/76; rebroadcast 8/31/76)

Cast: Mason Adams (Phil O'Hara); Ann Shepherd (Carol O'Hara); Guy Sorel (Dr. Fritz Heinemann); Robert Phelps (Joey O'Hara); Mandel Kramer (Ross Randall). Written by Roy Winsor.

Lifeboat Landing, New York, reputedly offers ideal conditions for those chosen to live there—no crime, clean air, beautiful homes, excellent recreational facilities, and so on. But when two men rob the Landing's bank, are caught, and then vanish, reporter Joey O'Hara is puzzled. He starts to investigate and finds the town run rigidly by three elders whose methods of governing—including dire threats to Joey—are far from ideal.

844. "The Public Avenger" (4/27/76; rebroadcast from 11/10/75)

845. "The Money Makers" (4/28/76; rebroadcast from 11/14/75)

846. "Two Plus Two Equals Death" (4/29/76; rebroadcast 9/1/76)

Cast: William Redfield (Peter Gerard); Marian Seldes (Francesca); Sam Gray (Marcel Roget); Bob Dryden (Mario Milan). Written by Alfred Bester.

Peter Gerard, who takes his late father's place as the Incredible Mechanical Man in a traveling circus, falls in love with Francesca, the ballerina who turns the key that starts his act. She is also smitten, but her identical twin sister can express only hatred for Peter. Unfortunately, he cannot tell the sisters apart and on the night of his marriage he finds himself alone with the twin who he thinks hates him.

847. "The Moonlighter" (4/30/76; rebroadcast from 11/17/75)

848. "Fear" (5/1/76; rebroadcast from 11/19/75)

849. "Lamps of the Devil" (5/2/76; rebroadcast from 11/20/75)

850. "The Cornstarch Killer" (5/3/76; rebroadcast 9/3/76)

Cast: Bob Dryden (Dennis Truffle); Earl Hammond (Officer Paderewski); Marian Seldes (Maude Menhaden). Written by Sam Dann.

Police are baffled by a series of murders—all the victims are men who made a practice of leering at women. The manager of a bus depot, a drunken professor who once was a heavyweight wrestler, and the policeman assigned to solve the murders of the first two all had a reputation of making lewd remarks to women and were found stabbed in the back, with a smudge of cornstarch just above the chin.

851. "The Hanging Judgment" (5/4/76; rebroadcast from 11/21/75)

852. "The Serpent's Tooth" (5/5/76; rebroadcast from 11/24/75)

853. "What a Change in Hilda" (5/6/76; rebroadcast 9/4/76)

Cast: Lois Nettleton (Hilda Turner); Nat Polen (Brad Turner); Robert L. Green (Dr. Satlu); Bryna Raeburn (Grace Hutchins). Written by Bob Juhren.

Hilda Turner is mightily impressed when an untalented friend emerges as a top concert singer after attending meditation sessions at the Center for Transposition Science. Hilda insists on visiting the center, where Dr. Satlu declares he can, through meditation, start Hilda on a new career as a model. He charges only $100 for this service, but doesn't tell Hilda what's in store for her in the long run.

854. "The Lap of the Gods" (5/7/76; rebroadcast from 11/25/75)

855. "The Dead, Dead Ringer" (5/8/76; rebroadcast from 11/27/75)

856. "The Frammis" (5/9/76; rebroadcast from 11/28/75)

857. "The Ghost of San Juan Hill" (5/10/76; rebroadcast 9/5/76)

Cast: Jack Grimes (Bobby Halstead); Marian Hailey (Mariah); Ian Martin (Billy Homestead); Bryna Raeburn (Aunt Milly); William Redfield (Woody Bennet). Written by Sam Dann.

Bobby Halstead was killed in Cuba while carrying Old Glory up San Juan Hill during the Spanish-American War. Mariah, Bobby's wife of a few days, now plans to marry Woody Bennet, who, even though he was Bobby's bosom pal, plotted with Mariah to get Bobby to enlist in the Rough Riders. The night before the wedding ceremony, Mariah sees Bobby's ghost. Nevertheless, Woody insists she go through with the wedding—until he, too, gets a glimpse of Bobby's apparition.

858. "With Malice Aforethought" (5/11/76; rebroadcast from 12/1/75)

859. "Promise to Kill" (5/12/76; rebroadcast from 12/3/75)

860. "The Secret Sharer" (5/13/76; rebroadcast 9/8/76)

Cast: Norman Rose (The Captain); Mandel Kramer (Leggatt); William Redfield (First Mate); Court Benson (Steward). Adapted by Elizabeth Pennell, based on the 1912 short story by Joseph Conrad.

While waiting for a breeze that will start him and his crew home to England, a ship's captain is startled to see a naked man hanging on to the ship's ladder. After coming aboard, Leggatt, a first mate from another ship, admits he had accidentally killed a sailor who refused to obey an order. The captain hides Leggatt in his cabin, knowing he is committing a crime. A strange power has overcome the captain, making him believe he must somehow save Leggatt's life.

861. "Portrait of a Killer" (5/14/76; rebroadcast from 12/4/75)

862. "Pharaoh's Daughter" (5/15/76; rebroadcast from 12/5/75)

863. "How Quiet the Night" (5/16/76; rebroadcast from 12/8/75)

864. "Blind Witness" (5/17/76; rebroadcast 9/11/76)

Cast: Patricia Elliott (Det. Julia Jedwick); Carmen Matthews (Aggie); Leon Janney (Chappie); Bryna Raeburn (Maggie); Earl Hammond (Lieutenant Sterling). Written by Sam Dann.

After shooting a druggist and store customer, Chappie, a hired killer, becomes alarmed when the newspapers report only one dead body. Detective Julia Jedwick, assigned to the case, suspects that because of the number of shots fired another person was in the store. That other person turns out to be Aggie, a blind, elderly woman who manages to stay under cover until her addicted sister needs more drugs.

865. "Stitch in Time" (5/18/76; rebroadcast from 12/9/75)

866. "You Can Change Your Life" (5/19/76; rebroadcast from 12/11/75)

867. "The Walking Dead" (5/20/76; rebroadcast 9/12/76)

Cast: Paul Hecht (James Valentine); Jack Grimes (Rex); Joan Shay (Dallas

Burton); Gilbert Mack (Nicholas Rostov); Rosemary Rice (Mari Sutton). Written by Alfred Bester.

Rex, an android grown chemically from proteins and minerals into human form, dislikes being the slave of James Valentine, whose every order he must obey. Though androids are not supposed to harm, lie or kill, and crime is unknown on the planet Paragon, Rex suddenly goes berserk, killing a woman. Valentine quickly flies him to another planet, Deneb-Alpha where a scientist, Nicholas Rostov, suspects that Rex has tired of his role and has resorted to violence to prove himself a man.

868. "Marry for Murder" (5/21/76; rebroadcast from 12/12/75)

869. "Burn, Witch, Burn" (5/22/76; rebroadcast from 12/15/75)

870. "The Eleventh Hour" (5/23/76; rebroadcast from 12/17/75)

871. "A Mexican Standoff" (5/24/76; rebroadcast 9/15/76)

Cast: Joseph Silver (George); Catherine Byers (Martha); Bob Dryden (Grady); Sam Gray (MacCarthy). Written by Ian Martin.

Shortly after George Adams, a small-town Nebraska mailman, is named "Mr. Good Citizen, USA" in a syndicated article, he and his wife, Martha, start getting more mail than George can deliver. In one letter, an anonymous admirer invites the couple on a Mexican vacation. It seems like a dream come true, until the Adamses meet their benefactor in Mexico City and George recognizes his face: it is from the "Ten Most Wanted" list on the post office's bulletin board.

872. "Fireball" (5/25/76; rebroadcast from 12/18/75)

873. "The Corpse Wrote Shorthand" (5/26/76; rebroadcast from 12/19/75)

874. "Demon Lover" (5/27/76; rebroadcast 9/18/76)

Cast: Mandel Kramer (Albert Morrison); Marian Seldes (Dr. Mallow); Bryna Raeburn (Maria Chiputchin); Earl Hammond (Clemmons). Written by Sam Dann.

Albert Morrison, a widower and professor of astronomy, is put in a mental institution because nobody believes that he killed a woman by mistake when she threatened to kill him if he did not fall in love with her at her command. A psychiatrist, Dr. Florence Mallow, is assigned to help him. During the course of the treatment she suddenly and violently expresses her love for him, threatening death if he doesn't respond.

875. "The Image" (5/28/76; rebroadcast from 12/22/75)

876. "The Murder Market" (5/29/76; rebroadcast from 12/23/75)

877. "License to Kill" (5/30/76; rebroadcast from 12/26/75)

878. "Ghost Town" (5/31/76; rebroadcast 9/19/76)
    Cast: Lois Nettleton (Sara Conway); Ralph Bell (Des Pogue); Nat Polen (Milburn Ross); Ian Martin (Sheriff Brenner); Russell Horton (Dr. Garvey). Written by Ian Martin.
    Des Pogue, who has escaped from a mental institution, sneaks into the back seat of schoolteacher Sara Conway's car, then orders her at gun-point to drive him to Bone Dry Gulch, a ghost town in Death Valley where Pogue's great-great-grandfather made a living 100 years ago as a hired killer. When they arrive, dazed from an auto accident, Sara finds herself a ghost in a bustling gold mining community and about to witness a killing by Pogue's infamous ancestor.

879. "The Memory Killers" (6/1/76; rebroadcast from 12/29/75)

880. "Sagamore Cottage" (6/2/76; rebroadcast from 12/31/75)

881. "Blue Justice" (6/3/76; rebroadcast 9/22/76)
    Cast: Leon Janney (Peter Littlefield); Jackson Beck (Miller); Evelyn Juster (Magda); Bob Dryden (John Helder). Written by Sam Dann.
    Peter Littlefield, the assistant minister of justice of a small totalitarian state, sentences to death every one of the 40 arrested during a street demonstration. By doing so, he feels he will soon replace his boss, whom he considers "too lenient." But one of the demonstrators was obviously innocent, a fact that has a profound effect on Littlefield's frenzied drive to reach the top job.

882. "One of the Missing" (6/4/76; rebroadcast from 1/1/76)

883. "Insight Into Murder" (6/5/76; rebroadcast from 1/2/76)

884. "Dig Me Deadly" (6/6/76; rebroadcast from 2/13/74)

885. "The Corpse That Would Not Die" (6/7/76; rebroadcast 9/25/76, 12/22/79)
    Cast: Patricia Elliott (Therese Raquin); Mary Jane Higby (Mme. Raquin); Roger De Koven (Inspector Michaude); William Redfield (Camille); Arnold Moss (Laurent Duchaine). Adapted by Arnold Moss, based on the 1867 novel *Therese Raquin* by Emile Zola.
    Therese Raquin and her lover, portrait painter Laurent Duchaine, murder Therese's husband, Camille. They do it so well that nobody suspects them, but instead of solidifying their relationship, the two are so filled with guilt that soon

they hate each other. Both have recurring dreams that Camille is still alive and begin to realize that he will haunt them for years to come, as will Camille's mother, who overhears them arguing about who is more guilty. She, however, is rendered speechless by a stroke and thus cannot tell anyone what she overheard.

886. "What the Shepherd Saw" (6/8/76; rebroadcast from 1/12/76)

887. "The Elixir of Death" (6/9/76; rebroadcast from 1/14/76)

888. "Free the Beast" (6/10/76; rebroadcast 9/26/76)

Cast: Paul Hecht (Dr. Thurman); Marian Seldes (Nurse Palmer); Joan Banks (Agatha); Ian Martin (Charles Connelly). Written by Ralph Goodman.

While touring the wards of Briarwood Sanitarium, Dr. Thurman hears a strange voice assuring a frightened, uncommunicative patient, Agatha Millford. Suddenly, Agatha's major enemy at Briarwood is killed, and all clues point to Agatha. Convinced that she is neither a murderer nor a schizophrenic, Dr. Thurman researches her background to discover the identity of the sinister "sister" of this only child.

889. "The Red Frisbee" (6/11/76; rebroadcast from 1/16/76)

890. "There's No Business Like" (6/12/76; rebroadcast from 1/19/76)

891. "The Lady of the Mist" (6/13/76; rebroadcast from 1/21/76)

892. "The Unthinkable" (6/14/76; rebroadcast 9/29/76)

Cast: Larry Haines (Walt Robinson); Teri Keane (Roxanne Robinson); Russell Horton (Phil); Robert Maxwell (Pop). Written by Sam Dann.

Walt Robinson, an electrical engineer out of work for 18 months, takes over the housework, begrudgingly, when his wife, Roxanne, gets a job as an assistant manager of a bank. While playing with his children in a park, Walt meets Phil, an unemployed architect, and together they start planning the heist of the bank where Roxanne works. They pull it off beautifully, except for one minor detail, which soon becomes a major one when the police start their investigation.

893. "The Slick and the Dead" (6/15/76; rebroadcast from 1/23/76)

894. "The Ferret" (6/16/76; rebroadcast from 1/26/76)

895. "Pension Plan" (6/17/76; rebroadcast 10/2/76)

Cast: Norman Rose (Stanley Haskins); Ann Pitoniak (Zelda); Leon Janney (Joe Jessup); William Redfield (Mr. Smith). Written by Sam Dann.

When he begins to plan his retirement days, Stanley Haskins is shocked to learn that his boyhood friend and boss, Joe Jessup, expects him to collect his own pension from kickbacks paid to him as Joe's office manager. Faced with a future of poverty because he was honest, Stanley threatens to kill Joe. However, the appearance of Mr. Smith, whose business is evil, soon changes the course of events for both Joe and Stanley.

896. "Mirror, Mirror" (6/18/76; rebroadcast from 1/28/76)

897. "Castle Kerfol" (6/19/76; rebroadcast from 1/30/76)

898. "First Prize—Death" (6/20/76; rebroadcast from 2/2/76)

899. "Checkmate" (6/21/76; rebroadcast 10/3/76)

Cast: Marian Hailey (Marian Trout); Bob Dryden (Sgt. Boles); Bryna Raeburn (Mrs. Apfelbaum); Court Benson (Slats). Written by Ian Martin.

Police detective Marian Trout gets a phone call from a man who says before dying that he's been murdered. Her superior, Sgt. Digger Boles, opposed to women police, scoffs when Marian tells him about the call but does agree to accompany her to the scene of the crime. The victim has been stabbed in the eye with a needle-like instrument. To Boles it's a cut-and-dry case: The murder was committed by a neighbor, an elderly lady who admits that she has at times used a hat pin to defend herself. Marian disagrees, demanding further investigation.

900. "The Dead Deserve to Rest" (6/22/76; rebroadcast from 2/3/76)

901. "The Children of Death" (6/23/76; rebroadcast from 2/5/76)

902. "Child of Fate" (6/24/76; rebroadcast 10/6/76)

Cast: Guy Sorel (James Trent); Jada Rowland (Halcyon Trent); Kenneth Harvey (Daniel); Anne Williams (Violet Tarcher). Written by Elspeth Eric.

Halcyon Trent spent her childhood alone, living in a secluded house, ignored by her ill mother and busy father, so she created an "imaginary" friend, Gerald. As teenagers, Halcyon and Gerald are still constant companions, until Violet Tarcher, a governess, comes to teach Halcyon. The two women become close friends. When Miss Tarcher is injured climbing a tree, Halcyon blames Gerald's jealousy and wonders if she should set him free before he does further harm to her new friend.

903. "Straight from the Horse's Mouth" (6/25/76; rebroadcast from 2/6/76)

904. "The Horror of Dead Lake" (6/26/76; rebroadcast from 2/9/76)

905. "You Owe Me a Death" (6/27/76; rebroadcast from 2/11/76)

906. "Forty-Five Minutes to Murder" (6/28/76; rebroadcast 10/9/76)

Cast: Larry Haines (Lt. Cooper); Leon Janney (Emmet Martindale); Joan Shay (Emma Martindale); Court Benson (Jim Raglan); Sam Gray (Barnaby). Written by Sam Dann.

On his birthday, Emmet Martindale, vice president of Carroway Chemicals, receives a $200 bottle of cognac from a disagreeable business associate, Jim Raglan. Martindale believes it is a reconciliation gift from Raglan, who for many years has coveted both Martindale's position and his wife, Emma. Emma's first swallow kills her, though, and all clues point to Raglan as the murderer until Lt. Cooper discovers a 45 minute time lapse when someone else could have poisoned the cognac.

907. "The Golden Chalices" (6/29/76; rebroadcast from 2/12/76)

908. "The Blue Roan Stallion" (6/30/76; rebroadcast from 2/13/76)

909. "Loser Takes All" (7/1/76; rebroadcast 10/10/76)

Cast: Patricia Elliott (Delphi Carr); Paul Hecht (Deke Roberts); Nat Polen (Bernie); Ian Martin (Jake Alexander). Written by Ian Martin.

When Jake Alexander, who considers himself the world's top theatrical agent, meets Dephi Carr, in his eyes the world's most beautiful woman, he tries his best to become her agent. He would also like her to become his wife. But before he can achieve his first wish, she gets married and suggests that Jake take her actor husband, Deke Roberts, as a client. Jake agrees, only because it will provide him with more opportunities to murder Deke, or have someone else do it.

910. "Angel of Death" (7/2/76; rebroadcast from 2/16/76)

911. "The Angry God" (7/3/76; rebroadcast from 2/17/76)

912. "Solid Gold Soldiers" (7/4/76; rebroadcast from 9/22/75)

913. "The Headless Hessian" (7/5/76; rebroadcast from 9/23/75)

914. "The Angels of Devil's Mountain" (7/6/76; rebroadcast from 9/24/75)

915. "The Black Whale" (7/7/76; rebroadcast from 9/25/75)

916. "Assassination in Time" (7/8/76; rebroadcast from 9/26/75)

917. "The Thomas Jefferson Defense" (7/9/76; rebroadcast from 9/27/75)

918. "The Other Self" (7/10/76; rebroadcast from 9/28/75)

919. "Good-Bye, Benjamin Flack" (7/11/76; rebroadcast from 2/19/76)

920. "Blood Red Roses" (7/12/76; rebroadcast 10/13/76)
    Cast: Bob Dryden (Nick Birko); Bryna Raeburn (Anna Birko); Arnold Moss (Jerry Bizett); Robert Kaliban (Sergeant Daly); William Redfield (Junior). Written by Sam Dann.
    When his son, Steve, a young priest, becomes an innocent victim of gangland war and the police make no arrests, Nick Birko sets out to make amends himself. He soon tracks down the head mobster, Jerry Bizett, and uses their mutual interest in growing roses—and Nick's "Blood Red Roses"—to get a job as Bizett's gardener. But it's the mobster's son, Junior, that revengeful Nick is after.

921. "The Bloody Legend" (7/13/76; rebroadcast from 2/20/76)

922. "The Patient Visitor" (7/14/76; rebroadcast from 2/23/76)

923. "The Last Trip of Charter Boat Sally" (7/15/76; rebroadcast 10/16/76)
    Cast: Teri Keane (Ruth Ordway); Mandel Kramer (Mike Phillips); Russell Horton (Tony Rose); Robert Dryden (Captain Hodges). Written by Roy Winsor.
    Captain Clint Hodges charters his tugboat, *Sally,* for fishing parties, but his best—and last—customers are Cecil Ordway and his business associates who do more gambling than fishing. When the *Sally* explodes at sea, Ordway is killed and, Captain Hodges makes it to shore. A tackle box full of money and Hodges' gun in the rescue dingy implicate him as a murderer, but the police discover that others also wanted to sink the *Sally.*

924. "General Laughter" (7/16/76; rebroadcast from 2/25/76)

925. "The Providential Ghost" (7/17/76; rebroadcast from 2/26/76)

926. "Half a Life" (7/18/76; rebroadcast from 2/27/76)

927. "Future Eye" (7/19/76; rebroadcast 10/17/76)
    Cast: Tony Roberts (John Quinn); Catherine Butterfield (Sono); Court Benson

(Macy); William Redfield (Oliver Wilson Wright); Evelyn Juster (Master Computer). Written by Alfred Bester.

Because the Mark 747 Digitary Master Control Computer malfunctioned, the memory data bank of the year 2976 is returned in time to 1976. John Quinn, chief intelligence officer for the sector, is dispatched by the embarrassed computer to retrieve it because its information, put in the wrong hands, could destroy the civilization of 2976. However, Oliver Wilson Wright, an enterprising 1976 earthling, realizing what possession of the data bank—the size of a matchbox—could mean to him, is in no mood to give it to Quinn.

928. "The Death Trail" (7/20/76; rebroadcast from 3/1/76)

929. "Afterward" (7/21/76; rebroadcast from 3/2/76)

930. "The Men with the Magic Fingers" (7/22/76; rebroadcast 10/20/76)

Cast: Mason Adams (Jack Youngblood); Catherine Byers (Leonora); Earl Hammond (Joe); Marian Seldes (Piety). Written by Sam Dann.

Talented carnival owner Jack Youngblood fabricates a lifelike female doll that, aided by the newly invented phonograph, can predict his customers' futures. The doll, Leonora, becomes the star of the carnival, replacing Jack's wife, Piety. Then suddenly, Leonora becomes alive and Jack falls in love with her, much to the consternation of Piety, who threatens to kill them both.

931. "The Monk and the Hangman's Daughter" (7/23/76; rebroadcast from 3/4/76)

932. "The Infernal Triangle" (7/24/76; rebroadcast from 3/5/76)

933. "The Queen of Spades" (7/25/76; rebroadcast from 3/8/76)

934. "The Brain Without Mercy" (7/26/76; rebroadcast 10/23/76)

Cast: Norman Rose (Dr. Diethardt); Bryna Raeburn (Mrs. Diethardt); Leon Janney (Willy); Ian Martin (Miguel Riveras). Written by Ian Martin.

When Dr. Werner Diethardt finds skyjacker Miguel Riveras on the hot Texas plain, the thief is near death. Having heard on the radio that Riveras had parachuted with his $2 million ransom, Dr. Diethardt, who needs the money for his advanced animal research project, allows Riveras' body to die, at the same time determining to keep his brain alive so that it will tell him the location of the cash. The brain, though, demands a new body before it will reveal the secret.

935. "I Thought I Saw a Shadow" (7/27/76; rebroadcast from 3/10/76)

936. "Pandora" (7/28/76; rebroadcast from 3/11/76)

937. "Shotgun Wedding" (7/29/76; rebroadcast 10/24/76)

Cast: Jack Grimes (Charley Demerest); Patricia Elliott (Elaine); Leon Janney (Gus Virko); Bill Griffis (Sheriff). Written by Sam Dann.

Machinist Gus Virko decides that Charley Demerest, a co-worker and respectable bachelor, is going to meet and marry the "girl of his dreams": Gus' daughter, Elaine. Despite Charley's protests, Gus insists on taking Charley at gunpoint to propose to Elaine, and as if in a dream, Charley falls instantly in love with her. But, suddenly, the whole affair becomes a nightmare when Charley discovers that ten years earlier, Elaine and her first fiancé were killed in a fire started by her jealous father.

938. "The Man Who Preyed on Widows" (7/30/76; rebroadcast from 3/12/76)

939. "The Aliens" (7/31/76; rebroadcast from 3/15/76)

940. "Crime Casts a Shadow" (8/1/76; rebroadcast from 3/16/76)

941. "Every Dog Has His Day" (8/2/76; rebroadcast 10/25/76)

Cast: Court Benson (Chadsworth); Ian Martin (Squire Rokesby); Russell Horton (Bishop); Morgan Fairchild (Antoinette). Written by Ian Martin.

Disappointed by his two sons—Bishop, whose only interest is making money, and Beauregard, who can only spend it—Squire Rokesby has just his dog, Whiskey, and his servant, Chadsworth, to console him. In fact, just before the squire's death, Bishop forces his father into willing the entire estate to him. Beauregard soon, accuses Bishop of deceiving and then murdering their father. Whiskey ends the family feud by making sure each son gets what is coming to him.

942. "The Other Side of the Coin" (8/3/76; rebroadcast from 3/18/76)

943. "A Matter of Love and Death" (8/4/76; rebroadcast from 3/19/76)

944. "Lovers and Killers" (8/5/76; rebroadcast 10/26/76)

Cast: Bob Dryden (David Miller); Marian Seldes (Myra Wilson); Robert Maxwell (Officer Lenz); Evelyn Juster (Vicky); Russell Horton (Howard). Written by Sam Dann.

Actor David Miller, a member of the jury, hears the testimony of a man who was arrested by the police, minutes after he allegedly shot and killed his lover's husband. He also hears the testimony of the woman involved. Both give very different versions of what actually happened. Miller, a very sympathetic person, believes both stories and cannot in good conscience declare the man either guilty or innocent. The rest of the jury members must also make up their minds.

945. "Stampede" (8/6/76; rebroadcast from 3/22/76)

946. "The Covered Bridge" (8/7/76; rebroadcast from 3/23/76)

947. "Brain Drain" (8/8/76; rebroadcast from 3/24/76)

948. "Overnight to Freedom" (8/9/76; rebroadcast 11/1/76)
Cast: William Redfield (George McAlester); Bob Dryden (Pal); Rosemary Rice (Ursula); Mandel Kramer (Schneider); Earl Hammond (Gerhardt). Written by Sam Dann.
Shortly after he flees a German POW camp, George McAlester, an American soldier with forged papers identifying him as a French machinist, boards a train for an overnight trip to freedom. Fearing he will be discovered, George seeks the help of a Frenchman who claims his work for the Germans allows him "to loosen fuses in their shells," and a German woman whose father owns the machine shop where his alias, Louis Cardinet, supposedly works. McAlester is afraid, though, of where their loyalties really lie.

949. "The Transformation of Joebee" (8/10/76; rebroadcast from 3/25/76)

950. "Extortion" (8/11/76; rebroadcast from 3/26/76)

951. "The Haliday Prediction" (8/12/76; rebroadcast 11/3/76)
Cast: Tony Roberts (Cash Haliday); Bob Dryden (Al Cosden); Ian Martin (Commander Bradley); Morgan Fairchild (Laura Fields). Written by Fielden Farrington.
Columnist Cash Haliday, who writes a weekly prediction about underworld crime, police corruption and government misdeeds, has such a high batting average that his secretary accuses him of making things happen, just by writing about them. Al Cosden, a gangster with good police connections, threatens to kill Cash if his fortune-telling continues. Cash tries to ward off the mobster by publishing a prediction that could make Al incapable of murdering him.

952. "The Saxon Curse" (8/13/76; rebroadcast from 3/29/76)

953. "The Intruders" (8/14/76; rebroadcast from 3/30/76)

954. "The Spit and Image" (8/15/76; rebroadcast from 3/31/76)

955. "Your Grade Is A" (8/16/76; rebroadcast 11/6/76)

Cast: Robert Kaliban (George Monroe); Joan Shay (Judith Palmer); Ralph Bell (Silas Butler); Joseph Silver (Captain Zachary). Written by Roy Winsor.

Silas Butler asks his correspondence school instructor, George Monroe, to listen to his idea for a murder mystery story. Monroe does, and offers a suggestion on how the murder should be committed: with carbon monoxide. After Butler finishes the story, his wife is found dead of carbon monoxide poisoning. The police explanation is suicide or accidental death, but Mrs. Butler's best friend, Judith Palmer, is not convinced they're right.

956. "The White Ghost" (8/17/76; rebroadcast from 4/1/76)

957. "Vanity Dies Hard" (8/18/76; rebroadcast from 4/2/76)

958. "The Golden People" (8/19/76; rebroadcast 11/7/76)

Cast: William Redfield (Richard Parradon); Bryna Raeburn (Sally); Marian Seldes (Louisa); Evelyn Juster (Jane). Written by Sam Dann.

Richard Parradon has been attracted to many beautiful, wealthy women and even engaged to a few, but never long enough to marry one. Then he meets and falls in love with Louisa, a schoolteacher who is neither rich nor pretty. Unimpressed, Louisa considers Richard to be one of "the golden people" born with the looks and luck to get what they want. But, finally, Louisa can't resist him any longer and agrees to marry, only to find out what a tarnished person Richard really is.

959. "Time Killer" (8/20/76; rebroadcast from 4/5/76)

960. "The Boy Wonder" (8/21/76; rebroadcast from 4/6/76)

961. "The Paradise Cafe" (8/22/76; rebroadcast from 4/7/76)

962. "The Train Stops" (8/23/76; rebroadcast 11/10/76)

Cast: Norman Rose (Dr. Barnes); Eugene Francis (Ben); Ann Shepherd (Woman); Jada Rowland (Mary). Written by Elspeth Eric.

Dr. Barnes' wife died during the birth of the first and only child, Mary, 18 years ago, and the doctor is acutely aware of his inability to deal with Mary's romantic problems. When Mary falls in love with a man who comes to her hometown, Dandridge, each week on the 5:15 train, she refuses to introduce him to her father or anyone else. Dr. Barnes becomes really alarmed when Dandridge is taken off the train schedule, and Mary is determined to make the train stop, even at the risk of her own life.

963. "Sleeping Dogs" (8/24/76; rebroadcast from 4/8/76)

964. "Fool's Gold" (8/25/76; rebroadcast from 4/9/76)

965. "The Man Who Could Work Miracles" (8/26/76; rebroadcast 11/13/76)

Cast: William Redfield (George McWhirter); Marian Hailey (Minnie McWhirter); Russell Horton (Charlie); Arnold Moss (Rev. Howell). Adapted by Arnold Moss, based on the 1898 short story by H.G. Wells.

George McWhirter, while drinking beer in Mike Brannigan's New York City saloon, discovers that he has suddenly been blessed with the power to perform miracles. He starts slowly, causing a kerosene lamp to burn while upside down and changing water into champagne. However, his newfound powers get the best of him—and everybody else—when he orders the world to stop turning and finds himself and his wife floating in space.

966. "Safe Judge" (8/27/76; rebroadcast from 4/12/76)

967. "Wishes Can Be Fatal" (8/28/76; rebroadcast from 4/13/76)

968. "Strange Passenger" (8/29/76; rebroadcast from 4/15/76)

969. "The Night Shift" (8/30/76; rebroadcast 11/14/76)

Cast: Howard Da Silva (Eddie O'Brien); Bryna Raeburn (Margie O'Brien); Earl Hammond (Jerry); William Griffis (Joe). Written by Sam Dann.

Wife Margie and best friend Jerry think Eddie O'Brien needs psychiatric care for the undue attention he pays to the new bus he drives #2792. He even leaves his wife every night at midnight to clean and repair it. When Jerry, who drives #2792 on the night shift, gets involved in a collision and causes excessive wear on the clutch, Eddie threatens to kill him if he's not more careful with the vehicle.

970. "The Three Elders of Lifeboat Landing" (8/31/76; rebroadcast from 4/26/76)

971. "Two Plus Two Equals Death" (9/1/76; rebroadcast from 4/29/76)

972. "The Magic Cay" (9/2/76; rebroadcast 11/24/76)

Cast: Paul Hecht (Tom Reynolds); Marian Seldes (Sunday); Ian Martin (Lieutenant Tarrant); Leon Janney (Doobie). Written by Ian Martin.

Tom Reynolds, fortyish, rich, but sick of the businessman's rat race, takes the advice of a psychiatrist friend and leaves for a two-week rest on uninhabited Bat Island. His first visitor is a beautiful woman who, near death, is washed up on the beach. Tom revives her and names her Sunday when she refuses to tell him who she is. The two begin an idyllic relationship which is brought to an abrupt halt when mainland police come looking for her.

973. "The Cornstarch Killer" (9/3/76; rebroadcast from 5/3/76)

974. "What a Change in Hilda" (9/4/76; rebroadcast from 5/6/76)

975. "The Ghost of San Juan Hill" (9/5/76; rebroadcast from 5/10/76)

976. "Graven Image" (9/6/76; rebroadcast 11/27/76)

Cast: Jack Grimes (Jodie Barnes); Bob Dryden (Craig Herbert); Hetty Galen (Lisa Barnes). Written by Bob Juhren.

Impressed by Jodie Barnes' singing at a small country fair, press agent Craig Herbert signs him to a long-term contract with the promise he'll make him a star. Jodie dutifully follows Herbert's every instruction, and in a short time he is the nation's number one country singer, his likeness appearing on T-shirts, lunch boxes, board games and hairdryers. But trouble begins when a manufacturer produces a Jodie Barnes singing doll that Jodie is certain will destroy both him and his career.

977. "Killer's Helper" (9/7/76; rebroadcast 11/28/76)

Cast: Michael Wager (Marty Carroway); Joan Banks (Margaret Masters); Evelyn Juster (Doreen Spellman); Bob Dryden (J.J. Masters). Written by Sam Dann.

J.J. Masters, president of a major Wall Street firm, has neglected his wife, Margaret, for years. On her birthday, he brings home Marty Carroway, whom he has just appointed number two man in the firm, and leaves the two alone while he conducts some business on the phone. Margaret flings herself at Carroway; not only does she want him to love her, but also to help in her scheme to end the life of her neglectful spouse.

978. "The Secret Sharer" (9/8/76; rebroadcast from 5/13/76)

979. "A Two-Bit Fortune" (9/9/76; rebroadcast 12/1/78)

Cast: Paul Hecht (Mike Wilson); Morgan Fairchild (Penny Wilson); Ian Martin (Amos Keane); Leon Janney (Stanford Spruce). Written by Ian Martin.

Mike Wilson, a skilled mechanic, takes an injured bum he picks up by the side of a highway to the hospital and lends him a quarter. Mike just laughs when the man says he is Stanford Spruce, a mysterious reclusive billionaire. However, when Mr. Spruce dies, Mike learns that he has inherited the man's fortune, his involuntary seclusion and his lawyer, Amos Keane, who threatens to kill Mike unless he does what he is told.

980. "A Magical Place" (9/10/76; rebroadcast 12/4/76)

Cast: William Redfield (Timothy Elkins); Anne Seymour (Mrs. Selby); Marian Seldes (Elinor). Written by Elspeth Eric.

Timothy and Elinor Elkins, both in their fifties, unhappy with their marriage and hoping to recapture the joys of their youth, visit the house they rented as newlyweds. Surprisingly, the house has changed little and is available again, so the Elkins rent it. They are delighted at first by the young voices they hear recalling their earlier pleasures, but become horrified when their efforts to restore the cottage are thwarted, and the voices persist.

981. "Blind Witness" (9/11/76; rebroadcast from 5/17/76)

982. "The Walking Dead" (9/12/76; rebroadcast from 5/20/76)

983. "The Tell-Tale Corpse" (9/13/76; rebroadcast 12/5/76)

Cast: Earl Hammond (Sid Sullivan); Court Benson (Ernie Blake); Catherine Byers (Aunt Grace); Guy Sorel (Hank). Written by Fielden Farrington.

Ernie Blake and Sid Sullivan, just out of jail, are the happy possessors of a key given them by a fellow inmate, now deceased. The dead man's Aunt Grace has the other key needed to open a chest that holds $100,000 in stolen cash. When they find the chest, with Aunt Grace's help, the two kill her and stuff her body into their auto's trunk. But Aunt Grace, who wanted her share of the loot, has no intention of allowing Sid and Ernie to keep it all for themselves.

984. "Journey to Jerusalem" (9/14/76; rebroadcast 12/8/76)

Cast: Vincent Gardenia (Elwood Jarvis); Joan Shay (Madame Salanis); Evelyn Juster (Miss Haskins); William Redfield (Doctor). Written by Sam Dann.

Elwood Jarvis, rich from the manufacture of filters, pleads with a $50-a-day psychiatrist to make him 25 years younger, so he can marry a woman who will love him, not his money, and have time to make real friends. It seems an impossible request—until Jarvis is accosted by a strange woman with raven black hair and deep black eyes. All that needs to be done, she says, is to find a robust, 30-year-old man willing to exchange bodies—and brains—with him.

Notes: Vincent Gardenia made his only appearance on *Theater* in this episode. Gardenia has appeared in numerous films including *The Super* (1991), *The Little Shop of Horrors* (1986), *Moonstruck* (1987), and *The Hustler* (1961).

985. "A Mexican Standoff" (9/15/76; rebroadcast from 5/24/76)

986. "Dr. Peterson's Pills" (9/16/76; rebroadcast 12/11/76)

Cast: Leon Janney (Dr. Emery Peterson); Rosemary Murphy (Daisy Peterson); Catherine Byers (Nicky Bell); Joseph Silver (Mayor Simms). Written by Fielden Farrington.

Dr. Emery Peterson, early in his career, had given up all hope of saving a dying boy. Off-handedly, he had muttered he would sell his soul to the devil in order to cure the youth. Miraculously, the boy survived, and now, 25 years later, the devil, in the form of attractive Nicky Bell, demands that the doctor live up to his end of the bargain. Not only does she want his soul, she wants all of him, even though he is a happily married middle-aged man.

987. "To Whom It May Concern" (9/17/76; rebroadcast 12/12/76)

Cast: Marian Seldes (Rebecca Owen); Ian Martin (Dr. Mandeville); Bryna Raeburn (Momma); Bob Dryden (Poppa); Earl Hammond (Walter Owen). Written by Sam Dann.

Rebecca Randolph Owen, a widow at 41 and beautiful, tells her psychiatrist that she often feels the presence of the Angel of Death. The spirit clutched her just before the Johnstown flood, the Iroquois Theater fire in Chicago, and the sinking of the Titanic, all of which she experienced and survived. She asks the psychiatrist, how she can make sure her presence will not cause any future disasters. The doctor thinks he has the answer.

988. "Demon Lover" (9/18/76; rebroadcast from 5/27/76)

989. "Ghost Town" (9/19/76; rebroadcast from 5/31/76)

990. "A Very Dear Ghost Indeed" (9/20/76; rebroadcast 12/15/76)

Cast: Court Benson (William Donovan); Patricia Elliott (Constance); Russell Horton (Padraic Duneen); Ian Martin (Sir Shamus). Written by Ian Martin.

William Donovan and his daughter, Constance, while traveling in Ireland at the turn of the century, are detained by a damaged bridge. While it is being repaired, they visit nearby Castle Carrickmoran, a moldering old building darkened by the ivy growing over it. They are surprised by a short, elderly man dressed all in green (except for square-buckled black shoes) who refuses to identify himself but proceeds to tell them a story they can scarcely believe.

991. "The Rainbow Man" (9/21/76; rebroadcast from 9/19/76)

Cast: Ralph Bell (Doc Meriweather); Russell Horton (Hank); Jada Rowland (Annie); Bob Dryden (Carter Billings). Written by Ian Martin.

When Doc Meriweather, known as the Rainbow Man, hears how Hank lost his small fortune gambling and now stands to lose the woman he loves to card shark Champ Rutledge, he vows to end the gambler's threat to the whole town. With Hank as his shill in a minor betting scheme, Doc works his way into a card game with Champ, where the stakes of which include not only the control of the town but also the gamblers' lives.

992. "Blue Justice" (9/22/76; rebroadcast from 6/3/76)

993. "Don't Play with Matches" (9/23/76; rebroadcast 12/19/76)

Cast: Mandel Kramer (Fire Chief); Earl Hammond (Jerry); Joan Shay (Anya); Gilbert Mack (Paul). Written by Sam Dann.

Fire Chief Delbert Casseroll's prevention program has snuffed out all the fires in Caswell Corners, so that the chief, when not appearing on television talk shows, just sits around the station. But on his day off, the usually conscientious chief becomes an arsonist—and eventually a murderer—creating work for other public servants. However, he soon discovers that when he plays with matches, he is bound to get burned.

994. "Queen of the Deadly Night" (9/24/76; rebroadcast 12/22/76)

Cast: Marian Seldes (Rachel); Arnold Moss (Asher); Bryna Raeburn (Bathsheba); Court Benson (Count Renaulf); Robert Kaliban (Isaac). Written by Sam Dann.

Immediately after Rachel ben Zi, who lived in France in the year 900, is married to Isaac, she is ordered by Count Renault, the lord of the castle, to spend her wedding night with the Count. Isaac objects, challenges Renault to a duel, and is killed by the Count's men-at-arms. While Rachel is in the Count's bedchamber, Isaac's apparition appears to inform her that she is destined to become the Queen of the Khazars—but only after she kills the Count.

995. "The Corpse That Would Not Die" (9/25/76; rebroadcast from 6/7/76)

996. "Free the Beast" (9/26/76; rebroadcast from 6/10/76)

997. "The Ghostly Private Eye" (9/27/76; rebroadcast 12/26/76)

Cast: Larry Haines (Flaxman Low); Paul Hecht (Professor Thierry); Ian Martin (Charles Volney); Guy Sorel (Sir George); Betty Winckler (Lady Cynthia). Written by Ian Martin.

Flaxman Low, a parapsychologist, is invited to spend a weekend in Land Manor in Surrey, whose owner, Sir George Blackburton, claims is cursed by a strange force that seems to be trying to crowd him and his wife out. While there, Low is shocked by the manner in which Sir George's nephew is murdered. Determined to find an explanation, Low volunteers to spend a night in the room where the terrifying incident took place.

998. "One Girl in a Million" (9/28/76; rebroadcast 12/29/76)

Cast: Michael Tolan (Frankie Falcon); Russell Horton (John Clock); Ralph Bell (Aldous Fisher); Evelyn Juster (Sima Morgan). Written by Alfred Bester.

John Clock, who has become a millionaire by helping corporate presidents make big decisions, has a major personal problem. Wherever he goes he keeps looking for his first and enduring love, a schoolteacher who died in a jet plane accident. Ultimately, a friend, ex-boxer Frankie Falcon, persuades a genetic biologist to make a duplicate of Clock's former flame, unaware that absence may not always make the heart grow fonder.

Notes: Michael Tolan has appeared in such films as *Night Terror* (1976), *Half Slave, Half Free* (1985), and *Presumed Innocent* (1990).

999. "The Unthinkable" (9/29/76; rebroadcast from 6/14/76)

1000. "Not for Sale" (9/30/76; rebroadcast 1/1/77)

Cast: Gordon Gould (Bryan Colfax); Rosemary Murphy (Faye Colfax); Court Benson (Carl Miller); Jack Grimes (Eddie). Written by Fielden Farrington.

When her Uncle Milo is murdered while tending his antique shop, Faye Colifax and the police assume the motive was robbery. However, Faye becomes suspicious when Carl Miller, the man who lives over the shop, offers to buy the building—at any price. When Uncle Milo's ghost asks Faye not to sell, she decides to go ahead with her plans to keep the building and run the antique shop herself, even as Miller's offer begins to sound more like a threat.

1001. "The Clairvoyant" (10/1/76; rebroadcast 1/2/77)

Cast: Tammy Grimes (Madame Sonya); Patricia Elliott (Laura); Ian Martin (Mr. Craig); Marian Seldes (Mother); Paul Hecht (John). Written by Elspeth Eric.

Madame Sonya, a well-respected clairvoyant in London in the 1930s and '40s, recalls how her career abruptly ended one day when an American woman asked her to do a reading for her daughter, Laura. Madame Sonya foresaw a happy enough life for Laura, but then Laura arranged a reading for her British fiancé, Anthony. Madame Sonya became confused and afraid during Anthony and his father's readings and could not tell anyone what horrifying events were in these Londoner's futures.

1002. "Pension Plan" (10/2/76; rebroadcast from 6/17/76)

1003. "Checkmate" (10/3/76; rebroadcast from 6/21/76)

1004. "The Midas Touch" (10/4/76; rebroadcast 1/5/77)

Cast: Bobby Morse (Jim Pangborn); Bryna Raeburn (Milly); Bob Dryden (Julius Trautwine); Jackson Beck (Sheriff). Written by Sam Dann.

Jim and Milly, his princess with mystical powers, make an easy $200 selling their Magic Hair Restorer to a bald-headed banker. Certain he can make more money from the banker, Jim tries to sell him the Midas touch, that is, the opportunity to read today, tomorrow's financial page with stock closings yet to be completed. The banker agrees to buy the financial page dated October 29, 1929, not knowing what losses he and Jim are about to experience.

1005. "Private Stock" (10/5/76; rebroadcast 1/8/77)

Cast: Ian Martin (Capt. Tom Turner); Catherine Byers (Ginnie Turner); Russell Horton (Bobby Lee); Earl Hammond (Chunky Chapman). Written by Sam Dann.

Ginnie Turner, beautiful, redheaded and a school teacher, knifes to death a rock 'n' roll singing star, Bobby Lee Armature, when he insists that she spend the night with his guitar player, Chunky Chapman. Ginnie's father, a police captain, investigates the slaying and smells, at the scene of the crime, the rare perfume his daughter uses. Additional evidence convinces him that she is guilty, but he can't bring himself to arrest his own daughter.

1006. "Child of Fate" (10/6/76; rebroadcast from 6/24/76)

1007. "Pool of Fear" (10/7/76; rebroadcast 1/9/77)

Cast: Morgan Fairchild (Beth Stillwell); William Redfield (Matt Brewster); Nat Polen (Lee Stillwell); Ann Shepherd (Milly Stillwell). Written by Fielden Farrington.

Beth Stillwell, who adored her mother, has nothing but contempt for her stepmother. She hires ex-con Matt Brewster to spend a weekend with her on her rich father's estate, pretending that she and Matt are engaged. She also wants Matt to drown her hated stepmother in the estate's swimming pool. Matt, who is broke, likes the $100,000 he is to receive for the murder, but when the time comes to do it, he can't escape the feeling that someone is watching him.

1008. "The Tortured Twins" (10/8/76; rebroadcast 1/18/77)

Cast: Marian Seldes (Joyce Adams/Janice Adams); Paul Hecht (Adam Duncan). Written by Ian Martin.

Adam Duncan knows he loves Joyce Adams from the first moment he set eyes on her at the off off Broadway theater where they both work, so he proposes to her right away. When the newlyweds move to Hollywood for Joyce's first movie role, Adam meets her twin sister, Janice. Suddenly he realizes he really should have married Janice, the more serious of the twins, and vows to make her his wife if it means that he has to kill Joyce first.

1009. "Forty-Five Minutes to Murder" (10/9/76; rebroadcast from 6/28/76)

1010. "Loser Takes All" (10/10/76; rebroadcast from 7/1/76)

1011. "My Wife Doesn't Understand Me" (10/11/76; rebroadcast 1/20/77)

Cast: Bob Dryden (Horace); Teri Keane (Marjory); Rosemary Rice (Ann). Written by Sam Dann.

Horace Bellows, 60 years old and dissatisfied with his work and his marriage, is enchanted by his new employee, Ann Jackson, a 30-year-old stenographer. While his wife, Marjory, spends her evenings at committee meetings, Horace spends his time with Ann, first complaining that his wife doesn't understand him and then talking incessantly about his chemical discoveries, for which he never really got due credit. But, when Marjory exposes the real reason for Ann's interest in him, Horace learns that his wife is the smart one after all.

1012. "The God Killer" (10/12/76; rebroadcast 1/22/77)

Cast: Tammy Grimes (Ursula Underwood); Earl Hammond (Lt. Czesticowitz); Ken Harvey (The Shiv); Leon Janney (Alistair Pollister). Written by Sam Dann.

Alistair Pollister, author of violent and murder-filled stories, is fatally knifed, and the police suspect his longtime secretary, Ursula Underwood. However, Miss Underwood claims that "The Shiv," one of Pollister's sinister characters, actually committed the murder. The police don't believe her story and try to make her sign a confession, but she refuses, saying to the baffled cops that Shiv will appear in person to verify her story.

1013. "Blood Red Roses" (10/13/76; rebroadcast from 7/12/76)

1014. "The Living Corpse" (10/14/76; rebroadcast 1/23/77)

Cast: Hurd Hatfield (Henry); Joan Shea (Mrs. Peabody); Patricia Elliott (Megan); Ian Martin (Lieutenant Quinn). Written by Ian Martin.

Henry Girard Flower Peabody VI, a member of Philadelphia society by birth and breeding, has always felt there was an element inside him that did not fit his sober side. As a young man, he kept his crazy, fun-loving girlfriend, Megan, a secret from his other friends and his strict but ailing mother. But, when Megan suggests that Henry end his mother's lingering life or else, Henry realizes he can no longer lead a double life and must kill one of them.

Notes: Hurd Hatfield made his only appearance in this episode. Hatfield has starred in numerous films, including a few from the horror-mystery genre: *The Picture of Dorian Gray* (1945), *The Boston Strangler* (1968), *Diary of a Chambermaid* (1946), and *Her Alibi* (1988).

1015. "A Point in Time" (10/15/76; rebroadcast 1/25/77)

Cast: Paul Hecht (Fred); Russell Horton (Don); Teri Keane (Zella); Court Benson (Karl). Written by Mary Jane Higby.

Fred and Don are hiking from Sante Fe to the Colorado border when they enter Silver Springs, a simulated 1920s mining town. They are immediately drugged and jailed. Two townspeople, Zella and Karl, explain that Silver Springs is an invasion base for the planet Agantha, which plans to take control of Earth and wipe out all earthlings. Zella, suspecting something is wrong with the mission, thinks Fred and Don can help.

1016. "The Last Trip of Charter Boat Sally" (10/16/76; rebroadcast from 7/15/76)

1017. "Future Eye" (10/17/76; rebroadcast from 7/19/76)

1018. "Killer's Appointment" (10/18/76; rebroadcast 1/27/77)

Cast: Marian Seldes (Lydia Prentiss); Bill Griffis (Sheriff); Bryna Raeburn (Momma); Michael Wager (Herb Larson). Written by Sam Dann.

Lydia Prentiss is so in love with Herb Larson that when he assaults a factory guard and empties the company safe, she tells the police she is the guilty one. She's willing to put off their wedding for three years if she can save Herb's reputation.

Suddenly, after a year, his daily letters stop coming to the jail, and so does he. When told by her mother that Herb has married his boss's daughter, Lydia swears she'll break out of prison and settle matters—with a gun.

1019. "The Mission of Atropos" (10/19/76; rebroadcast 1/29/77)

Cast: Mason Adams (Al Marks); Joan Banks (Dr. Louisa); Robert Maxwell (Spaulding); Jackson Beck (Lt. Carey); Joan Shay (Mrs. Drake). Written by Sam Dann.

Dr. Louisa Mandeville, plant physician for a company working on a top-secret project, is mystified by the unexplainable deaths of two workers. After some investigation, she suspects that an illegal substance used in production, KCV 144, caused the two to die. When she confronts the company's president with her suspicions, he offers her $50,000 to keep quiet. She refuses and becomes the third victim. The case seems closed until a nosy reporter starts investigating.

1020. "The Men with the Magic Fingers" (10/20/76; rebroadcast from 7/22/76)

1021. "To Hang by the Neck" (10/21/76; rebroadcast 1/30/77)

Cast: Marian Seldes (Becky Pryor); Robert Kaliban (Teague Whitman); Ann Pitoniak (Mother); Martha Greenhouse (Carrie); Bill Griffis (Chad). Written by Ian Martin.

Becky Pryor decides, after the end of the Civil War, to return to the C-Circle-C Ranch in Texas, just a year after she went there for what she thought was going to be Carrie Conway's wedding, but turned out to be her friend's funeral. Carrie's invalid mother now complains to Becky that the truth is not known about her daughter's death. A suspiciously quiet ranch hand, a Northerner, offers to help Becky find out why Carrie might have hanged herself—if indeed she did.

1022. "Somebody Help Me!" (10/22/76; rebroadcast 2/1/77)

Cast: Howard Da Silva (Bert); Larry Haines (Charlie); Bryna Raeburn (Charlie's Mom); Evelyn Juster (Inez). Written by Sam Dann.

Two policemen—Bert, the unattractive but sincere one, and Charlie, the handsome-but-married one, think Inez is the prettiest woman they have ever seen. But when she refuses a date with Bert, saying he is homely, Bert makes sure she never sees his face again—he kills her. Finally, after murdering several other pretty women who turn down his invitations, Bert confesses to Charlie, the officer assigned to the case. But Charlie, who already has a suspect, doesn't believe him.

1023. "The Brain Without Mercy" (10/23/76; rebroadcast from 7/26/76)

1024. "Shotgun Wedding" (10/24/76; rebroadcast from 7/29/76)

1025. "**Every Dog Has His Day**" (10/25/76; rebroadcast from 8/2/76)

1026. "**Lovers and Killers**" (10/26/76; rebroadcast from 8/5/76)

1027. "**The Deathly White Man**" (10/27/76; rebroadcast 2/3/77)

Cast: Betsy Palmer (Linda Barclay); Ian Martin (Mr. Rensevelt); Russell Horton (Ted); Bryna Raeburn (Mrs. Greaves). Written by Ian Martin.

Linda Barclay, 23 and in need of a job, is hired by wealthy Carther Rensevelt to nurse his invalid wife. Mrs. Rensevelt is confined to Broomwegen, a mansion perched on the rocks of a small island. She can hardly speak, thus can give no explanation of the deathly white man whose visits from the mansion's turret in the dead of night make life for Linda a most frightening experience.

Notes: Witches (young and old), ghosts, the Devil and grave robbers all show up in five consecutive broadcasts in observance of Halloween, which host E.G. Marshall says, "Evil spirits abound—ghouls and ghosts, pariahs and phenomena, witches and warlocks, vampires, werewolves, poltergeists and crawling things too awful to imagine—all the outcasts from the natural world, not only the supernatural and dead, but the half-dead, the haunting army of the lost between two worlds." This was the first of the five episodes in memorance to Halloween.

1028. "**Absolute Zero**" (10/28/76; rebroadcast 2/5/77)

Cast: Jada Rowland (Linda Russell); Ian Martin (Dr. Miles Hendon); Bryna Raeburn (Mrs. Hendon); Court Benson (Rev. Armbruster); Russell Horton (Digger Welles). Written by Ian Martin.

Linda Russell hurriedly returns from Paris to her stepfather's Cape Cod home when she learns of her mother's sudden death. Overcome by guilt for not having been at her mother's bedside when she died, Linda rushes to the mausoleum containing her mother's coffin. She is unable to open it. Later, a strange young man pries it open, and when Linda is told what he discovered—that it is empty—she suspects foul play and determines to find out who is responsible—and why.

1029. "**The Unborn**" (10/29/76; rebroadcast 2/6/77)

Cast: Mercedes McCambridge (Margo Baranya); Bob Dryden (Count Stavrianos); Robert Kaliban (Mike Burns). Written by Ian Martin.

Duchess Margo Baranya, nearing 60, cares not a whit that her husband has just died. She yearns for a return to her youth, a wish that is granted by Count Demetrios Stravrianos—financier, international broker, ship owner and puller of strings who is really the Devil. Margo will gradually become younger if she gives herself to the Count. She is satisfied with the deal—until she meets a much younger man, a playboy whom she much prefers to the Count.

1030. "**Witches' Sabbath**" (10/30/76; rebroadcast 2/12/77)

Cast: Larry Haines (Perry Harnishfeger); Leon Janney (Prince of Darkness); Marian Hailey (The Blonde); Evelyn Juster (The Brunette). Written by Sam Dann.

Though he wants to say no, shy Perry Harnishfeger shouts, "What are we waiting for!" when two beautiful women—a blonde and brunette—invite him to a night of fun. They take him to a party, dress him in a special robe, put him before a fountain of burning champagne, and introduce him to the Prince of Darkness. The Prince proclaims that in order to serve his royal highness, Perry must kill three times—his hated boss, his unfaithful wife and her lover. Perry obeys, but then wants to believe it was all a dream.

1031. "The Queen of Cats" (10/31/76; rebroadcast 2/13/77, 10/31/78)

Cast: Tammy Grimes (Sarah Taylor); Jack Grimes (Tony Readick); Joseph Silver (Sheriff); Betsy Beard (Carrie). Written by Ian Martin.

The townspeople are certain that Sarah Taylor's 63 cats are responsible for the gruesome maulings and deaths of three teenaged girls. They want the sheriff to run her out of town, but he hires a young, handsome lawyer, Tony Readick, to defend her. His fiancée, Carrie Chisolm, a student of parapsychology, suspects Mrs. Taylor is a witch and needs the blood of young girls to pursue her malevolent career. Carrie urges Tony to drop the case, but he won't listen.

1032. "Overnight to Freedom" (11/1/76; rebroadcast from 8/9/76)

Note: Because of election coverage, Mystery Theater *was not broadcast on November 2, 1976, the first day in almost three years since the series premiered that* Mystery Theater *was not broadcast.*

1033. "The Haliday Prediction" (11/3/76; rebroadcast from 8/12/76)

1034. "City of the Dead" (11/4/76; rebroadcast 2/9/77)

Cast: Earl Hammond (Sam Elstead); Kristopher Tabori (Starr Norton); Court Benson (Dr. Weybridge); Catherine Byers (Doris Elstead). Adapted by Arnold Moss, based on the 1896 short story by H.G. Wells.

Sam Elstead and Starr Norton, among history's first marine biologists, volunteer to dive four miles beneath the sea's surface in a eight-foot-in-diameter globe for a look at the Cayman Trough. Much of what they see and encounter are remarkably similar to those experienced in February of 1976 by three men who dove into the trough in a craft called *Alvin.*

1035. "The Secret Chamber" (11/5/76; rebroadcast 2/16/77)

Cast: Ian Martin (Thomas T. Tattersall); Marian Seldes (Felicity Hargreaves); Leon Janney (Dumont Hargreaves); Joan Shay (Countess Deejinarah). Written by Sam Dann.

Realtor Thomas T. Tattersall, to help the executor of Judge Hargreaves' will sell the Hargreaves house, agrees to try and convince the Judge's daughter, Felicity, who has remained in her room since her fiancé was killed at Chateau-Thierry, to leave. Before he can do so, Felicity disappears, and thereafter the house seems haunted—at least to potential buyers. Tattersall doesn't believe in ghosts—especially Felicity's—until he accompanies the executor to the house.

1036. "Your Grade Is A" (11/6/76; rebroadcast from 8/16/76)

1037. "The Golden People" (11/7/76; rebroadcast from 8/19/76)

1038. "The Graveyard" (11/8/76; rebroadcast 2/19/77)

Cast: Norman Rose (Pierre); Guy Sorel (Priest); Evelyn Juster (Terese); Ralph Bell (Henri); Jada Rowland (Simone). Adapted by Elspeth Eric, based on the short story *Was It a Dream?* by Guy de Maupassant.

Pierre goes to a confessional and blurts out the story of his love for Simone, whom he describes as an "angel with the insouciance, grace and beauty of a wood nymph." It was a love to which he dedicated everything: his worldly goods, his thoughts, his life, himself. Then one day Simone becomes mysteriously ill and soon dies. Not until he visits her grave does the heartbroken Pierre learn, to his horror, the reason for her death.

1039. "The Colony" (11/9/76; rebroadcast 2/20/77)

Cast: Tony Roberts (Michael Duncan); Morgan Fairchild (Mary Duncan); Frances Sternhagen (Mae Norton); Jackson Beck (Thad); Guy Sorel (Arnold Stebbins). Written by Fielden Farrington.

While on an automobile vacation, Michael and Mary Duncan sight a UFO on the highway, on the edge of a town called Colony. Unsure that anyone will believe them, the Duncans stop and report it to Colony's sheriff, who surprisingly takes them seriously—too seriously. However, when the sheriff puts them in jail, the Duncans realize that they had better find a way to escape this town, where all the people seem to be possessed—before it's too late.

1040. "The Train Stops" (11/10/76; rebroadcast from 8/23/76)

1041. "Strike Force" (11/11/76; rebroadcast 3/2/77)

Cast: Michael Wager (Dr. Sanderson); Court Benson (Bob Watson); Gilbert Mack (Captain Carey); Mary Jane Higby (Andrea); Patricia Elliott (Alice). Written by Sam Dann.

When Dr. Orville Sanderson examines a new corpse, he sees tattooed on its arm the emblem of the regiment in which his father, supposedly dead for 31 years, served. Eventually he determines that the corpse is his father. But when he confronts his mother and stepfather with this fact, the doctor becomes convinced that his family is like that in *The Illiad*—comprised of a warrior, his unfaithful wife, her lover, and a revengeful son.

1042. "A Question of Identity" (11/12/76; rebroadcast 3/5/77)

Cast: Joan Banks (Hilary Cummings); Bob Dryden (Bob One); Ian Martin (Bob Two); Joseph Silver (Bob Three). Written by Murray Burnett.

Hilary Cummings, on her way to work as a court stenographer, is kidnapped and taken to a country mansion where a U.S. government intelligence agent demands that she identify her ex-husband, Bob Christie, from among three spies posing as Bob. She ultimately agrees (the nation's security is involved), but there are two problems: Bob has undergone radical facial surgery, and she hasn't seen him for 12 years.

1043. "The Man Who Could Work Miracles" (11/13/76; rebroadcast from 8/26/76)

1044. "The Night Shift" (11/14/76; rebroadcast from 8/30/76)

1045. "Tom Sawyer, Detective" (11/15/76; rebroadcast from 1/5/76)

1046. "Is He Living or Is He Dead?" (11/16/76; rebroadcast from 1/6/76)

1047. "The Russian Passport" (11/17/76; rebroadcast from 1/7/76)

1048. "A Connecticut Yankee in King Arthur's Court" (11/18/76; rebroadcast from 1/8/76)

1049. "The Man That Corrupted Hadleyburg" (11/19/76; rebroadcast from 1/9/76)

1050. "The Stolen White Elephant" (11/20/76; rebroadcast from 1/10/76)

1051. "The Mysterious Stranger" (11/21/76; rebroadcast from 1/11/76)

1052. "Meeting by Chance" (11/22/76; rebroadcast 2/23/79)
Cast: Mandel Kramer (He); Marian Seldes (She); Robert Readick (Man). Written by Elspeth Eric.
Caught in a frightening thunderstorm, a man and a woman leave their automobiles and meet in an abandoned yet well-kept house. Unsure of each other's motives, they are drawn together when they hear the mewing of a white cat they soon discover is blind. Only when a man comes to feed the cat do they learn the astonishing yet compassionate story of why the animal has lost its sight and become the house's only inhabitant.

1053. "The Awakening" (11/23/76; rebroadcast 2/26/77)
Cast: Kim Hunter (Dr. Amelia Zeltner); Earl Hammond (Lieutenant Katz); Bryna Raeburn (Beatrice Boyers); Leon Janney (Ben Bentley). Written by Sam Dann.

The only clue police have in the murder of a psychiatrist is a tape recording of the murderer's conversation with his victim, before the murder took place, and the sounds of the murder itself. The tape doesn't help the police at all until another psychiatrist, Dr. Amelia Zeltner, is brought into the case. She listens to the tape and finds motives for murder in it that the police were unable to comprehend.

1054. "The Magic Cay" (11/24/76; rebroadcast from 9/2/76)

1055. "M-U-R-D-E-R" (11/25/76; rebroadcast 2/27/77)

Cast: Ralph Bell (Max Pickett); Larry Haines (Kyle Abbot); Marian Hailey (Maude); Teri Keane (Helen Picket); Marian Seldes (Gwen Abbot). Written by Fielden Farrington.

Max Picket's business is in shambles. His partner walked off with nearly $100,000 of the company's funds and then, according to Max, committed suicide. While visiting their friends the Abbots one evening, Max and his wife, for fun, agree to work the ouija board Gwen Abbot recently bought at a garage sale. When the board spells out M-U-R-D-E-R, no one takes it seriously until later, when it predicts that Max will M-U-R-D-E-R three more people.

1056. "Blood Will Tell" (11/26/76; rebroadcast 3/6/77)

Cast: Mason Adams (Norman Claymore); Bryna Raeburn (Mummy); Evelyn Juster (Melisande Resnik); Ken Harvey (Enoch Pennypacker). Written by Sam Dann.

Norman Claymore is ordered by a blonde, beautiful personnel department clerk at his office to explain, for life insurance purposes, how his father died. Norman's doting mother has never told him and now suspects that the personnel women's only purpose, in pressing for an answer, is to lure Norman away from his Mummy. But Norman determines to find out what happened. And when he does, he becomes a changed man, contemplating murder, with even his mother as a possible victim.

1057. "Graven Image" (11/27/76; rebroadcast from 9/6/76)

1058. "Killer's Helper" (11/28/76; rebroadcast from 9/7/76)

1059. "The Man Who Couldn't Get Arrested" (11/29/76; rebroadcast 3/9/77)

Cast: Fred Gwynne (Hector Freemont Carnehan); Court Benson (Ben); Bill Griffis (Dale); Joan Shay (Penelope Carnehan). Written by Sam Dann.

A Wall Street broker can't figure out whether he's dreaming or awake when his wife tries to tell him somebody's going to murder her. Wherever he goes one evening, Hector Freemont Carnehan keeps hearing a plea from his wife, Penelope, to save her—somebody's trying to kill her. The next day Penelope—alive and unharmed—visits Hector at his office and assures him that her life has not been threatened. But later that night Hector is told by his boss that Penelope has been found dead at their country home.

1060. "Now You See Them, Now You Don't" (11/30/76; rebroadcast 3/12/77)

Cast: Bob Dryden (Professor Harry Scrim); Leon Janney (General Eubie Harp); Martha Greenhouse (Lela Tibbett); Earl Hammond (Clive Hammer); Ian Martin (Captain Edward Edsel). Written by Alfred Bester.

Professor Harry Scrim, serving 20 years of hard labor in Alcatraz, which has been reactivated for conscientious objectors to World War V (2175 A.D.), is released temporarily to help solve the mystery of the 24 shock casualties confined to Ward J of a military hospital. They don't eat or sleep and, when confronted by doctors or military officers, disappear with a champagne cork–like pop.

1061. "A Two-Bit Fortune" (12/1/76; rebroadcast from 9/9/76)

1062. "How to Kill Rudy" (12/2/76; rebroadcast 3/13/77)

Cast: Paul Hecht (Rudy Slaymaker); Patricia Elliott (Ramona Slaymaker); Ralph Bell (Jack Jessup); Ian Martin (Mr. Tallow). Written by Sam Dann.

Rudy Slaymaker, who reads every Mace Hacker mystery novel, acquires one in which Hacker writes that a man named Rudy will soon be the victim of a murder plotted by his wife, Ramona, and his boss, Jack. Because his real-life wife and boss are named Ramona and Jack, and all of Hacker's stories eventually come true, a terrified Rudy takes steps he hopes will prevent the two from killing him.

1063. "Child of Misfortune" (12/3/76; rebroadcast 3/16/77)

Cast: Norman Rose (Dr. Sam Taylor); Joan Copeland (Jane Taylor); Court Benson (Dr. Holcombe); Jada Rowland (Jenny Taylor). Written by Ian Martin.

Jenny Taylor, 16, following the peculiar death of her parents, comes to live with her uncle, Dr. Sam Taylor, and his family. Jenny is a stunning young woman whose attention to Dr. Sam turns his head. But when his wife comes down with the strange ailment that killed Jenny's mother and Jenny admits that she, with her unusual powers, is responsible, Dr. Sam realizes that she must go—even if it means murdering her.

1064. "A Magical Place" (12/4/76; rebroadcast from 9/10/76)

1065. "The Tell-Tale Corpse" (12/5/76; rebroadcast from 9/13/76)

1066. "Child of the Sea" (12/6/76; rebroadcast 3/19/77)

Cast: Tony Roberts (David Wells); Evelyn Juster (Alonay); Bryna Raeburn (Ellen); Earl Hammond (Father). Written by Bob Juhren.

While scuba diving off California's Laguna Beach, playboy David Wells is trapped by a tentacle of an enormous squid. Only the quick action of a beautiful young woman with long, flowing blonde hair saves his life. She calls herself Alonay and David falls madly in love with her. Their relationship is doomed, however. Alonay must live in the ocean much of the time, and her father—half-man, half-fish—will not allow her to see David.

1067. "Enough Rope" (12/7/76; rebroadcast 3/20/77)

Cast: Russell Horton (Billy Baxter); Evelyn Juster (Alida); Bob Dryden (Jethro). Written by Sam Dann.

"Bunco" Billy Baxter has swindled a group of gullible miners out of $10,000 by selling them 100,000 acres of desert for one cent an acre. About to be hanged by the enraged men, Billy is rescued by a beautiful gun-toting woman who says she has lived for nearly four centuries. Later, she urges Billy to return the money, promising that if he does, she will help him pull off the biggest swindle in history.

1068. "Journey to Jerusalem" (12/8/76; rebroadcast from 9/14/76)

1069. "Nobody Dies" (12/9/76; rebroadcast 3/23/77)

Cast: Teri Keane (Alice); Ann Shepherd (Mrs. Holt); Jack Grimes (Jamie); Morgan Fairchild (Verity). Written by Elspeth Eric.

When Mrs. Holt hires Alice to care for her house and her just-born daughter, Verity, she is delighted that Alice's young son, Jamie, will be Verity's playmate. But as the years pass and the children become teenagers and then college students, Mrs. Holt is determined not to let Verity and Jamie marry. However, her determination destroys not only the closeness the four shared, but also leads to a haunting experience and death.

1070. "Identity Crisis" (12/10/76; rebroadcast 3/26/77)

Cast: Gordon Gould (Dr. Peters); Ann Williams (Jane Hollis); Bob Dryden (Carl Dunlap); Joseph Silver (Paul Morrison); Bryna Raeburn (Esther Kemperer). Written by Fielden Farrington.

When Senator Andrew Hollis suffers massive internal injuries in an auto accident and Ralph Kemperer is afflicted with brain cancer, Dr. Peters performs a brain transplant to save one of them. Dr. Peters and both men's wives and friends are concerned about the identity Hollis-Kemperer will take. Two of the senator's business associates, fearing he will talk about their corrupt dealings, try to get to Hollis-Kemperer and kill him.

1071. "Dr. Peterson's Pills" (12/11/76; rebroadcast from 9/16/76)

1072. "To Whom It May Concern" (12/12/76; rebroadcast from 9/17/76)

1073. "Hit Me Again" (12/13/76; rebroadcast 3/27/77)

Cast: Paul Hecht (Jerry Dykman); Patricia Elliott (Virginia Dykman); Ian Martin (Ace Drew); Jackson Beck (Dr. Drexel). Written by Ian Martin.

Jerry Dykman, a financial wizard, genius with numbers, and shoo-in for the vice-presidency at his brokerage firm, suddenly resigns. He is certain that by applying his mathematical talents he can beat the house at the blackjack table. Obsessed with his dream, he leaves his wife and heads for Las Vegas. His system works—so well, in fact, that house owners start thinking of fitting him for concrete boots and dumping him into a lake before they go broke.

1074. "The Smoking Pistol" (12/14/76; rebroadcast 3/30/77)

Cast: Howard Da Silva (Lt. Harry Reinfield); Robert Kaliban (George Mason); Ann Pitoniak (Bessie Mason); Rosemary Rice (Leona Lewis). Written by Sam Dann.

Jerry Reinfield, a young undercover cop, is murdered while trying to bust a drug ring, and George Mason is apprehended near the scene with the murder weapon, drugs and Jerry's wallet. Even to Jerry's father, Police Lt. Harry Reinfield, it seems like an open and shut case, since Mason was caught holding "the smoking pistol." But Mrs. Mason claims her son didn't do it and haunts the lieutenant until he opens an investigation of his son's horrible death.

1075. "A Very Dear Ghost Indeed" (12/15/76; rebroadcast from 9/20/76)

1076. "The Doctor's Evidence" (12/16/76; rebroadcast 4/2/77)

Cast: Frances Sternhagen (Ellen Robertshaw); Tony Roberts (Bruce Ellis); Ralph Bell (Ken Robertshaw); Guy Sorel (Dr. Croft); Catherine Butterfield (Kay Tyler). Written by Roy Winsor.

Businessman Ken Robertshaw has been having an affair with his secretary, Kay Tyler, for two years. Robertshaw's wife, Ellen, who has unusual powers of ESP, knows about their relationship and foresees trouble for her—and them. When Ellen falls to her death from an eighth story window, the police consider it a suicide, but her son, also with powers of telepathy, received a different message from his mother while she was still alive.

Notes: Frances Sternhagen won a Tony Award for her performance as the mother in *Equus*, and she was soon to begin an outing in Broadway's short-lived musical *Angel*.

1077. "A Quiet Evening at Home" (12/17/76; rebroadcast 4/3/77)

Cast: Tammy Grimes (Alicia Merriwether); Bob Dryden (Lieutenant Berger); Earl Hammond (Albert Merriwether); Earl Hammond (Bruce Pennington). Written by Sam Dann.

Alicia Merriwether and Bruce Pennington agree to run away together, leaving their wealthy spouses. They plan to meet at night at a railroad station and take a train to New York, but Bruce doesn't show up. While waiting, Alicia witnesses a murder, and the cabbie who drives her home afterward tells the police he picked her up at the scene of the crime. Accused of involvement in the killing, Alicia faces a dilemma. No matter what she tells the police, her life will be ruined.

1078. "The Rainbow Man" (12/18/76; rebroadcast from 9/21/76)

1079. "Don't Play with Matches" (12/19/76; rebroadcast from 9/23/76)

1080. "Date of Death" (12/20/76; rebroadcast 4/6/77)

Cast: Norman Rose (Dr. Matt Porter); Larry Haines (Dave Jensen); Joan Copeland (Janet Jensen); Evelyn Juster (Deidre). Written by Elspeth Eric.

David Jensen, who is recovering from a simple posterior infarction, reads all the books he can find on heart disease and soon convinces himself that he will die, at any moment, from a massive aneurysm, the bursting of the aortic artery at a crucial spot. His doctor assures him this will not happen, but Jensen accuses him of lying, claiming that the doctor visited him one night at home to warn him about the aneurysm.

1081. "The Lone Survivor" (12/21/76; rebroadcast 4/9/77)

Cast: Russell Horton (Theodore Williams); Ian Martin (Dr. Sedgefield); Bryna Raeburn (Jackie Williams); Kenneth Harvey (J.P. Henderson). Written by Ian Martin.

The combination of a hole in its fuselage and clear air turbulence causes the crash of a plane en route to Hawaii. All on board are killed, except one man found swimming in the nude in the ocean. The man, hospitalized, seems to be suffering from a severe case of amnesia, is unable to identify himself or explain why he was on the plane. He is a cooperative patient—until the police try to fingerprint him and have his photograph taken.

1082. "Queen of the Deadly Night" (12/22/76; rebroadcast from 9/24/76)

1083. "Double Zero" (12/23/76; rebroadcast 4/10/77)

Cast: Bob Dryden (Lt. Kramer); Bryna Raeburn (Sarinda); Joan Shay (Dolly Munson); Earl Hammond (Ronald Fairchild); Bill Griffis (Mr. Corliss). Written by Sam Dann.

Police find five twenty-dollar bills, each marked with two zeroes written in red, in the wallet of murdered private eye Luther Bendow. When, on television, private citizens are asked to provide any information they might have on the killing, a man tells police he gave the marked bills to his landlord. He says he always marks such bills so cashiers can't cheat him when making change. Little does he know how important these bills are to become in apprehending the murderer.

1084. "A Christmas Carol" (12/24/76 rebroadcast from 12/24/75)

1085. "The Magus" (12/25/76; rebroadcast 4/13/77)

Cast: Fred Gwynne (Adrian Storm); Carol Teitel (Mother); Russell Horton (Larry); Jada Rowland (Elly). Written by Elspeth Eric.

The cook in the mansion owned by Adrian Storm is upset because of the influence he has over her daughter, Elly, whose job it is to wait on the master's table. One day he asks Elly to carry a full-length mirror to his bedroom, claiming he will show her how he can cause his reflection in it to disappear. When he does, Elly panics and rushes to her mother, who calls his doctor, apparently the only one who can offer a rational explanation of Storm's supernatural powers.

1086. "The Ghostly Private Eye" (12/26/76; rebroadcast from 9/27/76)

1087. "The Mark of Cain" (12/27/76; rebroadcast 4/16/77)

Cast: Ralph Bell (Kaintuck); Robert Kaliban (Enoch); Ian Martin (Jared); Marian Seldes (Sharon). Written by Ian Martin.

In the Old West shortly after the Civil War, Kaintuck owns the fastest gun in Colorado and the worst reputation. He has killed his own brother, Abe, over a woman they both wanted. Nevertheless, the V Bar C ranch owner hires him to keep the sheepherders off his vast cattle grazing lands. All goes well until Kaintuck's son Enoch, whom he has never known, challenges him to a gunfight—over a young woman who prefers the father, not the son.

1088. "The Artist" (12/28/76; rebroadcast 4/17/77)

Cast: Michael Wager (Marc Harrison); Court Benson (Professor de la Croix); Partricia Elliott (Mlle. Fifi); Ann Pitoniak (Mother). Written by Sam Dann.

Marc Harrison is astounded when he first sees Professor Raoul de la Croix throw a knife that lands under his wife Mlle. Fifi's arm and right next to her heart. Marc is convinced that this is an act showing the ultimate faith one human being can have in another. But when Marc becomes the professor's friend and Mlle. Fifi's lover, he realizes that her life is in *real* danger every night.

1089. "One Girl in a Million" (12/29/76 rebroadcast from 9/28/76)

1090. "Your Move, Mr. Ellers" (12/30/76; rebroadcast 4/20/77)

Cast: Roger De Koven (Edward Ellers); Jack Grimes (Jeff Powers); Bob Readick (Tim Whelan); Jackson Beck (Will Minton). Written by Roy Winsor.

Tim Wheelan is assigned by his insurance company to investigate the continuing robberies at the Maudley and Son jewelry emporium. Even though convinced the heists are inside jobs, Whelan can find no verification until a daily lunchtime chess game between the store's most respected employee and a new salesman attracts his attention. What interests him even more is an evening chess game in which one of the players is a former fence, but now a respectable importer-exporter.

Notes: Roger De Koven is no stranger to horror and mystery. He played numerous supporting roles in other anthology radio programs such as *Suspense*, *Yours Truly, Johnny Dollar*, *The Mysterious Traveler*, *Tales of Tomorrow*, *Dimension X*, and *X Minus One*. He has also played supporting characters in such radio series as *Against the Storm*, *The Voice of Firestone*, and *This Is Nora Drake*.

1091. "Tomorrow's Murder" (12/31/76; rebroadcast 4/23/77)

Cast: Bob Dryden (Harold Starbright); Earl Hammond (Fred); Evelyn Juster (Gretchen); Court Benson (Man). Written by Sam Dann.

Harold K. Starbright, while walking in Morrison City Memorial Park, meets a man whose interest is cemetery sculpture. The man points out several unusual examples, including one tombstone with Starbright's name, birthdate and date of death, March 15, 1978. His wife Gretchen and his doctor, who is Gretchen's lover, don't take him seriously, but Starbright knows he must do something to stop the countdown.

1092. "Not for Sale" (1/1/77; rebroadcast from 9/30/76)

1093. "The Clairvoyant" (1/2/77; rebroadcast from 10/1/76)

1094. "Whose Little Girl Are You?" (1/3/77; rebroadcast 4/24/77)

Cast: Marian Seldes (Minnie Maxwell); William Griffis (Pop); Russell Horton (Bob Clone). Written by Sam Dann.

Minnie Maxwell, unbeatable on the tennis court, loses a big match to a woman she had easily beaten before because her strongest stroke, her backhand, seems to have failed her. Interviewed afterward by sports reporter Bob Clone, Minnie startles him with the admission that she has sold her backhand to the devil. But she doesn't tell Clone what form this devil has taken or why she agreed to make a deal with such a demon.

1095. "This Breed Is Doomed" (1/4/77; rebroadcast 4/27/77)

Cast: Howard Da Silva (Red Harrison Kendall); Ian Martin (Eubie Barken); Gilbert Mack (Kupperman); Bryna Raeburn (Sarah). Written by Ian Martin.

Red Harrison Kendall, an old-time confidence man usually one step ahead of the law, gets arrested in a small North Carolina town. He talks his way out of a jail sentence and starts to head west when he is befriended by a little old lady on her way to the bank to pay off her $1,000 mortgage in cash. Thinking Red a reverend, she asks him to hold her pocketbook for a moment—a mistake both she and he soon regret.

1096. "The Midas Touch" (1/5/77; rebroadcast from 10/4/76)

1097. "The Man from Ultra" (1/6/77; rebroadcast 4/30/77)

Cast: Court Benson (Solon Aquila); Robert Burr (Jeffrey Hale); Mandel Kramer (James Graham); Roberta Maxwell (Judith Field). Written by Alfred Bester.

Solon Aquila regrets that his unguarded glance sent talented artist Jeffrey Hall to the insane asylum, where doctors say he has withdrawn into childhood. Solon realizes that he can undo the spell if he helps Jeff live out all his childhood dreams. Not knowing that Jeff's fantasies will cast him as a scientist working on a dangerous experiment, a courageous private detective, a circus giant and a hunter on an African safari, Solon sends Jeff into a world of nightmares, not dreams.

Notes: Robert Burr is no stranger to other worlds and nightmares, having appeared in such films as *The Possession of Joel Delaney* (1972) and *Netherworld* (1990).

1098. "Conquest of Fear" (1/7/77; rebroadcast 5/1/77)

Cast: Tammy Grimes (Elizabeth Welch); Sam Gray (Juan Materos); Ian Martin (El Gitano); Rosemary Rice (Mercedes). Written by Ian Martin.

Elizabeth Welch, being chauffeured through the Pyrenees Mountains in order to be on time for her wedding in Madrid, is taken prisoner by bandits who demand a ransom of $100,000. Elizabeth recognizes the bandit leader as one of Spain's great bullfighters who, she says to his face, must have become a bandit because of his fear of the bulls. An accusation like this, she knows, could mean a bullet in her pretty head.

1099. "Private Stock" (1/8/77; rebroadcast from 10/5/76)

1100. "Pool of Fear" (1/9/77; rebroadcast from 10/7/76)

1101. "Two Renegades" (1/10/77; rebroadcast 8/1/77, 10/7/79)

Cast: Bob Dryden (O. Henry); Ralph Bell (Bernard O'Keefe); Leon Janney (Doc Milliken); Bryna Raeburn (Rosalia); Ian Martin (El Tigre). Adapted by Sam Dann, based on the 1904 short story by O. Henry.

Bernard O'Keefe, one of the most expert United States confidence men, is himself conned into leading an army of peasants against Panama's tyrannical General Pomposo. But they turn out to be an army of deserters, and when the charge begins, O'Keefe finds himself alone. He is taken prisoner and given three weeks to live. Only Dr. Milliken can save him, but he is an unreconstructed rebel and O'Keefe must take the oath of the Confederacy before the doctor will lift a finger on his behalf.

Notes: In recognition of *Theater*'s fourth year on the air, Himan Brown decided to broadcast seven consecutive episodes, all adaptations of short stories by O. Henry, and all adapted by Sam Dann. Bob Dryden starred as O Henry in all seven of the broadcasts.

1102. "The Passing of Black Eagle" (1/11/77; rebroadcast 8/2/77, 9/29/79)

Cast: Bob Dryden (O. Henry); Larry Haines (Chicken); Earl Hammond (Barkeeper); Evelyn Juster (Faith-Hope Alabaster). Adapted by Sam Dann, based on the 1901 short story by O. Henry.

New York City's foremost panhandler—whom everyone calls Chicken, because he looks like one—is a meek fellow when drunk, but when sober has delusions of grandeur. Forced to sober up while wintering in the sunny southwest, Chicken is mistaken by people in Texas for legendary outlaw Black Eagle and is feared by everyone—until the leader of a band of outlaws decides to challenge him.

1103. "Tobin's Palm" (1/12/77; rebroadcast 8/3/77, 8/5/79)

Cast: Bob Dryden (O. Henry); Fred Gwynne (Malone); Gilbert Mack (Cop); Jack Grimes (Daniel Tobin); Marian Seldes (Madame Zozo). Adapted by Sam Dann, based on the 1906 short story by O. Henry.

Daniel Tobin, saddened because he can't locate his forgetful bride, Katie Mahorner, just arrived from Ireland, visits, at the suggestion of his friend Malone, one Madame Zozo. She reads his palm and tells an unbelieving Tobin that an ocean voyage, a fire, a fat man, a blond woman, a man with a silver ornament, white horses, steel, steam, stone, a red-haired woman, a bald-headed man and a fellow with a crooked nose would, in sequence, lead him to his beloved Katie.

1104. "Don't Die Without Me" (1/13/77; rebroadcast 8/4/77, 8/25/79)

Cast: Bob Dryden (O. Henry); Marian Seldes (Eloise); Russell Horton (Sgt. O'Donoghue); Joan Shay (Mrs. Purdy). Adapted by Sam Dann, based on the 1906 short story *The Furnished Room* by O. Henry.

O. Henry, always the curious writer-reporter, witnesses police taking out the bodies of a golden-haired young woman and a dark-haired young man who rented, at different times, the same room in a run-down New York City boarding house. Intrigued, he tries to find out the reasons for their deaths, apparent suicides. While doing so, he spends a night alone in the room where they both had lived—and died.

1105. "A Departmental Case" (1/14/77; rebroadcast 8/5/77, 10/21/79)

Cast: Bob Dryden (O. Henry); Joseph Silver (Luke Standifer); Earl Hammond (Benton Sharp); Carol Teitel (Coralee Sharp). Adapted by Sam Dann, based on the 1902 short story by O. Henry.

O. Henry, living in New York, travels to Austin, Texas, to get the full story of why Luke Standifer, 65, now working as Texas's commissioner of insurance, statistics and history, challenged and shot to death a notorious desperado, Benton Sharp. Standifer claims he did it because Sharp had been mistreating his wife, the daughter of a Texas hero. But O. Henry soon discovers the story is much more complicated than that.

1106. "Cherchez la Femme" (1/15/77; rebroadcast 8/6/77, 4/14/79)

Cast: Bob Dryden (O. Henry); Ian Martin (Gaspard Morin); Bill Griffis (Gumbo Charley); Bryna Raeburn (Madame Tibault). Adapted by Sam Dann, based on the 1903 short story by O. Henry.

Madame Ottilie Tibault, owner of a prosperous little cafe in the French quarter of New Orleans, gives the $25,000 she has been keeping under her mattress to Gaspard Morin, one of her customers, for "investment." But, before he can tell her what he has invested in, Morin dies. O. Henry agrees to help Madame Tibault find out what happened to the money. His most promising clue is the name of a woman Morin uttered just before he died: "Miss Liberty."

1107. "Jimmy Valentine's Gamble" (1/16/77; rebroadcast 8/7/77, 9/22/79)

Cast: Bob Dryden (O. Henry); Paul Hecht (Jimmy Valentine); Catherine Byers (Annabelle Adams); Court Benson (Mike); Kenneth Harvey (Ben Price). Adapted by Sam Dann, based on the 1902 short story *A Retrieved Reformation* by O. Henry.

Jimmy Valentine, whom O. Henry met while both were serving time in an Ohio penitentiary, is released and returns immediately to his chosen profession: safecracking. Pursued by the feds, he lands in the small town of Elmore, Arkansas, and prepares to rob its only bank. But when he meets the bank president's daughter, Annabelle, Jimmy decides to go straight. He opens a shoe store and becomes engaged to Annabelle, hoping, mistakenly, the feds will never find him.

Notes: This episode was originally titled "Jimmy Valentine's Guilt," but the script title was changed just a couple of hours before the actual episode was recorded.

1108. "Son of Satan" (1/17/77; rebroadcast 5/4/77)

Cast: Gordon Gould (Tony Marsh); Ralph Bell (Cato Van Camp); Joan Banks (Ravena Marsh). Written by Elspeth Eric.

Tony and Ravena Marsh revive their old-time friendship with Sam (now Cato) Van Camp, with whom they once shared a beach house. They are startled by the change that has come over Cato, now a member of an exclusive sect, the Sons of Satan, dedicated to the gratification of the ego. They are even more startled at Cato's current project: the creation of an monumculus, a tiny artificial man who he hopes will someday rule the world.

1109. "The Tortured Twins" (1/18/77; rebroadcast from 10/8/76)

1110. "The Woman in Red" (1/19/77; rebroadcast 5/7/77)

Cast: Robert L. Green (Ledyard Larue); Bob Dryden (Lieutenant Birdwell); Earl Hammond (Krueger); Evelyn Juster (Detective Rodriguez); Bryna Raeburn (Angela). Written by Sam Dann.

"The Woman in Red," a valuable portrait on loan from Holland, is stolen from a museum by an expert thief who is identified in a documentary film, shot just before the theft occurred. But when the police track him down, the thief is dead. Two others suspected of being involved in the robbery are also killed before the police can question them. That, however, doesn't faze a woman detective, Maria Rodriguez, who majored in art while in college.

Notes: The original title of this episode, "The Lady in Red," was changed to "The Woman in Red," the same name as the painting described in the episode.

1111. "My Wife Doesn't Understand Me" (1/20/77; rebroadcast from 10/11/76)

1112. "Happy Death Day" (1/21/77; rebroadcast 5/8/77)

Cast: Marian Seldes (Marge Verner); Mandel Kramer (Paul Verner); Carol Teitel (Valerie); Kenneth Harvey (Dr. Stowe). Written by Ian Martin.

Paul Verner, married to an overweight but wealthy Marge, is secretly courting her half sister, Valerie. Scheming to do away with Marge, Paul concocts an elaborate plot involving hypnosis, under the influence of which Marge begins to believe that she will commit suicide on her next birthday. Convinced she is going mad, Marge visits a psychiatrist who, after several interviews, is able to get an inkling of what Paul and Valerie are up to.

1113. "The God Killer" (1/22/77; rebroadcast from 10/12/76)

1114. "The Living Corpse" (1/23/77; rebroadcast from 10/14/76)

1115. "License to Kill" (1/24/77; rebroadcast 5/18/77)

Cast: Tony Roberts (Chappie Chapman); Fred Gwynne (Coach Bradshaw); Marian Seldes (Louisa); Robert Maxwell (Brunner). Written by Sam Dann.

Billy (Chappie) Chapman, a six-foot, 260-pound defensive end, is cut from the football squad because he lacks the "killer" instinct. But when his wife is seriously injured in an auto accident and the medical bills start piling up, Chappie asks the coach for another chance. Only, the coach says, if he renames himself "The Chopper" and goes on the field ready to "chop down" and "kill" the quarterback. Unfortunately, Chappie takes his coach—and screaming fans—literally.

1116. "A Point in Time" (1/25/77; rebroadcast from 10/15/76)

1117. "The White Wolf" (1/26/77; rebroadcast 5/21/77)

Cast: Kristoffer Tabori (Herman Krantz); Norman Rose (Wilhem Krantz); Jada Rowland (Marcella Krantz); Ann Shepherd (Christina); Paul Tripp (Doctor Baum). Written by Ian Martin.

Wilhem Krantz, who in anger killed his unfaithful wife, now lives in isolation with his three children deep in Germany's Hartz Mountains. Out one day trying to shoot a white wolf that has been bothering them, Wilhem is surprised by a beautiful woman, dressed in a flowing white cape, emerging from the woods. He takes her in, then marries her, but his children are frightened especially when they see their new stepmother wolfing down food in a wolf-like manner.

1118. "Killer's Appointment" (1/27/77; rebroadcast from 10/18/76)

1119. "My Fair Lady-Killer" (1/28/77; rebroadcast 5/22/77)

Cast: Michael Tolan (Lt. Frank Lister); Ian Martin (Captain Tate); Bryna Raeburn (Juanita Rawlingson); William Griffis (Terence Falmouth). Written by Sam Dann.

During their investigation of the murders, all of which took place in the same neighborhood, police are told by their psychiatrist to look for a shy, middle-aged, repressed unmarried man who lives alone or with his mother and has been singularly unsuccessful with women. But their prime suspect is just the opposite—a young, married, flamboyant landscape gardener who, in the eyes of many women, is as handsome as a Greek god.

1120. "The Mission of Atropos" (1/29/77; rebroadcast from 10/19/76)

1121. "To Hang by the Neck" (1/30/77; rebroadcast from 10/21/76)

1122. "Casual Affair" (1/31/77; rebroadcast 5/25/77)

Cast: Mason Adams (Richard Pomeroy); Evelyn Juster (Cressida Harlow); Bob Dryden (Mr. Darling). Written by Sam Dann.

Richard Pomeroy, an engineer who troubleshoots for his motor manufacturing company, meets beautiful Cressida Harlow while spending an evening in a bar, away from home. Though happily married for fifteen years, Pomeroy falls madly in love with Cressida, a traveling researcher, and rearranges his schedules so he can secretly meet her in various cities throughout the country. He is deliriously happy—until he learns that Cressida is a front for a ring of smugglers who threaten blackmail unless he joins them.

1123. "Somebody Stop Me!" (2/1/77; rebroadcast from 10/22/76)

1124. "The Cat Is Dead" (2/2/77; rebroadcast 5/28/77)

Cast: Marian Seldes (Nicole Maynard); Ian Martin (Josh Maynard); Court Benson (Jean Barrere). Written by Ian Martin.

His code name in the underground was Jean Barrere. After World War II, in the Normandy town of Moncarnet, Barrere chose burglary as a profession. Because of his techniques, he was nicknamed "Le Cat" by the gendarmes. While being chased after one of his heists, Barrere is hidden by another former underground member, Nicole Maynard, now engaged to an American flyer they had saved. Her fiancé doesn't understand why Nicole would protect a thief—but Nicole does.

1125. "The Deathly White Man" (2/3/77; rebroadcast from 10/27/76)

1126. "The Ripple Effect" (2/4/77; rebroadcast 6/5/77)

Cast: Les Tremayne (Emerson Maitland); Bob Dryden (Lt. Quince); Bryna Raeburn (Lena); Earl Hammond (Honest John); Martha Greenhouse (Lolly). Written by Sam Dann.

Emerson Maitland, who wants his district's nomination for the House of Representatives, assures his party's chairman that there are no scandals in his past. But Maitland is lying. A married man, he once had an affair with a younger woman to whom he wrote many passionate love letters. He hires a common thief to retrieve the letters, a move that sets in motion a rapid succession of events that results in three murders Maitland had no intention of committing.

Notes: Les Tremayne's radio career spanned many years as star and supporting performer on numerous radio programs. Most notably he was featured performer on *Grand Hotel* during the 1936-37 season and host of *The Radio Reader's Digest* from 1947-48. He also served six years on *The First Nighter Program* opposite Barbara Luddy, and played the male lead in *Brownstone Theatre* for half a season.

Les Tremayne is no stranger to science-fiction and horror, having appeared in such films as *The War of the Worlds* (1953), *The Slime People* (1963), *The Monster of Piedras Blancas* (1957), *Creature of Destruction* (1967), *The Angry Red Planet* (1959), and *The Monolith Monsters* (1957).

1127. "Absolute Zero" (2/5/77; rebroadcast from 10/28/76)

1128. "The Unborn" (2/6/77; rebroadcast from 10/29/76)

1129. "I Pronounce You Dead" (2/7/77; rebroadcast 5/29/77)

Cast: Morgan Fairchild (Helen); Russell Horton (Billy); Mary Jane Higby (Mother); Robert Kaliban (Brother). Written by Elspeth Eric.

Helen Todd, a plain high school senior, doesn't really like her parents, her brother, or her boyfriend Billy. But she doesn't say anything until she meets Caesar Smith, who convinces Helen she is a goddess with the ability to cast spells on people who annoy her. When Billy breaks a date with her, Helen tests her powers by wishing him dead, but soon she becomes afraid that he and her parents and brother may really succumb to her evil wishes.

1130. "The Aurora Group" (2/8/77; rebroadcast 6/4/77)

Cast: Larry Haines (Zachery Eberhardt); Ann Williams (Emma Eberhardt); Bryna Raeburn (Stella); Joe Di Santis (Ethan Allen Plotz); Leon Janney (Mr. Stebbins). Written by Sam Dann.

Zachery Taylor Eberhardt cannot understand why the pocket of his new suit contains a 25-cent piece minted in 1986. But soon things begin to happen that give him an idea why. He loses his job when the Aurora group takes over his company; his nagging wife gets a job and lords it over him; he falls in love with a waitress; and, most significant of all, he dreams that he is an unfaithful husband in court in 1986, accused of having stabbed his wife to death.

Notes: Actress Anne Williams was recently murdered on *Search for Tomorrow*, a television day-time soap opera, after ten years as Eunice Martin. In this episode, her first for *Theater*, she was murdered, too, coincidentally by a character played by Larry Haines, who as Stu Bergman was her dearest friend on *Search for Tomorrow*.

1131. "City of the Dead" (2/9/77; rebroadcast from 11/4/76)

1132. "The Recluse" (2/10/77; rebroadcast 6/1/77)

Cast: Tony Roberts (Dr. Tom Lodge); Patricia Elliott (Nancy Lodge); Frances Sternhagen (Lil Meggs); Court Benson (Rufus Boggs). Written by Roy Winsor.

Dr. Tom Lodge, while settling the estate of his recently deceased grandmother, tells his wife, Nancy, a family secret he has kept for six years—that his father had stolen $75,000 from the bank in which he worked and disappeared. While inspecting his grandfather's large home, Tom discovers his father's skeleton, the head of which had been bashed in. Patricia sees it as a clear case of murder and points out that if Tom can solve it, he might be able to clear his father's name.

1133. "Masquerade" (2/11/77; rebroadcast 6/8/77)

Cast: Marian Seldes (Lucia Perrugini); Paul Hecht (Cabot Godwin); Ian Martin (Conte Degli Cappeto); Earl Hammond (Policeman). Written by Ian Martin.

Shortly after opera singer Lucia Perrugini performs at the Conte Degli Capetto's masked ball, the countess's valuable necklace is stolen. All clues lead to Lucia's date, Cabot Godwin, but Lucia knows he didn't do it because she bumped into the thief as she left the stage and he kissed her. To convince the police of Cabot's innocence, she is forced to find the real thief.

1134. "Witches' Sabbath" (2/12/77; rebroadcast from 10/30/76)

1135. "The Queen of Cats" (2/13/77; rebroadcast from 10/31/76)

1136. "Stamped for Death" (2/14/77; rebroadcast 6/11/77)

Cast: Russell Horton (Jeremy Taylor); Lloyd Battista (Gordon Taylor); Bob Dryden (Uncle Morgan); Ann Pitoniak (Aunt Martha). Written by Elizabeth Pennell.

Gordon and Jeremy Taylor, expecting a large cash inheritance from their father, get only his valuable stamp collection. While taking the collection to be appraised, their plane crashes. They survive, but the stamps are burned to a crisp. All that's left is what they think is one very valuable stamp willed to their uncle. Gordon and Jeremy devise various devious ways of acquiring the stamp, not knowing the real reason why their father left it to his brother.

1137. "The Star Killers" (2/15/77; rebroadcast 6/12/77)

Cast: Mercedes McCambridge (Dr. Marrisset); Court Benson (Dr. Abelard); Judith Light (Dora Shelton); Norman Rose (Eric Marshall). Written by Sam Dann.

Dr. Mary Jane Marrisset, a Nobel Prize–winning physicist, helps a stranger fix his stalled automobile. When he learns who she is, Eric Marshall proposes marriage, and she accepts. Later, he admits he's an advance man from the planet Arshanah, looking for a place for his four billion people to move. He has betrayed them, though, by marrying an earthling. When he is murdered by another Arshanahan, Mary Jane becomes the chief suspect.

Notes: Mercedes McCambridge made numerous radio appearances on *Everything for the Boys, Suspense, The Mercury Theatre of the Air, Screen Director's Playhouse, I Love a Mystery, Inner Sanctum Mysteries, Lights Out!, This Is Nora Drake, Murder at Midnight,* and *This Is Judy Jones.*

Commenting on McCambridge's work in *Inner Sanctum Mysteries,* Himan Brown said: "Mercedes McCambridge was wonderful. She had to appear in every show because in those days, it paid the rent for a lot of people, and McCambridge was not that rich. One week I didn't call her and she called me and said, 'What happened? I didn't get a call from *Inner Sanctum.*' And I said, 'Well, we don't have any women on this week. It's an all-male cast.' She said, 'What difference does that make? I'm coming and I'm playing an elevator operator!'" Brown didn't recall if she ever played an elevator operator, but he does remember that she showed up and did the program.

1138. "The Secret Chamber" (2/16/77; rebroadcast from 11/5/76)

1139. "If Mischief Follow" (2/17/77; rebroadcast 6/15/77)

Cast: Anne Williams (Dr. Marian Trevor); Gordon Gould (Dr. Brian Douglas); Ralph Bell (Craig Trevor); Bryna Raeburn (Nurse); Bob Readick (Dr. Jerry Wilson). Written by Ian Martin.

Dr. Marian Trevor and Dr. Brian Douglas' wedding plans have to be postponed when Marian's husband, Craig, who has supposedly been dead for five years, returns. Craig not only wants to live with his wife and son, but he wants Marian to diagnose his illness. However, when he needs an emergency operation that only Dr. Douglas can perform, Craig claims they are trying to kill him—and Dr. Douglas suspects that if Craig lives or dies, it can only mean trouble.

1140. "A Heart of Gold" (2/18/77; rebroadcast 6/18/77)

Cast: Frances Sternhagen (Miriam Purcell); Russell Horton (Arthur Purcell); William Griffis (Jason Anderson); Ann Shepherd (Helene Connors). Written by Bob Juhren.

Miriam Purcell, an elderly philanthropist, decides to have her remaining gold melted down and made into commemorative coins, with her image on them. While sitting for her portrait, draped in her gold jewelry, she recalls how she betrayed her friends—even at the expense of one's life—to accumulate her gold. But when the coins are completed, she is shocked to find they reveal all of her past.

1141. "The Graveyard" (2/19/77; rebroadcast from 11/8/76)

1142. "The Colony" (2/20/77; rebroadcast from 11/9/76)

1143. "Orient Express" (2/21/77; rebroadcast 6/19/77)

Cast: Mandel Kramer (Jake Shaw); Marian Seldes (Lili Vardas); Hans Conried

(P.M. Barnes); Earl Hammond (Konrad); Leon Janney (Muller). Written by Ian Martin.

Lili Vardas, en route to Berlin for a singing engagement, and reporter Jake Shaw, who is doing a story on the trail of Jan Stepanek, are reunited on the Orient Express. Lili is willing to do anything to save Jan's life, so when a man who claims to be his brother asks her to smuggle documents into Russia, she agrees. But Jake and Lili soon suspect that Jan may already be dead and that they themselves may not make it home alive.

1144. "Jane Eyre" (2/22/77; rebroadcast 6/22/77, 6/10/79)

Cast: Patricia Elliott (Jane Eyre); Arnold Moss (Mr. Rochester); Ann Pitoniak (Mrs. Fiarfax); Lloyd Battista (Mason). Adapted by Elizabeth Pennell, based on the 1847 novel by Charlotte Bonte.

Jane Eyre, whose own childhood was very unhappy, is a perfect governess to Mr. Rochester's ward, Adele Varens, at Thornfield. Mr. Rochester is so pleased that he himself falls in love with Jane and proposes marriage. But on their wedding day, Jane learns that he is already married—to the mad woman who is confined to Thornfield's tower, the same woman Jane has heard screaming and seen hovering over her bed. Distraught, Jane leaves Thornfield, only to be haunted by the memory until she returns.

1145. "Meeting by Chance" (2/23/77; rebroadcast from 11/22/76)

1146. "Last Judgment" (2/24/77; rebroadcast 6/25/77)

Cast: Norman Rose (Henry Smith); Carmen Mathews (Adele Smith); Michael Wager (Jan Wall); Nat Polen (Leo Smith); Teri Keane (Maria Smith). Written by Roy Winsor.

Henry Smith suffers from recurring nightmares so frightening, that he refuses to discuss them with his immediate family. But his daughter-in-law, a former nurse, is able, by careful questioning, to extract from him the essence of his dreams which seem to take place in a city of canals, where he orders his soldiers to kill the "resisters." Smith is so guilt ridden by the dreams, which he cannot explain, that he is sure he will soon die.

1147. "Legend of Phoenix Hill" (2/25/77; rebroadcast 6/26/77)

Cast: Howard Da Silva (Dr. Samuel Arnold); Robert Kaliban (Lee Arnold); Ian Martin (Dr. Herbert Stern); Evelyn Juster (Jessie Arnold). Written by Ian Martin.

Dr. Samuel Arnold, an archeologist at Wyndham University, tries to discourage his 20-year-old adopted son, Lee, from accompanying him, in the early 1900s, to China's Hunan province to dig for human remains over 2,000 years old. Others in the group believe that the presence of Lee, of Oriental extraction, will bring the expedition bad luck. But Lee prevails, and so does bad luck in the forms of a railroad wreck, an earthquake and a typhoon.

Himan Brown has said of the series: "The enthusiastic response of scores of writers, actors and actresses has helped us achieve this milestone. Not only do they continually let me know of the delight they find in their roles, they keep asking for more."

1148. "The Awakening" (2/26/77; rebroadcast from 11/23/76)

1149. "M-U-R-D-E-R" (2/27/77; rebroadcast from 11/25/76)

1150. "The Light That Failed" (2/28/77; rebroadcast 6/29/77, 8/12/89)

Cast: Tony Roberts (Dick Heldar); Mason Adams (Gilbert Torpenhow); Jackson Beck (Mr. Valdemar); Bryna Raeburn (Bessie). Adapted by Sam Dann, based on the 1891 novel by Rudyard Kipling.

Artist Dick Heldar makes a name for himself covering a war in the Anglo-Egyptian Sudan. During a battle, he is struck on the head by the broad side of a sword. The blow doesn't bother him until some years later when, painting a portrait of a woman who looks like his childhood sweetheart, his eyesight begins to fail. Doctors say he has little time to finish what his friends consider to be his finest work.

Notes: Mason Adams' voice might be familiar to listeners of this episode. Adams narrated the Cadbury Easter Bunny commercials on television, which are still broadcast each year.

1151. "The Hound of the Baskervilles" (3/1/77; rebroadcast 7/2/77, 6/24/79)

Cast: Kevin McCarthy (Sherlock Holmes); Lloyd Battista (Dr. Watson); Court Benson (Dr. Mortimer); Carol Teitel (Beryl Stapleton); Bob Dryden (Sir Henry Baskerville). Adapted by Murray Burnett, based on the 1902 novel by Sir Arthur Conan Doyle.

Sir Charles Baskerville is murdered, and Sherlock Holmes and Dr. Watson move in to solve the crime. The murderer apparently used an old superstition of death on the moor, by applying a gigantic hound to cover his misdeed. But when Selden, an escaped convict, is killed by mistake—the murderer thinking him to be Sir Charles' heir—Holmes and Watson can begin deducting who the guilty person is.

1152. "Strike Force" (3/2/77; rebroadcast from 11/11/76)

1153. "The Overcoat" (3/3/77; rebroadcast 7/3/77, 10/27/79)

Cast: Hans Conried (Akaky Akalievich); Bryna Raeburn (Landlady); Ian Martin (Director); Bob Dryden (Ivan); Leon Janney (Petrovich). Adapted by Ian Martin, based on the 1842 short story by Nikolay Vasilyevich Gogol.

Akaky Akalievich is an underpaid governmental clerk who, the humblest of his kind and the butt of cruel jokes by his fellow workers, manages to subsist on his tiny salary, nursing the single ambition of saving enough for a new overcoat.

After excessive privation, he saves enough to have a tailor make him an expensive new one, only to have it stolen in the middle of winter on the first evening he goes out.

1154. "Answer Me" (3/4/77; rebroadcast 7/6/77)

Cast: Larry Haines (Paul); Danny Ocko (Bartender); Joan Banks (Sylvia); Rosemary Rice (Susan). Written by Elspeth Eric.

Paul, upset by the death of his wife, sets out for Mexico on foot. On the way, an attractive, strong-willed woman, Sylvia, stops and insists that he get into her car. Paul is immediately convinced that she is an extraordinary person, but is not prepared for what he finds when he meets and falls in love with her daughter, Susan, whose every action is controlled telepathically by her mother.

1155. "A Question of Identity" (3/5/77; rebroadcast from 11/12/76)

1156. "Blood Will Tell" (3/6/77; rebroadcast from 11/26/76)

1157. "Beyond the Barrier" (3/7/77; rebroadcast 7/9/77)

Cast: Russell Horton (Dr. Harrow); Evelyn Juster (Cora); William Griffis (Dr. Blanchard); Arnold Moss (Guide). Written by Stella Moss.

Dr. Curry Harrow, a young research scientist, is seriously injured in a car accident. When he arrives at the hospital, he thinks he is still alive, yet he can't communicate by voice or body movement with his surgeons or his friends and is pronounced dead. He is terrified by the series of experiences that he can't explain—a floating sensation and strange communications with his father and his girlfriend, both dead. When he is led down a long dark passageway, he starts thinking that he, too, is now really dead.

1158. "The Sign of Four" (3/8/77; rebroadcast 7/10/77)

Cast: Kevin McCarthy (Sherlock Holmes); Court Benson (Dr. Watson); Jackson Beck (Major Sholto); Earl Hammond (Athelney Jones); Joan Shay (Mary Morstan). Adapted by Murray Burnett, based on the 1890 novel by Sir Arthur Conan Doyle.

Since her father disappeared, Mary Morstan has mysteriously received a valuable pearl on each birthday. Finally she is called by her benefactor, Thaddeus Sholto, who explains her father's death and her inheritance of a chest of jewels. But before Mary can claim her fortune, Thaddeus' brother is murdered and the jewels are stolen. Holmes and Watson disagree with Scotland Yard that Thaddeus did it, and they set out to find the real culprit and the jewels for Mary, whom Watson now wants to marry.

1159. "The Man Who Couldn't Get Arrested" (3/9/77; rebroadcast from 11/29/76)

1160. "The Pleading Voice" (3/10/77; rebroadcast 7/13/77)

Cast: Corrine Orr (Claire Bancroft); William Griffis (Dr. Simpson); Bryna Raeburn (Emma); Bob Dryden (Father Larkin); Gordon Gould (Clem Bancroft). Written by Roy Winsor.

Claire Bancroft, alone with the caretakers of her family's mansion in the sparsely settled Maine woods, becomes bedridden with a fever her doctor cannot diagnose. She insists her illness is caused by the fear that overtakes her when she hears a child's voice coming from the doorframe of a ruined gatehouse. Her sanity is questioned until one of the caretakers hears the same sound and vows never to walk past the gatehouse again after the sun goes down.

1161. "Till Death Do Us Part" (3/11/77; rebroadcast 7/16/77)

Cast: Tammy Grimes (Miriam Mallory); Ian Martin (Irwin Pomeroy); Evelyn Juster (Valerie). Written by Sam Dann.

Given a summons for speeding by a motorcycle cop, an angry Miriam Mallory, homely and still single at 45, resigns when her boss, Irwin Pomeroy, raises his voice at her. He, however, pleads with her to reconsider, saying that though married, he has been secretly in love with her for 15 years. She is so happy over finally being loved that she even volunteers to shoot Pomeroy's wife—until she's caught for speeding again by the same cop.

1162. "Now You See Them, Now You Don't" (3/12/77; rebroadcast from 11/30/76)

1163. "How to Kill Rudy" (3/13/77; rebroadcast from 12/2/76)

1164. "Look Backward Sometimes" (3/14/77; rebroadcast 7/17/77)

Cast: Roberta Maxwell (Susan Talbot); Russell Horton (Tony Marquis); Earl Hammond (Juan Miron); Martha Greenhouse (Mrs. Roder); Kristoffer Tabori (Pepe Silvera). Written by Ian Martin.

The plane that is taking Susan Talbot to compete in a Rome tennis tournament is caught in a sudden downdraft and crashes into the Swiss Alps. Of the five who are still alive, Susan and Juan Miron, an official of a despotic government, are uninjured. Juan who is carrying a gun, orders Susan to leave the others and help him climb down the mountains to safety.

1165. "The Shining Man" (3/15/77; rebroadcast 7/20/77)

Cast: Robert Kaliban (Don Campbell); Morgan Fairchild (Gigi Campbell); Ralph Bell (Dr. Low); Ian Martin (Thomas Niven). Adapted by Ian Martin, based on a short story by E. and H. Heron.

Don Campbell, just awarded the job of headmaster in a Scottish school, and his wife, Gigi, prepare to move into the Old Connor House which they have been told is haunted by "the shining man," but which had a price tag within their reach. The former owner and his daughter had both died in the house from mysterious causes. Nevertheless, the Campbells are undaunted, until the man sent to clean the house for them is also found dead—cause unknown.

Notes: Morgan Fairchild later appeared in such films as *Invitation of Sarah* (1978), *The Concrete Cowboys* (1979), *Deadly Illusion* (1987), *Haunting of Sarah Hardy* (1989), *Test Tube Teens from the Year Zero* (1993), and *Body Chemistry 3: Point of Seduction* (1993).

1166. "Child of Misfortune" (3/16/77; rebroadcast from 12/3/76)

1167. "Jobo" (3/17/77; rebroadcast 7/23/77)

Cast: Earl Hammond (Jobo); Russell Horton (David Leyton); William Griffis (Professor Tilletson); Evelyn Juster (Alma Tilletson). Written by Henry Slesar.

After reading a newspaper article about Jobo Haley, a Tennessee hillbilly who looks like one of the very tall, very slender stone statues found only on Easter Island, archeologist John Tilletson organizes an expedition to the Pacific paradise, while his daughter Alma heads for Tennessee. Both discover identical objects: shiny silver medallions previously unknown to archeologists. Only Jobo and an Easter Island common thief are able to explain the historical significance and the astonishing relationship of the two strange objects.

1168. "Little Green Death" (3/18/77; rebroadcast 7/24/77)

Cast: Kim Hunter (Adelaide Gordon); Nat Polen (Elmer Baker); Carol Teitel (Lucy Baker); Bob Dryden (Phil Hastings). Written by Sam Dann.

Phil Hastings, the best friend of bookstore owner Elmer Baker, hires Adelaide Gordon to defend Elmer, charged with the murder of Robert Curtland. Elmer had borrowed a large sum of money from Curtland to keep his shop solvent, and Curtland had refused to give him an extension on the loan. Gordon faces a rough trial because Elmer was on his yearly drinking spree and cannot remember whether or not he fired the gun that killed Curtland.

1169. "Child of the Sea" (3/19/77; rebroadcast from 12/6/76)

1170. "Enough Rope" (3/20/77; rebroadcast from 12/7/76)

1171. "The Eighth Deadly Sin" (3/21/77; rebroadcast 7/27/77)

Cast: Patricia Elliott (Diane Summers); Ian Martin (Francesco); Larry Haines (Gary Winters). Written by Ian Martin.

Gary Winter, a writer, meets and falls in love with actress Diane Summers, but their romance is constantly interrupted by the travel involved in their careers. While in Italy interviewing a jailed gambler, Gary finds that the gambler is also in love with Diane, who has assured him his eventual freedom. Thinking that there is more to their relationship than either Diane or the gambler will admit, Gary, irrational with jealousy, considers murder or suicide to be the only answer.

1172. "The Imposter" (3/22/77; rebroadcast 7/30/77)

Cast: Don Scardino (Ted); Norman Rose (Norman); Bryna Raeburn (Dortha); Ann Pitoniak (Kay).Written by Elspeth Eric.

After a first reading of the script, Ted Harris and Norman Gelb decide to produce a play written by an unknown playwright, Kay Mehaffey. Certain it is going to be a blockbuster, the producers hire a top-name cast and director. But on opening night, Kay wants to cancel the whole thing because she fears that the real author—an actor who has been dead for 50 years but has been communicating spiritually with her—is trying to kill her.

1173. "Nobody Dies" (3/23/77; rebroadcast from 12/9/76)

1174. "The Gift of Doom" (3/24/77; rebroadcast 7/31/77, 12/15/79)

Cast: Kim Hunter (Medeekah); Mason Adams (Jason Cobb); Russell Horton (Phineas Cobb); Arnold Moss (Cannibal Joe); Bryna Raeburn (Watonah). Adapted by Arnold Moss, based on the Euripedes' classic Greek tragedy.

Jason Cobb leaves his farm in the northwest United States to seek his fortune in the Klondike. He returns home a wealthy man, married to Meedekah (Medea), whose powers of sorcery not only saved his eyesight but led him to a fortune in gold. When Jason is offered an opportunity to run for Congress, his benefactor insists he send Meedekah back to the Klondike and marry again. This is when Jason learns of feminine human nature, the powerful will of a woman scorned.

1175. "A Study in Scarlet" (3/25/77; rebroadcast 8/9/77)

Cast: Kevin McCarthy (Sherlock Holmes); Court Benson (Dr. Watson); Mary Jane Higby (Miss Charpentier); Earl Hammond (John Rance); Ian Martin (Inspector Lestrade). Adapted by Murray Burnett, based on the 1887 novel by Sir Arthur Conan Doyle.

Watson, recently returned wounded from war service, meets Sherlock Holmes, and the two bachelors agree to share rooms at No. 221 B. Baker Street. Their first case is the mystery at Lauriston Garden where two men are murdered. These crimes of revenge confound Inspector Lestrade of Scotland Yard, who makes all the wrong assumptions while Watson watches in amazement as his new friend methodically and with apparent ease tracks down the guilty.

Notes: Two Sherlock Holmes novels were already adapted for *Theater*, both previously starring Kevin McCarthy in the lead role of Holmes, and Lloyd Battista played Watson for the first broadcast, Court Benson taking over thereafter. This was the third of the Sherlock Holmes episodes and was the first novel written by Doyle that featured the origin of the two sleuths.

1176. "Identity Crisis" (3/26/77; rebroadcast from 12/10/76)

1177. "Hit Me Again" (3/27/77; rebroadcast from 12/13/76)

1178. "The Warriors from Loanda" (3/28/77; rebroadcast 8/11/77, 9/8/79)

Cast: Bob Dryden (Kayerts); William Griffis (Carlier); Joen Arliss (Wife); Joseph Silver (Makola). Written by Roy Winsor.

Kayerts and Carlier are assigned by the Great Trading Company to an isolated post in the African jungle to collect ivory tusks. They are assisted by the natives, led by Makola. When they are initially unsuccessful, Makola arranges to sell the other natives who work at the post to hostile warriors from Loanda—payment to be made in ivory. Later, their assignment complete, but without employees to care for them, Kayerts and Carlier become feverish and quarrelsome, threatening to kill each other, and Makola does nothing to stop them.

Notes: Actress Joen Arliss is the daughter of actor George Arliss, who appeared in such films as *The Man Who Played God* (both 1922 and 1932 versions), *Alexander Hamilton* (1931), *Transatlantic Tunnel* (1935), and *Dr. Syn* (1937). Joen's mother, Florence Arliss, appeared in numerous films as well. Her brother, Leslie Arliss, went from screenwriter to director, directing such films as *The Night Has Eyes* (1942), *A Man About the House* (1947), and *Miss Tulip Stays the Night* (1955).

1179. "The Coldest Killer" (3/29/77; rebroadcast 8/13/77)

Cast: Bob Readick (Edward Coffin); Joan Shay (Mrs. Nafferton); Lloyd Battista (Joseph Nafferton); Gilbert Mack (Dr. Spurlock); Joan Banks (Melisande Nafferton). Written by Sam Dann.

Edward Coffin and Joseph Nafferton are successful business partners and good friends. Ed, still a bachelor, has for years been having a secret affair with Joe's wife, Melisande. When Joe's mother informs the two that she knows of their relationship and orders Ed to leave the country—or else—Ed and Melisande work out a "clean" way of killing her. They succeed—but now they must get rid of Joe, too.

1180. "The Smoking Pistol" (3/30/77; rebroadcast from 12/14/76)

1181. "Death Is Blue" (3/31/77; rebroadcast 8/14/77)

Cast: Frances Sternhagen (Julia Hoffman); Ralph Bell (Edward Mascomb); Ian Martin (Paul Darrieux); Bryna Raeburn (Baby); Marian Seldes (Matilda Darrieux). Written by Sam Dann.

Julia Hoffman, private eye, is unable to stop the marriage of Matilda Bascomb, whose face is blemished by a large blue birthmark, to playboy Paul Darrieux, who admits he likes her money. Matilda's brother Edward, who has squandered his half of the family fortune on fast women and slow horses, also likes his sister's money. With her dead, he would get it. But now that she is married, her husband would get it—unless he dies first.

1182. "You Bet Your Life" (4/1/77; rebroadcast 8/16/77)

Cast: Paul Hecht (Doug); Ray Owens (Mr. Fawcett); Evelyn Juster (Phyllis); Morgan Fairchild (Liz); Earl Hammond (Stretch Collins). Written by Ian Martin.

When Doug Hart loses his job, just as his wife Liz is about to have their first child, he heads to the racetrack with their savings. For four weeks he is able to "make a living" by betting on the favorites, but his luck soon changes. As Liz is rushed to the maternity ward, Doug makes a big bet he can't cover—he knows he *has* to win because he has bet his life.

1183. "The Doctor's Evidence" (4/2/77; rebroadcast from 12/16/76)

1184. "A Quiet Evening at Home" (4/3/77; rebroadcast from 12/17/76)

1185. "So Shall Ye Reap" (4/4/77; rebroadcast 8/18/77, 12/2/79)

Cast: Russell Horton (Don Edipo); Teri Keane (Iocasta); Ann Pitoniak (Cora); John Beal (Christiano); Arnold Moss (Tiresio). Adapted by Arnold Moss, based on the 427 B.C. Greek tragedy *Oedipus the King* by Sophocles.

The year is 1851, and Don Edipo is serving as mayor of the town of Thebes, New Mexico, which is suffering from a dread pestilence. Edipo has summoned his deputy, Don Christiano, for advice. Christiano calls on a blind old Indian, Tiresio, a prophet who says that the murderer of Don Luis, a former mayor of Thebes, is in their midst and must be driven from Thebes before the pestilence will pass. Then he reveals that Edipo was the unwitting slayer of his father, who was Luis, and that he is the incestuous husband of his own mother. The suddenness of these revelations makes them incredible to all.

1186. "The Sensitive" (4/5/77; rebroadcast from 3/20/77)

Cast: Gordon Gould (Philo Dency); Teri Keane (Sally Dency); Nat Polen (Dr. Frank Hayes); Ralph Bell (Karl Maynard); Marian Hailey (Joan Maynard). Written by Elspeth Eric.

At his wife Sally's insistence, Philo Dency agrees to attend a seance at the home of his boss. It's a trying session, especially for Philo, who manages to entice from his grave a French soldier who says he was killed fighting the Russians at Borodino. Hailed by his wife and boss as "a true sensitive," Philo becomes frightened when his doctor discovers he lost ten pounds during the séance and that his blood pressure has gone up alarmingly.

1187. "Date of Death" (4/6/77; rebroadcast from 12/20/76)

1188. "The High Priest" (4/7/77; rebroadcast 8/21/97)

Cast: Bob Dryden (Bennet Markowitz); William Griffis (Curly Peterson); Ian Martin (Martin Hollinbeck); Bryna Raeburn (Maggie O'Neill). Written by Sam Dann.

Martin Hollinbeck, who has just bribed his way out of prison, relieves a Mideast art counterfeiter of his latest work, a "perfect" Rembrandt. All Hollinbeck needs to rake in millions for the painting is to get art critic Bennet Markowitz's word that it is authentic. Instead, Markowitz declares it a fake, a statement that Hollinbeck and fellow hood Curly Peterson determine to force Markowitz to change, even if it requires a touch of murder.

1189. "Blood, Thunder and a Woman in Green" (4/8/77; rebroadcast 8/23/77)

Cast: Mandel Kramer (Abner Colbridge); Jackson Beck (Mr. Shakespeare); William Griffis (Dickie); Bob Dryden (Carl); Patricia Elliott (Miriam Taylor). Written by Fletcher Markle.

Abner Colbridge, a glib private detective, gets a phone call for help from his photographer friend who calls himself Bo Peep. Bo claims to have taken a photograph of a street murder and wants Abner to act as his bodyguard while he develops it. By the time Abner gets to Bo's apartment, however, his friend is dead. Abner starts a frantic search for the film, but is interrupted and put out of commission by a well-placed blow from a blackjack.

Notes: Fletcher Markle's radio credits stretched many years on such programs as *The Ford Theatre* and *Studio One*, both of which he produced and directed. He also occasionally adapted novels and plays for programs such as *The Red Badge of Courage, Ah, Wilderness, Dodsworth,* and *A Tree Grows in Brooklyn.*

1190. "The Lone Survivor" (4/9/77; rebroadcast from 12/21/76)

1191. "Double Zero" (4/10/77; rebroadcast from 12/23/76)

1192. "The Meteorite" (4/11/77; rebroadcast 8/25/77)

Cast: John Beal (Al Wilson); Marian Seldes (Carrie Wilson); Joseph Silver (Garret Smith); Evelyn Juster (Kruck); Russell Horton (Professor Dana). Written by Roy Winsor.

While returning home from an evening church service, Al Wilson and his wife, Carrie, see a cone of light in the sky and what they think is a meteorite land behind their barn. When the object, about 12 feet long, opens up, Al calls a scientist friend, Garret Smith. Together, they discover inside a person about the size of a 6-year-old boy with the face of an old man and elongated ears. He calls himself Kruck and says anyone who touches his "capsule" will be destroyed.

1193. "Man-Sized in Marble" (4/12/77; rebroadcast 8/27/77)

Cast: Paul Hecht (Jed Burgess); Roberta Maxwell (Lorna Burgess); Frances Sternhagen (Bunty); Fred Gwynne (Dr. McCondochie). Written by Ian Martin.

Lorna Burgess, whose maiden name was Campbell, takes her husband, Jed, to Scotland where her mother has just died, under circumstances Lorna had predicted. The couple settle near a church where two 1,000-year-old man-sized marble statues of Scottish knights are the main attraction. Villagers startle Jed with stories that the knights come alive once a year and kill anyone who gets in their way—just like one of them killed a woman named Lorna Campbell a thousand years ago.

1194. "The Magus" (4/13/77; rebroadcast from 12/25/76)

1195. "The Phantom House" (4/14/77; rebroadcast 8/28/77)

Cast: Marian Seldes (Mary Ann Stacey); Mason Adams (Bridge); Ian Martin (Judge Thurmond); Ann Pitoniak (Hattie); Patricia Elliott (Betty Lou Stacey). Written by Ian Martin.

While visiting their uncle, Judge Thurmond, Mary Ann and Betty Lou Stacey sight a house under Tully Ridge, but nervously the judge claims there is no house there. Still, Mary Ann, who can't find anyone who will discuss the house and its occupants with her, is drawn to the site, which she soon realizes explains how her "adopted" cousin, Bridge, came to live with the judge. Bridge, too, tries to uncover the true story, until he learns it may lead to Mary Ann's death.

1196. "Borderline Case" (4/15/77; rebroadcast 8/30/77)

Cast: Merry Flershem (Janie); Bryna Raeburn (Mom); Kenneth Harvey (Sheriff); Russell Horton (Tom Barlow); Ray Owens (Perkins). Written by Sam Dann.

When the flamboyant Mrs. Tottenham arrives at a quiet upstate New York hotel, the desk clerk, Janie, daughter of the local sheriff, is entranced by the grey pearl—the Star of Dehli—she wears. Janie is frightened by her own desire to possess the jewel, which for 100 years has meant death to its owner. But when Mrs. Tottenham turns up dead and minus the jewel, Janie tries to help her father solve the case before the new owner is killed, too.

1197. "The Mark of Cain" (4/16/77; rebroadcast from 12/27/76)

1198. "The Artist" (4/17/77; rebroadcast from 12/28/76)

1199. "A House Divided" (4/18/77; rebroadcast 9/1/77, 12/23/79)

Cast: Larry Haines ("Big" Jim Allen); Joan Banks (Claire Mennen); Rosemary Rice (Ellie Mennen); Russell Horton (Augie Mennen); Earl Hammond (Corey). Adapted by Arnold Moss, based on the 415 B.C. Greek drama *Electra* by Sophocles.

The time is World War I, and "Big" Jim Allen, one of Chicago's most powerful gangsters, plots with District Attorney Augie Mennen's wife, Claire, to mow him down. Mennen's son Aaron and daughter Ellis determine to take the law into their own hands and avenge their father's death. But they must wait until Aaron's return from military service. The facial disfigurement he suffered from a bomb blast in France is most helpful. "Big" Jim does not recognize him nor does his mother.

1200. "The Book of Abaca" (4/19/77; rebroadcast 9/3/77)

Cast: Allen Swift (Lieutenant Foster); Bryna Raeburn (Mrs. Miller); Bob Dryden (Tarrier); Court Benson (Officer Leoni). Written by Sam Dann.

The captain of the *Abaca* dies of a heart attack when the ship splits apart and dumps 3 million gallons of oil off the New Jersey coast. Before he dies, the captain gives the *Abaca's* chief engineer the ship's log which itemizes the many violations purposely overlooked by the ship's owners. But the engineer is murdered before he can present the book to the authorities. Without it, they have no case, and the owners know they can never be prosecuted unless it is found.

1201. "Your Move, Mr. Ellers" (4/20/77; rebroadcast from 12/30/76)

1202. "Come Away Death" (4/21/77; rebroadcast 9/4/77)

Cast: William Griffis (Simon Brokar); Marian Seldes (Nita Brokar); Norman Rose (Mr. Morris); Ian Martin (Mr. Rensalaer); Joan Shay (Mrs. Marples). Written by Ian Martin.

Simon Brokar, a bachelor millionaire, lies deathly ill in his huge, gloomy mansion. He has no intention of dying, until one night he is visited by a Mr. Morris, who says he is Death and has come to take Brokar away. But Mr. Morris also offers a way out from the inevitable. To avoid dying, Brokar can exchange places with him and enjoy a fling with his beautiful secretary, Bunny Huggins. But Brokar's lawyer is annoyed. He sees his client's entire fortune winding up in Bunny's bank account.

1203. "The Prisoner of Zenda" (4/22/77; rebroadcast 9/6/77, 4/22/79)

Cast: Howard Ross (Rudolf Rassendyll); Evelyn Juster (Flavia); Leon Janney (Colonel Sapt); Lloyd Battista (King Rudolf); Danny Ocko (Rupert Hentzau). Adapted by Robert Newman, based on the 1894 novel by Anthony Hope.

Rudolf Rassendyll arrives in Ruritania on the eve of the coronation of his cousin Rudolf. The king-to-be has an enemy in his brother, Duke Michael, who aspires to the throne. During festivities at Zenda Castle, the Duke drugs King Rudolf, and Rassendyll, who looks like the king, is persuaded to impersonate him and is crowned in his stead. The real king remains a prisoner in Zenda Castle, and many dramatic escapades, duels and intrigues are required to rescue him.

1204. "Tomorrow's Murder" (4/23/77; rebroadcast from 12/31/76)

1205. "Whose Little Girl Are You?" (4/24/77; rebroadcast from 1/3/77)

1206. "Bound East for Haiti" (4/25/77; rebroadcast 9/8/77)

Cast: Mason Adams (Dr. Philip Armstead); Fred Gwynne (Captain Pete Johnson); Ian Martin (Buku); Evelyn Juster (Lily). Written by Roy Winsor.

Dr. Philip Armstead, just out of medical school, boards the tramp steamer *Molly Moran* for a four-week voyage in the Caribbean. After a few days at sea, the ship's captain, Pete Johnson, soon to marry a beautiful native girl, Lily, suddenly becomes ill. Dr. Armstead is unable to help him, but Lily realizes that the first mate, Buku Chinn, an Arawak Indian who also loves her, has cast a spell on the captain. She knows he will die unless she can somehow break the evil spell.

1207. "The Adventure of the Red-Headed League" (4/26/77; rebroadcast 9/10/77, 8/18/79)

Cast: Kevin McCarthy (Sherlock Holmes); Court Benson (Dr. Watson); Bob Dryden (Vincent Spaulding); Ian Martin (Jabez Wilson). Adapted by Murray Burnett, based on the 1891 short story by Sir Arthur Conan Doyle.

Jabez Wilson, a tobacconist, comes to Holmes and Dr. Watson with a story about how he was hired, because he was red-headed, to copy the *Encyclopedia Britannia*, working from 10:00 A.M. until 2:00 P.M., six days a week. There was, however, one condition: He was not to leave his desk during those four hours. Watson thinks the story is preposterous, but Holmes, using his keen sense of deduction, sees a horrible fate for Wilson unless he follows Holmes' instructions to the letter.

1208. "This Breed Is Doomed" (4/27/77; rebroadcast from 1/4/77)

1209. "The Second Chance Lady" (4/28/77; rebroadcast 9/11/77)

Cast: Marian Seldes (Sarah-Ruth Arban); Teri Keane (Milly Smith); William Griffis (Jojo); Mandel Kramer (Ralph). Written by Sam Dann.

Sarah-Jane Arban, selling door-to-door for the Second Chance Cosmetic Co., talks her way into the home of Milly Smith and starts to demonstrate how her company's products can make Milly young and beautiful again. They are interrupted by the arrival of Milly's boyfriend, Jojo, who with two cronies has just robbed a factory of its $750,000 payroll. Jojo suspects Sarah-Ruth is a cop and makes it clear that to insure his and his friend's getaway, she must be eliminated.

1210. "Wuthering Heights" (4/29/77; rebroadcast 9/14/77, 7/15/77)

Cast: Paul Hecht (Heathcliff); Lloyd Battista (Edgar Linton); Bryna Raeburn (Nelly Dean); Russell Horton (Linton); Robert Maxwell (Catherine). Adapted by Elizabeth Pennell, based on the 1847 novel by Emily Bronte.

All the elements of this literary masterpiece are here, beginning with Heathcliff's arrival at Wuthering Heights and the disruption he causes. Catherine soon forms a passionate attachment for the boy, which continues until she dies, even though she marries a neighbor, Edgar Linton. Heathcliff ultimately marries Linton's sister, and the gothic drama moves on to involve the next generation: Heathcliff's sickly son and Catherine's daughter and nephew.

1211. "The Man from Ultra" (4/30/77; rebroadcast from 1/6/77)

1212. "Conquest of Fear" (5/1/77; rebroadcast from 1/7/77)

1213. "Much Too Much" (5/2/77; rebroadcast 9/17/77)

Cast: Bob Dryden (King); Earl Hammond (Minister of Justice); Ian Martin (Prisoner); Court Benson (Captain). Adapted by Gerald Keane, based on a story by Leo Tolstoy.

When a Monegasque kills his wife while trying to do away with her lover, the King sentences him to death. The Ministers, realizing that the small kingdom has never held an execution, then try to rent a guillotine, but the price is too high. So they borrow one, with the prisoner's intercession, from Sweden, but it arrives rusted beyond repair. Meanwhile the prisoner, who is eating every meal as if it were his last, demands gourmet cooking from the kitchen. The King wonders if Monaco can afford the execution or if he should commute the prisoner's sentence to life in prison.

1214. "The Luck Sisters" (5/3/77; rebroadcast 9/18/77)

Cast: Fred Gwynne (Mayor McDowell); Bryna Raeburn (Marie McDowell); Carol Teitel (Janice Hollings); Russell Horton (Reporter). Written by Sam Dann.

All the residents of Bullwer (pop. 100) look forward to becoming millionaires. Gold has been discovered in an abandoned mine that they own together. But Mayor Jeff McDowell and the town's councilmen are worried. In the past, whenever something good was about to happen to the town, it didn't—because, they sincerely believe, of Janice Hollings, a "bad luck" woman. When she can't be persuaded to leave, they vote to take her life by dynamiting the house.

1215. "Son of Satan" (5/4/77; rebroadcast from 1/17/77)

1216. "Reunion Fever" (5/5/77; rebroadcast 9/21/77)

Cast: Phyllis Newman (Dr. Norma Schwartz); Bob Kaliban (Maynard Tarbell); Evelyn Juster (Cressida Tarbell); Joseph Silver (Bunner); Paul Hecht (Lieutenant Rayfield). Written by Sam Dann.

The James Bowie Hotel has the best reputation in town until its grand ballroom is hired for a reunion dinner by a 1960 high school class. Afterward, 64 are hospitalized and 13 die, apparently poisoned by something they ate. Medical authorities are baffled. But then one nonhospitalized member of the class, Maynard Tarbell, receives an anonymous letter demanding $10,000 for the only known antidote. Unless he takes the antidote, the letter warns, Tarbell will die, too.

1217. "Bottom of the World" (5/6/77; rebroadcast 9/24/77)

Cast: Tony Roberts (Bob McDonald); Kristoffer Tabori (J.J. Porter); William Griffis (Mike Gonzalez); Robert Maxwell (Dr. Burns). Written by Arnold Moss.

J.J. Porter and Bob McDonald of the Strategic Sea Command are assigned to the South Polar Region to uncover the planet's last source of energy which is under an ice sheet miles thick. But the project is sabotaged by an enemy who dislodges the ice sheet, freezing the whole globe. Porter and McDonald, who board a spaceship filled with the world's leading citizens, think that they are saved, until some strange goings-on suggest that they are flying toward their own disintegration.

1218. "The Woman in Red" (5/7/77; rebroadcast from 1/19/77)

1219. "Happy Death Day" (5/8/77; rebroadcast from 1/21/77)

1220. "Murder Most Foul" (5/9/77; rebroadcast from 4/19/76)

1221. "The Assassination" (5/10/77; rebroadcast from 4/20/76)

1222. "The Love Song of Death" (5/11/77; rebroadcast from 4/21/76)

1223. "The Green-Eyed Monster" (5/12/77; rebroadcast from 4/22/76)

1224. "Long Live the King Is Dead" (5/13/77; rebroadcast from 4/23/76)

1225. "The Prince of Evil" (5/14/77; rebroadcast from 4/24/76)

1226. "The Serpent of the Nile" (5/15/77; rebroadcast from 4/25/76)

1227. "Mayerling Revisited" (5/16/77; rebroadcast 9/25/77)
Cast: Marian Seldes (Kitty Scott); Paul Hecht (David Carlton); Joan Shay (Liz Carlton); Ian Martin (Frank Carlton). Written by Nancy Moore.
Kitty Scott has long felt a kinship for Marie Vetsera who, betrothed to Archduke Rudolph, heir to the throne of Austria-Hungary, died with the Archduke in the village of Mayerling before they could go through with their wedding plans. The cause of their deaths is still a matter of speculation, but Kitty is sure that she, a penniless schoolteacher, and her betrothed, David Carlton, son of a tyrannical Texas oil millionaire, are destined to repeat the courtship of the Archduke and Marie and will ultimately meet the same fate.

1228. "The Child's Cat Paw" (5/17/77; rebroadcast 9/28/77)
Cast: Sarah Jessica Parker (Dinah); Bryna Raeburn (Mother); Guy Sorel (Uncle Willie); Earl Hammond (Father); Evelyn Juster (Fammy). Written by Ian Martin.
Ten-year-old Dinah has moved to an isolated farm with her parents and her ailing Uncle Willie. Her father wants to write a novel, her mother wants to paint. When cold weather sets in, they pay little attention to Dinah, whose cat Fammy, named after a familiar, the alter ego of a witch, becomes her closest friend. She has long conversations with Fammy, who suddenly starts talking back. Dinah's mother overhears them, but not distinctly enough to know what they are conjuring up for Uncle Willie.

Notes: Sarah Jessica Parker later had quite a good film career after her *The-ater* appearance, in such films as *Ed Wood* (1994), *L.A. Story* (1991), *Girls Just Want to Have Fun* (1985), *Footloose* (1984), *Hocus Pocus* (1993), and *Flight of the Navigator* (1986).

1229. "License to Kill" (5/18/77; rebroadcast from 1/24/77)

1230. "A Matter of Customs" (5/19/77; rebroadcast 10/1/77)

Cast: Mary Jane Higby (Millie Gordan); Court Benson (Sam Gordon); Joan Copeland (Wanda Rivers); Leon Janney (Howie Rivers). Written by Ian Martin.

Millie Gordon and her husband, Sam, celebrating their 35th wedding anniversary, set out on a cruise in the Caribbean. Because she has read so many mystery stories, Millie occasionally thinks of herself as an amateur detective, and she grows suspicious of Wanda and Howie Rivers, who seldom leave their stateroom. She becomes certain the two are involved in some kind of criminal activity when they go ashore in Venezuela and Millie returns with another man disguised as her husband.

1231. "Wine, Women and Murder" (5/20/77; rebroadcast 10/2/77)

Cast: Bob Dryden (Elias Breckenridge); Carol Teitel (Maude Bexlar); William Griffis (Inspector Schmidt); Robert Kaliban (Cabbie). Written by Sam Dann.

Los Angeles book shop owner Elias Breckenridge, planning a trip to Cologne to attend a meeting of the International Coleridge Society, is persuaded by one of his customers, Maude Bexlar, to do her a favor. She asks him to deliver a deed to her cousin, Dr. Karl Bexlar, a professor at Cologne University. Breckenridge does so and, upon returning to his hotel, is told by the police that Dr. Bexlar has been murdered and that he (Breckenridge) is the chief suspect.

1232. "The White Wolf" (5/21/77; rebroadcast from 1/26/77)

1233. "My Fair Lady-Killer" (5/22/77; rebroadcast from 1/28/77)

1234. "The Briefcase Blunder" (5/23/77; rebroadcast 10/4/77)

Cast: Paul Hecht (Harry Owens); Ian Martin (Sloane); Anne Williams (Molly); Jackson Beck (Lt. Bender). Written by Karen Thorsen.

Harry Owens discovers a briefcase containing $50,000 in cash on the back seat of his cab and takes it home. He sees a trip to Paris for him and his wife, Molly, and a new cab for himself. But Molly insists he return it to its owner, a man Harry remembers picking up at a downtown squash club. The man, named Sloane, stops his game to see Harry, seems annoyed, and refuses to take the briefcase. Molly then insists that Harry take it to the police. Harry agrees and gives it to a lieutenant, who turns out to be Sloane's squash partner.

1235. "Transmutation, Inc." (5/24/77; rebroadcast 10/6/77)

Cast: Bob Dryden (Bones Terwilliger); Norman Rose (Apple); Bryna Raeburn (Gussie Schultz). Written by Sam Dann.

While visiting his girlfriend Gussie in the diner she recently inherited from her uncle, small-time gambler Bones Terwilliger magnanimously picks up the $1.97 check one of her customers claims he can't pay. The customer introduces himself as Apple (admitting later that he is Satan) and offers, because of Bone's kindness, to help him become a millionaire. All Bones must do is what Apple tells him to do—first with his bookie, then with a stockbroker.

1236. "Casual Affair" (5/25/77; rebroadcast from 1/31/77)

1237. "The Countess" (5/26/77; rebroadcast 10/8/77, 11/24/77)

Cast: Marian Seldes (Countess Josephine); Robert Maxwell (Rosalie); William Griffis (Carlos); Court Benson (Count de Merret); Russell Horton (Charles). Adapted by Gerald Keane, based on the short story by Honore de Balzac.

Countess Josephine de Merret, despite her much older husband's orders, takes their newborn baby to a Parisian park where she meets a young Spanish nobleman, Carlos. It's love at first sight. Later the Count, drunk most of the time, interrupts a tryst in Josephine's bedroom. Carlos hides in a closet, and even though Josephine swears there is no one inside, the Count orders it bricked up. Then, with a gun at his side, he sets up a vigil outside the closet. If Carlos manages to get out, Josephine knows it will be the end for both of them.

1238. "Guilty Secret" (5/27/77; rebroadcast 10/9/77)

Cast: Mandel Kramer (Sen. Melvin Blaisdell); Evelyn Juster (Gloria Blaisdell); Teri Keane (Emily Hawkins); Leon Janney (Jim). Written by Sam Dann.

Sen. Melvin Blaisdell, just 42 and certain to be his party's choice for president, assures his backers there will be no "surprises" that might hurt his chances to win. But he is not telling the truth. He's the father of a child born out of wedlock, by a pretty librarian in his hometown. She swears she will never tell anyone about it. But that doesn't mean the taxi driver who used to take him to the library or the child's nosy nursery school teacher will keep their mouths shut.

1239. "The Cat Is Dead" (5/28/77; rebroadcast from 2/2/77)

1240. "I Pronounce You Dead" (5/29/77; rebroadcast from 2/7/77)

1241. "The Silent Witness" (5/30/77; rebroadcast 10/11/77)

Cast: Ralph Bell (Gordon Davis); Earl Hammond (Chung Lee Yung); Lloyd Battista (Tony Blessing); Marian Seldes (Jill). Written by Roy Winsor.

Gordon Davis, a successful banker, once gave up the love of a married woman, Helen Drumley, because he feared it would end his banking career. Now Davis is haunted by the memory of Helen, who died in Hawaii shortly after her husband

and two daughters returned to the United States. When showing Helen's grave to his new employee, Tony Blessing, Gordon is shocked to see a grave being dug nearby. When no one else sees it, Gordon begins to assume it is *his* grave.

1242. "The Boscombe Pool Mystery" (5/31/77; rebroadcast 10/13/77, 4/29/79)

Cast: Kevin McCarthy (Sherlock Holmes); Ian Martin (Inspector Lestrade); Court Benson (Dr. Watson); Dallas Coke (James McCarthy); Patricia Elliott (Susan Turner). Adapted by Murray Burnett, based on the 1891 short story *The Boscombe Valley* by Sir Arthur Conan Doyle.

Sherlock Holmes is called to Boscombe Valley by Susan Turner, James McCarthy's fiancé, to investigate the murder of his father, for which he is charged. James, seen arguing with his father near Boscombe Pool minutes before the murder, won't say what they were arguing about or why he had just returned from Bristol. But Holmes and Watson are able to deduce some likely answers, pointing them in the direction of the real murderer.

1243. "The Recluse" (6/1/77; rebroadcast from 2/10/77)

1244. "A God Named Smith" (6/2/77; rebroadcast 10/15/77)

Cast: Russell Horton (Smith); Norman Rose (Luke Wingate); Evelyn Juster (Evelyn); Robert Kaliban (Reporter). Written by Henry Slesar.

Smith, just 12 years old and a college senior, is asked by his upper classmates, as a joke, to build something man has always needed—a left-handed monkey wrench. He does and proceeds to develop, in the laboratory, a small planet. After more work, he is able to launch the materials necessary to construct another planet, 3,000 miles in diameter, in space. This causes a panic as most of the earth's best scientists, business leaders, artists and writers decide to migrate to Smith's world, billed as true paradise.

1245. "The Two-Dollar Murders" (6/3/77; rebroadcast 10/16/77)

Cast: Larry Haines (Gordon Morrison); Bob Dryden (Lieutenant Gomez); Joan Shay (Rowena Morrison); Bryna Raeburn (Molly Goldstein). Written by Sam Dann.

The only lead the police have for two murders is that both victims were shot by the same revolver. No one in the neighborhood is of much help, and the publisher is certain he won't be caught. But he doesn't know what the policeman told a diner waitress before he was killed or that his wife suspects him—not only of having cheated on her but also, for reasons she can't figure out, of having fired the .38 he always carries at both the women and the cop.

1246. "The Aurora Group" (6/4/77; rebroadcast from 2/8/77)

1247. "The Ripple Effect" (6/5/77; rebroadcast from 2/4/77)

1248. "The Blood Red Wine" (6/6/77; rebroadcast 10/18/77)

Cast: Ralph Bell (Joel); Joan Banks (Myra); Bob Dryden (Sheriff); Marian Seldes (Lorraine). Written by Sam Dann.

Joel, an honest but unsuccessful salesman, tries to help a stranger who comes to his door in the midst of a storm, suffering from a heart attack. Joel helps the man, who identifies himself as J.B. Lucas, by loosening his clothes and giving him his wife Myra's special boysenberry wine. But when Lucas dies, Myra convinces Joel to put his body back in his car and keep Lucas' money ($250,000), even though Joel knows a clue and a guilty conscience will lead the sheriff to him.

1249. "The Curse of Conscience" (6/7/77; rebroadcast 10/20/77)

Cast: Tony Roberts (Simon Berman); Mary Jane Higby (Cousin Anne); Bryna Raeburn (Candy); Earl Hammond (Ted Slade). Written by Ian Martin.

No good Simon Berman, nearly penniless in Cleveland, meets an 85-year-old spinster at a church social. Cousin Anne, as she calls herself, takes him home, gets him a job and promises to make him her heir. But when an old buddy shows up, Simon agrees to join him in a bank heist. They fail and Si heads for New York. Soon in trouble with some loan sharks, he asks Cousin Anne for money. When she refuses, he shoots her and lands in jail, with her ghost a constant companion.

1250. "Masquerade" (6/8/77; rebroadcast from 2/11/77)

1251. "Dialogue with Death" (6/9/77; rebroadcast 10/22/77)

Cast: Paul Hecht (Dr. George Cudworth); Fred Gwynne (Father); Evelyn Juster (Jenny). Written by Elspeth Eric

Dr. George Cudworth joins his father's medical practice in Marble Point and immediately falls in love with Jenny, a young woman the elder Dr. Cudworth has raised since her parents died in a fire. Soon George realizes that Jenny is discussing their wedding plans with her dead parents and that she sees them and her dead horse. Certain that she needs some medical treatment, George is shocked when his father threatens to kill him if he confronts Jenny with his diagnosis.

1252. "The Night We Died" (6/10/77; rebroadcast 10/23/79)

Cast: Bob Readick (Toby Kane); William Griffis (Captain Moffett); Joan Shay (Vanessa); Jackson Beck (Sam Thumbs). Written by Henry Slesar.

Toby Kane is called back to Earth from Mars by Sam Thumbs, who needs his help in selling a rich woman some phony asteroid mine stock. Kane changes his name and his face (by plastic surgery), but becomes suspicious when the women seems too easily convinced she should part with her money. When he learns that she and Thumbs are members of a group plotting a revolution on the moon, Kane joins the interplanetary police in a scheme to stop them.

Notes: Jackson Beck was no stranger to science fiction radio by the time he played his role of Sam Thumbs in this episode. He was the announcer for the 1952 juvenile sci-fi series *Tom Corbett, Space Cadet.* He also made a few appearances on the NBC anthology series *X Minus One,* which featured different tales from different sci-fi writers during the late 1950s. His voice was used as a radio announcer for Woody Allen's 1987 film *Radio Days*.

1253. "Stamped for Death" (6/11/77; rebroadcast from 2/14/77)

1254. "The Star Killers" (6/12/77; rebroadcast from 2/15/77)

1255. "First Woman in Space" (6/13/77; rebroadcast 10/26/77)

Cast: Phyllis Newman (Margo Gordon); Lloyd Battista (Professor Harry Freeman); Hans Conried (Owen); Marian Seldes (Alien). Written by Sam Dann.

Astronaut Margo Gordon, a heroine after her successful *Athena One* flight, suffers, for some strange reason, from the heat—although it's midwinter. She now also has the strength of ten men. Her body chemistry has changed. And she keeps hearing a voice saying, "Our planet is gone. I survive in this body." She knows she must rid herself of this alien force or else she'll never qualify for *Athena Two*.

1256. "Murder One" (6/14/77; rebroadcast 10/29/79)

Cast: Tammy Grimes (Madge Telford); Teri Keane (Harriet); Leon Janney (Dr. Arthur Cotter). Written by G. Frederic Lewis.

Madge Telford, whose rich elderly husband allegedly died from a strange African disease, becomes convinced of Telford's death: poison administered by Madge and hushed up by a friendly doctor. Determined to stop any attempts at blackmail by Harriet, Madge starts feeding herself small amounts of arsenic. By doing so she hopes to pin an attempted-murder charge on Harriet. But Marge must be very careful not to give herself an overdose.

1257. "If Mischief Follow" (6/15/77; rebroadcast from 2/17/77)

1258. "Little Lucy's Lethal Libation" (6/16/77; rebroadcast 10/30/77)

Cast: Larry Haines (Tom Raglan); Joan Shea (Dr. Margaret Paskow); Earl Hammond (Terence Ingram); Bryna Raeburn (Little Lucy). Written by Sam Dann.

Tom Raglan, whose advertising campaign sold $32 million worth of Yum-Yummy dog food, is being transferred by his woman boss to the Little Lucy's Lively Libation account. The product is owned by a woman who tells him she needs no advertising; the drink sells itself. Tom sees this as a plot to get him fired, which is what is happening to other men in his agency. He winds up in a mental institution under the care of a woman psychiatrist assigned to him by the managing director, a woman appointed by the governor, also a woman.

1259. "Two Motives for Murder" (6/17/77; rebroadcast 11/2/77)

Cast: Don Scardino (Bill Davis); Evelyn Juster (Carol Davis); Bob Dryden (Burton Wall); Ian Martin (Frank Turner).Written by Roy Winsor.

One hundred thousand dollars worth of ATL stock is missing from a firm owned by Burton Wall, who insinuates that one of his employees, Bill Davis, has stolen it. Wall invites Davis for an afternoon cruise on his yacht, drugs him and has him pushed overboard into shark-infested waters, claiming afterward that Davis was distraught because he was guilty of the theft and wanted to commit suicide. Unfortunately for Wall, Davis is rescued by a passing tanker.

1260. "A Heart of Gold" (6/18/77; rebroadcast from 2/18/77)

1261. "Orient Express" (6/19/77; rebroadcast from 2/21/77)

1262. "The Birthmark" (6/20/77; rebroadcast 11/5/77, 11/18/79)

Cast: Gordon Heath (Aminadab); Tony Roberts (Aylmer); Marian Seldes (Georgianna). Adapted by Elspeth Eric, based on the 1843 short story by Nathaniel Hawthorne.

Aylmer, one of the great scientists of the late 1700s, marries beautiful Georgianna. But soon he cannot stand to look at her because of a strange birthmark which glows whenever she turns pale. Though Alymer's lab assistant, Aminadab, would accept Georgianna just as she is, Aylmer is haunted by the desire to erase the blemish, no matter what the consequence. Georgianna consents, knowing that perhaps whatever he does will mean her death.

1263. "Tomorrow, Cloudy and Cold" (6/21/77; rebroadcast 11/6/77)

Cast: Norman Rose (Dr. Herman Bruno); Russell Horton (Rick Slander); Bryna Raeburn (Mrs. Borden); Morgan Fairchild (Robin Fowler); Ralph Bell (John Fowler). Written by Bob Juhren.

After several months of hypnosis and the ingestion of various herbs, 22-year-old Rick Slander is made capable by Dr. Herman Bruna of affecting weather changes by his changing moods. When Rick is happy, it's warm and sunny; when he is unhappy, it's cold and rainy. Because he's been made a virtual prisoner, Rick becomes sulky and, when he ultimately escapes, Dr. Bruno correctly predicts that wherever Rick goes storms and floods are bound to occur—with disastrous results.

1264. "Jane Eyre" (6/22/77; rebroadcast from 2/22/77)

1265. "The Red Circle" (6/23/77; rebroadcast 11/9/77)

Cast: Catherine Byers (Min Wolkins); Ann Pitoniak (Laura Vear); Bob Dryden (Will Vear); Joseph Silver (Dr. Reagan). Written by Roy Winsor.

Nobody believes Laura Vear's story that Min Wilkins paid her a visit, (because Min died); under mysterious circumstances three weeks ago. But when Laura tells her husband, Will, what Min told her about a will and some hidden cash, minds begin to change. The police call Min's death a suicide, but Laura is convinced she was murdered and that the culprit is either Min's husband Clyde, his best friend, or the next-door widow Clyde has been seeing regularly.

1266. "Fan Mail" (6/24/77; rebroadcast 11/12/77)

Cast: Anne Williams (Margo); Mandel Kramer (Perry Stanhope); Teri Keane (Irma Burkett); Ian Martin (Payton Forsney); William Griffis (Sergeant Freeman). Written by Sam Dann.

Perry Stanhope, starring as Joe in "Crossroads," a popular television daytime serial, kills his wife Margo, an actress the producer wants written out of the continuing story. Margo, who in real life is also Perry's wife, is furious because Perry didn't try to save her job and threatens to kill him. In the next installment of "Crossroads," the police seem to believe Joe's alibi and, when he's murdered in real life, the real police are convinced his wife did it.

1267. "Last Judgment" (6/25/77; rebroadcast from 2/24/77)

1268. "Legend of Phoenix Hill" (6/26/77; rebroadcast from 2/25/77)

1269. "Come, Fill My Cup" (6/27/77; rebroadcast 11/13/77)

Cast: Larry Haines (Jerry Garland); Russell Horton (Don Jorgenson); Earl Hammond (Lou Vitry); William Griffis (Frank Durham). Written by Sam Dann.

Don Jorgenson, who has been playing poker on the 7:49 out of Westville for years, decides to quit; he's lost so much money his wife is threatening to divorce him. But one of the other players, Jerry Garland, persuades him to play one more time, guaranteeing to cover any of his losses. Reluctantly, Don agrees and, just as the game is becoming intense, Jerry drinks a cup of coffee he himself has brought to the card table. Within minutes he is dead, poisoned by a drug in the strychnine family.

1270. "The Adventure of the Speckled Band" (6/28/77; rebroadcast 11/20/77, 11/3/79)

Cast: Kevin McCarthy (Sherlock Holmes); Court Benson (Dr. Watson); Patricia Elliott (Helen Stoner); Jackson Beck (Dr. Roylott). Adapted by Murray Burnett, based on the 1892 short story by Sir Arthur Conan Doyle.

Helen Stoner arouses Holmes and his associate, Dr. Watson, in the middle of the night. Trembling with fright, she tells them about the death of her twin sister, who was strangled in their stepfather's home. Holmes agrees to help Helen when she explains that, like her sister, she plans to get married and fears that her stepfather, who is subject to violent rages, will somehow try to stop the wedding from taking place.

1271. "The Light That Failed" (6/29/77; rebroadcast from 2/28/77)

1272. "Dead Men Do Tell Tales" (6/30/77; rebroadcast 11/16/77)

Cast: Mason Adams (Sam Small); Howard Ross (Captain Ben Trock); Marian Seldes (Landlady); Ian Martin (Guido Nette); Robert Kaliban (Sergeant Rico Alvira). Written by Ian Martin.

A man wearing a money belt containing nearly $9,000 is murdered in his room at a rundown boarding house by two shots fired from a short-barreled .38 revolver. One piece of evidence found at the scene of the crime is an explosive linen handkerchief monogrammed with the initials H-R-M. From the manufacturer the police learn, much to their consternation, that the handkerchief belongs to one of their own: their boss, the commander.

1273. "Revenge" (7/1/77; rebroadcast 11/19/77)

Cast: Gordon Heath (The Stranger); Bob Dryden (Jade Wanamaker); Leon Janney (The Sheriff); Gilbert Mack (Clem); Bryna Raeburn (Esther Wanamaker). Written by Percy Granger.

Jade Wanamaker, a quiet domestic man, and Herbert Beall, a hard-drinking bachelor addicted to nightly poker games, have each acquired a small fortune. They're living the grand life until a stranger comes to town and lets it be known he has some business to settle with them. Determined to make both pay for their transgressions, he plans to use an old Oriental principle to force them to attack him and then use their own energy against them.

1274. "The Hound of the Baskervilles" (7/2/77; rebroadcast from 3/1/77)

1275. "The Overcoat" (7/3/77; rebroadcast from 3/3/77)

1276. "Boomerang" (7/4/77; rebroadcast 11/22/77)

Cast: Ann Shepherd (Celia); Corinne Orr (Carol); Michael Wager (Robin); Norman Rose (John). Written by Elspeth Eric.

Away at boarding school when her father became ill, 16-year-old Carol was not asked to be at home with him when he died. She has not forgiven her mother for this, has spent much of her time in her room, and has fallen in love with a much older man, an English novelist, whom she met at the beach. When he does not respond, she tries to cast a spell over him. But she suffers more than he does: first in an auto accident, then with a self-inflicted bullet wound in her shoulder.

1277. "Hexed" (7/5/77; rebroadcast 11/24/77)

Cast: Roberta Maxwell (Lisa Peters); Paul Hecht (Craig Peters); Ian Martin (Gary Hutchins). Written by Nancy Moore.

After marrying the English owner of a tea estate in Ceylon, Lisa Peters becomes fascinated by devil dances, fire walking and other native magic. When told that her husband's male servant may become jealous of an upstart American giving orders in the household, Lisa fears he might practice some black magic on her. She becomes terrified when she finds a scorpion in her shoe, is attacked by a bat, and is nearly killed by a falling statue of Buddha.

1278. "Answer Me" (7/6/77; rebroadcast from 3/4/77)

1279. "A Stranger Among Us" (7/7/77; rebroadcast 11/26/77)

Cast: Marian Seldes (Lisa Stallings); Lloyd Battista (Dr. Bruce Dunlap); Court Benson (Sergeant Obanion). Written by Elspeth Eric.

The police ask the help of psychologist Bruce Dunlap when Lisa Stallings comes to them with a bizarre story. A firm believer in the existence of UFOs, she has told Sergeant Dave Obanion about being taken to the landing site, near Carmel, California, of a spaceship from a distant star galaxy and meeting the people on board. She is unable to recollect all the details, and Obanion hopes that through hypnosis Dr. Dunlap will help her remember everything that happened to her.

1280. "The Gift" (7/8/77; rebroadcast 11/27/77)

Cast: Ralph Bell (Dennis Holland); Bob Dryden (Walter Powers); Evelyn Juster (Rita Holland); Sam Gray (Lieutenant Savage). Written by by Sam Dann.

Rita Holland and Walter Powers accomplish a murder they have been planning for some time. They go to Rita's apartment, and after she turns up the hi-fi to its loudest pitch, Walter shoots her husband, Dennis. Their explanation to the police is that Dennis was killed by a burglar trying to steal his valuable coin collection. The police begin a routine investigation, so routine, and thorough that Walter, subject to hallucinations, starts believing they know he's guilty.

1281. "Beyond the Barrier" (7/9/77; rebroadcast from 3/7/77)

1282. "The Sign of Four" (7/10/77; rebroadcast from 3/8/77)

1283. "A Scandal in Bohemia" (7/11/77; rebroadcast 11/29/77)

Cast: Kevin McCarthy (Sherlock Holmes); Court Benson (Dr. Watson); Marian Seldes (Irene Adler); William Griffis (The King). Adapted by Murray Burnett, based on the 1891 short story by Sir Arthur Conan Doyle.

Disguised as Count von Kramm, the King of Bohemia pays a visit to Holmes and Dr. Watson, explaining that if his affair with the beautiful Irene Adler, an American opera singer, ever becomes public knowledge, his imminent marriage to a Scandinavian princess will be jeopardized—with serious international complications. He instructs Holmes, at any cost, to retrieve a photograph Miss Adler refuses to give up, of the King and her together.

1284. "The Colonel Chabert" (7/12/77; rebroadcast 12/1/77, 12/9/79)

Cast: Alexander Scourby (Colonel Chabert); Larry Haines (Master Derville); Lori March (Countess Ferraud); Danny Ocko (Blanchet). Adapted by Karen Thorsen, based on the novella *Colonel Chabert* by Honore de Balzac.

By using the arm bone of a dead soldier, Colonel Chabert manages to dig his way out of a common grave, in which he found himself after the French cavalry charge at Eylau. It takes him ten years to get back to Paris, where a lawyer, Master Derville, agrees to help him retrieve his fortune, now in his remarried wife's name. But instead of heeding Derville's advice, Chabert tries to negotiate directly with his wife, who much prefers that he remain dead.

Notes: For 25 years, Larry Haines had been seen as Stu Bergman on the television soap opera *Search for Tomorrow*, and his radio career spanned an even longer period. Haines claims to have appeared in some 15,000 radio broadcasts, a tradition he continues with frequent appearances on *Mystery Theater*. "But," he says, "they are really two different media: television daytime drama with its everyday social problems and radio drama with its whodunits. I enjoy them both, but radio is my 'pet love.'"

1285. "The Pleading Voice" (7/13/77; rebroadcast from 3/10/77)

1286. "A Matter of Conscience" (7/14/77; rebroadcast 12/3/77, 12/1/79)

Cast: Kristoffer Tabori (Parker Addison); Evelyn Juster (Mrs. Addison); Earl Hammond (Hasterlick); Bob Dryden (Colonel Brayle); Arnold Moss (General). Adapted by Arnold Moss, based on the 1891 short story by Ambrose Bierce.

Despite his mother's pleas to reconsider, young Addison Parker leaves his home in the South and joins the Fourth Indiana Infantry because, he says, his sympathies are with the North. Immediately he is ordered to don a Confederate uniform and go as a spy behind the Southern lines. His mission seems successful until a Confederate medic demands that he remove the bandage from the head wound he doesn't have.

1287. "The Kingdom Below" (7/15/77; rebroadcast 12/4/77)

Cast: Fred Gwynne (Ben Stebbins); Phyllis Newman (Mayetta Stebbins); Roger Baron (Thurman Trueblood); Bryna Raeburn (Momma Stebbins); Paul Hecht (The Prince). Written by Sam Dann.

Benjamin Franklyn Stebbins, one of the 50 richest men in America, is dragged to Rome by his wife and daughter, Mayetta, to buy some paintings and sculpture for their mansion back home and a titled foreign nobleman for Mayetta: the Prince of Portocorvo, said by the peasants to be the Devil himself. But that doesn't stop the senior Stebbins or Mayetta, who immediately falls in love with the Prince.

Notes: Phyllis Newman has appeared in such films as *Picnic* (1955), *Follies in Concert* (1985), and *A Secret Space* (1988).

1288. "Till Death Do Us Part" (7/16/77; rebroadcast from 3/11/77)

1289. "Look Backward Sometimes" (7/17/77; rebroadcast from 3/14/77)

1290. "The Bisara of Pooree" (7/18/77; rebroadcast 12/6/77, 11/10/79)

Cast: Paul Hecht (Major John Churton); Ralph Bell (Tom Fewton); Marian Seldes (Millicent Hollis); William Griffis (Captain Pack). Adapted by Sam Dann, based on the 1888 short story by Rudyard Kipling.

British Major John Churton, serving in India, runs into a streak of bad luck, including the decision of his fiancée, the colonel's daughter, to break their engagement. All of Churton's troubles have come about, according to his friend Tom Fewton, a student of Indian customs, because he had bought a silver box, the Bisara of Pooree. If he had stolen it, Fewton explains, he would have his heart's desire. Now Churton must figure a way to get rid of the box and then steal it back.

1291. "The Mysterious Island" (7/19/77; rebroadcast 12/8/77)

Cast: Leon Janney (Captain Pencroft); Jackson Beck (Captain Harding); Roger Baron (Neb); Earl Hammond (Gideon Spillett). Adapted by Ian Martin, based on the 1874 novel by Jules Verne.

Captain Harding, a Union engineer often rough with his men, contains enough spirit bottled up to give his men hope. Gideon Spillett, a newspaperman, claims the pen is mightier than the sword. Pencroft, a sailor by trade with a nose for navigation, has spawned a young son named Neb. All four men are amazed when they find, on a seemingly deserted island, a chest of supplies and new tools. Their life improves in other unexpected ways, as if some higher being were on the island, until a ship appears on the horizon, flying a Jolly Roger.

1292. "The Shining Man" (7/20/77; rebroadcast from 3/15/77)

1293. "Rendezvous with Death" (7/21/77; rebroadcast 12/10/77)

Cast: Kristoffer Tabori (Mike Thurston); Roberta Maxwell (Laura Willow); Arnold Moss (Dr. Paul Baxter); Ann Pitoniak (Mrs. Thurston); Mandel Kramer (Mr. Thurston). Written by Ian Martin.

Mike Thurston, a college football star suffering from terminal cancer, convinces his parents that he should spend his last days in the mountains of New Mexico. While horseback riding one day and contemplating suicide, he encounters a girl named Laura Willow. They fall in love but she refuses to let him meet her parents and declines to meet his. They see each other frequently at a secret spot in the mountains, and Mike's health, for some unknown reason, starts to improve.

1294. "The Secret of the Aztecs" (7/22/77; rebroadcast 12/11/79)

Cast: Mason Adams (Jim Hudson); Bob Dryden (Wesley Parman); Court Benson (Quetzal); Kenneth Harvey (Charley Parks). Written by Percy Granger.

When his car stalls in the middle of the Jim Hudson is picked up by a man named Quetzal. Hudson has been warned that a killer is loose in the area, and Quetzal tells him that he, not Hudson, may be the killer's next victim. He takes Hudson to a mountaintop cave where Montezuma's treasure has been hidden. Quetzal, an old Aztec, explains that only he knows the hiding place, and according to tradition he must show someone else its location before he dies. Hudson soon wishes that the privilege never came to be.

1295. "Jobo" (7/23/77; rebroadcast from 3/17/77)

1296. "Little Green Death" (7/24/77; rebroadcast from 3/18/77)

1297. "The Adventure of the Blue Carbuncle" (7/25/77; rebroadcast 12/13/77, 11/25/79)

Cast: Kevin McCarthy (Sherlock Holmes); Court Benson (Dr. Watson); William Griffis (Inspector Lestrade); Lloyd Battista (Ryder). Adapted by Murray Burnett, based on the 1892 short story by Sir Arthur Conan Doyle.

So often proved wrong by the astute Holmes, Inspector Lestrade feels a measure of satisfaction when he arrives at 221 B. Baker Street with a warrant for the private detective's arrest for the possession of stolen goods. Holmes has in hand the Countess of Morcar's priceless stone, a blue carbuncle, found in the crop of a goose that was dropped by a slightly intoxicated man when accosted by a bunch of toughs. After some debate, however, Lestrade agrees not to go through with the arrest until Holmes has had a chance to catch the real thief.

1298. "The Rocket's Red Glare" (7/26/77; rebroadcast 12/15/77)

Cast: Mason Adams (Sergeant Mangle); Catherine Byers (Daisy Magle); Sam Gray (Captain Suggs); Bob Dryden (Lomas). Written by Percy Granger.

Sergeant Fritz Mangle is ordered to investigate the apparent suicide of nuclear scientist Jeff Simpson, working on Lomas Industries' new Pentagon project, the deadly Scorpio missile. Soon after he concludes that Simpson may not have killed himself, Mangle is told to stop his investigation; the case has been closed. But Mangle disobeys and sends his wife to apply for a job at the Lomas plant. What she learns supports her husband's belief of what really happened.

1299. "The Eighth Deadly Sin" (7/27/77; rebroadcast from 3/21/77)

1300. "The Secret of Laurels" (7/28/77; rebroadcast 12/17/77)

Cast: Norman Rose (Philip Hudson); Don Scardino (Rob Hudson); Evelyn Juster (Margo); Anne Williams (Rose Grove). Written by Roy Winsor.

At his trial, Philip Hudson staunchly maintained he had not killed his wife's lover even though, after the murder, he was found on the floor unconscious, gun in hand. Out of jail, he returns to his former home, Laurels, now in a dilapidated condition, and confronts his house keeper, still living there. She refuses to change her mind about his guilt and tries to keep him out of the room where the murder took place, a move that strengthens Hudson's belief in his innocence.

1301. "The Thousand and First Door" (7/29/77; rebroadcast 12/18/77)

Cast: Russell Horton (Art Hollis); Carol Teitel (Elaine Hollis); Jackson Beck (Dan Fenton); Earl Hammond (Tom Hollis). Written by Ian Martin.

Art Hollis, whose aim in life is to be a doctor, quits medical school to take over his ailing father's drugstore. He marries Elaine, "the prettiest, nicest" girl in the neighborhood who turns out to be a real shrew. But he sticks with her and their only child for 20 years. Then his friend, Dan Fenton, points out how simple it would be for Art, as a druggist, to murder Elaine. They carefully plan it, Art not realizing why Dan is so interested in seeing Elaine eliminated.

1302. "The Imposter" (7/30/77; rebroadcast from 3/22/77)

1303. "The Gift of Doom" (7/31/77; rebroadcast from 3/24/77)

1304. "Two Renegades" (8/1/77; rebroadcast from 1/10/77)

1305. "The Passing of Black Eagle" (8/2/77; rebroadcast from 1/11/77)

1306. "Tobin's Palm" (8/3/77; rebroadcast from 1/12/77)

1307. "Don't Die Without Me" (8/4/77; rebroadcast from 1/13/77)

1308. "A Departmental Case" (8/5/77 rebroadcast from 1/14/77)

1309. "Cherchez la Femme" (8/6/77; rebroadcast from 1/15/77)

1310. "Jimmy Valentine's Gamble" (8/7/77; rebroadcast from 1/16/77)

1311. "Hope Springs Eternal" (8/8/77; rebroadcast 12/20/77)
    Cast: Court Benson (Reuben Thompson); Anne Williams (Alice Pennington); Russell Horton (Edgar Pennington); Robert Maxwell (Alistair Hodge). Written by Percy Granger.
    Just two weeks after his marriage, back in 1942, Edgar Pennington disappeared from a deserted New England beach during the few minutes his wife, Alice, went back to their house to give some instructions to their servant. Because they were so deeply in love, Alice cannot believe Edgar won't return, despite the local constable's feeling he committed suicide and a U.S. government agent's claim he was a German spy taken aboard a U-boat. For 35 years she has waited, certain he'll be back at any moment.

1312. "A Study in Scarlet" (8/9/77; rebroadcast from 3/25/77)

1313. "Case Closed" (8/10/77; rebroadcast 12/22/77)
    Cast: Mandel Kramer (Chester Jones); Evelyn Juster (Joanna Butler); Joan Shay (Helen Jones); Joseph Silver (Lt. Fitzmaurice); Earl Hammond (J.R. Trowbridge).Written by Sam Dann.

Chester Jones, fired after 20 years as chief engineer at Trowbridge Industries and deeply in debt, hears a police siren as he points a gun at the head of bank teller Joanna Butler. He orders all other bank employees and customers out, but keeps Joanna as a hostage, threatening to kill her if the police try to storm the building. When his demand that Trowbridge rehire him is met, he still refuses to release Joanna who, after a while, begins to understand what he really wants.

1314. "The Warriors from Loanda" (8/11/77; rebroadcast from 3/28/77)

1315. "For Want of a Nail" (8/12/77; rebroadcast 12/25/77)

Cast: Betsy Palmer (Armina Saunders); Ian Martin (Ralph Saunders); Bryna Raeburn (Dolores); Bob Dryden (Cabbie). Written by Sam Dann.

Stuck in Marsden City, South Carolina, when the plane makes a forced landing, Armina Saunders decides to visit the Audley Company, which her husband has told her is the major purchaser of the sophisticated starter engine he has designed. The company turns out to be a small office manned by a lone secretary. Her husband finds this hard to believe, but Armina insists on an explanation, especially when she learns that the taxi driver who took her to the Audley address has been murdered.

Notes: Betsy Palmer has appeared in such films as *Friday the 13th* (1980), *Friday the 13th Part II* (1981), *The Last Angry Man* (1959), *The Long Gray Line* (1955), *The Tin Star* (1957), and *Still Not Quite Human* (1992).

1316. "The Coldest Killer" (8/13/77; rebroadcast from 3/29/77)

1317. "Death Is Blue" (8/14/77; rebroadcast from 3/31/77)

1318. "The Together Place" (8/15/77; rebroadcast 12/27/77)

Cast: Norman Rose (Dr. Leahey); Rosemary Rice (Rose Craven); Mary Jane Higby (Mary Mahaffey); Marian Seldes (Mother). Written by Elspeth Eric.

Rose Craven, whose mother is under the care of Dr. Ed Leahey, arouses his curiosity when he overhears her conversing with Lily, the nonexistent twin sister. He becomes concerned upon learning that Rose has not left her room for three days. Lily is in Kama Loca, "The Together Place," Rose explains, where people's souls go—but for a brief time. They don't drown or burn up or go to jail there, she adds, but they die. Unless somebody helps her, Lily is going to die, too.

1319. "You Bet Your Life" (8/16/77; rebroadcast from 4/1/77)

1320. "In the Fog" (8/17/77; rebroadcast 12/29/77)

Cast: Gordon Gould (Captain O'Reilly); Ian Martin (Dr. Henry); Martha Greenhouse (May Collard); William Griffis (Jeff Collard). Written by Roy Winsor.

Captain Terry O'Reilly is told by his doctor that he is well enough to visit some friends on Boston's Beacon Hill. Emerging from the subway, O'Reilly walks into a dense fog and meets a strange, beautiful woman. Together they grope their way to Beacon Hill. She enters a house, and when O'Reilly hears a scream he follows her in, only to find her lying on a bed, stabbed to death. He rushes away in a panic, leaving his hat in the bedroom.

1321. "So Shall Ye Reap" (8/18/77; rebroadcast from 4/4/77)

1322. "The Instrument" (8/19/77; rebroadcast 12/31/77)

Cast: Ralph Bell (Tony Warlock); Robert Kaliban (Dick Harrison); Evelyn Juster (Ruth Warlock). Written by Sam Dann.

Anthony Warlock, who specializes in writing supernatural or occult mystery stories, met his literary agent, Dick Harrison, when Dick saved him from drowning. Subsequently, actions taken by Dick prevent Tony from being killed by a crashing plane, a fiery cruise ship and a malfunctioning automobile. As a result, Tony starts to think that Dick has the ability to make him immortal. To test it, he decides to deliberately jump in front of an onrushing auto.

1323. "The Sensitive" (8/20/77; rebroadcast from 4/5/77)

1324. "The High Priest" (8/21/77; rebroadcast from 4/7/77)

1325. "Return to Pompeii" (8/22/77; rebroadcast 1/1/78)

Cast: Marian Seldes (Jennifer Matthews); Patricia Elliott (Olga Peterson); Paul Hecht (Paulus); Larry Haines (Milos). Written by Victoria Dann.

Jennifer Matthews, depressed by the death of her husband, half heartedly agrees to take a summer tour of Italy with her friend, Olga Peterson. One minute they are standing in the midst of the ancient ruins of Pompeii and, in the next moment, Olga is gone, the ruins have disappeared and in their place stands the old town, alive again. Jennifer tries to warn her new friends about the impending destruction of Pompeii, but nobody believes her.

1326. "Blood, Thunder and a Woman in Green" (8/23/77; rebroadcast from 4/8/77)

1327. "The Adventures of Don Quixote" (8/24/77; rebroadcast 1/3/78, 12/29/79)

Cast: Arnold Moss (Don Quixote); Bob Dryden (Sancho Panza); Bryna Raeburn (Esmeralda); Court Benson (Innkeeper). Adapted by Arnold Moss, based on the 1605 novel *Don Quixote of La Mancha* by Miguel de Cervantes.

Don Quixote becomes so deeply involved reading romances of chivalry that he finally believes them to be true and, considering himself a knight-errant, goes forth in the world to defend the oppressed and undo wrongs. With the good-natured, middle-aged peasant Sancho Panza as his squire, the Don finds many opportunities for knightly combat, but he is forever transforming the common into the extraordinary: windmills become giants inns, castles chain gangs, oppressed gentlemen.

Notes: Arnold Moss can be seen in such films as *The Fool Killer* (1965), *The 27th Day* (1957), *Viva Zapata!* (1952), *Reign of Terror* (1949), and *The Loves of Carmen* (1948).

1328. "The Meteorite" (8/25/77; rebroadcast from 4/11/77)

1329. "Area Thirteen" (8/26/77; rebroadcast from 1/5/77)

Cast: Mandel Kramer (Vignor); Ian Martin (Dr. Keith Lewton); Marian Seldes (Celia Newson); Joan Banks (Marissa Finlayson). Written by Murray Burnett.

In a world of computer-chosen marriages and professions, programmed personalities and reproduction by artificial insemination exists, a handful of human beings live under the constant surveillance of the Provost. When the computers detect an unreported individualistic 9-year-old son belonging to humans, Dr. Keith Lewton and his wife, who live in Area Thirteen, undercover agent Vignor is ordered to find the boy and take him to the accommodators for brainwashing. The emotionless robots who govern society by computer in the year 2176 feel endangered by the minority of free-thinking human beings.

1330. "Man-Sized in Marble" (8/27/77; rebroadcast from 4/12/77)

1331. "The Phantom House" (8/28/77; rebroadcast from 4/14/77)

1332. "To Be a Rose" (8/29/77; rebroadcast 1/14/78)

Cast: Leon Janney (Curly); Joan Shay (Nurse); Earl Hammond (Jackie Thorpe); Catherine Byers (Pammy Puckett). Written by Sam Dann.

Elwood "Curly" Quentin is lured into marriage by beautiful Pammy Sue Puckett, an editor who turns his talent for writing poetry into a fortune. During promotional campaigns for Curly, Pammy Sue often travels with Curly's agent and friend, Jackie Thorpe. When the two are found dead in a Chicago hotel room, Curly is accused of their murder. Put under psychiatric care, he regresses into a state of amnesia, refusing to believe that Pammy Sue and Jackie are dead, or that he killed them.

1333. "Borderline Case" (8/30/77; rebroadcast from 4/15/77)

1334. "The Reunion" (8/31/77; rebroadcast 1/15/78)

Cast: Paul Hecht (Louis Simons); Mildred Clinton (Janie Simons); William Griffis (Inspector Malraux); Sam Gray (Hank Murphy/Henri Jones). Written by Sam Dann.

When Louis Simons meets his old buddy, Hank Murphy, in a Paris bar, his greeting is a sock in the jaw. A few minutes later, when they meet again in Louis' room, Hank is surprised when Louis hits him. They resolve their differences once they discover that a schizophrenic man named Henri Jones, who looks like Hank, is loose in the city, and they agree he must have been the one who hit Louis. But later, when Hank (or Henri?) is found murdered, the police accuse Louis of the crime.

1335. "A House Divided" (9/1/77; rebroadcast from 4/18/77)

1336. "Olive Darling and Morton Dear" (9/2/77; rebroadcast 1/18/78)

Cast: Fred Gwynne (Morton Miller); Bryna Raeburn (Olive Miller); Ralph Bell (Elrod P. Smith); Bob Dryden (Sheriff). Written by Sam Dann.

While driving to the Alverada Mountains, Morton Miller is stopped by a sheriff who searches his car for a stolen $109,000 payroll. When the sheriff finds no money, Miller drives on until his car breaks down near a cottage whose occupant, Elrod P. Smith, forces Miller at gunpoint to move in with him and to cook his meals. Smith claims to be a writer seeking privacy, but his gun is the same type that was used to heist the payroll.

1337. "The Book of Abaca" (9/3/77; rebroadcast from 4/19/77)

1338. "Come Away Death" (9/4/77; rebroadcast from 4/21/77)

1339. "The Waiting Room" (9/5/77; rebroadcast 1/21/78)

Cast: Larry Haines (Robert Carson); Marian Seldes (Rhoda); Russell Horton (Bert Thomas); Don Scardino (Marty Lannings); Jada Rowland (Charlotte). Written by Bob Juhren.

Robert and Rhoda Carson invite Bert Thomas and Marty and Charlotte Lannings to their lush home, which is guarded by hostile pet birds. As the guests enjoy the Carsons' luxurious home and pool, they become annoyed by the spying birds and their host's insistent inquiries about their health. Then Bert, Marty and Charlotte learn to their horror that the Carsons intended to have their bodies inhabited by evil spirits, so history's deceased villains can be reincarnated.

1340. "The Prisoner of Zenda" (9/6/77; rebroadcast from 4/22/77)

1341. "Silent Shock" (9/7/77; rebroadcast 1/22/78)

Cast: Mercedes McCambridge (Kathy); Ralph Bell (Doctor); Ian Martin (Father); Teri Keane (Harriet). Written by Elspeth Eric.

Although improving, Kathy still imagines conversations with her husband, her lover and her father—none of whom have visited her in the 15 years she has been hospitalized. Now, at a beach house with her private doctor, Kathy is intrigued and frightened by the sea, which brings her last memory of her father leaving by ship. When she imagines the ship returning, she walks out into the sea to meet it. Her doctor does nothing to stop her, even as she risks drowning.

1342. "Bound East for Haiti" (9/8/77; rebroadcast from 4/25/77)

1343. "The Woman in the Green Dress" (9/9/77; rebroadcast 1/25/78)

Cast: Michael Tolan (Paul Maiden); Lois Kibbee (Jenny Morrison); Earl Hammond (Andrew Scott); Guy Sorel (Kirby Small). Written by Roy Winsor.

Photographer Paul Maiden becomes fascinated with an old portrait of a beautiful young woman wearing a green dress. He learns that the portrait is of Melanie Brent, who was killed by a jealous suitor the day before she was to be married by Andrew Scott, now 90. The murderer, Scott claims, was acquitted, but later committed suicide. He also claims that Melanie still visits him often, which causes his younger relatives to consider him mentally unstable.

1344. "The Adventure of the Red-Headed League" (9/10/77; rebroadcast from 4/26/77)

1345. "The Second Chance" (9/11/77; rebroadcast from 4/28/77)

1346. "First Childhood" (9/12/77; rebroadcast 1/28/78)

Cast: Eileen Heckart (Regina); Bryna Raeburn (Belle Marshak); Bob Dryden (Judge Sterling); Paul Hecht (Walter Owens).Written by Sam Dann.)

While staying at an ocean resort, Walter Owens, a lawyer, meets Regina Summerfield, a philosophical but strange woman who invites him to her mansion to meet her husband, Everett. Owens soon realizes that Everett was killed at Pearl Harbor, although Mrs. Summerfield still talks to him, and the "mansion" is a dilapidated old house. But when Mrs. Summerfield's niece tries to have her committed to an institution and take her house, Owens attempts to defend the eccentric lady, and it's her strange childhood that provides the key to her defense.

1347. "The Way to Dusty Death" (9/13/77; rebroadcast 1/29/78, 12/30/79)

Cast: Arnold Moss (Captain Webb); Gilbert Mack (Judge Calvin); Evelyn Juster (Isabel Carpenter); Don Scardino (Harmon Webb); Marian Seldes (Amanda Carpenter). Adapted by Stella and Arnold Moss, based on 441 B.C. story *Antigone* by Sophocles.

When Civil War captain Crane Webb kills Paul Carpenter, the war between the Webbs and the Carpenters flares up again. But Amanda Carpenter is determined to bury her brother's body, which still lies on Webb property, and she seeks the help of the captain's son, Harmon, whom she hopes to marry someday, ending the families' fighting. But Harmon's plea has no effect on his father, so the young couple proceed to move Paul's body at the risk of both their lives.

1348. "Wuthering Heights" (9/14/77; rebroadcast from 4/29/77)

1349. "Passport to Freedom" (9/15/77; rebroadcast 2/1/78)

Cast: Paul Hecht (Andy); Martha Greenhouse (Carol); Ian Martin (C.K. Halliday); Bryna Raeburn (Diana Barau). Written by Ian Martin.

Andy and Carol Lake, on what Andy promises will be their last assignment for the U.S. government, join a tour group in Romania, where they are to exchange identities with a scientist, Anton Zotescu, who looks just like Andy. The plan is for Zotescu and his wife to take the Lakes' places in the group, and to bring the energy formula to the U.S. government. However, when Mimi, Zotescu's lab technician and mistress, kills his wife, the whole plan and the Lakes' safe return seem in danger.

1350. "Death on Project X" (9/16/77; rebroadcast 2/4/78)

Cast: Larry Haines (Eli Hews); Bob Dryden (Colonel); Court Benson (Dr. Hilary); Catherine Byers (Dr. Baylor). Written by Victoria Dann.

The only thing government account Eli Hews knows about Project X, a top-secret research center working on the ultimate weapon, is the size of its tremendous budget. But Project X seems to be run efficiently, and Hews is ready to file a positive report until he receives a note saying "Beware, the end is near," and then discovers that the project's psychiatrist is insane. However, when he tries to recommend Project X's termination, Hews faces his greatest threat: death.

1351. "Much Too Much" (9/17/77; rebroadcast from 5/2/77)

1352. "The Luck Sisters" (9/18/77; rebroadcast from 5/3/77)

1353. "The Wind and the Flame" (9/19/77; rebroadcast 2/5/78)

Cast: Celeste Holm (Sabina); Norman Rose (Arthur Randolf Hale); Earl Hammond (Lieutenant Bauer). Written by Sam Dann.

Sabina arrives at Arthur Randolf Hale's door, announcing that her mistress and Hale's longtime love, Penelope Terwilliger, is now free to marry him—but only after Sabina, a housekeeper, reorganizes his disorderly, bachelor life. Certain that marriage to Mrs. Terwilliger would be bliss, Hale agrees. But suddenly Sabina tells him that he is receiving mysterious and threatening phone calls from Wesley Carradine, Hale's former partner who was recently murdered, and the old man begins to wonder who Sabina really is.

1354. "The Tunnel Man" (9/20/77; rebroadcast 2/8/78)

Cast: Ralph Bell (Mr. Mole); Robert Maxwell (Mayor Gibbs); Earl Hammond (Commissioner Hankla); Court Benson (George Trilby). Written by Percy Granger.

A West Coast town is threatened by a massive earthquake when a planetary alignment is expected to unleash such combined gravitational pulls that all fault lines will be activated. While the mayor considers evacuating the city, another threat arises. Mr. Mole, a former scientist who, in a wheelchair contraption, robs banks and then escapes from jail, always by mysteriously tunneling underground. Mole, head of a subterranean nation, plans to make sure the earthquake wipes out the entire West Coast.

1355. "Reunion Fever" (9/21/77; rebroadcast from 5/5/77)

1356. "The Plan" (9/22/77; rebroadcast 2/11/78)

Cast: Kim Hunter (Rebecca Russell); Bob Dryden (Robert Russell); Russell Horton (Officer Ulman); Evelyn Juster (Marybelle). Written by Sam Dann.

When Marybelle, the Russells' domestic, is killed in a freak taxicab accident while going to work, Mrs. Russell blames herself. As a birthday present to Marybelle, her employer arranged to pay her cabfare rather than give her the day off she requested. However, when Mr. Russell suggests that Marybelle's death was part of a master plan, his wife becomes determined to find out why the girl and the cabdriver had to die.

1357. "The Burning Whirlwind" (9/23/77; rebroadcast 2/12/78)

Cast: Michael Tolan (Sid Wicks); Bryna Raeburn (Candy Barr); Ian Martin (Mr. Prouty); Mary Jane Higby (Mrs. Hartley Loring). Written by Ian Martin.

When Mrs. Hartley Loring, wealthy widow of the ex-governor, withdraws her $8 million fortune, no one at the bank knows where she is storing it or what she plans to do with it. Then Sid Wicks, the security guard and a former flim flam artist, bumps into his old girlfriend, who happens to be Mrs. Loring's fortune-teller. Soon he has a plan to swindle the distraught widow, who expects the money to go to heaven on a chariot of fire in a whirlwind like Elijah.

1358. "Bottom of the World" (9/24/77; rebroadcast from 5/6/77)

1359. "Mayerling Revisited" (9/25/77; rebroadcast from 5/16/77)

1360. "The Guy De Maupassant Murders" (9/26/77; rebroadcast 2/15/78)

Cast: Marian Seldes (Martha Mullins); Fred Gwynne (Hydge Wilmot); Nat Polen (Lieutenant Altman); Martha Greenhouse (Dorcas). Adapted by Sam Dann, based on a short story by Guy De Maupassant.

When eight bloody murders are committed, police lieutenant Altman receives notes from the killer claiming that nature has commanded him to kill because "the more she destroys, the more she renews herself." The note left behind with each new victim quotes the Bible, "Thou shalt not kill." Once a description of the killer is obtained, Altman consults Judge Wilmot, who theorizes that the killer has a dual personality like Jekyll and Hyde. So Altman suspects just about everyone except the judge who fits the description perfectly and owns a gun like the assassin's.

1361. "The Wintering Place" (9/27/77; rebroadcast 2/18/78)

Cast: Bob Dryden (Franklin Bering); Evelyn Juster (Robyn); Earl Hammond (Sheriff). Written by Sam Dann.

After the death of his wife Emily, Frank Bering acquires a nasty disposition, until he meets Robyn, a young woman who reminds him of Emily. Delighted at his find, Frank makes a pass at Robyn, but she resists him. Unable to accept her rejection, Frank forces himself on her, causing her to fatally strike her head. Later, when someone else is accused of the murder, Robyn reappears to insist that Frank confess, convincing him that she now embodies Emily's spirit as well as her own.

1362. "The Child's Cat Paw" (9/28/77; rebroadcast from 5/17/77)

1363. "The Solitary" (9/29/77; rebroadcast 2/19/78)

Cast: Larry Haines (The Man); Fred Gwynne (The Warden); Ralph Bell (Don); Nat Polen (Karl). Written by Elspeth Eric.

A man who is jailed for battering his disloyal girlfriend assaults a prison guard named Karl and is placed in solitary confinement. Once in an isolated pitch-black cell, the man alternates between nightmares and insomnia, sometimes doubting his own existence. Then Don, a sympathetic guard, tries to comfort him with fabricated good news. However, when Karl returns and accidentally shatters this pretense, the man assaults Karl again, insuring that his stay in solitary will be extended.

1364. "Trilby" (9/30/77; rebroadcast 2/22/78)

Cast: Marian Seldes (Trilby); Ian Martin (Svengali); Mandel Kramer (Billy); Gordon Gould (Sandy). Adapted by James Agate, Jr., based on the 1894 novel by George du Maurier.

While Trilby is modeling for some painters, she gets a migraine headache which a man named Svengali relieves by putting her in a trance. Then Trilby is fine, until years later she again needs him to cure her. But this time, when Svengali hypnotizes her, he makes her into a marvelous singer. Then, Trilby's future depends on Svengali, who suddenly drops dead on stage, leaving her unable to sing and uncertain of her identity and the origin of the bruises on her body.

Notes: Du Maurier's novel, *Trilby,* has been adapted for the big screen more than once, but all under the title of *Svengali.* The 1931 version featured John Barrymore as the mad hypnotist and Marian Marsh as Trilby. In 1955, a British version was released in the theaters with Hildegarde Neff as the victimized singer and Donald Wolfit as Svengali. In 1983, Peter O'Toole starred as Svengali with Jodie Foster as Trilby. The 1983 version was released as a made-for-television film.

1365. "A Matter of Customs" (10/1/77; rebroadcast from 5/19/77)

1366. "Wine, Women and Murder" (10/2/77; rebroadcast from 5/20/77)

1367. "Mother Knows Best" (10/3/77; rebroadcast 2/25/78)

Cast: Bryna Raeburn (Maggie Dawson); Russell Horton (Joe Dawson); Court Benson (Lt. Cassello); Robert Kaliban (Mr. Jedwick). Written by Sam Dann.

When Joe Dawson can't find a job, two hoods offer to let him in on their get-rich-quick scheme, providing he invest a grand. So Joe goes to his wealthy but miserly Uncle Frank to ask for a loan, but becomes outraged by his uncle's patronizing attitude and is overheard by neighbors as he threatens to kill him. Shortly after returning home with the money, Joe is arrested for robbing and murdering his uncle. But Joe swears that when he left his uncle he was alive—a story only his mother believes.

1368. "The Briefcase Blunder" (10/4/77; rebroadcast from 5/23/77)

1369. "The Sea Nymph" (10/5/77; rebroadcast 2/26/78)

Cast: Norman Rose (Morgan Childs); Jada Rowland (Susan Gentry); Paul Hecht (Scott Fallon). Written by Ian Martin.

Morgan Childs, a rich old man who is obsessed with owning beautiful ornaments, hires a driver named Scott Fallon to scan the sea for an ancient statue of a supposedly immortal sea nymph called Thallassia who died as a result of a triangular love affair. When Scott meets Susan Gentry, Morgan Childs' ward, and they fall in love, Morgan is outraged and refuses to release her from his island. Both men know that when Thallassia faced the same choice it ended tragically, and Scott fears the same fate for Susan.

1370. "Transmutation, Inc." (10/6/77; rebroadcast from 5/24/77)

1371. "The Adventure of the Beryl Coronet" (10/7/77; rebroadcast 3/1/78)

Cast: Kevin McCarthy (Sherlock Holmes); Court Benson (Dr. Watson); Russell Horton (Arthur Holder); Catherine Byers (Mary Holder). Adapted by Murray Burnett, based on the 1892 short story by Sir Arthur Conan Doyle.

After a noble family pawns their coronet to a bank in exchange for a 50,000 pound loan, banker Alexander Holder brings it home and locks it up for safe keeping, telling only his immediate family of its hiding place. Holder is later awakened by a noise, and he discovers his son Arthur holding the crown, which is now mangled and missing three stones. Holder infers that Arthur's gambling debts account for his motive, but Holmes thinks Arthur is innocent.

1372. "The Countess" (10/8/77; rebroadcast from 5/26/77)

1373. "Guilty Secret" (10/9/77; rebroadcast from 5/27/77)

1374. "The Actress" (10/10/77; rebroadcast 3/4/78)

Cast: Tammy Grimes (Lorna Barrett); Arnold Moss (Max); Bryna Raeburn (Mother); Larry Haines (Ted Barrett). Written by Elspeth Eric.

Lorna Barrett is playing the lead role in *Medea*, Euripede's tragedy about a woman who kills her sons to spite her husband after he deserted her for another woman. With each performance Lorna becomes more engrossed in her role, subconsciously substituting her present family for Medea's and reaching a point where her husband, Ted, discovers her standing over their 5-year-old son's bed, a knife poised in her hand.

1375. "The Silent Witness" (10/11/77; rebroadcast from 5/30/77)

1376. "The Case of Chateau-Margaux" (10/12/77; rebroadcast 3/5/78)

Cast: Jackson Beck (Charley Nash); William Griffis (Noah Greeley); Bob Dryden (Edgar); Lloyd Battista (Phillip Cramer). Adapted by James Agate, Jr., based on a story by Edgar Allan Poe.

Horace Cramer agrees to house his nephew Phillip because of their kinship, although he dislikes him. After telling Phillip he plans to eliminate him from his will, Cramer sets out for Boston to see his lawyer. Three days later Cramer's horse arrives back to town, riderless and wounded. Charley Nash, Cramer's buddy, takes a search party into the woods to find Cramer, but, mysteriously, Charley is the only one who finds any clues, all of them incriminating Phillip.

1377. "The Boscombe Pool Mystery" (10/13/77; rebroadcast from 5/31/77)

1378. "The People of Sissora" (10/14/77; rebroadcast 3/8/78)

Cast: Ralph Bell (Professor Martin Struve); Evelyn Juster (Regina); William Griffis (Mr. Simpkins). Written by Sam Dann.

While Professor Martin Struve is dining out with his wife Regina, he notices a stranger wearing a scarabaeus pinned to his lapel. The professor tells his disbelieving wife that the scarabaeus is the emblem of Sissora, a hostile society from another galaxy. Struve also insists that he came to Earth on a Sissorian spaceship centuries ago and that, because of his allegiance to mankind, he must kill the stranger to protect the world. Regina thinks her husband has gone mad.

1379. "A God Named Smith" (10/15/77; rebroadcast from 6/2/77)

1380. "The Two-Dollar Murders" (10/16/77; rebroadcast from 6/3/77)

1381. "Return Engagement" (10/17/77; rebroadcast 3/11/78)

Cast: Fred Gwynne (Roy Rayburn); Ann Pitoniak (Gertrude Rayburn); Bob Dryden (Driver); Court Benson (Schmidt). Written by James Agate, Jr.

Roy Rayburn, once a famous Shakespearean actor, is found wandering in his pajamas on the George Washington Bridge. He manages to slip away from the police and purchase some fire tongs in a Manhattan antique shop. Later on, he heads for the Long Island estate owned by his mother whom, he sincerely believes, like Queen Gertrude in *Hamlet*, murdered his father and now must pay for the crime.

Notes: Ann Pitoniak has been in numerous films including *House of Cards* (1992), *Old Enough* (1984), *Best Seller* (1987), *The Wizard of Loneliness* (1988), and *Agnes of God* (1985).

1382. "The Blood Red Wine" (10/18/77; rebroadcast from 6/6/77)

1383. "The Island on Silver Tree Lake" (10/19/77; rebroadcast 3/12/78))

Cast: Patricia Elliott (Pamela Allen); Teri Keane (Vonnie); Earl Hammond (Leroy Larue); Lloyd Battista (Charlie). Written by Victoria Dann.

Pamela Allen fails to heed a policeman's advice and drives too fast on a wet, curvy road. She is knocked unconscious when her car skids into an embankment and, when she awakens, is taken by motorboat to an island resort in Silvertree Lake. The next day she tries to return to her car, but is stopped by a vicious German shepherd dog. She will never, she is told by the resort owners, be allowed to leave the island.

1384. "The Curse of Conscience" (10/20/77; rebroadcast from 6/7/77)

1385. "Sorry to Let You Go" (10/21/77; rebroadcast 3/15/78)

Cast: Mandel Kramer (Walter Hayes); Joan Shay (Birdie); Bryna Raeburn (Louise Hayes); Leon Janney (Ed Portman); Arnold Moss (Mr. Swanson). Written by Ian Martin.

Walter Hayes, told he's being let go in three months because a computer has taken the job he has held for 20 years, hasn't the courage to tell his wife or friends about his predicament. Too old for another job in his field and with family bills piling up, he considers suicide, but he must do it before the three months pass in order for his family to collect his company-financed life insurance.

Notes: Mandel Kramer, who played police chief Bill Marceau on television's *The Edge of Night* for 18 years, commented: "Unlike the parts I play on *Mystery Theater*, Marceau is as honest as the day is long. In television, you are cast according to the way you look, but in radio it's how you sound. I'm not the popular concept of a heavy, yet on *Mystery Theater* I can be. It's the theater of the imagination."

1386. "Dialogue with Death" (10/22/77; rebroadcast from 6/9/77)

1387. "The Night We Died" (10/23/77; rebroadcast from 6/10/77)

1388. "Trial for Murder" (10/24/77; rebroadcast 3/18/78)

Cast: Paul Hecht (Charles); Earl Hammond (William); Court Benson (Mr. Harker); Robert Maxwell (Judge). Adapted by James Agate, Jr., based on the 1865 short story *To Be Taken With a Grain of Salt* by Charles Dickens.

In their murder-mystery, two authors plan to have the victim's throat slit from ear-to-ear by a razor. As they begin work on the book, both are called as jurors to a case in which the accused allegedly committed his crime in the same manner. They have already had visions of the victim pursuing the murderer down a London street. As the trial progresses, the spirit of the victim will not let them alone, not only in the courtroom but every night as they go to bed.

1389. "Just to Keep Busy" (10/25/77; rebroadcast 3/19/78)

Cast: Bob Dryden (Frank Gilmore); Judy Lewis (Lizzie Wentworth); Larry Haines (Woody Wallace); Evelyn Juster (Sally Schaefer). Written by Sam Dann.

Woody Wallace, engaged to Sally Schaefer, a dress designer living in Paris, has an affair, "just to keep busy," with Lizzie Wentworth, the secretary of his best friend, Frank Gilmore. Woody even asks Lizzie to marry him, knowing that Sally is soon coming home for their wedding. When Lizzie learns the truth, she jumps overboard from a sailboat at night, and Woody is accused of her murder. He hopes Sally will be the chief witness in his defense.

1390. "First Woman in Space" (10/26/77; rebroadcast from 6/13/77)

1391. "The House by the Seine" (10/27/77; rebroadcast 3/22/78)

Cast: Marian Seldes (Marianne Duvier); Hetty Galen (Annette); Gilbert Mack (Inspector Tirot); William Griffis (Armand Claudet). Written by Ian Martin.

Marianne Duvier, a beautiful French actress idolized by all men, is surprised when she arrives at her home near the Seine River by an unexpected birthday party. She is more surprised when she receives a box containing orchids and a recently fired revolver. But, for some reason, she is not surprised by the arrival of a police inspector, suggesting that she may be responsible for the death, earlier in the evening, of her leading man.

1392. "A Question of Identity" (10/28/77; rebroadcast 3/25/78)

Cast: Russell Horton (Paul Chapin); Ian Martin (Bernard); Jackson Beck (Hans Koppell); Bryna Raeburn (Hulda). Written by Roy Winsor.

Paul Chapin, in Amsterdam to deliver 1,000 uncut diamonds, arranges for the jewels to be locked in his hotel's safe for the night. While in his room resting before dinner, drugged wine is delivered by his chambermaid, and he awakens in the morning to find his clothes, passport and the diamonds missing. Because he cannot identify himself, he is accused of being an imposter who probably had a hand in the theft of the jewels.

1393. "Murder One" (10/29/77; rebroadcast from 6/14/77)

1394. "Little Lucy's Lethal Libation" (10/30/77; rebroadcast from 6/16/77)

1395. "Trial by Fire" (10/31/77; rebroadcast 3/26/78)

Cast: Michael Tolan (Brad Stuart); Evelyn Juster (Christine); Norman Rose (Tom Hendricks). Written by Nancy Moore.

After reading how the natives of an Indian island are expecting a white man to come and walk across a bed of burning coals, thus becoming their high priest, con man Brad Stuart talks his scientist friend, Tom Hendricks, into inventing a potion to protect his bare feet from intense heat. Stuart goes to the island, certain that after he fire-walks the natives will not only make him their high priest, but will also present him with their solid gold, richly jeweled, fire-god idol.

1396. "Last Train Out" (11/1/77; rebroadcast 3/29/78)

Cast: Anne Williams (Diana Sherwood); Ian Martin (Dr. Akduz); Bob Dryden (Serpiakov); Earl Hammond (Bob Hart). Written by Ian Martin.

Star television reporter Diana Sherwood and her favorite cameraman, Bob Hart, working on a documentary about Turkey, are given medical aid after an auto accident in a remote part of the country by a Turkish doctor, Bulent Akduz. Another guest (in hiding) at the doctor's house is Serpiakov, a top man in the Russian politburo. Wanted by both Communists and anti–Communists, Serpiakov appeals to the Americans to help him escape to Paris and ultimate freedom in the United States.

1397. "Two Motives for Murder" (11/2/77; rebroadcast from 6/17/77)

1398. "Land of the Living Dead" (11/3/77; rebroadcast 4/1/78)

Cast: Don Scardino (Kenty Floyd); Arnold Moss (Hans Schneider); Carol Teitel (Lilith); Russell Horton (Terry Bridgewater). Written by Arnold Moss.

Kent Floyd and Terry Bridgewater fly their plane to Cuyaba to pick up supplies for their trip into the Brazilian jungle, where a tribe of white-skinned Indians is said to live. They are told that these Indians possess a powerful magic that causes a person to see the most unusual things. To be sure, the anthropologists first see a modern airport in the middle of the jungle. After they land they see an arrivals gate, but, to their horror, no departure gate.

Notes: Don Scardino can be seen in the films *Squirm* (1976) and *He Knows You're Alone* (1980).

1399. "The Final Judgment" (11/4/77; rebroadcast 4/2/78)

Cast: Gordon Heath (King Solomon); Bryna Raeburn (Bathsheba); Ralph Bell (Abiel); Nat Polen (Benjamin); Roger De Koven (Joseph). Written by Sam Dann.

Three merchants—Joseph, Abiel and Benjamin—returning together from Damascus to Jerusalem and afraid of being robbed, put their coins and jewels in a purse which they bury each night. One morning the purse is gone, and each swears he did not dig it up. King Solomon, Israel's top dispenser of justice, has trouble determining who is guilty until he comes up with a ploy he's certain will unmask the culprit.

Notes: Unbeknownst to most listeners, this story, involving the biblical King Solomon, was not taken directly from the Bible.

1400. "The Birthmark" (11/5/77; rebroadcast from 6/20/77)

1401. "Tomorrow, Cloudy and Cold" (11/6/77; rebroadcast from 6/21/77)

1402. "The Therapeutic Cat" (11/7/77; rebroadcast 4/5/78)

Cast: Fred Gywnne (Henry Joyce); Bryna Raeburn (Mrs. Bingham); Jada Rowland (Denny Bingham); Paul Hecht (Jack Joyce). Written by Elspeth Eric.

Henry Joyce, a wealthy man, initially thinks his son Jack has gone bananas, but when his condition worsens he follows Jack's advice: to get a cat and imitate it, because a cat is the most relaxed of all animals. Miraculously, Henry begins to feel better and ultimately becomes so fond of the cat that, much to his son's consternation, he decides to change his will, leaving much of his fortune to the therapeutic feline.

1403. "The Haunted Mill" (11/8/77; rebroadcast 4/8/78)

Cast: Ralph Bell (Dr. James Patmore); Russell Horton (Charley Royce); Court Benson (John Royce); Patricia Elliott (Hannah Bliss). Adapted by James Agate, Jr., based on a story by Richard Donovan.

Dr. James Patmore refuses to believe the story of young Charley Royce, back home after three years at sea. Charley comes to the doctor one dark night, suffering from a severe head wound. He says he was hit while passing an abandoned mill which, he claims, has been inhabited for years by ghosts. Dr. Patmore has no use for such stories of the supernatural, but he does agree to accompany Charley on a midnight visit to the run-down building.

1404. "The Red Circle" (11/9/77; rebroadcast from 6/23/77)

1405. "A Tale of Two Worlds" (11/10/77; rebroadcast 4/9/78)

Cast: Robert Kaliban (Eddie Smith); Augusta Dabney (Marcia Bryce); Ian Martin (Brock Chalmers); Bob Dryden (Henley Davis). Written by Ian Martin.

Eddie Smith, who has played Timmy Brice in the soap opera *For All Seasons,* for 13 years (since he was 7), is shocked to learn that he's going to be "killed" on the program. Because his mother ran away with another man and his father committed suicide, Eddie's only life has been the one he has led in his role on *For All Seasons.* He becomes so distraught that he threatens violence—either to the show's producer or to himself.

1406. "We Meet Again" (11/11/77; rebroadcast 4/12/78)

Cast: Teri Keane (Anne Kovacs); Larry Haines (Harry Kovacs); Lloyd Battista (Lieutenant Jordan); Catherine Byers (Carrie Drake); Earl Hammond (Dick). Written by Sam Dann.

Anne Kovacs is shocked when her detective husband Harry tells her he has, after three months of leg work, solved the murder of a well-known actress. Although Harry doesn't know it, Anne was once engaged to Jeff Parker, the man Harry has arrested. Anne realizes that Jeff has long been a playboy, but is certain that he is incapable of committing murder. Without telling Harry, she starts her own investigation to prove Jeff innocent.

1407. "Fan Mail" (11/12/77; rebroadcast from 6/24/77)

1408. "Come, Fill My Cup" (11/13/77; rebroadcast from 6/27/77)

1409. "The Gloria Scott" (11/14/77; rebroadcast 4/15/78)

Cast: Kevin McCarthy (Sherlock Holmes); Court Benson (Dr. Watson); Paul Hecht (Victor Tervor); William Griffis (Sir James Trevor). Adapted by Ralph Goodman, based on the 1893 short story by Sir Arthur Conan Doyle.

Sherlock Holmes is challenged by elderly, wealthy Sir James Trevor, during their first meeting, to put his fabled deductive powers to a test—to tell what he can about Sir James' hidden past. Holmes is so accurate that Sir James turns pale and demands to be put to bed. What Holmes has begun to uncover is why the *Gloria Scott*, on which Sir James was a passenger, was mysteriously lost at sea.

1410. "A Point in Time" (11/15/77; rebroadcast 4/16/78)

Cast: Norman Rose (General Morgan); Jackson Beck (Dr. Otto Segrim); Ralph Bell (Colonel Paul); Evelyn Juster (Leta). Written by Victoria Dann.

Dr. Otto Segrim makes sure that he is arrested for treason by Gen. Franklin Ulysses Morgan's elite guard. He then plots to have his sister, Leta, trick the general into shaking her poisoned-gloved hand. The general will die within hours unless he accepts the professor's offer to send him back to a point in time where he can have a chance to decide not to become a dictator.

1411. "Dead Men Do Tell Tales" (11/16/77; rebroadcast from 6/30/77)

1412. "Hunted Down" (11/17/77; rebroadcast 4/19/78)

Cast: Gordon Heath (Edgar Simpson); Bob Dryden (Julius Slinkton); Patricia Elliott (Marguerite); Earl Hammond (Meltham). Adapted by James Agate, Jr., based on the 1850 short story by Charles Dickens.

Julius Slinkton has purchased insurance policies from London Life for his two nieces and a friend, in each case naming himself the beneficiary. When one of his nieces, only 23, dies while with him in Italy, Slinkton is suspected of foul play by the London Life agent who sold him the policy. The agent must not only prove his assumption but prevent Slinkton from doing away with the other two policyholders.

1413. "A Grain of Salt" (11/18/77; rebroadcast 4/22/78)

Cast: Teri Keane (Katie O'Neil); Fred Gwynne (Terence O'Neil); Bryna Raeburn (Bridget O'Neil); Lloyd Battista (Sergeant Smith). Written by Sam Dann.

Sgt. Smith, himself half-Irish, doesn't quite believe Katie O'Neil's story about her loss of a salt shaker, from which salt always flows freely. He's much more interested in taking her to a concert by John Philip Sousa's band. But when he hears how her father, Terrence, acquired the salt shaker in Ireland, thinking it was going to make him rich for life, the sergeant agrees to lend a hand in its recovery.

1414. "Revenge" (11/19/77; rebroadcast from 7/1/77)

1415. "The Adventure of the Speckled Band" (11/20/77; rebroadcast from 6/28/77)

1416. "She" (11/21/77; rebroadcast 4/23/78)

Cast: Gordon Gould (Leo Vincey); Joan Shay (She); William Griffis (Job); Gordon Heath (Uncle Holly). Adapted by Roy Winsor, based on the 1887 novel by H. Rider Haggard.

Leo Vincey, 25, and his uncle Holly open a small iron chest containing Leo's father's legacy, ordering Leo to go to Africa and slay the queen who had murdered Killikrates, dead for over 2,000 years and a direct ancestor of Leo's. Holly and Leo set sail and after much adventure come face-to-face with She, the very old but young-looking and beautiful Queen whom the natives say must be obeyed. But instead of killing the beguiling woman, Leo falls in love with her.

Notes: H. Rider Haggard wrote numerous fantasy and adventure stories, most notably *The Ghost Kings* and *King Solomon's Mines. She* was adapted for the big screen as a silent film in 1917 and later remade in 1926 and 1935 (with Helen Gahagan in the role of eternal queen). Hammer Studios in Britain filmed the fourth version in 1965 with Ursula Andress as the queen, teaming with Peter Cushing and Christopher Lee. This was followed by a sequel-remake three years later titled *The Vengeance of She.* In Italy, Sandahl Bergman played the queen role, filmed in 1982 and released in 1985.

1417. "Boomerang" (11/22/77; rebroadcast from 7/4/77)

1418. "The Pinkerton Method" (11/23/77; rebroadcast 4/26/78)

Cast: Ian Martin (William Pinkerton); Lloyd Battista (Robert Pinkerton); Nat Polen (Harold Black); Earl Hammond (George Newton). Adapted by James Agate, Jr., based on actual files from the Pinkerton Agency.

The true story of the first private detective force in the United States. A Rock

Island train carrying $22,000 in cash is robbed, and the express car's agent murdered. William Pinkerton, son of the founder of the Pinkerton National Detective Agency and a passenger on the train, agrees to track down the guilty. After leaving for a few days to investigate another train robbery, he returns to the Rock Island case to put to work, in a seemingly casual manner, the Pinkerton method: "diligence, doggedness, studying character, knowing your man."

Notes: Nat Polen played Dr. James Craig, chief of staff of Llandview Hospital and a pillar of strength in the community on the daytime television soap opera *One Life to Live*.

1419. "Hexed" (11/24/77; rebroadcast from 7/5/77)

1420. "Indian Giver" (11/25/77; rebroadcast 4/29/78)

Cast: Fred Gywnne (Spencer Smallwood); Mary Jane Higby (Victoria Soames); Bob Dryden (Jitters); Bryna Raeburn (Miss Dowdy). Written by Sam Dann.

Haughty Mrs. Victoria Soames foresees disaster for her social standing when a ghost scares away not only her servants, but worse, all of her socialite friends. Though she refuses to believe in ghosts, Mrs. Soames does hire private investigator Spencer Smallwood to drive out whatever's haunting her house. Her main fear: that before he does so, her archrival, Mrs. Van Poundsworth, will have taken her place at the top of the social register.

1421. "A Stranger Among Us" (11/26/77; rebroadcast from 7/7/77)

1422. "The Gift" (11/27/77; rebroadcast from 7/8/77)

1423. "The Man Is Missing" (11/28/77; rebroadcast 4/30/78)

Cast: Anne Williams (Mia McLaughlin); Larry Haines (Ben Chase); Teri Keane (Irma Chase); Ralph Bell (Captain Caldwell). Written by Elspeth Eric.

Ben Chase is assigned to find the missing husband of photographic model Mia McLaughlin. Ben's wife, Irma, has long been fascinated by psychographology, the study of handwriting, and when Mia receives a note from her missing spouse, Irma analyzes it and declares he could be paranoid. When a second note arrives, Irma deduces from it that its writer is also capable of committing murder, with either Ben or Mia the intended victim.

1424. "A Scandal in Bohemia" (11/29/77; rebroadcast from 7/11/77)

1425. "The Teddy Bear" (11/30/77; rebroadcast 5/3/78)

Cast: Michael Wager (Jack Woods); Court Benson (Bob Buckley); Martha Greenhouse (Dr. Kessler); Ian Martin (Ambassador). Written by James Agate, Jr.

Jack Woods' editor suspects that the Russians were somehow involved in the mysterious explosion of a U.S. spacecraft as it descended toward the Pacific Ocean; all that landed was a teddy bear. During an interview with the Russian ambassador, Woods learns about a newly arrived Russian scientist, Dr. Gerda Kessler, an expert in psychic warfare. His interview with her concludes when he walks through what he thinks is her front door and gets locked in a detaining room.

1426. "The Colonel Chabert" (12/1/77; rebroadcast from 7/12/77)

1427. "Neatness Counts" (12/2/77; rebroadcast 5/6/78)

Cast: Ralph Bell (Aeneas Carlyle); Joan Shay (Harriet Paulson); Robert Maxwell (Lieutenant Rienzo); Evelyn Juster (Joanna); Earl Hammond (Bowers). Written by Sam Dann.

In just one morning, Aeneas Carlyle callously tosses a faithful servant into the street, provokes his valuable housekeeper into quitting, infuriates a highly idealistic young man, and tightens the screws on a business associate. The next morning he is found murdered in his study. Two of these people admit they wanted to kill the despicable Carlyle and are arrested, but the police soon realize they don't have the right person.

1428. "A Matter of Conscience" (12/3/77; rebroadcast from 7/14/77)

1429. "The Kingdom Below" (12/4/77; rebroadcast from 7/15/77)

1430. "The Lost Tomorrows" (12/5/77; rebroadcast 5/7/78)

Cast: Mandel Kramer (Matthew Karling); Anne Williams (Rena Karling); Arnold Moss (Hunac); Elizabeth Lathram (Maria). Written by Stella Moss.

Despite the warnings of elderly Hunac and his granddaughter Maria, Matthew and Rena Karling, in search of Mayan artifacts, make plans to explore the Cave of Lost Tomorrows, a cavers' paradise in the Mexican state of Yucatan. Hunac, who claims he can speak to his dead ancestors, fears for the Karlings' safety. "Things you take from caves," he says, "belong to dead ancestors. ... not the living world."

1431. "The Bisara of Pooree" (12/6/77; rebroadcast from 7/18/77)

1432. "Fire and Ice" (12/7/77; rebroadcast 5/10/78)

Cast: Fred Gwynne (J.J. Trelawney); Marian Haley (Marcella Trelawney); Earl Hammond (William Stillman); Lloyd Battista (Edward Wilson). Written by Sam Dann.

Marcella Trelawney, living in 1912, is ordered by her rich father, J.J., to marry his business associate, William Stillman. But she loves Edward Wilson, an astronomer. To help him decide who should have her hand, J.J. asks Wilson and Stillman to accompany him on a trip to the Arctic, rugged enough to test any man.

J.J., testing himself, disappears in a blizzard. Wilson finds him, frozen to death, and his diary, which contains his decision on who should marry Marcella.

Notes: Lloyd Battista noted,"Radio gives the actor a flexibility that rarely occurs in television or film. Few actors can play a 40-year-old man one day and then a 90-year-old man the next ... except in radio."

1433. "The Mysterious Island" (12/8/77; rebroadcast from 7/19/77)

1434. "This Time Around" (12/9/77; rebroadcast 5/13/78)

Cast: Gordon Heath (Kenneth B. Sturgis); William Griffis (Steven J. Tread-well); Teri Keane (Della Downing); Bryna Raeburn (Miss Magruder). Written by Sam Dann.

Kenneth B. Sturgis, one of the ten most powerful businessmen in America, is fired because of his scandalous private life and failure to cooperate with his board of directors. At the same time, he hears voices telling him that because of high crimes against the people, he—a Middle Ages nobleman—has been condemned to die. In both lives, real and illusory, he vows to fight back, even if he must commit murder.

1435. "Rendezvous with Death" (12/10/77; rebroadcast from 7/21/77)

1436. "The Secret of the Aztecs" (12/11/77; rebroadcast from 7/22/77)

1437. "The Ten Million Dollar Heist" (12/12/77; rebroadcast 5/14/78)

Cast: Joseph Silver (Big Jake); Skip Hinnant (Tommy); Bob Dryden (Big Tom). Written by James Agate, Jr.

Big Tom Noonan, just out of Sing Sing, meets Big Jake Erdman in Philadelphia during the U.S. Centennial and, with him, makes plans to break through the walls of the Customs House clock room into the adjoining Sub-Treasury building's vault. Their aim: to heist ten million in gold, silver and bills. Noonan's son, Tommy, is invited to join them (he needs some experience). But his one swing with a sledgehammer is a near disaster. He not only hits his father's hand, but the chisel files into the clock's works and stops it.

1438. "The Adventure of the Blue Carbuncle" (12/13/77; rebroadcast from 7/25/77)

1439. "The Death Shot" (12/14/77; rebroadcast 5/17/78)

Cast: Michael Tolan (Bob Paisley); Ann Williams (Diana Paisley); Jackson Beck (Major Malas); Court Benson (Dean Canby). Written by Ian Martin.

Bob Paislety sets up his camera to photograph the Parthenon. As he begins to shoot, a man falls from the top of the temple's ruins. Bob's new wife, Diana, claims the man was pushed. When the films are developed, Diana is proven to be correct. The pusher is shown to be Major Constantin Malas, chief hatchet man of the new dictatorship. The Paisleys realize what might happen to them if they take the photos to the authorities, but they do so anyway.

1440. "The Rocket's Red Glare" (12/15/77; rebroadcast from 7/26/77)

1441. "The Ghost with a Knife" (12/16/77; rebroadcast 5/20/78)

Cast: Arnold Moss (Bryce Bond); Patricia Elliott (Rebecca Green); Robert Kaliban (David Enters); Gordon Gould (Leo Green). Written by James Agate, Jr.

Leo and Rebecca Green, a young couple living in Mineola, New York, request that Bryce Bond, a well-known psychic scientist and investigator of the supernatural, help them rid their house of a six-foot-tall ghost who, they say, has a beard, wears olive green pants and carries a long knife in his hand. What happened one night while Bond and a friend, who was both a medium and a photographer, were inside the Greens' house is dramatized during this broadcast.

1442. "The Secret of Laurels" (12/17/77; rebroadcast from 7/28/77)

1443. "The Thousand and First Door" (12/18/77; rebroadcast from 7/29/77)

1444. "Brothers of the Angle" (12/19/77; rebroadcast 5/21/78)

Cast: Ralph Bell (Billy Falcon); Joan Shea (Mrs. Buttweiser); Evelyn Juster (Sally Magruder). Written by Sam Dann.

Henrietta Augusta Buttweiser, rich and widowed, takes pity on "down-trodden" door-to-door salesperson Sally Magruder and invites her in. Mrs. Buttweiser believes her dead husband, Charles, is desperately trying to reach her and tells Sally so. She also describes in detail her late husband's habits, information that Sally takes to Billy Falcon, her con-man boyfriend. Billy wants to use it when he tries to convince Mrs. Buttweiser that he has been in contact with Charles and can serve as a conduit between them—for a price, or course.

1445. "Hope Springs Eternal" (12/20/77; rebroadcast from 8/8/77)

1446. "The Big Ten-Cent Hustle" (12/21/77; rebroadcast 5/24/78)

Cast: Earl Hammond (The Dime); Bob Dryden (Joe); Bryna Raeburn (Maggie); William Griffis (Mr. Treskit); Russell Horton (The Philanthropist). Written by Sam Dann.

The "talking" dime, fresh from the mint, goes from a bank to a philanthropist, who gives it to Joe and Maggie, a broke and unemployed couple. On their way to take a job as a chauffeur and maid, Joe gives the dime, their last, to a beggar, who realizes the coin's value. When Joe and Maggie learn that their new boss has heard about the coin and is willing to pay $2,500 for it, Joe vows to take it back from the beggar—even if it means he has to murder him to get it.

1447. "Case Closed" (12/22/77; rebroadcast from 8/10/77)

1448. "The Witching Well" (12/23/77; rebroadcast 5/27/78)

Cast: Paul Hecht (Patrick Kinsella); Carol Teitel (Boann Connaught); Ian Martin (Ephraim Wyatt). Written by Ian Martin.

Patrick Kinsella is instructed in a letter from his recently deceased father to continue paying $800 a month to one Boann Connaught, who lives in Branwell, Ireland. Because such a payment amounts to nearly $10,000 a year and because he has no idea who Boann Connaught is, Patrick journeys to the Emerald Isle. In Branwell, he meets Boann, a little wisp of a woman who reluctantly tells him a story he can scarcely believe.

1449. "A Christmas Carol" (12/24/77; rebroadcast from 12/24/76)

1450. "For Want of a Nail" (12/25/77; rebroadcast from 8/12/77)

1451. "The Ghosts of Yesterday" (12/26/77; rebroadcast 5/28/78)

Cast: Teri Keane (Marge Stafford); Russell Horton (Steve Stafford); Leon Janney (Valarius Koslo); Mandel Kramer (Harry Warren). Written by Victoria Dann.

Marge Stafford, wife of a successful American businessman, is urged by a former member of the World War II underground to identify one Harry Warren as former SS Captain Hans Dietrich. Marge, at the age of 8, was the only one not killed when Dietrich ordered the entire population of Hammenbiere annihilated. Even though she has withheld her past from her husband, Marge is willing to cooperate if she is not asked to do it publicly. But then her husband announces he just concluded a major business deal with one Mr. Harry Warren.

1452. "The Together Place" (12/27/77; rebroadcast from 8/15/77)

1453. "The Missouri Kid" (12/28/77; rebroadcast 5/31/78)

Cast: Lloyd Battista (C.J. and Dan Schumacher); Evelyn Juster (Nellie); Russell Horton (Sheriff); Ian Martin (William Pinkerton); Robert Maxwell (The Missouri Kid). Written by James Agate, Jr.

A Pinkerton detective attempts to apprehend, in the early 1900s, Missouri's most-wanted criminal. Rudy Randolph, also known as "The Missouri Kid," robbed the Union, Missouri, bank of $28,000. C.J., the detective, tracks The Kid to his sister Nellie's place, identifies him, and later returns with a posse. In the ensuing gunfight, C.J. is wounded and then killed in cold blood by The Kid. His brother vows to shoot the murderer on sight, but is reminded that Pinkerton men always observe the law in their pursuit of criminals.

1454. "In the Fog" (12/29/77; rebroadcast from 8/17/77)

1455. "The Ninth Volume" (12/30/77; rebroadcast 6/3/78)

Cast: Michael Wager (John Perk); Court Benson (Milo Hawkins); Bob Dryden (Sharkey). Written by Percy Granger.

While drilling for oil on the western slopes of the Rocky Mountains in the year 1998, geologist John Perk is amazed by the reddish dust drawn up from 19,967 feet. When it reaches the earth's surface, the dust evaporates. Reaching through caves the spot where the drilling stopped, Perk is even more astonished by what he sees: a modern house encased in rock with bedrooms, bathroom, books, even a TV set, all of which he figures must be over 12 billion years old.

Notes: Michael Wager has appeared in such films as *Hill 24 Doesn't Answer* (1955), *Exodus* (1960), and *Jane Austen in Manhattan* (1980).

1456. "The Instrument" (12/31/77; rebroadcast from 8/19/77)

1457. "Return to Pompeii" (1/1/78; rebroadcast from 8/22/77)

Cast: Marian Seldes (Jennifer Matthews); Patricia Elliott (Olga Peterson); Paul Hecht (Paulus); Larry Haines (Milos). Written by Victoria Dann.

Jennifer Matthews, depressed by the death of her husband, half heartedly agrees to take a summer tour of Italy with her friend, Olga Peterson. One minute they are standing in the midst of the ancient ruins of Pompeii and, in the next moment, Olga is gone, the ruins have disappeared and in their place stands the old town, alive again. Jennifer tries to warn her new friends about the impending destruction of Pompeii, but nobody believes her.

1458. "Peter, Peter, Pumpkin Eater" (1/2/78; rebroadcast 6/4/78)

Cast: Fred Gwynne (Peter Perkins); Bryna Raeburn (Charity); Arnold Moss (Bartender); Earl Hammond (Fats Fergonzie). Written by Sam Dann.

Peter Perkins, whom people keep calling Peter Pumpkin, is a daydreamer. He imagines himself, at different times, a military hero, a miracle-working surgeon and baseball's leading home-run hitter. When he is approached in a saloon by a beautiful blonde, he thinks it's just another dream. But this is for real, and mobster Fats Fergonzie warns him to walk away from her—or else. Perkins laughs in his face. He who laughs in the face of danger...

1459. "The Adventures of Don Quixote" (1/3/78; rebroadcast from 8/24/77)

1460. "Family Album" (1/4/78; rebroadcast 6/7/78)

Cast: Paul Hecht (Joe Smith); Nat Polen (Ned Powers); William Griffis (Andre Canuet); Ray Owens (Marco Hestos). Written by Roy Winsor.

Reporter Joe Smith gets the scoop on a drowning in New York's Pelham Bay of Marco Hestos, the most-wanted international crook. Because little is known of Hestos' past, Smith is sent by his newspaper to Europe to find out all he can.

He quickly learns that certain people don't want him to conduct such an investigation. He manages to outwit them, but while in Nicosia discovers the fact about his own early life he finds hard to believe.

1461. "Area Thirteen" (1/5/78; rebroadcast from 8/26/77)

1462. "Dracula" (1/6/78; rebroadcast from 7/27/74)

1463. "Frankenstein Revisited" (1/7/78; rebroadcast from 12/6/74)

1464. "Dr. Jekyll and Mr. Hyde" (1/8/78; rebroadcast from 9/4/74)

1465. "The Picture of Dorian Gray" (1/9/78; rebroadcast from 10/5/74)

1466. "The Black Room" (1/10/78; rebroadcast from 12/21/74)

1467. "The Hand" (1/11/78; rebroadcast from 7/14/74)

1468. "Goodbye, Karl Erich" (1/12/78; rebroadcast from 11/18/75)

1469. "The Laughing Maiden" (1/13/78; rebroadcast 6/10/78)
Cast: Norman Rose (Jason Hanesworth); Arnold Moss (Tom Cooper); William Griffis (Ernie Chowders). Written by Percy Granger.
Three men in the charter boat business set out for the Bahamian island of Caicos, on which Captain Kidd reputedly buried the single richest prize ever taken by a pirate on the Spanish Main. They make several trips to Caicos and each time, shortly after their arrival, espy a large ship's mast on the horizon. They're sure the ship belongs to the Syndicate, which, they fear, is making plans to seize the treasure, if and when they find it.

1470. "To Be a Rose" (1/14/78; rebroadcast from 8/29/77)

1471. "The Reunion" (1/15/78; rebroadcast from 8/31/77)

1472. "In Another Place" (1/16/78; rebroadcast 6/11/78)
Cast: Fred Gwynne (Sheriff Morrison); Evelyn Juster (Tamar Hartsfield); Court Benson (Ben Blakenship); Gilbert Mack (Percy). Written by Sam Dann.
Tamar Hartsfield and her boyfriend, Ben Blakenship, are outraged when Sheriff Joe Morrison tells them he knows, but can't prove, they murdered Tamar's rich, elderly husband. Both have perfect alibis: They were somewhere else when the crime was committed. But Morrison persists and ultimately comes upon a tiny, insignificant loose end that Tamar and Ben failed to realize could be their undoing.

1473. "A Model Murderer" (1/17/78; rebroadcast 6/13/78)

Cast: Larry Haines (Lew Richmond); Marian Seldes (Phoebe Richmond); Ian Martin (Sergeant Quinn); Earl Hammond (Lieutenant Matthews); Catherine Byers (Athena Blackwell). Written by Ian Martin.

Lew Richmond, known in police headquarters across the country as Phil the Flash, has used the line on 17 beautiful young women that he is a famous photographer who can make them even more famous than he. At the same time, he has taken them for some 35 to 40 grand. But when he tries it on number 18, she fights back, and during a struggle in his hotel room he accidentally kills her. Now the police vow to put a quick end to his career.

1474. "Olive Darling and Morton Dear" (1/18/78; rebroadcast from 9/2/77)

1475. "Sophia and the Pilgrim" (1/19/78; rebroadcast 6/15/78)

Cast: Gordon Heath (Ivan Trepolov); Jada Rowland (Sophia); Russell Horton (Abdrei); Bryna Raeburn (Madame Karpovna); Bob Dryden (Boris). Adapted by C. Frederic Lewis, based on a story by Ivan Turgenev.

Ivan Trepolov, a census taker from Moscow, visits his former university classmate, Boris, whose daughter, Sophia, is intrigued by the powers of an illiterate "holyman" who, for a price, can show people their deceased friends and relatives. Boris is concerned because the eldest daughters of the two of his closest friends consulted this man and, three days later, disappeared forever.

1476. "The Enchanted Child" (1/20/78; rebroadcast 6/17/78)

Cast: Ralph Bell (Ed Bristol); Teri Keane (Maida Bristol); Evelyn Juster (Grandma); Adam Ross (Mark Bristol); Don Scardino (Pastor). Written by Elspeth Eric.

Every time young Mark Bristol hears disparaging remarks about someone, he excuses himself and goes to his room. Within minutes the person who was being discussed dies. First, it's his grandfather, then his grandmother and then his father's boss. Concerned over these strange happenings, Mark's father, Ed, visits the family's minister to ask for advice. After the meeting, Ed, not feeling well, staggers into the path of an oncoming truck. Ten-year-old Mark, thinks he is God, but seems to have more of the devil in him than he knows.

Notes: Teri Keane "Whether or not you look the part, you can portray it on radio. You just have to have it *in* you."

1477. "The Waiting Room" (1/21/78; rebroadcast from 9/5/77)

1478. "Silent Shock" (1/22/78 rebroadcast from 9/7/77)

1479. "The Forgetful Ghost" (1/23/78; rebroadcast 6/18/78)

Cast: Mandel Kramer (Sam Gordon); Martha Greenhouse (Eve Gordon); Ian Martin (Peter Pruitt); Jackson Beck (Cop). Written by Ian Martin.

Sam Gordon hopes he and his wife Eve will celebrate their 40th wedding anniversary before she dies. While preparing a cup of hot chocolate for her one evening, Sam is accosted by Peter Pruitt, who claims he's a ghost. Sam fears Pruitt has been sent to take Eve, but Pruitt is not so sure. But he does save Sam's life, helps him win back $10,000 from a crooked gambler, and then makes him an offer he cannot refuse.

Notes: Mandel Kramer, veteran of numerous radio shows, stars as Sam in this hauntingly good episode of *Theater*. Kramer played insurance detective Johnny Dollar for a while on CBS's *Yours Truly, Johnny Dollar*. He often played the roles of police officers on such shows as *Gangbusters*, *The Shadow*, and *Inner Sanctum*.

1480. "The Ranee of Rajputana" (1/24/78; rebroadcast 6/20/78)

Cast: Kevin McCarthy (Leander Garrison); Marian Seldes (The Ranee); Joan Shay (Mrs. MacNiece); Earl Hammond (Sergeant Cassano). Written by Sam Dann.

Socialite Mrs. MacNiece calls on her investment counselor, the brilliant Leander Garrison, and demands he return her $2 million. She accuses him of being a common thief, because the night before during a party at her apartment she saw him put a small statue in his pocket. The statue is of the Ranee of Rajputana, the Queen of Thieves. Later, the statue comes to life and points out to the penniless Garrison that the only way he can settle with Mrs. MacNiece is to kill her.

1481. "The Woman in the Green Dress" (1/25/78; rebroadcast from 9/9/77)

1482. "The Safety Match" (1/26/78; rebroadcast 6/22/78)

Cast: Bob Dryden (Chubikoff); Russell Horton (Dukovski); Court Benson (Andrei); Bryna Raeburn (Maria). Adapted by Percy Granger, based on a short story by Anton Chekhov.

Informed of the murder of Major Klausoff, a retired officer of the Horse Guards, a small Russian town's pompous examining magistrate and his discerning secretary immediately begin an investigation. They know Klausoff was an infamous drunkard, philanderer and gambler who could have been murdered by any number of people. Their most important clue is a safety match, a rarity 100 years ago in Russia.

1483. "The Defectors" (1/27/78; rebroadcast 6/24/78)

Cast: Fred Gwynne (Sen. Hotchkiss); Bryna Raeburn (Chickie); Robert Kaliban (Milrose); Kenneth Harvey (Comrade Snapper). Written by Sam Dann.

Sen. Luther K. Hotchkiss and his paramour, Chickie Paradise, are picked up when their car breaks down outside Washington by John J. Milrose, an agent for a Communist country. Hotchkiss doesn't know it, but his wife, Marguerite, is having an affair with Milrose, who has been sent to America to somehow blackmail Hotchkiss into introducing a bill in the Senate which would give back to Mexico the states of Texas, California, and Arizona.

1484. "First Childhood" (1/28/78; rebroadcast from 9/12/77)

1485. "The Way to Dusty Death" (1/29/78; rebroadcast from 9/13/77)

1486. "Yesterday's Giant" (1/30/78; rebroadcast 6/25/78)

Cast: Norman Rose (Jim MacLane); Howard Ross (Captain Arthur Fairfield); Ralph Bell (Richard Gidding). Written by G. Frederic Lewis.

Amateur anthropologist Richard Gidding excitedly tells his old friend, naturalist Jim MacLane, that a recent underground nuclear explosion in Nevada had flushed out from a remote cave a family of giant prehistoric Neanderthals. Gidding wants Jim to go back to the cave area with him during the next test blast. Jim agrees, but is greatly disappointed when Giddings admits his prime purpose is to capture the family alive so he can make money exhibiting them.

1487. "The Ice Palace" (1/31/78; rebroadcast 6/27/78)

Cast: Tony Roberts (Captain Joe Gates); Earl Hammond (Kullabak); Ian Martin (Colonel Edward Champ); Arnold Moss (Raven). Written by Percy Granger.

While trying to find the reasons for the sudden appearance of open water in many normally frozen sections of the Arctic, causing Russia and the United States to hurl verbal charges at each other, Captain Joe Gates and his Eskimo friend, Kullabak, fall into a deep crevasse. They are met below by a man living in an ice palace who calls himself Raven and who claims he has invented a machine, using the laser beam principle, with which he plans to flood the entire Earth.

Notes: Tony Roberts, who plays Captain Joe Gates in this episode, was currently on the big screen in Woody Allen's Oscar-winning *Annie Hall*, and was in rehearsal for the Berkshire Theater Festival production of *Let 'Em Eat Cake*. Roberts had previously co-starred in another of Woody Allen's films, *Play It Again, Sam* (1972), playing the ghost of Humphrey Bogart.

1488. "Passport to Freedom" (2/1/78; rebroadcast from 9/15/77)

1489. "Don't Look Back" (2/2/78; rebroadcast 6/29/78)

Cast: Don Scardino (Renfro Tibbit); Bob Dryden (Arthur Guggenheimer); Marian Seldes (Doree). Written by Sam Dann.

While stopped for gas, rock star Renfro Tibbit offers Doree, the young woman who runs the garage, a free ticket to his next concert. When Doree doesn't show, Renfro drives back to the garage and proposes to her, the first woman who has ever refused his favors. Doree admits she is in love with him, but fears if she married him his career would be over—his millions of women fans would never forgive him—and his dollar-happy manager would surely kill her.

1490. "The Postmistress of Laurel Run" (2/3/78; rebroadcast 7/1/78)

Cast: Marian Seldes (Betsy Barker); Robert Kaliban (Stanton Green); Ray Owens (Harry Home); William Griffis (Charley). Adapted by G. Frederic Lewis, based on the 1894 short story by Bret Harte.

Betsy Barker, a widow, was named postmistress of Laurel Run, Montana, in

1890. Because of her attractiveness, men spent a lot of money buying postage stamps they didn't need. Every day she was sent an expensive present on the mail stage by Stanton Green, postmaster of nearby Hickory Hill. This was fine until a federal mail inspector is dispatched from San Francisco to find out why mailed money orders are disappearing somewhere between Hickory Hill and Laurel Run.

1491. "Death on Project X" (2/4/78; rebroadcast from 9/16/77)

1492. "The Wind and the Flame" (2/5/78; rebroadcast from 9/19/77)

1493. "The Talking Women" (2/6/78; rebroadcast 7/2/78)

Cast: Ed Ames (Robert Bazewell); Evelyn Juster (Julie Palmer); Sam Gray (Sergeant Delucca); Bryna Raeburn (Lolly Harbison). Written by Sam Dann.

Robert Bazewell keeps telling his wife Martha how boring those business trips to New York have become for him. He wants to stop them, but beautiful Lolly Harbison, the reason for his visits to the Big Apple, but won't hear of it. She threatens to commit suicide if he stays home. He tries to stop her from shooting herself but, during a struggle for possession of the gun, it goes off. Lolly is killed, and Robert fears that someday he'll be accused of murder. He is absolutely correct.

1494. "Dr. Heidegger's Experiment" (2/7/78; rebroadcast 7/4/78)

Cast: Gordon Heath (Dr. Heidegger); Guy Sorel (Charles Medbourne); Bob Dryden (Colonel Killegrew); Mary Jane Higby (Clara Wycherly). Adapted by Percy Granger, based on the 1837 short story by Nathaniel Hawthorne.

Dr. Heidegger, an eccentric New Englander, invites four old friends to his laboratory and entices them into drinking glasses of water a friend has sent him from Florida's fabled Fountain of Youth. The three men and one woman become much younger, but, instead of realizing the fallacies of their youth, the three men start fighting amongst themselves for the attention of the woman, just as they did 50 years before.

1495. "The Tunnel Man" (2/8/78 rebroadcast from 9/20/77)

1496. "All Unregistered Aliens" (2/9/78; rebroadcast 7/6/78)

Cast: Anne Williams (Dr. Anna Quiller); Court Benson (Uncle Stefan); Earl Hammond (Lieutenant McKeegan). Written by Victoria Dann.

Dr. Anna Quiller has set up her practice in the slum area in which she was born. "I'm needed here," she says. The area is home for many unregistered aliens, and when one of them, dying from a bullet wound, is brought to her she neglects to report his death to the police. One reason for this is that after the boy died, the body disappeared. Dr. Quiller can't figure out why or how this could have happened.

1497. "Reflected Terror" (2/10/78; rebroadcast 7/8/78)

Cast: Marian Seldes (Emily Falkirk); Court Benson (Joseph Royston); Bryna Raeburn (Mrs. Klemper); Russell Horton (James Royston). Written by Ian Martin.

A gothic tale, says host Marshall, is "a style noted by a gloomy setting, grotesque or violent events, and an atmosphere of degeneration and decay." Emily Falkirk faces all of these conditions when she goes to work for Joseph Coning Royston, a sad recluse living in a large, desolate mansion. He has become a victim of consuming depression since the untimely death of his beloved wife who looked, when she was alive, very much like Emily, a reflection he never wants to see again.

1498. "The Plan" (2/11/78; rebroadcast from 9/22/77)

1499. "The Burning Whirlwind" (2/12/78; rebroadcast from 9/23/77)

1500. "Night Eyes" (2/13/78; rebroadcast 7/9/78)

Cast: Ralph Bell (Richard Starbright); Earl Hammond (Nate Forrest); Joan Banks (Lorna Starbright); Sam Gray (Joe). Written by Sam Dann.

Former prizefighter and now track employee Nate Forrest informs wealthy racehorse owner Richard Starbright that his never-win thoroughbred, Turkish Taffy, with whom Forrest says he has talked a lot, has been replaced in its stall by another horse that's a double, for T.T. Starbright knows all about it—he hopes to, and does, win a bundle with the substitute steed. But neither he nor his trainer can afford to let Forrest spread the word about the new horse. The trainer says he knows an excellent way to keep Forrest from talking.

1501. "Revenge Is Sweet" (2/14/78; rebroadcast 7/12/78)

Cast: Mandel Kramer (Peter); Bob Dryden (Harry); William Griffis (Claiborne); Lloyd Battista (Roberts). Adapted by G. Frederic Lewis, based on the short story *A Piece of String* by Guy de Maupassant.

Peter, given the job of orderly in a men's health club despite his 20 years in jail, is wrongfully accused of having stolen a wallet from the locker of one of the club's patrons. Even though the wallet is later spotted behind a radiator, Peter is fired. When he finds he cannot get another job, he vows to give his accuser an anxious moment or two; he still has a pass key to all the health club's lockers.

1502. "The Guy De Maupassant Murders" (2/15/78; rebroadcast from 9/26/77)

1503. "Something in the Air" (2/16/78; rebroadcast 7/15/78)

Cast: Gordon Heath (Max Avery); Corrine Orr (Nina Avery); Ralph Bell (Dan Fogarty); Anne Williams (Hester). Written by Elspeth Eric.

Destitute middle-aged artist Dan Fogarty calls on wealthy painter Max Avery for reasons he can't explain. Max, also for reasons he can't explain, suspects Dan and his daughter Nina, only 18, have fallen in love. Learning later he's right about Dan and Nina, a relationship he's against, Max becomes agitated by Nina's ability to know what Dan is doing no matter where he is and Dan's capacity for knowing Nina's every move. Somehow he must put a stop to all this clairvoyancy.

1504. "The Church of Hell" (2/17/78; rebroadcast 7/16/78)

Cast: Paul Hecht (David Francis); Roberta Maxwell (Jane Francis); Lloyd Battista (Lieutenant Price); Roger De Koven (Dr. Wharton). Written by Ian Martin.

Just back in their city apartment after two weeks in Europe, David and Jane Francis get a telephone call from the police in the town where they have a country home. They're told the lease has been broken by the untimely and unexplainable death of their tenant, an elderly widow. When they reach their home, they find an unwanted tenant has taken possession, a tenant who may be difficult, if not impossible, to evict.

1505. "The Wintering Place" (2/18/78; rebroadcast from 9/27/77)

1506. "The Solitary" (2/19/78; rebroadcast from 9/29/77)

1507. "Angel from England" (2/20/78; rebroadcast 7/19/78)

Cast: Marian Seldes (Edith Cavell); Court Benson (Phillipe Baucq); Bob Dryden (Colonel Boger); Bryna Raeburn (Sister White); Earl Hammond (The Reverend). Adapted by G. Frederic Lewis, based on a short story by Ambrose Bierce.

Several years before the start of World War I, British-born Edith Cavell was named head of a nursing school in Belgium. When the Germans occupied the country, she knew she would be needed to care for the many wounded in a Red Cross hospital in Brussels. While there she began to work with the Belgian underground, helping Allied soldiers in the hospital to escape to Holland. She was very successful until the fall of 1915, when she was arrested by German authorities.

1508. "A Phantom Yesterday" (2/21/78; rebroadcast 7/22/78)

Cast: Kim Hunter (Lilo Dichter); Michael Tolan (Gil Blake); Arnold Moss (Mark Dana); Ray Owens (Emil Bruchner). Written by Ian Martin.

Lilo Dichter, against the advice of her agent, accepts a nightclub engagement in Berlin at a time when the neo–Nazis were still trying through terrorism to make a comeback. She also wants to be with the only man she has ever loved: American reporter Gil Blake. But Blake, working on an explosive story, has been kidnapped. Only with the help of her former underground friends is she able to rescue him.

1509. "Trilby" (2/22/78; rebroadcast from 9/30/77)

1510. "Vanishing Lady" (2/23/78; rebroadcast 7/23/78)

Cast: Tony Roberts (Peter Carlsen); Russell Horton (Len Grey); Evelyn Juster (Lois Free); Nat Polen (Police Sergeant). Written by Murray Burnett.

In the midst of making plans for his wedding, Peter Carlsen discovers, to his dismay, that his intended, Lois Free, has vanished. Neither her parents, the police nor the local newspaper are of any help to him. When he finally breaks into her apartment, he meets one of her high school boyfriends, who intimates that because of her extrasensory perception, Lois has been sent on a secret mission for the U.S. government, and that he, Peter, had better not interfere.

1511. "Loser Take All" (2/24/78; rebroadcast 7/26/78)

Cast: Paul Hecht (Will Dudley); Patricia Elliott (Hannah Peabody); Russell Horton (Ben Greene); Arnold Moss (Sergeant Driscoll). Adapted by Arnold Moss, based on the 1891 short story *George Thurston.*

No matter how they compete, Ben Greene always bests Will Dudley. This so provokes Dudley that he vows on the day of their college graduation it will never happen again. An officer in the Ohio militia, Dudley is soon called to Civil War duty. During the battle at Preservation Ridge, he is sent much needed replacements. Among them is Private Ben Greene, whom Captain Dudley immediately orders to carry out a dangerous mission that can only result in Private Greene's death.

1512. "Mother Knows Best" (2/25/78; rebroadcast from 10/3/77)

1513. "The Sea Nymph" (2/26/78; rebroadcast from 10/5/77)

1514. "Second Sight" (2/27/78; rebroadcast 7/29/78)

Cast: Court Benson (Glen Paxton); Earl Hammond (Larry Milland); Robert Kaliban (Detective Rambo); Bryna Raeburn (Judith Paxton). Written by Percy Granger.

Larry Millard, a drifter with a police record, is found guilty of murdering a farmer who was, in reality, killed by respected businessman Glen Paxton. The farmer has refused to sell Paxton his land for a planned reservoir. On the eve of his execution Millard is asked if he wishes to donate any of his organs to science. Knowing that Paxton needs an eye transplant, Millard says he will gladly give him his eyes, anonymously, so that Paxton will be condemned to see for the rest of his life with eyes that know the truth about the murder.

1515. "A Message from Space" (2/28/78; rebroadcast 7/30/78, 3/18/79)

Cast: Tony Roberts (Pete Herron); Bryce Bond (himself); Jada Rowland (Maru); Joe Silver (R.X. Riley). Written by Ian Martin.

An American newspaper sends an ace reporter, Pete Herron, to Warminister, England, with orders to make those who claim to be seeing UFOs look foolish. While there, Herron runs into Bryce Bond, an authority on ufology, and to his astonishment, witnesses with Bond the landing of a flying saucer in a wheat field. What makes completing his assignment even more difficult is his meeting Maru, one of the spaceship's crew members, with whom he immediately falls in love.

Notes: Bryce Bond, former radio and television commentator and now an investigator of reported UFO sightings and landings, plays himself in this episode.

1516. "The Adventure of the Beryl Coronet" (3/1/78; rebroadcast from 10/7/77)

1517. "You Tell Me Your Dream" (3/2/78; rebroadcast 8/1/78)

Cast: Teri Keane (Dr. Lucy Abelson); Ralph Bell (John Joseph Hill); Bob Dryden (Morley Sutledge). Written by Sam Dann.

Construction company owner John Joseph Hill describes to Dr. Lucy Abelson his recurring dream: Morley Sutledge, a man whom he has never met but has learned does exist, is going to kill him in a hunting accident. Soon Dr. Abelson also begins dreaming about Sutledge—his car keeps hitting hers and pushing it into an abutment. To prevent both dreams from coming true, Dr. Abelson makes plans to confront Sutledge at the hunting lodge, before he can kill Mr. Hill.

1518. "The Assassin" (3/3/78; rebroadcast 8/3/78)

Cast: Larry Haines (Executioner Kyle); Earl Hammond (Signor Messina); Marian Seldes (Elena); Jackson Beck (Mr. Jones). Written by Murray Burnett.

Plans are carefully made for executioner Kyle to fly to Aragona and assassinate its dictator, General Louis Rey Saturnino. However, while traveling to the airport, Kyle's taxi is hit by a truck. When he regains consciousness, Kyle has no idea who he is or why he has tickets to Aragona. He also doesn't know—never did, in fact—that his contacts in Aragona have instructions to kill him right after the assassination.

1519. "The Actress" (3/4/78; rebroadcast from 10/10/77)

1520. "The Case of Chateau-Margaux" (3/5/78; rebroadcast from 10/12/77)

1521. "The House and the Brain" (3/6/78; rebroadcast 8/5/78)

Cast: Gordon Heath (Harold Rumsford); Bob Dryden (Walter Garrison); Court Benson (Cheevers). Adapted by Percy Granger, based on the short story by Edward Bulwer-Lytton.

Harold Rumsford, a lifelong student of supernatural phenomena, is intrigued by eyewitness accounts of a house near Leiscester Square in which no one, except the housekeeper, dares to live. He determines to spend a night there with his manservant and dog. What happens in those terrifying few hours convinces him that the house is haunted by a powerful and evil will that somehow has its origin in a living, human mind.

1522. "The Red Scarf" (3/7/78; rebroadcast 8/6/78)

Cast: Ralph Bell (Alan Standish); Teri Keane (Erika Standish); Bryna Raeburn (Gerry); Russell Horton (Tom Turner). Written by Sam Dann.

Movie queen Erika Standish kills her longtime lover, actor Tom Turner, when he orders her replaced as costar of his next film. Erika's husband, Alan, offers to take the blame for the crime, certain he will never be convicted because of what he calls "the unwritten law," which gives him the right to kill a man who has deceived him. But once he is jailed, Erika proclaims that Alan is the real murderer. Only a red scarf he has purchased can save him from life imprisonment.

1523. "The People of Sissora" (3/8/78; rebroadcast from 10/14/77)

1524. "The Instant Millionaires" (3/9/78; rebroadcast 8/8/78)

Cast: Robert Kaliban (Mick Berrigan); Roy Owens (Kurt Wiener); Ian Martin (Sal Caccio); Ralph Bell (Gino Marino); Evelyn Juster (Emma Wiener). Written by Ian Martin.

Because more space is needed in the warehouse, three employees are told to send out for an auction, a trunk unclaimed for 20 years. As they start to move it, the trunk falls open, spilling out books and $3 million in cash. Each takes $1 million and sets out to do what he's always dreamed of doing. The only trouble is a hood knows about the trunk and the money. He believes he has more right to the cash than any of them.

1525. "Who Is George Williams?" (3/10/78; rebroadcast 8/10/78)

Cast: Larry Haines (George Williams); Court Benson (George Teller); Bob Dryden (Dr. Bertram); Joan Shay (Connie). Written by G. Frederic Lewis.

While playing chess during a blinding blizzard, Anchorage's police chief, George Teller, and his friend Dr. William Bertram hear a cry for help. They find a man in a snowdrift who doesn't know who he is or how he got there. They name him George Williams, and Teller gives him a job. He soon becomes an excellent policeman, but still cannot remember his real name—until he is sent to help the Juneau police unravel the mystery of a human skeleton found in a deep well.

1526. "Return Engagement" (3/11/78; rebroadcast from 10/17/77)

1527. "The Island on Silver Tree Lake" (3/12/78; rebroadcast from 10/19/77)

1528. "The Wheel of Life" (3/13/78; rebroadcast 8/12/78)

Cast: Russell Horton (Joe); Bryna Raeburn (Jenny); Lloyd Battista (Rudy Kastner). Written by Sam Dann.

Rudy Kastner, saved from dying in a jungle by Vietnamese monks, looks up his wartime buddy, Joe, now a cab driver. Rudy recalls his experience with the holy men who he claims control the Wheel of Life and who had promised him the U.S. presidency in 1995. Rudy wants Joe to become his right-hand man in the Forward America crusade that will take him to the White House. Joe is tempted, until he realizes how Rudy plans to run the country.

1529. "The Impossible Is True" (3/14/78; rebroadcast 8/13/78)

Cast: Anne Williams (Corey Sterret); Michael Wager (Phil Sterret); Catherine Byers (Linda Venner); Earl Hammond (Jareth); Paul Hecht (Mark Gentry). Written by Ian Martin.

After wealthy old Fulton Sterret commits suicide, his mansion becomes haunted by the ghost of his wife. At least his daughter, Corey, keeps seeing her mother's image, some think perhaps because she sincerely believes she murdered her mother. Determined to find out what Corey has been seeing, the family doctor and valet hide near her room one night. When Corey's mother's ghost calls out to her, they see it too.

1530. "Sorry to Let You Go" (3/15/78; rebroadcast from 10/21/77)

1531. "The Time Fold" (3/16/78; rebroadcast 8/15/78)

Cast: Paul Hecht (Chad Stevens); Ian Martin (Jake Slade); Evelyn Juster (Meg Chatham); Fred Gwynne (J. Bruce Proctor). Written by Ian Martin.

On a flight to New York, a twin-engine corporate jet hits such strong clear-air turbulence that it is tossed into space. Weightless inside the plane, the passengers and crew face death within 24 hours. But they are saved by people on *Goodspeed One*, a space station orbiting the moon 1,000 years in the future. Their civilization is a near utopia. The jet's crew wants to settle there, but its owner demands to be taken back to New York so he can attend a very important business meeting.

1532. "Identified Flying Objects" (3/17/78; rebroadcast 8/17/78)

Cast: Bryna Raeburn (Molly); Earl Hammond (Mor El); Court Benson (Dr. Nudell); Gilbert Mack (Officer Pinchot). Written by Sam Dann.

Officer Pinchot arrests the space machine's pilot for obstructing traffic. The pilot, who has no registration or driver's license and whose only words are "voor ee amana," infuriates the judge, who orders him committed to an institution for the insane. There he meets Molly, a cleaning lady, who is able to understand his language and who learns, to her horror, that his planet, Ayvora, has plans to conquer and colonize the Earth, killing all of its inhabitants in the process.

1533. "Trial for Murder" (3/18/78; rebroadcast from 10/24/77)

1534. "Just to Keep Busy" (3/19/78; rebroadcast from 10/25/77)

1535. "All Things Are Beautiful" (3/20/78; rebroadcast 8/19/78)

Cast: Paul Hecht (John Agar); Martha Greenhouse (Virginia Agar); William Griffis (Billy West); Ian Martin (Brennan). Adapted by G. Frederic Lewis, based on the 1872 short story *God Sees the Truth, But Waits* by Leo Tolstoy.

Despite the protests of his wife, who dreams the next time she sees him he will be old and gray, up-and-coming store owner John Agar heads to Toledo to attend a menswear convention. He is met by a local detective who says Agar is the prime suspect in the murder of a salesman en route to the convention. An astonished Agar claims his innocence, but the detective finds a blood-stained knife in his suitcase. A laboratory analysis of the blood proves it to be the same as that of the dead salesman.

1536. "The Golden Amulet" (3/21/78; rebroadcast 8/20/78)

Cast: Tony Roberts (Hagawara); Bob Dryden (Dr. Shijo); Joan Shay (Monay); Evelyn Juster (Tsuyu). Based on a Japanese ghost story, and adapted by Roy Winsor.

Young Hagawara loves Tsuyu, but she is of a higher class and her samurai father will never permit them to marry. When Tsuyu dies, a grief-stricken Hagawara goes to her tomb, knowing this could mean his death. Tsuyu's ghost greets him, and they embrace. Tsuyu wishes him to return, but Hagawara has no recollection of their meeting. Only if death also comes to him can they possibly ever be happy.

Notes: During the rehearsal of this broadcast, a television camera filmed the *Theater* for a segment in *Razzmatazz*, a CBS news magazine for young viewers on television. The program, hosted by Barry Bostwick, was broadcast on Thursday, May 11, 1978, from 4–4:30 P.M., ET, on CBS.

1537. "The House by the Seine" (3/22/78; rebroadcast from 10/27/77)

1538. "The Judas Kiss" (3/23/78; rebroadcast 8/22/78)

Cast: Fred Gwynne (Oskar Aptheker); Teri Keane (Enid Grant); Lloyd Battista (Luke); Don Scardino (Robert). Written by Elspeth Eric.

Oskar Aptheker, who lives in the valley town of Tipton, offers to help attractive, middle-aged Enid Grant get settled in a remote mountainside cabin for the summer. Soon she is visited by a much younger man. Oskar, who brags about his clairvoyancy and is appalled as he "watches" the young man become bored with Enid, who ultimately murders him. When her husband arrives and refuses her for her affair, she shoots him, too—at least that's what Oskar "saw" happening.

Notes: Fred Gwynne can be seen in such films as *The Littlest Angel* (1969), *Sanctuary of Fear* (1979), *The Cotton Club* (1984), *Fatal Attraction* (1987) and *Pet Cemetery* (1989).

1539. "Wise Child" (3/24/78; rebroadcast 8/24/78)

Cast: Ralph Bell (Calvin Spurlock); Anne Williams (Joyce Spurlock); Jackson Beck (Mr. Rossler); Hetty Galen (Eunice). Written by Sam Dann.

Calvin and Joyce Spurlock are deliriously happy with their sudden parenthood. But, as the months go by and the baby doesn't gain an ounce, they become frightened. Their fears mount when they read in a newspaper that the town near where they found the child is a dumping ground for atomic waste. Radioactivity may be preventing the baby from growing, but it—or the child—is strangely enough providing the Spurlocks with a power of insight they never had before.

1540. "A Question of Identity" (3/25/78; rebroadcast from 10/28/77)

1541. "Trial by Fire" (3/26/78; rebroadcast from 10/31/77)

1542. "The Pretend Person" (3/27/78; rebroadcast 8/26/78)

Cast: Teri Keane (Woman); Ian Martin (Father); Bob Dryden (Friend); Bryna Raeburn (Mother). Written by Elspeth Eric.

A woman near death after open heart surgery gets little sympathy from her family, but lots from someone only she can see. The woman is visited in the hospital by her mother, father, brother and husband, none of whom seem to know what to say about her postoperative condition. Her employer telephones frequently, only to ask when she expects to return to work. But when she is alone, the woman has another visitor, a friend no one else can see. Only she knows why this friend has become such an important part of her life.

1543. "The Ghost in the Well" (3/28/78; rebroadcast 8/27/78)

Cast: Tony Roberts (James Taxon); Patricia Elliott (Guliana Sands); Court Benson (Aaron Burr); William Griffis (Levi Weeks). Written by Murray Burnett.

Artist Jim Taxon's friends think he has gone mad when he tells them why he has painted the same subject several times in order to get a good likeness. His subject is Guliana Sands, who died in 1799 when she fell into a well—pushed, she tells Jim, by her betrothed Levi Weeks. She has come back, not only to be painted, but to clear herself of the sins Levi's lawyers—Alexander Hamilton and Aaron Burr—claimed she was guilty of.

Notes: William Griffis was currently portraying Harlan Tucker, the friendly retired banker on the daytime television series *All My Children.* He had been appearing on *Theater* for the past two years, playing everything from a 16-year-old boy to a 90-year-old Tibetan lama. Griffis commented, "I love the versatility of radio acting, particularly the opportunity to 'double'—that is, play two people in one drama and maybe even talk to myself."

1544. "Last Train Out" (3/29/78; rebroadcast from 11/1/77)

1545. "Big City Blues" (3/30/78; rebroadcast 8/29/78)

Cast: Russell Horton (Harold Conners); Marian Hailey (Marge Conners); Earl Hammond (Ron); Mandel Kramer (Dln Purvis). Written by G. Frederic Lewis.

Shortly after they settle down in the honeymoon suite of a big city hotel, Harold and Marge Conner of Barrows Point, Maine, are robbed of everything they brought with them. A television program host puts them on the air, and soon the Conners have everything they lost and much more. But their new-found good fortune comes to an abrupt halt when the Barrows Point police chief arrives with a warrant for their arrest for having written a bad check back home.

1546. "Shark Bait" (3/31/78; rebroadcast 8/31/78)

Cast: Tony Roberts (Randolf Watson); Joan Shay (Aunt Ethel); Lloyd Battista (Rudolf Watson); Earl Hammond (Lieutenant Ferret). Written by Sam Dann.

Randolf Watson owes the syndicate $50,000. He must pay it in a few days, or else. His wealthy Aunt Ethel refuses to help, even though she is most generous to his twin brother, Rudolf. Murdering both Aunt Ethel and Rudolf and thus becoming heir to the family fortune is Randy's solution to his predicament. In order to get away with the crime, Randy plans to first convince the police that his look-alike brother is the one who really owes the syndicate the fifty grand.

1547. "Land of the Living Dead" (4/1/78; rebroadcast from 11/3/77)

1548. "The Final Judgment" (4/2/78; rebroadcast from 11/4/77)

1549. "Fortune's Favorite" (4/3/78; rebroadcast 9/2/78)

Cast: Mary Jane Higby (Felicia Palisade); Earl Hammond (Harvey); Joan Shay (Martha); William Griffis (Alonzo Fortune). Written by Sam Dann.

Felicia Palisade, who lives alone in a large, remote house in Maine, at first refuses the offer of a representative of rich Alonzo T. Fortune, who says she has been chosen as one of "Fortune's Favorites," which means a trip to Mexico. However, she accepts when another Fortune representative presents her with tickets. She becomes suspicious of the whole deal, though, when Fortune himself offers to put a call through from Mexico to her hometown sheriff, which she later learns the sheriff never received.

1550. "Delusion of Reprieve" (4/4/78; rebroadcast 9/3/78)

Cast: Paul Hecht (Lt. Mike Bernstein); Norman Rose (Captain Tony Nolan); Evelyn Juster (Maria Heindrich); Ian Martin (Peter Fleming). Written by Percy Granger.

Four men are murdered in less than two months. Police investigation reveals the four did not know one another, all were killed in the same manner with the same gun; none were robbed; all had been arrested on minor charges; and all were post–World War II immigrants from Europe. These leads produce no suspects until information from Interpol notes that all four were members of the Hitler elite corps that was in charge of the Nazi concentration camps.

Notes: Himan Brown journeyed to Provo, Utah, and was presented the Distinguished Service Award in Communications at the Brigham Young University's Department of Communications on April 4, 1978.

1551. "The Therapeutic Cat" (4/5/78; rebroadcast from 11/7/77)

1552. "A Tragedy of Error" (4/6/78; rebroadcast 9/5/78)

Cast: Tammy Grimes (Hortense Bernier); Bob Dryden (Charles Bernier); Russell Horton (Louis de Mayrau); Fred Gwynne (Emil). Adapted by G. Frederic Lewis, based on the 1864 novel by Henry James.

Charles Bernier, who left his wife, Hortense, and France five years ago after embezzling 500,000 francs, writes that he is soon to return. Hortense well remembers the beatings the lame Charles gave her with his cane and has found herself a new man, Louis de Mayrau. She hires an ex-sailor to meet Charles' ship and kill him while rowing ashore. But the sailor, by mistake, picks up Louis, who also uses a cane and who has gone aboard the ship to confront Charles.

1553. "The Parasite" (4/7/78; rebroadcast 9/7/78)

Cast: Norman Rose (Gilbert Gilroy); Robert Kaliban (Colin Wilson); Bryna Raeburn (Helen Penclosa); Hetty Galen (Agatha Marden). Adapted by G. Frederic Lewis, based on the 1894 story by Sir Arthur Conan Doyle.

Physiology professor Gilbert Gilroy is invited by one of his colleagues, Colin Wilson, to meet Helen Penclosa, a practitioner of the black arts. Gilroy has no patience with hypnotists or mesmerism, but when he watches Miss Penclosa put his favorite lady, Agatha Marden, the dean's daughter, into a trance, he agrees to conduct a scientific study of Miss Penclosa's powers. Soon she has him in her grasp, and he can find no means of escape.

1554. "The Haunted Mill" (4/8/78; rebroadcast from 11/8/77)

1555. "A Tale of Two Worlds" (4/9/78; rebroadcast from 11/10/77)

1556. "Childish Laughter" (4/10/78; rebroadcast 9/10/78)

Cast: Alexander Scourby (Hugh Montrose); Lori March (Thyra Bordenave); Court Benson (Mr. Crenshaw). Written by Sam Dann.

While driving along a deserted road, chemist Hugh Montrose, trying to avoid a little girl, crashes into a tree. When he regains consciousness, Montrose frantically searches for the girl, whom he can hear laughing but cannot see. Later he learns she is dead, but not because she was hit by his automobile. She had died from eating a body-building health food he had invented, a food which, while being manufactured, was somehow contaminated with a deadly poison.

1557. "Blackmail" (4/11/78; rebroadcast 9/12/78)

Cast: Larry Haines (Tony Carbo); Teri Keane (Maxine); Jada Rowland (Maidey Rambeau); Bob Dryden (Eddie Small). Written by Roy Winsor.

Three blackmailers try to extract a fortune from a young movie star with a photo they have of her embracing a notorious mobster. Maidey Rambeau, a fast-rising young film star, can't figure out how the blackmailers obtained the photo. She doesn't want to pay the $100,000 being demanded, but her good friend, her hairdresser, believes that if she doesn't, her image as "Miss Clean" will be destroyed. Tony Carbo, wanted for hijacking and murder, claims he can straighten everything out. Maidey is interested.

1558. "We Meet Again" (4/12/78; rebroadcast from 11/11/77)

1559. "The Shriek of the Mandrake" (4/13/78; rebroadcast 9/14/78)

Cast: Anne Williams (Virginia Stewart); Ian Martin (Denton Norris); Ray Owens (Inspector Havisham); Paul Hecht (Peaser). Written by Percy Granger.

Beautiful actress Virginia Stewart is in England to make a film. But before long both the film's male lead and director, after the shrill shriek of a mandrake plant is heard, are found dead near the base of the tower attached to "haunted" Wicklow Manor, where the film is being made. However, it is Virginia, not the ghost, who is suspected, since she was the last person to see each of the two men alive.

1560. "Chapter of Errors" (4/14/78; rebroadcast 9/17/78)

Cast: Court Benson (Gustave Pinochet); Bryna Raeburn (Jeanne Pinochet); Ian Martin (The Professor); Russell Horton (Augie). Written by Ian Martin.

The Professor and his sidekick, Augie, heist two Picasso etchings worth $100,000 from the Pinochet Gallery. Pinochet puts a sign in the gallery's front window offering $5,000 for their return. The Professor will give them up—after enjoying them for a few days in his apartment—for nothing less than $20,000. But two young punks, seeing the sign in the window, pretend they have the etchings and agree to give them to Pinochet for his original offer.

1561. "The Gloria Scott" (4/15/78; rebroadcast from 11/14/77)

1562. "A Point in Time" (4/16/78; rebroadcast from 11/15/77)

1563. "Murder at Troyte's Hill" (4/17/78; rebroadcast 9/19/78)

Cast: Marian Hailey (Loveday Brooke); Bob Dryden (Inspector Griffiths); Ray Owens (Dr. Hector Craven); Earl Hammond (Coroner). Written by G. Frederic Lewis.

In 1870, Loveday Brooke, Scotland Yard's first lady detective, is sent to the town of Grenfall in Cumberland to help the local constable in a murder case. The victim is Alexander Henderson, the elderly lodgekeeper of retired Dr. Hector Craven, owner of Troyte's Hill. After attending the inquest, Loveday agrees with the constable that the investigation should be conducted from inside the Troyte Hill mansion and volunteers to take a job as Dr. Craven's secretary until the murderer is apprehended.

1564. "Uncle Louis" (4/18/78; rebroadcast 9/21/78)

Cast: Tony Roberts (Terry Smith); Anne Williams (Helen Pauli); Kenneth Harvey (Joe); Ralph Bell (Father Burke); Jackson Beck (Harry George). Written by Sam Dann.

Reporter Arnold Miller, about to expose corruption in the mayor's office, is shot to death by a hired assassin while sitting on a park bench. First to see Miller's body and to call the police is a widow, Helen Pauli, who after questioning by detective Terry Smith is suspected of withholding certain crucial facts. One is that her 5-year-old daughter witnessed the shooting. But Helen in no way wants her little girl involved in the investigation.

Notes: This episode was originally titled "Say Goodbye to Uncle Louis," but was changed shortly before the actual episode was recorded.

1565. "Hunted Down" (4/19/78; rebroadcast from 11/17/77)

1566. "The Avocado Jungle" (4/20/78; rebroadcast 9/24/78)

Cast: Larry Haines (Silas); Lois Kibbe (Joan Edmonds); Teri Keane (Angela); Howard Ross (Jerry Winkler). Written by Elspeth Eric.

Silas Love takes on the assignment of writing an "as told to" book about once famous actress Joan Edmonds. While interviewing Ms. Edmonds, Love becomes fascinated with her daughter, Angela, who adores her mother and whose bedroom is cluttered with a "jungle" of avocado trees, the largest of which is growing in soil once stepped on by her mother. In a moment of weakness, Ms. Edmonds tells Love that Angela is an adopted daughter, which she never wants Angela to know.

1567. "Bet with Angels" (4/21/78; rebroadcast 9/26/78)

Cast: Mason Adams (Jason Clark); Marian Seldes (Hilary Jones); Mandel Kramer (Lew Marvin). Written by Murray Burnett.

Advertising executive Jason Clark, as a show of friendship to his longtime pal, Lew Marvin, often joins him in his betting sprees, putting up a few dollars to Lew's hundreds. Suddenly, Lew dies and Jason stops his wagering, until he begins to hear Lew's voice instructing him how to bet. Soon he has made so much money (he never loses a wager) that his bookmakers get rough. They demand to know what he knows—or else.

1568. "A Grain of Salt" (4/22/78; rebroadcast from 11/18/77)

1569. "She" (4/23/78; rebroadcast from 11/21/77)

1570. "The Grandee of Terra Loco" (4/24/78; rebroadcast 9/28/78)

Cast: Paul Hecht (Richard Leach); Earl Hammond (Fred Perkins); Joan Shay (Mrs. Stevens); Bob Dryden (Sheriff Pickard). Written by Percy Granger).

Dallas newspaper reporter Richard Leach convinces his editor he should be sent to Rylan, Texas, to write a feature story about an honest politician, Rylan's mayor, who ruled the town unchallenged for over 40 years and who recently died. But when Leach starts questioning the town's manager, the coroner, the mayor's doctor and the mayor's widow, he is told to get out—quick. When he refuses, the sheriff locks him up without giving him a chance to call his editor.

Notes: Himan Brown was the honored guest at the University of Florida's annual Broadcast Day on April 24, 1978. He mentioned, "Knowing that all of these young people, who never before experienced drama on radio, are tuning us in and, at the same time, want to learn how it is done, gives me a great deal of satisfaction. I'll continue to accept as many campus-speaking dates as my schedule permits."

1571. "International Dateline" (4/25/78; rebroadcast 10/1/78)

Cast: Michael Tolan (Steve Catlett); Evelyn Juster (Lisa); Ian Martin (Alfie). Written by Ian Martin.

Captain Steve Catlett, his crippled B-17 ready for ditching after a bombing run over Germany, orders his crew to bail out. He crash-lands the plane and is seriously injured, remaining in a coma for several weeks. After recovering, he marries his nurse, but soon becomes restless and volunteers for duty in the Philippines, where a jealous native woman tries, but fails, to kill him. Now, like the legendary cat, he has used up eight lives and has only one more to go.

1572. "The Pinkerton Method" (4/26/78; rebroadcast from 11/23/77)

1573. "The Queen of Palmyra" (4/27/78; rebroadcast 10/3/78)

Cast: Fred Gwynne (Charles Carswell); Court Benson (Dudley MacIlhenny); Jack Grimes (Fatso); Bryna Raeburn (Zenobia). Written by Sam Dann.

Zenobia, who claims to be the ancient Queen of Palmyra but who in reality is a convicted forger, has millionaire Dudley MacIlhenny believing the world is soon coming to an end. To insure his salvation, Zenobia convinces him to turn his holdings into gold and to give the gold to her. Trying to put a stop to this madness, MacIlhenny's nephew, Fatso, enlists the aid of private detective Charles Carswell. Soon Carswell is also convinced the world's days are numbered.

1574. "The House on Chimney Pot Line" (4/28/78; rebroadcast 10/6/78)

Cast: Marian Seldes (Marian Sage); Earl Hammond (Jim Sage); Teri Keane (Georgia Kane); Sam Gray (Elliot Mann). Written by Bob Juhren.

After ignoring the realtor's warning and buying a house whose former occupants either completely disappeared or tried unsuccessfully to burn it down, Marian and Jim Sage begin to redecorate it. Their biggest mistake is to put a large photo mural of an African jungle scene on one wall. In it is a lion that one day leaps roaring from the photo while a telephone repairman is at work. Afterward, neither the Sages nor the police can find any trace of him.

1575. "Indian Giver" (4/29/78; rebroadcast from 11/25/77)

1576. "The Man Is Missing" (4/30/78; rebroadcast from 11/28/77)

1577. "A Drink with Dionysius" (5/1/78; rebroadcast 10/8/78)

Cast: Fred Gwynne (Sprinkles Magoon); Bryna Raeburn (Boston Sadie); Ian Martin (Mumbles Pennyfeather); Bob Dryden (Sergeant Flummer). Written by Sam Dann.

Boston Sadie's shady husband enlists the aid of two other crooks, one being a professional pickpocket, in a clever plot to steal 50 Army revolvers. The job is done well, but when the three thieves open the wooden crate at their fence's hideout, they find it contains the Army's latest nuclear warhead—the Dionysius—but no guns. They now face a *major* problem: how to dispose of such a powerful weapon of destruction.

1578. "The Figure in the Moonlight" (5/2/78; rebroadcast 10/10/78)

Cast: Paul Hecht (Ted Norris); Patricia Elliott (Diana Norris); Ralph Bell (Homer Knowles); Tony Roberts (Ben Ware). Written by Roy Winsor.

Ted and Diana Norris, asked to evaluate an art collection willed to a New Hampshire university, come across a 25-year-old engraving of a mansion near which a murder had been committed. The couple is fascinated by a crouching man who appears in a corner of the engraving but then disappears. Next they see the man on the mansion's porch, then climbing through an open window. The Norrises consider taking up residence on the island of St. Croix, or anywhere away from New Hampshire.

1579. "The Teddy Bear" (5/3/78; rebroadcast from 11/30/77)

1580. "Journey to Somewhere" (5/4/78; rebroadcast 10/12/78)

Cast: Norman Rose (Henry Thorpe); Carol Teitel (Julie Conrad); Evelyn Juster (Linda Snow); Russell Horton (Duke Fallow). Written by Ian Martin.

Five persons—a lady who is being railroaded into an old folks home against her will; a woman who feels her life is already over; a man who has turned from the living to the dead; a self-confessed punk who cares about nothing but himself; and a young girl whose secret lies behind two dark and frightened eyes—are all headed for Skeffington Junction, until the train carrying them starts crossing a bridge that has been weakened by the winter's worst storm.

1581. "Cool Killer Karl" (5/5/78; rebroadcast 10/15/78)

Cast: Mason Adams (Karl Hefner); Marian Seldes (Shirley Cable); William Griffis (Bartender); Ian Martin (Officer Cramer). Written by G. Frederic Lewis.

Brandishing two loaded .44s, a man described as "very young, very calm, very cool," stages a series of holdups at bars, usually near closing time. Twice the police seem to have him trapped, but twice he shoots his way out, killing one officer in the process. But he's no match for Mrs. Shirley Cable, a mother of two young children and, by profession, a guidance counselor with an uncanny talent for handling all types of people—even killers.

1582. "Neatness Counts" (5/6/78; rebroadcast from 12/2/77)

1583. "The Lost Tomorrows" (5/7/78; rebroadcast from 12/5/77)

1584. "Death and Desire" (5/8/78; rebroadcast 10/17/78)

Cast: Mercedes McCambridge (Madame Melba); Arnold Moss (Rafferty); Bob Dryden (Orville); Joen Arliss (Woman). Written by Elspeth Eric.

Madame Melba, a former circus fat lady, and her husband Orville, a former circus human skeleton, now conduct sèances, usually for the very rich. Orville—the ghost, table rapper, musician, voice thrower, and so forth—does most of the work. After one very trying sèance, he becomes sick and dies, and a few days later returns as a real ghost to comfort his wife. Now she can claim without fear of contradiction that she has the capability of communicating with the dead.

Notes: Mercedes McCambridge can be seen in such films as *All the King's Men* (1949), *Giant* (1956), *The President's Plane Is Missing* (1971), *The Sackets* (1979), and *Echoes* (1983).

1585. "Room 418" (5/9/78; rebroadcast 10/19/78)

Cast: Michael Tolan (Kent Farrady); Carol Teitel (Elizabeth Farrady); Teri Keane (Gloria); Nat Polen (Cabbie). Written by Sam Dann.

Kent Farrady is at first told there are no rooms available in the resort hotel where he stayed the previous day. But the night clerk, Gloria, is taken by his deep blue eyes and gives him the key to room 418, whose occupant has mysteriously disappeared. The occupant is Kent's wife, whose body he had stuffed in a closet after shooting her twice. Strangely, she becomes alive and awakens him in the middle of the night. They have words, and he is compelled to shoot her again twice.

1586. "Fire and Ice" (5/10/78; rebroadcast from 12/7/77)

1587. "The Guilt of the Innocent" (5/11/78; rebroadcast 10/22/78)

Cast: Fred Gwynne (Grishka); Robert Kaliban (Ivan); Earl Hammond (Alexei); Jackson Beck (Ship's Captain). Adapted by G. Frederic Lewis, based on the 1923 short story *The Hermit* by Maxim Gorky.

Ivan Ivanovitch, in an innocent country with hopes of striking it rich, is hired by an old, experienced dock thief, Grishka Chelkash, to row a load of stolen goods to a steamship waiting outside the harbor. Ivan doesn't realize what he's getting into until it's too late. But when he sees how much Grishka has been paid for the loot, he demands a larger share.

1588. "The Secret of Shen-Si" (5/12/78; rebroadcast 10/24/78)

Cast: Carol Teitel (Mady Neale); Arnold Moss (Joshua Neale); Robert Kaliban (Dr. Carlos Moran). Written by Arnold Moss.

Professor Joshua Neale, an historian in his fifties who considers himself an expert on past catastrophes, is amazed when his new, young wife, Mady, a former actress, recounts in the minutest detail the sinking of the *Titanic*, the guillotining of the aristocracy during the French Revolution, and the world's most destructive earthquake, in China's Shen-Si province in 1556. She is unable to explain this most unusual talent; he hopes a psychiatrist will.

Notes: Arnold Moss not only acts in this episode, he wrote the script. Moss has appeared on such shows as *Suspense, Lights Out!, Tales of Tomorrow,* and *The Time Tunnel.*

1589. "This Time Around" (5/13/78; rebroadcast from 12/9/77)

1590. "The Ten Million Dollar Heist" (5/14/78; rebroadcast from 12/12/77)

1591. "Edmund Orme" (5/15/78; rebroadcast 10/26/78)

Cast: Lamont Johnson (David Delano); Gordon Gould (John Clements); Mary Jane Higby (Ann Marsden); Jada Rowland (Charlotte Marsden). Adapted by Roy Winsor, based on the 1892 story *Sir Edmund Orme* by Henry James.

Ann Marsden suffers from moments of dizziness whenever she sees the ghost of the man, Sir Edmund Orme, she jilted years ago. Whoever falls in love with her beautiful daughter, Charlotte, is also affected by Sir Edmund's specter. One of these young men, David Delano, tries, with Mrs. Marsden's consent, to propose to Charlotte. But she cannot take him seriously; every time he is about to express his love to Charlotte, he sees the ghost, his eyes glaze over, and he loses his wits.

Notes: Lamont Johnson makes his first appearance as David Delano. Johnson's previous radio credits range as a regular on *The Adventures of Frank Merriwell, The Six Shooter,* and *Suspense.* Johnson was Wendy Warren's first love before World War II separated them on *Wendy Warren and the News,* and starred in the title role of *Tarzan,* which ran from 1951 to 1953 by Commodore Productions.

1592. "Girl Talk" (5/16/78; rebroadcast 10/29/78)

Cast: Teri Keane (Edna Everly); Bob Dryden (James Everly); Anne Williams (Marcella Borden). Written by Sam Dann.

Marcella Borden, now a U.S. senator and in town for a hearing, phones her college roommate of 30 years ago, Edna Everly, now a housewife and mother suffering from the ravages of middle age. Edna has long hated Marcella for her success and for having introduced her to her husband, James, whom she now despises. Edna takes a gun to Marcella's hotel room, ready to murder her, but she's not ready for Marcella's reaction to the pointed pistol.

1593. "The Death Shot" (5/17/78; rebroadcast from 12/14/77)

1594. "Time Out of Mind" (5/18/78; rebroadcast 10/30/78)

Cast: Russell Horton (Scott Pittman); Ian Martin (Col. Gilpin); Lloyd Battista (Theo Puttman). Written by Percy Granger.

As Scott Pittman is driving through Kansas on his way back to college, his father, Theo, tells him about his uncle, after whom he was named. The uncle was killed during the invasion of Italy, and Theo often wondered if the uncle had received a letter Theo sent him, apologizing for the way he had mistreated him. Moments after their car crash, Scott wakes up in Italy in 1949, learning that his uncle had received the letter and had written a reply, hoping against hope he would live long enough to send it to Theo.

1595. "The Hundred Dollar Difference" (5/19/78; rebroadcast 11/2/78)

Cast: Mason Adams (Thad Moffet); Carol Teitel (Wyona Caldwell); Evelyn Juster (Aunt Sarah Jane); Gilbert Mack (Rembert). Written by Sam Dann.

Rich and elderly Sarah Jane Moffet wants her playboy nephew, Thad, to settle down and get married. In fact, she even picks out the bride: her lawyer's secretary, Wyona Caldwell. During their first meeting, Wyona agrees to marry Thad, but only after he murders his aunt, who is planning, Wyona reveals, to rewrite her will, setting up a foundation and leaving Thad with hardly enough to live on.

1596. "The Ghost with a Knife" (5/20/78; rebroadcast from 12/16/77)

1597. "Brothers of the Angle" (5/21/78; rebroadcast from 12/19/77)

1598. "The Girl He Left Behind" (5/22/78; rebroadcast 11/5/78)

Cast: Anne Williams (Janie Raymond); Jack Grimes (Andy Nelson); Bryna Raeburn (Eleanor Raymond); Bob Dryden (Dr. Harper). Written by Percy Granger.

In the army just four months, Andy Nelson comes home on leave to give Janie Raymond, his girlfriend since their high school days, an engagement ring. Janie's mother, however, objects, and Janie turns down Andy's proposal, but, at his insistence, keeps the ring. On the way back to his base, Andy is killed in an auto accident. Soon, his ring starts turning on Janie's finger, cutting it. She sees his specter in her room. She can't eat or sleep, and her mother fears for her sanity.

1599. "Window to Oblivion" (5/23/78; rebroadcast 11/7/78)

Cast: Russell Horton (Lt. Billy Howard); Teri Keane (Joan Howard); Ian Martin (Major Gil Shane); Bryce Bond (Bryce Bond). Written by Ian Martin.

World War II has just ended, and Lt. Billy Howard is stationed at the U.S. Marine air base at Fort Lauderdale, Florida. He's getting ready to fly a routine sea patrol, but his wife, Joan, pleads with him not to. She's sure he'll never return, but Billy reassures her and takes off. His mission: to fly patrol over an area of the Atlantic Ocean that years later became known as the Bermuda Triangle.

1600. "The Big Ten-Cent Hustle" (5/24/78; rebroadcast from 12/21/77)

1601. "The Spy and the Traitor" (5/25/78; rebroadcast 11/9/78)

Cast: Gordon Heath (Benedict Arnold); Catherine Byers (Peggy Arnold); Earl Hammond (Stansbury); Howard Ross (Major John Andre). Written by G. Frederic Lewis.

Benedict Arnold, a proud and ambitious officer in General George Washington's army, becomes embittered by the threat of a court-martial and Washington's reluctance to make him a general. After a severe reprimand from Washington, Arnold is appointed commandant of the fort at West Point, whose surrender to the British he later plots with Major John Andre—for a price: 20,000 pounds.

Notes: A national park in New York is maintained in the memory of the Battle of Saratoga, a turning point in the War of Independence. One of the heroes of that war, unfortunately, went on to become a traitor. That fact created a problem: How to honor the heroic deeds without honoring the man who did them? The Saratoga monument was built for that purpose, the same shape as the Washington Monument (only 1/4 the actual size), with a self-portrait statue of each hero on each side. Philip Skyler, Horatio Gates, Daniel Morgan, and for the last side, there remains no statue at all. The man who would have been represented there, had his bravery not been matched by his treachery was Benedict Arnold. This episode dramatizes one of the earliest acts of treason in the United States.

1602. "Arctic Encounter" (5/26/78; rebroadcast 11/12/78)

Cast: Mason Adams (Chappie); Mandel Kramer (Pappy); Bryna Raeburn (Olga). Written by Sam Dann.

Lts. Stewart "Chappie" Chapman and George "Pappy" Padadopolis, on patrol over the Arctic, see a crashed Russian plane on the ice below. While investigating, their plane strangely loses power, their radio goes dead and they crash-land near the Russian plane. Chappie ventures out in the 70-below temperature and meets Olga, who has survived the crash of her plane. Neither can explain what had happened, but both know they can live for no more than two or three hours.

1603. "The Witching Well" (5/27/78; rebroadcast from 12/23/77)

1604. "The Ghosts of Yesterday" (5/28/78; rebroadcast from 12/26/77)

1605. "The Rich Ostrich" (5/29/78; rebroadcast 11/14/78)

Cast: Don Scardino (Jack Simon); Patricia Elliott (Julie Hendricks); Leon Janney (Big Bill); Earl Hammond (Sir Zafrullah). Written by G. Frederic Lewis.

Despite the warning of Julie Hendricks, a circus owner's daughter, Sir Zafrullah Muhmed gets too close to the circus's ostrich cage, and one of the six birds reaches out and plucks a $250,000 diamond from his turban. Nobody knows which bird took the jewel because the one that did immediately rushes back to join the others. Reporter Jim Simon's story of the incident makes national headlines, and Julie's father, Big Bill, sees a way to make big money for his failing enterprise. The only stumbling block is Sir Zafrullah, who wants his diamond back.

1606. **"The Bittersweet Honeymoon"** (5/30/78; rebroadcast 11/16/78)

Cast: Jada Rowland (Mary Shelton); Russell Horton (Jim Shelton); Ian Martin (Purser); Gordon Heath (Enzio). Written by Ian Martin.

Because of a mix-up in the booking of their passages from Italy, honeymooners Jim and Mary Shelton are given the ship's most expensive suite, vacated at the last minute by a Middle Eastern shah. As Jim carries Mary into the sumptuous quarters, he is knocked unconscious by an assailant who manages to get away before Mary can get a good look at him. The ship's purser figures the shah was the assailant's intended victim, but Jim and Mary are not at all convinced.

1607. **"The Missouri Kid"** (5/31/78; rebroadcast from 12/28/77)

1608. **"The Silent Woman"** (6/1/78; rebroadcast 11/18/78)

Cast: John Beal (Franz Komar); Carol Teitel (Veile); Bob Dryden (Leyb Narr); Joan Shay (Bettel Komar); Norman Rose (Rabbi Mendi); Based on a story by Leopold Kompert, and adapted by Percy Granger.

Within moments after her marriage to a prosperous young merchant, Veile Komar becomes silent. She says not a word to her husband on their wedding night, during the births of her two children, nor even during the marriage of her daughter. Her friends and relatives are convinced she is under some kind of evil spell. Only her rabbi knows the real reason, and he is pledged to secrecy until after Veile dies.

1609. **"Diamond Cut Woman"** (6/2/78; rebroadcast 11/21/78)

Cast: Norman Rose (Sir Charles); Fred Gwynne (Colonel Clay); Earl Hammond (Sy Wentworth); Barbara Sohmers (Mrs. Picard). Written by G. Frederic Lewis.

Sir Charles Vandrift, who has made a fortune in diamonds, is attracted during a stay on the French Riviera by a woman who constantly wins at roulette. She tells Sir Charles that she gets her winning numbers from a guru, Mara Mishi, who has many other remarkable powers. Sir Charles demands to be introduced to Mishi, who is known to the police as the slippery Colonel Clay, a master swindler. The colonel finds Sir Charles a most gullible victim—not once, but twice.

1610. **"The Ninth Volume"** (6/3/78; rebroadcast from 12/30/77)

1611. **"Peter, Peter, Pumpkin Eater"** (6/4/78; rebroadcast from 1/2/78)

1612. **"The Undying Heart"** (6/5/78; rebroadcast 11/23/78)

Cast: Mandel Kramer (Sid Parks); Bryna Raeburn (Alice Parks); Joan Shay (Aunt Esther); Ian Martin (Parker Wilson). Written by Ian Martin.

Instead of delivering the $50,000 his bookie owes to a gangster, Sid Parks goes to the roulette wheels in Vegas and loses the entire bundle. His wife, Alice, points out that Sid's life is not for long if he doesn't get up the cash in a hurry. Sid's only hope is his 86-year-old Aunt Esther, owner of a large life insurance policy naming him the beneficiary. But Aunt Esther is not ready to die, at least from natural causes. Sid must overcome that little problem within a week.

1613. "Miracle in Sharon City" (6/6/78; rebroadcast 11/25/78)

Cast: Joan Beal (Frank Spencer); Ann Williams (Marie Spencer); Ray Owens (Will Johnson); Bob Dryden (Elwood Starbright). Written by Sam Dann.

Frank Spencer, mayor of Sharon City, is a hero. He has gone to Chicago and convinced the Miller-Basford Corporation to build a new factory in Sharon City, creating 800 new jobs and prosperity for all. But then a former employee of the corporation comes to town and tells Frank that in its reduction process the factory will emit Amphoran, which, if inhaled over a few years, can turn people into homicidal maniacs. Frank wants to listen, but his fellow citizens don't.

Notes: John Beal's film credits include *Les Misérables* (1935), *Madame X* (1937), *Edge of Darkness* (1943), *Amityville 3: The Demon* (1983), and *The Kid Who Loved Christmas* (1990).

1614. "Family Album" (6/7/78; rebroadcast from 1/4/78)

1615. "Death Spell" (6/8/78; rebroadcast 11/28/78)

Cast: Ralph Bell (Tom Craven); Joan Banks (Helen Craven); Gordon Heath (Bart Crowley); Teri Keane (Roslyn Crowley). Written by Elspeth Eric.

Struggling artist Tom Craven meets an old friend from his art school days, Bart Crowley, now too rich to worry about painting. Bart offers Tom and his wife, Helen, the use of the studio on his estate—for free. The Cravens are suspicious of this sudden generosity and soon find their suspicions are not unfounded. Bart is afraid that his beautiful Trinidadian wife has cast a death spell over him and needs the Cravens to try and help him overcome it.

Notes: Theater went live at the Garden State Art Center in New Jersey on this date. WOR in New York went live that day, from 5:30 A.M. to 10 P.M. *Theater* did not run its usual show on WOR that night. Instead, Gene Klavan announced the show in place of E.G. Marshall, who was at the Theater doing *The Gin Game.* Himan Brown showed the versatility of radio actors when Carol Teitel and Bob Dryden (playing dual roles) did a scene from "Silent Woman," an upcoming episode. Teitel did a scene from *The Glass Menagerie,* a play she did when she was 18. Then she played the role of Laura; now she played the part of the mother. Ian Martin did a speech from the revival of *Inherit the Wind.* The episode "Death Spell" as described above, was broadcast nationally, while the local origination, WOR, broadcasted this live special instead. WOR listeners were able to catch this episode a few months later when it was repeated in November.

1616. "A Long Way from Home" (6/9/78; rebroadcast 11/30/78)

Cast: Russell Horton (Youth); Evelyn Juster (Girl); Arnold Moss (Dr. Malson); Lloyd Battista (Sam). Adapted by Arnold Moss, based on the 1891 short story *The Mocking-Bird* by Ambrose Bierce.

In 1862 a young man and his friend, Sam, enlist in the Union Army. During their first taste of battle, Sam is fatally wounded and the young man panics. While running from the battlefield, he receives a head wound, which is treated at an army hospital. Later, he finds himself wandering around the Tennessee countryside, trying to find his regiment and explain why his wound was in the back—not in the front—of his head.

1617. "The Laughing Maiden" (6/10/78; rebroadcast from 1/13/78)

1618. "In Another Place" (6/11/78; rebroadcast from 1/16/78)

1619. "Alias Mr. Aladdin" (6/12/78; rebroadcast 12/5/78)

Cast: Bob Dryden (David McNell); Teri Keane (Walt Hollins); Roberta Maxwell (Ann Baker); Joan Beal (Ben Baker). Written by Roy Winsor.

When his young wife, Millie, asks David McNell, her elderly husband, where he gets his money, he says it comes from a genie in a lamp. She and her boyfriend, Walt Hollins, want the money, all of it—after Dave dies, of course. But they realize they can't get rid of him until he tells them the truth about the money's hiding place. Dave has told only one person—his best friend, County Prosecutor Ben Baker—who also has some ideas about who should get Dave's bank roll.

1620. "A Model Murderer" (6/13/78; rebroadcast from 1/17/78)

1621. "Charlie, the Actor" (6/14/78; rebroadcast 12/7/78)

Cast: Leon Janney (Bouncer Dugan); Earl Hammond (The Sergeant); Bryna Raeburn (Molly). Written by Sam Dann.

Bouncer Dugan, nearing retirement as one of New York City's finest, is sent to guard King Zophrana of Murania during his visit to the United Nations. Dugan soon becomes suspicious of the king's regal qualifications, certain he's seen his face before—as Carleton Billingham Drake, otherwise known as "Charlie," the Actor, an escaped murderer. His young sergeant thinks Dugan is wrong, until Dugan manages to get the "king's" fingerprints on a drinking glass.

1622. "Sophia and the Pilgrim" (6/15/78; rebroadcast from 1/19/78)

1623. "The Unholy Miracle" (6/16/78; rebroadcast 12/12/78)

Cast: Mandel Kramer (Harry Kemp); Barbara Sohmers (Sara Kemp); Carol Teitel (Natasha Baronchev); Betsy Beard (Susan Kemp); Ian Martin (Colonel Jim Stein). Written by Ian Martin.

Harry and Sarah Kemp are distressed by a phone call for their adopted daughter, Susan, whose picture recently appeared in newspapers. The caller claims she is Susan's mother they look exactly alike, she says, because Susan is a clone, the result of parthenogenesis, the development of an egg without fertilization. The Kemps, who believe that the miracle of birth should not be tampered with, swear they'll never allow this woman to come anywhere near their beloved daughter.

1624. "The Enchanted Child" (6/17/78; rebroadcast from 1/20/78)

1625. "The Forgetful Ghost" (6/18/78; rebroadcast from 1/23/78)

1626. "Dr. Jekyll and Mrs. Hyde" (6/19/78; rebroadcast 12/14/78)

Cast: William Prince (Sheriff Ed Blake); Earl Hammond (Sam Teller); Evelyn Juster (Mary Teller); Bryna Raeburn (Mrs. Jessie Teller); Earl Hammond (Arthur Courtney). Written by G. Frederic Lewis.

Sam Teller even permits ex-con Arthur Courtney to wed his daughter, Mary, after he allows Arthur to run his business. Within five years Courtney is able to expand Teller's business into 22 thriving steak houses and, in recognition of this accomplishment, is elected president of the Junior Chamber of Commerce. But suddenly he disappears, as does Mary. A piece of cloth torn from her dress is found in a remote area. She is presumed to be dead, and all evidence gathered by Sheriff Ed Blake points to Courtney as her murderer.

1627. "The Ranee of Rajputana" (6/20/78; rebroadcast from 1/24/78)

1628. "A Matter of Faith" (6/21/78; rebroadcast 12/19/78)

Cast: Michael Wager (Vernon McCabe); Gordon Heath (Efran Limon); Ian Martin (Marcos Valdez); Carol Teitel (Carla Jemne). Written by Percy Granger.

Sent to Rio de Janeiro to ascertain why shipments of rosewood ordered by his company have suddenly come to a halt, Vernon McCabe meets, by chance, a woman who looks like Carla Jemne, a friend who was executed 12 years ago by revolutionary leader Marcos Valdez. Because of a birthmark and possession of a locket he gave her, McCabe is certain she is Carla, But he can't figure out how she could still be alive.

1629. "The Safety Match" (6/22/78; rebroadcast from 1/26/78)

1630. "The Black Door" (6/23/78; rebroadcast 12/21/78)

Cast: Kevin McCarthy (John Albermarle); Guy Sorel (Mr. Cartwright); Russell Horton (Michael Torrance). Adapted by G. Frederic Lewis, based on the 1908 short story *The Sealed Room* by Sir Arthur Conan Doyle.

Solicitor John Albermarle assists young Michael Torrance who, on a foggy London night, has been run down by a speeding horse and carriage. Albermarle accompanies Michael to his home, his rich father's mansion in which he now lives alone. Michael tells the lawyer about a sealed black door upstairs which his father, in his instructions, says Michael shall open when he reaches 21. But when the time comes, Michael is too frightened to enter the room.

1631. "The Defectors" (6/24/78; rebroadcast from 1/27/78)

1632. "Yesterday's Giant" (6/25/78; rebroadcast from 1/30/78)

1633. "Lady Bluebeard" (6/26/78; rebroadcast 12/26/78)

Cast: Fred Gwynne (Raymond Poindexter); Marian Hailey (Luana Pilbeam); Bob Dryden (Dr. Braithwaite). Written by Sam Dann.

Raymond Poindexter, an insurance investigator, is sent by his company to call on Luana Pilbeam, 35 and very attractive, because she has been the beneficiary of six now-deceased elderly men, all of whom were married to her for less than two years. Poindexter sincerely believes that she poisoned them all. He becomes convinced she is guilty of murder when he drinks some of her lemonade "with a secret ingredient," causing both his temperature and heartbeat to rise dangerously.

Notes: Marian Hailey can be seen in the films *Jenny* (1970) and *Lovers and Other Strangers* (1970).

1634. "The Ice Palace" (6/27/78; rebroadcast from 1/31/78)

1635. "The Quadruple" (6/28/78; rebroadcast 12/28/78)

Cast: Michael Tolan (Vittorio Basso); Evelyn Juster (Lilo); Ian Martin (Lou Cypher); Court Benson (Papa). Written by Ian Martin.

Vittoria Basso, determined to perfect a triple somersault in his circus trapeze act, gets some unexpected encouragement from fire-eater "The Amazing Diavolo" (real name Lou Cypher). Lou, who says he's also a psychiatrist, maintains that Vittorio can accomplish the feat if he is willing to risk everything. Vittoria succeeds and now wants to learn the quadruple, only this time he doesn't have complete support of the man he considers to be the devil.

1636. "Don't Look Back" (6/29/78; rebroadcast from 2/2/78)

1637. "The Good Times Express" (6/30/78; rebroadcast 1/2/79)

Cast: Ralph Bell (Alvin Smith); Roberta Maxwell (Polly); Bob Dryden (Max). Written by Sam Dann.

Calvin Smith, a cynical, disillusioned science teacher, en route to Boston to sell a children's game he calls Bomb-O, is detained when his plane comes down for minor repairs. While waiting, Smith is told the flight has been canceled because of snow in Boston. He refuses to believe this since it is June 15, so he boards the Good Times Express, a train that, according to a taxi driver, is bound for Boston. But a fellow passenger tells Smith it is the Boston of 1775, not 1978.

1638. "The Postmistress of Laurel Run" (7/1/78; rebroadcast from 2/3/78)

1639. "The Talking Women" (7/2/78; rebroadcast from 2/6/78)

1640. "King Bankrobber" (7/3/78; rebroadcast 1/3/79)

Cast: Mason Adams (Michael Emerson); Earl Hammond (Sam Horton); Ray Owens (Red Wilson); Jackson Beck (Charlie Harris). Written by G. Frederic Lewis.

Michael Emerson, holder of an architectural degree, is enraged at the light probationary sentence given the 18-year-old youth who, while driving a stolen car, killed Emerson's parents. In a personal vendetta against society, Emerson becomes the world's best bank robber by utilizing his architectural skills. No one suspects him, not even after he retires.

1641. "Dr. Heidegger's Experiment" (7/4/78; rebroadcast from 2/7/78)

1642. "My Kingdom for a Horse" (7/5/78; rebroadcast 1/29/79)

Cast: Joe Silver (Fishface Harnishfegger); Mandel Kramer (Swifty); Bryna Raeburn (Blue Streak); Bryna Raeburn (Cupcake). Written by Sam Dann.

Fishface Harnishfegger, taking $300 of his fiancée's money to buy her a wedding ring, spends it on a horse instead. Swifty, the seller, has conned Fishface into believing all horseplayers should own a steed. This one, named Blue Streak, turns out to be a 20-year-old bag of bones. But Blue Streak can talk, and Fishface foresees millions for them on television. But when Fishface brings his bride-to-be to meet Blue Streak, the horse refuses to say a word.

1643. "All Unregistered Aliens" (7/6/78; rebroadcast from 2/9/78)

1644. "The Four-Fifteen Express" (7/7/78; rebroadcast 1/31/79)

Cast: William Prince (William Langford); Ian Martin (John Dwerhouse); Anne Williams (Amanda Jelf); Earl Hammond (Augustus Raikes). Adapted by Elizabeth Pennell, based on the short story by Amelia B. Edwards.

William Langford is given the railroad company's compartment for his trip on the 4:15 express from London. Though told he will be traveling alone, he is joined by John Dwerhouse, who says he is carrying 75,000 pounds of the company's money in cash. When Langford reaches his destination and tells his friends about Dwerhouse and the money, he is ordered to stay in his room. His friends fear he may be somehow involved with Dwerhouse, who absconded with the money three months ago.

1645. "Reflected Terror" (7/8/78; rebroadcast from 2/10/78)

1646. "Night Eyes" (7/9/78; rebroadcast from 2/13/78)

1647. "Sound Advice" (7/10/78; rebroadcast 2/2/79)

Cast: Carol Teitel (Doreen); Martha Greenhouse (Mavis Gumbler); Court Benson (Freddy Gumbler); Arnold Moss (Sheriff). Written by Victoria Dann.

Doreen, whose syndicated column is read by millions, sincerely believes she has never given the wrong answer to any question sent in by her readers. But when a woman she told to leave her husband is drowned in an auto accident, Doreen has a suspicion that the woman's husband, who managed to survive, may have intentionally driven the car into the water. She takes a few days leave from her desk to find out if her suspicion has any merit.

1648. "Guardian Angel" (7/11/78; rebroadcast 2/3/79)

Cast: Jada Rowland (Doreen); John Beal (Dr. Alden); Russell Horton (David); Guy Sorel (Father). Written by Elspeth Eric.

David, who has taken over his family's truck body plant, is smitten by a teenager named Jane whom he sees sitting under a tree on his father's vast estate.

Jane—brilliant, mystical and comfortable with inmates of the local asylum—is unlike any female David has known. She wanders a lot, sees things that others don't, but declares she is always protected by her guardian angel, someone, she says, David must find if he is ever to know the real meaning of life.

1649. "Revenge Is Sweet" (7/12/78; rebroadcast from 2/14/78)

1650. "The Village of Fools" (7/13/78; rebroadcast 4/5/79)

Cast: Fred Gwynne (Mendele-Moishe); Bob Dryden (Baron Rothschild); Bryna Raeburn (Soureh-Rivkah). Written by Sam Dann.

Baron Rothschild, a man of great wealth, dispatches Mendele-Moishe to find the town of Chellem, whose location is known to no one. Mendele will know it, the Baron says, when he finds it; it is a village of fools. Mendele is sure he has located such a place when he meets a man searching for a ruble he lost in some mud. He is looking for it on hard, dry ground which, he says, should make it much easier to find.

1651. "The Hanging Judge" (7/14/78; rebroadcast 4/6/79)

Cast: Court Benson (Judge Moor); Teri Keane (Margaret Browne); Earl Hammond (Edgar Browne); William Griffis (Jack Powell). Based on actual court records of London's Old Bailey, and written by G. Frederic Lewis.

After firing his assistant for stealing six silk shirts from his store, Edgar Browne is so upbraided by his creditors that he closes his shop and prepares to sail for America. While waiting in Plymouth to embark, he is accused of theft, based on circumstantial evidence. But he fears the man who will judge him, a man who, people say, has no qualms about sentencing 20 men to death at Margate before he eats his lunch. And in those days, robbery was punishable by death.

1652. "Something in the Air" (7/15/78; rebroadcast from 2/16/78)

1653. "The Church of Hell" (7/16/78; rebroadcast from 2/17/78)

1654. "The Tell-Tale Scar" (7/17/78; rebroadcast 4/3/79)

Cast: Tony Roberts (Ted Brooks); Russell Horton (Webb Morrison); Ralph Bell (Paul Galvano); Ray Owens (Mike Larkin). Written by Roy Winsor.

The *Forum*'s ace reporter, Ted Brooks, is certain that restaurant owner Paul Galvano is really Mobster Tony Campo, who was supposedly killed in a shoot-out. He is sure because both men have the same tell-tale scar on their faces. District Attorney Webb Morrison agrees, but the records show that Campo was pronounced dead by a doctor and buried by a reputable undertaker. Defying the law, Brooks and Morrison disinter Campo's casket. They find no body, only a sealed gold box containing the gangster's ashes.

1655. "The Absent-Minded League" (7/18/78; rebroadcast 4/10/79)

Cast: Norman Rose (Eugene Valmont); Bob Dryden (Podgers); Lloyd Battista (Inspector Hale). Adapted by Gerald Keane, based on a story by Robert Barr.

Inspector Spenser Hale of Scotland Yard seeks the assistance of the famed Eugene Valmont in putting behind bars the leaders of a gang, minting fake five-shilling silver coins. As Valmont hearts up his investigation, he discovers Scotland Yard has been tracking the wrong people, ones involved in an entirely different racket: taking advantage of anyone who is absent-minded.

1656. "Angel from England" (7/19/78; rebroadcast from 2/20/78)

1657. "The Further You Go, the Less You Know" (7/20/78; rebroadcast 1/16/79)

Cast: Mandel Kramer (Bridges Barzell); Bryna Raeburn (Dimples Kovacs); Ian Martin (Leonard Kovacs). Written by Sam Dann.

Bridges Barzell, a hustler downcast because the gullible population is rapidly decreasing, meets up with an old girlfriend, Dimples Kovacs, who's worried about her husband, Leonard. Also a veteran hustler, Leonard has been conned by a guru into believing he is the reincarnation of Leonardo da Vinci. Under the guru's influence, Leonard is painting a second portrait of Mona Lisa, which the conniving guru figures will put millions into his pocket.

1658. "The Locked Trunk" (7/21/78; rebroadcast 1/18/79)

Cast: Patricia Elliott (Rosalind Wingate); Russell Horton (Arthur Lloyd); Betsy Beard (Perdita Wingate); Gordon Gould (Bernard Wingate); Ann Pitoniak (Mrs. Wingate). Adapted by Roy Winsor, based on the 1868 short story *The Romance of Certain Old Clothes* by Henry James.

Beautiful Rosalind Wingate vows she will make life miserable for her plain-Jane sister, Perdita, when wealthy and handsome Arthur Lloyd chooses Perdita for his wife. Rosalind is very successful. Perdita dies after giving birth to a daughter, and Rosalind snares Arthur. But Perdita still has an ace in the hole: a locked trunk full of her best clothes that Rosalind desperately desires.

1659. "A Phantom Yesterday" (7/22/78; rebroadcast from 2/21/78)

1660. "Vanishing Lady" (7/23/78; rebroadcast from 2/23/78)

1661. "Close Shave" (7/24/78; rebroadcast 1/20/79)

Cast: Larry Haines (Algernon Pepper); Evelyn Juster (Lolly Dankowitz); Earl Hammond (Elwood Fenris). Written by Sam Dann.

Algernon Pepper gets the ear of billionaire Elwood Fenris by offering him the crown of Dalzeel and marriage to Dalzeel's beautiful princess, ineligible to the throne because of the Salic law. Aided by his confederate, Lolly Dankowitz, who pretends she's the princess, and Dalzeel's ambassador to the UN, who agrees to promote the hoax because of his many personal debts, Pepper convinces Fenris to sign a million-dollar contract. But his plans begin to falter when Fenris and Lolly fall in love.

1662. "The Stranger Inside" (7/25/78; rebroadcast 1/21/79)

Cast: Ralph Bell (Lieutenant Jerry Garfield); Ian Martin (Downs); Carol Teitel (June Wicklow). Written by Sam Dann.

Monica Wicklow's dead body and handbag containing $5,000 in small bills are found in a slum area. Knowing that Monica had once been picked up for drug possession, Lt. Jerry Garfield presumes she was killed for pushing on someone's turf. Unwilling to accept this, Monica's stepmother decides to case the slum area herself, searching for witnesses. She soon thinks she's found one: a girl who looks just like Monica and who is running for her life.

1663. "Loser Take All" (7/26/78; rebroadcast from 2/24/78)

1664. "The Cabinet of the Unsolved" (7/27/78; rebroadcast 1/23/79)

Cast: Bob Dryden (Inspector Hilliard); Ray Owens (Mack McGuire); Lloyd Battista (Edwin); Robert Kaliban (Timothy). Adapted by G. Frederic Lewis, based on a short story by Sir Arthur Conan Doyle.

Timothy, who has never made it as an actor, uses his thespian training and skills at disguise to help him and his partner, Mack McGuire, make a fortune playing fixed poker games with gentlemen of means. But Timothy's brother Edwin is determined to put a stop to these deceptions. When lecturing doesn't work, Edwin interrupts one of the card games to expose his brother's methods of cheating. Nothing, however, seems to discourage Timothy, until he turns up dead.

1665. "Double-Take" (7/28/78; rebroadcast 1/25/79)

Cast: Marian Seldes (Ellie Reynolds); Patricia Elliott (Susan Powell); Charles Irving (Jack Reynolds/Powell); Robert Maxwell (Joe Crim). Written by Percy Granger.

As small-time writer Susan Powell is accusing renowned novelist Ellie Reynolds of stealing her story, they discover an uncanny number of parallels in their plots. Each has written about what her husband probably does on extended business trips; each has come up with a story of a man who has two wives. After comparing more notes, they find they are the wives of the same bigamist. So, to taunt him, they agree to switch homes and to sit back and enjoy his reactions. But, on her way to Susan's house, Ellie disappears.

1666. "Second Sight" (7/29/78; rebroadcast from 2/27/78)

1667. "A Message from Space" (7/30/78; rebroadcast from 2/28/78)

1668. "The Vanishing Point" (7/31/78; rebroadcast 1/27/79)

Cast: Fred Gwynne (Dr. William Carstairs); Court Benson (Kellner); Earl Hammond (Inspector Mueller); Bryna Raeburn (Erika Bauer). Written by Sam Dann.

Dr. William Carstairs, in Munich to deliver a paper on dislocated ionic particles in a negatively charged nucleus, tries to locate a Dr. Franz Wilhelm Klust who, in the 1930s, wrote a monograph on the disappearance of matter. While conducting his search, Carstairs is kidnapped, beaten and threatened with death. Klust, it seems, is a captive of Germany's new National Restoration Party which is demanding that he develop the ultimate weapon that will give Germany another try at conquering the world.

1669. "You Tell Me Your Dream" (8/1/78; rebroadcast from 3/2/78)

1670. "The Devil's Brew" (8/2/78; rebroadcast 1/28/79)

Cast: Russell Horton (Dusty Lane); Rosemary Rice (Sally Mae); Ian Martin (Mr. Conjureman); Leon Janney (Stacey Engel). Written by Ian Martin.

Nineteen-year-old Dusty Lane, against his parents' wishes, has signed a big league baseball contract with the Cougars. With a batting average of .392, he's soon everybody's hero. But then he's knocked unconscious by a baseball. While in a coma, he meets a Mr. Conjureman, who says he has failed "to honor thy father and thy mother." Furthermore, Mr. C. says, Dusty must either sign with *his* team, the Hellcats, or never get another major league hit.

1671. "The Assassin" (8/3/78; rebroadcast from 3/3/78)

1672. "The Avenging Shot of Kitty Morgan" (8/4/78; rebroadcast 2/6/79)

Cast: Mandel Kramer (Joseph Chesny); Bryna Raeburn (Aunt Sylvia); Sam Gray (Tom Bullen); Evelyn Juster (Julie Miller). Written by Sam Dann.

Shortly after Kitty Morgan killed herself in the Chesny mansion nearly 100 years ago, her unfaithful lover, Robert Chesny, died there, his cause of death "unknown." Since then the mansion has been vacant, because Kitty's ghost is said to lurk there. Now, a century later, Robert Chesny's great-grandson, Joseph, decides to transform the mansion into a resort hotel. He goes there unaware that Kitty's ghost has vowed to murder any male descendant of Robert's who enters the old mansion.

1673. "The House and the Brain" (8/5/78; rebroadcast from 3/6/78)

1674. "The Red Scarf" (8/6/78; rebroadcast from 3/7/78)

1675. "The Sixth Commandment" (8/7/78; rebroadcast 2/8/79)

Cast: Teri Keane (Ginnie); Gilbert Mack (Lawyer Ridges); Ian Martin (Clem); Russell Horton (Jody). Written by Ian Martin.

Clem is furious when he learns that his deceased father has willed the family farm to his younger brother, Jody, always his father's favorite. Clem figures the only way to get what is "rightfully" his is to murder Jody. When Jody returns from agricultural college with his new bride, Ginnie, Clem decides he wants her too. But Clem is so brutal in his approach that Ginnie starts thinking the only way to stop him is to somehow arrange his murder, maybe even doing it herself.

1676. "The Instant Millionaires" (8/8/78; rebroadcast from 3/9/78)

1677. "The Versegy Case" (8/9/78; rebroadcast 2/9/79)

Cast: Bob Dryden (Sandor Versegy); Arnold Moss (Detective Plaut); William Griffis (Commissioner Franz); Carol Teitel (Helena Versegy). Written by Gerald Keane.

The Budapest police are visited by a nervous and very excited Sandor Versegy, a professor who claims he was robbed of securities worth 150,000 gulden and most of his wife's jewelry. All the evidence the police collect make it appear that Versegy robbed himself so he could claim the insurance. But Detective Richard Plaut, after a trip to Vienna, thinks otherwise, even after the professor seems to admit his own guilt by committing suicide.

1678. "Who Is George Williams?" (8/10/78; rebroadcast from 3/10/78)

1679. "Doctor Eduardo" (8/11/78; rebroadcast 2/13/79)

Cast: Norman Rose (Dr. Eduardo Columbo); Betsy Beard (Susan Greeley); Bob Dryden (Mayor Greeley); Earl Hammond (Matthew Greeley); Lloyd Battista (Defense Counsel). Adapted by Gerald Keane, based on the 1908 short story *The Black Doctor* by Sir Arthur Conan Doyle.

Strangers are always looked upon with suspicion in the small fishing village of Winter Harbor, and the arrival of Portuguese-born doctor Eduardo Columbo proves to be no exception. But Columbo turns out to be an excellent physician, and until he proposes to Mayor Horace Greeley's daughter, there is no attempt made to run him out of town. However, shortly after he seeks Susan Greeley's hand, he is found murdered in his new home, and Susan's brother, Matthew, is the chief suspect.

1680. "The Wheel of Life" (8/12/78; rebroadcast from 3/13/78)

1681. "The Impossible Is True" (8/13/78; rebroadcast from 3/14/78)

1682. "The Black Sheep and the Captain" (8/14/78; rebroadcast 2/15/79)

Cast: Jack Grimes (William Hutchens); Jackson Beck (Captain Tanner); Ian Martin (Sailor); Ray Owens (Uncle Arthur). Adapted by G. Frederic Lewis, based on the 1894 short story *The Winning Shot* by Sir Arthur Conan Doyle.

William Hutchens, a 20-year-old college student, is summoned from Land's End, England, by his Uncle Arthur who, ten years ago, moved in a hurry to the desolate moors of northern England. Arthur had left after being badly beaten up by a sailor who claimed Arthur had cheated him. Now out of jail, the sailor is again after Arthur, who asks his nephew to bring a gun and lots of ammunition.

1683. "The Time Fold" (8/15/78; rebroadcast from 3/16/78)

1684. "Raptures of the Deep" (8/16/78; rebroadcast 2/16/79)

Cast: Michael Tolan (Steve Carr); Ray Owens (J. Calvin Hunter); Catherine Byers (Ariadne); Sam Gray (Cobb Straker). Written by Ian Martin.

Two former U.S. Navy frogmen—Steve Carr and Cobb Straker—agree to dive for treasure hunter J. Calvin Hunter, who claims he knows the exact location of a Spanish ship sunk in the Atlantic in 1663. Carr is able to dive the deepest, and what he discovers he can't believe. A beautiful woman surrounded by man-shaped scaly creatures takes him much deeper—to what he later learns is the lost island of Atlantis and a very advanced underwater civilization.

1685. "Identified Flying Objects" (8/17/78; rebroadcast from 3/17/78)

1686. "Our Own Jailer" (8/18/78; rebroadcast 2/20/79)

Cast: John Beal (Howard Spurlow); Bryna Raeburn (Marla); Ian Martin (Mr. Gordon); Robert Kaliban (Davis). Written by Sam Dann.

Howard Spurlow, who draws designs for food can labels, and Mr. Gordon, a teacher of poetry in a junior college, meet in a bar. Both agree they should free themselves of their responsibilities and become, respectively, a great artist and a great poet. Spurlow manages, in what seems to be a dream, to fulfill his ambition with the help of a beautiful woman. But later, when Gordon refuses to help him find a way to rejoin the woman, a furious Spurlow pulls a gun and kills him.

1687. "All Things Are Beautiful" (8/19/78; rebroadcast from 3/20/78)

1688. "The Golden Amulet" (8/20/78; rebroadcast from 3/21/78)

1689. "Cross Fire" (8/21/78; rebroadcast 2/21/79)

Cast: Russell Horton (Frank Grove); Ann Williams (Lucy Grove); Court Benson (Langston); Earl Hammond (Lieutenant Thompson). Written by Percy Granger.

Frank Grove, because it's a slow day, agrees to drive a well-dressed businessman to an address in the South Bronx, a trip a lot of cabbies refuse to make. It wasn't such a good decision, however, because Grove soon realizes he's trapped between two gangs of diamond thieves, one expecting him to deliver a bag containing $250,000 of the jewels, the other watching every move he makes.

1690. "The Judas Kiss" (8/22/78; rebroadcast from 3/23/78)

1691. "The Eavesdropper" (8/23/78; rebroadcast 2/23/79)

Cast: Teri Keane (Myrtle Chapman); Charles Irving (Martin Chapman); Ralph Bell (Charlie); Morleen Rouse (Woman). Written by Elspeth Eric.

Myrtle Chapman, married for eight years to a man who pays little attention to her (he likes to read), eavesdrops as he calls another woman on the phone. Their conversation is about Hermes, the Greek god who helped people. According to legend, his statue could be asked a question, the answer coming later in the very first thing the questioner heard anyone say. Knowing there's a small statue of Hermes in a neighborhood bar, Myrtle goes there alone to ask it whether her husband still loves her. The answer is startling.

1692. "Wise Child" (8/24/78; rebroadcast from 3/24/78)

1693. "The Other Soul" (8/25/78; rebroadcast 2/27/79)

Cast: Russell Horton (Dr. Adam Parks); Mandel Kramer (Dr. Larry Cain); Anne Williams (Gabriella); Jackson Beck (Mario). Written by Gerald Keane.

Dr. Adam Parks, in Rome for a convention, tries to help a beautiful woman who appears ready to faint as they tour the catacombs. She hands him her business card, on the back of which is a message in Latin written with red ink. When he asks the manager of his hotel to translate it for him, Parks is ordered to leave the hotel—and Rome. When he returns to Long Island, his wife leaves him, as does the doctor with whom he shares his practice. He is even shot at by the local police. Does he have a severe case of the black plague?

1694. "The Pretend Person" (8/26/78; rebroadcast from 3/27/78)

1695. "The Ghost in the Well" (8/27/78; rebroadcast from 3/28/78)

1696. "Will the Real Amy Stand Up?" (8/28/78; rebroadcast 3/1/79)

Cast: Jennifer Harmon (Amy Trowbridge); Ian Martin (Ephraim Clough); Ray Owens (Hedley Spence); Bryna Raeburn (Hester Spence). Written by Ian Martin.

Amy Trowbridge, just past 21, suddenly finds herself alone and ill-equipped to care for herself after years of nursing her invalid and tyrannical father. Shortly after his death, two kindly and compassionate cousins—Hedley and Hester Spence—turn up and offer to live with Amy in her spacious country mansion. But their interest is more in Amy's large fortune than in her well-being.

1697. "Big City Blues" (8/29/78; rebroadcast from 3/30/78)

1698. "The Biggest Fish in the World" (8/30/78; rebroadcast 3/2/79)

Cast: Joan Shay (Agatha Porcelain); Leon Janney (Digby Porcelain); Earl Hammond (Luther Flensing); William Griffis (Mr. Follansbee). Written by Sam Dann.

Digby Porcelain, whose occupation is even unknown to his wife Agatha, is swallowed by Spartacus, the prize catch of Agatha's whale-loving society, the Cetaceans. Outraged when Agatha, their president, insists that Spartacus be sliced open, the Cetaceans launch a massive "Save Spartacus" campaign. Meanwhile, Digby secretly returns to Agatha to explain that his being swallowed by Spartacus was in the line of duty and why Spartacus must not be destroyed.

1699. "Shark Bait" (8/31/78; rebroadcast from 3/31/78)

1700. "Flash Point" (9/1/78; rebroadcast 3/13/79)

Cast: Kevin McCarthy (John Roth); Court Benson (Mr. Horrocks); Felicia Farr (Sarah Horrocks). Adapted by Gerald Keane, based on a story by H.G. Wells.

Writer John Roth is sent by his editor to a Pennsylvania steel town to capture in words the "beauty" of the place. While doing his research, he meets and falls in love with Sarah Horrocks, wife of the man who runs the blast furnaces. They don't think her husband realizes what is happening until he forces Roth to take a walk with him to the steel mill's dangerous areas where many others have had fatal accidents.

Notes: Felicia Farr has appeared in many films over the years, most notably: *Jubal* (1956), *3:10 to Yuma* (1957), *Kiss Me, Stupid!* (1964), *Kotch* (1971), and *Charley Varrick* (1973).

1701. "Fortune's Favorite" (9/2/78; rebroadcast from 4/3/78)

1702. "Delusion of Reprieve" (9/3/78 rebroadcast from 4/4/78)

1703. "Devil's Gold" (9/4/78; rebroadcast 3/8/79)

Cast: Russell Horton (Rusty West); Lloyd Battista (Frank Barth); Betsy Beard (Kim Morgan); Earl Hammond (Guy Fowler). Written by Bob Juhren.

While souvenir shopping, Rusty West visits an antique shop known as The Devil's Boutique because it mysteriously appears, vanishes and then reappears in another location. Inside, he scares off a thief and, in gratitude, the shopkeeper gives Rusty a gold coin which, he says, can never belong to anyone else. This is confirmed when Rusty loses the coin in a gamble to a man who is later killed, and the coin turns up again in Rusty's possession, implicating him in a murder.

1704. "A Tragedy of Error" (9/5/78; rebroadcast from 4/6/78)

1705. "Dead Wrong" (9/6/78; rebroadcast 3/9/79)

Cast: Jack Grimes (Elmer Potts); Ralph Bell (Peter Bell); Teri Keane (Marge Bell); Court Benson (Peter Pell). Written by Ian Martin.

Debutante ghost Elmer Potts is ordered to summon the spirit of Peter B. Pell of 25 Sperling Drive and to accompany him in his departure. But, en route to Mr. Pell's house, Potts mislays the invoice and ends up at Peter P. Bell's home at 25 Sterling Street. Despite Bell's resistance, Potts claims his soul. However, on the way to heaven, Potts finds the invoice and, realizing his blunder, knows that he must either convince the unwilling Bell to play dead or convince the unassuming Pell that he is better off dead.

1706. "The Parasite" (9/7/78; rebroadcast from 4/7/78)

1707. "Ignorant Armies" (9/8/78; rebroadcast 3/6/79)

Cast: Mandel Kramer (Walter Patterson); Evelyn Juster (Doctor); Bryna Raeburn (Marina); Ray Owens (Orlov). Written by Sam Dann.

Walter Patterson is a man who works hard at his job as a food chemist, lives with his mother, and has few vices. Yet, suddenly he finds himself held captive by German officers who remind him of a story he told a Fraulein in a bar in Glassenheim, Germany, ten years ago. Trying to impress her, Walter, then a young soldier, claimed that he was in American Intelligence, and now Patterson is threatened with death if he doesn't turn over U.S. government secrets to the Germans.

1708. "Time and Again" (9/9/78; rebroadcast from 3/30/74)

1709. "Childish Laughter" (9/10/78; rebroadcast from 4/10/78)

1710. "End of a Memory" (9/11/78; rebroadcast 3/15/79)
Cast: Tony Roberts (Gilbert Vaughn); Carol Teitel (Pauline March); Ian Martin (Dr. Baker); John Lithgow (Kenyon Grant). Written by Gerald Keane.

Two years before his marriage to Pauline March, Gilbert Vaughn witnessed a murder but was spared by the killer because he was blind. Now, his eyesight restored, he has wed Pauline, who describes herself as someone with no past. Soon, Gilbert discovers that he can't bear her condition, which sometimes makes her forget even yesterday's events. So he investigates her past and finds, to his astonishment, that she, too, was present at the murder.

1711. "Blackmail" (9/12/78; rebroadcast from 4/11/78)

1712. "High Caqueta" (9/13/78; rebroadcast 3/16/79)
Cast: John Beal (Don Bledsoe); Marian Seldes (Margaret Bledsoe); Earl Hammond (Carl Cobb). Written by Percy Granger.

New Hampshire residents Don and Margaret Bledsoe get little response from their congressman, senator or the State Department regarding the disappearance of their daughter, who last wrote that she was in Equador and planning to climb Mt. Caqueta in the Andes. So they go to South America to conduct their own research. However, when the American consulate there reveals that other Americans have been lost on Mt. Caqueta and offers to join the Bledsoes on their climb, Don suspects that this is all part of a sinister plot he can't quite explain.

1713. "The Shriek of the Mandrake" (9/14/78; rebroadcast from 4/13/78)

1714. "The Secret of Crow's Nest" (9/15/78; rebroadcast 3/20/79)
Cast: Mandel Kramer (James Burns); Carol Teitel (Martha Burns); Ian Martin (Slade Brown). Written by Gerald Keane.

It was 30 years ago that James and Martha Burns invited their college chum Slade Brown to their lodge for a weekend of hiking and trail-blazing. Shortly after his arrival, Slade was found dead in front of the fireplace, with James standing over him dangling a rifle. His mind completely blank, James could not defend himself. Now, one prison term later, he returns to confront Slade's ghost who is said to haunt the vacant lodge and to find out what really happened.

1715. "The Fall of the House of Usher" (9/16/78; rebroadcast from 6/8/74)

1716. "Chapter of Errors" (9/17/78; rebroadcast from 4/14/78)

1717. "It's Hard to Be Rich" (9/18/78; rebroadcast 3/22/79)
Cast: Lloyd Battista (Stephen Brooks); Jada Rowland (Jenny); William Griffis (O'Malley); Martha Greenhouse (Hilda). Written by Sam Dann.

When writer Stephen Brooks rents a room in a dingy, dilapidated building, the meddlesome superintendent, Hilda, can't understand why such an obviously wealthy man would tolerate such a seedy place. Her suspicions are further aroused by his complaints that he's being bothered by the piano playing of Jenny Cartwright, who, Hilda knows, had lived there before she was murdered almost a century ago. Hilda takes her worries to the police, who look up Brooks' file and discover that he was the prime suspect in the recent murder of his wife, who was also named Jenny.

1718. "Murder at Troyte's Hill" (9/19/78; rebroadcast from 4/17/78)

1719. "The Beheading" (9/20/78; rebroadcast 3/23/79)

Cast: Teri Keane (Joyce); Grace Matthews (Hester); Court Benson (Doctor); Bryna Raeburn (Nurse). Written by Elspeth Eric.

After seeing a variety of medical practitioners without success, Joyce is still very distressed by her frequent asthma attacks. Then she meets an elderly physician who immediately wins her confidence. In fact, Joyce is so at ease with him that at their first session she agrees to let him perform a head transplant to relieve her discomfort. Now all they have to do is locate a spare head.

1720. "Uncle Louis" (9/21/78; rebroadcast from 4/18/78)

1721. "The Conversation Factor" (9/22/78; rebroadcast 3/27/79)

Cast: Norman Rose (Dr. Frederick Lanners); Jada Rowland (Darlene Jones); Bryna Raeburn (Momma); Earl Hammond (Mr. Carsons). Written by Sam Dann.

En route to resign from what he considers a dead-end project, research scientist Frederick Lanners leaves his attaché case in a diner. Frantically, he returns there, hoping the teenaged cashier, Darlene Jones, has found it. But before he can ask, she says she knows what he wants and hands him the case. Testing her further, Lanners finds that she has ESP and can be the key to his project's success. But Darlene wants no part of it, not even for $50,000.

1722. "The Suicide Club" (9/23/78; rebroadcast from 7/28/74)

1723. "The Avocado Jungle" (9/24/78; rebroadcast from 4/20/78)

1724. "A Table for Two" (9/25/78; rebroadcast 3/29/79)

Cast: Larry Haines (Henri); Court Benson (Herbie Lister); Anne Williams (Helen); Catherine Byers (Margaret). Written by Sam Dann.

Henri de la Tour, the maitre d' at the fashionable Cafe Tremblay, is really Henry Smith, a reformed ex-con with a well-hidden past. One day Henri's old cell mate, Herbie Lister, barges into the cafe and, without a reservation, insists on being served. Henri complies, but Herbie wants more. Unless Henri agrees to help him burglarize the homes of the cafe's wealthiest patrons, Herbie will tell Henri's boss about his past.

1725. "Bet with Angels" (9/26/78; rebroadcast from 4/21/78)

1726. "The Headhunters" (9/27/78; rebroadcast 3/30/79, 5/22/81, 8/27/81)

Cast: Tony Roberts (Tim Lang); Evelyn Juster (Mary Lang); Ian Martin (Dondoc); Mary Jane Higby (Sister Bergeron). Written by Ian Martin.

Newlyweds Tim and Mary Lang return to their native Philippine island to find that Tim's grandmother, Lola, is determined to have him avenge the murder of her husband, Tali, by beheading Mary's grandfather, Dondoc. Claiming that Tali's spirit will be condemned to wander until Dondoc's skull is buried in Tali's grave, Lola summons her voodoo powers to force Tim into beheading Dondoc. When Tim refuses, Tali's ghost threatens to harm the baby Mary is expecting.

1727. "The Grandee of Terra Loco" (9/28/78; rebroadcast from 4/24/78)

1728. "A Thousand-Year-Old Story" (9/29/78; rebroadcast 4/12/79)

Cast: Ralph Bell (Sir Dabney); Carol Teitel (Lady Dabney); Russell Horton (Clive Chubb); Gordon Heath (Jim Trees). Written by Percy Granger.

Sir Dabney is found dead on his yacht soon after it enters a small port in the Marianna Islands. Everyone on board assumes Sir Dabney died of a heart attack, but Dr. Charles Duggin, at the request of police inspector Jim Trees, performs an autopsy, which proves that the 68-year-old millionaire had been poisoned. Trees is convinced the murder was committed by Sir Dabney's secretary, Clive Chubb, whom he discovers, had been having an affair with Dabney's young wife. But Dr. Duggin, an old school chum of Chubb's, refuses to go along with Trees' theory.

1729. "Diary of a Madman" (9/30/78; rebroadcast from 6/15/74)

1730. "International Dateline" (10/1/78; rebroadcast from 4/25/78)

1731. "The Forever Alley" (10/2/78; rebroadcast 4/13/79)

Cast: Larry Haines (Lt. Joe Mulvaney); Catherine Byers (Henrietta); Robert Kaliban (Fred); Marian Seldes (Dr. Martha Underhill). Written by Sam Dann.

The night Bobby Clover vanished, his brother-in-law, police lieutenant Joe Mulvaney, had met him in the bowling alley to discuss a personal matter. According to Joe, Bobby told him to wait in his car while he paid his bill, but Bobby neither left the alley nor remained inside—he just disappeared. After conducting an investigation, Joe believes he knows where Bobby is—only his theory is so incredible he fears he has lost his sanity. Dr. Martha Underhill, a police psychiatrist, doesn't quite agree. She thinks Joe may have murdered his brother-in-law.

1732. "The Queen of Palmyra" (10/3/78; rebroadcast from 4/27/78)

1733. "Shadow of Love" (10/4/78; rebroadcast 4/17/79)

Cast: Norman Rose (Father Murchison); Bob Dryden (Professor Guildea).

Adapted by James Agate, Jr., based on the short story *How Love Came to Professor Guildea* by Robert Hichens.

Professor Guildea, who cringes at the thought of giving or receiving love and affection, leads an isolated, complacent life. Then, one day, he senses that his home has been invaded by an invisible presence. Guildea fears that the being is an evil spirit that wishes to harm him. But he soon realizes that, whatever it is, it wants to smother him with love. Frantic, he turns to his friend, Father Murchison, for help.

1734. "The House on Chimney Pot Line" (10/5/78; rebroadcast from 4/28/78)

1735. "The Captain of the PoleStar" (10/6/78; rebroadcast 4/19/79)

Cast: Paul Hecht (Dr. John Ray); Court Benson (Captain Cragie); Joan Shay (Flora); Earl Hammond (Bruce). Adapted by Murra Burnett, based on the 1890 short story by Sir Arthur Conan Doyle.

John Ray, a young medic, signs on as doctor of the *Polestar*, a whaling ship. He is warned that the voyage will be dangerous and that the ship's captain, David Cragie, is so temperamental that he allows no one in the cabin, not even the steward. Now, after six weeks of searching for whales in the Arctic, Dr. Ray and the crew are terrified by the strange noises emanating from the captain's quarters and by the ice that is closing in around them.

1736. "The Chinaman Button" (10/7/78 rebroadcast from 3/15/74)

1737. "A Drink with Dionysius" (10/8/78; rebroadcast from 5/1/78)

1738. "The Triple Crown" (10/9/78; rebroadcast 4/24/79)

Cast: Ian Martin (Paddy Devlin); Jackson Beck (Morton Oakes); Joen Arliss (Mrs. Oakes); Jack Grimes (Stevie Oakes). Written by Ian Martin.

Paddy Devlin, who has somehow acquired a very fast colt he calls Malachi, meets a small, young farmhand, Stevie Oakes, who, Paddy believes, can be trained to ride Malachi to the Triple Crown. Stevie's stepfather, Morton, agrees to allow the penniless Paddy to live in his barn with Malachi and teach Stevie how to ride after the boy has finished his chores. But when boy and horse are ready to race, Morton serves Paddy with legal papers stating that he now owns Malachi as payment for all the board and feed he has provided.

1739. "The Figure in the Moonlight" (10/10/78; rebroadcast from 5/2/78)

1740. "The Man in Black" (10/11/78; rebroadcast 4/26/79)

Cast: Kim Hunter (Gail Howard); Earl Hammond (Lt. Graham); Bryna Raeburn (Jackie). Written by Victoria Dann.

"I was walking to my car," Gail Howard tells the police. "A man came out of nowhere. He said, 'Help me. I've been shot by the man in black.' There was blood on his shirt. A couple of minutes later he was dead." The police, after combing the area and finding no evidence of foul play, think Gail has an overactive imagination. They won't listen to her, even after a man named Smith tells her she's going to be the next victim of the man in black.

1741. "Journey to Somewhere" (10/12/78; rebroadcast from 5/4/78)

1742. "How Much Land Does a Man Need?" (10/13/78; rebroadcast 4/27/79)

Cast: Paul Hecht (Tom Morgan); Gordon Heath (Peter Porter); Ray Owens (Chief Great Eagle); Patricia Elliott (Sally). Adapted by Sam Dann, based on the 1886 short story by Leo Tolstoy.

This adaptation takes place in colonial Virginia, not Tolstoy Russia. Tom Morgan, industrious but also grasping, lends people money and, when they cannot repay him, takes their land. He now owns thousands of acres and is hated by almost everyone. One day he is approached by an agent for an Indian chief who is willing to sell him, for 100 pounds, all the land he can walk around in a day. It's an intriguing proposition, but disastrous for one as greedy as Tom.

1743. "Mother Love" (10/14/78; rebroadcast from 3/31/74)

1744. "Cool Killer Karl" (10/15/78 rebroadcast from 5/5/78)

1745. "The Winds of Time" (10/16/78; rebroadcast 4/20/79)

Cast: Carol Teitel (Carol Ormsby); Ian Martin (Adolf Hitler); Bob Dryden (Fritz); Bryce Bond (himself). Written by Ian Martin.

When parapsychologist Bryce Bond takes Carol Ormsby into his care, he senses that a deep-rooted guilt or fear is causing her severe headaches. Disbelieving, but desperate, Carol lets Bond take her back, through hypnosis, to her previous lives. Two of the regressions return her to incidents where she was behind a gun barrel, contemplating murder. But it's not until the third regression that they locate the shocking origin of her headaches.

1746. "Death and Desire" (10/17/78; rebroadcast from 5/8/78)

1747. "Never Answer an Advertisement" (10/18/78; rebroadcast 5/1/79)

Cast: Russell Horton (Dr. Richard Brooke); Evelyn Juster (Sarah Brooke); John Beal (John Faraday); Court Benson (Hugh Faraday). Adapted by James Agate, Jr., based on the 1908 short story *The Beetle-Hunter* by Sir Arthur Conan Doyle.

Richard Brooke, a struggling young doctor in need of money, reads that a law firm is looking for the services of a robust medical man with a background in entomology. Because he had once collected beetles and is strong physically, Dr. Brooke applies and is hired for 100 pounds a day. But not until he is taken to a remote country estate and faces a homicidal maniac does the doctor realize that he has made a very serious mistake.

1748. "Room 418 (10/19/78; rebroadcast from 5/9/78)

1749. "The Outside Girl" (10/20/78; rebroadcast 5/3/79)

Cast: Paul Hecht (Charles Dryer); Ann Pitoniak (Mother); Ralph Bell (Philip); Catherine Byers (Cassandra). Written by Elspeth Eric.

Geraldine, the Dryers' household maid, calls with the news that because of her mother's illness she will have to send someone to take her place. Cassandra, who calls herself an "outside girl," arrives and immediately opines that the subject for a portrait in the Dryer library looks "dead." While working, she talks to it sympathetically and later it seemingly, talks back to Charles Dryer, who painted it. It's a portrait of his late father, whom he disliked, and it says to Charles: "Help, please help me."

Notes: Paul Hecht was featured in the television movie *The Savage Bees* in 1976, and was soon to be seen in another television movie, *Mary and Joseph: A Story of Faith* (1979), which also featured another *Theater* "performer," Lloyd Bochner.

1750. "The Horla" (10/21/78; rebroadcast from 5/17/74)

1751. "The Guilt of the Innocent" (10/22/78; rebroadcast from 5/11/78)

1752. "The Lazarus Syndrome" (10/23/78; rebroadcast 5/4/79)

Cast: Mandel Kramer (Perry Marston); Lloyd Battista (George Gotham); Anne Williams (Abigail Marston); Bryna Raeburn (Mrs. Flume). Written by Sam Dann.

Perry Marston, whose company has been swallowed up by a merger, now works for a man who's 24 years his junior. Against the advice of wife and doctor, Marston keeps accepting challenges at tennis from the younger man, until he suffers a heart attack on the court. Despite the efforts of his doctor, Marston is declared clinically dead for a few moments. However, after he is brought back to life he begins to wonder whether he was not better off dead.

1753. "The Secret of Shen-Si" (10/24/78; rebroadcast from 5/12/78)

1754. "Family Ties" (10/25/78; rebroadcast 5/8/79)

Cast: Russell Horton (Lt. Warren); Evelyn Juster (Janet Pendennis); Ray Owens (Gilbert Klieg). Written by Percy Granger.

Janet Pendennis asks the police to locate her husband, Robert, an accountant who always came home every night after work but now has been missing for two days. The only clue she has is a piece of blank note paper on which the pressure of Robert's pen has left a clear indentation of an address. However, when they visit the address, which turns out to be a one-room apartment of an elderly lady, Janet and the police find only evidence of a fierce fight, an empty picture frame and Robert's tie clasp.

1755. "Edmund Orme" (10/26/78; rebroadcast from 5/15/78)

1756. "The Sound of Terror" (10/27/78; rebroadcast 5/10/79)

Cast: Patricia Elliott (Betsy Grant); Larry Haines (Sergeant Ed Ritter); Ian Martin (Lieutenant Jerry Reimer); Earl Hammond (Achmed). Written by Ian Martin.

While returning from a day in the country with his girlfriend, Betsy Grant, police Sgt. Ed Ritter is ordered, over his car's radio, to proceed at once to his precinct headquarters—an Arabian ambassador to the United Nations has been kidnapped. Betsy volunteers to take a bus to her apartment. While waiting for one to arrive, she hears a public phone ringing. She answers it, setting off for her a chain of very terrifying events.

Notes: Mystery Theater received tens of thousands of letters from its listeners. The one Himan Brown liked the best said, "Thank you for giving my child back the world of fantasy."

1757. "The Creature from the Swamp" (10/28/78; rebroadcast from 6/1/74)

1758. "Girl Talk" (10/29/78; rebroadcast from 5/16/78)

1759. "Time Out of Mind" (10/30/78; rebroadcast from 5/18/78)

1760. "The Queen of Cats" (10/31/78; rebroadcast from 2/13/77)

1761. "The Midas of Castle Hill" (11/1/78; rebroadcast 5/11/79)

Cast: Norman Rose (Eugene Valmont); Russell Horton (James Hill III); Bob Dryden (Browning). Adapted by James Agate, Jr., based on a story by Robert Barr.

Valmont is offered half the inheritance of James Hill III if he can locate it. Hill's millionaire father had left him a note saying the money could be found "between a couple of sheets in the library." While Hill and Valmont are searching for it, Browning the butler is hit on the head with a hammer, later claiming he was attacked by two men. Valmont deduces that Browning hit himself. Why he did so, Valmont thinks, may have a bearing on the money's hiding place.

1762. "The Hundred Dollar Difference" (11/2/78; rebroadcast from 5/19/78)

1763. "The Man with the Claret Mark" (11/3/78; rebroadcast 5/22/79)

Cast: Teri Keane (Agnes de Lacey); Lloyd Battista (Ultor de Lacey); Evelyn Juster (Una de Lacey); Ian Martin (Larry Sullivan). Adapted by Ian Martin, based on the 1872 short story *Dickon the Devil* by J. S. Lefanu.

The specter of a man with a sarcastic leer, a drooping nose and a great purplish stain across his face sent fear into the hearts of all male members of the de Lacey clan. They knew they were destined to die whenever the specter appeared. After the last de Lacey male has expired, there is still Agnes, an elderly, dying nun, and Una, a young girl who doesn't know that the specter has planned the same fate for her.

1764. "Honeymoon with Death" (11/4/78; rebroadcast from 2/27/74)

1765. "The Girl He Left Behind" (11/5/78; rebroadcast from 5/22/78)

1766. "Hit and Run" (11/6/78; rebroadcast 5/24/79)

Cast: Anne Williams (Ruletta); Ralph Bell (Lieutenant Dreyfus); Court Benson (Sid); Earl Hammond (Paul Foster). Written by Sam Dann.

Ruletta Pound, who posed as witness to the "accident," tries to blackmail Congressman Paul Foster, driver of the fancy red sports car that killed Louie LaPeer, the Flopper. Because he had his mistress with him, the congressman fled the scene. Though the scandal could ruin his career, he has no intention of paying the $150,000 Ruletta demands to keep quiet. Instead, he concocts another way of dealing with her.

1767. "Window to Oblivion" (11/7/78 rebroadcast from 5/23/78)

1768. "Second Sight" (11/8/78; rebroadcast 5/25/79)

Cast: Michael Tolan (Allan Harvey); Bob Dryden (Jacob Greer); Earl Hammond (Dr. Kingsley); Joan Shay (Peg Johnson). Written by James Agate, Jr.

Allan Harvey, grounded because he has seen things in the sky no other pilot has witnessed, is urged by a psychiatrist to pursue his hobby of painting. In an art class Allan draws pictures of three deaths—two murders and a suicide—of his teacher, a fellow student and the class's model. The next day all three are dead, and Allan's worried psychiatrist demands to see him immediately.

1769. "The Spy and the Traitor" (11/9/78; rebroadcast from 5/25/78)

1770. "A Better Mousetrap" (11/10/78; rebroadcast 5/15/79)

Cast: Joan Beal (Lieutenant Barth); Ian Martin (Ralph Lester); Joan Banks (Lucy Lester); Bryna Raeburn (Gloria). Written by Ian Martin.

When Lucy Lester confronts her husband Ralph with the fact that he not only has been unfaithful but also has squandered her insurance, he panics and unintentionally chokes her to death. Then he plots with his secretary girlfriend to make it seem that Lucy has been kidnapped and killed by her abductors. The police seem to buy this explanation for the moment.

1771. "The Return of the Moresbys" (11/11/78; rebroadcast from 2/20/74)

1772. "Arctic Encounter" (11/12/78; rebroadcast from 5/26/78)

1773. "The Pilgrim Soul" (11/13/78; rebroadcast 5/17/79)

Cast: Carol Teitel (Ann Jesperson); Bryna Raeburn (Mrs. Carden); Gordon Gould (Greg Davis); Gordon Heath (Dr. Raynolds). Written by Percy Granger.

Ann Jesperson, who grew up unhappily in a Madison, Wisconsin, orphanage, goes to London during the World War II blitzkrieg to help nurse the wounded back to health. She works long hours, dispassionately, even refusing to go into a shelter during air raids. Nevertheless, she is ultimately attracted to a seriously wounded American aviator who, despite Ann's round-the-clock attention, dies just moments before she receives the mysterious call that saves her life.

1774. "The Rich Ostrich" (11/14/78; rebroadcast from 5/29/78)

1775. "The Conspiracy" (11/15/78; rebroadcast 5/18/79)

Cast: Teri Keane (Anne Logan); Court Benson (Simon Ashton); Grace Matthews (Mona Ashton). Written by Elspeth Eric.

Mona Ashton, divorced from renowned photographer Simon Ashton, demands that her ex-husband make some portraits of Anne Logan, who, 20 years ago, had been so hurt emotionally by Simon that she wound up in an insane asylum. Simon reluctantly agrees. He doesn't recognize Anne, whose years in the institution have changed her facial features, but he is so shaken at what his photographs of her reveal that he begins to think he is in need of psychiatric treatment.

1776. "The Bittersweet Honeymoon" (11/16/78; rebroadcast from 5/30/78)

1777. "The Favor of Women" (11/17/78; rebroadcast 5/29/79)

Cast: Lloyd Battista (Captain Victor); Evelyn Juster (Queen Lura); Ray Owens (Orvo); William Griffis (Admiral Refern). Written by Sam Dann.

Because Earth has only a 15-day supply of selko left, Captain Victor, a man who captivates women, is ordered to fly a spaceship to the planet Arana, which is the universe's main source of this type of energy. Arana is ruled by the beautiful Queen Lura, who allows no foreigners on her planet. Victor, pretending that engine trouble necessitates a landing, is captured and brought before Lura, who decrees he must be sacrificed at the Temple of All the Gods.

1778. "The Silent Woman" (11/18/78; rebroadcast from 6/1/78)

1779. "You Can Die Again" (11/19/78; rebroadcast from 3/10/74)

1780. "The Thing at Nolan" (11/20/78; rebroadcast 5/31/79)

Cast: Russell Horton (John May); Court Benson (Charles May); Bryna Raeburn (Elvira May); Arnold Moss (Harry Odell). Adapted by Arnold Moss, based on the short story by Ambrose Bierce.

John May, living with his father Charles and mother Elvira in the Ozark Mountains in 1879, is the first member of the family to learn how to read, a skill that causes him to develop some new-fangled notions: that women should not be mistreated and that he doesn't have to help his father seven days a week. The result is a fatherly punch in the face, which John vows his father will soon regret.

1781. "Diamond Cut Woman" (11/21/78; rebroadcast from 6/2/78)

1782. "The Grey Slapper" (11/22/78; rebroadcast 6/1/79)

Cast: Carol Teitel (Dolly Morrison); Gordon Heath (Tony Pringle); Bob Dryden (John Joseph Harrigan). Written by Sam Dann.

Dolly Morrison, in love with 60-year-old Tony Pringle from the time he was a 30-year-old idealistic professor, claims she has been talking to his younger self. Pringle is now a shady politician who has forsaken his ideals in his lust for power and success. Dolly, who has seemingly appeared from out of nowhere, warns Pringle that his younger self is going to kill him for having abandoned his ideals. Tony thinks she's crazy until he meets his younger self face-to-face.

1783. "The Undying Heart" (11/23/78 rebroadcast from 6/5/78)

1784. "Night Visitor" (11/24/78; rebroadcast 6/5/79)

Cast: Teri Keane (Charito); Evelyn Juster (Phillinnion); Earl Hammond (Machates); Ray Owens (Demonstratus). Adapted by Elspeth Eric, based on the 200 short story by Phlegon.

Machates, a friend of King Philip II and on state business in Macedonia, visits his old friends, Demonstratus and Charito. During his first night in the guest bedroom, Melissa, the household maid, looks in and discovers a woman in bed with him. She insists it is Phillinnion—Demonstratus and Charito's daughter who has been dead for several months. But Machates swears it was a living woman who had visited him during the night.

1785. "Miracle in Sharon City" (11/25/78; rebroadcast from 6/6/78)

1786. "The Girl Who Found Things" (11/26/78; rebroadcast from 3/8/74)

1787. "Alien Presences" (11/27/78; rebroadcast 6/7/79)

Cast: John Beal (Jem Hardin); Joan Shay (Ruth Hardin); John Lithgow (Moses Hardin); Ian Martin (Woody). Written by Ian Martin.

While Jem and Ruth Hardin are driving in a thunderstorm, they see a flying object crash-land and burn. Looking for survivors, they find a baby boy Ruth wants to adopt. Jem says okay unless they hear news of a missing infant. They don't and, after years of raising the child (they've named him Moses), all is going well with the Hardins. But they do begin to worry about Moses' normality when he reaches seven feet, six inches and is still growing.

Notes: John Lithgow, who plays Kenyo Grant in this episode, has a large list of film credits to his name, including *Twilight Zone—The Movie* (1983), *2010* (1984), *Santa Claus: The Movie* (1985), *The Manhattan Project* (1986), *Harry and the Hendersons* (1987), *Memphis Belle* (1990), and *Cliffhanger* (1993). Lithgow later starred as an extraterrestrial in the NBC comedy, *3rd Rock from the Sun*.

1788. "Death Spell" (11/28/78; rebroadcast from 6/8/78)

1789. "The Romany Revenge" (11/29/78; rebroadcast 6/8/79)

Cast: Earl Hammond (William Harrow); Court Benson (Dwight Mason); Bryna Raeburn (Beatrice). Written by James Agate, Jr.

Joseph Millbourn, who made his fortune in diamonds from land in Brazil stolen from gypsies, leaves his estate to his two nieces—Beatrice and Margaret—his nephew Clifford and his right-hand man, Jose Silva. During the sea voyage back home from Brazil, Margaret dies from an unknown poison and Clifford's body is found in a funeral pyre in Brazil. This leaves Jose, whose whereabouts are unknown, and Beatrice, whose husband, Dwight, fears she will be the next to die.

1790. "A Long Way from Home" (11/30/78; rebroadcast from 6/9/78)

1791. "Squaring the Triangle" (12/1/78; rebroadcast 6/12/79)

Cast: Ian Martin (D. J. Prior); Felicia Farr (Beatrice Oliver); William Griffis (Richie); Paul Hecht (Ernest Oliver). Written by Sam Dann.

D. J. Prior, chairman of multinational D. J. Prior Industries, is forced because of bad weather to land his company plane in Central City, Illinois home of one of his subsidiaries. It is run by Ernest Oliver, whom he has never met. Invited to dinner by the Olivers, Prior is taken by Ernest's wife, Beatrice. Bored with life in Central City, she is intrigued by Prior's offer to take her away from it all. But she is not so intrigued with his plans for her husband—an accidental death in the jungles of Brazil.

1792. "The Old Ones Are Hard to Kill" (12/2/78; rebroadcast from 3/1/74)

1793. "I Warn You Three Times" (12/3/78; rebroadcast from 2/7/74)

1794. "The Serpent of Saris" (12/4/78; rebroadcast 6/14/79)

Cast: Fred Gwynne (Lt. Jerry Roman); Russell Horton (Dapper Danny Malloy); Ray Owens (Solly Stillson); Evelyn Juster (Jeannie). Written by Sam Dann.

Immediately after an aspiring middleweight boxer, Dapper Danny Malloy, is found dead in his bed, a beautiful chorus girl, Jeannie Barr, and a big-time, much-in-debt gambler, Andy Blue, claim they had murdered him: Jeannie, because Danny had jilted her Blue, hoping to be jailed and thus safe from his many creditors. But police detective Jerry Roman believes neither of them. He knows something about Danny, a longtime friend, that nobody else does.

1795. "Alias Mr. Aladdin" (12/5/78; rebroadcast from 6/12/78)

1796. "The Devil's Bargain" (12/6/78; rebroadcast 6/15/79)

Cast: Bob Dryden (Otto Glaser); Gordon Heath (Lord Carnovan); Joan Shea (Lady Carnovan); Jackson Beck (Marvello). Adapted by James Agate, Jr., based on a short story by Guy Boothby.

Lord Carnovan, a member of English nobility, hires Otto Glaser, the renowned psychic detective, to recover Lady Carnovan's precious diamond necklace worth, according to the Lord, some $2 million. Little does he know that Glaser, disguised as an Iranian sheik, had, with the aid of a retired magician, stolen the diamonds, or that Glaser has earned his reputation for retrieving stolen goods because, in every case, he has been the thief.

1797. "Charlie, the Actor" (12/7/78; rebroadcast from 6/14/78)

1798. "The Exploding Heart" (12/8/78; rebroadcast 6/19/79)

Cast: Robert Kaliban (Dr. Matt Bard); Evelyn Juster (Kim Bard); Gordon Gould (Jay Norton); Ian Martin (Dr. Harkness). Written by Ian Martin.

Jay Norton, a seemingly healthy young man, asks Dr. Matt Bard to give him a complete physical check-up before his marriage to the doctor's sister, Kim. When chest X-rays reveal an aneurysm, Dr. Bard is faced with a difficult decision: Should he tell Jay and Kim? He does tell Jay, who demands an operation, knowing he only has a 50-50 chance of survival. But the hospital's chief surgeon says no, because a failure on the operating table could mean the end of financial support from Jay's father, the richest man in town.

1799. "Cold Storage" (12/9/78; rebroadcast from 1/3/76)

1800. "The Resident" (12/10/78; rebroadcast from 12/1/74)

1801. "A Horror Story" (12/11/78; rebroadcast 6/21/79)

Cast: Bob Dryden (Donnet/Feraud); Ian Martin (Poncet); Mary Jane Higby (Camille). Written by Elspeth Eric.

Gaston Donnet—or is he Lucien Feraud?—is a gourmet cook, restaurateur and expert cobbler. That all sounds okay, until the ingredients of his most famous and best-liked recipe and the material he uses to make his finest slippers become known.

Notes: Bob Dryden is a radio actor with many different qualities to his voice as a ventriloquist. He is often asked to "double" or "triple" and has even been called upon to play all the parts in a scene. Here, he plays a double role.

1802. "The Unholy Miracle" (12/12/78; rebroadcast from 6/16/78)

1803. "Ward Six" (12/13/78; rebroadcast 6/22/79)

Cast: Norman Rose (Dr. Andrei Yefimych); Eugene Troobnick (Mikhail); Earl Hammond (Ivan Dmitrick); Russell Horton (Dr. Knobotov); Bryna Raeburn (Daryushka). Adapted by Percy Granter, based on the 1892 short story *Ward Number Six* by Anton Chekov.

Dr. Andrei Yefimych is assigned to take over the hospital of a small village in the Russian heartland. There is filth and vermin everywhere, but the villagers don't seem to care—they're too poor and ignorant. What upsets the doctor most is the condition of Ward Six, where the insane are locked up, but where the doctor finds the one man with whom he can carry on an intelligent conversation. All this does is start the villagers thinking the doctor is also insane.

1804. "Dr. Jekyll and Mrs. Hyde" (12/14/78; rebroadcast from 6/19/78)

1805. "The Search for Myra" (12/15/78; rebroadcast 6/26/79)
Cast: Mandel Kramer (George Hastings); Carol Teitel (Myra); Court Benson (Dr. Rayer); Marian Seldes (Ruth Hastings). Written by Sam Dann.
George Hastings' secretary is less concerned than his wife, Ruth, when he calls her Myra. Ruth demands that he visit a psychiatrist. With some prodding the doctor gets Hastings to admit that 30 years ago a girl named Myra was his boyhood sweetheart, but that he married Ruth instead for her money. When Ruth hears this and leaves him, Hastings searches out Myra, who looks as if she is still 21 years old. Hastings is amazed, until he finds out why.

1806. "The Ring of Truth" (12/16/78; rebroadcast from 3/29/74)

1807. "A Very Old Man" (12/17/78; rebroadcast from 3/22/74)

1808. "The Familiar Ghost" (12/18/78; rebroadcast 6/28/79)
Cast: Charles Irving (Dr. Hesselius); Gordon Heath (Captain James Barton); Teri Keane (Viola Montague); Ian Martin (General Montague). Written by Ian Martin.
James Barton, who served in His Majesty's navy during the American Revolution, is readily accepted by beautiful Viola Montague, but she must wait for the return of her father, a retired general. In the meantime, Barton starts believing he is being followed, but only he can hear the footsteps of his pursuer who, the famous psychic detective Dr. Hesselius declares, is a "familiar," someone who is holding Barton "in a supernatural tie." Why he is being held so must be determined before the wedding ceremony can take place.
Notes: This episode's rebroadcast on June 28, 1979, marked the 2,000th broadcast of the *CBS Radio Mystery Theater.* The show had been broadcast every day since its premiere (except once on election night of 1976). Its first broadcast was carried by 79 stations; the June 28 drama was transmitted by 234. By this episode, the series had presented 1,035 first-run programs, with 965 repeats; 875 were original scripts, and there were 160 adaptations. A team of 15 writers had produced the 1,035 stories.

1809. "A Matter of Faith" (12/19/78; rebroadcast from 6/21/78)

1810. "It Has to Be True" (12/20/78; rebroadcast 6/29/79)
Cast: Joan Beal (James Correll); Earl Hammond (Walter Sturgess); Joan Shay (Della Correll); Bob Dryden (Inspector Luther). Written by Sam Dann.
While driving to Chicago, James Correll, assistant sales manager of an electronics company, is stopped by two highway patrolmen, searched, and taken to police headquarters. There he is accused of having murdered a woman he has never even met; his clothes and gun were found in her room. He swears he's innocent, but a police psychiatrist puts together so plausible a story of Correll's "involvement" that he starts believing he did commit the crime.

Notes: Sam Dann has twice been awarded the Writers Guild of America Award for "the best radio dramatic script" of the year.

1811. "The Black Door" (12/21/78; rebroadcast from 6/23/78)

1812. "The Power of Evil" (12/22/78; rebroadcast 7/3/79)

Cast: Lloyd Battista (Jack Pantay); Evelyn Juster (Agnes Keith); Gordon Gould (Arthur Myland); Ray Owens (Jeweler). Written by James Agate, Jr.

Jack Pantay, an employee of the U.S. consulate in Hong Kong, spends all his time gambling at a casino in nearby Macao. A constant loser, he is startled one day when an older woman, who says she's Agnes Keith, offers to lend him some cash and teach him how to beat the roulette wheels. A winning streak is the result, but Pantay is not prepared to pay the price Ms. Keith starts asking for her services.

1813. "A Very Private Miracle" (12/23/78; rebroadcast from 12/25/75)

1814. "A Christmas Carol" (12/24/78; rebroadcast from 12/24/77)

1815. "If I Can't Have You" (12/25/78; rebroadcast 7/5/79)

Cast: Robert Kaliban (Victor Volovsky); Anne Williams (Praskovya Suslove); Carol Teitel (Marina Trigorin); Russell Horton (Sergei Berdayev). Written by Sam Dann.

Victor Volovsky plays the violin; Praskovya Suslove is the cellist; Sergei Berdayev is at the piano. Praskovya is engaged to Victor, but Sergei also loves her. Their music is not affected by this inner turmoil, but the "people's" government is. It wants Victor to spy on Sergei, who has expressed some reservations about the government. Victor becomes jealous when Praskovya, upset by his infatuation with a buxom, blonde television interviewer, pretends she prefers Sergei. This causes Victor to do something he later terms "despicable."

1816. "Lady Bluebeard" (12/26/78; rebroadcast from 6/26/78)

1817. "No Way Out" (12/27/78; rebroadcast 7/6/79)

Cast: Earl Hammond (Mark Evans); Charles Irving (Edgar Evans); Roberta Maxwell (Mimi Magowan). Written by Elspeth Eric.

Ne'er-do-well Mark Evans introduces his rich Uncle Edgar, a widower, to his current girlfriend, but Mimi Magowan, and soon wishes he hadn't. Edgar not only takes up with Mimi, starts believing in her faith in numerology. The numbers 12172 take on a significant meaning in life, popping up in all kinds of situations, to a point where he becomes convinced he had been the cause of his wife's death. She died on 12172: January 21, 1972. (The numbers also total 13!)

1818. "The Quadruple" (12/28/78; rebroadcast from 6/28/78)

1819. "The Dead House" (12/29/78; rebroadcast 7/10/79)

Cast: Bob Dryden (Mark Twain); Leon Janney (Karl Ritter); Ian Martin

(Adler); Bryna Raeburn (Nell Ritter). Adapted by Ian Martin, based on the 1883 short story from *Life on the Mississippi* by Mark Twain.

Mark Twain meets Karl Ritter while researching a story in Germany about Munich's "dead house," where corpses were kept until it became clear they were really dead. Ritter, now dying, had worked in the "dead house" and reveals to Twain his successful attempt to divert the mighty Mississippi River and his killing of a Union cavalryman who not only murdered his wife and baby daughter, but also stole $25,000 from him. Ritter asks Twain to perform a "small" favor.

1820. "Lost Dog" (12/30/78; rebroadcast from 2/11/74)

1821. "And Nothing but the Truth" (12/31/78; rebroadcast from 3/17/74)

1822. "Complete Recovery" (1/1/79; rebroadcast 1/22/80)

Cast: Mary Jane Higby (Eleanor Houston); Joan Shay (Nurse); Russell Horton (Dr. James). Written by Percy Granger.

While recovering from injuries sustained when struck by an auto, Eleanor Houston becomes psychologically paralyzed, fearing the color blue. Shaken from her paralysis when her wheelchair drops down a flight of stairs, Mrs. Houston is able to explain why she fears blue—it was the color of the car that hit her. That car was driven by her money-hungry son-in-law who, she fears, will make another attempt on her life. But this time, she vows, she'll be ready for him.

1823. "The Good Times Express" (1/2/79; rebroadcast from 6/30/78) 1/2/79)

1824. "King Bankrobber" (1/3/79; rebroadcast from 7/3/78)

1825. "The Look" (1/4/79; rebroadcast 7/12/79)

Cast: Michael Tolan (Sen. Frank Stoddard); Carol Teitel (Irma Stoddard); Teri Keane (Justine Dorian); Earl Hammond (Al Dorian). Written by Sam Dann.

Senator Frank Stoddard is causing headlines with his subcommittee's investigation of organized crime in the United States. The committee's chief witness, Al Dorian, constantly takes the Fifth Amendment, but suddenly agrees to meet the senator secretly. When Stoddard arrives at their rendezvous, he finds Dorian dying from a bullet wound. But the gangster manages to tell Stoddard something that will make his road to the presidency a rocky one.

1826. "Deadly Honeymoon" (1/5/79; rebroadcast from 3/23/74)

1827. "The Man Who Heard Voices" (1/6/79; rebroadcast from 4/5/74)

1828. "Three Women" (1/7/79; rebroadcast from 1/28/74)

1829. "Nefertiti Part I: The Vulture Screams" (1/8/79; rebroadcast 8/6/79)

Cast: Tammy Grimes (Nefertiti); Russell Horton (Akhenaton); Evelyn Juster (Tiy); Ian Martin (Horenrab); Bob Dryden (Aye). Written by Gerald Keane.

When they were children, Nefertiti, the daughter of Egyptian Prime Minister Aye, frightened the Pharaoh's son, Akhenaton, and also made fun of him. Nevertheless, when Akhenaton, after his father's death, is named the new pharaoh, it is arranged for Nefertiti to be his queen. He's still afraid of her, complaining of an upset stomach on their wedding day. She considers him immature, but when she learns of her father's plan to have him murdered, she vows to make sure it doesn't happen.

Notes: To celebrate *Theater's* start of the sixth season on the air, Himan Brown presented five interrelated stories, all written by contributing writer Gerald Keane, titled "Nefertiti." *Theater* at this time was being broadcast on 232 radio stations across the country. The program premiered six years earlier on 218 radio stations.

Several years before the *CBS Radio Theater* presentation in January of 1979, "Nefertiti" was written in script form for an epic motion picture. The film never was produced, apparently because of its stupendous expense. Instead, Gerald Keane, the author of the original film script, decided to put his story of the queen of ancient Egypt to radio.

1830. "Nefertiti Part II: To Kill a Pharaoh" (1/9/79; rebroadcast 8/7/79)

Cast: Tammy Grimes (Nefertiti); Russell Horton (Akhenaton); Evelyn Juster (Marianni); Bob Dryden (Aye); Ian Martin (High Priest). Written by Gerald Keane.

Akhenaton, like all new pharaohs before him, must enter the tomb of his ancestors and pray for guidance. He almost suffocates when the statues in the tomb start falling on him, but he follows the light he sees at an entrance to the tomb and is saved. He thanks the Sun God, Aton, for having shown him how to escape and proclaims that from now on Egyptians will worship only one God, Aton, instead of many. Aye, the prime minister and Nefertiti's father, sincerely believes that Akhenaton has gone mad. He persuades the young pharaoh to drink some drugged wine and, when it has put Akhenaton to sleep, Aye places him in a coffin, which he plans to throw into the Nile River. But Nefertiti, while searching for her favorite cat, sees her father driving off in the coffin-bearing chariot and demands to know what he is up to.

1831. "Nefertiti Part III: The Cobra Strikes" (1/10/79; rebroadcast 8/8/79)

Cast: Tammy Grimes (Nefertiti); Russell Horton (Akhenaton); Court Benson (Commander); Earl Hammond (Horenrab). Written by Gerald Keane.

When he hears reports from Egypt's top general, Horenrab, that the son of the Hittite king, Prince Zannanza, has set out for Egypt with an armed escort,

Akhenaton says to welcome him with open arms. Horenrab, fearing Egypt may be conquered, executes a hit and run attack on the prince, who was merely bringing gifts to Akhenaton. Nefertiti, who made no attempt to stop Horenrab because she believed his fears of an attack, now feels the general should be punished. He is assigned a corporal's job of guarding Nefertiti and Akhenaton as they pursue their newest project—building an entirely new city of truth, hope and prosperity—Amarna—where only one god, Aton, will be worshipped.

Notes: Himan Brown commented: "Egyptology has truly captured our imaginations these days. Just look at the crowds who have been drawn to the King Tut exhibition as it has traveled across the country. Certainly the exhibit has great significance, but it must be said, as *The New York Times* has pointed out, that Nefertiti's husband, Akhenaton, is, in the eyes of educated Egyptians, a person of 'infinitely greater consequence' than Tut."

1832. "Nefertiti Part IV: The Head with One Eye" (1/11/79; rebroadcast 8/9/79)

Cast: Tammy Grimes (Nefertiti); Russell Horton (Akhenaton); Evelyn Juster (Marianni); Earl Hammond (Horenrab). Written by Gerald Keane.

Amarna, the city of truth, is nearing completion along eight miles of the Nile River. Nefertiti assumes new duties in governing the city and, at the same time, starts sitting for a sculpture for herself, the first to be done realistically (copies of which are now in many museums across the world). Akhenaton continues spending Egypt's gold on the city, refusing to appropriate more money for the army. He also insists that his 5-year-old daughter, Mekataton, worship only Aton, the Sun God. One day he leaves her kneeling in the hot sun, long enough for her to collapse and die. A heartbroken Nefertiti accuses both Aton and her husband of representing all that is evil and refuses to return to the palace.

1833. "Nefertiti Part V: The Curse of the Scarab" (1/12/79; rebroadcast 8/10/79)

Cast: Tammy Grimes (Nefertiti); Russell Horton (Akhenaton); Evelyn Juster (Marianni); Earl Hammond (Horenrab). Written by Gerald Keane.

Akhenaton, with his obstinate belief in one god, has become a religious fanatic. Because he has denied their daughter, Mekataton, a proper Egyptian funeral, Nefertiti stows away on a Nile River barge headed for Thebes, carrying with her Mekataton's embalmed body. But, just as the funeral ceremony is about to begin, Akhenaton appears. He stops the proceedings, takes away his daughter's coffin and decrees that Nefertiti will from now on be treated as a common slave. Later, when he proclaims he has become Aton, his one god, and Nefertiti calls him a fool, he attacks her with a palette knife. But he accidentally falls on it and kills himself, leaving Nefertiti and the young Tutankhamen to rule Egypt.

Notes: According to Himan Brown: "Our story, based on archeological discoveries, was written by Gerald Keane, who was well-prepared for this monumental task. Several years ago he did a movie scenario about Nefertiti, which, fortunately for me, is still waiting to be produced. His five one-hour scripts make for a series of dramatic, meaningful and entertaining mystery stories, which all locked together when Tammy Grimes said she would love to star as Nefertiti."

"It [the original film script] never got of the ground," continued Brown. "I surmise because of the great expense involved. Keane was able to translate this script into five hour-long segments, each a self contained show ... It's [the radio play] something that can only be done on radio ... I can give you pyramids thousands of feet high, I can give you hundreds of thousands of Egyptians. It's all in your imagination, and you bring as much to this as I bring to it in the studio."

1834. "Dead Ringer" (1/13/79; rebroadcast from 4/6/74)

1835. "The Sign of the Beast" (1/14/79; rebroadcast from 4/13/74)

1836. "The Long, Long Sleep" (1/15/79; rebroadcast 7/13/79)

Cast: Larry Haines (Norman Hill); Ian Martin (Dr. Forrest Haddon); Ann Williams (Laurie Hill). Written by Arnold Moss.

Norman Hill, science fiction writer and advertising executive, is experiencing more frequent pains in his chest. His doctor advises an immediate operation, explaining that such surgery is usually only 50 percent successful. Hill is certain he is going to die and, while under the anesthesia, dreams his doctor has made a fatal mistake. He starts his journey to death, which he finds most interesting.

Notes: Arnold Moss has appeared in a few television programs, even in one episode of *The Monkees*. He also designed crossword puzzles for *The New York Times*.

1837. "The Further You Go, the Less You Know" (1/16/79; rebroadcast from 7/20/78)

1838. "The Wandering Wind" (1/17/79; rebroadcast 7/17/79)

Cast: Joan Beal (John Masters); Gordon Gould (Simon Cascia); Teri Keane (Doreen Dawkins). Written by Elspeth Eric.

John Masters, 63 but still deathly afraid of other people, is enticed into marriage by Doreen Dawkins. When John invites 18-year-old Simon Cascia, who is afraid of other people, to live with them, Doreen strenuously objects. John understands when she explains why, but he persists, and only when she learns why Simon wants to live with them does she relent.

1839. "The Locked Trunk" (1/18/79; rebroadcast from 7/21/78)

1840. "Side Effects" (1/19/79; rebroadcast 7/19/79)

Cast: Bob Dryden (Paul Rutledge); Joseph Silver (Nick Gorgas); Mandel Kramer (Melvin Arvin); Bryna Raeburn (Rita Arvin). Written by Sam Dann.

Drug company owner Paul Rutledge sees a fortune coming his way when he starts producing Alderson, a new miracle antibiotic developed by his friend, Melvin Arvin. But additional tests indicate that the drug might be lethal to 10 percent of those who take it. When Arvin tells this to Rutledge, Rutledge shoots him in what appears to be a hunting accident. A jury finds Rutledge innocent, and it seems that Alderson, which has passed all government tests, will soon be on the market.

1841. "Close Shave" (1/20/79; rebroadcast from 7/24/78)

1842. "The Stranger Inside" (1/21/79; rebroadcast from 7/25/78)

1843. "Let the Buyer Beware" (1/22/79; rebroadcast 7/20/79)

Cast: Joan Banks (Marcy Virtue); Earl Hammond (Alex Virtue); Bryna Raeburn (Martha); Bob Dryden (Sheriff Phillips). Written by Sam Dan.

Marcy Virtue brings home an antique table she thinks is worth much more than the $25 she paid for it. Her husband brings her back to Earth when he proves it is a U.S. mass-produced piece of furniture. But then she discovers the table has a secret drawer containing a .38 revolver with the owner's name and address engraved on it. Marcy insists on returning the gun to its owner—a mistake, because she immediately finds herself involved in an unsolved murder.

1844. "The Cabinet of the Unsolved" (1/23/79; rebroadcast from 7/27/78)

1845. "The Burning Bough" (1/24/79; rebroadcast 7/24/79)

Cast: Norman Rose (Uncle George); Grace Matthews (Madelyn Hunter); Russell Horton (Jimmy Hunter); Catherine Byers (Mrs. Miller). Written by Sam Dann.

Madelyn Hunter, a teacher and a widow, resorts to superstition to save the life of her dying baby, Jimmy. Like Althea of Calydon in Greek mythology, she pulls a blazing log from a fireplace. Althea was told that until the log was consumed her son would live. Jimmy turns into a spoiled brat, causing the deaths of five others. Madelyn's brother, George, insists that she throw the log back into the fire, but she, always a loving mother, refuses to do so.

1846. "Double-Take" (1/25/79; rebroadcast from 7/28/78)

1847. "The Dominant Personality" (1/26/79; rebroadcast 7/26/79)

Cast: Roberta Maxwell (Olivia Talbert); Ralph Bell (Rod Talbert); Gordon Heath (Professor Leo Hertel); Charles Irving (Sheriff Russ). Written by Percy Granger.

Rod Talbert, who has lived alone in the woods for years, startles his few neighbors by marrying Olivia, an ex-waitress. A few days later, a dog is poisoned, then its master murdered. The sheriff suspects Rod, who has always hated the dead man. Olivia fears that she may have made a mistake marrying Rod, who, she now realizes, is able to dominate her. What she doesn't know is that someone else is dominating Rod.

1848. "The Vanishing Point" (1/27/79; rebroadcast from 7/31/78)

1849. "The Devil's Brew" (1/28/79; rebroadcast from 8/2/78)

1850. "My Kingdom for a Horse" (1/29/79; rebroadcast from 7/5/78)

1851. "Speak of the Devil" (1/30/79; rebroadcast from 3/24/74)

1852. "The Four-Fifteen Express" (1/31/79; rebroadcast from 7/7/78)

1853. "The Man Who Asked for Yesterday" (2/1/79; rebroadcast from 4/7/74)

1854. "Sound Advice" (2/2/79; rebroadcast from 7/10/78)

1855. "Guardian Angel" (2/3/79; rebroadcast from 7/11/78)

1856. "A Ghostly Game of Death" (2/4/79; rebroadcast from 2/2/74)

1857. "Love After Death" (2/5/79; rebroadcast 7/27/79)
Cast: Norman Rose (Andrei Daninoff); Evelyn Juster (Marta Daninoff); Ralph Bell (Max Breck); Ian Martin (Father Quinn). Written by Ian Martin.
Each of Marta Daninoff's piano concerts seem to get better. The reason, her agent and friends believe, is that she is playing for her husband, Andrei, whom she loves deeply but hasn't seen since 1946, when he returned to their native land. Authorities there announced his "elimination" in 1959 because of his political activities against the state. Marta, who keeps playing despite a serious illness, is certain he's still alive. But every lead she receives concerning his whereabouts turns out to be a dead end.

1858. "The Avenging Ghost of Kitty Morgan" (2/6/79; rebroadcast from 8/4/78)

1859. "Everybody Does It" (2/7/79; rebroadcast 7/31/79)
Cast: Bob Dryden (Wilson Crawford); Carol Teitel (Margaret Constant); Earl Hammond (Perry Gulliver). Written by Sam Dann.
Critic William Crawford, divorced from his actress wife Margaret Constant, learns she is going to star in a new production of *Joan of Arc*. He warns he will pan her performance, no matter how well she acts; he doesn't think it is a suitable role for her. True to his word, Crawford writes a scathing review. An angry Margaret storms into his apartment and threatens to kill him with a letter opener, but

she can't go through with it. Later, however, Crawford is found murdered, and Margaret is accused of the crime.

1860. **"The Sixth Commandment"** (2/8/79; rebroadcast from 8/7/78)

1861. **"The Versegy Case"** (2/9/79; rebroadcast from 8/9/78)

1862. **"The Lady Was a Tiger"** (2/10/79; rebroadcast from 4/19/74)

1863. **"Here Goes the Bride"** (2/11/79; rebroadcast from 4/14/74)

1864. **"The Sinister Shadow"** (2/12/79; rebroadcast 8/2/79)

Cast: Teri Keane (Dorrie); Grace Matthews (Double); Joan Shay (Mother). Written by Elspeth Eric.

Instead of going directly home from the bank as she has every other afternoon, Dorrie stops at a bar and grill and meets a woman who looks just like her. Dorrie, who has always been afraid of her mother, changes her drab clothing and hair styles to those her double prefers. They keep meeting at the bar, and Dorrie keeps arriving home late. When Dorrie finally explains why she is being detained, her mother becomes infuriated. Dorrie retaliates by threatening to kill her. But her double tells her not to worry—she has already committed the dastardly act.

1865. **"Doctor Eduardo"** (2/13/79; rebroadcast from 8/11/78)

1866. **"The Missing Day"** (2/14/79; rebroadcast 8/3/79)

Cast: Russell Horton (Art Cummings); Hetty Galen (Bonnie Cummings); Court Benson (Sheriff); Ray Owens (Simon). Written by Percy Granger.

Art Cummings, the plant's chief executive, while on his way home to celebrate his wedding anniversary, is hailed by a stranger who shoots him with a strong anesthetic. Cummings misses a whole day of his life during which a truckload of high-grade uranium being shipped from his plant is hijacked. Cummings, one of two people who knew about the shipment, can't remember telling anyone about it. The local sheriff, though, is mighty suspicious: There was enough uranium in the truck to build half a nuclear bomb.

1867. **"The Black Sheep and the Captain"** (2/15/79; rebroadcast from 8/14/78)

1868. **"Raptures of the Deep"** (2/16/79; rebroadcast from 8/16/78)

1869. **"The Deadly Hour"** (2/17/79; rebroadcast from 4/26/74)

1870. **"Dead Man's Mountain"** (2/18/79; rebroadcast from 4/27/74)

1871. "The Shock of His Life" (2/19/79; rebroadcast 8/14/79)

Cast: Larry Haines (Herbie Boggs); Ian Martin (Dr. Bains); Joan Shea (Sadie Boggs). Written by Ian Martin.

Bar and grill owner Herbie Boggs, furious because his television set goes black just as a Sunday football game is about to begin, tries to fix the set himself The result is an electric shock that sends him to the hospital. When he recovers, he discovers that he can predict what will happen the next day. Sadie, his wife, without being electrified, but with a woman's intuition, foresees nothing but trouble ahead for both of them. It doesn't take long for her prediction to come true.

1872. "Our Own Jailer" (2/20/79; rebroadcast from 8/18/78)

1873. "The Great Brain" (2/21/79; rebroadcast 8/16/79)

Cast: Gordon Heath (Dr. Gregory March); Earl Hammond (Herbert); Ian Martin (Warden); Russell Horton (Jason). Adapted by James Agate, Jr., based on the 1905 short story *The Problem of Cell 13* by Jaques Futrelle.

Dr. Gregory March, who never played chess in his life, defeats the grandmaster champion in four of five matches. "I'm just trying to show that anything is possible with human brain power," he says. To prove his thesis further, he wagers with two of his colleagues that he can break out of the best-guarded cell in the state prison in no more than a week. All he asks the warden is for some tooth powder, one five-dollar and two ten-dollar bills, and permission to have his shoes shined before he enters the cell.

1874. "Cross Fire" (2/22/79; rebroadcast from 8/21/78)

1875. "The Eavesdropper" (2/23/79; rebroadcast from 8/23/78)

1876. "After the Verdict" (2/24/79; rebroadcast from 4/20/74)

1877. "Blizzard of Terror" (2/25/79; rebroadcast from 5/10/74)

1878. "Hickory, Dickory, Doom" (2/26/79; rebroadcast 8/17/79)

Cast: Tony Roberts (Charlie Tucker); Patricia Elliott (Charlotte Tucker); Joan Shea (Agnes Lee); Sam Gray (Paul Carlton). Written by Bob Juhren.

Charlie and Charlotte Tucker, intending to buy a lamp at a garage sale, wind up with a 100-year-old grandfather's clock that doesn't chime. When they get it home, though, it immediately starts chiming—no matter what time it is. It also emits cold air when its door is opened, scares the family cat and, finally, catches fire. Frightened, the Tuckers call in a psychic investigator, who discovers the word "Sargatanas" etched inside the clock. Sargatanas, the investigator tells the horrified Tuckers, is none other than the devil's locksmith.

1879. "The Other Soul" (2/27/79; rebroadcast from 8/25/78)

1880. **"Shadows from the Grave"** (2/28/79; rebroadcast 8/21/79)

Cast: Kristoffer Tabori (Xavier Zenith); Betsy Beard (Catherine); Court Benson (Father Daly); Fred Gwynne (Uncle George). Adapted by James Agate, Jr., based on a story by Wilkie Collins.

Xavier Zenith, a Hollywood still photographer and just recently married, inherits his Uncle George's 59-acre estate. But, in order to keep the property, he must live on it and every day check his uncle's mausoleum to make certain there's been no tampering with its locks. Xavier's wife, Catherine, is not too happy with the prospect of such a confining existence and expresses her opinion to Xavier, who soon wishes he had listened to her.

1881. **"Will the Real Amy Stand Up?"** (3/1/79; rebroadcast from 8/28/78)

1882. **"The Biggest Fish in the World"** (3/2/79; rebroadcast from 8/30/78)

1883. **"The Locked Room"** (3/3/79; rebroadcast from 6/28/74)

1884. **"The Walking Corpse"** (3/4/79; rebroadcast from 5/5/74)

1885. **"The Fall of Gentryville"** (3/5/79; rebroadcast 8/23/79)

Cast: Michael Tolan (Pete); Jackson Beck (Gomez); Ray Owens (Sheriff); Evelyn Juster (Jennie Towers). Written by Sam Dann.

A reporter named Pete, in order to redeem himself, is assigned to write a story about why the little town of Gentryville and all its residents have vanished without a trace. The geologists and engineers blame it on an earth fault but, after he interviews the town's sole survivor, a spinster named Jennie Powers, Pete comes up with a different theory that, if printed, will either land him in a nuthouse or win him a Pulitzer Prize.

1886. **"Ignorant Armies"** (3/6/79; rebroadcast from 9/8/78)

1887. **"Watcher of the Living"** (3/7/79; rebroadcast 8/24/79)

Cast: Tony Roberts (Fred Plattner); Gilbert Mack (Dr. Bendiner); Bob Dryden (Professor Lidgett); Bryna Raeburn (Mrs. Carson). Based on a short story by H.G. Wells, and adapted by James Agate, Jr.

Teacher Fred Plattner, at his doctor's office for a physical, is told that all the bodily organs usually on his left side have moved to his right side. Plattner blames it on an explosion in his chemistry class when he put a match to some green powder brought in by one of his students. This overworked teacher in the small grammar school believes that he has exploded himself into the World of the Dead.

Notes: E.G. Marshall said: "H.G. Wells wrote with two words in mind. The two words are: 'Could be!' With extraordinary resourcefulness and creativity, Wells brought life to the incredible."

1888. "Devil's Gold" (3/8/79; rebroadcast from 9/4/78)

1889. "Dead Wrong" (3/9/79; rebroadcast from 9/6/78)

1890. "Sea Fever" (3/10/79; rebroadcast from 5/11/74)

1891. "A Dream of Death" (3/11/79; rebroadcast from 4/28/74)

1892. "All the Time in the World" (3/12/79; rebroadcast 8/28/79)

Cast: Ralph Bell (Harry); Ray Owens (Lucas); Joan Shea (Rose). Written by Sam Dann.

While serving time, Harry meets a man named Lucas, who was in for 99 years because of the murder he committed during an armed robbery. When Lucas is released, Harry goes to pick him up. A doctor validates Lucas' physical age at around 35. Prison records show he was jailed nearly 100 years ago. In the mind of con man Harry, there's a million to be had in what he plans to call "Lucas' Elixir of Eternal Life"—if Harry can only find a millionaire who wants to live forever.

1893. "Flash Point" (3/13/79; rebroadcast from 9/1/78)

1894. "The Love God" (3/14/79; rebroadcast 8/30/79)

Cast: Court Benson (Bahadur Khan); Grace Matthews (Pamela); William Griffis (Willis Foster); Marian Seldes (Louise). Written by Sam Dann.

Willis Foster, a British district commissioner in India, is a confirmed bachelor. His sister Pamela, eager to remedy this, invites from England her longtime friend Louise. Pamela, wise to the local superstitions, arranges to have a native, Bahadur Khan, offer Louise a charm from the love god Aumeera. It's an offer Louise can't afford to refuse, for Willis is a difficult man to catch.

1895. "End of a Memory" (3/15/79; rebroadcast from 9/11/78)

1896. "High Caqueta" (3/16/79; rebroadcast from 9/13/78)

1897. "The Horse That Wasn't for Sale" (3/17/79; rebroadcast from 5/18/74)

1898. "A Choice of Witnesses" (3/18/79; rebroadcast from 5/22/74)

1899. "The Unseen Watcher" (3/19/79; rebroadcast 8/31/79)

Cast: Earl Hammond (Sam Bendix); Mandel Kramer (Morgan Denning); Evelyn Juster (Cheryl Denning); Sam Gray (Captain Fuchs). Written by Ian Martin.

Flying his helicopter toward a traffic tie-up, reporter Sam Bendix takes a peek at the roof where a woman he and the boys in the radio newsroom call "Suntan Sue" often sunbathes in the nude. But this time, instead of waving at the helicopter, she is thrown down by a man and smothered with a pillow. It is a case of murder, for sure, but Sam's testimony, say the police, will be no good in court. He was 600 feet above the scene of the crime.

1900. "The Secret of Crow's Nest" (3/20/79; rebroadcast from 9/15/78)

1901. "Masks" (3/21/79; rebroadcast 9/4/79)

Cast: John Beal (John Fountain); Court Benson (Inspector Davis); Ray Owens (Ralph Glass); Joan Shea (Ada Norell). Adapted by Gerald Keane, based on a story by Richard Marsh.

While riding a train from Dover to London, John Fountain, former head of Fountain Pictures, is offered a shot of whiskey by a young man. It knocks him unconscious. Later, at London House, a woman offers to show him the Tower of London. While there, she locks him in the dungeon. He also keeps getting brief glimpses of another woman with a badly disfigured face. John Fountain's desire to retire and live quietly in London is off to a bad start.

1902. "It's Hard to Be Rich" (3/22/79; rebroadcast from 9/18/78)

1903. "The Beheading" (3/23/79; rebroadcast from 9/20/78)

1904. "The Edge of Death" (3/24/79; rebroadcast from 5/19/74)

1905. "Out of Sight" (3/25/79; rebroadcast from 5/24/74)

1906. "Enemy from Space" (3/26/79; rebroadcast 9/6/79)

Cast: Mandel Kramer (President Alexander); Russell Horton (Colonel Harris); Evelyn Juster (Ginny Alexander). Written by Ian Martin.

U.S. President Winston Alexander is kidnapped in the year 2729 by robots from a giant ship cruising through space in search of a planet to colonize. They transform the president into one of them, a machine wrapped in a simulacrum, which gives the machine the semblance of a human. Twenty-four hours later, they return the president to Earth, programmed to push the button that will start the long-dreaded nuclear war. Once all human life has been obliterated, the simulacrums will move in and set up their own society.

1907. "The Conversation Factor" (3/27/79; rebroadcast from 9/22/78)

1908. "Waste Paper" (3/28/79; rebroadcast 9/7/79)

Cast: Kim Hunter (Detective Millrose); Earl Hammond (Stanley J. Drone); Lloyd Battista (Captain Williams). Written by Sam Dann.

Detective Gertrude Millrose is finally given, by her sexist superiors, a chance to investigate a murder. Captain Roger Williams considers the killing of a chairwoman a routine case and allows Millrose just one day to work on it. But he is forced to give her an extension when the clues she turns up—a noisy vacuum cleaner, unexplained donations of money and the chairwoman's interest in waste paper—transform the case into one of more than passing interest.

1909. "A Table for Two" (3/29/79; rebroadcast from 9/25/78)

1910. "The Headhunters" (3/30/79; rebroadcast from 9/27/78)

1911. "Diary of a Madman" (3/31/79; rebroadcast from 6/15/74)

1912. "The Mysterious Stranger" (4/1/79; rebroadcast from 11/21/76)

1913. "Voyage of Intrastar" (4/2/79; rebroadcast 9/11/79)

1914. "The Tell-Tale Scar" (4/3/79; rebroadcast from 7/17/78)

1915. "The Believers" (4/4/79; rebroadcast 9/13/79)

Cast: Kristoffer Tabori (Alan Pearson); John Beal (Eban Bolivar); Joan Shea (Agatha Pearson). Written by Percy Granger.

Agatha Pearson has been watching the house of her neighbor, Eban Bolivar, for days. In the evenings people leave their own cars in Bolivar's driveway, enter his house, and are not seen again. Later in the evening, Bolivar drives the cars away. Finally, her curiosity getting the better of her, Agatha sends her 30-year-old son, Alan, to investigate. Alan has a friendly conversation with Bolivar, who concludes it by inviting Alan to come to his house that evening.

1916. "The Village of Fools" (4/5/79; rebroadcast from 7/13/78)

1917. "The Hanging Judge" (4/6/79; rebroadcast from 7/14/78)

1918. "The Green-Eyed Monster" (4/7/79; rebroadcast from 5/12/77)

1919. "The Canterville Ghost" (4/8/79; rebroadcast from 9/21/74)

1920. "The Permanent Man" (4/9/79; rebroadcast 9/14/79)

Cast: Robert Dryden (Dr. Vigo); Russell Horton (Tech); Teri Keane (Mrs. Vigo). Adapted by Gerald Keane, based on a story by William Morrow.

Dr. Vigo, whose office and laboratory are located very near Neptune's spaceport in the year 2020, is visited one day by a 25-year-old man, Tech, who wants to donate his body to science right now. Tech is willing to be kept alive (so Vigo won't be accused of murder), but he wants the doctor to experiment with his brain. Vigo can hardly turn down such an offer, but Tech without a brain becomes a monster who will probably never die if properly fed. He also becomes almost impossible to handle.

1921. "The Absent-Minded League" (4/10/79; rebroadcast from 7/18/78)

1922. "The Charnel House" (4/11/79; rebroadcast 9/18/79)

Cast: Roberta Maxwell (Jane Pryor); Gordon Gould (Dr. Stephen Garrick); Grace Matthews (Nurse Banyon); Court Benson (Dr. Mandley). Written by Ian Martin.

Concerned because she hasn't heard from her father, who has been a patient at the prestigious Chisholm Clinic, for three months, Jane Pryor leaves her voice school in Vienna and heads for Cape Ann, Massachusetts the clinic's location. She finds Dr. Chisholm incapacitated, her father dead, and the clinic in the hands of an unscrupulous doctor and nurse with nefarious schemes on how to keep getting money for the cure of patients already dead. Neither patients nor Miss Pryor can escape because of a pair of vicious Doberman pinschers.

1923. "A Thousand-Year-Old Story" (4/12/79; rebroadcast from 9/29/78)

1924. "The Forever Alley" (4/13/79; rebroadcast from 10/2/78)

1925. "Cherchez la Femme" (4/14/79; rebroadcast from 8/6/77)

1926. "Is He Living or Is He Dead?" (4/15/79; rebroadcast from 11/16/76)

1927. "Ring of Evil" (4/16/79; rebroadcast 9/20/79)

Cast: Kathleen Quinlan (Helena); Earl Hammond (Arthur); Norman Rose (Colonel Bill). Adapted by James Agate, Jr., based on a story by B. H. Maxwell.

While vacationing with her father in Taxco, 18-year-old Helena witnesses the murder of a Mexican woman. What she saw was a man's hand drive a knife into the woman's chest as she stood in a window. On one of his fingers was a ring with a blood-red stone. Later, Helena sees the same ring on the finger of a business associate of her father, a man he calls Colonel Bill. She immediately faints. She becomes even more fearful of the ring when the colonel tells her its history.

Notes: Kathleen Quinlan made her radio acting debut in this episode. She had just opened the stage production of *Taken in Marriage* and was starring in the film *The Promise*. Her television debut was in *Little Ladies of the Night*.

1928. "Shadow of Love" (4/17/79; rebroadcast from 10/4/78)

1929. "The Golden Girl" (4/18/79; rebroadcast 9/21/79)

Cast: Earl Hammond (Arthur M. Stillman); Evelyn Juster (Raya); Gordon Heath (Messenger Lawrence). Written by Sam Dann.

Raya not only tells her lawyer, Arthur M. Stillman, about the computer, but why she was sent to Earth from the planet Serenity to kill Messenger Lawrence, an earthly religious despot. The elders of Serenity—a world without violence, only happiness and beauty—fear the spread of Lawrence's evil throughout the universe and, much against their nature, sent Raya to kill him. Stillman can hardly believe Raya's story, but he can't wait to have her tell it to a jury.

1930. "The Captain of the PoleStar" (4/19/79; rebroadcast from 10/6/78)

1931. "The Winds of Time" (4/20/79; rebroadcast from 10/16/78)

1932. "Long Live the King Is Dead" (4/21/79; rebroadcast from 5/13/77)

1933. "The Prisoner of Zenda" (4/22/79; rebroadcast from 9/6/77)

1934. "The Glass Bubble" (4/23/79; rebroadcast 9/25/79)

Cast: Teri Keane (Doris); Patricia Elliott (Joan); Tony Roberts (Tom Struthers). Written by Elspeth Eric.

Doris has lived alone in a room she calls her glass bubble for 43 years. She has come out for meals, her father's death and to tell Tom Struthers to forget about marrying her. Later, Tom marries Doris' sister, Joan, a marriage that doesn't work out because according to Joan, Tom is jealous of the many other men in her life. But these men are only a figment of Joan's imagination, men created by the devil who, in Joan's life, has taken the form of a big black dog that never leaves her side.

1935. "The Triple Crown" (4/24/79; rebroadcast from 10/9/78)

1936. "Letter of Love, Letter of Death" (4/25/79; rebroadcast 9/27/79)

Cast: Michael Tolan (Lt. Leoni); Martha Greenhouse (Sara Jean Taylor); Bob Dryden (Inspector); Ian Martin (Edward Larsen). Written by Sam Dann.

Police Lt. Leoni is convinced that theatrical producer William K. Crandall was murdered by playwright Edward Larsen, whose latest script Crandall had turned down. But someone else's fingerprints are on the letter opener that killed him. A mousy middle-aged woman who typed Crandall's scripts calls Leoni to say that she had killed the producer. But Leoni refuses to believe her, even though he later learns the prints on the letter opener are hers.

1937. "The Man in Black" (4/26/79; rebroadcast from 10/11/78)

1938. "How Much Land Does a Man Need?" (4/27/79; rebroadcast from 10/13/78)

1939. "Murder Most Foul" (4/28/79; rebroadcast from 5/9/77)

1940. "The Boscombe Pool Mystery" (4/29/79; rebroadcast from 10/13/77)

1941. "War of Angels" (4/30/79; rebroadcast 9/28/79)
Cast: Ann Williams (Lillian Bryant); Russell Horton (Lucifer); Bryna Raeburn (Cissie Patterson); Mandel Kramer (Archangel Michael). Written by Ian Martin.
Lillian Bryant, since the death of her husband, has become the hard-driving, ruthless head of his publishing house. She has alienated her son and daughter and the one man who really loved her. When she suffers a massive stroke, Lucifer and the Archangel Michael appear at the hospital, both wanting to claim her soul. It becomes a toss-up as the many good things she has done may possibly offset the many aspects of her life people have considered evil.

1942. "Never Answer an Advertisement" (5/1/79; rebroadcast from 10/18/78)

1943. "The Fabulous Pillow" (5/2/79; rebroadcast 10/2/79)
Cast: Tony Roberts (Tom Porter); Ralph Bell (Lieutenant Hogan); William Griffis (John Sutter); Teri Keane (Claire Porter). Written by Roy Winsor.
Tim Porter, forced to resign after he testified on behalf of a bank guard suspected of involvement in a heist of $500,000, can find employment only as a high-school math teacher. But now, ten years later, when knocked unconscious in an auto accident, Tom dreams of again meeting the guard who admits he was involved in the crime, and offers Tom $60,000 of the stolen money. Not even Tom believes the dream, until the sixty grand, stuffed in a pillow, arrives in the mail.

1944. "The Outside Girl" (5/3/79; rebroadcast from 10/20/78)

1945. "The Lazarus Syndrome" (5/4/79; rebroadcast from 10/23/78)

1946. "The Lodger" (5/5/79; rebroadcast from 5/13/74)

1947. "The Assassination" (5/6/79; rebroadcast from 5/10/77)

1948. "Search for Eden" (5/7/79; rebroadcast 10/4/79)

Cast: Lloyd Battista (Carlos); Jackson Beck (Murray); Evelyn Juster (Eva); Ian Martin (Eduardo). Adapted by Gerald Keane, based on the 1911 short story *The Country of the Blind* by H. G. Wells.

While guiding two Americans on a climb in the Andes, Carlos, an Ecuadorian, is trapped in an avalanche that sweeps him down into an unknown valley. All of its inhabitants are blind, but their environment is a veritable paradise, an Eden. Carlos, the only one in the valley who can see, is able to adapt himself to their way of life. He falls in love with their leader's daughter, Eva, and wants to marry her. She agrees on the condition that Carlos accept a life of blindness like everyone else in the valley.

1949. "Family Ties" (5/8/79; rebroadcast from 10/25/78)

1950. "The Hole in the Sky" (5/9/79; rebroadcast 10/5/78)

Cast: Mandel Kramer (Roger Thorp); Joan Shea (Dinara); Earl Hammond (Curly); Russell Horton (Ardi). Written by Sam Dann.

Roger Thorp, who makes a living flying illegal goods to distant planets, reluctantly agrees to take a cargo of women's cosmetics (considered contraband) to the planet Bacchus. To reach Bacchus in the required six days means flying through the dreaded hole in the sky, something like the Bermuda Triangle back on Earth. Thorp has been through it once before and is almost certain no one can make it twice.

1951. "The Sound of Terror" (5/10/79; rebroadcast from 10/27/78)

1952. "The Midas of Castle Hill" (5/11/79; rebroadcast from 11/1/78)

1953. "The Cask of Amontillado" (5/12/79; rebroadcast from 3/19/75)

1954. "The Picture of Dorian Gray" (5/13/79; rebroadcast from 10/5/74)

1955. "Virtue Is Its Own Reward" (5/14/79; rebroadcast 10/9/79)

Cast: Fred Gwynne (Junius K. Barley); Bob Dryden (Mr. Lamb); Bryna Raeburn (Dolly); Ray Owens (Mr. Nimbus). Written by Sam Dann.

Junius K. Barley makes his living by inserting small-print items in legal agreements that people don't read carefully and pay dearly for later. But what he makes from this kind of skullduggery is peanuts to what he is offered by a very beauti-ful woman who realizes what Barley could do in the big time if given the oppor-tunity. But first, she says, he must divorce his wife. Though a plain-Jane type, Mrs. Barley is not one to back away from this kind of competition.

1956. "A Better Mousetrap" (5/15/79; rebroadcast from 11/10/78)

1957. "Messenger from Yesterday" (5/16/79; rebroadcast 10/11/79)

Cast: Norman Rose (Ramsey West); Teri Keane (Gloria West); Gordon Gould (Frank); Russell Horton (The Pharaoh). Written by Gerald Keane.

Ramsey West, who teaches Egyptology at Imhotep College, near Boston, gives his wife, Gloria, a life-size statue of an Egyptian Pharaoh as a birthday pre-sent. When Gloria leaves for Chicago to care for her ill sister, the statue takes over her housework, including the vacuuming. It even prepares a steak dinner for Ramsey and his psychologist friend Frank. It's a real treat; the Wests haven't had a steak on their table since the beginning of a double-digit inflation.

1958. "The Pilgrim Soul" (5/17/79; rebroadcast from 11/13/78)

1959. "The Conspiracy" (5/18/79; rebroadcast from 11/15/78)

1960. "The Horla" (5/19/79; rebroadcast from 5/17/74)

1961. "The Phantom of the Opera" (5/20/79; rebroadcast from 7/18/75)

1962. "Help Wanted" (5/21/79; rebroadcast 10/12/79)

Cast: Tony Roberts (Lt. Arthur MacRae); Carol Teitel (Aunt Millie); Bryna Raeburn (Mrs. Colfax); Earl Hammond (Mr. Diaz). Written by Sam Dann.

Detective Lt. Arthur MacRae is told that unless he solves the murders of the five women it's back on the street beat for all members of his department. MacRae learns that each of the women, all living alone and lonely, had charge accounts at a corner grocery store owned by a Mexican American named Diaz, and that each had a violent argument with Diaz over money before they were killed. He also learns two more facts: that Diaz is in the country illegally, and that his own Aunt Millie was in the store during each of the arguments.

1963. "The Man with the Claret Mark" (5/22/79; rebroadcast from 11/3/78)

1964. "Dreams" (5/23/79; rebroadcast 10/16/79)

Cast: Kristoffer Tabori (Ben Bailey); Bob Dryden (Doctor Fleisher); Evelyn Juster (Gloria Bailey). Written by Elspeth Eric.

Ben Bailey, a bass guitarist, married Gloria over the objection of her parents, who wanted a son-in-law with a steady income. But Ben is able to provide Gloria with all the modern comforts as long as he wins at roulette, which he does when Gloria's dreams tell him which numbers to bet. But when she suffers a shock (a dream of her mother's death) and becomes comatose, Ben's source of income, which he needs to pay the doctor's bills, suddenly dries up.

1965. "Hit and Run" (5/24/79; rebroadcast from 11/6/78)

1966. "Second Sight" (5/25/79; rebroadcast from 11/8/78)

1967. "Dracula" (5/26/79; rebroadcast from 1/6/78)

1968. "The Fall of the House of Usher" (5/27/79; rebroadcast from 9/16/78)

1969. "The Outsider" (5/28/79; rebroadcast 10/18/79)

Cast: John Beal (Doug Watson); Joan Shea (Gail Harrison); Robert Maxwell (Russ Harrison); Ray Owens (Walter Cummings). Written by Bob Juhren.

In the late 1940s, the citizens of Hanover Hills felt a terrific rumbling underground, resulting in a giant fissure opening up on a nearby hill, from which came a curious vapor. Since then, not a person, car, truck, train or bus has entered or left Hanover Hills. No one has grown a day older; no one has died; not a single child has been born. Doug Watson's arrival causes a joyous celebration. Hanover Hill's residents are sure he has been sent to lead them back into the real world.

1970. "The Favor of Women" (5/29/79; rebroadcast from 11/17/78)

1971. "A Curious Experience" (5/30/79; rebroadcast 10/19/79)

Cast: Bob Dryden (The Major); Kristoffer Tabori (Robert Wicklow); Jackson Beck (Sgt. Rayburn); Bryna Raeburn (Lady Strathclyde). Adapted by Sam Dann, based on the 1881 short story by Mark Twain.

It's 1862 and a pale, ragged 16-year-old, Robert Wicklow, who claims he's a homeless Southerner, tries to enlist in a Union fort in New London, Connecticut. The major in charge, a man with feelings, permits Wicklow to join the fort's musicians. But soon Wicklow is caught writing suspicious notes and is accused of spying. He finally confesses, but in doing so, implicates half of the fort's troops as well as several prominent civilians living in New London.

1972. "The Thing at Nolan" (5/31/79; rebroadcast from 11/20/78)

1973. "The Grey Slapper" (6/1/79; rebroadcast from 11/22/78)

1974. "The House of Seven Gables" (6/2/79; rebroadcast from 8/31/74)

1975. "The Golem" (6/3/79; rebroadcast from 2/22/75)

1976. "Willy and Dilly" (6/4/79; rebroadcast 10/23/79)

Cast: Fred Gwynne (Dilly); Evelyn Juster (Willy); Lloyd Battista (Norman). Written by Sam Dann.

Harrison Dillard Wentworth, nicknamed Dilly, is smitten by the charms of Wilhelmina Zurich, nicknamed Willy, when she pleads with him to invest prudently her entire savings of $5,000. Long-married Dilly starts seeing Willy secretly until her brother, Norman, threatens to blackmail him. Norman says he'll keep quiet if Dilly can arrange for him to steal $1 million in negotiable bonds. Dilly agrees, but he has a surprise for Norman. The attaché case he steals contains no bonds, just blank sheets of paper.

1977. "Night Visitor" (6/5/79; rebroadcast from 11/24/78)

1978. "The Pardon" (6/6/79; rebroadcast 10/25/79)

Cast: Larry Haines (Jack); Russell Horton (Angus); Ray Owens (Judge); Carol Teitel (Anna). Adapted by Gerald Keane, based on a story by Emil Bazan.

Jack, who's been disabled in a coal mine accident, is given a 20-year sentence for the murder of his stingy mother-in-law who refused to lend him money to start a business of his own. He swears her death was accidental and vows to come back some day and get his revenge on those who testified against him. His wife, Anna, realizes she did little to help him during the trial and fears she will be the victim of his anger. Then the dreaded word comes: Jack has been pardoned by the governor.

1979. "Alien Presences" (6/7/79; rebroadcast from 11/27/78)

1980. "The Romany Revenge" (6/8/79; rebroadcast from 11/29/78)

1981. "The Murders in the Rue Morgue" (6/9/79; rebroadcast from 3/15/75)

1982. "Jane Eyre" (6/10/79; rebroadcast from 6/22/77)

1983. "Look Who's Coming" (6/11/79; rebroadcast 10/26/79)

Cast: Teri Keane (Flo Betts); Earl Hammond (Mark); Martha Greenhouse (Grace); Joseph Silver (Harry Betts). Written by Ian Martin.

Harry Betts likes science-fiction programs while his wife Flo goes for daytime serials. One afternoon Flo is startled when her favorite show is interrupted by pictures of two humanoids who seem to be in some kind of electronic work-shop. They warn Earth not to resist when their spaceship tries to land otherwise earthlings will face annihilation. At first Flo thinks the station has broadcast a portion of a science-fiction show by mistake, but the two humanoids keep reap-pearing, at least on Flo's television set, repeating the same warning.

1984. "Squaring the Triangle" (6/12/79; rebroadcast from 12/1/78)

1985. "The Copenhagen Connection" (6/13/79; rebroadcast 10/30/79)

Cast: Ralph Bell (Sam Kellogg); Lloyd Battista (George); Bryna Raeburn (Mrs. Rusk); Earl Hammond (Jerry Harvey). Written by Gerald Keane.

All three occupants of a small chartered plane that crashed into the San Bernardino Mountains are burned beyond recognition, but one, Donald Harvey, is identified by a small unburned bit of a necktie. Harvey was about to put the finger on a Dane known as "The Viking," the chief of the Copenhagen Connec-tion. Thus begins a tale of skullduggery never equaled in the annals of crime.

1986. "The Serpent of Saris" (6/14/79; rebroadcast from 12/4/78)

1987. "The Devil's Bargain" (6/15/79; rebroadcast from 12/6/78)

1988. "The Suicide Club" (6/16/79; rebroadcast from 7/28/74)

1989. "The Oblong Box" (6/17/79; rebroadcast from 3/9/75)

1990. "The Unquiet Tomb" (6/18/79; rebroadcast 11/1/79)

Cast: Fred Gwynne (Captain Jack O'Shea); Bob Dryden (Nick); Teri Keane (Nellie). Written by Elspeth Eric.

An old salt, Captain Jack O'Shea, appropriates a small remote island on which he builds a house of coral and a large tomb for himself. As people living with him die, he permits their coffins to be put in the tomb—first, his house-keeper, then the two children and wife of a very close friend. But for no apparent reason, the children's lead coffins are often found moved to different places, and the housekeeper's wooden coffin starts to deteriorate. The captain also faces another problem: wondering why ships he sees headed for his island never land.

1991. "The Exploding Heart" (6/19/79; rebroadcast from 12/8/78)

1992. "The Spaces on the Wall" (6/20/79; rebroadcast 11/2/79)

Cast: Kevin McCarthy (Tom Westerly); Court Benson (Halsey Crawford); Ray Owens (Copper); Carol Teitel (Ursula Derringer). Written by Sam Dann.

A millionaire art collector buys four paintings by a famous German artist, but his agent, Ursula Derringer, maintains they are fake—the owner had promised the originals to her. To track down the forger, Mrs. Derringer hires private investigator Tom Westerly, who quickly becomes irritated when she refuses to answer his more pertinent questions. She, in turn, shows much irritation when he includes her among five possible suspects.

1993. "A Horror Story" (6/21/79; rebroadcast from 12/11/78)

1994. "Ward Six" (6/22/79; rebroadcast from 12/13/78)

1995. "The Diamond Necklace" (6/23/79; rebroadcast from 9/3/75)

1996. "The Hound of the Baskervilles" (6/24/79; rebroadcast from 7/2/77)

1997. "Mission from Zython" (6/25/79; rebroadcast 11/6/79)
Cast: John Beal (John Bergstrom); Russell Horton (Ralph Bergstrom); Ian Martin (Rotar); Kristoffer Tabori (Professor Mulloy). Written by Roy Winsor.
A creature who calls himself Rotar first lands near the Iowa farm of John Bergstrom. Young Ralph demands both film and camera after paralyzing the elder Bergstrom with a low-level electrical charge from his eyes. Then he explains his mission: the destruction of all atomic warheads because those that have already been exploded have polluted the atmosphere of his planet, Zython, even though it's millions of miles from Earth.

1998. "The Search for Myra" (6/26/79; rebroadcast from 12/15/78)

1999. "The Giuseppe Verdi Autobus" (6/27/79; rebroadcast 11/8/79)
Cast: Tammy Grimes (Norma Davis); Bob Dryden (Charley Wilson); Lloyd Battista (Detective Stern); Gilbert Mack (Gildo). Written by Sam Dann.
Norma Davis, a widow for five years, meets a divorced American, Charley Wilson, in Florence. It's a great day for both of them—they fall in love. As they head for home, intending to get married, she agrees to carry in her suitcase a music box he has bought for one of his children. At New York's Kennedy Airport, a customs officer discovers the music box is filled with $1 million in heroin. When he does, Charley disappears and Norma is arrested.

2000. "The Familiar Ghost" (6/28/79; rebroadcast from 12/18/78)

2001. "It Has to Be True" (6/29/79; rebroadcast from 12/20/78)

2002. "The Masque of the Red Death" (6/30/79; rebroadcast from 3/8/75)

2003. "The Tell-Tale Heart" (7/1/79; rebroadcast from 3/16/75)

2004. "The Rivalry" (7/2/79; rebroadcast 11/9/79)

Cast: John Beal (Inspector James); Kristoffer Tabori (Sgt. Holloway); Earl Hammond (Police Surgeon); Court Benson (Andrew Wolf). Adapted by James Agate, Jr., based on a short story by Maurice Leblanc.

Andrew Wolf, who has gone straight, gives his old nemesis, Inspector James, a number of material clues which make it apparent that a man once high in political office may have caused the death of a music-hall dancer. The inspector, however, wants to solve the case without any help from an ex-felon. The only problem is he can't find anyone who will testify that the suspect has ever had anything to do with the victim.

2005. "The Power of Evil" (7/3/79; rebroadcast from 12/22/78)

2006. "The Great White Shark" (7/4/79; rebroadcast 11/13/79)

Cast: Michael Tolan (Capt. Gunner Trent); Ian Martin (J. H. Burden); Joan Banks (Eve Burden). Written by Ian Martin.

Captain Gunner Trent agrees to take Texas millionaire J. H. Burden and his much younger wife, Eve, fishing for a 1,200-pound marlin. Burden turns out to be a drunken bully, suspicious of everyone—including Trent, whom he thinks has a yen for Eve. When they make their first strike, it's not a marlin, but the white shark Trent has vowed to kill. Burden hooks the shark and it pulls him overboard. Trent dives in to save him and to settle his score with the great fish.

2007. "If I Can't Have You" (7/5/79; rebroadcast from 12/25/78)

2008. "No Way Out" (7/6/79; rebroadcast from 12/27/78)

2009. "Dr. Jekyll and Mr. Hyde" (7/7/79; rebroadcast from 1/8/78)

2010. "The Pit and the Pendulum" (7/8/79; rebroadcast from 5/25/75)

2011. "Smile at a Homely Girl" (7/9/79; rebroadcast 11/15/79)

Cast: Larry Haines (Will Bennett); Teri Keane (Sarah Lewis); Evelyn Juster (Marcia Bennett); Ray Owens (George). Written by Sam Dann.

Will and Marcia Bennett, their high school's handsomest pair, find their marriage near a breaking point. She accuses him of having an affair with his partner's secretary and swears he will pay dearly for it. When Marcia suddenly dies, the coroner finds she had been poisoned, and Will is accused of her murder. But Sarah Lewis, the homely town librarian who has never forgotten that Will had asked her to dance at the senior prom, volunteers some evidence that could save Will's life.

2012. "The Dead House" (7/10/79; rebroadcast from 12/29/78)

2013. "The Fools" (7/11/79; rebroadcast 11/16/79)

Cast: Russell Horton (Vanya Kuzin); Bryna Raeburn (Mother); Ray Owens (Nikolai); Fred Gwynne (Ivan Salakin). Adapted by Gerald Keane, based on the short story *One Autumn Night* by Maxim Gorki.

Two ragged, homeless Russians, Vanya Kuzin and Ivan Salakin, have come to the city in the winter looking for work. Vanya spends all his money on vodka Ivan sells his precious boots for a miserable two rubles. Blue with cold, they roam the streets, hired sometimes, but not too often, to split wood or chop ice for a few kopecks (pennies). Vanya is reduced to begging Ivan, to stealing. Frustrated, they set out in a blizzard for the next town to filch anything they can carry from Ivan's former employer. This could mean Siberia for both of them, which, they reason, will be no worse than their present situation.

2014. "The Look" (7/12/79; rebroadcast from 1/4/79)

2015. "The Long, Long Sleep" (7/13/79; rebroadcast from 1/15/79)

2016. "Frankenstein Revisited" (7/14/79; rebroadcast from 12/6/74)

2017. "Wuthering Heights" (7/15/79; rebroadcast from 9/14/77)

2018. "The House of Dead Heart" (7/16/79; rebroadcast 11/20/79)

Cast: Kristoffer Tabori (Paul Wyant); Gordon Gould (Professor Dalton); Court Benson (Dr. Lombard); Evelyn Juster (Sybilla Lombard). Adapted by James Agate, Jr., based on the 1904 short story *The House of the Dead Hand* by Edith Wharton.

Sybilla Lombard, 17, spends, at her father's insistence, all of her inheritance for a Leonardo da Vinci original. But her father, an eccentric art connoisseur, takes possession of the painting, allowing only a chosen few to see it. He also makes Sybilla a virtual prisoner, not even permitting her to see her boyfriend. When Paul Wyant arrives from Cincinnati with a note from his art teacher, he's invited to see the da Vinci. Sybilla begs him to help her escape, but he refuses—a decision he soon regrets having made.

2019. "The Wandering Wind" (7/17/79; rebroadcast from 1/17/79)

Notes: John Beal has acted in numerous films over the years, ranging from the early Hollywood years to the current nineties. He has appeared in such films as *Les Misérables* (1935), *Madame X* (1937), *Edge of Darkness* (1943), *Ten Who Dared* (1960), *Amityville 3: The Demon* (1983), and *The Firm* (1993).

2020. "The Case of the Forced Divorce" (7/18/79; rebroadcast 11/22/79)

Cast: Bob Dryden (Andrew Wolf); Ian Martin (Inspector James); Paul Hecht (George); Roberta Maxwell (Countess Lila). Adapted by James Agate, Jr., based on the short story by Maurice Leblanc.

George Beufort plays upon his wife Lila's fears of scandal to force her into giving him a divorce. His weapon is her wedding ring that is inscribed with another man's name. He also demands custody of their 10-year-old son, who will inherit a fortune when he turns 21. He has already kidnapped the child and won't release him until his demands are met. Lila frustratedly turns to her ex-boyfriend, Andrew Wolf, king of deception, who boasts that "an amateur cheat is no match for a professional."

2021. "Side Effects" (7/19/79; rebroadcast from 1/19/79)

2022. "Let the Buyer Beware" (7/20/79; rebroadcast from 1/22/79)

2023. "The Black Cat" (7/21/79; rebroadcast from 6/22/74)

2024. "The 36th Man" (7/22/79; rebroadcast from 1/3/75)

2025. "No Man's Land" (7/23/79; rebroadcast 11/23/79)

Cast: Tony Roberts (Craig); Earl Hammond (Rooster); William Griffis (Jackson); Carol Teitel (Aimee). Written by Percy Granger.

It is 1944 and the Allied drive for Berlin is moving ahead in full force when Sergeant Craig's squad of U.S. soldiers is ambushed near the Somme River in France, the sight of one of the bloodiest battles of World War I. The surviving members of the squad seek refuge in a small village, where they quickly find themselves on trial. The village people, who feel that they had nothing to do with starting the war yet are its principal victims, have decided to execute all soldiers with their own weapons. The men's fate depends on Craig's convincing them that the soldiers are on their side.

2026. "The Burning Bough" (7/24/79; rebroadcast from 1/24/79)

2027. "Catch a Falling Star" (7/25/79; rebroadcast 11/27/79)

Cast: Carol Teitel (Miss Mamie); Teri Keane (Grace Browning); Kathleen Quinlan (Hallie Browning); Ralph Bell (David Browning). Written by Nancy Moore.

The 70-year-old Miss Mamie, a seamstress since age 15 and a recluse even then, doesn't sew well, but her many customers delight in the tales she weaves about herself, them and the dresses she alters. Then, painter David Browning gives Miss Mamie her first chance for real-life prominence when he begins her portrait for his upcoming show in New York. But the sittings end abruptly and the dreams turn to nightmares when Browning's daughter offers the never-married Miss Mamie her ultimate fantasy: to sew a wedding gown.

2028. "The Dominant Personality" (7/26/79; rebroadcast from 1/26/79)

2029. "Love After Death" (7/27/79; rebroadcast from 2/5/79)

2030. "The Hand" (7/28/79; rebroadcast from 1/11/78)

2031. "Berenice" (7/29/79; rebroadcast from 3/11/75)

2032. "Relax and Enjoy It" (7/30/79; rebroadcast 11/29/79)

Cast: Norman Rose (Curtis Alexander Arnold); Paul Hecht (Caro); Earl Hammond (Goral); Roberta Maxwell (Marla). Written by Sam Dann.

Curtis Alexander Arnold, wealthy president of Arnold Industries, is abducted by members of the People's Revolutionary Movement of Lasia, a small island off an unknown coast. He finds himself in the midst of a financial gun-wielding woman, Marla, and her passive, Harvard-educated accomplice, Caro. Arnold immediately realizes that the key to his escape lies with Caro so he quickly creates a rift between he and Marla. But before Arnold can get away, they reach the hideout where the third kidnapper, Goral, reveals his intention to kill Arnold.

2033. "Everybody Does It" (7/31/79; rebroadcast from 2/7/79)

2034. "The Love Goddess Caper" (8/1/79; rebroadcast 11/30/79)

Cast: Court Benson (Mark Twain); Russell Horton (Frank Walcott); Gordon Gould (George); Bryna Raeburn (Mary). Adapted by Sam Dann, based on a story by Mark Twain.

Frank Walcott, who has made his fortune designing bathroom fixtures, says the recently excavated statue is of his wife, Mary, not Venus—and he knows because he is the sculptor. The Italian government, thinking Frank is crazy, sends him to an asylum. But Twain, who agrees there is a resemblance, offers to help Frank and Mary claim their right to the statue. The author begins by trying to prove, much to the Walcotts' consternation, that they are the reincarnated sculptor and model.

Notes: Host E.G. Marshall announced this episode as "The Goddess Caper," the original title of the script before it was changed to "The Love Goddess Caper."

2035. "The Sinister Shadow" (8/2/79; rebroadcast from 2/12/79)

2036. "The Missing Day" (8/3/79; rebroadcast from 2/14/79)

2037. "The Serpent of the Nile" (8/4/79; rebroadcast from 5/15/77)

2038. "Tobin's Palm" (8/5/79; rebroadcast from 8/3/77)

2039. "Nefertiti Part I: The Vulture Screams" (8/6/79; rebroadcast from 1/8/79)

2040. "Nefertiti Part II: To Kill a Pharaoh" (8/7/79; rebroadcast from 1/9/79)

2041. "Nefertiti Part III: The Cobra Strikes" (8/8/79; rebroadcast from 1/10/79)

2042. "Nefertiti Part IV: The Head with One Eye" (8/9/79; rebroadcast from 1/11/79)

2043. "Nefertiti Part V: The Curse of the Scarab" (8/10/79; rebroadcast from 1/12/79)

2044. "Tom Sawyer, Detective" (8/11/79; rebroadcast from 11/15/76)

2045. "The Light That Failed" (8/12/79; rebroadcast from 6/29/77)

2046. "Tiger, Tiger, Shining Bright" (8/13/79; rebroadcast 12/4/79)
    Cast: Bob Dryden (Dr. Lewis Robey); Patricia Elliott (Charlotte Banning); William Griffis (Dr. Ray Taylor). Written by Roy Winsor.
    Charlotte Banning begs her psychologist Lewis Robey to hypnotize her because, she tells him, there's "a demon churning around inside me." While under hypnosis she reveals an event that took place 100 years ago: the horrible slaying of an ancestor, also named Charlotte, by a tiger. Dr. Robey tells Mrs. Banning that the key to ridding herself of this spirit is to trace and confront the experience. But, before she can act on his advice, she unwittingly visits a zoo where she has her own encounter with a tiger.

2047. "The Shock of His Life" (8/14/79; rebroadcast from 2/19/79)

2048. "Body and Soul" (8/15/79; rebroadcast 12/6/79)
    Cast: Teri Keane (Laura); Mandel Kramer (Robert); Martha Greenhouse (Nurse); Ray Owens (Doctor). Written by Elspeth Eric.
    Laura Burton, who is chronically sick, suddenly discovers her spiritual body separated from her physical one. In this new spiritual realm, she experiences peacefulness and deep internal satisfaction. She likes this state of being until she

realizes that it causes pain for others; she sees her husband weeping over her inert body and her daughter, whom she hasn't seen in months, rushing to her bedside. Laura realizes she must decide which is better—life or death.

2049. "The Great Brain" (8/16/79; rebroadcast from 2/21/79)

2050. "Hickory, Dickory, Doom" (8/17/79; rebroadcast from 2/26/79)

2051. "The Adventure of the Red-Headed League" (8/18/79; rebroadcast from 9/10/77)

2052. "Markheim: Man or Monster?" (8/19/79; rebroadcast from 9/9/75)

2053. "Taboo Means Death" (8/20/79; rebroadcast 12/7/79)

Cast: Russell Horton (Mac Calder); Earl Hammond (Digger Browne); Evelyn Juster (Noelani). Written by Ian Martin.

Mac Calder learns from his intended Noelani that she can't wed him because she must marry another pure-blood Samoan. Unable to persuade her to reject the island's "ethnic purity," he appeals to her mother who tells him they will go against the gods if they marry. Still resolved to make Noelani his bride, he charters a small plane and they make their escape. But when they encounter a thunderstorm and are unable to establish ground control, Noelani begins to fear the curse of the gods—death.

2054. "Shadows from the Grave" (8/21/79; rebroadcast from 2/28/79)

2055. "Stranger from Nowhere" (8/22/79; rebroadcast 12/11/79)

Cast: Paul Hecht (Charley Robinson); Carol Teitel (Mary); Court Benson (Joshua Pride); Gordon Heath (Dr. Latrobe). Written by Gerald Keane.

For two years, Charley Robinson's espionage on Earth for his planet, Tycho Brahe, has been extremely successful. But suddenly he is confronted by Mary, the wife of the real Charley Robinson, whose body the spy is using. Then a science-fiction writer—a former teacher of Mary's—reveals on a television talk show the existence of Tycho Brahe, which he describes in detail in his new book. Charley knows he must act or his mission will be jeopardized.

2056. "The Fall of Gentryville" (8/23/79; rebroadcast from 3/5/79)

2057. "Watcher of the Living" (8/24/79; rebroadcast from 3/7/79)

2058. "Don't Die Without Me" (8/25/79; rebroadcast from 1/13/77)

2059. "The Sire de Maletroit's Door" (8/26/79; rebroadcast from 4/22/75)

2060. "A Cup of Bitter Chocolate" (8/27/79; rebroadcast 12/13/79)

Cast: Paul Hecht (Ted Poindexter); Joan Shea (Mrs. Poindexter); Bob Dryden (Miles). Written by Ian Martin.

Ted Poindexter, heir to his mother's vast fortune but desperate for money right now, is urged by his greedy girlfriend to poison his mother. But Miles, the family butler, prevents Ted from slipping pills into her nightly hot chocolate, warning that as long as he's around Ted won't get away with murder. At his girlfriend's prodding, Ted makes plans to do away with his mother and Miles. Nearly the victim of an auto accident involving Ted's car, Miles decides he must do something about Ted before Ted can do something about him.

2061. "All the Time in the World" (8/28/79; rebroadcast from 3/12/79)

2062. "Ninety Lives" (8/29/79; rebroadcast 12/14/79)

Cast: Fred Gwynne (Muldoon); Teri Keane (Shirley); Russell Horton (Dr. Sidney LaFleur). Written by Sam Dann.

Just as Muldoon and his sister Shirley are about to close up their diner for the night, a well-dressed but penniless man walks in. Shirley, whose leg was badly mangled in an auto accident, takes an immediate liking to the man, even though she doesn't know who he is. When her brother learns that the stranger is a noted linguist who has murdered his wife, Shirley defends him, making it clear to her brother that if the police are to be notified, she will be the one to do it.

2063. "The Love God" (8/30/79; rebroadcast from 3/14/79)

2064. "The Unseen Watcher" (8/31/79; rebroadcast from 3/19/79)

2065. "A Connecticut Yankee in King Arthur's Court" (9/1/79; rebroadcast from 11/18/76)

2066. "The Premature Burial" (9/2/79; rebroadcast from 3/2/75)

2067. "Tomorrow Will Never Come" (9/3/79; rebroadcast 12/18/79)

Cast: Bob Dryden (Charlie Henkle); Grace Matthews (Patricia Hartley); Earl Hammond (Fred Johnson); Ray Owens (Henry Greene). Written by Nancy Moore.

Charlie Henkle, a 70-year-old elevator operator, talks and listens to Nellie, an antique, mahogany-paneled people lifter. When Henry Greene, owner of the building, tells Charlie that he and Nellie will soon be replaced by a steel and plastic push-button model, Charlie and the building's tenants are outraged. Despite a tenants' petition demanding that Nellie be kept running, a wrecking crew arrives, a day ahead of the scheduled demolition. But Charlie and Nellie are ready with a deadly scheme they hope will insure them their jobs.

2068. "Masks" (9/4/79; rebroadcast from 3/21/79)

2069. "The Man in the Black Cap" (9/5/79; rebroadcast 12/20/79)

Cast: Paul Hecht (John Morgan); Ian Martin (Mr. Higgins); Carol Teitel (Hester Morgan). Adapted by James Agate, Jr., based on the 1932 short story *A Glimpse* by Edith Wharton.

John and Hester Morgan sell their copper mine—some say fraudulently—and buy a rustic seaside home in Maine, despite the real estate agent's warning that all previous inhabitants have reported the presence of an unusual variety of ghost—the kind people bring with them. The Morgans scoff at such "nonsense," but, two months later, when a man in a black cap keeps appearing and disappearing, John starts behaving strangely, then vanishes without a trace. Hester begins to have second thoughts about the real estate man's warning.

2070. "Enemy from Space" (9/6/79; rebroadcast from 3/26/79)

2071. "Waste Paper" (9/7/79; rebroadcast from 3/28/79)

2072. "The Warriors from Loanda" (9/8/79; rebroadcast from 8/11/77)

2073. "The Venus d'Ile" (9/9/79; rebroadcast from 7/19/74)

2074. "The Odyssey of Laura Collins" (9/10/79; rebroadcast 12/21/79)

Cast: Betsy Beard (Laura Collins); Evelyn Juster (Ellen Collins); Court Benson (Dr. Wade); Don Scardino (Jerry Marfay). Written by Bob Juhren.

Laura Collins, still mentally scarred by her boyfriend's sudden decision to call off their wedding six months ago, coolly tells her mother she is going to kill herself. Alarmed, Mrs. Collins rushes to psychiatrist Dr. Wade, who hypnotizes Laura and tells her that she must "express herself." But the next day, when Laura mysteriously lapses into a coma and Mrs. Collins starts receiving phone calls from a woman in New York who claims to be Laura, Dr. Wade becomes convinced that the young woman is experiencing a form of mind-travel.

2075. "Voyage of Intrastar" (9/11/79; rebroadcast from 4/2/79)

2076. "The Two Sams" (9/12/79; rebroadcast 12/26/79)

Cast: Russell Horton (Sam Jacobs); Fred Gwynne (Samson O'Malley); Evelyn Juster (Moira Flynn); Ian Martin (Howard Brice). Written by Gerald Keane.

Private detective Samson O'Malley and lawyer Sam Jacobs investigate the kidnapping of eight-month-old Billy Brice, son of wealthy Howard and Gloria Brice. Billy was abducted while under the housekeeper's care, but she only remembers a black limousine and someone with long fingers, wearing a gold ring with a square turquoise in the middle. O'Malley discovers that Billy is Gloria's illegitimate son and, digging further, learns that Billy's father runs a limousine service and owns a gold ring with a square turquoise in the center.

2077. "The Believers" (9/13/79; rebroadcast from 4/4/79)

2078. "The Permanent Man" (9/14/79; rebroadcast from 4/9/79)

2079. "An Occurrence at Owl Creek Bridge" (9/15/79; rebroadcast from 8/24/74)

2080. "The Garden" (9/16/79; rebroadcast from 11/10/74)

2081. "The Guillotine" (9/17/79; rebroadcast 12/28/79)

Cast: Paul Hecht (Gottfried); Don Scardino (Karl); Bryna Raeburn (Woman). Adapted by Elspeth Eric, based on the 1824 short story *The Adventure of the German Student* by Washington Irving.

Gottfried, brooding and lonely, turns to his friend Karl for solace. Karl suggests a trip to Paris. Gottfried agrees, arriving there at the start of the Revolution when hundreds of people are being guillotined. In his loneliness, he creates a woman he tells Karl "exists only in my mind." Nevertheless, he meets her one stormy night—in the flesh—when he is inexplicably drawn to the site of the guillotine. He invites her to his room, but the next morning finds her dead, a victim of the giant blade.

2082. "The Charnel House" (9/18/79; rebroadcast from 4/11/79)

2083. "You're Better Off Guilty" (9/19/79; rebroadcast 1/1/80)

Cast: Kristoffer Tabori (Ralph Westfield); Joan Shea (Miss Reymer); Ray Owens (Inspector Thorstad); Marian Hailey (Sylvia). Written by Sam Dann.

On his way to work one morning, mild-mannered Ralph Westfield discovers the murdered body of rock 'n' roll star Jill Joris. Immediately, he's a public figure, the press, public and police linking him romantically with the star. His paycheck increases, and women start fawning over him. At the same time, the police try to pin the murder on him, so relentlessly that he almost begins believing he committed it.

Notes: Richard M. Brescia commented: "We've decided to showcase this highly praised drama series on the evenings it has performed best for us. The *Mystery Theater* is now carried by more stations [253] than ever before. But they've found that peak listening to the series continues to occur during the Monday-thru-Friday broadcasts. Station clearances are also at their best during those five nights."

2084. "Ring of Evil" (9/20/79; rebroadcast from 4/16/79)

2085. "The Golden Girl" (9/21/79; rebroadcast from 4/18/79)

2086. "Jimmy Valentine's Gamble" (9/22/79; rebroadcast from 8/7/77)

2087. "The Beach of Falesa" (9/23/79; rebroadcast from 10/11/74)

2088. "The Gettysburg Address" (9/24/79; rebroadcast 1/3/80)
    Cast: Bob Dryden (Andrew Wolf); Earl Hammond (Inspector James); Lloyd Battista (Jeffrey Knox). Adapted by Gerald Keane, based on a story by Maurice Leblanc.
    Wealthy Jeffrey Knox shows retired thief Andrew Wolf (Arsene Lupin) one of two paintings dated July 4, 1863, and tells him it is the key to an unsolved mystery involving hidden treasure. It seems the hiding place is somewhere depicted in the painting, the other copy of which is owned by a woman in an apartment across the street from Knox. When she's found dead a day later and Knox disappears without a trace, Wolf is sure there's more to the painting than meets the eye.

2089. "The Glass Bubble" (9/25/79; rebroadcast from 4/23/79)

2090. "The Eighth Day" (9/26/79; rebroadcast 1/15/80)
    Cast: Mandel Kramer (Roger Criswell); Evelyn Juster (Julia Criswell); William Griffis (Stebbins); Court Benson (Lou Paradell). Written by Sam Dann.
    Roger Criswell has been waiting for years for his father-in-law, Lou Paradell, to die so he can inherit the lucrative Paradell Paint Company. After Paradell's death, it doesn't take very long for Criswell to ruin the flourishing enterprise. His only way out is to hire someone to blow up the paint factory. Criswell has no intention of being in his office when the big bang occurs, but the hired dynamiter is very secretive about his plans, much to Criswell's consternation.

2091. "Letter of Love, Letter of Death" (9/27/79; rebroadcast from 4/25/79)

2092. "War of Angels" (9/28/79; rebroadcast from 4/30/79)

2093. "The Passing of Black Eagle" (9/29/79; rebroadcast from 8/2/77)

2094. "The Love Song of Death" (9/30/79; rebroadcast from 5/11/77)

2095. "The Beast" (10/1/79; rebroadcast 1/17/80)

Cast: Norman Rose (Henry Trevor); Carol Teitel (Martha Trevor); Russell Horton (Bartholomew); Bob Dryden (Wayne). Adapted by James Agate, Jr., based on the 1910 short story *The Blonde Beast* by Edith Wharton.

Henry Trevor has so many personal problems he refuses to be bothered by the fact he killed a man while driving to his summer home on Cape Cod. Trevor has lost most of his wife's money in bad investments) she has fallen in love with the family lawyer. Trevor is able to convince his wife to keep quiet about the accident, but the son of the man who was killed wants revenge. A blood-stained dent in Trevor's car may be the evidence he needs.

2096. "The Fabulous Pillow" (10/2/79; rebroadcast from 5/2/79)

2097. "The Finger of God" (10/3/79; rebroadcast 1/24/80)

Cast: Kristoffer Tabori (Chad Roberts); Ian Martin (J. B. Randall); Catherine Byers (Carey Randall); Russell Horton (Rusty Roberts). Written by Ian Martin.

Chad Roberts, a poor ranch hand, and Carey Randall are very much in love. Standing in their way is Carey's rich and powerful father, J. B., who arranges a match for Carey with a man twice her age. When Chad and Carey decide to elope, Chad's brother, Rusty, gives them a large sum of money he's stolen from J. B., and the three head for Nevada with J. B.'s men in pursuit. It looks like they'll make it until Chad is bitten by a rattlesnake and they must decide whether to go back or continue on. Either decision could prove fatal to Chad.

2098. "Search for Eden" (10/4/79; rebroadcast from 5/7/79)

2099. "The Hole in the Sky" (10/5/79; rebroadcast from 5/9/79)

2100. "The Russian Passport" (10/6/79; rebroadcast from 11/17/76)

2101. "Two Renegades" (10/7/79; rebroadcast from 8/1/77)

2102. "Wilhelmina Wilson" (10/8/79; rebroadcast 1/29/80)

Cast: Paul Hecht (Sgt. Joe Keller); Bryna Raeburn (Mollie Truesdale); Joan Shea (Wilhelmina Wilson); Ray Owens (Sid Truesdale). Written by Sam Dann.

A distraught couple, Sid and Mollie Truesdale, plead with Sgt. Joe Keller of the Missing Persons Bureau to find their daughter, Margy, who has been missing for only four hours. Because Margy is beautiful and in training for the Olympics as a swimmer, Keller works extra hard on the case. The Trusedales offer little help, but a librarian does. She reveals that Margy's favorite book is *William Wilson and Other Stories* by Edgar Allan Poe. "Brush up on your Poe…"

2103. "Virtue Is Its Own Reward" (10/9/79; rebroadcast from 5/14/79)

2104. "At the End of the Passage" (10/10/79; rebroadcast 1/31/80)
Cast: John Beal (Hummil); Court Benson (Spurstow); Earl Hammond (Lowndes). Adapted by Roy Winsor, based on the 1890 story by Rudyard Kipling.
A British engineer in charge of building a railroad in the hot, disease-ridden interior of India faces an adventure of a lifetime. The unrelenting heat was debilitating. Life was temporary and cheap. To the credit of the British, they worked hard to improve the lot of the natives, at the same time trying to cling to their own more civilized ways. Sometimes they cracked up...

2105. "Messenger from Yesterday" (10/11/79; rebroadcast from 5/16/79)

2106. "Help Wanted" (10/12/79; rebroadcast from 5/21/79)

2107. "The Stolen White Elephant" (10/13/79; rebroadcast from 11/20/76)

2108. "The Man That Corrupted Hadleyburg" (10/14/79; rebroadcast from 11/19/76)

2109. "Out of the Mist" (10/15/79; rebroadcast 2/5/80)
Cast: Russell Horton (Harry Steers); Bob Dryden (Calvin Bell); Carol Teitel (Mrs. Peters); Jada Rowland (Anne Campbell). Written by Elspeth Eric.
When he earns enough money to buy himself a motorcycle, city-born Harry Steers heads for the countryside. There he meets an old man, Calvin Bell, who tells him all about wilderness and offers to send him to college to study botany. One misty morning en route to school, Harry meets a pretty young girl, Anne Campbell. It's love at first sight until Anne insists he take her to the house where she was born. It's a house everyone insists is haunted by a young girl as an old man.
Notes: According to Jada Rowland: "Radio is thrilling for actors. With soaps [on television], we rehearse all day, then film. But with radio drama, you have to be a real pro and rapid in your performance. You read through once and then go right to the microphone to record the program."
Jada Rowland was featured on the television daytime drama *The Doctors* as nurse and mother Carolee. From 1956 to 1974 she portrayed Amy on television's *Secret Storm*. Rowland has also appeared as a child on such radio series as *The Road of Life* and *The Second Mrs. Burton*, which has allowed her to perfect the technique of various voice characterizations for the numerous roles on *Mystery Theater*.

2110. "Dreams" (10/16/79; rebroadcast from 5/23/79)

2111. "Jerry, the Convincer" (10/17/79; rebroadcast 2/7/80)
Cast: Paul Hecht (Carter Ellsworth); Mandel Kramer (Stu Nelson); Ray

Owens (Jerry, the Convincer); Evelyn Juster (Sarajean Howell). Written by Sam Dann.

Wealthy Carter Ellsworth can't turn down an offer of $25,000 in cash from Jerry, the Convincer. All Ellsworth has to do is lend his cabin cruiser to take ashore a load of marijuana. But the boat's landing is interrupted by a policeman who takes a bullet in the head from Jerry's revolver. He's the same cop who recently had given Ellsworth a speeding ticket and whom Ellsworth jokingly and publicly said he would have killed had he had a gun.

2112. "The Outsider" (10/18/79; rebroadcast from 5/28/79)

2113. "A Curious Experience" (10/19/79; rebroadcast from 5/30/79)

2114. "The Monk and the Hangman's Daughter" (10/20/79; rebroadcast from 7/23/76)

2115. "A Departmental Case" (10/21/79; rebroadcast from 8/5/77)

2116. "Sheer Terror" (10/22/79; rebroadcast 2/12/80)

Cast: Teri Keane (Betty Campbell); Larry Haines (Captain Jim Campbell); Ian Martin (Sergeant Wartkovsky); Earl Hammond (Sidney Prout). Written by Ian Martin.

Sidney Prout has followed the television soap opera life of Betsy Campbell for more than three years. He's fallen in love with the character she portrays and is upset because she will "wed" her leading man in an upcoming broadcast. Because he wants to marry her, Prout kidnaps Betty, takes her to an isolated building, keeps her quiet with chloroform and starts making preparations for their wedding.

Notes: Ingenious sound effects are created to simulate the most simplest of things. Take one *Mystery* script for example: A man has been transformed into a spider and is speaking from inside a bottle. Some experimentation led to a plastic film can over the mike, with the actor speaking directly into the bottom of the can from a few inches away, and some filtering in the mike channel.

2117. "Willy and Dilly" (10/23/79; rebroadcast from 6/4/79)

2118. "Dangerous Memory" (10/24/79; rebroadcast 2/14/80)

Cast: Larry Haines (Richard Carey); Catherine Byers (Wendy); Court Benson (Dr. Perkins); Arnold Moss (Detective Gannon). Adapted by James Agate, Jr., based on a short story by Jacques Futrelle.

Richard Carey is unable, after 15 years, to forget the horror of his war experiences in Vietnam especially the needless killing of innocent Vietnamese by his sergeant. Carey's fiancée hopes a psychiatrist can find a way to stop his recurring nightmares, but before the treatment can begin, Carey's old sergeant shows up and is murdered with Carey's service revolver. He's accused of the crime, even though he swears he has never touched the gun since the war's end.

Notes: Catherine Byers' voice has been used for many foreign-dubbed animation films. Under the name of Bobby Byers, she starred as the bunny rabbit in *The Amazing Three*, and in the lead role of *Prince Planet*.

2119. "The Pardon" (10/25/79; rebroadcast from 6/6/79)

2120. "Look Who's Coming" (10/26/79; rebroadcast from 6/11/79)

2121. "The Overcoat" (10/27/79; rebroadcast from 7/3/77)

2122. "The Queen of Spades" (10/28/79; rebroadcast from 7/25/76)

2123. "The Alien Guest" (10/29/79; rebroadcast 2/19/80)

Cast: Paul Hecht (Hector de Brissac); Bob Dryden (Maurice); Patsy Bruder (Eveline). Adapted by Elspeth Eric, based on a story first published in 1862.

Hector de Brissac, a soldier most of his life, kills his cousin Andre in revenge for having stolen a woman from him. As he dies, Andre promises, when Hector least expects it, to come between him and all he holds fairest and dearest, his ghostly hand "to drop a poison in Hector's cup of joy." Andre stays away until Hector is happily married and living a life of luxury in his dead cousin's chateau.

2124. "The Copenhagen Connection" (10/30/79; rebroadcast from 6/13/79)

2125. "Who Has Seen the Wind?" (10/31/79; rebroadcast 2/21/80)

Cast: Michael Tolan (Gary Stewart); Teri Keane (Kitty Stewart); Carol Teitel (Mona Clayton). Written by Nancy Moore.

Theatrical agent Gary Stewart and his actress wife, Kitty, are awakened at 6:00 A.M. by a frantic phone call from Mona Clayton, who pleads with them to come and open her stuck bedroom door. Kitty volunteers to go but takes her time getting to Mona, a claustrophobic who fears the bedroom walls are closing in on her. Gary finally has to help, but it's too late—Mona has jumped sixteen stories to her death. Only Gary thinks he knows why.

2126. "The Unquiet Tomb" (11/1/79; rebroadcast from 6/18/79)

2127. "The Spaces on the Wall" (11/2/79; rebroadcast from 6/20/79)

2128. "The Adventure of the Speckled Band" (11/3/79; rebroadcast from 11/20/77)

2129. "One of the Missing" (11/4/79; rebroadcast from 6/4/76)

2130. "The Terrorist" (11/5/79; rebroadcast 2/26/80)

Cast: Russell Horton (Halik Yaman); Ian Martin (Bulent Yaman); Grace Matthews (Grace Carlino); Jada Rowland (Jane Travis). Written by Ian Martin.

Bulent Yaman, otherwise known as Saladin the Butcher (his latest terrorist act was the killing of an American peace envoy in Athens), finds his brother, Halik, on the small Aegean island of Cesme. Halik is working for a rich, elderly and widowed author, Grace Carlino, and her niece, Jane Travis. Bulent promises the two women the same treatment he gave the American envoy unless they agree to hide him from the authorities.

2131. "Mission from Zython" (11/6/79; rebroadcast from 6/25/79)

2132. "Davey Jerrold's Jacket" (11/7/79; rebroadcast 2/28/80)

Cast: Russell Horton (Curly); Ian Martin (Davey Jerrold); Ray Owens (President); Betsy Beard (Little Sister). Written by Sam Dann.

On April 29, 1803, Col. Davey Jerrold, as President Jefferson's emissary, gave the Hopisake Indians the land between the Mississippi and the Rockies in return for their land east of the river. The agreement was written on the back of Jerrold's buckskin jacket, now worn by Little Sister, the Hopisakes' last survivor. She just wants to wander around the land, enjoying it—until she meets a con man named Curly, who has ideas on how both can get rich—quick.

2133. "The Giuseppe Verdi Autobus" (11/8/79; rebroadcast from 6/27/79)

2134. "The Rivalry" (11/9/79; rebroadcast from 7/2/79)

2135. "The Bisara of Pooree" (11/10/79; rebroadcast from 12/6/77)

2136. "The Saxon Curse" (11/11/79; rebroadcast from 8/13/76)

2137. "House Without Mirrors" (11/12/79; rebroadcast 3/4/80)

Cast: Paul Hecht (Man); Bob Dryden (Mr. Macy); Bryna Raeburn (Maid); Norman Rose (Dr. Garden). Adapted by Elspeth Eric, based on the 1866 short story *The Compensation House* by Charles Collins.

A man accustomed to walking daily along a riverbank becomes intrigued by another who emerges from a house every day at the same time to gaze into the flowing river. The man, Mr. Macy, who performs this daily ritual, explains why: It is to check on his appearance, since the master of the house, whose servant he is, cannot abide mirrors. Wishing to pursue the origin of this idiosyncrasy, the questioner is advised by Macy to call at the house next door where a Dr. Garden, physician to the man who abhors mirrors, lives. What he learns from the doctor is enough to make anyone think twice before peering into a looking glass.

2138. "The Great White Shark" (11/13/79; rebroadcast from 7/4/79)

2139. "The $999,000 Error" (11/14/79; rebroadcast 3/6/80)

Cast: Jackson Beck (Narcisso Esmilla); Carol Teitel (Chareng Magpali); Ian Martin (Josh Slocum); Ralph Bell (J.M. Forrest). Written by Ian Martin.

A letter arrives from the United States addressed to Chareng Magpali, who lives in the wilds of the Philippines. Narcisso Esmilla, a lawyer and neighbor, translates it. Chareng's sister has died, and her estate has sent a Manila bank a $1,000 check made out to Chareng. The lawyer volunteers to pick up the money, but when he sees the check is worth $1 million—a computer error—he gives Chareng $1,000 and heads for Brazil with what's left: $999,000.

2140. "Smile at a Homely Girl" (11/15/79; rebroadcast from 7/9/79)

2141. "The Fools" (11/16/79; rebroadcast from 7/11/79)

2142. "The Death of Halpin Fraser" (11/17/79; rebroadcast from 7/13/75)

2143. "The Birthmark" (11/18/79; rebroadcast from 11/5/77)

2144. "The God That Failed" (11/19/79; rebroadcast 3/11/80)

Cast: Fred Gwynne (Sen. Bob Blaisdell); William Griffis (Sen. Everett); Gilbert Mack (Mahlo); Evelyn Juster (Aureela). Written by Sam Dann.

Sen. Bob Blaisdell (Blaze, for short) is sent by his committee chairman to visit Alesser, a new nation in Asia. Blaze tries his best to suggest ways to modernize the land, but its people have no use for supermarkets or oil refineries. They do have one decrepit airplane, and Blaze is taken on a sightseeing trip which ends when the plane crashes in a remote jungle. The people who rescue him think he must be some kind of a god descended from the sky and expect him to heal the sick, stop the floods and end the wars. "But I can't even do that in the United States Senate," wails Blaze, whose only wish is to get back to Washington—fast.

2145. "The House of Dead Heart" (11/20/79; rebroadcast from 7/16/79)

2146. "By Word of Mouth" (11/21/79; rebroadcast 3/13/80)

Cast: Court Benson (Rudyard Kipling); Russell Horton (Dr. Edward Dumoise); William Griffis (Rutton Singh); Carol Teitel (Lallah). Adapted by Sam Dann, based on the 1888 short story *The Phantom Rickshaw* by Rudyard Kipling.

Dr. Edward Dumoise, a young surgeon, forces his way into an Indian temple where Lallah, a 20-year-old priestess, lies near death. He cures her, but because she has been touched by an unbeliever, Lallah is thrown into the street. Dumoise takes her in and later marries her, despite the misgivings of Kipling and all his other friends. The young couple enjoy several years of happiness until Lallah suddenly falls ill again and Dumoise is unable to help her.

2147. "The Case of the Forced Divorce" (11/22/79; rebroadcast from 7/18/79)

2148. "No Man's Land" (11/23/79; rebroadcast from 7/23/79)

2149. "The Countess" (11/24/79; rebroadcast from 10/8/77)

2150. "The Adventure of the Blue Carbuncle" (11/25/79; rebroadcast from 12/13/77)

2151. "Strange New Tomorrow" (11/26/79; rebroadcast 3/18/80)

Cast: Teri Keane (Una); Ian Martin (Emperor Condor); Gordon Heath (General Vardon); John Beal (Dr. Ralph Tremayne). Written by Ian Martin.

The holocaust on Earth has taken place countless generations ago. The few remaining humans survive by capturing from other planets a constant supply of healthy bodies, hoping they can be used to weed out Earth's radioactive poison. But the population continues to dwindle, and Gen. Vardon orders Earth's one major scientist, Dr. Ralph Tremayne, to build an army of war-like robots with which to conquer a clean planet. If the reluctant Tremayne refuses, Vardon swears he will have the doctor's beautiful young wife, Una, a humanoid created by Tremayne, destroyed and buried in a forgotten grave.

2152. "Catch a Falling Star" (11/27/79; rebroadcast from 7/25/79)

2153. "The Philosopher's Stone" (11/28/79; rebroadcast 3/20/80)

Cast: Fred Gwynne (Harry Lawson); Ray Owens (Denis Lawson); Bryna Raeburn (Mrs. Jeffries); Earl Hammond (Janitor). Written by Sam Dann.

Harry Lawson has trouble paying his rent because, even though he works in a bank, he often lends his own money to persons be believes really need it. For a piece of stone that looks like a marble kids play with, Harry lends a man $100— of bank money this time—much to the consternation of his older brother, the bank's president who thinks Harry's turned crazy. The borrower says the marble is the Philosopher's Stone and should change Harry's life in many ways.

Notes: Bryna Raeburn's voice may sound a little familiar to some listeners, not only for her role as Mrs. Jeffries in this episode, but that of Mrs. Butterworth in the maple syrup television commercials.

2154. "Relax and Enjoy It" (11/29/79; rebroadcast from 7/30/79)

2155. "The Love Goddess Caper" (11/30/79; rebroadcast from 8/1/79)

2156. "A Matter of Conscience" (12/1/79; rebroadcast from 12/3/77)

2157. "So Shall Ye Reap" (12/2/79; rebroadcast from 8/18/77)

2158. "The Specter Bridegroom" (12/3/79; rebroadcast 3/25/80)
Cast: Paul Hecht (Hendrik); Patsy Bruder (Herta); Bob Dryden (Baron Van Landshort); Grace Matthews (Aunt Matilda). Adapted by Elspeth Eric, based on the 1819 short story by Washington Irving.
The husband-to-be of an 18-year-old baroness announces on their wedding day that he is dead and must return to his castle for burial. She thinks him most handsome and is certain his sudden departure means he did not want her after all. But what she believes to be his specter starts appearing in her castle's garden every night, and Herta makes sure he can see her in her bedroom window. She blossoms, she's happy, and her health improves until one night she disappears without a trace.

2159. "Tiger, Tiger, Shining Bright" (12/4/79; rebroadcast from 8/13/79)

2160. "Appointment at Sarajevo" (12/5/79; rebroadcast 3/27/80)
Cast: Tony Roberts (Archduke Ferdinand); Court Benson (Emperor); Bob Dryden (Dr. Eisenmanger); Roberta Maxwell (Countess Sophie). Written by Sam Dann.
Archduke Franz Ferdinand, heir apparent to the Austro-Hungarian throne, commits the unpardonable sin: He marries the woman he loves, Countess Sophie Shutnek, who in his family's opinion is only a glorified maid servant. Their tragic, trouble-filled life is detailed in this dramatization, from their meeting at a grand ball in Prague, given in the honor of Franz, until their assassination on June 28, 1914, by a Serbian nationalist in Sarajevo.

2161. "Body and Soul" (12/6/79; rebroadcast from 8/15/79)

2162. "Taboo Means Death" (12/7/79; rebroadcast from 8/20/79)

2163. "The Third Person" (12/8/79; rebroadcast from 2/21/76)

2164. "The Colonel Chabert" (12/9/79; rebroadcast from 12/1/77)

2165. "If a Body" (12/10/79; rebroadcast 4/1/80)
Cast: Fred Gwynne (Sheriff Bolan); Earl Hammond (Edmund Vail); Ray Owens (Tattersall); Bryna Raeburn (Maria McKibben). Written by Sam Dann.
Maria McKibben begs Sheriff Joseph T. Bolan to find her husband, Clarence, who, she claims, walked into a field near his farm some 20 miles from Detroit and

just vanished. The sheriff is sympathetic, though he cannot believe her story. But he does believe Clarence was murdered and soon gathers enough evidence to prove it. The town prosecutor, however, refuses to take the case to court unless the sheriff can produce Clarence's body which, try as he might, he is unable to do.

2166. "Stranger from Nowhere" (12/11/79; rebroadcast from 8/22/79)

2167. "The Movie Makers" (12/12/79; rebroadcast 4/3/80)

Cast: Marian Seldes (Vera Saville); Russell Horton (Martin); Earl Hammond (Howard Frank); Norman Rose (Dr. John Saville). Written by Henry Slesar.

Dr. John Saville, whose space heat theory which, if utilized, could destroy entire planets, is invited to Life Films headquarters, some 18 miles outside Boston. There he is placed in a darkened room and shown, on a screen, replays of any moment in his life he wishes to see—in beautiful color. He can't believe the films were made without his knowing it. He also doesn't know that whatever he sees on the screen he will completely forget—forever.

2168. "A Cup of Bitter Chocolate" (12/13/79; rebroadcast from 8/27/79)

2169. "Ninety Lives" (12/14/79; rebroadcast from 8/29/79)

2170. "The Gift of Doom" (12/15/79; rebroadcast from 7/31/77)

2171. "The Damned Thing" (12/16/79; rebroadcast from 2/5/75)

2172. "Beyond Belief" (12/17/79; rebroadcast 4/8/80)

Cast: Jada Rowland (Amnesiac); Carol Teitel (Anna Vesela); Ralph Bell (Dan); Gerald Hiken (Cop). Written by Elspeth Eric.

Neither the policeman nor Anna Vesela and her notion shop partner, Dan, can, despite much questioning, find out anything about a young woman who can't even remember her name. Anna and Dan, both of whom lost their families in catastrophes they are trying to forget, provide room and food for the amnesiac and take her for treatment to the local hospital clinic, which does nothing but ask her to return in three weeks. Only when Dan discovers eight newly made keys in the young woman's pocketbook does the mystery begin to unravel.

2173. "Tomorrow Will Never Come" (12/18/79; rebroadcast from 9/3/79)

2174. "Shadow of a Lover" (12/19/79; rebroadcast 4/10/80)

Cast: Michael Tolan (Lt. Miller); Bryna Raeburn (Mayetta Mosby); Evelyn Juster (Melissa Merriweather); Russell Horton (Clovis Hollister). Written by Sam Dann.

After seeing her umpteenth Clovis Hollister film, mousy Mayetta Mosby flies to Hollywood to be with him; "the look in his eye" is calling for her. She manages to sneak undetected into his apartment, but when he makes a pass at her, Mayetta retaliates by hitting him with a poker and unintentionally leaving her M. M. initialed handkerchief beside his dead body. The police immediately suspect Hollister's jealous leading lady, whose initials are also M. M.

2175. "The Man in the Black Cap" (12/20/79; rebroadcast from 9/5/79)

2176. "The Odyssey of Laura Collins" (12/21/79; rebroadcast from 9/10/79)

2177. "The Corpse That Would Not Die" (12/22/79; rebroadcast from 9/25/76)

2178. "A House Divided" (12/23/79; rebroadcast from 9/1/77)

2179. "A Christmas Carol" (12/24/79; rebroadcast from 12/24/78)

2180. "Death Is a Woman" (12/25/79; rebroadcast 4/15/80)

Cast: Gordon Heath (Gregory Chalmers); William Griffis (Norman Whiteside); Bob Dryden (Emory Blaine). Written by Elspeth Eric.

Bachelor Gregory Chalmers invites two college chums whom he hasn't seen in 20 years to join him for a weekend. Norman Whiteside's wife has left him for another man whom he has never met and whom he intends to kill if he does. Widower Emory Blaine has fallen for a divorced woman he intends to marry. The trouble begins when the portrait says she loves both men and they believe she's talking for Evelyn, the woman who has left Whiteside and will soon marry Blaine.

2181. "The Two Sams" (12/26/79; rebroadcast from 9/12/79)

2182. "Between These Worlds" (12/27/79; rebroadcast 4/17/80)

Cast: Tony Roberts (Garth Victor); Bob Dryden (Trock); Carol Teitel (Pat McGlade). Written by Ian Martin.

Captain Garth Victor, imprisoned on food-poor Kronek for his unpopular methods of producing energy, is released so he can fly to Earth to plan its invasion by Kronek's astral fleet. His spaceship, out of control, falls into the Atlantic Ocean. Rescued by two fishermen, he offers to help Earth build space ships using his radical energy techniques. But he intends to fly the first craft made back to Kronek so he personally can lead the attack on Earth.

2183. "The Guillotine" (12/28/79; rebroadcast from 9/17/79)

2184. "The Adventures of Don Quixote" (12/29/79; rebroadcast from 1/3/78)

2185. "The Way to Dusty Death" (12/30/79; rebroadcast from 1/29/78)

2186. "The One-Thousand Pound Gorilla" (12/31/79; rebroadcast 4/22/80)

Cast: Mandel Kramer (Franklyn J. Wilkinson); Teri Keane (Wendy); Earl Hammond (Haskins). Written by Sam Dann.

All of his business associates are jealous of Franklyn J. Wilkinson, who has the most beautiful, understanding wife imaginable. He's a very happy man until one day, during a company-sponsored afternoon of golf, he is accosted by a man named Haskins who claims he had been married to Wilkinson's wife, Wendy, and that he had left her because she had tried to murder him. "Leave her," Haskins insists, "before she kills you." Wilkins doesn't believe him, but Haskins is persistent, so persistent that Wilkinson is soon not sure what to believe.

Notes: Beginning with this episode, Monday, December 31, 1979, the *CBS Radio Theater* began broadcasting five nights a week (Mon. thru Fri.) instead of seven. On December 10, Richard M. Brescia, Vice President and General Manager of the CBS Radio Network announced to the press the reason for the schedule change.

2187. "You're Better Off Guilty" (1/1/80; rebroadcast from 9/19/79)

2188. "Revenge Is Not Sweet" (1/2/80; rebroadcast 4/24/80)

Cast: Bob Dryden (Dr. Van Dusen); Jada Rowland (Elizabeth Devan); Jackson Beck (Hutchinson Hatch); Gordon Gould (John Stockton). Adapted by G. Frederic Lewis, based on the 1906 short story *The Lost Radium* by Jacques Futrelle.

Dr. Van Dusen, "The Thinking Man," is called upon for help by Elizabeth Devan. Miss Devan is much disturbed by the recent death of her stepfather, inventor Pomeroy Stockton. She claims his death was not due to heart failure, as the newspapers reported, nor was it a suicide as the doctor wrote on a false death certificate. She firmly believes her stepfather was murdered.

2189. "The Gettysburg Address" (1/3/80; rebroadcast from 9/24/79)

2190. "Ring a Ring of Roses" (1/4/80; rebroadcast from 12/3/74)

2191. "The Last Days of Pompeii, Part One: The City of the Dead" (1/7/80; rebroadcast 7/21/80)

Cast: Russell Horton (Marcus Rufus); Earl Hammond (Arbaces); Kristoffer Tabori (Apaecides); Evelyn Juster (Oriana). Adapted by Gerald Keane, based on the 1843 novel *The Last Days of Pompeii* by Lord Edward George Earle Bulwer-Lytton.

Marcus Aurelius Rufus, a young Athenian architect who makes his home in Pompeii, saves a blind slave girl, Lydia, from being crushed by a runaway chariot. Along with Diomed, the ship owner, they visit the temple of Arbaces, whom Bulwer-Lytton describes as "half prophet, half fiend." For a sizable donation, Arbaces will guarantee the safe return of Diomed's fleet of ships and Marcus the opportunity to meet a beautiful woman: Oriana, the sister of a young priest in Arbaces' temple. Outside the temple, muggers continue to roam the streets, Christians meet secretly in underground tunnels, and tavern owners try to sell watered wine.

Notes: To help celebrate *Theater*'s seventh year on the air, Lord Edward Bulwer-Lytton's classic novel was adapted into a five-part mini-series. Starring in the lead role is longtime *Theater* performer Russell Horton, who was featured in several Woody Allen movies of the 1990s.

This five-part adventure was rebroadcast on July 21, 1980. Russell Horton, the star of this grand adventure, is well known for supplying the voice of Toucan Sam for Kellogg's Froot Loops commercials.

2192. "The Last Days of Pompeii, Part Two: Thrown to the Lions" (1/8/80; rebroadcast 7/22/80)

Cast: Russell Horton (Marcus Rufus); Earl Hammond (Arbaces); Kristoffer Tabori (Apaecides); Evelyn Juster (Oriana); Valecka Gray (Julia). Adapted by Gerald Keane, based on the 1843 novel *The Last Days of Pompeii* by Lord Edward George Earle Bulwer-Lytton.

Oriana, who has been drugged and imprisoned inside his temple by the Egyptian high priest, Arbaces, escapes with the help of Marcus when the building is destroyed by an earthquake. A few hours later, Julia, the daughter of ship owner Diomed, offers gold to Arbaces to help restore his temple if he will work out a way of drugging Marcus, whom she would like to marry. Arbaces slips a potion into Marcus' wine glass during a party at Diomed's home, and the young architect runs screaming into the street. When found later that evening, he is standing over the dead body of Oriana's brother, Apaecides, a bloody dagger in his hand.

2193. "The Last Days of Pompeii, Part Three: Half Prophet, Half Fiend" (1/9/80; rebroadcast 7/23/80)

Cast: Russell Horton (Marcus Rufus); Earl Hammond (Arbaces); Ian Martin (Calvus); Evelyn Juster (Lydia). Adapted by Gerald Keane, based on the 1843 novel *The Last Days of Pompeii* by Lord Edward George Earle Bulwer-Lytton.

Because the Senate cannot come to a decision on Marcus' guilt, its members decree he will be tried by the king of beasts in the public arena. Diomed, the ship owner, makes an abortive attempt to help his friend. But only Calvus, the tavern keeper, can save him. He was an eyewitness to the murder and saw the high priest, Arbaces, not Marcus, wield the dagger. When he tries to blackmail Arbaces, Calvus is tricked and locked into a dungeon in the priest's temple. Lydia, the blind slave girl, is thrown in with him, but she manages to escape through a narrow opening. She rushes to the arena to tell the senators of Arbaces' guilt, but it is too late. Marcus has already been shoved into the arena with the lion.

Notes: Pompeii was a favorite Italian vacation town for Romans, Greeks and Egyptians until that fateful third week in August, 79 A.D., when it was hit first by an earthquake and followed, four days later, by the eruption of Mount Vesuvius, which buried the beautiful metropolis under 30 feet of volcanic ash. The eruption was described by Roman author Pliny as "a cloud like a huge pine tree, shooting up in great height, a tall trunk of fire and smoke with branches of falling cinders ... a terrible sight to behold."

2194. "The Last Days of Pompeii, Part Four: Danger, Love and Death" (1/10/80; rebroadcast 7/24/80)

Cast: Russell Horton (Marcus Rufus); Earl Hammond (Arbaces); Ian Martin (Calvus); Evelyn Juster (Lydia); Patricia Elliott (Oriana). Adapted by Gerald Keane, based on the 1843 novel *The Last Days of Pompeii* by Lord Edward George Earle Bulwer-Lytton.

The crowd in the arena cheers when the king of beasts slinks back into his cage, thus proving Marcus did not kill Oriana's brother. The real murderer, the Egyptian high priest Arbaces, does his best to convince the crowd he's innocent, but they won't listen. In the confusion, Arbaces manages to sneak back to his temple and to start haranguing anyone who will listen. Oriana has also left the arena, and Marcus is certain Arbaces has imprisoned her. Marcus and the slave girl, Lydia, search in vain in the temple's catacombs, finally finding Oriana, safe in her own home. By then, however, Mount Vesuvius, dormant for 1,000 years, has erupted; its cloud of ashes, cinders and flaming rocks darken the sky, falling on everyone as they run for their lives.

2195. "The Last Days of Pompeii, Part Five: The Buried City" (1/11/80; rebroadcast 7/25/80)

Cast: Russell Horton (Marcus Rufus); Earl Hammond (Arbaces); Evelyn Juster (Lydia); Patricia Elliott (Oriana). Adapted by Gerald Keane, based on the 1843 novel *The Last Days of Pompeii* by Lord Edward George Earle Bulwer-Lytton.

Marcus, Oriana and Lydia huddle in Oriana's garden as Pompeii's terror-stricken populace clog the city's streets, now knee-deep in ashes. It's pitch dark, but Lydia says she can find her way to Pompeii's dock area where an undamaged boat might be found. Marcus and Oriana, following her, convince ship owner Diomed, who has lost both his wife and daughter, to join them. They find one of Diomed's boats ship-shape and start rowing toward the bay. Arbaces, the high priest and murderer, calling from the shore, begs them to return and take him aboard. Marcus says no, but Diomed insists they go back and give him a set of oars. But Arbaces, instead of accepting the oars, grabs Oriana, whom he has long wanted as a wife or mistress, and threatens to choke her to death if Marcus makes a move to save her.

Notes: Archaeologists have uncovered virtually everything in the buried city of Pompeii and found proof that even in the 2,000-year-old Italian town, gambling was legal. There were gamblers and crooked gamblers. Not too surprisingly, archaeologists uncovered 2,000-year-old dice, six sided cubes with dots. And a few were loaded, fixed to always come up winners!

2196. "The Better Half" (1/14/80; rebroadcast 4/29/80)

Cast: Tony Roberts (Bobby Boyle); Patricia Elliott (Jeannie Frye); Fred Gwynne (Jack Martin); Valeka Gray (Lieutenant Pollock). Written by Sam Dann.

Bobby Boyle and Jeannie Frye are married partners in a prosperous public relations business. Jeannie possesses the real creative ability, though, and when this becomes evident to their clients, Bobby, in a fit of rage, shoots her. That night he sees and hears her. She hasn't come back from the dead for revenge. Because she still loves him, she has come back to make sure he doesn't get accused of her murder.

2197. "The Eighth Day" (1/15/80; rebroadcast from 9/26/79)

2198. "Prisoner of the Machines" (1/16/80; rebroadcast 5/1/80)

Cast: John Lithgow (Major John Gulliver); Earl Hammond (Captain 174-B); Ray Owens (Colonel Drummond); Ian Martin (Private Morley). Written by Henry Slesar.

In the year 2085, 1,400 Earth soldiers, are captured in a battle with the Indasian rebels, who make their headquarters on the moon. The men are flown to an asteroid and guarded by Maks, mechanical foot soldiers who are unaffected by cold, hunger, fatigue, despair and homesickness. To top it all, the Maks have been programmed to allow no prisoners to leave the asteroid, even if the war with the Indasians comes to an end.

2199. "The Beast" (1/17/80; rebroadcast from 10/1/79)

2200. "Dig Me Deadly" (1/18/80; rebroadcast from 2/13/74)

2201. "Once Upon an Island" (1/21/80; rebroadcast 5/6/80)

Cast: Norman Rose (Jaspar Lowe); Russell Horton (Jack Turner); Diana Kirkwood (Betty Turner). Written by Elspeth Eric.

Young Jack Turner, a psychiatrist disturbed by what he considers his new wife's hallucinations, goes alone to the old house to investigate the plausibility of the mysterious light seeming to shine from the library window and the improbable presence of a man who shines in the dark. When he doesn't return, his wife Betty and her Uncle Jaspar walk to the house and find Jack stretched out on the library floor. He babbles unintelligibly for a moment or two and then lapses into insensibility.

2202. "Complete Recovery" (1/22/80; rebroadcast from 1/1/79)

2203. "The Forty-Four" (1/23/80; rebroadcast 5/8/80)

Cast: John Beal (Sheriff Scobie); Court Benson (Doc); Bryna Raeburn (Aunt Emma); Carol Teitel (Alexandrea Edison). Written by Sam Dann.

Alexandrea Edison, single and a person of considerable wealth, calls Sheriff Harry Scobie, whom she's known since their high school days, to tell him she's shot and killed a lawyer named Martin K. Beasley. As everyone in town knows, Beasley has been representing a firm intent on buying Miss Edison's estate and turning it into a development of hamburger stands and cheap shops. Sheriff Scobie can't believe Miss Edison is capable of murder, but nevertheless, in case he's wrong, he orders her to claim she was forced to shoot in self-defense.

2204. "The Finger of God" (1/24/80; rebroadcast from 10/3/79)

2205. "The Ghost Driver" (1/25/80; rebroadcast from 7/13/74)

2206. "The God Machine" (1/28/80; rebroadcast 5/13/80)

Cast: Lloyd Battista (Thomas); Patricia Elliott (Emma); Teri Keane (Myra); Robert Kaliban (Paul). Written by Sam Dann.

Thomas and Emma, a thousand years into the future, are ordered by a computer, the "god" of their society, to get married. The computer knows their genes will produce a master mathematician, whom the society sorely needs. Even though they've never met before, the young couple discover they have many common interests—"archaic" books and popular music of the twentieth century—and they fall in love, which is forbidden. The unhappy computer issues another order: get divorced.

2207. "Wilhelmina Wilson" (1/29/80; rebroadcast from 10/8/79)

2208. "The Crystal Gazer" (1/30/80; rebroadcast 5/15/80)

Cast: Bob Dryden (Dr. Van Dusen); Ian Martin (Howard Varick); Evelyn Juster (Jadeh Singh); Ray Owens (Hatch). Adapted by G. Frederic Lewis, based on the 1906 short story by Jacques Futrelle.

Howard Varick has, for years, asked an Indian mystic for advice on how to play the stock market. Always, the mystic, by looking into his crystal ball, has told Varick when to buy and when to sell. The result is a small fortune. But when the crystal ball shows Varick being murdered—stabbed in the back by someone he doesn't even know—the businessman panics. His only hope is consultation with Dr. Augustus Van Dusen, the world's great private investigator.

2209. "At the End of the Passage" (1/31/80; rebroadcast from 10/10/79)

2210. "The Horror Within" (2/1/80; rebroadcast from 4/17/74)

2211. "That's What Friends Are For" (2/4/80; rebroadcast 5/20/80)

Cast: Tony Roberts (Lt. Tesser); Russell Horton (Lieutenant Horrocks); Earl Hammond (Ahmed Din); Diana Kirkwood (Melisanda). Adapted by Sam Dann, based on the 1887 short story *A Friend's Friend* by Rudyard Kipling.

No matter how hard he tries, Lt. James Eddington Tesser, in the service of Her Majesty's government in India, cannot silence a noisy Scottish bagpipe-playing ghost who is haunting his house. His fiancée, Melisanda, a major's daughter, vows she'll never marry him until he does. A real Scottish bagpiper ultimately tells Tesser how to handle the ghost, but the lieutenant has no intention of following the piper's instructions.

2212. "Out of the Mist" (2/5/80; rebroadcast from 10/15/79)

2213. "The Deserter" (2/6/80; rebroadcast 5/22/80)

Cast: John Lithgow (Tom Roberts); Evelyn Juster (Eve Roberts); Ralph Bell (Chad Walker). Written by James Agate, Jr.

Tom Roberts, a newspaper reporter, is driving his wife, Eve, and 1-year-old son, Johnny, through the rugged California Sierras. Suddenly, they find themselves isolated by a landslide. While trying to prevent the family camper from rolling off a cliff, Tom is pinned beneath it. A mountaineer, Chad Walker, comes to their aid, sets Tom's damaged legs, builds a fire and a lean-to, provides food, but refuses absolutely to take them down the mountain to the nearest open road.

2214. "Jerry, the Convincer" (2/7/80; rebroadcast from 10/17/79)

2215. "Sea of Troubles" (2/8/80; rebroadcast from 6/9/74)

2216. "Talk to Me" (2/11/80; rebroadcast 5/27/80)

Cast: John Beal (John Marlow); Bryna Raeburn (Mrs. Serafin); Jack Grimes (Benny Serafin); Paul Hecht (Lieutenant Stillwagen). Written by Sam Dann.

John Marlow, who sometimes thinks his memory is failing, tells police lieutenant Frank Stillwagen he saw a youth running from the scene of a murder. Using Marlow's description, the lieutenant picks up Benny Serafin, a young punk with a prison record, and finds the murdered man's wallet in his pocket. Later, when Marlow learns that Benny is the son of the woman from whom he buys his groceries, he tries to change his story. But the lieutenant refuses to listen to him.

2217. "Sheer Terror" (2/12/80; rebroadcast from 10/22/79)

2218. "Crime of Passion" (2/13/80; rebroadcast 5/29/80)

Cast: Mandel Kramer (Phil Wilcox); Earl Hammond (Tom Cartwright); Ian Martin (George Parrish); Carol Teitel (Margaret Wilcox). Written by Sam Dann.

Attorney Phil Wilcox is hired to take the case of George Parrish, a middle-aged night watchman who came home one night to discover his wife, half-dressed, with another man. Parrish then shot her. Wilcox, prone to spend many hours in the office away from his wife, works hard on the case. His wife, meanwhile, spends more and more time with a man at the art gallery where she works. Wilcox, hearing rumors from his friends, begins to wonder what he'll have to do to stop her.

2219. "Dangerous Memory" (2/14/80; rebroadcast from 10/24/79)

2220. "A Sacrifice in Blood" (2/15/80; rebroadcast from 6/5/74)

2221. "The Time Box" (2/18/80; rebroadcast 6/3/80)

Cast: Russell Horton (Jake Howard); Bob Dryden (Dr. Dryden Harper); Diana Kirkwood (Priscilla Harper). Written by G. Frederic Lewis.

Jake Howard, doing research for his newspaper on an inventor named Dryden Harper who lived in the late 19th century, discovers a wooden box in an excavation being dug on a site which once was the location of Harper's laboratory. The box explodes in his hands, and Howard finds himself in 1880 talking to Harper's daughter, Priscilla. She takes him to her father, who shows the reporter several of his inventions and also asks for one favor. Because he is from the future, Howard is asked whether Priscilla's current boyfriend is to be apprehended for the murders of ten young women. Dr. Harper thinks he will be.

2222. "The Alien Guest" (2/19/80; rebroadcast from 10/29/79)

2223. "The Vampire Plant" (2/20/80; rebroadcast 6/5/80)

Cast: Bob Dryden (Hubbard Quint); Teri Keane (Dolores Masterson); Ian Martin (Dr. Harwich); Joan Shea (Mrs. Quint). Written by Ian Martin.

Hubbard Quint, tied to his widowed mother's apron strings, secretly writes letters to female pen pals, one of whom, Dolores Masterson, determines to marry him. He's the heir to a lucrative burglar alarm business, but his mother has always kept it from him. Dolores makes Mrs. Quint a present of a haemoederentus plant which she puts beside her bed. Within hours she's dead. A few days later, the burglar alarm factory manager meets the same fate. Dolores now has only Hubbard to get rid of before she can take over the business.

2224. "Who Has Seen the Wind?" (2/21/80; rebroadcast from 10/31/79)

2225. "The Murder Museum" (2/22/80; rebroadcast from 6/29/74)

2226. "The Unseen and the Seen" (2/25/80; rebroadcast 6/16/80)

Cast: Paul Hecht (Donald); Carol Teitel (Mona); Court Benson (Henry). Written by Elspeth Eric.

Donald, a widower with three children, lives with his mother-in-law, Mona, and her personal maid, Selma. He is shocked one morning to find his wedding picture, which has been on the mantelpiece for 20 years, lying on the floor. Then he finds it on a windowsill, behind a chair, in a wastebasket. When no one will admit having moved the photo, Donald sends them all away. Nothing happens for six nights, but during the seventh the photo gets moved to a coffee table and, as Donald confides to a friend, he's "scared to death."

2227. "The Terrorist" (2/26/80; rebroadcast from 11/5/79)

2228. "The Intruder" (2/27/80)

Cast: Norman Rose (Phillip Melville); Grace Matthews (Dorothy Melville); Russell Horton (Robby). Adapted by James Agate, Jr., based on a story by Jules Verne.

Dr. Phillip Melville, a nationally famous astro-electronic engineer, and his bride, Dorothy, a leading author, discover that their son, Robby, home from college, is not their son. He looks like Robby, but he's from another dimension, representing a planet whose race is dying out. He has been instructed to return to his planet with Dorothy, whose body and brains will insure the continuation of his species. If she refuses, the Melvilles will never see their son again.

2229. "Davey Jerrold's Jacket" (2/28/80; rebroadcast from 11/7/79)

2230. "Men Without Mouths" (2/29/80; rebroadcast from 7/6/74)

2231. "Laundry Money" (3/3/80; rebroadcast 6/17/80)

Cast: Larry Haines (Simon Wilson);Earl Hammond (Charlie Wentworth); Evelyn Juster (Ramona Wilson). Written by Sam Dann.

Simon Wilson discovers, by accident, that his longtime lawyer friend, Charlie Wentworth, is arranging for large sums of money to be laundered in Mexico. But he hasn't discovered that his wife, Ramona, is involved with Charlie in the get-rich-quick scheme. When she tells Charlie that Simon knows not about them, but about the money, the big boys decree that Simon must go. But Simon bests a hit man ready to kill him with an automatic revolver and miraculously evades a speeding auto. Angered by these failures, the big boys order Charlie and Romana to do the job themselves.

2232. "House Without Mirrors" (3/4/80; rebroadcast from 11/12/79)

2233. "A Matter of Identity" (3/5/80; rebroadcast 6/19/80)

Cast: Heather McCray (Clare Reed); Lloyd Battista (Professor Homer Reed); Russell Horton (Luke Calloway). Written by Roy Winsor.

When Antoinette Duchamps fails to return from a drive into the hill country of Haiti, her worried cousin, Clare Reed, flies down to investigate. Aided by a man from the U.S. embassy, Luke Calloway, and the local police, Clare learns that the car in which Antoinette was driving with a female guide was struck by a rock slide caused by a torrential downpour. Both women have disappeared in a country where believers in voodoo and human sacrifice reign supreme.

2234. "The $999,000 Error" (3/6/80; rebroadcast from 11/14/79)

2235. "Where Fear Begins" (3/7/80; rebroadcast from 9/8/74)

2236. "You're Going to Like Rodney" (3/10/80; rebroadcast 6/24/80)

Cast: Tony Roberts (Edgar Carpenter); Patricia Elliott (June Carpenter); Bryna Raeburn (Mrs. Nathanson); Earl Hammond (Dugan). Written by Bob Juhren.

Edgar and June Carpenter offer to care for a 12-year-old boy, Rodney, while Edgar's brother goes on a business trip to Switzerland. Rodney is an orphan whose grandmother died in a mysterious fall from her bedroom window and whose parents were killed in an unusual auto accident. Rodney, unable to speak, communicates only by writing notes. His first to the Carpenters is "Your cat Sylvester will die." Shortly after the cat is found dead, Rodney writes another note: "You're next."

2237. "The God That Failed" (3/11/80; rebroadcast from 11/19/79)

2238. "The Secret of the Fifth Bell" (3/12/80; rebroadcast 6/26/80)

Cast: Earl Hammond (Dr. Van Dusen); Joyce Gordon (Norma Phillips); Ian Martin (Inspector Mallory); Arnold Moss (Frank Phillips). Adapted by G. Frederic Lewis, based on a story by Jacques Futrelle.

Norma Phillips gives her wealthy industrialist husband Frank a set of six Japanese bells on a silken cord. Frank is pleased to add the gift to his collection of valuable curios, until the fifth bell on the cord starts ringing every so often for no apparent reason. The mysterious ringing frightens Frank, even more so when the woman who sold it to Norma is found murdered in Frank's study. He calls in the famed Dr. Van Dusen to solve the murder and to silence the bell.

2239. "By Word of Mouth" (3/13/80; rebroadcast from 11/21/79)

2240. "The Trouble with Ruth" (3/14/80; rebroadcast from 8/11/74)

2241. "The Evil Eye" (3/17/80; rebroadcast 7/1/80)

Cast: Mandel Kramer (John Bates); Carol Teitel (Louise Bates); Teri Keane (Kathy Corrigan). Written by Elspeth Eric.

Louise Bates, the country's best-known female author, is spurred into writing her next novel when she learns that a $1 million advance has been paid to her British competitor. She orders her tax accountant husband John to allow no one to disturb her for ten days. But John, who has been cheating on Louise, leaves home for 30 minutes one day to visit his lady friend. While he's gone, one of his frantic clients tries to enter the house. Later, the client is found dead. Then the British writer dies. A barking dog down the street dies. John's girlfriend is certain that Louise possesses an evil eye and that they might be next to die if Louise learns about their relationship.

2242. "Strange New Tomorrow" (3/18/80; rebroadcast from 11/26/79)

2243. "The Death Wish" (3/19/80; rebroadcast 7/3/80)

Cast: Ralph Bell (George Solway); William Griffis (Dr. Philip Eagan); Ian Martin (Mahareeshi Ranjit); Carol Teitel (Mary Solway). Written by Ian Martin.

George Solway, who is nearing the breaking point because of overwork, hypertension and too much alcohol, rejects his wife's suggestion that he seek medical help. Instead he listens to some commuter train advice from an Indian mystic who advocates "rhapsodic meditation." It works for a while, until Solway begins dreaming, while meditating, that he needs another woman because his wife is secretly seeing her high school sweetheart again.

2244. "The Philosopher's Stone" (3/20/80; rebroadcast from 11/28/79)

2245. "Hurricane" (3/21/80; rebroadcast from 9/13/74)

2246. "The Blue Tiger" (3/24/80; rebroadcast 7/8/80)

Cast: Larry Haines (Leo); Bryna Raeburn (Alice); Earl Hammond (The Man); Ray Owens (Drury). Written by Sam Dann.

Known only as Leo, a gunman for hire keeps a step ahead of federal authorities. One agent, Drury, vows to bring him in singlehandedly. This is a mistake, because even though Drury is able to gain the confidence of Leo's girlfriend, the gunman is able, at the last minute, to learn of Drury's plans for capturing him and to fell him with a single shot. But Leo is not so successful with his next assignment: posing as the missing son of an elderly woman whose valuable land the syndicate wants at almost any price.

2247. "The Specter Bridegroom" (3/25/80; rebroadcast from 12/3/79)

2248. "Conspiracy" (3/26/80; rebroadcast 7/10/80)

Cast: Kevin McCarthy (John Wilkes Booth); Court Benson (Captain Surratt); Arnold Moss (Dr. Samuel Mudd); Russell Horton (Abraham Lincoln). Written by G. Frederic Lewis.

Booth, an actor who won fame for his Shakespearean roles and an ardent Confederate sympathizer, first tried to abduct President Lincoln and take him to Richmond, there to hold him until the North gave up the war. When that failed, Booth, a few weeks later, managed to enter the presidential box at Washington's Ford Theater unobserved, to shoot and kill the president. How he plotted both these incidents is dramatized in this broadcast.

2249. "Appointment at Sarajevo" (3/27/80; rebroadcast from 12/5/79)

2250. "The Dream Woman" (3/28/80; rebroadcast from 9/22/74)

2251. "The End of the Rainbow" (3/31/80; rebroadcast 7/15/80)

Cast: Teri Keane (Carlotta Armiston); Robert Kaliban (Terry); Mandel Kramer (James Armiston). Written by Sam Dann.

Fed up with her husband's frequent and lengthy business trips, Carlotta Armiston timidly visits a singles bar. There she meets a man named Terry, who says he's away from his wife on a business trip. Terry offers to take Carlotta to a posh night spot, but while driving an ambulance, Carlotta must think fast—for her own sake as well as Terry's.

2252. "If a Body" (4/1/80; rebroadcast from 12/10/79)

2253. "The Fateful Bell" (4/2/80; rebroadcast 7/17/80)

Cast: Kristoffer Tabori (Ming-Yee); Ian Martin (Kouan-Fu); Evelyn Juster (Ko-Nagai). Suggested by the short stories of Lafcadio Hearn, and written by Ian Martin.

A prominent mandarin of 15th century China is ordered by the emperor to cast a bell big enough to be heard for 100 li (33 miles)—or be beheaded. Kuoan-Fu is petrified when the order to build the bell arrives. He sees it as an almost impossible task. Even with the aid of China's top artisans, two casting attempts fail. His only hope seems to be young Ming-Yee, a commoner who is seeking the hand of his daughter, Ko Nagai. Only Ko knows of the sacrifice that must be agreed to—with a witch—if the casting of the giant bell is to be successful.

2254. "The Movie Makers" (4/3/80; rebroadcast from 12/12/79)

2255. "The Headstrong Corpse" (4/4/80; rebroadcast from 10/6/74)

2256. "Madame Sirocco" (4/7/80; rebroadcast 7/29/80)

Cast: Bryna Raeburn (Madame Sirocco); William Griffis (Johannes Svetic); Joyce Gordon (Maria Svetic); Earl Hammond (Lieutenant Luther). Written by Sam Dann.

Maria Svetic is aghast when her old-fashioned thinking father, Johannes, tells her she is going to marry a man more than twice her age. Even though she has never disobeyed her father, Maria runs away, and a frantic Johannes calls the police. Lt. Luther, with very little help from either Johannes or Maria's friends, gets nowhere in his search. Frustrated, Johannes enlists the aid of a psychic, Madame Sirocco, whom Lt. Luther knows as Thelma Hoffinger, a true-blue con artist.

2257. "Beyond Belief" (4/8/80; rebroadcast from 12/17/79)

2258. "Kitty" (4/9/80; rebroadcast 7/31/80)

Cast: Teri Keane (Kitty Methune); Robert Kaliban (Lieutenant Dan McKenzie); Russell Horton (Professor Gilmore); Catherine Byers (Holly Methune). Written by Henry Slesar.

Holly Methune, on her way home after a night of dancing at the Kit Kat Club, fights off a man trying to pick her up. Because his doctor says he might lose an eye from scratches inflicted by Holly, the man charges her with assault. Later, he is found dead in his apartment, his throat scratched wide open. Three more deaths by scratching follow, and the police begin to wonder whether Holly and her sister, Kitty, a cat lover, could in any way be involved.

2259. "Shadow of a Lover" (4/10/80; rebroadcast from 12/19/79)

2260. "My Sister—Death" (4/11/80; rebroadcast from 9/24/74)

2261. "Star Sapphire" (4/14/80; rebroadcast 8/5/80)

Cast: Fred Gwynne (Dan Ferris); Carol Teitel (Bessie Ferris); Evelyn Juster (Edna Kelly); Court Benson (Paul). Written by Elspeth Eric.

Dan and Bessie, both 52, live on a farm they inherited, but have never had children. Dan arranges with a foundling home to adopt a teenager, Edna Kelly, to help Bessie, an invalid for the past ten years, and some day to inherit the farm. Edna is fascinated by Dan's star sapphire ring, and he discovers that when she stares at it, he can hypnotize her. He uses his new power discreetly, and all goes well until he teaches her, while under hypnosis, to become a crack shot with a .22 rifle.

2262. "Death Is a Woman" (4/15/80; rebroadcast from 12/25/79)

2263. "The Face in the Coffin" (4/16/80; rebroadcast 8/7/80)

Cast: Kristoffer Tabori (Tim Doyle); Robert Kaliban (Mr. Starewell); Fred Gwynne (Senator Henderson); Roberta Maxwell (Cathy Doyle). Written by James Agate, Jr.

Tim and Cathy Doyle visit a funeral parlor late one night to pay their respects to his deceased Aunt Emma. Somehow they manage to enter the wrong room and see in an open coffin not Aunt Emma, but a man who Tim, a member of the U.S. Justice Department, thinks, but is not certain, is a famous judge soon to hand down a decision on the building of a controversial gambling casino. What is certain, though, is that their inadvertent peek is going to kill them both.

2264. "Between These Worlds" (4/17/80; rebroadcast from 12/27/79)

2265. "The Hit Man" (4/18/80; rebroadcast from 10/2/74)

2266. "The Fourth Reason" (4/21/80; rebroadcast 8/12/80)

Cast: John Lithgow (Purvis); Teri Keane (Irene Thatcher); Court Benson (Congressman); Arnold Moss (Tom Thatcher). Written by Sam Dann.

Irene Thatcher turns to her congressman for help when her husband, an oil engineer on the verge of a major technological breakthrough, does not return—much to her chagrin—from a trip to Paris. The congressman orders his assistant, Purvis, to investigate, hoping he is stepping into an international oil plot that will turn him into a national figure. But Tom Thatcher has disappeared for reasons only he knows and can control.

2267. "The One-Thousand Pound Gorilla" (4/22/80; rebroadcast from 12/31/79)

2268. "The Dead You Can't Bury" (4/23/80; rebroadcast 8/14/80)

Cast: Jada Rowland (Amanda Harrow); Carol Teitel (Mrs. Trevelyan); Ian Martin (Ralph Harrow); Lloyd Battista (Andrew Trevelyan). Written by Ian Martin.

At her brother's instigation, Amanda, still in mourning over their father's death, marries wealthy lumberman Andrew Trevelyan. Amanda consented to the marriage even though a woman in her dreams (who turns out to be Andrew's first wife) warned her that by doing so she will seal her doom. Soon after the wedding, Amanda suffers a serious—but not fatal, this time—fall from a horse due to an unbuckled stirrup.

2269. "Revenge Is Not Sweet" (4/24/80; rebroadcast from 1/2/80)

2270. "The Bride That Wasn't" (4/25/80; rebroadcast from 11/19/74)

2271. "Portrait of a Memory" (4/28/80; rebroadcast 8/19/80)

Cast: Norman Rose (Justin Court); Marian Seldes (Amelia North); Carol Teitel (Maria-Helena). Adapted by James Agate, Jr., based on the 1899 short story *The Real Thing* by Henry James.

Amelia North, a wealthy American residing in Paris, commissions Maria-Helena, through her painter friend Justin Court, to produce a portrait of an unknown man for which she agrees to pay an exorbitant sum. She refuses to explain why she wants the picture but, as fate would have it, the portrait Maria-Helena paints turns out not to be of an unknown man, but someone from the pasts of both Amelia and Maria-Helena.

2272. "The Better Half" (4/29/80; rebroadcast from 1/14/80)

2273. "How Can I Ever Thank You" (4/30/80; rebroadcast 8/21/80)

Cast: Mandel Kramer (Algernon Barraclough); Joyce Gordon (Margaret); Russell Horton (Malcolm Tinsley); Earl Hammond (Jefferson Winslow). Written by Sam Dann.

Algernon Barraclough, author of ten successful novels, is so impressed with the first manuscript of young Malcolm Tinsley that he persuades his publisher to buy it. The story, even though Barraclough later describes it "a grubby potboiler for sex-starved neurotics," is an immediate best-seller, and soon Tinsley has replaced Barraclough as the publisher's favorite author. When Tinsley is found murdered, Barraclough becomes the logical—and only—suspect.

2274. "Prisoner of the Machines" (5/1/80; rebroadcast from 1/16/80)

2275. "Journey Into Terror" (5/2/80; rebroadcast from 10/13/74)

2276. "The Inner Eye" (5/5/80; rebroadcast 8/26/80)

Cast: Roberta Maxwell (Betsy); Gordon Gould (Carl Ashton); Teri Keane (Mother); Court Benson (Doctor). Written by Elspeth Eric.

Carl Ashton swears he's been destroyed when Betsy refuses to go off to Europe with him in search of fame and fortune. Betsy is deeply hurt when he leaves her and becomes overwrought when she sees, in a series of visions, that he is carrying a gun and plans to use it on himself. Accompanied by a psychiatrist, her mother and a police sergeant, Betsy sets out to stop Carl, but wherever her visions lead them, they always arrive a few minutes too late.

2277. "Once Upon an Island" (5/6/80; rebroadcast from 1/21/80)

2278. "Wanted, a Husband" (5/7/80; rebroadcast 8/28/80)

Cast: Fred Gwynne (Jeff Peters); Ian Martin (Andy Tucker); Bryna Raeburn (Wilhemina Trotter); Ray Owens (P.J. Nethersole). Adapted by G. Frederic Lewis, based on the 1908 short story *The Exact Science of Matrimony* by O. Henry.

Jeff Peters and Andy Tucker, thrown off a freight train in Cairo, Illinois, meet Wilhemina Trotter, a widow slinging hash in a rundown restaurant. Together they plan a scam for men seeking a mate, with Wilhemina and a $2,000 bank account as lures. Everything moves briskly and the cash rolls in, but Wilhemina soon becomes a fly in the ointment. She falls for one of the applicants and wants to marry him.

2279. "The Forty-Four" (5/8/80; rebroadcast from 1/23/80)

2280. "The Final Vow" (5/9/80; rebroadcast from 10/16/74)

2281. "Tomorrow Is Never" (5/12/80; rebroadcast 9/2/80)

Cast: Marian Seldes (Caroline Spencer); Larry Haines (Larry Stanford); Ray Owens (Cousin George). Adapted by James Agate, Jr., based on the 1888 novel *The Aspern Papers* by Henry James.

Caroline Spencer has taught her pupils for many years while daydreaming of all the places she has never been and saving her money so that one day she could actually travel. Her daydreams continue until she meets Laurence Stanford at a party and he encourages her to pack her bags. But on her first trip to France, Caroline gets involved with an unscrupulous cousin.

2282. "The God Machine" (5/13/80; rebroadcast from 1/28/80)

2283. "On the Side of the Angels" (5/14/80; rebroadcast 9/4/80)

Cast: Earl Hammond (Hank Boone); Evelyn Juster (Lucy Stubbs); Ian Martin (Curly Stubbs). Written by Ian Martin.

Lucy Stubbs has been worked so hard by her father and two brothers on their ranch that at first glance she looks like one of the boys, unless one could see that beneath the grime and worn clothes she was a truly pretty girl. But a peddler with a secret enters her life and unalterably changes it—along with his own—during the town's biggest dance. He does it with a magic wand that packs bullets.

2284. "The Crystal Gazer" (5/15/80; rebroadcast from 1/30/80)

2285. "The Hand That Refused to Die" (5/16/80; rebroadcast from 11/1/74)

2286. "Two of a Kind" (5/19/80; rebroadcast 9/9/80)

Cast: Kristoffer Tabori (Wally); Russell Horton (Casey); Martha Greenhouse (Aunt Louise). Written by Henry Slesar.

Because his Aunt Louise is sure to cut off his allowance upon her imminent release from a sanitarium, free-spending Wally starts making plans to ensure she will soon be recommitted to the institution. With $25,000 of her money, he rents two identical adjacent apartments and furnishes each in the very same manner. What he plans to do with them, he hopes, will make his Aunt Louise react so violently that the men in the white coats will demand to make her a patient again.

2287. "That's What Friends Are For" (5/20/80; rebroadcast from 2/4/80)

2288. "Private Demon" (5/21/80; rebroadcast 9/11/80)

Cast: Norman Rose (Professor Soames); Robert Kaliban (David Porter); Carol Teitel (Portia Porter). Written by Sam Dann.

Shortly after he is told he can expect a Nobel Prize for his lifelong research on the people of ancient Chaytor, Professor Jerimiah Soames is confronted by a young instructor, David Porter, who's also researched Chaytor and who points out a major flaw in the older man's work. In a rage, Soames stabs him to death with a Chaytorian knife and makes it appear that Porter had been mugged in his car. The police are convinced this is what happened, but the dead man's wife isn't.

2289. "The Deserter" (5/22/80; rebroadcast from 2/6/80)

2290. "Medium Rare" (5/23/80; rebroadcast from 10/25/74)

2291. "Phantom Paradise" (5/26/80; rebroadcast 9/16/80)

Cast: Marian Seldes (Lady Castleton); Robert Maxwell (Pascal); Court Benson (Lord Castleton); Lloyd Battista (Lieutenant Maybury). Written by Ian Martin.

The only two survivors of the sunken H.M.S. *Arabella*, Lady Valerie Castleton—accustomed to living a life of luxury—and Lt. Giles Maybury—who murdered his superior officer—manage to swim to a small island. With the help of the island's lone inhabitant, a former French sailor, they manage to learn to live quite comfortably. They also fall in love and conduct their own wedding ceremony, swearing that under no circumstances would they return to civilization. But after a year, a British frigate sails into the island's harbor. It is captained by the legal husband of the now-pregnant Lady Castleton.

2292. "Talk to Me" (5/27/80; rebroadcast from 2/11/80)

2293. "The Bluff" (5/28/80; rebroadcast 9/18/80)

Cast: Larry Haines (Rick Pearson); Earl Hammond (Joe Trager); Roberta Maxwell (Evvy Trager). Written by Henry Slesar.

Since being blinded by acid thrown in his face by a punk mobster, former police captain Joe Trager has improved his sense of hearing so he can tell, by the creaking of the floor boards, where anyone is in his living room. He puts out a phony story about an operation he has agreed to that will restore his eyesight. He hopes this will lure the acid-thrower, fearing recognition, to his living room and give the former cop a chance to shoot him. His family and old friend, Rick Pearson, think he's crazy, but this is how Trager wants to exact his revenge.

2294. "Crime of Passion" (5/29/80; rebroadcast from 2/13/80)

2295. "Murder to Perfection" (5/30/80; rebroadcast from 11/17/74)

2296. "Let George Do It" (6/2/80; rebroadcast 9/23/80)

Cast: Russell Horton (Perry Foster); Ian Martin (Sid Rawlings); Evelyn Juster (Eleanor Crosbie). Written by Sam Dann.

Perry Foster, an unhappily married traveling salesman, is forced to spend an afternoon in a sleepy New England village when the accelerator clip on his car snaps. While waiting for a local mechanic to locate a new clip, Foster meets gift shop owner Eleanor Crosbie and immediately falls for her. She is willing to marry him if he will help her murder her elderly husband, whose quarter-million life insurance policy is hers when he dies. Foster is tempted, until he has another conversation with the mechanic.

Notes: Nick Pryor has appeared in such films as *The Happy Hooker* (1975), *Smile* (1975), *Night Terror* (1976), *Last Song* (1980), *Into Thin Air* (1985), *Pacific Heights* (1990), and *Hoffa* (1992).

2297. "The Time Box" (6/3/80; rebroadcast from 2/18/80)

2298. "Obsession" (6/4/80; rebroadcast 9/25/80)

Cast: Bob Dryden (Emmett O'Hara); Teri Keane (Muriel Chase); Carol Teitel (Rosalie); Mandel Kramer (David Chase). Written by Elspeth Eric.

Emmett O'Hara pleads with his longtime friend, police chief David Chase, to put him in jail. If he doesn't, O'Hara is sure he'll commit a perfect—and horrible—crime. Chase refuses and urges his friend to see a psychiatrist about his obsession. But it's not long before the chief realizes he has made a big mistake: He should have locked O'Hara up and thrown away the key.

2299. "The Vampire Plant" (6/5/80; rebroadcast from 2/20/80)

2300. "Trapped" (6/6/80; rebroadcast from 11/27/74)

2301. "That Magic Touch" (6/9/80; rebroadcast 9/30/80)

Cast: Marian Seldes (Annalee); Kristoffer Tabori (Ronald); Ray Owens (Dr. Shawn); Michael Tolan (Ted Samson). Written by G. Frederic Lewis.

Unable to have children of their own, producer Ted Samson and his leading lady wife, Annalee, adopt a son whom they name Ronald. Ted, always seeking more fame and fortune for both himself and Annalee, drives her to a nervous breakdown and continues to mistreat her even after her release from a sanitarium. During a struggle in their home, Annalee falls over a banister and down a flight of stairs, disfiguring her face for life. Ronald then declares he could easily murder his father.

2302. "The Unseen and the Seen" (6/10/80; rebroadcast from 2/25/80)

2303. "Legacy of Guilt" (6/11/80; rebroadcast 10/2/80)

Cast: Roberta Maxwell (Angie Barr); Russell Horton (Tom Barr); Bryna Raeburn (Ghost). Written by Ian Martin.

Tom and Angie Barr, young New York actors and parents of a brand-new baby, are refurbishing an old Victorian house some 40 miles up the Hudson River. They're having a wonderful time, hammering and sanding, until they discover in the attic an old three-quarter-length oval mirror. It's a rare antique, but it turns sinister when Angie starts seeing in it, a young woman crying for help and demanding that Angie give up her young child.

2304. "The Intruder" (6/12/80; rebroadcast from 2/27/80)

2305. "The Sighting" (6/13/80; rebroadcast from 1/19/75)

2306. "Voice from the Grave" (6/16/80; rebroadcast 10/7/80)

Cast: Earl Hammond (Captain Norman Burgess); Court Benson (Dr. Toon Hoy); Carol Teitel (Charlena Lee). Written by Roy Winsor.

Captain Norman Burgess, without a clue in his investigation of the brutal murder of a Chinese woman, is intrigued by information provided by Dr. Toon Hoy, whose wife was a friend of the victim. While sleeping, Mrs. Hoy, with a voice sounding much like the murdered woman's, described the last moments of her friend's life. Burgess is skeptical of this psychic phenomenon, but he's willing to accept any help he can get in his attempts to discover the murderer's identity.

2307. "Laundry Money" (6/17/80; rebroadcast from 3/3/80)

2308. "In the Name of Love" (6/18/80; rebroadcast 10/9/80)

Cast: Teri Keane (Celeste Manning); Bob Dryden (Joe); Evelyn Juster (Maureen Lovell); Norman Rose (Roger Carlson). Written by Sam Dann.

Advertising mongul, Celeste Manning, meets a billionaire industrialist, Roger Carlson, on a flight from Paris and tells him a personal secret: She has a daughter, but it's only an illusion. The "daughter" is really movie star Maureen Lovell, whom Celeste, who has never found time to get married, has admired since she was a child actress. When Maureen, who has taken to using drugs, disappears, Celeste panics and begs Carlson to help her and Maureen.

2309. "A Matter of Identity" (6/19/80; rebroadcast from 3/5/80)

2310. "The Fatal Connection" (6/20/80; rebroadcast from 2/1/75)

2311. "Life Blood" (6/23/80; rebroadcast 10/14/80)

Cast: John Beal (Arthur Moore); Gordon Gould (Jarrell Thornton); Ralph Bell (Harry Burton); Marian Seldes (Amelia). Written by Murray Burnett.

After ten years of experimentation with computers, sound waves, and unheard of advances in physics and chemistry, Jarrell Thornton has created a most beautiful, "perfect" woman, Amelia, a robot. He hopes to lure Harry Burton, a scientist he hates, into marrying her without knowing her background, but he doesn't count on the interference of another scientist, Arthur Moore, who also falls in love with Amelia and doesn't want her to be hurt.

2312. "You're Going to Like Rodney" (6/24/80; rebroadcast from 3/10/80)

2313. "The Sweet Smell of Murder" (6/25/80; rebroadcast 10/16/80)

Cast: Bryna Raeburn (Momma); Joseph Silver (Lieutenant Sims); Evelyn Juster (Maudie); Bob Dryden (Thomas T. Granby). Written by Sam Dann.

Thomas Taylor Granby, a retired chauffeur, buys his wife, whom he calls Momma, a cashmere coat she's always wanted and a $42,000 ship-to-shore radio for their aging powerboat. Next thing Momma knows, her husband is in jail, accused of stealing $30,000. First, he said he won the money in a lottery, then that he had found it in a shopping bag on their dock. He has never lied to his wife before, but the police, figuring the case closed, point out there's always a first time.

2314. "The Secret of the Fifth Bell" (6/26/80; rebroadcast from 3/12/80)

2315. "Picture on the Wall" (6/27/80; rebroadcast from 11/30/74)

2316. "The Old Maid Murders" (6/30/80; rebroadcast 10/21/80)

Cast: Tammy Grimes (Laura McRae); Earl Hammond (Dr. Waller); Norman Rose (Dr. Morgan Lowecraft); Court Benson (Colonel). Written by Sam Dann.

Laura McRae devoted the best years of her life to serving the eminent Dr. Morgan Lowecraft, intimate to presidents and privy to the country's most delicate national secrets. When Lowecraft asks the dedicated Laura to hand-deliver an annotated manuscript to its author in Florida, an airport mix-up allows Laura the chance to examine the document. What Laura reads convinces her that Lowecraft may be betraying national secrets.

2317. "The Evil Eye" (7/1/80; rebroadcast from 3/17/80)

2318. "Maud-Evelyn" (7/2/80; rebroadcast 10/23/80)

Cast: Paul Hecht (Peter Harkness); Carol Teitel (Lavinia); Lloyd Battista (George). Adapted by G. Frederic Lewis, based on the 1900 short story by Henry James.

Lavinia sets a strict condition for agreeing to marry English heir Peter Harkness: He must pursue a career with a future. Harkness takes up the challenge by becoming a travel companion to an unusual London couple who draw Harkness into a strange intrigue.

2319. "The Death Wish" (7/3/80; rebroadcast from 3/19/80)

2320. "Concerto in Death" (7/4/80; rebroadcast from 3/30/75)

2321. "Silent Partners" (7/7/80; rebroadcast 10/28/80)

Cast: Marian Seldes (Margaret Tracy); Mandel Kramer (Sylvester Burley); Gilbert Mack (Goodloe). Written by Sam Dann.

Sylvester Burley, chairman of the board of Burley Industries, accompanied by his faithful if unappreciated secretary, Margaret Tracy, arrives in a Latin American country to develop its untapped resources for his corporation. Their trip takes a hazardous turn when they are abducted by revolutionaries, and Burley, with all his corporate cunning, is unable to escape the situation. It then falls to Miss Tracy to prove that she can do more than just type.

2322. "The Blue Tiger" (7/8/80; rebroadcast from 3/24/80)

2323. "Sierra Alpha 638" (7/9/80; rebroadcast 10/30/80)

Cast: Bob Dryden (Reverend Joy/Commander Bill Shane); Russell Horton (Captain Mike Torrez/Lieutenant Doug Breck); Ray Owens (Ham Jesson/Harvey); Diana Kirkwood (Anita Silvera). Written by Ian Martin.

Sierra Alpha 638, under the command of Captain Mike Torrez, is abruptly taken over by Reverend Joy of the Temple of the Angelical Revelation. Before the captain and crew can make a move, the hijacker and his hired cohorts cut off all radio and radar contact. Only when Reverend Joy is in complete control do they discover the "true communion" of his church.

2324. "Conspiracy" (7/10/80; rebroadcast from 3/26/80)

2325. "Sleepy Village" (7/11/80; rebroadcast from 4/2/75)

2326. "Nightmare in Gillette Castle" (7/14/80; rebroadcast 11/4/80)

Cast: Kevin McCarthy (William Gillette); Jada Rowland (Pamela Watson); Carol Teitel (Mrs. Hudson); Russell Horton (Jim Watson). Written by Elizabeth Pennell.

Jim Watson, a Sherlock Holmes aficionado, has a special interest in visiting Gillette Castle, the dank home of long-dead Sherlock Holmes actor William Gillette. But when Jim and his wife Pamela are separated from the castle tour group, they take a wrong turn down a corridor called "Baker Street" and come face to face with the castle's builder, dead since 1937.

Notes: Kevin McCarthy plays William Gillette in this episode, a character who was supposedly once a Sherlock Holmes actor. Kevin McCarthy played Sherlock Holmes in a handful of *Theater* episodes.

A November 4, 1980, rebroadcast of this episode was preempted in some areas due to the presidential election coverage.

2327. "The End of the Rainbow" (7/15/80; rebroadcast from 3/31/80)

2328. "Murder Preferred" (7/16/80; rebroadcast 11/6/80)

Cast: Tony Roberts (Tom Hendricks); Teri Keane (Adrian Haven); Court Benson (Dr. Sims). Written by Henry Slesar.

The police had Tony Gerard imprisoned as the murderer of Walter Haven, who was found shot to death in his study on the eve of announcing his campaign for the Senate. But Haven's widow believes in Gerard's innocence, and she asks lawyer Tom Hendricks to defend him. Hendricks accepts the challenge, only to find that more than one person may share the guilt in Haven's death.

2329. "The Fateful Bell" (7/17/80; rebroadcast from 4/2/80)

2330. "Death on Skiis" (7/18/80; rebroadcast from 4/19/75)

2331. "The Last Days of Pompeii, Part One: The City of the Dead" (7/21/80; rebroadcast from 1/7/80)

2332. "The Last Days of Pompeii, Part Two: Thrown to the Lions" (7/22/80; rebroadcast from 1/8/80)

2333. "The Last Days of Pompeii, Part Three: Half Prophet, Half Fiend" (7/23/80; rebroadcast from 1/9/80)

2334. "The Last Days of Pompeii, Part Four: Danger, Love and Death" (7/24/80; rebroadcast from 1/10/80)

2335. "The Last Days of Pompeii, Part Five: The Buried City" (7/25/80; rebroadcast from 1/11/80)

2336. "A Ton of Gold" (7/28/80)

Cast: Ralph Bell (Prof. Edwin Doughty); Carol Teitel (Ruth Doughty); Earl Hammond (Crazy Joe); Gordon Gould (Walter Stafford). Written by Sam Dann.

Dr. Edwin Doughty, his wife Ruth, and his assistant Walter Stafford arrive in western New Mexico to uncover a treasure in gold dust, hidden centuries before the Yawe Indians. Their Indian guide agrees to lead them to the riches on one condition: that first they hear about the curse of the Zamora gold.

2337. "Madame Sirocco" (7/29/80; rebroadcast from 4/7/80)

2338. "The Death Disk" (7/30/80; rebroadcast 11/13/80)

Cast: Tammy Grimes (Selma Pruitt); Norman Rose (Elwood Townsend); Mandel Kramer (Joe Stovall). Written by Sam Dann.

Selma Pruitt feels she is perfect for the job of executive director of the Martindale Foundation, and thought her interview with wealthy Elwood Townsend, the foundation's trustee, was progressing smoothly until he suddenly turned her down. To her consternation, she discovers that he believes she stole a small gold disc during the interview. No one accepts her vehement claims of innocence, and soon she begins to doubt her own sanity.

2339. "Kitty" (7/31/80; rebroadcast from 4/9/80)

2340. "A Small Question of Terror" (8/1/80; rebroadcast from 4/30/75)

2341. "This Deadly Fraternity" (8/4/80; rebroadcast 11/18/80)

Cast: Jack Grimes (Harry Clark); Valeka Gray (Helen Clark); Court Benson (M.J. Trimble); Russell Horton (Buck Stanley). Written by Ian Martin.

Harry Clark reluctantly returns to his alma mater under pressure from a very important fellow alumni: his boss. There he meets classmate and fraternity brother Buck Stanley, who shares Clark's queasiness about the campus: Both were present during the Tau Alpha Gamma initiation that years earlier killed pledge Phil Fowler. Every other brother who participated in that fatal ceremony—except Harry and Buck—has died mysteriously on an anniversary of Fowler's death, and the next October 15 is coming up soon.

2342. "Star Sapphire" (8/5/80; rebroadcast from 4/14/80)

2343. "The Mysterious Hanging of Squire Huggins" (8/6/80; rebroadcast 11/20/80)

Cast: Paul Hecht (Dominicus Pike); Bob Dryden (Sheriff); Ray Owens (Bartender); Patricia Elliott (Sarah Pike). Adapted by James Agate, Jr., based on the 1834 short story *Mr. Higginbotham's Catastrophe* by Nathaniel Hawthorne.

Dominicus and Sarah Pike, en route to the home of Huggins, meet a stranger who claims the squire was hanged by brigands. But when Dominicus repeats the tale, the squire is discovered alive and well, and the peddler is put in jail. Sarah arranges his escape, and during their flight another stranger reports the hanging anew. Dominicus now hatches a plot to get at the bottom of this mystery.

2344. "The Face in the Coffin" (8/7/80; rebroadcast from 4/16/80)

2345. "The Strange Case of Lucas Lauder" (8/8/80; rebroadcast from 5/17/75)

2346. "The Master Minds" (8/11/80; rebroadcast 11/25/80)

Cast: Russell Horton (Bradley Leighton); Court Benson (Inspector Conway); Carol Teitel (Diana Lake). Adapted by G. Frederic Lewis, based on the 1906 short story *The Missing Necklace* by Jacques Futrelle.

American police detective Diana Lake combines her talents with those of Inspector Conway of Scotland Yard in a chase across the ocean to search for a necklace believed stolen by dashing Bradley Leighton. Lake and Conway are convinced that Leighton has hidden the jewels somewhere on the luxury liner H.M.S. *Romantic*. To recover them, Diana attempts to divert ladies' man Leighton from the necklace to herself.

2347. "The Fourth Reason" (8/12/80; rebroadcast from 4/21/80)

2348. "The Return of Edward Blair" (8/13/80; rebroadcast 11/27/80)

Cast: John Lithgow (Edward Blair); Earl Hammond (Jack Manning); Joan Shay (Sarah); Bob Dryden (Andrew). Written by Roy Winsor.

One rainy night, a young drifter pounds on the door of a quiet ranch house, and the answering servants, Andrew and Sarah, believe their master Edward Blair has come home at last. When Blair later is unable to understand the hostility with which his hometown greets him, Sarah begins to suspect that perhaps this man is not Blair at all. The real Blair might never have returned to Lost Cabin.

2349. "The Dead You Can't Bury" (8/14/80; rebroadcast from 4/23/80)

2350. "The Eye of Death" (8/15/80; rebroadcast from 5/31/75)

2351. "Human Error" (8/18/80; rebroadcast 12/1/80)

Cast: Larry Haines (Harry Margolies); Jack Grimes (Friend); Evelyn Juster (Isabel). Written by Elspeth Eric.

Planning a rare trip to the track, Harry Margolies is so engrossed in conversation with a close friend that he runs a red light and knocks down a pedestrian, who turns out to be a pretty young woman. Harry wonders if this is the golden opportunity to put some excitement back into his life, especially when the girl gives him her phone number. But his all-knowing friend reminds him of a complication: his wife, Isabel.

2352. "Portrait of Memory" (8/19/80; rebroadcast from 4/28/80)

2353. "Kill Now—Pay Later" (8/20/80; rebroadcast 12/2/80)

Cast: Fred Gwynne (Sheriff); Tony Roberts (Stuart Belden); Bryna Raeburn (Aunt Melisande); Teri Keane (Maude Henderson). Written by Sam Dann.

When Stuart Belden, spineless scion of the first family of Belden Corners, declares his love for local waitress Maude Henderson, Sheriff Hollister predicts a violent clash of wills between Stuart and his powerful Aunt Melisande. After the murder, Sheriff Hollister vows to bring Stuart to justice. The lone deterrent is the disappearance of the murder weapon, and only Maude knows where it is.

2354. "How Can I Ever Thank You" (8/21/80; rebroadcast from 4/30/80)

2355. "Sting of Death" (8/22/80; rebroadcast from 7/27/75)

2356. "Poor Lester" (8/25/80; rebroadcast 12/3/80)

Cast: Teri Keane (Juliet); Earl Hammond (Lester); Joyce Gordon (The Queen); Norman Rose (Zeus). Written by Sam Dann.

With the crunch of metal and the shattering of glass, Juliet Keyworth loses the one inspiration in her life: her husband, famed agronomist Dr. Lester Keyworth. Grief stricken, she rushes from the hospital wishing she could have died in his stead. The great god Zeus appears to her and with some reluctance grants her request, so long as she see how "Poor Lester" fares without her.

2357. "The Inner Eye" (8/26/80; rebroadcast from 5/5/80)

2358. "A Feast of Death" (8/27/80; rebroadcast 12/4/80)

Cast: Jada Rowland (Yvette); Bob Dryden (Jacques); Joan Banks (Danielle); Ray Owens (Andre). Written by Elspeth Eric, which was based on a true story.

In Paris during the tumultuous years of World War I, a penniless seamstress meets a charming and mysterious entrepreneur who vows undying lover for her. Beautiful Yvette is so entranced when she is swept off her feet into the arms and sumptuous lifestyle of her new lover, Jacques, that she thinks little about the origin of his incredible wealth. When he is arrested suddenly, Yvette turns to his friend Andre for help. As she pours out her story it becomes apparent to them that perhaps Jacques is not at all who he presents himself to be.

2359. "Wanted, a Husband" (8/28/80; rebroadcast from 5/7/80)

2360. "The Intermediary" (8/29/80; rebroadcast from 7/19/75)

2361. "The Power of Zeus" (9/1/80; rebroadcast 12/8/80)

Cast: Russell Horton (Jonathan Troy); Earl Hammond (President); Patricia Elliott (Miranda). Written by James Agate, Jr.

In a future world split into two halves—the Anglos and the Asiatics—early prophecies about the ozone layer have come true, and food production is severely jeopardized. Renowned scientists Jonathan and Miranda Troy must race against time to formulate a soil compound able to withstand the destructive power of the sun's unfiltered rays. But while on their special mission to the planet Zeus they accidentally discover another formula that has the power both to save and destroy the world.

2362. "Tomorrow Is Never" (9/2/80; rebroadcast from 5/12/80)

2363. "Leave Well Enough Alone" (9/3/80; rebroadcast 12/9/80)

Cast: John Beal (Guy de Maupassant); Court Benson (Henri Lantin); Tracey Ellis (Celeste). Adapted by Sam Dann, based on a story by Guy de Maupassant.

De Maupassant swallows his natural cynicism when neighbor Henri Lantin, a middle-aged government clerk, marries 18-year-old Celeste in an apparently happy match. His uncharacteristic optimism is reinforced when Henri, acting on an anonymous note, spies on his wife during one of her frequent solo trips to the opera and finds Celeste in the company of a woman friend. When de Maupassant discovers the truth about Celeste's penchant for cheap jewelry his faith is restored.

2364. "On the Side of the Angels" (9/4/80; rebroadcast from 5/14/80)

2365. "Roses Are for Funerals" (9/5/80; rebroadcast from 7/6/75)

2366. "Hand in Glove" (9/8/80; rebroadcast 12/10/80)

Cast: Russell Horton (Dr. Dan Crane); Diana Kirkwood (Lairel Blair); Mandel Kramer (Dr. Stewart Courtney). Written by Nancy Moore.

When a blazing shootout in the halls of a university hospital leaves murderer Jed Gant dead and Dr. Dan Crane with an irreparably damaged hand, head surgeon Stewart Courtney performs a daring transplant using the dead man's hand. The transplant is successful, but Dan is haunted by Gant's dying vow to curse him from beyond the grave. His new hand seems to fulfill that curse: With a will of its own, it threatens to bring the killer back to life.

2367. "Two of a Kind" (9/9/80; rebroadcast from 5/19/80)

2368. "Ocean of Emptiness" (9/10/80; rebroadcast 12/10/80)

Cast: Paul Hecht (Ned Miller); Teri Keane (Chloe Miller); Arnold Moss (Voice). Written by Arnold Moss.

Chloe and Ned Miller, piloting the spaceship *Hyperion*, leave Earth in the year 1995 to explore uncharted areas of the galaxy. Their expected dangers become even more terrifying once they reach the planet. In Jupiter's orbit they receive a radio transmission that they've been dead for 100 years.

2369. "Private Demon" (9/11/80; rebroadcast from 5/21/80)

2370. "Bullet Proof" (9/12/80; rebroadcast from 8/2/75)

2371. "Number One" (9/15/80; rebroadcast 12/15/80)

Cast: Larry Haines (Bart Wallace); Earl Hammond (Numbero Uno); Evelyn Juster (Ruth Wallace). Written by Sam Dann.

Movie star Bart Wallace insists his wife Ruth accompany him on location for a new picture. She knows it will co-star his latest beautiful "protégé" and is prepared for yet another long, lonely siege. But as the company begins to shoot in the isolated mountain ranges of a Latin American country, a roving band of revolutionaries suddenly appears. Their freedom will be given on the condition that Ruth spend the night with the darling leader of the bandits, Numbero Uno.

2372. "Phantom Paradise" (9/16/80; rebroadcast from 5/26/80)

2373. "The Threshold" (9/17/80; rebroadcast 12/16/80)

Cast: Fred Gwynne (Jeff Tanner); Bob Dryden (Shane Boggs); Ian Martin (Charles Fairly); Bryna Raeburn (Mrs. Fairly). Written by G. Frederic Lewis.

Scientist turned hardware store owner Jeff Tanner and his friend, Shane Boggs, seem to be the only people in Mercury, Montana, who know or care about the strange goings-on at Dry Lake, the ghost town in some nearby mountains. An enigmatic couple has bought up the whole town, a waste-land since it was contaminated by radioactivity 40 years before. Half the Dry Lake population died from that contamination. But then who is doing all the construction work Tanner and Boggs hear each night?

2374. "The Bluff" (9/18/80; rebroadcast from 5/28/80)

2375. "Through the Looking Glass" (9/19/80; rebroadcast from 7/23/75)

2376. "The Mysterious Rochdale Special" (9/22/80; rebroadcast 12/17/80)

Cast: Ralph Bell (Herbert Lernac); Ian Martin (Clement Roget); Court Benson (Superintendent Potter); Bob Dryden (Inspector Collins). Adapted by Murray Burnett, based on the 1908 short story *The Lost Special* by Sir Arthur Conan Doyle.

Herbert Lernac, a proud French master criminal in prison for a crime beneath his dignity, importunes lawyer Clement Roget to hear out his claim to have master minded the greatest unsolved mystery in England. The disappearance of the Rochdale Special, a private train traveling from Liverpool to London in 1893, has baffled Scotland Yard and railroad officials for nearly a decade. Lernac thinks his knowledge of the affair will get him off the hook from his current charge: the coldblooded murder of a green grocer in front of three witnesses.

2377. "Let George Do It" (9/23/80; rebroadcast from 6/2/80)

2378. "The Murder of Caesar" (9/24/80; rebroadcast 12/18/80)

Cast: Earl Hammond (Caesar); Joan Shay (Calpurnia); Gordon Gould (Cicero); Paul Hecht (Brutus). Written by G. Frederic Lewis, based on writings of Plutarch.

An exhausted, aging Caesar returns home from the Roman conquest of Spain to the acclaim of citizens and the suspicions of senators. He confides a death wish to his best friend, Brutus. A clique of senators led by Cassius and Cicero may make that wish come true, but first they must lure Caesar from his home.

2379. "Obsession" (9/25/80; rebroadcast from 6/4/80)

2380. "Where Angels Fear to Tread" (9/26/80; rebroadcast from 8/26/75)

2381. "The Ruby Lamp" (9/29/80; rebroadcast 12/22/80)

Cast: Mandel Kramer (Paul Morrison); Joan Beal (Matthew Horner); Teri Keane (Edith Morrison). Written by Elspeth Eric.

The marriage of Paul and Edith Morrison is suffering from the strain of a secret Paul withholds from his wife "for her own good." While visiting Professor Matthew Horner to avoid Edith's constant efforts to learn the secret, Paul learns of a process that can photograph thoughts, using a ruby lamp and unexposed film. He agrees to experiment with it, and the resulting image changes his marriage forever.

2382. "That Magic Touch" (9/30/80; rebroadcast from 6/9/80)

2383. "Hero's Welcome" (10/1/80; rebroadcast 12/23/80)

Cast: Tony Roberts (Russ Anderson); Russell Horton (Frank Evans); Joyce Gordon (Dotty Anderson); Robert Kaliban (The Chief). Written by Sam Dann.

Russ Anderson became a hero when his friends saw him dive from a lifeboat to save a drowning woman, and thought he never came up. In reality, he suffered amnesia and drifted to a Pacific atoll, later becoming son-in-law to the island's chief. When his memory finally returned, Russ decided to go home to his wife and friends. But he finds that a dead hero was easier for them to cope with.

2384. "Legacy of Guilt" (10/2/80; rebroadcast from 6/11/80)

2385. "Key to Murder" (10/3/80; rebroadcast from 6/28/75)

2386. "Second Sight" (10/6/80; rebroadcast 12/26/80)

Cast: Fred Gwynne (Sgt. James Greenwood); Earl Hammond ("Fingers" Dickson); Carol Teitel (Zelda Ginestera); Robert Maxwell (P.J. Ginestera). Written by Sam Dann.

Arthur "Fingers" Dickson, to whom no safe is safe, is caught by millionaire P. J. Ginestera in the act of burglarizing his mansion. Fingers escapes empty-handed and unharmed. So when the police arrest him for Ginestera's murder, Fingers claims it's a set-up. But only Sergeant James Greenwood, who was forced to retire when he was blinded in the course of arresting Fingers on another caper, can get Fingers off the hook.

2387. "Voice from the Grave" (10/7/8; rebroadcast from 6/16/80)

2388. "Portrait of an Assassin" (10/8/80; rebroadcast 12/29/80)

Cast: John Lithgow (Charles Guiteau); Patricia Elliott (Anna Guiteau); Bob Dryden (Morland Finley). Written by James Agate, Jr., based on actual historical facts and documents.

Fast-talking and full of schemes for success in America, Charles Guiteau believes himself on the way to the top when he marries Anna, a wealthy lawyer's niece. But the marriage sours as the pair flee creditors from city to city. Guiteau flings himself into politics with visions of earning a grand appointment. He is crushed when his candidate, James Garfield, ignores him after the successful campaign. Guitreau feels betrayed, and his deadly response makes history.

2389. "In the Name of Love" (10/9/80; rebroadcast from 6/18/80)

2390. "The Rise and Fall of the Fourth Reich" (10/10/80; rebroadcast from 8/31/75)

2391. "Napoleon and the Queen of Sheba" (10/13/80; rebroadcast 12/30/80)

Cast: Kristoffer Tabori (Eddie); Evelyn Juster (Inez Garcia); Court Benson (Little Napoleon); Ian Martin (Tom Garcia). Written by Sam Dann.

Eddie, fresh from serving a two-year prison sentence, seems to be heading right back when he attempts to hold up a neighborhood grocery run by Tom Garcia and his sister, Inez. After Tom overpowers him, Inez prevails upon the grocer to release Eddie. But it will take more than a casual kindness to help Eddie, who works for "Little Napoleon," the tough local mobster who keeps very close tabs on his employees.

2392. "Life Blood" (10/14/80; rebroadcast from 6/23/80)

2393. "The Bright Golden Murders" (10/15/80; rebroadcast 12/31/80)

Cast: Tammy Grimes (Doria Payne); Russell Horton (Stanley Platte); Martha Greenhouse (Mrs. Talmadge); Ray Owens (Ellsworth Payne). Written by Sam Dann.

The death of Ellsworth Payne, an atomic scientist who parlayed his knowledge into a successful business, seemed to be an act of revenge for fooling around with the wrong guy's girl. But his shocked widow Doris begins to think differently when his secretary starts talking about Ellsworth's revolutionary discovery and a mysterious "they" who wanted the secret. Doris' list of "plotters" soon grows to include everyone who denies this theory.

2394. "The Sweet Smell of Murder" (10/16/80; rebroadcast from 6/25/80)

2395. "The Executioner" (10/17/80; rebroadcast from 9/14/75)

2396. "Honest Mistake" (10/20/80; rebroadcast 1/5/81)

Cast: Earl Hammond (Eddie Pond); Ian Martin (Roderick T. Hammersmith); Evelyn Juster (Frances Pond). Written by Sam Dann.

Eddie Pond and his wife Frances would be an ordinary suburban couple if it weren't for one thing: Eddie is a killer for hire. But Eddie has been in the business too long, and even his employer thinks Eddie should retire. Nevertheless, Eddie agrees to silence a witness before he can testify. The intended victim should be very easy to find—he's the only Roderick T. Hammersmith in the phone book. But is he really the only R.T. Hammersmith?

2397. "The Old Maid Murders" (10/21/80; rebroadcast from 6/30/80)

2398. "Confession" (10/22/80; rebroadcast 1/7/81)

Cast: Paul Hecht (David Saville); Norman Rose (John Guest); Fred Gwynne (Edgar Saville); Valeka Gray (Laura Guest). Written by G. Frederic Lewis.

Easygoing David Saville hardly knows his wheeler-dealer stepbrother Edgar, more than twice his age. So, when David invites his older brother to join him at a resort, he has no idea that Edgar will turn the vacation into a bitter confrontation with a slightly dishonest business associate. Edgar forces David to join the confrontation, not knowing that the businessman's daughter has become the object of his affection.

2399. "Maud-Evelyn" (10/23/80; rebroadcast from 7/2/80)

2400. "Return to Shadow Lake" (10/24/80; rebroadcast from 9/7/75)

2401. "The Gilbert Stuart" (10/27/80; rebroadcast 1/9/81)

Cast: Gordon Gould (John Rose); Carol Teitel (Mrs. Fontaine); Lloyd Battista (Jefferson Rose); Tracey Ellis (Eleanor). Adapted by James Agate, Jr., based on the 1901 short story *The Rembrandt* by Edith Wharton.

John Rose knows perfectly well that the painting poor Mrs. Cecily Fontaine wants him to buy is not the Gilbert Stuart she claims. As curator of a small museum Mrs. Fontaine's brother founded, he is too kind to tell her it's a fake and too professional to buy it. So his brother Jeff and Eleanor, his fiancée, try to be helpful, and end up forcing John to acquire the painting with money he is not authorized to spend.

2402. "Silent Partners" (10/28/80; rebroadcast from 7/7/80)

2403. "Bloodline" (10/29/80; rebroadcast 1/19/81)

Cast: John Lithgow (Lewis Olcutt); Ray Owens (J. R.); Bryna Raeburn (Rozika); Russell Horton (Kevin). Written by Sam Dann.

Lewis Olcutt, of a prominent investment family, is caught reducing his firm's bank account by several million dollars. He claims his once-magic touch with money declined into embezzlement from the shock of discovery that he was adopted into, not descended from, the Olcutt financial dynasty. The missing millions are in the hands of two con artists who convinced him to steal the money for his true heritage: a Balkan kingdom.

2404. "Sierra Alpha 638" (10/30/80; rebroadcast from 7/9/80)

2405. "Dracula" (10/31/80; rebroadcast from 5/26/79)

2406. "Guilty" (11/3/80; rebroadcast 1/21/81)

Cast: Paul Hecht (Henry Graham); Lloyd Battista (Peter Ashton); Joyce Gordon (Robin Draper); Ray Owens (D.A.). Adapted by G. Frederic Lewis, based on the 1908 short story *The Verdict* by Edith Wharton.

Henry Graham hasn't written a hit play in ten years. When he tells his lawyer, Peter Ashton, that his plays have failed since then because that's when he murdered his rich uncle, Ashton thinks the man is crazy, as does the D. A. Graham ends up in a sanitarium until Ashton locates a witness who can put him in the jail cell his conscience prefers.

2407. "Nightmare in Gillette Castle" (11/4/80; rebroadcast from 7/14/80)

2408. "The Question" (11/5/80; rebroadcast 1/23/81)

Cast: Kristoffer Tabori (Jamie); Bob Dryden (Joshua); Teri Keane (Mary Mannering). Written by Elspeth Eric.

Actress Mary Mannering abruptly leaves her starring role in a long-running Broadway play to return to her family's seaside estate. At the old mansion, abandoned except for its faithful caretaker, Joshua, she hopes to recapture the sense of self years of acting have worn away. But the empty home seems to hold more ghosts than answers until a strange young man named Jamie brings the past to life.

2409. "Murder Preferred" (11/6/80; rebroadcast from 7/16/80)

2410. "Frame-Up" (11/7/80; rebroadcast from 10/26/75)

2411. "The Dagger of Almohades" (11/10/80; rebroadcast 1/26/81)

Cast: Patricia Elliott (Jennifer Wilson); John Lithgow (Lord Andreas); Earl Hammond (Sir Gilbert Stone); Court Benson (Major Lytton). Adapted by Murray Burnett, based on the 1908 short story *The Brown Hand* by Sir Arthur Conan Doyle.

The beauty of Jennifer Wilson, an English adventuress in Colonial India, breaks hearts and causes duels until her marriage to Lord Andreas brings her back to London and conventional society life. But there her scandalous involvement with famed surgeon Sir Gilbert Stone incites Lord Andreas to a vicious act of revenge that pits Stone's modern blade against the ancient dagger of Indian assassins.

Notes: Himan Brown noted: "As in the past, we are proving that radio drama is a potent, meaningful form of entertainment and the most personal form of theater. Radio drama isn't a stunt. It isn't nostalgia. More than seven years on the CBS Radio Network, and an audience of over one million prove this."

2412. "A Ton of Gold" (11/11/80; rebroadcast from 7/28/80)

2413. "Natural Sugar" (11/12/80; rebroadcast 1/28/81)

Cast: Fred Gwynne (Captain Altman); Evelyn Juster (Louisa Brundage); Russell Horton (Fred Bantom). Written by Sam Dann.

Actor Emmett Brundage, co-starring with his wife Louisa in a play about murder, is actually poisoned on stage. The investigation of police Captain Altman uncovers a whole cast of suspects who would like the cranky actor dead. But one suspect has the most convincing motive of all: self-defense.

2414. "The Death Disk" (11/13/80; rebroadcast from 7/30/80)

2415. "That Hamlet Was a Good Boy" (11/14/80; rebroadcast from 10/25/75)

2416. "The Eleventh Plague" (11/17/80; rebroadcast 1/30/81)

Cast: Russell Horton (Captain Joel Taylor); Lloyd Battista (Corsini); Ian Martin (Lieutenant Esquilla). Written by Henry Slesar.

In the year 2065, Captain Joel Taylor of the U.S. Space Command has carefully chosen his crew for a three-year mission to Planet A-15 in the Antares System. But as soon as they erect a base camp, the planet's mysterious lone inhabitant—Corsini—threatens the team. The crew rallies to destroy the dangerous creature, only to confront a more powerful threat to their existence.

2417. "This Deadly Fraternity" (11/18/80; rebroadcast from 8/4/80)

2418. "The Iron Horse" (11/19/80; rebroadcast 2/3/81)

Cast: Norman Rose (Mendel); Bob Dryden (Bandit); Earl Hammond (Avrum); Evelyn Juster (Malke). Written by Sam Dann.

Mendel, a dealer of horses in a small Central European village in the early 1800s, owes the local lord 250 kroner, and, to make matters worse, his inability to come up with a dowry loses his daughter's suitor. It seems like more bad luck when a bandit catches him alone in the forest, but the clever bandit has a scheme he claims will make them both rich.

2419. "The Mysterious Hanging of Squire Huggins" (11/20/80; rebroadcast from 8/6/80)

2420. "The Widows' Auxiliary" (11/21/80; rebroadcast from 11/15/75)

2421. "The Killer Instinct" (11/24/80; rebroadcast 2/5/81)

Cast: Ralph Bell (Harrison Craig); Martha Greenhouse (Marlene Craig); Teri Keane (Lieutenant Ruth Barry); Court Benson (Dr. Bardel). Written by Sam Dann.

Harrison Craig has begged his wife, Marlene, to give him her $50,000 inheritance to invest in a new business venture. It was a sad coincidence that it took her death for him to get the money. Her physician, Dr. Bardel, goes straight to police lieutenant Barry, claiming Harry murdered his patient. When two more deaths help Harry's new business venture, the case seems stacked against him. But then, one other possibility arises.

2422. "The Master Minds" (11/25/80; rebroadcast from 8/11/80)

2423. "Breakout" (11/26/80; rebroadcast 2/10/81)

Cast: Paul Hecht (Anselme Marchal); Robert Kaliban (Roland Garros); Ray Owens (Colonel); Bryna Raeburn (Renata). Written by James Agate, Jr., based on a true story.

Anselme Marchal and Roland Garros, boasting dozens of air victories between them, find themselves locked inside Germany's Scharnhorst prison. A month of careful planning gets the pair outside the prison gates and halfway to the Dutch border. But the Germans are close on their trail. Will that farm house ahead be their only hope for safety, or hold a German enemy?

2424. "The Return of Edward Blair" (11/27/80; rebroadcast from 8/13/80)

2425. "The Master Computer" (11/28/80; rebroadcast from 8/13/75)

2426. "Human Error" (12/1/80; rebroadcast from 8/18/80)

2427. "Kill Now—Pay Later" (12/2/80; rebroadcast from 8/20/80)

2428. "Poor Lester" (12/3/80; rebroadcast from 8/25/80)

2429. "A Feast of Death" (12/4/80; rebroadcast from 8/27/80)

2430. "The Eavesdropper" (12/5/80; rebroadcast from 1/22/76)

2431. "The Power of Zeus" (12/8/80; rebroadcast from 9/1/80)

2432. "Leave Well Enough Alone" (12/9/80; rebroadcast from 9/3/80)

2433. "Hand in Glove" (12/10/80; rebroadcast from 9/8/80)

2434. "Ocean of Emptiness" (12/11/80; rebroadcast from 9/10/80)

2435. "You're Only Young Twice" (12/12/80; rebroadcast from 2/22/76)

2436. "Number One" (12/15/80; rebroadcast from 9/15/80)

2437. "The Threshold" (12/16/80; rebroadcast from 9/17/80)

2438. "The Mysterious Rochdale Special" (12/17/80; rebroadcast from 9/22/80)

2439. "The Murder of Caesar" (12/18/80; rebroadcast from 9/24/80)

2440. "Stay Out of Dutchman's Woods" (12/19/80; rebroadcast from 3/13/76)

2441. "The Ruby Lamp" (12/22/80; rebroadcast from 9/29/80)

2442. "Hero's Welcome" (12/23/80; rebroadcast from 10/1/80)

2443. "A Christmas Carol" (12/24/80; rebroadcast from 12/24/79)

2444. "A Holiday Visit" (12/25/80; rebroadcast 12/25/81)
Cast: Lloyd Battista (Skip Bartram); Diana Kirkwood (Joan Bartram); Bob Dryden (Dad); Bryna Raeburn (Mother). Written by Bob Juhren.
A business trip gives Skip and Joan Bartram a company-paid opportunity for a long-delayed Christmas reunion with Joan's family. But as they near Joan's hometown, their car skids off the icy road on a lonely strip of highway. The couple find shelter in a deserted small town that brings forgotten memories back to Joan.

2445. "Second Sight" (12/26/80; rebroadcast from 10/6/80)

2446. "Portrait of an Assassin" (12/29/80; rebroadcast from 10/8/80)

2447. "Napoleon and the Queen of Sheba" (12/30/80; rebroadcast from 10/13/80)

2448. "The Bright Golden Murders" (12/31/80; rebroadcast from 10/15/80)

2449. "Catch the Smallest Devil" (1/1/81; rebroadcast 1/1/82)
Cast: Fred Gwynne (J. Barnabus Whitney); Court Benson (Dr. Fowler); Norman Rose (Chaplain Peterson); Teri Keane (Nurse Lydia Mae Stewart). Written by Nancy Moore.
Wealthy, tight-fisted J. Barnabus Whitney, hospitalized for heart surgery, wakes up New Year's Day in typical fashion: He insults his nurse, scorns his

doctor and turns the visiting chaplain out of his room. But under sedation, he has a troubling dream and wakes up full of resolutions to do good before it's too late.

2450. "Sins of the Fathers" (1/2/81; rebroadcast 2/12/81)

Cast: Patricia Elliott (Felice Powers); Mandel Kramer (Dad); Ian Martin (Joe Blackwood); Carol Teitel (Jennie Carroll). Written by Sam Dann.

When reporter Felice Powers obtains an interview with grand jury witness Jennie Carroll—a local bar owner—the talkative innkeeper unwittingly reveals that Felice was really born to one of her waitresses 26 years ago. Powers immediately takes up a new assignment: to discover her real parents.

Notes: Richard M. Brescia commented: "Several other radio drama formats have been attempted during the seven-year period we've been presenting *Theater*. However, only the *Theater* has been able to stand up to the test of time imposed by both the listener and the affiliate. I hope more developments in radio drama will be tried. We believe that drama can play a vital role in future programming …[this success] is a testimony to the skill of Hi Brown, *Theater* creator and executive producer, and to the great actors who perform in the series."

2451. "Honest Mistake" (1/5/81; rebroadcast from 10/20/80)

2452. "The Tenth Life" (1/6/81; rebroadcast 2/17/81)

Cast: Paul Hecht (Luke Harvey); Russell Horton (Harry); Amanda Plummer (Karima); Earl Hammond (Landlord). Written by G. Frederic Lewis.

Top reporter Luke Harvey falls in love at first sight with a beautiful, sloe-eyed woman he bumps into while riding home on the subway. His curiosity is piqued when his editor, Harry, assigns Luke to a murder story that leads to the woman's apartment, amazingly right above his own, from which he hears loud cat sounds all night long.

Notes: Acclaim for *CBS Radio Theater* and Hi Brown was forthcoming since its first broadcast. The series was honored with coveted Peabody and Mystery Writers of America awards, among others. Brown himself has received "Broadcaster of the Year" accolades from San Francisco State University, Brigham Young University and Texas Tech, and just weeks before the eighth season started he was singled out by New York City's The New School with a special commendation for his contributions to radio drama for the past half-century.

2453. "Confession" (1/7/81; rebroadcast from 10/22/80)

2454. "In the Dark" (1/8/81; rebroadcast 2/19/81)

Cast: Teri Keane (Karen Antek); Ralph Bell (Max); Carol Teitel (Mrs. Antek); Ray Owens (Benjamin Antek). Written by Elspeth Eric.

Karen Antek comes home from a month's vacation with her mother-in-law to discover that her husband, an unassuming musician, has been taken away by the secret police. All her efforts to learn his whereabouts are worse than discouraging: Authorities deny he ever existed. Only when she finds out that her best friend's husband also was meaninglessly carried away does she appreciate the true meaning of totalitarianism.

2455. "The Gilbert Stuart" (1/9/81; rebroadcast from 10/27/80)

2456. "The Legend of Alexander, Part One: Courage"
(1/12/81; rebroadcast 6/22/81)

Cast: Russell Horton (Alexander); Court Benson (King Phillip); Evelyn Juster (Queen Olympias); Bob Dryden (Philonicus). Written by Gerald Keane, based on historical material.

Young Alexander begins his apprenticeship to become king, while his parents battle over his future. Alexander longs to exchange his mother's mystical influence for his father's exciting life on the battlefields of Europe. But before he can become a warrior, he must win a private battle: to have the courage to set himself apart from his parents' conflicting wishes.

Notes: According to Himan Brown: "We begin our eighth year with the greatest excitement because the entire form of the theater of the imagination—radio drama—has literally become alive in the last eight years. Listener response to *Theater* has been overwhelming. For instance, last year, the National Education Association gave *Theater* their seal of approval."

2457. "The Legend of Alexander, Part Two: Assassination"
(1/13/81; rebroadcast 6/23/81)

Cast: Russell Horton (Alexander); Court Benson (King Phillip); Evelyn Juster (Queen Olympias); Ian Martin (Demosthenes). Written by Gerald Keane, based on historical material.

The assassination of King Phillip by a cousin of Queen Olympias catapults a 20-year-old Alexander to the throne of the embattled kingdom of Macedonia. His inheritance brings with it an unfinished war. But a terrible suspicion weakens Alexander's resolve to complete his father's effort. He suspects his mother had a hand in his father's death.

2458. "The Legend of Alexander, Part Three: Divide and Conquer" (1/14/81; rebroadcast 6/24/81)

Cast: Russell Horton (Alexander); Earl Hammond (Jason); Evelyn Juster (Queen Olympias); Ian Martin (Demosthenes). Written by Gerald Keane, based on historical material.

King Alexander has inherited a piecemeal realm held together by tribute and loyalty to his father. The new Macedonian leader's first challenge is to unite his kingdom. His second goal is to bring the world under his rule, and to do that he must conquer Athens and bring Greek influence to all corners of the world.

Notes: Russell Horton, who starred in the last five-part mini-adventure, returns as Alexander in this historical epic, based on the life of Alexander the Great. Horton also supplied the voice for the crazy rabbit in the General Mills Trix cereal commercials.

Himan Brown commented: "The spectacular setting and scope of 'The Legend of Alexander' are particularly suited to the possibilities offered by radio. Only in radio can you have the opportunity to paint the canvas of the story of Alexander the Great. Through the voices of radio we can soar into the sky, move backward and forward in time, and share the lives of kings, villains and heroes. Or, in the case of Alexander, ride elephants and traverse continents, all through the magic of radio."

2459. "The Legend of Alexander, Part Four: The Oracle"
(1/15/81; rebroadcast 6/25/81)

Cast: Russell Horton (Alexander); Earl Hammond (Cyrus); Lloyd Battista (Parmenio); Marian Seldes (The Oracle). Written by Gerald Keane, based on historical material.

Alexander, now conqueror of the Mediterranean (as well as Athens), turns his sights east to Persia. But Persian king Darius commands a million troops, versus Alexander's small, if highly trained, force of 10,000. The Macedonian king consults the Oracle at Delphi to determine his fate. What the Oracle decides could change forever the face of Europe.

2460. "The Legend of Alexander, Part Five: The Legend Begins" (1/16/81; rebroadcast 6/26/81)

Cast: Russell Horton (Alexander); Ray Owens (Lysander); Lloyd Battista (Darius); Mandel Kramer (Parmenio). Written by Gerald Keane, based on historical material.

Alexander faces every campaigner's dilemma: After the victory, what next? Alexander's dream of uniting the world under a common rule and culture is realized. At age 30, he rules the Mediterranean, Europe to the borders of modern Russia, all of Serbia and the vast kingdom of Persia. Now, his singleminded pursuit of a world state faces its most critical test. Will absolute power corrupt Alexander absolutely?

Notes: Ancient lives and times have enjoyed a renaissance of interest with the American public, evidenced by the success of the then-recent Pompeii and King Tutankhamen exhibits across the country. The current historic discovery during this five-part broadcast was believed to be the tomb of King Phillip, father of Alexander the Great, which became part of the touring exhibition "The Search for Alexander," then displayed at the National Gallery.

2461. "Bloodline" (1/19/81; rebroadcast from 10/29/80)

2462. "The Fountain of Truth" (1/20/81; rebroadcast 2/24/81)

Cast: Fred Gwynne (Pedro de Zamora); Joan Shay (Isabella); Earl Hammond (Diego Alvarado). Written by Sam Dann, based on actual historical facts and documents.

Two Spanish adventurers in the New World scheme to discover enormous wealth. Pedro de Zamora, a clever sergeant in the service of Ponce de Leon, and his reluctant aide, Diego Alvarado, join in a plot to convince their leader that they have discovered the Fountain of Youth. A weary but hopeful de Leon agrees to sail to unexplored Florida to find the fabled elixir. The Spaniards find their water, but instead of youth de Leon finds something else.

2463. "Guilty" (1/21/81; rebroadcast from 11/3/80)

2464. "The Final Mind" (1/22/81; rebroadcast 2/26/81)

Cast: Norman Rose (Justin Day); Anne Williams (Elizabeth Day); Paul Hecht (Max Freeman); Bob Dryden (Charley Wall). Written by G. Frederic Lewis.

When scientist Justin Day's "protection curtain" over the United States saves the country from nuclear devastation in the 30th century, he is elected president on a tide of popular appreciation. At the height of his successful administration, Day turns up as a voice in his wife's mind, claiming to have invented a computer that will be the perfect president.

2465. "The Question" (1/23/81; rebroadcast from 11/5/80)

2466. "The Dagger of Almohades" (1/26/81; rebroadcast from 11/10/80)

2467. "Small Money" (1/27/81; rebroadcast 3/3/81)

Cast: Tony Roberts (Stan Standish); Evelyn Juster (Suzy Standish); Larry Haines (Lieutenant Shafer); Ian Martin (Pete). Written by Sam Dann.

Professional golfer Stan Standish regretted the day he taught his librarian wife, Suzy, to swing a club. Her native ability soon overshadowed his own, and he dropped out of the circuit to become her manager. When Suzy is found murdered, no one suspects Stan. But then he can't resist making a few dollars more, using something only the murderer would have available.

2468. "Natural Sugar" (1/28/81; rebroadcast from 11/12/80)

2469. "The Vanishing Herd" (1/29/81; rebroadcast 3/5/81)

Cast: John Beal (Sherlock Holmes); Ian Martin (Duke of Holderness); Ray Owens (James Wilder); Court Benson (Dr. Watson). Adapted by Murray Burnett, based on the 1904 short story *The Priory School* by Sir Arthur Conan Doyle.

Holmes and his trusted companion Dr. Watson travel to England's moor country to solve a kidnapping case involving the son of the Duke of Holderness. Holmes and Watson manage to trace the route of the boy's abductors, but they are baffled by the number of cow prints they find in an area where only sheep graze.

2470. "The Eleventh Plague" (1/30/81; rebroadcast from 11/17/80)

2471. "The Man Who Saw Martians" (2/2/81; rebroadcast 3/10/81)

Cast: Jack Grimes (Amos Jones); Earl Hammond (Horace Bailey); Russell Horton (Jack); Jada Rowland (Susan Bailey). Written by G. Frederic Lewis.

Amos Jones, in love with the daughter of his newspaper's publisher, Susan Bailey, concocts a story about UFO sightings to impress his boss, and therefore Susan. What he doesn't count on is the elder Bailey's enthusiasm. He orders Amos to man an all-night UFO watch, leaving Susan free to receive the attentions of Amos's roommate, Jack.

2472. "The Iron Horse" (2/3/81; rebroadcast from 11/19/80)

2473. "Who Is Jessica Worth?" (2/4/81; rebroadcast 3/12/81)

Cast: Marian Seldes (Jessica Worth); Paul Hecht (Dr. Bob Curran); Bob Dryden (Uncle Albert); Joan Shay (Aunt Emily). Written by James Agate, Jr., based on a true story.

Jessica Worth wakes from a coma with no memory of her life since the death of her parents some ten years earlier. A second coma two years later not only fails to restore her memory but creates a series of new personalities that take over Jessica's mind: a psychic, an artist, a shrew and a baby girl. Dr. Bob Curran tries to help the troubled woman; he wants her many personalities to meet each other.

2474. "The Killer Instinct" (2/5/81; rebroadcast from 11/24/80)

2475. "Is Venice Drowning?" (2/6/81; rebroadcast 3/17/81)

Cast: Kim Hunter (Margaret McClain); Mandel Kramer (Arthur Williston); Lloyd Battista (Antonio Donatelli); Carol Teitel (Venus). Written by Sam Dann.

Margaret McClain, a young engineer, is assigned to an international project to save Venice from drowning. She abandons her conventional solutions when the goddess Venus suddenly appears in one of Venice's ancient plazas. Margaret becomes convinced the only way to save the stricken city is to build a temple to its namesake, Venus.

2476. "Transplant" (2/9/81; rebroadcast 3/19/81)

Cast: Marian Seldes (Celia Grey); Patricia Elliott (Janet Barclay); Earl Hammond (James Barclay); Robert Kaliban (Michael Grey). Written by G. Frederic Lewis.

Celia Grey and Janet Barclay become friends when their husbands undergo coronary bypass operations together. Comparing notes a few months later, the women agree: Both husbands have changed drastically since the operations, and for the worse. But they don't realize how much worse until Celia's husband tries to strangle her.

2477. "Breakout" (2/10/81; rebroadcast from 11/26/80)

2478. "The Shadow of a Killer" (2/11/81; rebroadcast 3/24/81)

Cast: Fred Gwynne (Mace Hacker); Bob Dryden (Perry); Ian Martin (Kazmeier); Joyce Gordon (Irene). Written by Sam Dann.

Mace Hacker, a tough cop in a television series, is confronted by a woman who begs him to solve an actual murder case. His producer thinks Mace has gone overboard in identifying with his television role. But then Mace always has felt a special obligation to his fans.

2479. "Sins of the Fathers" (2/12/81; rebroadcast from 1/2/81)

2480. "Behind the Blue Door" (2/13/81; rebroadcast 3/26/81)

Cast: Jada Rowland (Emily); George Furth (Paul); Russell Horton (Man); Anne Williams (Mother). Written by Elspeth Eric.

Emily knows she has a good man in Paul, but before she can say yes to his marriage proposal she decides to spend a month of freedom in Europe. When she meets a strange man in a romantic Parisian bistro, Emily thinks maybe the loyal Paul isn't the perfect man for her after all.

2481. "Troubled Waters" (2/16/81; rebroadcast 3/31/81)

Cast: Ralph Bell (Joe Carpenter); Robert Kaliban (Frank Perkins); Evelyn Juster (Alice Carpenter). Written by Sam Dann.

Once at the top of his craft, Joe Carpenter hasn't had an engineering assignment since the collapse of his bridge in India years ago. His wife, Alice, finds a job for him in the Amazon. Joe reluctantly accepts, only to endanger the job by delaying work on a key bridge: He tells Alice that before he can build it, he has to wait for a sign from the Great River God he angered in India.

2482. "The Tenth Life" (2/17/81; rebroadcast from 1/6/81)

2483. "Stand-In for Murder" (2/18/81; rebroadcast 4/2/81)

Cast: Paul Hecht (Dr. Gray Hall); Teri Keane (Dr. Jean Thurston); Carol Teitel (Phyllis Hall). Written by Ian Martin.

Dr. Gray Hall longs to leave his wife, Phyllis, in order to marry his attractive associate, Dr. Jean Thurston. His solution is to invent a clone of himself that will murder his wife. His horrified associate reveals Hall's scheme to Phyllis, who quickly makes her own plans for the second Dr. Hall.

2484. "In the Dark" (2/19/81; rebroadcast from 1/8/81)

2485. "The Gift House" (2/20/81; rebroadcast 4/7/81)

Cast: Joyce Gordon (Nancy Pryor); Paul Hecht (Ted Pryor); Ian Martin (Mr. Montgomery); Bob Dryden (Peter Prouty). Written by Ian Martin.

Recently fired Ted Pryor and his pregnant wife, Nancy, are delighted to find that Nancy has inherited a house from an unknown uncle. But when they visit the unexpected property, they find the big old house ransacked. Then the IRS shows up, ready to collect the missing thousands of dollars old Uncle Chris won at the track just before he died.

2486. "The Frog Prince" (2/23/81; rebroadcast 4/9/81)

Cast: Robert Kaliban (Paul Rigg); Patricia Elliott (Betsy Ring); Gordon Heath (Mr. Gabriel). Written by G. Frederic Lewis.

Betsy and Paul King are the sensations of the race circuit until Paul crashes into a wall. His body mends, but the recovery of his racing reflexes seems to be taking a long time—too much so for his wife, who yearns to be back on the track. So Paul calls on the couple's long-time Haitian mechanic, Mr. Gabriel, to work a little magic.

2487. "The Fountain of Truth" (2/24/81; rebroadcast from 1/20/81)

2488. "A God Named Henry" (2/25/81; rebroadcast 4/14/81)

Cast: Ralph Bell (Henry Clay Fitzsimmons); Joan Shay (Dora); Ray Owens (Bart). Written by Sam Dann.

Henry Clay Fitzsimmons is in trouble at both ends: His boss exploits him mercilessly, and his wife Dora won't stop nagging him for being such a doormat. But when Henry's sailboat is caught in a storm and beached in an uncharted cove, things change for the better. He encounters a primitive tribe that thinks he is a god and transforms him into a tiger.

2489. "The Final Mind" (2/26/81; rebroadcast from 1/22/81)

2490. "Love Me, Don't Leave Me" (2/27/81; rebroadcast 4/16/81)

Cast: John Beal (Ed Harvey); Teri Keane (Mary Harvey); Ian Martin (Tom Gorman); Evelyn Juster (Angie Gorman). Written by Ian Martin.

Ed Harvey still can't believe he's alone after so many wonderful years with his late wife, Mary. Their daughter, Angie, and her husband, Tom, urge Ed to carry out his wife's last request: to look for a new Mrs. Harvey. Ed agrees, and a computer dating service turns up a very mysterious candidate.

2491. "The Raft" (3/2/81; rebroadcast 4/21/81)

Cast: Norman Rose (Peter Ordway); Mandel Kramer (Ben Holderby); Marian Seldes (Mrs. Harper); Russell Horton (Frederick Walpole). Adapted by G. Frederic Lewis, based on a story by Jacques Futrelle.

Peter Ordway, a millionaire many times over, suddenly begins receiving strange messages that say only "one million dollars." His staff, thinking it's the work of a crackpot, is mystified when Ordway buys a gun. What they don't know is that Ordway made a million-dollar deal many years ago, and now someone wants to collect.

2492. "Small Money" (3/3/81; rebroadcast from 1/27/81)

2493. "Her Long Blonde Hair" (3/4/81; rebroadcast 4/23/81)

Cast: Lloyd Battista (Lieutenant Sikorsky); Martha Greenhouse (Magda Sikorsky); Arnold Moss (Benjamin). Written by Sam Dann.

Magda Sikorsky, wife of a police lieutenant, is fascinated by her course in Medieval English, taught by renowned professor Damon Mildood. But when one of the poems she is studying seems to resemble a murder case her husband can't solve, she decides to do a little sleuthing of her own and finds the professor may be more than a teacher.

2494. "The Vanishing Herd" (3/5/81; rebroadcast from 1/29/81)

2495. "Heads You Love, Tails You Die" (3/6/81; rebroadcast 4/28/81)

Cast: Court Benson (Count Stephan Morenyi); Evelyn Juster (Alma Collins); Marian Seldes (Countess Elena); Russell Horton (Harry Collins). Written by Sam Dann.

The world knows Countess Elena Morenyi as a gracious, talented European aristocrat. Only she and Count Stephan, the man who adopted her, know she once was Gertrude Schmitt, daughter of a murdered shopkeeper. Despite the luxury of her new life, the countess swears she'll avenge her father's death. But when the moment comes, she hesitates: She is in love with her father's killer.

2496. "Murder on the Space Shuttle" (3/9/81; rebroadcast 4/30/81)

Cast: Gordon Heath (Capt. Charlie C-17); Paul Hecht (Jack JB-4); Gilbert Mack (Dr. Maher); Valeka Gray (Jennifer J-13). Adapted by G. Frederic Lewis, based on the a story by Jacques Futrelle.

The death of a U.S. space shuttle communications officer may be murder, but Dr. Maher lacks the lab space to prove or refute it. Captain Charlie C-17 has no choice but to lock up his first officer, Jack JB-4, on suspicion of murder. But then another suspect turns up on the small spacecraft—a woman claiming to be the dead man's fiancée.

Notes: Jacques Futrelle was born in Georgia in 1875, of French Huguenot stock. Futrelle did a great deal of newspaper work while living in Richmond, Virginia, and was a theatrical stage manager for a short time. Futrelle eventually moved north, settling in the Boston area. At the time that he created The Thinking Machine (a fictional detective whose stories were often adapted on *Theater*) he was a member of the editorial staff of the *Boston American*, the local Hearst newspaper. Futrelle and his wife May, herself a writer, were on the *Titanic* on the fateful night of April 14-15, 1912. Futrelle pushed his wife into a lifeboat, but refused to get in himself, and went down with the ship. His stories rank as some of the best-remembered on *Theater*.

2497. "The Man Who Saw Martians" (3/10/81; rebroadcast from 2/2/81)

2498. "Last Act" (3/11/81; rebroadcast 5/5/81)

Cast: Court Benson (Commissioner McCloud); Carol Teitel (Mrs. Redfield); Earl Hammond (Joseph Barton); Bob Dryden (Peter Gaunt). Written by Elspeth Eric.

Barrister Peter Gaunt made his reputation with the flamboyant if unsuccessful defense of Joseph Barton, accused of strangling his wife. Yarmouth Police Commissioner McCloud also advanced his career with the case. But both men find their faith in the law shaken when, years later, another woman is found dead in the same strange circumstances as Mrs. Barton.

2499. "Who Is Jessica Worth?" (3/12/81; rebroadcast from 2/4/81)

2500. "The Heel of Achilles" (3/13/81; rebroadcast 5/7/81)

Cast: Arnold Moss (Roland K. Palfrey); Earl Hammond (Mr. Martin); Joyce Gordon (Marian Palfrey); Joan Shea (Dr. Pleskow). Written by Sam Dann.

At 60, Roland K. Palfrey had never made a mistake: His business acumen parlayed a small company into an international conglomerate. Then he met Marian—lovely, gracious and half his age—and married her on the spot. Was it a mistake to think the beautiful Marian would stay faithful to a man old enough to be her father?

2501. "Maiden Ladies" (3/16/81; rebroadcast 5/12/81)

Cast: Teri Keane (Emma Penrose); Michael Tolan (Paul Bennett); Carol Teitel (Janet Rouse); Russell Horton (Lieutenant Settles). Written by Sam Dann.

Police Lt. Settles dismisses Paul Bennett as a suspect in the murder of his business partner because the same gun was used to kill a young Eagle Scout, seeming to exonerate Bennett. But the dead youth's aunt, Emma Penrose, isn't convinced. Concerned the police aren't getting anywhere, she takes it upon herself to crack the case.

2502. "Is Venice Drowning?" (3/17/81; rebroadcast from 2/6/81)

2503. "Pretty Polly" (3/18/81; rebroadcast 5/14/81)

Cast: Tony Roberts (Joe Gaffney); Paul Hecht (Walter Evans); Evelyn Juster (Lieutenant Marker); Marian Seldes (Polly Simmons). Written by Sam Dann.

Joe Gaffney, an analyst in Walter Evans' securities firm, falls in love with a client's secretary, Polly Simmons, whom he has met only on the phone. Evans encourages his shy employee to date the woman, and Gaffney invents a fantasy romance to satisfy his boss. The only trouble is that the dream girl is found murdered one evening that Gaffney claimed to have been with her.

2504. "Transplant" (3/19/81; rebroadcast from 2/9/81)

2505. "The Million Dollar Scam" (3/20/81; rebroadcast 5/19/81)

Cast: Jennifer Harmon (June Henderson); Joan Shay (Mrs. Billie Worth); Ray Owens (Detective Conroy); Mandel Kramer (Stanley). Written by G. Frederic Lewis.

June Henderson had been thoroughly trained in the art of thievery by Stanley, ever since he found her as a promising pickpocket. June thinks she has the perfect mark for her first solo scam: the dotty widow of millionaire Fred Worth. But then June makes a fatal mistake. Old Fred Worth didn't get rich playing fair, and he taught his widow Billie every trick in the book.

2506. "The First Day of Eternity" (3/23/81; rebroadcast 5/21/81)

Cast: Norman Rose (Bob Stuart); Bob Dryden (Cardinal Dennison); Tracey Ellis (Miss Mott); Earl Hammond (Rupert Reston). Written by Sam Dann.

Bob Stuart, a ruthless capitalist, turns away the request of a childhood friend, now Cardinal Dennison, for a donation to the church. Stuart vows he'll find a way to live forever instead. All his meticulous research leads only to charlatans and fanatics. Then Stuart suffers a near–fatal heart attack, and discovers a totally unexpected way to eternal life.

2507. "The Shadow of a Killer" (3/24/81; rebroadcast from 2/11/81)

2508. "The Ghost-Grey Bat" (3/25/81; rebroadcast 5/26/81)

Cast: Don Scardino (Alec Grant); Jennifer Harman (Moira Grant); Bob Dryden (Dr. Koenig); Joan Shay (Frau Zauber). Written by Ian Martin.

Alec and Moira Grant seize an opportunity to trade their Manhattan apartment for a remote Austrian chalet for a summer. The gingerbread house–like cabin turns out to have everything they dreamed of, including a grandmotherly housekeeper, Frau Zauber. But a huge grey bat appears nightly in their bedroom, and it bears an uncanny resemblance to the kindly Frau.

2509. "Behind the Blue Door" (3/26/81; rebroadcast from 2/13/81)

2510. "Did I Say Murder?" (3/27/81; rebroadcast 5/28/81)

Cast: Tammy Grimes (Eleanor of Aquitane); Norman Rose (Thomas Beckett); Michael Wager (Henry II); Lloyd Battista (Louis VII). Written by Sam Dann, based on actual historical facts from English history.

Eleanor of Aquitane, the outstanding woman of her age, leaves her husband, Louis VII of France, for the love of Henry VII, king of England. But Eleanor senses trouble in her new English paradise when Henry introduces her to his new friend, Thomas Beckett. Henry disregards her warnings and is sorry years later when four of his liegemen kill the saintly Beckett, now archbishop of Canterbury, thinking they are acting on Henry's orders.

Notes: Himan Brown offered: "The enthusiasm we have created in an age group of 12–28 is remarkable, since that is a generation that never knew the excitement of a 'theater of the mind.' They absolutely are television children, born and raised to that medium, and never had to think about words as they were being entertained. And of course, all the older generation fondly remembers the fun of radio and have found they can recapture the joys of their youth through the dramas we present on *CBS Radio Theater*."

2511. "The Dead Come Alive" (3/30/81; rebroadcast 6/2/81)

Cast: Ralph Bell (Carey Windom); Marian Seldes (Martha Windom); Earl Hammond (Prof. Marvelli); Ray Owens (Lucas Kane). Written by Murray Burnett.

Professor Marvelli's claim to be able to raise the dead meets general skepticism in Vesalia. But when Marvelli's life is threatened by an anonymous "committee," Mayor Lucas Kane realizes someone in town must believe Marvelli's ability—perhaps the murderer of Peggy Thatcher, whose name she could reveal if brought back to life.

2512. "Troubled Waters" (3/31/81; rebroadcast from 2/16/81)

2513. "Down the Garden Path" (4/1/81; rebroadcast 6/4/81)

Cast: Gordon Gould (Niccolo Machiavelli); Mandel Kramer (Piero Soderini); Joyce Gordon (Caterina di Modena); Russell Horton (Alfredo Petrucci). Written by Sam Dann.

Duke Cesare Borgia, threatening to conquer Florence, wants to have killed a young Florentine who has been seeing the duke's mistress. So Machiavelli convinces Alfredo Petrucci to die in order to live forever as an immortal martyr to the city. But Florence governor Piero Soderini decides Petrucci must live, and now Machiavelli must turn a "hero" back into an ordinary citizen.

2514. "Stand-In for Murder" (4/2/81; rebroadcast from 2/18/81)

2515. "Somewhere Else" (4/3/81; rebroadcast 6/9/81)

Cast: Marian Seldes (Edith Nelson); Earl Hammond (Theriff); Lloyd Battista (Dr. Miller). Written by Sam Dann.

In Edith Nelson's increasingly vivid dream life, Theriff, a fiery Viking, wants to take her away to adventures unknown. Edith's psychiatrist, Dr. Miller, assumes the disturbing dreams stem from her anxiety about impending marriage to solid, if dull, Harold. But the strange dreams soon intrude on Edith's daily life, and she must choose from two compelling realities: Theriff or Harold.

2516. "The Gratitude of the Serpent" (4/6/81; rebroadcast 6/11/81)

Cast: Paul Hecht (Hernando Cortez); Ian Martin (Montezuma); Robert Kaliban (Francisco Jaramillio); Evelyn Juster (Marina). Written by Sam Dann.

Marina, sold into slavery by her father to avoid certain death as a human sacrifice to Aztec gods, learns Spanish and becomes the mistress of a renegade soldier named Cortez. Cortez's blond hair and fire-breathing metal tubes convince the innocent Marina that he is really the god Quetzalcoatl, and she leads him straight to Montezuma's fabled capital.

2517. "The Gift House" (4/7/81; rebroadcast from 2/20/81)

2518. "The Doll" (4/8/81; rebroadcast 6/30/81)

Cast: Kristoffer Tabori (Bob); Russell Horton (Don); Joan Beal (Dad); Teri Keane (Mom). Written by Elspeth Eric.

Identical twins, Bob and Don, share a mysterious telepathic link that tells one exactly what the other is thinking. On the anniversary of their younger sister's death, Don disappears, and for the first time Bob has to survive as an individual.

2519. "The Frog Prince" (4/9/81; rebroadcast from 2/23/81)

2520. "The Empty Coffin" (4/10/81; rebroadcast 7/2/81)

Cast: Tony Roberts (Hal Brooks); Court Benson (Ross Luddington); Carol Teitel (Ethel Brooks); Gordon Gould (Ralph Nelson). Written by Roy Winsor.

Ethel Brooks has been troubled right into adulthood by vivid dreams of England, her home before she was adopted by an American couple after World War II. Then one day, she receives a letter from England naming her heiress to an estate. Her strange dreams now carry a new threat.

2521. "Stampede" (4/13/81; rebroadcast 7/7/81)

Cast: Jennifer Harmon (Judith Ann Royce); Court Benson (Colonel Royce); Lloyd Battista (Edward Malden); Ian Martin (Chet Holmes). Written by Ian Martin.

Colonel Royce returns to Texas from a visit to the Wyoming Territory, convinced he can drive cattle through the desert and past Indians, to the lush grasslands of the north. With the aid of his spirited daughter, Judith Ann, and a quiet mysterious Easterner, he embarks on his scheme to drive 2,500 longhorns 3,000 miles through hostile territory.

Notes: This episode was originally titled "Death Trail" before being changed to "Stampede" during the recording rehearsals.

2522. "A God Named Henry" (4/14/81; rebroadcast from 2/25/81)

2523. "The Fatal $50,000" (4/15/81; rebroadcast 7/9/81)

Cast: Mandel Kramer (Robert Arthur Moresby); Earl Hammond (Russ Haley); Marian Seldes (Rita Moresby). Written by Sam Dann.

Robert Arthur Moresby, a businessman accustomed to having his way, fires Russ Haley for embezzling $50,000. Soon after Haley commits suicide. Moresby's wife Rita turns against him and he begins to receive phone calls from the dead Haley that no one else can hear.

2524. "Love Me, Don't Leave Me" (4/16/81; rebroadcast from 2/27/81)

2525. "But with Blood" (4/17/81; rebroadcast 7/14/81)

Cast: Fred Gwynne (John Brown); Teri Keane (Mary Anne Brown); Bob Dryden (John Unseld); Russell Horton (Oliver Brown). Written by James Agate, Jr., based on an historical incident.

A God-fearing Bible-quoting abolitionist, John Brown becomes convinced he can end slavery in the United States. In June 1859, Brown decides to go underground. He changes his name and, together with his family and an army of a dozen men, begins plotting an attack on the U.S. government that leads to a deadly showdown at the federal munitions stronghold in Harper's Ferry, West Virginia.

2526. "The Power of Ode" (4/20/81; rebroadcast 7/16/81)

Cast: Kristoffer Tabori (Michael Lipton); Jada Rowland (Lorna Deering); Norman Rose (Hans von Drucker); Robert Kaliban (Frank Cabot). Written by Elspeth Eric.

Lorna Deering, a quiet 20-year-old with an aversion to bright lights, is gently courted by Michael Lipton, who finds her reticence charming. But he finds she also is being pursued by Frank Cabot, his college buddy, plus an enigmatic older man who espouses a mysterious 19th century philosophy.

2527. "The Raft" (4/21/81; rebroadcast from 3/2/81)

2528. "The Terrifying Gift" (4/22/81; rebroadcast 7/21/81)

Cast: Roberta Maxwell (Martha Herriot); Carol Teitel (Signora Buonafortuna); Ian Martin (Dr. Phillips); Russell Horton (Don Herriot). Written by Ian Martin.

Martha Herriot, entering a fortuneteller's parlor on a lark, is greeted by the owner as her long-lost granddaughter. After telling a nonplused Martha she now will have the ability to tell the future the old woman abruptly dies. Martha finds her new power so terrifying she threatens to kill herself to get rid of the rare talent.

Notes: Ian Martin, one of the most prolific writers and actors for *Theater*, died of a heart attack during the week of this episode's rebroadcast on July 21, 1981, at his Westport, Connecticut, home. Himan Brown, creator, director and executive producer of the series, called Martin's death "a sad loss to the creativity of *Theater*." Martin had written more than 250 dramas and acted in some 500 episodes during the eight years of *Theater* broadcasts on the *CBS Radio Network*. Brown added: "He was a gifted writer for the arts, including films, novels, television and magazines. But he always felt that radio was a special medium, and it was the one he most enjoyed writing for. Some of Ian's adaptations of the classics are among the best ever done for *Theater*."

2529. "Her Long Blonde Hair" (4/23/81; rebroadcast from 3/4/81)

2530. "The Long Blue Line" (4/24/81; rebroadcast 7/28/81)

Cast: Mandel Kramer (Inspector O'Neill); Earl Hammond (Lieutenant O'Neill); Marian Seldes (Leda Jones). Written by Sam Dann.

Lieutenant Terence O'Neill, the latest in 100 years of O'Neill policemen, is assigned to the recently reopened case of a murdered Broadway actor, previously worked on by his father, Inspector O'Neill. As the younger O'Neill reconstructs the past, he begins to realize his father may have had more than a professional interest in the case.

2531. "Big Momma" (4/27/81; rebroadcast 7/30/81)

Cast: Paul Hecht (Harry Simmons); Joan Shay (Sarajean Crawley); Earl Hammond (P. Monroe Hastings); Evelyn Juster (Trisha MacDowell). Written by Sam Dann.

Harry Simmons refuses to allow a large company to locate in the small community he serves as town planner. Suddenly his cherished manuscript, rejected 20 times before, is accepted by the country's most prestigious publisher. Its successful release makes him a happy celebrity until he discovers that the publisher, a talk-show hostess and famous reviewer all work for the company he spurned: Big Momma.

2532. "Heads You Love, Tails You Die" (4/28/81; rebroadcast from 3/6/81)

2533. "The Man of Two Centuries" (4/29/81; rebroadcast 8/4/81)

Cast: Len Cariou (Jack Carter); Diana Kirkwood (Mary Carter); Lloyd Battista (Donnaconna); Bob Dryden (P. C. Jones). Written by James Agate, Jr.

Jack Carter, researching colonial Canadian history on a houseboat on the St. Lawrence River while his wife Mary has an artist's studio on the dock, befriends a full-blooded Huron, Donnaconna. Donnaconna's detailed knowledge of Indian culture is invaluable to Carter. Then, the Huron offers to share the source of his extraordinary information by taking Carter 300 years back through time.

Notes: Len Cariou has appeared in numerous films including *Dying Up the Streets* (1976), *The Four Seasons* (1981), *Who'll Save Our Children?* (1982), *The Lady in White* (1988), and *Witness to the Execution* (1994).

2534. "Murder on the Space Shuttle" (4/30/81; rebroadcast from 3/9/81)

2535. "The Voices" (5/1/81; rebroadcast 8/6/81)

Cast: Amanda Plummer (Jeanne); Norman Rose (Pierre Cauchon); Earl Hammond (Hans). Written by G. Frederic Lewis.

Pierre Cauchon, collaborating with the Nazi occupation forces during World War II, is obsessed by a young woman, Jeanne, who is brought in for interrogation after hiding an American soldier on her farm in Domremy. Cauchon is

convinced the voices she speaks of hearing—Catherine, Margaret and Michael—
are Resistance aliases. He orders her held and tortured, if necessary, until she
reveals her allies in the Resistance.

2536. "Garden of the Moon" (5/4/81; rebroadcast 8/11/81)

Cast: Kim Hunter (Yolanda Westerville); Paul Hecht (Bill Westerville); Ralph
Bell (Dr. Lunestra); Evelyn Juster (Roxy). Written by Bob Juhren.

Yolanda Westerville finds her frayed nerves pleasantly restored by a skin cream
available only at a new health store, Garden of the Moon. The proprietor, Dr.
Lunestra, claims his products derive their power from moonlight. Westerville's
chemists say this is impossible, but she still can't resist taking up Lunestra's offer
to visit the New Hampshire farm where the products are made.

2537. "Last Act" (5/5/81; rebroadcast from 3/11/81)

2538. "The Apparition" (5/6/81; rebroadcast 8/12/81)

Cast: Kristoffer Tabori (Danny Mercer); Marian Seldes (Mrs. Mercer); Bob
Dryden (Warden Davola); Lloyd Battista (Officer Quinn). Written by Elspeth
Eric.

Danny Mercer is in prison because his father turned him in for check forgery.
Now, Danny is convinced his stern father will die before he completes his sentence, to the increasing alarm of his mother and Warden Davola. Sniffles eventually kill his father, but when the Warden attempts to tell the boy, Danny already
seems to know.

2539. "The Heel of Achilles" (5/7/81; rebroadcast from 3/13/81)

2540. "Is the Doctor In?" (5/8/81; rebroadcast 8/13/81)

Cast: Tony Roberts (Dr. Harold Smiley); Joyce Gordon (Suann); Ray Owens
(Pop Waldo). Written by Sam Dann.

Dr. Harold Smiley is ready to go home from his office when three men force
their way into his office. Smiley recognizes Pop Waldo, who, with the aid of two
cohorts, forces Smiley to operate on an abdominal wound. By some miracle, the
improvised surgery is a success, But Waldo isn't satisfied. The gangster wants to
turn himself in, and he wants Smiley's help to do it.

2541. "End of a Queen" (5/11/81; rebroadcast 8/18/81)

Cast: Tammy Grimes (Marie Antoinette); Norman Rose (Prosecutor
Georges); Robert Kaliban (de Busne); Russell Horton (Louis XVI). Written by
James Agate, Jr., based on documented historical events.

Marie Antoinette, despised by the French people for her extravagance and
political meddling, is brought to trial in 1793 at the height of the French Revolution. Guarded by sympathetic lieutenant de Busne, she faces the wrath of Prosecutor Georges, a man she once sentenced to exile for a trifle. She accepts the inevitable

outcome with dignity, or is it vindictiveness that refuses to show the French people a cringing queen?

2542. "Maiden Ladies" (5/12/81; rebroadcast from 3/16/81)

2543. "Diogenes, Inc." (5/13/81; rebroadcast 8/19/81)

Cast: Jack Grimes (Alfredo Pinto); Ray Owens (Max Maximilian); Court Benson (Chief Maloney); Evelyn Juster (Selma Sylvester). Adapted by James Agate, Jr., based on a story by Jacques Futrelle.

Alfredo Pinto, a pint-sized clown, and Selma Sylvester, the "Lady Hercules," are out of work when their show burns down. The clever Alfredo decides to become a private eye and invites Selma to join him in the venture Diogenes, Inc. Then police chief Maloney offers the pair their first case: to investigate their former boss.

2544. "Pretty Polly" (5/14/81; rebroadcast from 3/18/81)

2545. "Cold Comfort" (5/15/81; rebroadcast 8/20/81)

Cast: Bob Dryden (Amos Crandall); Carol Teitel (Emily Crandall); Earl Hammond (Mr. Trent). Written by Sam Dann.

Amos Crandall, an enemy collaborator as a POW in Korea, has been blackmailed ever since into working with a nest of spies. His request to retire is denied by the group's leader, Mr. Trent. But when the mild-mannered optometrist makes a mistake that could expose them all, he inadvertently stumbles on a chance to finally free himself.

2546. "A Shocking Affair" (5/18/81; rebroadcast 8/25/81)

Cast: Joseph Silver (Mill Fram); Patricia Elliott (Judy Fuller); Michael Wager (Jerry Fuller); Ian Martin (El Generaliffe). Written by Ian Martin.

Killer-for-hire Mill Fram finds Judy and Jerry Fuller's vacant Fifth Avenue apartment offers the perfect vantage point from which to assassinate a Central American dictator staying in New York. But the young couple's unexpected return from a canceled ocean cruise threatens Fram's set-up and starts a battle of wits between a mild general practitioner and a professional murderer.

Notes: Joe Silver has appeared in numerous films including *The Apprenticeship of Duddly Kravitz* (1974), *Rabid* (1977), *The Gig* (1985), *Switching Channels* (1988), and *Mr. Nice Guy* (1986).

2547. "The Million Dollar Scam" (5/19/81; rebroadcast from 3/20/81)

2548. "Insomnia" (5/20/81; rebroadcast 8/26/81)

Cast: Teri Keane (Anita Dwyer); Carol Teitel (Sheila Corey); Russell Horton (Bill Dwyer). Written by Elspeth Eric.

Anita Dwyer, left alone for the first time in many years when her husband moves out to be with a younger woman, begins to suffer extreme insomnia. Her morbid anxieties increase despite all sorts of cures suggested by her neighbor and son. She even buys a canary to keep her company, but it soon dies under very mysterious circumstances.

Notes: "Working in New York City these past eight years has been very exhilarating for me because it is the heart of theater," stated Himan Brown. "Hardly any Broadway star has turned down a role in the series. They all want to do radio. As actress Tammy Grimes—a prolific performer on *Theater*—stressed: 'It's instant acting.' Radio drama is the most potent form of theater I know. It is an art form, a means of communication and, above all else, entertainment. It gives you an experience no other form of theater—movies and television included—can duplicate."

2549. "The First Day of Eternity" (5/21/81; rebroadcast from 3/23/81)

2550. "The Headhunters" (5/22/81; rebroadcast 8/27/81)

Cast: Len Cariou (Stearns); Earl Hammond (Carver); Tracey Ellis (Erna Stearns); Paul Tripp (Robert). Written by Sam Dann.

Erna Stearns is a reactionary in the year 2100: She prefers natural food and still believes in true love. When her fiancé abruptly cancels their engagement, she asks her father, a professional "changer" who alters criminal personalities into more acceptable characters, to investigate. He discovers a conspiracy that could be reshaping society.

2551. "The Innocent Face" (5/25/81; rebroadcast 9/1/81)

Cast: Roberta Maxwell (Wanda Beasley); Ian Martin (Hartley Sanders); Evelyn Juster (Sherry); Paul Hecht (Eugene Harper). Written by Victoria Dann.

Wanda Beasley, late of Pulaski Pond, Arkansas, labored in the shipping department of a Southern California firm for just two weeks until Vice President Hartley Sanders, impressed by her innocent good looks, made her his receptionist. Eugene Harper also is taken by her sweet face. In fact, on their first date, a drive to Tiajuana, he insists that *she* take a special piòata across the American border.

2552. "The Ghost-Grey Bat" (5/26/81; rebroadcast from 3/25/81)

2553. "Little Richard" (5/27/81; rebroadcast 9/2/81)

Cast: Kristoffer Tabori (Richard Mell); Joan Shea (Frau Brunehilda); Bernard Grant (Inspector); Bob Dryden (Mayor). Written by Sam Dann.

Richard Mell, just released from prison for forging an insignificant check in the name of the mayor's father-in-law, is sent straight back to jail because the corrupt inspector needed to arrest a surrogate armed robber. Free again, he's convinced by his friend Frau Brunehilda to rob the mayor's accumulated bribe money from a secret safe.

2554. "Did I Say Murder?" (5/28/81; rebroadcast from 3/27/81)

2555. "Out of the Past" (5/29/81; rebroadcast 9/3/81)

Cast: Paul Hecht (Barry Jordan); Mandel Kramer (Duke); Evelyn Juster (Meg Jordan); Russell Horton (Lieutenant Sloan). Written by Ian Martin.

Barry Jordan, who has been supported by his wife Meg, a lawyer, is asked by a television station to draw sketches during a trial of three men accused of armed robbery and murder. The trial was set up to draw out the missing fourth man in the crime and, during a recess, Jordan idly begins to sketch the crowd, which contains a frighteningly familiar face.

2556. "The Runaway General" (6/1/81; rebroadcast 9/8/81)

Cast: Norman Rose (Henri Giraud); Ian Martin (Lieutenant Georges Martin); Earl Hammond (Captain Von Meist); Tudi Wiggens (Mrs. Giraud). Written by G. Frederic Lewis.

Henri Giraud escaped from a German prison in World War I. Now 62 and commander of the French Army, he's captured again. But this time, he is inside one of Germany's fiercest prisons and on a steep cliff 720 feet above the raging Elbe River.

2557. "The Dead Come Alive" (6/2/81; rebroadcast from 3/30/81)

2558. "The Cat's Paw" (6/3/81; rebroadcast 9/9/81)

Cast: Larry Haines (Dr. Samuel Jeffreys); Robert Kaliban (Ross Parker); Joan Shay (Edith Duncan); Marian Seldes (Alfreda Chase). Written by Roy Winsor.

Ross Parker asks his top agent to play the role of Dr. Samuel Jeffreys, the nation's leading nuclear physicist, as a lure to draw out a double agent in the national security system. There's just one catch: If captured, will the ersatz Jeffreys be able to fake his way through a certain dose of sodium pentothal?

2559. "Down the Garden Path" (6/4/81; rebroadcast from 4/1/81)

2560. "Matched Pair for Murder" (6/5/81; rebroadcast 9/10/81)

Cast: Arnold Moss (Judge Landsdowne); Kristoffer Tabori (Joe Talley); Bernard Grant (Marvin Stroud); Evelyn Juster (Marietta Winslow). Written by Sam Dann.

Judge Marshall Taney Landsdowne believes Marietta Winslow when she tells him her fiancé, Joe Talley, did not commit the murder he's been charged with. So Landsdowne directs the jury to a verdict of innocent, then discovers new evidence showing Talley's guilt. The only problem: Talley is protected by the rule of double jeopardy.

2561. "Stranded" (6/8/81; rebroadcast 9/15/81)

Cast: Gordon Gould (Major Raymin); Marian Seldes (Dr. Reya); Bernard Grant (Colonel Perri). Written by Victoria Dann.

Colonel Perri and Major Raymin, on the last leg of an extended space mission, are forced to crashland on an alien planet when their spacecraft is gutted during a meteor storm. They are captured by beings surprisingly similar to themselves and well cared for, until Raymin realizes why.

2562. "Somewhere Else" (6/9/81; rebroadcast from 4/3/81)

2563. "Second Look at Murder" (6/10/81; rebroadcast 9/16/81)

Cast: Roberta Maxwell (Lizzie Borden); Russell Horton (John Howard); Bob Dryden (Sergeant McCauley); Jada Rowland (Louisa). Written by G. Frederic Lewis.

When John Howard, a Boston newspaper reporter, discovers a rusty hatchet blade in the woods outside Fall River, Massachusetts, he decides to tackle the sensational 19th-century Lizzie Borden murder case. He comes up with a new scenario for the still-unsolved murders of Andrew and Abby Borden, and finds he may have more than one relative who played a role in the famous case.

2564. "The Gratitude of the Serpent" (6/11/81; rebroadcast from 4/6/81)

2565. "When in Rome" (6/12/81; rebroadcast 9/17/81)

Cast: Fred Gwynne (Henry Cahill); Joan Shea (Livy Cahill); Ian Martin (King Zulan); Ray Owens (Count Rosporo). Written by Sam Dann.

Henry Cahill wins an ambassador's post to the minute kingdom of Lavaria because his millions helped elect President Hayes. The blunt, enterprising Cahill throws himself into his new assignment. He soon discovers the queen is in love with her minister, who wants Europe in war.

2566. "Two's a Crowd" (6/15/81; rebroadcast 9/22/81)

Cast: Earl Hammond (Len Brock); Mandel Kramer (Phil Henderson); Evelyn Juster (Mrs. Henderson). Written by Ian Martin.

Len Brock is about to hold up a New York pharmacy when he realizes the proprietor is a mirror image of himself. So instead of stealing the money he needs to pay his bookie, he decides to hit up his newly discovered wealthy twin brother, Phil Henderson, for a loan. The only problem is that Phil has been dabbling in a few illegalities of his own.

2567. "The Young Die Good" (6/16/81; rebroadcast from 7/4/74)

Cast: Patricia Elliott (Lisa Bissonette); Carol Teitel (Clarice Wenderby); Ira Lewis (Ray Bissonette); Dan Ocko (Cooper). Written by Murray Burnett.

Lisa Bissonette, just married, meets the lady next door, Clarice Wenderby, a woman of 38. Lisa's husband, Ray, also meets her. But this time she's Clarissa, 38, beautiful and beguiling. Clarice urges Lisa to move away Clarissa urges Ray to take her out. The Bissonettes have their first marital spat which can be resolved only if they see Clarice and Clarissa together, but for some reason they never are.

2568. "The Final Step" (6/17/81; rebroadcast 9/23/81)

Cast: Marian Seldes (Naomi Berger); Earl Hammond (Karl Durer); Roberta Maxwell (Ann Durer); Norman Rose (Jacob Berger). Written by G. Frederic Lewis.

Naomi Berger, who lived through Auschwitz, has made a pact with her husband Jacob to kill Dr. Karl Durer, the man whose experiments killed her parents and sister. Her 20-year search finds Durer in a small New Jersey town. But she discovers her resolve may not be as strong as her conscience.

2569. "Having a Horrible Time" (6/18/81; rebroadcast from 8/21/74)

Cast: Lynn Lorring (Amy Hastings); Ralph Bell (Ralph Cooke); Mandel Kramer (Fred Russell); Frances Sternhagen (Lois Wilson); Nat Polen (George Smith). Written by Bob Juhren.

A vacation is in order for Amy Hastings, after turning in the mobster who handled most of the city's illegal drugs. But when Amy and her friend Lois arrive at a singles resort they are watched by two men (one, Ralph Cooke, a police detective the other, unknown, a mobster out to murder Amy). So many men approach Amy that it's impossible to know which of them is the would-be murderer, until Ralph realizes that she's in more imminent danger than anyone thought.

2570. "Henrietta's Revenge" (6/19/81; rebroadcast 9/24/81)

Cast: Patricia Elliott (Henrietta Tufts); Joyce Gordon (Jill Kramer); Mandel Kramer (Sergio Varese); Robert Kaliban (Tom Hayward). Written by James Agate, Jr.

Henrietta Tufts, on her way to the top of a Detroit car company, falls in love with Sergio Varese during a three-week Caribbean cruise. The dashing Brazilian passes himself off as a wealthy shipping magnate, when in reality he just needs a rich woman to pay off his gambling debts. Love is blind, but Henrietta's secretary isn't, and his fiancée has just made detective sergeant in the local police force.

2571. "The Legend of Alexander, Part One: Courage"
(6/22/81; rebroadcast from 1/12/81)

2572. "The Legend of Alexander, Part Two: Assassination"
(6/23/81; rebroadcast from 1/13/81)

2573. "The Legend of Alexander, Part Three: Divide and Conquer" (6/24/81; rebroadcast from 1/14/81)

2574. "The Legend of Alexander, Part Four: The Oracle"
(6/25/81; rebroadcast from 1/15/81)

2575. "The Legend of Alexander, Part Five: The Legend Begins" (6/26/81; rebroadcast from 1/16/81)

2576. "Waking and Sleeping" (6/29/81; rebroadcast 9/29/81)

Cast: Michael Tolan (Man); Teri Keane (Woman); Amanda Plummer (Girl); Bob Dryden (Servant). Written by Elspeth Eric.

A 60-year-old businessman takes up residence in tiny Ungerville to try to restore some meaning to a life that now seems empty to him. But his cherished solitude is broken by a chance remark to a young girl. His comment convinces the girl that he is a god, and Ungerville residents want to ride him out of town.

2577. "The Doll" (6/30/81; rebroadcast from 4/8/81)

2578. "The Fourth Bullet" (7/1/81; rebroadcast 9/30/81)

Cast: Bernard Grant (Humbert Ferrand); Russell Horton (Hector Berlioz); Ian Martin (The Colonel); Evelyn Juster (Camille Moke). Written by Sam Dann.

They dreamed that she would play the beautiful music he composed for her, but Camille Moke breaks her engagement to volatile romantic Hector Berlioz. Berlioz draws his close friend, Humbert Ferrand, into a wild scheme to kill Camille, her new fiancé and her scheming mother. There is only one flaw in Berlioz's plan: The fourth bullet he has reserved to kill himself.

2579. "The Empty Coffin" (7/2/81; rebroadcast from 4/10/81)

2580. "A Second Chance" (7/3/81; rebroadcast 10/1/91)

Cast: Paul Hecht (George Carswell); Robert Kaliban (Dr. Hall); Joan Shea (Grace Marlin); Marian Seldes (Janet Carswell). Written by Bob Juhren.

George Carswell, who went into the hospital unconscious, wakes claiming he is Henry Marlin, a St. Louis architect. Skeptical doctors think Carswell suffered brain damage, but a phone call to St. Louis proves a Henry Marlin died three days earlier. Marlin decides to use his new insight to warn of a dangerous flaw in one of his firm's buildings, but Carswell's feeble body may not hold out.

2581. "My Good Name" (7/6/81; rebroadcast 10/6/81)

Cast: Tammy Grimes (Helen Harper); Russell Horton (Waldo Trent); Earl Hammond (Jerry Kenwood). Written by Sam Dann.

Waldo Trent was at the top of the fashion world when he was found shot to death in his Manhattan apartment, apparently having surprised a burglar. But reporter Helen Harper, a friend of Waldo's since he was an unknown artist, suspects something else. The only problem is finding some evidence to support her instinct.

2582. "Stampede" (7/7/81; rebroadcast from 4/13/81)

2583. "Death and the Dreamer" (7/8/81; rebroadcast 10/7/81)

Cast: Mandel Kramer (Garibaldi); Ian Martin (Antonio Meucci); Evelyn Juster (Leonora Meucci). Written by Sam Dann.

With his army defeated, Garibaldi is working in a Staten Island candle factory, convinced his dream of leading his country will be realized by someone else. His employer, Antonio Meucci, notices Garibaldi's strange trips to the docks every morning, seeking a berth on a sailing ship. But when he refuses to admit to these visits, the Meucci family fears the great general is losing his mind.

2584. "The Fatal $50,000" (7/9/81; rebroadcast from 4/15/81)

2585. "A Man of Honor" (7/10/81; rebroadcast 10/8/81)

Cast: John Beal (Arthur); Teri Keane (Emma); Bernard Grant (Paul); Patricia Elliott (Enid). Written by Elspeth Eric.

One week from receiving the prestigious Braithwaite Award for his latest novel, Arthur decides to spend an hour alone after a beautiful day picnicking with his family. But when his wife calls him into the house, he is suddenly and radically different, and says he will refuse to accept his latest honor.

2586. "The Good Shepherds" (7/13/81; rebroadcast 10/13/81)

Cast: Bob Dryden (Msgr. Jean Auguste); Russell Horton (Reverend Corot); Evelyn Juster (Nurse Anne-Marie); Ray Owens (Father Rodier). Written by G. Frederic Lewis.

When Msgr. Jean-Auguste's Sunday Mass is shattered by Nazi gunfire, the elderly curate immediately makes plans to hide the children whose parents died in the massacre. His work grows to include a network of doctors, farmers and the clergy of France that hides children of those rounded up for concentration camps. Then Jean-Auguste himself is captured, and his friends fear the old man will break under SS pressure.

2587. "But with Blood" (7/14/81; rebroadcast from 4/17/81)

2588. "Alice" (7/15/81; rebroadcast 10/14/81)

Cast: Marian Hailey (ALICE); Court Benson (MacIntosh); Bernard Grant (KGB Agent). Written by G. Frederic Lewis.

Harold Haberman turns his chess-playing computer into a full-scale robot on a dare from his journalist friend MacIntosh. His invention, the Artificial, Life-designed, Integrated Circuit Extender, or ALICE, catapults Haberman into national prominence because, as it turns out, ALICE has some friends in very high places.

2589. "The Power of Ode" (7/16/81; rebroadcast from 4/20/81)

2590. "Pie in the Sky" (7/17/81; rebroadcast 10/15/81)

Cast: Robert Kaliban (Luther Temple); Teri Keane (Aggie Temple); Bernard Grant (Professor Tonneau). Written by Sam Dann.

Luther Temple's plan to put his wife's inheritance in the bank at a comfortable

5 percent interest runs into a snag when he meets Professor Tonneau. The professor's prediction of millions to be made in the new fields of automobiles and airplanes tempts Temple until he has a vision of what his potential wealth could do to his happy marriage.

2591. "The Eye of the Idol" (7/20/81; rebroadcast 10/20/81)

Cast: Tony Roberts (Jack Farnsworth); Earl Hammond (Dunnoo); Roberta Maxwell (Penelope). Written by Sam Dann.

Jack Farnsworth has nothing but pawn tickets to show for his addiction to gambling. His declining fortunes break up his engagement. In desperation, Farnsworth's faithful servant Dunnoo seeks out a witch doctor to turn his master's fate around. She agrees, but not before warning Farnsworth of the consequences of never losing a bet.

2592. "The Terrifying Gift" (7/21/81; rebroadcast from 4/22/81)

2593. "Toy Death" (7/22/81; rebroadcast 10/21/81)

Cast: Patricia Elliott (Isabella Trevelyan); Court Benson (Captain Hugh Trevelyan); Marian Seldes (Mrs. Fowler); Kristoffer Tabori (Tony Parker). Adapted by James Agate, Jr., based on the short story *The Doll* by Algernon Blackwood.

As Captain Hugh Trevelyan records his memoirs with the help of his secretary, Tony Parker, strange things are happening to his daughter Isabella. First she can't be parted from her collection of "dollies." Then she believes she can talk to her long-dead mother. But when a turbaned gentleman gives her a strange straw doll, her mysterious behavior takes a lethal turn.

2594. "Help Somebody" (7/23/81; rebroadcast from 8/18/75)

Cast: William Redfield (Anthony Price); Danny Ocko (Leong Long); Joan Shay (Claudia Crisi); Court Benson (Clark McKay). Written by Elspeth Eric.

Anthony Price, an unsuccessful writer living in Rome, finds his world changed when his wealthy father dies and leaves his entire inheritance to his only son. With all the money he can spend, a novel that's suddenly very popular, and the beautiful woman he desires, Anthony has everything he thought he wanted, but he's inexplicably unhappy. Not until he meets a nameless girl, an old man, and a mongrel dog can he begin living again.

2595. "Once a Thief" (7/24/81; rebroadcast 10/22/81)

Cast: Fred Gwynne (Frank Ellsworth); Bernard Grant (Morton Sanford); Bob Dryden (Dick Van Walken); Joan Shay (Bridget Ellsworth). Written by Sam Dann.

Frank Ellsworth, an ex-cop in charge of security for a large corporation, suspects trouble when he is introduced to Morton Sanford, the firm's new efficiency expert: whom arrested years before for stealing, but Sanford's money squelched the incident. Ellsworth isn't surprised when Morton's analysis finds his job superfluous. He is convinced Morton plans a major theft, but everyone thinks the old man is bitter over his forced retirement.

2596. "The Silver Medal" (7/27/81; rebroadcast 10/30/81)

Cast: Russell Horton (Charles West); Roberta Maxwell (Theodora West); Earl Hammond (Dr. Carl Cheney). Written by James Agate, Jr.

New Englander Charles West takes his Mississippi-born wife Theodora to a cozy lodge at the base of a glacier. A little champagne and a charming scientist, Dr. Carl Cheney, convince West and his acrophobic wife to venture up to the glacier by cable car. But the Wests' marriage looks like it is going to take a dangerous turn when the car stops in midair, dangling thousands of feet over the mountainside.

2597. "The Long Blue Line" (7/28/81; rebroadcast from 4/24/81)

2598. "Postage Due" (7/29/81; rebroadcast 10/27/81)

Cast: Ralph Bell (George MacCreedy); Teri Keane (Martha MacCreedy); Ian Martin (Postmaster); Robert Kaliban (Elroy Winters). Written by Douglas Dempsey.

When mailman George MacCreedy appears at a house with a World War II–vintage letter, he finds the addressee's brother surprisingly eager to get his hands on it. At the sender's posh mansion, an old servant would only be too happy to take the missive. George decides to turn it over to the dead letter office, but a late night phone call advises him otherwise.

2599. "Big Momma" (7/30/81; rebroadcast from 4/27/81)

2600. "A Penny for Your Thoughts" (7/31/81; rebroadcast 10/28/81)

Cast: Michael Tolan (Jack Wilshire); Bernard Grant (Potter); Marian Seldes (Penthesilea Cummings); Mandel Kramer (Bill Cummings). Written by Sam Dann.

When Penthesilea Cummings' book of poetry soars to the top of the charts, the media clamor for more information about the enigmatic author. But "Penny" will see only Pulitzer Prize–winning reporter Jack Wilshire. No sooner does he arrive at her retreat than she tells him her husband plans to kill her, and Bill Cummings cheerfully admits she's right.

2601. "Honor Among Thieves" (8/3/81; rebroadcast 11/3/81)

Cast: Fred Gwynne (Teach); Ian Martin (Wally); Evelyn Juster (Sarah); Earl Hammond (Sweets). Written by Ian Martin.

Septuagenarians Teach and Sweets, tired of the desperation of living from pension check to pension check, convince Wally to go along with their plan to rob a bank. The three cronies miraculously make off with the loot. But Wally's wife Sarah sees them counting it and wants to give it back. The gang agrees and now has to pull off the robbery in reverse.

2602. "The Man of Two Centuries" (8/4/81; rebroadcast from 4/29/81)

2603. "The Orphaned Heart" (8/5/81; rebroadcast 11/4/81)

Cast: Roberta Maxwell (Susan Martin); Teri Keane (Aunt Tim); Bob Dryden (Dr. Levy); Gordon Gould (David Clark). Written by Nancy Moore.

Susan Martin remains paralyzed from a car accident caused by her new husband, Dr. David Clark. Guilt—Susan's for forcing the marriage, and David's for causing the accident—makes their marriage a living nightmare. So Susan coerces her Aunt Tim to arrange her "death" to find out how much David really loves her.

2604. "The Voices" (8/6/81; rebroadcast from 5/1/81)

2605. "Let No Man Put Asunder" (8/7/81; rebroadcast 11/5/81)

Cast: Michael Wager (Paul Raymond); Russell Horton (Mark Young); Joyce Gordon (Janice). Written by James Agate, Jr.

Paul Raymond, imprisoned on suspicion of killing his wife, has spent the last ten New Year's Eves with best friend Mark Young, and this one is no different. Despite Raymond's seeming lack of remorse about his wife's death in a fire, Young believes his old college roommate is innocent in her death, but a murderer nonetheless.

2606. "Hostage to Terror" (8/10/81; rebroadcast 11/10/81)

Cast: Roberta Maxwell (Fran Warren); Ian Martin (Achmed); Earl Hammond (Rick Warren). Written by Ian Martin.

Fran and Rick Warren think Israel may be a letdown after the wonders of Egypt and beauty of Jordan. But a sudden knock on the hotel door insures they'll have an exciting visit: An Arab plans to hold them hostage so he can deliver a bomb to a traitor in the Israeli government.

2607. "Garden of the Moon" (8/11/81; rebroadcast from 5/4/81)

2608. "The Apparition" (8/12/81; rebroadcast from 5/6/81)

2609. "Is the Doctor In?" (8/13/81; rebroadcast from 5/8/81)

2610. "Lovely People" (8/14/81; rebroadcast 11/11/81)

Cast: Kim Hunter (Tamara); Russell Horton (Harold Herman); Joan Shay (Esther). Written by Elspeth Eric.

Whether it is her readings of the future or her self-taught psychoanalysis, Tamara's salon is crowded by the wealthy. Tamara tries to aid the forlorn male secretary of one of her unhappy rich female clients by pairing them. But what Harold doesn't suspect is that the pastries Tamara gives him to woo his boss contain a special ingredient: arsenic.

2611. "The Thracian Lovers" (8/17/81; rebroadcast 11/12/81)

Cast: Marian Seldes (Dr. Myra); Michael Tolan (Harold Simmons); Robert Kaliban (Leon); Jennifer Harmon (Andrea Simmons). Written by Sam Dann.

Thracian King Eurebus paid the Oracle at Delphi with a gold clasp for the knowledge that his wife and lieutenant were betraying him. Then Eurebus killed the lovers. Generations later, Harold Simmons has plotted the deaths of his cheating wife and best friend. But he can't explain his irrational behavior to his psychiatrist, Dr. Myra, until she develops a special interest in his unusual gold tie clasp.

2612. "End of a Queen" (8/18/81; rebroadcast from 5/11/81)

2613. "Diogenes, Inc." (8/19/81; rebroadcast from 5/13/81)

2614. "Cold Comfort" (8/20/81; rebroadcast from 5/15/81)

2615. "The Left Hand of God" (8/21/81; rebroadcast 11/17/81)

Cast: Norman Rose (Samuel Clements); Bob Dryden (Dudley Everett); Evelyn Juster (Martha); Kristoffer Tabori (Tom Ditson). Written by Sam Dann.

Dudley Everett arrives at his friend Sam Clements' apartment desperate for help: Tom Ditson, a character in his latest short story, refuses to die as plotted. Clements, fearing for the man's sanity, agrees to finish the tale. He gets Tom to the scaffold, only to find the fictional murderer refusing to go one step further.

2616. "The Leopard Man" (8/24/81; rebroadcast 11/18/81)

Cast: Norman Rose (Rudyard Kipling); Robert Kaliban (Strickland); Earl Hammond (Fleete). Adapted by James Agate, Jr., based on the 1890 short story *The Mark of the Beast* by Rudyard Kipling.

Police Chief Strickland and writer Rudyard Kipling become increasingly annoyed by the rude behavior of Strickland's house guest, Fleete. Fleete insults the club gin, then refuses to share his Cuban cigars. Finally, he stubs out a stogie in the eye of a sacred Indian idol and brings the wrath of the mysterious East down on all three.

2617. "A Shocking Affair" (8/25/81; rebroadcast from 5/18/81)

2618. "Insomnia" (8/26/81; rebroadcast from 5/20/81)

2619. "The Headhunters" (8/27/81; rebroadcast from 5/22/81)

2620. "Hidden Memory" (8/28/81; rebroadcast 11/19/81)

Cast: Kristoffer Tabori (Evan); Teri Keane (Mother); Bob Dryden (Doctor); Elspeth Eric (Grandmother). Written by Elspeth Eric.

Sodium amyl, taken to relive the traumatic moment that cost Evan the use of his legs, totally cures his paralysis. But the medication also leaves him with a remarkable side effect: Evan now has total recall not only of his own past but that of his strange family as well.

2621. "The Musgrave Ritual" (8/31/81; rebroadcast 11/24/81)

Cast: Gordon Grant (Sherlock Holmes); Bernard Grant (Reginald Musgrave); Court Benson (Dr. Watson); Marian Seldes (Rachel Howells). Written by Murray Burnett.

Reginald Musgrave brings to Sherlock Holmes the missing persons case of Burton, head of Musgrave's household staff, and Rachel Howells, the woman to whom he was engaged. On the eve of Burton's disappearance he was discovered stealing a family document recording a meaningless, old, family ritual.

Notes: Among the handful of Sherlock Holmes episodes, "The Musgrave Ritual" is the only episode not based on a Sir Arthur Conan Doyle story. Murray Burnett, who adapted many of the earlier Holmes episodes, wrote this original adventure for *Theater.*

2622. "The Innocent Face" (9/1/81; rebroadcast from 5/25/81)

2623. "Little Richard" (9/2/81; rebroadcast from 5/27/81)

2624. "Out of the Past" (9/3/81; rebroadcast from 5/29/81)

2625. "Double-Cross Death" (9/4/81; rebroadcast 11/25/81)

Cast: Fred Gwynne (Bill Watts); Russell Horton (Jimmy McCall); Ray Owens (Charley); Mandel Kramer (Ed Watts). Written by James Agate, Jr.

Bill Watts, facing a retirement he doesn't want, convinces his boss to let him stay for one more job: investigating the shooting death of his niece as she and her husband were held up in their apartment building. He corrals her father, Ed, into the case on the basis of a hunch: the bewildered look on the face of the supposed murderer, killed by the woman's enraged husband.

2626. "Episode of the Terror" (9/7/81; rebroadcast 11/26/81)

Cast: Marian Seldes (Sister Marguerite); Earl Hammond (Father Laurent); Sam Gray (The Vendor); Arnold Moss (Stranger). Adapted by G. Frederic Lewis, based on a short story by Honore de Balzac.

Sister Marguerite and Father Laurent continue to perform secret masses for the faithful despite the revolutionaries' edict banning church services. The pair's safety is provided for by a kind stranger they see only twice during "The Terror." But, free at last from hiding as the revolution ends, they discover the secret of their savior's horrible identity.

2627. "The Runaway General" (9/8/81; rebroadcast from 6/1/81)

2628. "The Cat's Paw" (9/9/81; rebroadcast from 6/3/81)

2629. "Matched Pair for Murder" (9/10/81; rebroadcast from 6/5/81)

2630. "The Senior Prom" (9/11/81; rebroadcast 12/1/81)

Cast: Larry Haines (Lieutenant Holman); Russell Horton (Marty); Evelyn Juster (Maggie Bridges). Written by Sam Dann.

City Hall and the morning papers are after Lieutenant Holman for his inability to solve the murders of four East Side women in their thirties. He appears to get a break in the case when an intended fifth victim fights off the killer. But although top fashion designer Maggie Bridges got a look at her attacker, her upper-crust British background just doesn't seem to fit the murderer's M.O.

2631. "Flower of Evil" (9/14/81; rebroadcast 12/2/81)

Cast: Arnold Moss (Jethro Procter); Russell Horton (Ethan Procter); Roberta Maxwell (Amanita Drysdale). Written by Arnold Moss.

Widower Jethro Procter's claim at Sutter's Mill provided everything he could want, except a wife. Despite his son Ethan's resistance, he marries a mail-order bride, Amanita Drysdale, of Salem, Massachusetts. The lovely young woman accepts the grizzled miner without a complaint, but skeptical Ethan soon notices some bizarre changes in campsite routines.

2632. "Stranded" (9/15/81; rebroadcast from 6/8/81)

2633. "Second Look at Murder" (9/16/81; rebroadcast from 6/10/81)

2634. "When in Rome" (9/17/81; rebroadcast from 6/12/81)

2635. "The Land of Dreams" (9/18/81; rebroadcast 12/3/81)

Cast: Kristoffer Tabori (Joe); Earl Hammond (The Computer); Marian Hailey (Priss). Written by Sam Dann.

Computers that once were the tools for mankind have taken on a life of their own in dominating the future Earth. What's left of the human race settles for synthetic food, while hooked on computer-programmed dream machines. But a band of rebels has a radical plan to destroy the computers: repopulate the Earth the old-fashioned way by having babies.

2636. "Diablo" (9/21/81; rebroadcast 12/8/81)

Cast: Marian Seldes (Carlotta Quintana); Mandel Kramer (Charlie Benson); Michael Tolan (Bruce Elliott). Written by Nancy Moore.

Carlotta Quintana has targeted the closed Diablo mines as her program's latest target. Her reports succeed in putting the miners back to work and net her the mine's owner, Bruce Elliott, as husband. Mild Elliott is thrilled by his famous wife's energy and ambitions for him until he learns of a very peculiar trait of Carlotta.

2637. "Two's a Crowd" (9/22/81; rebroadcast from 6/15/81)

2638. "The Final Step" (9/23/81; rebroadcast from 6/17/81)

2639. "Henrietta's Revenge" (9/24/81; rebroadcast from 6/19/81)

2640. "The Judge's House" (9/25/81; rebroadcast 12/9/81)

Cast: Gordon Gould (Brian Stokes); Lloyd Battista (Mark Mason); Bob Dryden (Andy). Adapted by Bob Juhren, based on the 1891 short story by Bram Stoker.

Englishman Brian Stokes and his American classmate Mark Mason cloister themselves in a remote cottage north of Liverpool to finish their paper on abnormal psychology. Local tales that the place is haunted by "Hanging Judge" Shelling only amuse the pair until they encounter some pretty convincing evidence that threatens both their lives.

2641. "The Liar" (9/28/81; rebroadcast 12/10/81)

Cast: Norman Rose (Oliver Lyon); Carol Teitel (Eve); Bernard Grant (Arthur Ashmore); Court Benson (Colonel Capadose). Adapted by James Agate, Jr., based on the 1888 short story by Henry James.

Oliver Lyon never got over the love of his student days, Eve, now married to a pompous prevaricator 15 years her senior, Colonel Capadose. The colonel agrees to sit for Oliver, never suspecting that behind the offer of a free portrait by England's leading painter is a most malicious purpose.

2642. "Waking and Sleeping" (9/29/81; rebroadcast from 6/29/81)

2643. "The Fourth Bullet" (9/30/81; rebroadcast from 7/1/81)

2644. "A Second Chance" (10/1/81; rebroadcast from 7/3/81)

2645. "Mata Hari" (10/2/81; rebroadcast 12/15/81)

Cast: Tammy Grimes (Mata Hari); Mandel Kramer (Von Jago); Lloyd Battista (Sir Basil); Arnold Moss (Gabriel). Written by G. Frederic Lewis.

Mata Hari, known throughout Europe for her exotic dance act, is recruited by the Kaiser's intelligence unit to spy on the Allies. Desperately in love with a Russian colonel, she offers her services as a double agent to France for a $1 million. France accepts, but now the dancer is trusted by no one and hunted by all. The race is not always to the swift, nor the battle to the strong.

2646. "The Solid Gold Scarf" (10/5/81; rebroadcast 12/16/81)

Cast: Larry Haines (James Madison Wilson); Earl Hammond (Harold H. Hubbell); Frances Sternhagen (Trudy Wilson); Bob Dryden (Dr. Soldis). Written by Sam Dann.

James Madison Wilson is in shock: No one can tell him why he has been fired from Transcontinental, Inc. His wife Trudy urges him to simply find another job, but that makes him feel unfaithful to Transcontinental. He finally hits on a solution to his despair: to demand an accounting from the company chairman, Harold H. Hubbell.

2647. "My Good Name" (10/6/81; rebroadcast from 7/6/81)

2648. "Death and the Dreamer" (10/7/81; rebroadcast from 7/8/81)

2649. "A Man of Honor" (10/8/81; rebroadcast from 7/10/81)

2650. "Sleeping Dogs" (10/9/81; rebroadcast 12/17/81)

Cast: Russell Horton (Etienne); Evelyn Juster (Nicole Martinet); Gordon Gould (Jean Martinet); Ray Owens (Louis XVI). Written by Sam Dann, based on actual historical events.

The conscripts Martinet assembles are a motley lot, and Louis XVI scoffs at his general's promise to turn 600 peasants into better soldiers, and, later, the king's own guards. Drills, swift punishment and more drills whip the new recruits into a crackerjack unit. The only thing Martinet doesn't count on is the possible effect of replacing the soldiers' minds with his will. General Jean Martinet commands with such harsh discipline that his name becomes part of the language.

2651. "The 500 Carats" (10/12/81; rebroadcast 12/18/81)

Cast: Gordon Gould (Philip Marsden); Lloyd Battista (Inspector Grace); Court Benson (Sir Hugh). Written by G. Frederic Lewis.

Mine operator, Sir Hugh, calls in Inspector Grace to find a 500-carat gem, which was somehow removed from its berth in an airtight room. Sir Hugh and his aides Marsden and Derwent were all in the room when the diamond was last seen, but Grace noticed more than their uneasiness when he interviews them there—a wind is carrying his cigar smoke toward an outer wall.

2652. "The Good Shepherds" (10/13/81; rebroadcast from 7/13/81)

2653. "Alice" (10/14/81; rebroadcast from 7/15/81)

2654. "Pie in the Sky" (10/15/81; rebroadcast from 7/17/81)

2655. "J'Accuse" (10/16/81; rebroadcast 12/21/81)

Cast: Roberta Maxwell (Lucy Dreyfuss); Alfred Dreyfuss (Louis Turenne);

Bob Dryden (Colonel Picquart); Earl Hammond (Major Henri); Bernard Grant (Emile Zola). Adapted by James Agate, Jr., based on the 1898 letter by Emile Zola.

A French spy in the Paris offices of the German Embassy brings evidence of a traitor in the army to France's Chief of Intelligence, Major Henri, and his aide Colonel Picquart. They railroad the conviction of an obscure Jewish officer, Alfred Dreyfuss and find an eloquent supporter in novelist Emile Zola and unexpected help from Picquart's wavering conscience.

2656. "The Equalizer" (10/19/81; rebroadcast 12/29/81)

Cast: Larry Haines (Don Henley); Evelyn Juster (Rosita Ramirez); Ray Owens (Major Baroja). Written by Sam Dann.

Don Henley's cool professionalism as a gun-for-hire is legendary. The beleaguered People's Revolutionary Army is happy to pay the steep price for his services to train their rag-tag troops. They provide him with a cover—as a major league baseball scout—and a contact to meet at the airport, Colonel Ramirez—Rosita Ramirez, that is.

2657. "The Eye of the Idol" (10/20/81; rebroadcast from 7/20/81)

2658. "Toy Death" (10/21/81; rebroadcast from 7/22/81)

2659. "Once a Thief" (10/22/81; rebroadcast from 7/24/81)

2660. "The Most Necessary Evil" (10/23/81; rebroadcast 12/30/81)

Cast: Michael Tolan (Eddie Blake); Carol Teitel (Dora Blake); Mandel Kramer (Tom Herrick); Ralph Bell (Lieutenant Crain). Written by Sam Dann.

Dora Blake knows something is coming up when she discovers her husband Eddie has paid all their bills in cash. She becomes furious when Eddie won't tell her where all the money is coming from. When Eddie is found murdered, she turns to his best friend for help and utterly refuses to believe his story of another woman.

2661. "Daddy's Girls" (10/26/81; rebroadcast 1/5/82)

Cast: Teri Keane (Clara); Carol Teitel (Mary); Bernard Grant (Bob Loomis). Written by Sam Dann.

Clara's gossip column is a force to be feared. Her invalid sister Mary puts up with it, even though Clara's unprincipled reporting would make their straight laced father roll over in his grave. When Clara's publisher Bob Loomis is found murdered, Mary suspects Clara knows more than she admits to and that father's strict teaching will overcome the gossiper's instincts.

2662. "Postage Due" (10/27/81; rebroadcast from 7/29/81)

2663. "A Penny for Your Thoughts" (10/28/81; rebroadcast from 7/31/81)

2664. "In Touch" (10/29/81; rebroadcast 1/6/82)

Cast: Amanda Plummer (Ellen Bartlett); Bob Dryden (Mr. Bartlett); Russell Horton (Daniel Post). Written by Elspeth Eric.

Ellen Bartlett's periodic attacks are beyond any prescription of Dr. Abramowitz. When medical student Daniel Post, vacationing with the doctor, tries his hand in curing her, his unexpected success makes a deep impression on the girl. But Post's career takes him far away, and when one of the attacks recurs, her father alone is left to help.

2665. "The Silver Medal" (10/30/81; rebroadcast from 7/27/81)

2666. "Between Two Mirrors" (11/2/81; rebroadcast 1/7/82)

Cast: Marian Seldes (Judy Horton); Lloyd Battista (James Horton); Joyce Gordon (Peggy Schofield); Sidney Slon (Reverend Smith). Written by Sidney Slon.

James Horton is alive only because one machine breathes for him and another circulates his blood. Dr. Rollins gently urges Judy Horton to permit her husband to die, but she's not so sure he's dead; she gets phone calls from Jim every night.

2667. "Honor Among Thieves" (11/3/81; rebroadcast from 8/3/81)

2668. "The Orphaned Heart" (11/4/81; rebroadcast from 8/5/81)

2669. "Let No Man Put Asunder" (11/5/81; rebroadcast from 8/7/81)

2670. "The Rescue" (11/6/81; rebroadcast 1/18/82)

Cast: Louis Turenne (Pierre Montand); Roberta Maxwell (Yvonne); Earl Hammond (Leon Van Stuwe). Written by G. Frederic Lewis.

Pierre Montand hides Leon Van Stuwe, fleeing from the Gestapo in Paris, and together they decide to steal a plane to England. A stray cat leads them to the one unbombed plane in an airport outside the city, and Pierre's skilled flying soon has the pair over the English Channel heading straight into a squadron of German aircraft.

2671. "Golden Time" (11/9/81; rebroadcast 1/20/82)

Cast: Larry Haines (Harvey Stillson); Evelyn Juster (Martha Stillson); Sally Fisher (Frankie); Earl Hammond (Armand). Written by Sam Dann.

An urgent late-night phone call turns into a bigger job than expected for plumber Harvey Stillson. But he agrees to fix a leaky water main in the basement for a neighbor in anticipation of racking up a lot of overtime or, "golden time." The only problem is that when Harvey locates the leak, he also finds a big plastic bag bulging with a mysterious white powder.

2672. "Hostage to Terror" (11/10/81; rebroadcast from 8/10/81)

2673. "Lovely People" (11/11/81; rebroadcast from 8/14/81)

2674. "The Thracian Lovers" (11/12/81; rebroadcast from 8/17/81)

2675. "The Presence" (11/13/81; rebroadcast 1/22/82)

    Cast: Norman Rose (Owen); Elspeth Eric (Nellie); Russell Horton (Gordon). Written by Elspeth Eric.

    Gordon claims his inability to complete his final exam resulted from the feeling of a mysterious presence behind him at his desk. Owen, his stern father, is furious, but accedes to his wife Nellie's wish to send Gordon on an ocean cruise. But the presence seems to follow Gordon, because he keeps sending postcards to his parents signed with someone else's initials: H.M.G.

2676. "Death Will Not Silence Me" (11/16/81; rebroadcast 1/25/82)

    Cast: Marian Seldes (Mary Todd Lincoln); John Beal (Abraham Lincoln); Lloyd Battista (Robert Todd Lincoln); Carol Teitel (Elizabeth Edwards). Written by Arnold Moss, based on actual historical events.

    Delicate and beautiful, Kentucky aristocrat Mary Todd thinks she caused her mother's death but, nevertheless, a rangy young lawyer named Abraham Lincoln falls in love with her. One by one, she sees her husband and each son except the oldest, Robert, die. Robert's decision to commit the grieving woman is condemned by the public, and Mary claims Robert will inherit the curse.

2677. "The Left Hand of God" (11/17/81; rebroadcast from 8/21/81)

2678. "The Leopard Man" (11/18/81; rebroadcast from 8/24/81)

2679. "Hidden Memory" (11/19/81; rebroadcast from 8/28/81)

2680. "A Handful of Dust" (11/20/81; rebroadcast 1/27/82)

    Cast: Paul Hecht (Hank Theodore); Teri Keane (Marsha Theodore); Ian Martin (Conrad Theodore); Jada Rowland (Vanessa). Written by Ian Martin.

    When renowned Egyptologist Conrad Theodore remarried, he chose beautiful, young, Egyptian Marsha, whose brief affair with his son Hank was long over. The elder Theodore can't figure out why she and her brother Selim discouraged him from excavating the ancient tomb of Queen Mersegret, until a young American volunteer realizes a shocking parallel from the past in the Theodore family triangle.

2681. "The Code" (11/23/81; rebroadcast 1/29/82)

    Cast: Russell Horton (Paul Wagner); Carol Teitel (Juanita); Bob Dryden (Sheriff); Evelyn Juster (Drusie). Written by Sam Dann.

    At 21, Paul Wagner convinces the mysterious Juanita to hire him as barker for her mind-reading act in a touring circus. He learns her code for clues in "reading" audience thoughts so well that the local sheriff asks Juanita to help solve a murder. Paul fears that without his "code" Juanita will be exposed for the charlatan she really is.

2682. "The Musgrave Ritual" (11/24/81; rebroadcast from 8/31/81)

2683. "Double-Cross Death" (11/25/81; rebroadcast from 9/4/81)

2684. "Episode of the Terror" (11/26/81; rebroadcast from 9/7/81)

2685. "Diana, the Huntress" (11/27/81; rebroadcast 2/2/82)
   Cast: Teri Keane (Diana Manley); Jada Rowland (Janet); Earl Hammond (Alan Manley); Arnold Moss (Dr. Ullman). Written by Sam Dann.
   Dr. Ullman's decision could save or condemn Diana Manley, nicknamed "Diana the Huntress" by local press after shooting her husband, a doctor. Dr. Ullman's dilemma: Did Diana shoot her husband the instant she found out about his infidelity, or had she really planned the shooting all along?

2686. "Vanity and Jane" (11/30/81; rebroadcast 2/4/82)
   Cast: Marian Seldes (Vanity Wilson/Jane Wilson); Ralph Bell (Dan Kirkpatrick); Paul Hecht (Charley Ingalls). Written by G. Frederic Lewis.
   Charley Ingalls is quite charmed by outgoing and athletic, Jane Wilson, but her twin sister Vanity is decidedly less friendly. Then, Charley discovers the "twins" are really split personalities in the same body, and that Vanity is trying desperately to murder her extroverted counterpart.

2687. "The Senior Prom" (12/1/81; rebroadcast from 9/11/81)

2688. "Flower of Evil" (12/2/81; rebroadcast from 9/14/81)

2689. "The Land of Dreams" (12/3/81; rebroadcast from 9/18/81)

2690. "The Dog-Walker Murders" (12/4/81; rebroadcast 2/9/82)
   Cast: Lloyd Battista (Randy Garfield); Carol Teitel (Sergeant Barbara Collins); Ian Martin (Lieutenant Cassidy); Martha Greenhouse (Shirley Cooper). Written by Ian Martin.
   Randy Garfield, raised in the circus, is an old hand at hypnosis. He finds the skill comes in handy at his new job managing a bank's safety contents. The only problem is to figure out what he will do with his unwitting benefactors once they learn they've been bilked.

2691. "The White Rabbit" (12/7/81; rebroadcast 2/11/82)
   Cast: Norman Rose (Forest Thomas); Louis Turenne (de Gaulle); Lloyd

Battista (Commander Passy); Earl Hammond (Winston Churchill). Written by James Agate, Jr.

Wing Commander Forest Thomas earns the respect of de Gaulle and Churchill for his brave exploits early in World War II. He therefore becomes the natural choice to rescue the radio voice of the Resistance, Commander Passy, held by the Germans. But although the noted agent has escaped from prison before, he has never tried to break into a well-guarded German camp.

2692. "Diablo" (12/8/81; rebroadcast from 9/21/81)

2693. "The Judge's House" (12/9/81; rebroadcast from 9/25/81)

2694. "The Liar" (12/10/81; rebroadcast from 9/28/81)

2695. "The Song of the Siren" (12/11/81; rebroadcast 2/16/82)

Cast: Mandel Kramer (Roy Rismond); Evelyn Juster (Arlene Davis); Ian Martin (Professor Davis); Joyce Gordon (Nurse). Written by Sam Dann.

Reports of Professor Davis' 125-pound weight loss and delirium during a desert expedition are too irresistible for Roy Rismond to ignore. The ambitious reporter decides to retrace the anthropologist's desert mission, knowing only that Davis believes reptilian creatures of the Age of the Dinosaurs are still alive.

2696. "Harry's Taxi and the 'T' Machine" (12/14/81; rebroadcast 2/18/82)

Cast: Larry Haines (Harry); Bob Dryden (Grandpa); Bernard Grant (Cornelius); Carol Teitel (Gladys). Written by G. Frederic Lewis.

An unemployed 21st-century scientist invents a transmigration machine. Harry and his wife's grandfather have successfully sent a chair and case of wine through space, but they really want to try their invention with a human subject. How was Harry to know his curious wife Gladys would accidentally send herself flying into intermolecular space?

2697. "Mata Hari" (12/15/81; rebroadcast from 10/2/81)

2698. "The Solid Gold Zarf" (12/16/81; rebroadcast from 10/5/81)

2699. "Sleeping Dogs" (12/17/81; rebroadcast from 10/9/81)

2700. "The 500 Carats" (12/18/81; rebroadcast from 10/12/81)

2701. "J'Accuse" (12/21/81; rebroadcast from 10/16/81)

2702. "Invited Guests" (12/22/81; rebroadcast 2/23/82)

Cast: Teri Keane (Louise); Russell Horton (Oliver); Lloyd Battista (Dr. Mabley). Written by Elspeth Eric.

Oliver's former girlfriend, Louise, asks church pastor Dr. Mabley to look into why Oliver has refused all her dinner invitations in the two years since she's been married. Mabley agrees, and finds out that Oliver has been entertaining his parents all the while. Louise is incredulous; she attended their funeral three years ago!

2703. "The Head of a Pin" (12/23/81; rebroadcast 2/25/82)

Cast: Robert Kaliban (Eddie Kincaid); Bernard Grant (Dr. Mecklenberg); Don Scardino (Robby Baxter); Valeka Gray (Sally Baxter). Written by Sam Dann.

Eddie Kincaid always got out of jams with the help of his sister Sally and her husband Robby Baxter, but he may be in over his head when he agrees with Robby to use their business to "wash" money for gangsters. Robby soon has an attack of conscience, and Eddie finds himself in the position of having to kill his friend or get killed.

2704. "A Christmas Carol" (12/24/81; rebroadcast from 12/24/80)

2705. "A Holiday Visit" (12/25/81; rebroadcast from 12/25/80)

2706. "The Silver Mirror" (12/28/81; rebroadcast 3/2/82)

Cast: Gordon Gould (Sir Arthur Conan Doyle); Ray Owens (Peter Matson); Earl Hammond (Dr. George Sinclair); Marian Seldes (Louise Doyle). Written by James Agate, Jr.

When Sir Arthur Conan Doyle decides to rid himself of the famous detective Sherlock Holmes in a final escapade, he has nightmares and visions. But when Doyle claims that he views the 300-year-old murder of David Riccio, minstrel to Mary, Queen of Scots, Doyle's wife and psychiatrist conspire to salvage the last remaining threads of Doyle's sanity.

2707. "The Equalizer" (12/29/81; rebroadcast from 10/19/81)

2708. "The Most Necessary Evil" (12/30/81; rebroadcast from 10/23/81)

2709. "Too Early Too Late" (12/31/81; rebroadcast 3/4/82)

Cast: Russell Horton (Jack Peterson); Arnold Moss (Voice); Marian Seldes (Ruth Peterson); Paul Hecht (Dave Bascom). Written by Elizabeth Pennell.

Jack and Ruth Peterson share more than old times with childhood chum Dave Bascom this New Year's morning. When a mysterious voice in their dreams instructs them to return to the grim playground, they decide to comply with its wishes, never anticipating that their date could alter the future of the world.

2710. "Catch the Smallest Devil" (1/1/82; rebroadcast from 1/1/81)

2711. "The Acquisition" (1/4/82; rebroadcast 3/9/82)

Cast: Tony Roberts (Jonas McDowell); Patricia Elliott (Estelle); Mandel Kramer (Taro). Written by Sam Dann.

Jonas McDowell, the "Wonder Boy" of Wall Street, is totally baffled when his magnanimous proposal for marriage is rejected. Believing that marriage could prolong his life, Jonas determines to find out why he was refused, never realizing that he could lose the very life he hopes to save.

2712. "Daddy's Girls" (1/5/82; rebroadcast from 10/26/81)

2713. "In Touch" (1/6/82; rebroadcast from 10/29/81)

2714. "Between Two Mirrors" (1/7/82; rebroadcast from 11/2/81)

2715. "The Last Orbit" (1/8/82; rebroadcast 3/11/82)

Cast: Larry Haines (Emmett Rockwell); Marian Seldes (Luna); Russell Horton (Wally Bruder). Written by Douglas Dempsey.

Astronaut Emmett Rockwell notices Luna during a bash thrown in his honor. When she reminds him of a long-forgotten promise he made to her, he has a nagging suspicion that she is telling the truth. But the valiant leader finds his life in jeopardy when he underestimates a woman's wrath and attempts to renege on the agreement.

2716. "Les Misérables, Part I: The Thief and the Bishop"
(1/11/82; rebroadcast 6/7/82)

Cast: Alexander Scourby (Jean Valjean); Bernard Grant (Inspector Javert); Mandel Kramer (The Bishop); Joan Shay (Madame Magloire); Earl Hammond (Gendarme). Adapted by Gerald Keane, based on the 1862 novel by Victor Hugo.

After 19 years in prison, Jean Valjean can hardly believe he is free again. But society seems unable to forget Valjean's past. Will one kindly "Monsignor Welcome" be able to win his soul, or will desperation drive this man to total madness?

Notes: To celebrate *Theater*'s ninth (and final) year on the air, Gerald Keane adapted Victor Hugo's novel *Les Misérables* as a five-part mini-series. Starring in the title role is Alexander Scourby as Jean Valjean, and Inspector Javert as Bernard Grant.

Alexander Scourby's film credits include *Affair in Trinidad* (1952), *The Redhead from Wyoming* (1953), and *The Big Heat* (1953).

Himan Brown noted: "This production is more important than anything I've done to date, in its vastness and production demands—from sound effects to casting the actors' interpretation of the roles. It was also quite challenging for me as the director."

2717. "Les Misérables, Part II: The Lawless and the Law"
(1/12/82; rebroadcast 6/8/82)

Cast: Alexander Scourby (Jean Valjean); Bernard Grant (Inspector Javert); Earl Hammond (The Bishop); Russell Horton (Prosecutor); Teri Keane (Fantine). Adapted by Gerald Keane, based on the 1862 novel by Victor Hugo.

The inexorable Inspector Javert has his doubts about the legitimacy of the new wealthy Mayor "Monsieur Madeleine," alias Jean Valjean. That is, until he sees a peasant arrested for pilfering apples who agrees to positively identify the man as Jean Valjean. If Valjean allows this to happen he will be free of his convict's shadow at last, but a nagging conscience imprisons him in another way.

2718. "Les Misérables, Part III: No Escape" (1/13/82; rebroadcast 6/9/82))

Cast: Alexander Scourby (Jean Valjean); Bernard Grant (Inspector Javert); Evelyn Juster (Cosette); Robert Kaliban (Paul); Lloyd Battista (Maurice). Adapted by Gerald Keane, based on the 1862 novel by Victor Hugo.

Valjean persuades orphan Cosette that she is his granddaughter and to go into hiding with him. If Cosette leaves the country with Valjean she will never again see Marius, the only man she loves, but Valjean suspects that Marius is not her love-struck suitor, but a spy instead.

2719. "Les Misérables, Part IV: Fear, Love and Death"
(1/14/82; rebroadcast 6/10/82)

Cast: Alexander Scourby (Jean Valjean); Bernard Grant (Inspector Javert); Lloyd Battista (Maurice); Earl Hammond (Henri); Robert Kaliban (Paul). Adapted by Gerald Keane, based on the 1862 novel by Victor Hugo.

As police roam the streets of Paris, Valjean and cohort Paul seek refuge in the crocodile-infested sewers, carrying the weakening Marius with them. A vow to Cosette's mother sustains an exhausted Valjean's efforts to unite Marius with his lover, but Paul fears all three are doomed.

2720. "Les Misérables, Part V: The Final Chapter" (1/15/82; rebroadcast 6/11/82)

Cast: Alexander Scourby (Jean Valjean); Bernard Grant (Inspector Javert); Robert Kaliban (Paul); Amanda Plummer (Cosette); Lloyd Battista (Maurice). Adapted by Gerald Keane, based on the 1862 novel by Victor Hugo.

Suspecting that Valjean has hoodwinked the young Cosette, Marius attempts to denounce the man who saved his life. Only Paul knows Valjean's true identity, but he has vowed to Valjean to never reveal it. Will he go back on his word?

Notes: According to Himan Brown: "We also have lots of new people to draw upon, like Amanda Plummer, Martin Balsam, Len Cariou and Richard Kiley, among others. We also have some new writers who've added more excitement to what we're doing. We have uncovered some new Sherlock Holmes stories, and several new classics in mystery and suspense from French, Russian and English literature. We look ahead to this new season not only with renewed commitment to the theater of the mind, but knowing that our work is more important than ever."

(Richard Kiley was unable to make another appearance on the series, as he did before. Martin Balsam was apparently scheduled for the series, but he never made an appearance on the program.)

2721. "The Rescue" (1/18/82; rebroadcast from 11/6/81)

2722. "The Real World" (1/19/82; rebroadcast 3/16/82)

Cast: Joyce Gordon (Sgt. Detective Millrose); Mandel Kramer (Captain Spencer); Ray Owens (Chester Dawkins); Evelyn Juster (Estelle Dawkins). Written by Sam Dann.

Sgt. Detective Millrose may have a degree in psychology, but she still can't figure out how to nail the murderer of a babyfaced night club singer. One suspect is an underworld kingpin, and the other is the distinguished scion of one of the country's finest families.

2723. "Golden Time" (1/20/82; rebroadcast from 11/9/81)

2724. "Gate 27" (1/21/82; rebroadcast 3/18/82)

Cast: Joe Driscoll (Fr. Gwynne); Teri Keane (Louise); C. Benson (Frank); Bernard Grant (Harry).Written by Sam Dann.

Joe Driscoll is a once proud cop whose instinct is aroused in a bum, when, after killing a small-time punk in dubious circumstances, turns to the demon: rum. But when his best shot for coffee money every morning—the lady in the blue dress who gets off at gate 27 at Grand Central Station—misses her train for two days, Joe cleans up his act and returns to the sharp detective he once was.

2725. "The Presence" (1/22/82; rebroadcast from 11/13/81)

2726. "Death Will Not Silence Me" (1/25/82; rebroadcast from 11/16/81)

2727. "To Be an Empress" (1/26/82; rebroadcast 3/23/82)

Cast: Amanda Plummer (Catherine); Russell Horton (Peter); Louis Turenne (Count Brummer); Joan Shay (Johanna). Written by James Agate, Jr.

Sophie, countess of Anhalt-Zerbst, was barely out of her teens when the mighty Empress Elizabeth of Russia chose her to marry the future czar, Peter III. Sophie changes her name, language and religion in her zeal to serve her new country well, a zeal which ambition may flame to murder.

Notes: Amanda Plummer has appeared in numerous films, playing a variety of roles from prostitutes to angels. Her film credits include *The World According to Garp* (1982), *Daniel* (1983), *Made in Heaven* (1987), *The Fisher King* (1991), *So I Married an Axe Murderer* (1993), *Pulp Fiction* (1994), and *Freeway* (1997).

2728. "A Handful of Dust" (1/27/82; rebroadcast from 11/20/81)

2729. "Dickens of Scotland Yard" (1/28/82; rebroadcast 3/25/82)

Cast: Paul Hecht (Charles Dickens); Robert Kaliban (Tom Thompson); Tudi Wiggens (Rosie Thompson); Earl Hammond (Inspector Field). Written by James Agate, Jr.

Inspector Field beefs up the fledging Scotland Yard force by enlisting the famous writer to help solve the mystery of "Tally-Ho" Thompson, a con man whose most recent caper included stealing horses. Dickens is delighted to help, but will his great insight into fictional characters translate into real-life deduction as well?

2730. "The Code" (1/29/82; rebroadcast from 11/23/81)

2731. "The Good Ship Aud" (2/1/82; rebroadcast 3/30/82)

Cast: Earl Hammond (Roger Casement); Lloyd Battista (Count Van Bethmann); Court Benson (King Leopold); Marian Seldes (Gee Gannister). Written by Sam Dann.

Sir Roger Casement's dedication and patriotism to his nation has reaped world recognition. But the freedom fighter is not given much rein to enjoy his reputation; his tactics are foiled and he is arrested for treason.

Notes: Beginning with this episode, Tammy Grimes took over the role as host of the *Theater*, replacing E.G. Marshall, who was forced to bow out due to various other projects. "I'm going to be provocative," Grimes announced, "just as E.G. was provocative as host. *Theater* brings back the kind of excitement that radio can offer, and it's getting stronger all the time. It's terrifically exciting to be part of the circle of magic that *Theater* creates."

2732. "Diana, the Huntress" (2/2/82; rebroadcast from 11/27/81)

2733. "The Mysterious Slumber" (2/3/82; rebroadcast 4/1/82)

Cast: Diana Kirkwood (Mary Reynolds); Mandel Kramer (John Reynolds); Don Scardino (Simon Reynolds); Elspeth Eric (Mother). Written by Elspeth Eric.

Teenager Mary baffles her family when she wakes up one morning with a spanking new personality and recognizes no one. Her family enjoys Mary's sweetened temperament but are horrified by the increasing frequency of these bizarre personality changes.

Notes: Commented E. G. Marshall on his resignation as series host: "I'm forced to bow out because of my difficult assignment schedule. Tammy [Grimes] and I are old colleagues and friends. She brings to *Theater* a wonderful voice that gives words resonance beyond the sum of their letters."

2734. "Vanity and Jane" (2/4/82; rebroadcast from 11/30/81)

2735. "The Cantankerous Ghost" (2/5/82; rebroadcast 4/6/82)

Cast: Marian Seldes (Estelle Logan); Lloyd Battista (Rex Blake); Earl Hammond (Eddie Rogers); Evelyn Juster (Myra Longdale). Written by Bob Juhren.

A headstrong ghost, Clayton Logan, finds he cannot rest in peace when he perceives that the old homestead has been run amok. The problem is that neither can anyone else when he decides to pitch in and get his relatives out of the jam.

Notes: Said Himan Brown of Tammy Grimes: "She's sensational. Tammy adds something so fresh and new it'll knock listeners on their ears. The creaking door and Tammy Grimes were just destined to meet at some point."

2736. "Change of Heart" (2/8/82; rebroadcast 4/8/82)

Cast: Louis Turenne (Roger Skipworth); Sam Gray (Pruit); Joan Shay (Mrs. Speckle); Patricia Elliott (Millicent Sanford). Written by Sam Dann.

Millicent Sanford's parting shot to corporate kingpin Roger Skipworth as she broke off their engagement was to call him a "pig." Not long afterwards, Roger is rushed into the hospital where an ailing heart valve is replaced by a porcine substitute, and Roger begins to think there may be something after all to Millicent's remark.

Notes: Tammy Grimes, the new host of the series, is a distinguished and versatile actress who had recently starred in the Broadway musical *42nd Street*. Her work on Broadway has been honored with two Tony Awards, for *The Unsinkable Molly Brown* and *Private Lives*. She has also appeared in numerous film and television productions and has recorded a number of records, including all of Maurice Sendak's works for Caedmon Records.

2737. "The Dog-Walker Murders" (2/9/82; rebroadcast from 12/4/81)

2738. "The Sand Castle" (2/10/82; rebroadcast 4/13/82)

Cast: Norman Rose (Jeremy Denham); Gordon Gould (Ralph Poole); Teri Keane (Elinor Hart); Jada Rowland (Maureen Hart). Written by Elspeth Eric.

Every day, Maureen Hart returns to the same spot on the beach to make endless intricate sand castles that each night are wiped away by the tides. It takes a kindly young poet who manages the nearby bird sanctuary and an elderly naturalist to unravel the mystery of her long afternoons at the shore.

2739. "The White Rabbit" (2/11/82; rebroadcast from 12/7/81)

2740. "The Bargain" (2/12/82; rebroadcast 4/15/82)

Cast: Russell Horton (Roger Ferris); Mandel Kramer (Marty Frasner); Tracey Ellis (Gloria Granville); Ray Owens (C. B. Granville); Robert Kaliban (Pete Marvin). Written by James Agate, Jr.

Pete Marvin, racked up in the hospital for the seventh time in one year, finally coaxes a yes out of Gloria Granville to his marriage proposal—if he'll leave racing. But there might be enough financial stake in his driving to want Gloria out of the way forever.

2741. "The .44 Connection" (2/15/82; rebroadcast 4/20/82)

Cast: Marian Seldes (Nellie Murdock); Fred Gwynne (Jack); Evelyn Juster (Liz Lewis); Lloyd Battista (Lieutenant Carson). Written by Sam Dann.

Jeremy Lewis had plenty of enemies who might have killed him with an antique Colt, including the wife he was trying to divorce and his blackmailing mistress. But then there's another possible suspect: Nellie Murdock, descendant of a Custer lieutenant, recently fired by Lewis after 25 years of devoted service.

2742. "The Song of the Siren" (2/16/82; rebroadcast from 12/11/81)

2743. "The Washington Kidnap" (2/17/82; rebroadcast 4/22/82)

Cast: Paul Hecht (Henry Dawkins); Robert Maxwell (Sergeant Thomas); Robert Kaliban (Isaac Young); Mandel Kramer (George Washington). Written by G. Frederic Lewis.

Henry Dawkins' great artistic talents are directed toward one goal: printing his own version of George III's legal tender. When his engraving operation lands him and friend Isaac Young in prison, they discover they serve time with a host of Tory sympathizers who are eager to use Henry's ability for their own Loyalist cause: bringing George Washington to England in chains.

2744. "Harry's Taxi and the 'T' Machine" (2/18/82; rebroadcast from 12/14/81)

2745. "The Victim" (2/19/82; rebroadcast 4/27/82)

Cast: John Lithgow (Joe Thompson); Russell Horton (Public Defender); Teri Keane (Helen Travis); Earl Hammond (Ferras). Written by Bryce Walton.

Joe Thompson's conviction for murder is based on such flimsy evidence that the great lawyer Ferras, defender of the downtrodden, is able to free Joe and get $2 million in damages in the bargain. Joe is so happy he's going to take off for Acapulco with the prosecution's main witness.

2746. "Nickels and Dimes" (2/22/82; rebroadcast 4/29/82)

Cast: Michael Tolan (Ray Vance); Ray Owens (Barney Smith); Earl Hammond (Big Joe); Joan Shay (Millie). Written by Sam Dann.

Ray Vance is so successful in infiltrating Big Joe's East Side organization, he becomes heir apparent to Joe's operation. The new apartment, salary and girlfriends reward Joe's talent in his new role, and suddenly the dowdy lifestyle of a cop seems pretty dull in comparison.

2747. "Invited Guests" (2/23/82; rebroadcast from 12/22/81)

2748. "Invaders from Atlantis" (2/24/82; rebroadcast 5/4/82)

Cast: Arnold Moss (Seth Cook); Don Scardino (Jason Cook); Court Benson (Mister Gorgon); Evelyn Juster (Catherine). Written by G. Frederic Lewis.

Strange three-eyed aliens, in control of major cities, finally get around to sending an agent to Parson's Corner to impose their rule. Mr. Gordon soon has the town under the alien's control, and along the way falls in love with the local school teacher who exercises a certain control of her own.

2749. "The Head of a Pin" (2/25/82; rebroadcast from 12/23/81)

2750. "The Blood Red Ink" (2/26/82; rebroadcast 5/6/82)

Cast: Fred Gwynne (Bert Gilbert); Teri Keane (Helen Gilbert); Robert Kaliban (Blass); Lloyd Battista (Mike Culligan). Written by Sidney Slon.

Bert Gilbert is in a deep funk, having just flunked the exam to make detective for the third time. So when a shady character named Blass offers Bert the chance to steal a pocketful of diamonds, he agrees to the plan. Is Bert really giving up on the force, or is he just trying another way to make detective?

2751. "The Blue Sedan" (3/1/82; rebroadcast 5/11/82)

Cast: Kim Hunter (Lucille Miller); Carol Teitel (June Delfat); Bernard Grant (Harold Soames); Earl Hammond (Lew Delfat). Written by Sam Dann.

To the police, the shooting death of Lew Delfat was no more than a routine investigation into the robbery and murder of a sleazy private detective. But homicide detective Lucille Miller saw it as much more, especially when anyone with information regarding Delfat's business met with a sudden and violent death.

2752. "The Silver Mirror" (3/2/82; rebroadcast from 12/28/81)

2753. "Death Star" (3/3/82; rebroadcast 5/13/82)

Cast: Marian Seldes (Liza Rountree); Russell Horton (Jim); Earl Hammond (Blake). Written by Sam Dann.

Liza Rountree prides herself on being a smart, sensible business executive. Yet, since the new newsstand attendant appeared on the scene, she mysteriously and without warning takes on the personality of Molly Tapely, a woman burned at the stake for adultery and witchcraft many years ago. Coming to grips with her dual personality leads Liza to solve the problem as Molly might have—with murder!

2754. "Too Early Too Late" (3/4/82; rebroadcast from 12/31/81)

2755. "Death at a Distance" (3/5/82; rebroadcast 5/18/82)

Cast: Norman Rose (Dr. John Best); Earl Hammond (Judge Moody); Bernard Grant (Dr. Barola). Written by Elspeth Eric.

Dr. John Best had all the knowledge modern medicine could impart when he set up shop in a remote west African village. But when one of the villagers, a hated hunter, is mysteriously plagued by pain and hallucinations, the young doctor is powerless against the overwhelming forces of native revenge, voodoo and death.

2756. "First Impressions" (3/8/82; rebroadcast 5/20/82)

Cast: Teri Keane (Det. Cynthia Weston); Carol Teitel (Mrs. Zelda Palmer); Mandel Kramer (Brooks); Keir Dullea (Bradley Palmer). Written by Victoria Dann.

Zelda Palmer is on the way to prison for the murder of her husband. Her claim that it was an accident is overshadowed by the testimonies of her butler and stepson. Only detective Cynthia Weston questions the *real* motive in the case: Why would Zelda murder John when she was madly in love with him?

2757. "The Acquisition" (3/9/82; rebroadcast from 1/4/82)

2758. "The Heart of Boadicea" (3/10/82; rebroadcast 5/25/82)

Cast: Marian Seldes (Queen Boadicea); Russell Horton (Vectis); Lloyd Battista (Cynwyn). Written by Sam Dann.

Boadicea, queen of the Inceni centuries ago, was left half control of her husband's kingdom upon his death. Nero, emperor of Rome, disregards the deathbed promise and seeks control of the entire British nation, unaware of the fact that Boadicea is willing to fight to the death for justice and vengeance.

2759. "The Last Orbit" (3/11/82; rebroadcast from 1/8/82)

2760. "The New Man at the Yard" (3/12/82; rebroadcast 5/27/82)

Cast: Paul Hecht (Charles Dickens); Court Benson (John Kent); Gordon Gould (Francis); Evelyn Juster (Constance). Written by G. Frederic Lewis.

Young Francis Kent is found hanged in the barn by his stepsister, Constance. It is a simple suicide until Scotland Yard solicits the help of author and neighbor Charles Dickens to assist in the investigation. First clue: Constance is a mass of cuts and bruises, inflicted by her dead stepbrother.

2761. "The Face of the Waters" (3/15/82; rebroadcast 6/1/82)

Cast: Paul Hecht (Arthur); Jada Rowland (Julia); Norman Rose (Roland Laverne); Lloyd Battista (Harrison Clay). Written by G. Frederic Lewis.

Roland Laverne had power, wealth and the guardianship of his beautiful niece, Julia—everything a man could desire. However, when a romance between Julia and the Laverne's chauffeur threatens to destroy Roland's ideal world, he must use any means to eliminate the young intruder.

2762. "The Real World" (3/16/82; rebroadcast from 1/19/82)

2763. "Tippecanoe and Tyler, Too" (3/17/82; rebroadcast 6/3/82)

Cast: Carol Teitel (Dorcas Downey); Cynthia Harris (Sally); Earl Hammond (Harry Tyler); Arnold Moss (Adam Cartwright). Written by Sam Dann.

Dorcas Downey's longtime friend, Adam Cartwright, has just married his secretary, a smart young lady less than half his age. His plan is to sell his company and sail around the world, her plan is to eliminate Adam and inherit the business. Dorcas can stop the murder, but no one will believe the lonely old spinster.

2764. "Gate 27" (3/18/82; rebroadcast from 1/21/82)

2765. "The Magic Stick of Manitu" (3/19/82; rebroadcast 6/15/82)

Cast: Keir Dullea (Idri); Fred Gwynne (Mr. Block); Sam Gray (Tashti); Marian Seldes (Arlena). Written by Victoria Dann.

Several centuries into the future, Arlena and her disagreeable companion, Mr. Block, are on an interplanetary trade and cultural affairs tour. Their first stop is the planet of Manitu, where Arlena finds love and mysterious music. The natives of the beautiful land have a secret means of producing their music while eliminating unwanted visitors!

2766. "The Tool Shed" (3/22/82; rebroadcast 6/17/82)

Cast: John Vickery (Robinson Crane); Evelyn Juster (Gwen); Bernard Grant (Martin Hazeltine). Written by G. Frederic Lewis.

Martin Hazeltine has earned a fortune writing books on black magic and the occult. When Robinson Crane is assigned to interview him, the young journalist finds the Hazeltine family steeped in mystery. Why is the son perfectly healthy yet mute? Why does Mrs. Hazeltine refuse her husband any contact with the boy? What is the age-old "mark of the devil" doing on the floor of the child's favorite playroom, the tool shed?

Notes: John Vickery can be seen in many films, including, *Rapid Fire* (1992), and *Deconstructing Sarah* (1994), to name a few.

2767. "To Be an Empress" (3/23/82; rebroadcast from 1/26/82)

2768. "The Old Country" (3/24/82; rebroadcast 6/22/82)

Cast: Paul Hecht (Gabriel Carson); Carol Teitel (Franceska); Joan Shay (Darinka); Court Benson (Colonel). Written by Sam Dann.

Gabriel Carson changes his name and disavows all connections with the homeland and heritage of his immigrant parents. But on a business trip to the "old country" young Carson finds himself mysteriously transported back to a time and place he never knew. It is now World War II. He has assumed the position his father held in his Nazi-occupied village and faces trial by the villagers for treason. The only sentence, if he is found guilty, is death!

2769. "Dickens of Scotland Yard" (3/25/82; rebroadcast from 1/28/82)

2770. "In the Cards" (3/26/82; rebroadcast 6/24/82)

Cast: Tammy Grimes (Josephine); Louis Turenne (Napoleon); Teri Keane (Theresa); Earl Hammond (Joseph). Written by G. Frederic Lewis, based on actual historical documents.

Empress Josephine of France has allowed "the cards" to foretell the fate of her first husband, her short and stormy marriage to Napoleon Bonaparte, and her ultimate fall from grace. Of course, the emperor finds this childish, especially when the cards dictate that if he and she were ever to divorce, that the almighty Bonaparte might die in battle—or worse, in exile.

2771. "On the Night of the Dead" (3/29/82; rebroadcast 6/29/82)

Cast: John Vickery (Pentheus); Tracey Ellis (Woman); Earl Hammond (Cadmus); Marian Seldes (Agave). Written by Sam Dann.

Pentheus, the young governor of an ancient Greek island, finds his people in the midst of a relentless drought. When all else fails, a "god" appears, seemingly from nowhere, with mysterious and miraculous powers. Is he really a god, sent to deliver the island from its scorching heat? The answer spells madness and murder.

2772. "The Good Ship Aud" (3/30/82; rebroadcast from 2/1/82)

2773. "I Am the Killer" (3/31/82; rebroadcast 7/1/82)

Cast: Keir Dullea (Dr. Semmelweis); Lloyd Battista (Dr. Johann Ciari); Evelyn Juster (Vera); Mandel Kramer (Dr. Klein). Written by Sam Dann.

It is the mid–1800s. Dr. Ignatz Semmelweis is a young, brash and dedicated obstetrician in one of Vienna's largest hospitals. The patients of the doctors on Ward I are dying at an alarming rate, yet the midwives of Ward II boast of nearly no deaths at all. Obviously, there is a killer loose in Ward I. But who or what is killing these young women?

2774. "The Mysterious Slumber" (4/1/82; rebroadcast from 2/3/82)

2775. "The Naval Treaty" (4/2/82; rebroadcast 7/6/82)

Cast: Gordon Gould (Sherlock Holmes); Lloyd Battista (Percy Phelps); Carol Teitel (Anne Harrison); Bernard Grant (Dr. Watson). Adapted by Murray Burnett, based on the 1894 short story by Sir Arthur Conan Doyle.

Young Percy Phelps is a bright, up-and-coming British diplomat who has been entrusted with a top-secret, multinational treaty. In a rare unguarded moment, the document is stolen, leaving Mr. Phelps in a state of shock. His only hope is to call Sherlock Holmes out of retirement to help solve the mystery of who stole the treaty, and why.

2776. "Widow Wonderland" (4/5/82; rebroadcast 7/8/82)

Cast: Elspeth Eric (Muffie Van Dreelan); Fred Gywnne (Detective Harry Warren); Evelyn Juster (Rosie Harris); Earl Hammond (Augustus Bishop). Written by Steve Lehrman.

Muffie Van Dreeland, Winnifred Croft and Rosie Harris are all wealthy, independent widows, left alone in the prime of their lives. Augie Bishop, alias

Andre Mercato and Armand Grenville, has succeeded in bilking each of these three lovely ladies out of their loneliness and $10,000. Detective Harry Warren is hot on Augie's trail, but the ladies have a better idea of how to put this charming gold digger in his place.

2777. "The Cantankerous Ghost" (4/6/82; rebroadcast from 2/5/82)

2778. "Change of Heart" (4/8/82; rebroadcast from 2/8/82)

Cast: Marian Seldes (Semiramis); Russell Horton (Adarmalik); Ray Owens (Ninus); Norman Rose (Menon). Written by Sam Dann.

Semiramis, really an ordinary woman, believes that she is the daughter of a mortal man and the goddess Dagon. With such an extraordinary bloodline, she schemes to rule Assyria, Babylon and all the provinces therein. She succeeds, but her husbands—all three of them—must pay a heavy price for her glory.

2779. "Change of Heart" (4/8/82; rebroadcast from 2/8/82)

2780. "You Tell Me Your Dream" (4/9/82; rebroadcast 7/15/82)

Cast: Michael Tolan (Ed Larsen); Robert Kaliban (Mark Howgate); Cynthia Adler (Ginny Larsen); Mandel Kramer (Bartender). Written by Mary Renwick.

Ed Larsen has been having a recurring dream in which he is viciously attacked by a faceless person. Mark Howgate, a stranger to Ed, is having the same dream on the same nights. When the two men finally meet, they decide to act out the dream in order to find the faceless murderer and put an end to their nightmares. The *real* nightmare, though, is just beginning.

2781. "His Fourth Wife" (4/12/82; rebroadcast 7/19/82)

Cast: Russell Horton (Hans Holbein); Norman Rose (Thomas Cromwell); Earl Hammond (Henry the VIII); Carol Teitel (Anne of Cleves). Written by Sam Dann, based on actual historical events.

Court painter, Hans Holbein is commissioned by Henry VIII to produce the portraits of Anne of Cleves and Christina of Denmark. From the two portraits, the king will choose his next wife. Hans' ability to paint the ladies' faces—as well as their innermost feelings—makes Henry's choice simple and deadly.

2782. "The Sand Castle" (4/13/82; rebroadcast from 2/10/82)

2783. "The Visions of Sir Philip Sidney" (4/14/82; rebroadcast 7/21/82)

Cast: Lee Richardson (Sir Philip Sidney); Russell Horton (Trevor Haight); Court Benson (Inspector Graham); Cynthia Harris (Margaret Sidney). Written by G. Frederic Lewis.

Sir Philip Sidney, a war hero, has experienced three very strange encounters with persons who may or may not truly exist. His "visions" are gradually becoming very much like his wife, best friend and house guest. Are they real, or is the shock brought on by his trauma from the war returning?

Notes: Cynthia Harris' film credits include *Edward and Mrs. Simpson* (1980), *Reuben and Reuben* (1983), *Izzy and Moe* (1985), *Three Men and a Baby* (1987), and *Pancho Barnes* (1988).

2784. "The Bargain" (4/15/82; rebroadcast from 2/12/82)

2785. "Something to Live For" (4/16/82; rebroadcast 7/23/82)

Cast: Fred Gwynne (Gus Barstow); Joan Shea (Anna Barstow); Bernard Grant (Commissioner Murphy); Earl Hammond (Jacob Kowalski). Written by Mary Renwick.

Gus Barstow, a retired detective, saves Jacob Kowalski from taking his own life. Once safe, Jacob confesses that he is wanted by the police for insurance fraud. Gus' nose for justice leads the two of them on a wild and dangerous investigation to clear Jacob's name.

2786. "Shelter" (4/19/82; rebroadcast 7/26/82)

Cast: Ralph Bell (Sloan Cunningham); Evelyn Juster (Petra Cunningham); Don Scardino (Warren Crisp); Robert Kaliban (Denton Barnes). Written by Henry Slesar.

Sloan Cunningham, his wife Petra, and her lover, Warren Crisp, meet to have a frank and civilized discussion of the Cunninghams' impending divorce. But a nuclear accident halfway around the earth triggers worldwide panic and leads to Sloan's only bargaining point: Petra and Warren may start their new life together with his blessing if they leave the safety of the "shelter."

2787. "The .44 Connection" (4/20/82; rebroadcast from 2/15/82)

2788. "The Jataka" (4/21/82; rebroadcast 7/28/82)

Cast: Marian Seldes (Geraldine MacElroy); Lloyd Battista (Jack Lowden); Earl Hammond (Inspector Selby). Written by Sam Dann.

Geraldine MacElroy has just finished lecturing at the University of Delhi where her old friend Professor Tankling is translating "The Jataka," the story of the birth of Buddha. When the professor disappears, the most obvious conclusion is to believe that Jack, his brilliant young assistant, has murdered him. Why? Because everyone knows that he's done it before.

2789. "The Washington Kidnap" (4/22/82; rebroadcast from 2/17/82)

2790. "The Whimpering Pond" (4/23/82; rebroadcast 7/30/82)

Cast: Norman Rose (Sam Fowler); Evelyn Juster (Diana Brooks); Mandel Kramer (Paul Brooks); Ralph Bell (Emmett Stark). Written by Roy Winsor.

Paul and Diana Brooks have bought their house from a heartbroken lawyer whose wife suddenly disappeared about seven years ago. Suddenly, while houseguest Sam Fowler, a distant relative of the missing woman, visits the Brooks', a shadowy figure across the pond appears, pleading for help. Is this just an illusion, brought about by the fog and evening mist, or could it be that someone is reaching out from the grave for vengeance?

2791. "The Hanging Sheriff" (4/26/82; rebroadcast 8/2/82)

Cast: Fred Gwynne (Sheriff Tom Bender); Elspeth Eric (Sarah Bender); Bernard Grant (Frank); Russell Horton (Jud). Written by Bryce Walton.

Sheriff Tom Bender never thought that he would be called upon to be chief executioner when a drifting salesman was accused, convicted and sentenced to hang for murder. In truth the drifter accidentally killed someone, but the town needs a hanging and needs a hangman. Tom must find a way of ridding himself of the job and his nagging wife.

2792. "The Victim" (4/27/82; rebroadcast from 2/19/82)

2793. "The Ghost of Andersonville" (4/28/82; rebroadcast 8/4/82)

Cast: Tony Roberts (Major Calvin Russell); Teri Keane (Mrs. Mary Cutler); Robert Kaliban (General Benjamin Cutler); Keir Dullea (Tim Forres). Written by James Agate, Jr.

Major Calvin Russell was wounded and imprisoned by the Confederates while following the orders of his commander, General Benjamin Cutler. Along with Russell, 1,500 other Union soldiers were killed or captured. Now, Russell has the opportunity to face the general and bring to light the details of that nightmare. But the general is found dead, and the only suspect, Major Russell, finds himself once more in a prisoner's irons.

2794. "Nickels and Dimes" (4/29/82; rebroadcast from 2/22/82)

2795. "The Last Duel" (4/30/82; rebroadcast 8/6/82)

Cast: Lee Richardson (Captain Nicholson); Bernard Grant (Colonel Sergio); Teri Keane (Marta); Russell Horton (Lieutenant Lawrence). Adapted by James Agate, Jr., based on the 1830 short story *The Shot* by Alexander Pushkin.

Colonel Sergio is an officer in the British forces stationed in nineteenth-century India. Although his bravery is legend, he has just backed out of a duel that someone knows he would have easily won. Was it cowardice, as some of the men in the ranks think? Or is Colonel Sergio merely intent upon finishing an old duel— with the man who took his fiancée away from him—before moving on to other challenges?

2796. "Guilty as Charged" (5/3/82; rebroadcast 8/9/82)

Cast: Michael Tolan (Gene Fowler); Carol Teitel (Jane Fowler); Lloyd Battista (Trooper Carson); Mandel Kramer (Sam Strauss). Written by G. Frederic Lewis.

Gene and Jane Fowler are hard-working, honest people who believe in the justice system and wouldn't think of stepping over the line. However, in a matter of just a few short hours, Gene is accused of armed robbery and kidnapping and placed in jail to face criminal charges. The burden of proof is on Gene, while his double is still free to commit more crimes.

2797. "Invaders from Atlantis" (5/4/82; rebroadcast from 2/24/82)

2798. "Dreamers and Killers" (5/5/82; rebroadcast 8/11/82)

Cast: Marian Seldes (Helen); Diane Kirkwood (Jo Anne); Gordon Gould (Richard). Written by Sam Dann.

Helen and Richard were engaged for five years, and it seemed that it would go on forever. However, when Richard met Louise, things changed. Everyone felt that Helen was taking the news particularly well, until Richard confided to her that he had been having some very close calls with death, just as Helen had been dreaming about since their engagement was broken.

2799. "The Blood Red Ink" (5/6/82; rebroadcast from 2/26/82)

2800. "The Wedding Present" (5/7/82; rebroadcast 8/13/82)

Cast: Ralph Bell (Oliver Tolliver); Earl Hammond (King Bohvrah); Patricia Elliott (Jennie). Written by Sam Dann.

Oliver, a semi-successful con man, has stumbled into a remote little country off the coast of Australia to find that an old buddy of his, Jake, has conned his way up to the throne of the little nation. In the process of using his old friend at the top, he falls in love with the young American artist who is painting the king's portrait, and finds a way to gain money, freedom and the lovely young artist in one fell swoop. But it is a long shot, and con artists do not take long shots.

2801. "Tourist Trap" (5/10/82; rebroadcast 8/16/82)

Cast: Paul Hecht (Harry Meeker); Earl Hammond (Hollis McAllister); Evelyn Juster (Kay McAllister); Teri Keane (Ruth Meeker). Written by Douglas Dempsey.

Harry and Ruth Meeker are on their way to a long overdue and well-deserved vacation when a slight accident and a wrong turn into the village of "Downsville," finds them mysteriously and frighteningly held against their wills. Harry wants some questions answered: Why can't he and Ruth leave? Why is everyone in Downsville related? And why are there two gravestones in the town's cemetery with Ruth and Harry's names on them?

2802. "The Blue Sedan" (5/11/82; rebroadcast from 3/1/82)

2803. "The Wound That Would Not Heal" (5/12/82; rebroadcast 8/18/82)

Cast: Ralph Bell (Mark Foresight); Bernard Grant (Sergeant Gentry); Cynthia Adler (Carol Foresight). Written by Sidney Slon.

Mark Foresight is trying to pull his marriage together, at least what there is left of it. His first step is to end his affair with Lorene Jessup. However, the day after they split, Lorene is found murdered. Mark had no reason to do it, but the constant sound of Lorene's voice, begging him to save her, has him believing that he is the only possible killer.

2804. "Death Star" (5/13/82; rebroadcast from 3/3/82)

2805. "The Hills of Arias" (5/14/82; rebroadcast 8/20/82)

Cast: Mandel Kramer (Francisco Canoyas); Marian Seldes (Emily); Robert Kaliban (Cypriano); Ray Owens (Dr. Kurtz). Written by Sam Dann.

Francisco Canoyas, a once-revered revolutionary hero, is now living a quiet American life, far from the turmoil in his old country. His mundane existence is interrupted by his 20-year-old godson, who urges Francisco to return to his country and again lead his people to victory. The young man's pleas are seconded by the spirits of those who fought with Francisco in the last revolution, including his first—and very dead—wife.

2806. "The Imperfect Crime" (5/17/82; rebroadcast 8/23/82)

Cast: Russell Horton (Inspector Charles Allan); Bob Dryden (Cornelius Spry); Carol Teitel (Matilda Allan). Written by James Agate, Jr.

Years ago, Inspector Charles Allan was in love with Jessie Havermeyer. Now, he is trying to find out who recklessly ran her down in the middle of the night. Thanks to the police officer's snooping wife, clues are appearing which indicate that Jessie might have been ruthlessly murdered.

2807. "Death at a Distance" (5/18/82; rebroadcast from 3/5/82)

2808. "The Brooch" (5/19/82; rebroadcast 8/25/82)

Cast: Paul Hecht (Andrei); Patricia Elliott (Mashenka); Anne Seymour (Fedosya); Earl Hammond (Igor). Adapted by G. Frederic Lewis, based on the a short story by Anton Chekhov.

Young Mashenka is a governess employed by a very wealthy and very strange Russian couple. Shortly after her arrival, she is subjected to some bizarre encounters, including the attempted suicide of the master and the accusation that she has stolen a priceless brooch from her mistress.

2809. "First Impressions" (5/20/82; rebroadcast from 3/8/82)

2810. "The 'Different' People" (5/21/82; rebroadcast 8/27/82)

Cast: Kristoffer Tabori (Bick Bixby); Jada Rowland (Susannah Partridge);

Russell Horton (Jerry Hansen); Arnold Moss (Timothy Partridge). Written by Arnold Moss.

"Bick" Bixby discovers an old letter written by a soldier to his wife about the special reason why he and only a few others were returning from the Civil War unharmed. His plan was to find a place where he and his family could start their own village in total seclusion. Now, more than a century later, Bick wants to find that village and learn the secret this small band of settlers discovered so long ago.

2811. "Your Desires, My Guilt" (5/24/82; rebroadcast 8/30/82)

Cast: Norman Rose (Maurice); Elspeth Eric (Dorothy); Teri Keane (Ursula). Written by Sam Dann.

Maurice and Ursula live the middle-class existence of a small-town college professor and his wife. Ursula wishes for wealth, and Maurice sincerely wishes he could provide her with it. Suddenly, as if from a fairy tale, their wishes are granted.

2812. "The Heart of Boadicea" (5/25/82; rebroadcast from 3/10/82)

2813. "Why Is This Lady Smiling?" (5/26/82; rebroadcast 9/1/82)

Cast: John Vickery (Leonardo Da Vinci); Diana Kirkwood (Mona Lisa Del Giocondo); Bernard Grant (Zanobi Del Giocondo). Written by Sam Dann.

Mona Lisa Del Giocondo's rich husband has commissioned the famed Leonardo da Vinci to paint a portrait of his wife. The fascinating thing about this lovely young woman is her hypnotic smile. However, after the artist displays his masterpiece, the model's husband and acquaintances take a sudden and violent dislike for her. Is it her new-found fame?

2814. "The New Man at the Yard" (5/27/82; rebroadcast from 3/12/82)

2815. "The Chess Master" (5/28/82; rebroadcast 9/3/82)

Cast: Paul Hecht (Charley Williams); Fred Gwynne (Chessman); Russell Horton (Ben Bradley); Lamis Farris (Susan Williams). Written by Murray Burnett.

Charley Williams gets fired from his job, plays a simple game of chess with a stranger, and finds himself $5,000 richer—all within the space of two days. A job offer and more games ensue, but why is everything happening so fast? And why does Charley have the feeling that each time he wins a game, he is losing a very important part of his life?

2816. "Lady Macbeth at the Zoo" (5/31/82; rebroadcast 9/6/82)

Cast: Larry Haines (Waldo); Teri Keane (Martha); Earl Hammond (Carl); Evelyn Juster (Edna). Written by Sam Dann.

Waldo and Edna, prize attractions at the Bronx Zoo, overhear Carl Carrol and Martha Tyson plan to kill his rich uncle. But what can two apes, behind bars, do to either stop the murder or bring the two killers to the attention of the police? The murder is committed, and now only two apes and two humans know whodunit. Can Waldo bring the killers to justice?

2817. "The Face of the Waters" (6/1/82; rebroadcast from 3/15/82)

2818. "Two Times Dead" (6/2/82; rebroadcast 9/8/82)

Cast: Lloyd Battista (Ezra Harper); Bernard Grant (Chadwick Pollister); Carol Teitel (Lydia); Ray Owens (Nathaniel Pollister). Written by Sam Dann.

Chadwick Pollister is discovered murdered on the road near home. James K. Selby has just been arrested, tried and convicted of the crime. However, Selby claims he is really Pollister and that he found Selby's body and switched identities. A visiting journalist finds too many unanswered questions in the situation: Why won't anyone in town identify him? And if he is Pollister, how can he hang for killing himself?

2819. "Tippecanoe and Tyler, Too" (6/3/82; rebroadcast from 3/17/82)

2820. "My First Rogue" (6/4/82; rebroadcast 9/10/82)

Cast: Lee Richardson (Arsene Lupin); Louis Turenne (Robert); Bob Dryden (Marcel); Robert Kaliban (Maurice LeBlanc). Adapted by G. Frederic Lewis, based on the a story by Maurice LeBlanc.

Frenchman Arsene Lupin, a master thief and gentleman, is in jail for having stolen the Gilbert Stuart portrait of George Washington. While there, a wealthy resident of his small village is robbed of several priceless art objects, in spite of the fact that the man had three detectives and a host of security devices guarding his home. Lupin takes full credit for the theft, having skillfully executed the entire operation from his jail cell.

Notes: Lee Richardson's film credits include *Prizzi's Honor* (1985), *The Believers* (1987), *Tiger Warsaw* (1987), and *The Fly II* (1989), and *A Stranger Among Us* (1992).

2821. "Les Misérables, Part I: The Thief and the Bishop" (6/7/82; rebroadcast from 1/11/82)

2822. "Les Misérables, Part II: The Lawless and the Law" (6/8/82; rebroadcast from 1/12/82)

2823. "Les Misérables, Part III: No Escape" (6/9/82; rebroadcast from 1/13/82)

2824. "Les Misérables, Part IV: Fear, Love and Death" (6/10/82; rebroadcast from 1/14/82)

2825. "Les Misérables, Part V: The Final Chapter" (6/11/82; rebroadcast from 1/15/82)

2826. "The Woman Who Wanted to Live" (6/14/82; rebroadcast 9/13/82)

Cast: Larry Haines (Ray Bardon); Roberta Maxwell (Lisa); Russell Horton (Freddy). Written by Bryce Walton.

Lisa has inadvertently walked in on escaped convict Ray Bardon as he robs and murders a young gas station attendant. In what should be a method of saving herself, she offers to protect him through police barricades and road blocks to find freedom. But why is Lisa so intent upon saving this ruthless murderer? A secret from Lisa's past keeps her and Bardon alive—for now.

2827. "The Magic Stick of Manitu" (6/15/82; rebroadcast from 3/19/82)

2828. "A Most Dangerous Animal" (6/16/82; rebroadcast 9/15/82)

Cast: Fred Gwynne (Tiger Vincent); Teri Keane (Laurie Vincent); Mandel Kramer (Jack Huggins); Bob Dryden (Dusty). Written by Sidney Slon.

Tiger Vincent is a ruthless heavyweight boxer who has already beaten one opponent to death and wouldn't mind repeating that performance if it means the title. Meanwhile, he practices this "manly" art by beating up his estranged wife and her present love. Can a slight-yet-crafty lover overcome a huge, professional fighter?

2829. "The Tool Shed" (6/17/82; rebroadcast from 3/22/82)

2830. "The Fifth Man" (6/18/82; rebroadcast 9/17/82)

Cast: Norman Rose (Everett Parker); Bernard Grant (William Jackson); Marian Seldes (Frances Jackson); Lloyd Battista (Karl Carson). Written by James Agate, Jr.

William Jackson has been murdered. He was a higher-up within the British secret intelligence, well known throughout international spy circles. The question is, was he killed by his own people, the enemy, or his best friend who was in love with his wife Frances? Or did he simply "accidentally" fall from a moving train?

2831. "Universe Hollow" (6/21/82; rebroadcast 9/21/82)

Cast: Patricia Elliott (Sheila Rogan); Joyce Gordon (Serena); Arnold Moss (Bard); Earl Hammond (Lewis). Written by Sam Dann.

Correspondent Sheila Rogan was at the top of her profession when her Pulitzer Prize–winning book was discovered to be based on lies. She hopes her report on a group that claims to communicate with other planets will serve to polish her tarnished reputation, only to find a disturbing credibility to that band's claims.

2832. "The Old Country" (6/22/82; rebroadcast from 3/24/82)

2833. "Matching Chairs" (6/23/82; rebroadcast 9/23/82)

Cast: Paul Hecht (Cary); Elspeth Eric (Mother); Carol Teitel (Jessie); Kristoffer Tabori (Troy). Written by Elspeth Eric.

Cary has been taught since his earliest memory to take care of "The Little One," younger brother Troy. Cary has his work cut out for him; despite his best intentions, Troy is always in a fix. Now Cary has to solve a new one: Troy is convinced his problems stem from one chair in a set of handsome family heirlooms.

2834. "In the Cards" (6/24/82; rebroadcast from 3/26/82)

2835. "Don't Kill Me" (6/25/82; rebroadcast 9/28/82)

Cast: Tony Roberts (Ted); Roberta Maxwell (Wilma); Joan Shay (Grace); Lee Richardson (George). Written by Sam Dann.

Wilma really couldn't help killing husband George. All it took was walking away when the sick man's breathing stopped. And besides, she got to marry rich Ted in the bargain. But Ted whisks her away to the Amazon, where he is searching for lost civilizations and where she contracts a wasting illness for which she is dependent on Ted for medicine to keep her alive just as George once depended on her.

2836. "Escape to Prison" (6/28/82; rebroadcast 9/30/82)

Cast: Marian Seldes (Liz Marlowe); Bernard Grant (Dr. Tom Souris); Earl Hammond (Lieutenant Ted Risman); Evelyn Juster (Ruth/Rose). Written by Sam Dann.

Cosmetics executive Liz Marlowe is up for a promotion, but colleagues, friends and even her psychiatrist seem to be blocking it. Clearing up the mystery surrounding her husband's death would put Liz in a better bargaining position. She enlists the aid of the police, but in the process brings some long-buried secrets to the surface.

2837. "On the Night of the Dead" (6/29/82; rebroadcast from 3/29/82)

2838. "Killer Crab" (6/30/82; rebroadcast 10/5/82)

Cast: Russell Horton (Joe Harkness); Ann Williams (Ruth); Bob Dryden (Povar); Mandel Kramer (Sam). Written by James Agate, Jr.

Joe Harkness, a "down to Earth" guy living on planet Vivian, doesn't seem to measure up to mate Ruth's ideals. Despite her desire to separate from Joe, Ruth insists on retaining her share of Joe's new weapon, K. C. What neither of them realize is the future price to be paid for this investment.

2839. "I Am the Killer" (7/1/82; rebroadcast from 3/31/82)

2840. "Bring Back My Body" (7/2/82; rebroadcast 10/7/82)

Cast: Kim Hunter (Tabitha); Carol Teitel (Mother/Ms. Dustan); Bernard Grant (Doctor/Father); Louis Turenne (Spencer). Written by Sam Dann.

Tabitha Riding, an educated, conservative engineer, knows she must murder Spencer Whitlow, a man she's never heard of. She consults a psychiatrist to help unravel this mystery, and suddenly past, present and future collide openly as Tabitha and Spencer meet face to face—again.

2841. "The Romance of Mary Oates" (7/5/82; rebroadcast 10/12/82)

Cast: Roberta Maxwell (Mary); Paul Hecht (Burt); Bob Dryden (Mr. Becker); Mandel Kramer (Father). Written by Bob Juhren.

When love first comes to lonely, middle-aged Mary Oates, the world seems rosy to her alone. For the first time she's trying all kinds of new things, including murder.

Notes: At the time of this broadcast Roberta Maxwell could be seen on the big screen in *Lois Gibbs and the Love Canal* (1982). She later appeared in *Psycho 3* (1986) and *Philadelphia* (1993).

2842. "The Naval Treaty" (7/6/82; rebroadcast from 4/2/82)

2843. "Code Word: Caprice" (7/7/82; rebroadcast 10/14/82)

Cast: Lloyd Battista (Alan Harper); Bernard Grant (Jack Clark); Joyce Gordon (Yvette); Earl Hammond (Tom Tully). Written by Roy Winsor.

The Mercury Express Company hauls food and ammunition—a hijacker's dream. One truck after another seems to be disappearing without a trace, until supposedly honest employee Tom Tully turns in $5,000 he received for cooperating with the hijackers.

2844. "Widow Wonderland" (7/8/82; rebroadcast from 4/5/82)

2845. "Come Back Next Week" (7/9/82; rebroadcast 10/21/82)

Cast: Teri Keane (Emma Dawson); Evelyn Juster (Carlotta); Fred Gwynne (Boomer); Sam Gray (Guard). Written by Sam Dann.

Millionairess Emma Dawson sets out to avenge her husband's death. Convicted hit man Boomer cautiously introduces her to the alien world of crime, but the cast of characters is surprisingly familiar to Emma. Were all saints first sinners or could it be that every cop is a killer?

2846. "The Hand of Amnesia" (7/12/82; rebroadcast 10/19/82)

Cast: Ralph Bell (Bill); Marian Seldes (Anny); Lloyd Battista (Foster); Carol Teitel (Judith). Written by G. Frederic Lewis.

A poor cook gets married to a wealthy matron very unexpectedly, rushing the services to top speed. But the marriage comes to a quick halt when the cook learns that he is the prime suspect in a murder investigation, of which his wife is the slab.

2847. "Only a Woman" (7/13/82)

Cast: Marian Seldes (Semiramis); Russell Horton (Adarmalik); Norman Rose (Menon); Ray Owens (Ninus). Written by Sam Dann.

Semiramis, a young and beautiful woman, is subject to flights of fantasy when she believes herself to be a goddess. Her demonic dreams get out of hand when she begins making plans to rule the world.

2848. "The Innocent Murderer" (7/14/82; rebroadcast 10/26/82)

Cast: Tony Roberts (John Seuratt); Bob Dryden (Conductor); Gordon Gould (Booth); Robert Kaliban (Henri). Written by James Agate, Jr.

The sole conspirator of the Abraham Lincoln assassination escapes and makes plans to travel the world, hoping he will never be recognized. But neither his guilt nor his capture can be assuaged.

2849. "You Tell Me Your Dream" (7/15/82; rebroadcast from 4/9/82)

2850. "The Great Catherine" (7/16/82; rebroadcast 10/28/82)

Cast: Tammy Grimes (Catherine); Russell Horton (Paul); Earl Hammond (Panin); Bernard Grant (Olaf). Written by G. Frederic Lewis.

Shakespeare's immortal *Hamlet* plot springs to mortal life when Catherine the Great's son and heir, Paul, discovers some ruthless dealings in the life of his mother.

Notes: On January 26, 1982, "To Be an Empress" was broadcast, concerning the early years of Catherine the Great, played by Amanda Plummer. In this episode, *Theater* presented the later years of Catherine the Great, and to play the role of Catherine this time, a woman with an older voice was needed. It was no surprise that Amanda's mother, Tammy Grimes, got the role. "There is a great deal of similarity between the life of Catherine and that of my daughter and me," noted Grimes. "She was passionate about art, culture and music and took her role in society very seriously."

2851. "His Fourth Wife" (7/19/82; rebroadcast from 4/12/82)

2852. "Formula Z—The Protector" (7/20/82; rebroadcast 11/1/82)

Cast: Patricia Elliott (Lieutenant Webster); Ray Owens (Joe Buhler); Mandel Kramer (Captain Kohler); Evelyn Juster (Lillian). Written by Sam Dann.

In order to fingerprint suspects and criminals in murder investigations, an ink pad is required. But when new wonder paint Formula Z is the main ingredient of such an investigation, the police stir up a batch of murder suspects that can't be covered over by international intrigue.

Notes: This episode, "Formula Z—The Protector," was originally titled "The Protector."

2853. "The Visions of Sir Philip Sidney" (7/21/82; rebroadcast from 4/14/82)

2854. "Yearbook" (7/22/82; rebroadcast 11/3/82)

Cast: Evelyn Juster (Rose Rossman); Lloyd Battista (Donald); Sam Gray (Chief Reading). Written by Douglas Dempsey.

Walter Laszlo still lives up to his high school nickname "Ladykiller," but he may be taking it all too seriously.

2855. "Something to Live For" (7/23/82; rebroadcast from 4/16/82)

2856. "Shelter" (7/26/82; rebroadcast from 4/19/82)

2857. "Adolf and Eva" (7/27/82; rebroadcast 11/5/82)

Cast: Roberta Maxwell (Eva Braun); Bob Dryden (Martin Borden); Louis Turenne (Jack Lowden). Written by Sam Dann.

A frightening vision of the future, and a new version of the Adam and Eve story. The final days in a confined bunker come alive for Eva as she attains all she's wanted for 16 years. But the Bible says, "Go forth and multiply."

2858. "The Jataka" (7/28/82; rebroadcast from 4/21/82)

2859. "Mind Over Mind" (7/29/82; rebroadcast 11/8/82)

Cast: Jada Rowland (The Girl); Bernard Grant (The Detective); Russell Horton (The Teller); Earl Hammond (The Manager). Written by Elspeth Eric.

A detective discovers more than just a grave coverup when he discovers that a young bank teller who is accused of robbery has been under hypnosis the entire time. When she is snapped out of her so-called trance, she discovers that it was *she* who was robbed.

2860. "The Whimpering Pond" (7/30/82; rebroadcast from 4/23/82)

2861. "The Hanging Sheriff" (8/2/82; rebroadcast from 4/26/82)

2862. "Redhead" (8/3/82; rebroadcast 11/10/82)

Cast: Fred Gwynne (Harry); Carol Teitel (Alice); Mandel Kramer (Joey). Written by Sam Dann.

Harry is a has-been prize fighter whose only major handicap is the color red. Like a raging bull, Harry goes crazy whenever this bright color shines his way, and he is driven to knock out his opponents, including innocent redheads he's never met.

2863. "The Ghost of Andersonville" (8/4/82; rebroadcast from 4/28/82)

2864. "Murder by Decree" (8/5/82; rebroadcast 11/12/82)

Cast: Marian Seldes (Ann Boleyn); Earl Hammond (Henry VIII); Carol Teitel (Rosalind); Bernard Grant (Norfolk). Written by James Agate, Jr., based on actual historical events.

Henry VIII's second wife, Ann Boleyn, cannot give him the son he wants so desperately, leading the king to contrive a plan to do away with his queen.

2865. "The Last Duel" (8/6/82; rebroadcast from 4/30/82)

2866. "Guilty as Charged" (8/9/82; rebroadcast from 5/3/82)

2867. "A Pair of Green Eyes" (8/10/82; rebroadcast 11/15/82)

Cast: Teri Keane (Lili); Robert Kaliban (Shep); Arnold Moss (Luis); Russell Horton (Cesar). Written by Arnold Moss.

A man uncovers a powerful stone that contains the force and ability to turn a man into an immortal god. A series of demonic events prove just what kind of god.

2868. "Dreamers and Killers" (8/11/82; rebroadcast from 5/5/82)

2869. "The Man with the X-Ray Eyes" (8/12/82; rebroadcast 11/17/82)

Cast: Fred Gwynne (Sheriff); Court Benson (Decker); Lloyd Battista (Dr. Golynska). Written by Bryce Walton.

Personal gain instead of justice blinds a law man from bringing a murderer to the stand.

2870. "The Wedding Present" (8/13/82; rebroadcast from 5/7/82)

2871. "Tourist Trap" (8/16/82; rebroadcast from 5/10/82)

2872. "Famous Last Words" (8/17/82; rebroadcast 11/19/82)

Cast: Kim Hunter (Irma); Mandel Kramer (Lew); Robert Kaliban (Dozier). Written by Sam Dann.

A respected engineer's credibility is questioned when she insists on having seen a dead body on a deserted street.

2873. "The Wound That Would Not Heal" (8/18/82; rebroadcast from 5/12/82)

2874. "Eleanora" (8/19/82; rebroadcast 11/22/82)

Cast: Marian Seldes (Eleanora); Lloyd Battista (Misha); Earl Hammond (Max); Evelyn Juster (Mrs. Flake). Written by James Agate, Jr.

A secret society persuades a famous actress to become a member and causes her to play the most deadly role of her career.

2875. "The Hills of Arias" (8/20/82; rebroadcast from 5/14/82)

2876. "The Imperfect Crime" (8/23/82; rebroadcast from 5/17/82)

2877. "Funeral Without a Corpse" (8/24/82; rebroadcast 11/24/82)
Cast: Norman Rose (Richard); Bernard Grant (Max); Teri Keane (Pauline); Ray Owens (Mack). Written by Sidney Slon.
A gubernatorial hopeful is haunted by ghosts from his past who return for their own personal agenda, putting his career and marriage in peril.

2878. "The Brooch" (8/25/82; rebroadcast from 5/19/82)

2879. "Barn Burner" (8/26/82; rebroadcast 11/26/82)
Cast: Patricia Elliott (Jodie); Russell Horton (Jed); Bob Dryden (Doc Townsend); Ralph Bell (Skeeter). Written by Steve Lehrman.
There's more to horse racing than training thoroughbreds, as two down-and-out equestrians quickly discover.

2880. "The 'Different' People" (8/27/82; rebroadcast from 5/21/82)

2881. "Your Desires, My Guilt" (8/30/82; rebroadcast from 5/24/82)

2882. "How Do You Like Those Apples?" (8/31/82; rebroadcast 11/29/82)
Cast: Mandel Kramer (John Crosswell); Carol Teitel (Louise Crosswell); Robert Kaliban (Professor Tolliver); Cynthia Adler (Jane). Written by Sam Dann.
John has been unfaithful to his wife, Louise, and life's just desserts catch up to him when he discovers that the events of a recurring nightmare suddenly become true.

2883. "Why Is This Lady Smiling?" (9/1/82; rebroadcast from 5/26/82)

2884. "The Rim of Eternity" (9/2/82; rebroadcast 12/1/82)
Cast: Larry Haines (Joe Morris); Mandel Kramer (Mr. Kaufman); Evelyn Juster (Elaine Starky). Written by Sam Dann.
Joe Morris, a down-and-out journalist, notices the new changes in his life when the solution to a seemingly routine murder investigation sheds new light on human fallibility.

2885. "The Chess Master" (9/3/82; rebroadcast from 5/28/82)

2886. "Lady Macbeth at the Zoo" (9/6/82; rebroadcast from 5/31/82)

2887. "Scenes from a Murder" (9/7/82; rebroadcast 12/3/82)

Cast: Russell Horton (Raskolnikov); Carol Teitel (Alyona); Joan Shay (Mother); Earl Hammond (Pestrakov). Adapted by G. Frederic Lewis, based on the 1886 novel *Crime and Punishment* by Fyodor Dostoyevsky.

A poor student commits a heinous crime in a far-fetched attempt to better himself, only to find he is tormented by self-induced punishment.

2888. "Two Times Dead" (9/8/82; rebroadcast from 6/2/82)

2889. "The Riddle" (9/9/82; rebroadcast 12/4/82)

Cast: Patricia Elliott (Penelope); Lloyd Battista (Barton); Elspeth Eric (Alicia). Written by Karen Thorsen.

An enterprising young couple help an old woman come to terms with her past, solving a riddle that dates back to her childhood.

2890. "My First Rogue" (9/10/82; rebroadcast from 6/4/82)

2891. "The Woman Who Wanted to Live" (9/13/82; rebroadcast from 6/14/82)

2892. "The Forbidden House" (9/14/82; rebroadcast 12/8/82)

Cast: Tony Roberts (Charles); Diana Kirkwood (Ellen); Bob Dryden (Doctor); Bernard Grant (Visitor). Written by Elspeth Eric.

A wandering circus comes to town, and everyone is talking about the elephants, clowns, trapeze artists, and fire-eaters. One of the circus attendants is drawn into a small unassuming house and, after paying the resident a visit, refuses to leave until the town's aging doctor reveals the truth about him.

2893. "A Most Dangerous Animal" (9/15/82; rebroadcast from 6/16/82)

2894. "Two Sisters" (9/16/82; rebroadcast 12/9/82)

Cast: Marian Seldes (Samantha); Patricia Elliott (Sophia); Earl Hammond (James Parker). Written by Sam Dann.

Murder does not quell the turbulence between two sisters, it simply leads to the undoing of them both.

2895. "The Fifth Man" (9/17/82; rebroadcast from 6/18/82)

2896. "The Way Station" (9/20/82; rebroadcast 12/10/82)

Cast: Norman Rose (Peter); Mia Dillion (Judith); Bernard Grant (Dr. Kodaly); Russell Horton (Stephan). Written by G. Frederic Lewis.

A grave digger is responsible for carrying out the final wishes of the dead—including those of his wife.

2897. "Universe Hollow" (9/21/82; rebroadcast from 6/21/82)

2898. "Pursuit of a Dream" (9/22/82; rebroadcast 12/13/82)

Cast: Carol Teitel (Marie Curie); Mandel Kramer (Pierre); Lloyd Battista (Jozef). Written by G. Frederic Lewis, based on actual historical events.

The life of scientist Marie Curie is dramatized, from her humble beginnings through her remarkable discovery of radioactive elements polonium and radium in the mineral pitchblende in 1898. After winning a Nobel Prize for chemistry in 1911, she died of leukemia, no doubt contracted in the course of her work with radioactive materials.

2899. "Matching Chairs" (9/23/82; rebroadcast from 6/23/82)

2900. "The Force of Evil" (9/24/82; rebroadcast 12/14/82)

Cast: Paul Hecht (Stanley); Teri Keane (Sarah); Diana Kirkwood (Kim); Mary Negro (Lucy); Court Benson (Father Francis). Written by Roy Winsor.

A broken heart leads to possession by the devil and a haunting plan to win back a love.

Notes: Mary Joan Negro had previously appeared in the film *The Family Man* in 1979, and was currently being filmed for *No Big Deal*, which was released in the theaters months later.

2901. "Roll Call of the Dead" (9/27/82; rebroadcast 12/15/82)

Cast: Russell Horton (Jimmy); Lloyd Battista (Clark); Bob Dryden (Berry Davis); Arnold Moss (Joe Broken Arrow). Written by Arnold Moss.

When two young Easterners out for an "adventure" in the Wild West ignore the advice of their Apache guide, they encounter four dead men with hair-raising tales to tell.

2902. "Don't Kill Me" (9/28/82; rebroadcast from 6/25/82)

2903. "The Million Dollar Leg" (9/29/82; rebroadcast 12/16/82)

Cast: Tony Roberts (Tom); Bernard Grant (Larry); Evelyn Juster (Jan); Carol Teitel (Helena). Written by Sam Dann.

An attempt to persuade an Iron Curtain football natural to defect to the United States causes an ex-player to engage in a series of battles with his conscience.

2904. "Escape to Prison" (9/30/82; rebroadcast from 6/28/82)

2905. "Escape from Anzio" (10/1/82; rebroadcast 12/17/82)

Cast: Gordon Gould (Jack Hastings); Sam Gray (Lieutenant); Cynthia Adler (Sophia); Robert Kaliban (Tony Morelli). Written by James Agate, Jr.

Two downed American World War II fliers test their mettle in the toughest mission of their careers: escaping from behind enemy lines.

2906. "The Ninth Commandment" (10/4/82; rebroadcast 12/20/82)

Cast: Michael Tolan (Dick); Teri Keane (Alicia); Earl Hammond (Lieutenant Kaplan). Written by Sam Dann.

A wealthy society woman falls in love with a burglar, but when he's accused of murder, there's much more at stake than just his life.

2907. "Killer Crab" (10/5/82; rebroadcast from 6/30/82)

2908. "The Abraham Lincoln Murder Trial" (10/6/82; rebroadcast 12/21/82)

Cast: Lloyd Battista (Abraham Lincoln); Patricia Elliott (Lily); Bob Dryden (Sheriff); Gordon Gould (Tom). Written by James Agate, Jr.

When a case of gambling and murder shines in the public's eye, a young Abe Lincoln, just starting out his career in court politics, demonstrates his uncanny knack for prosecution.

2909. "Bring Back My Body" (10/7/82; rebroadcast from 7/2/82)

2910. "The Pale Horse" (10/8/82; rebroadcast 12/22/82)

Cast: Earl Hammond (Dr. Eaton); Marian Seldes (Donna); Mandel Kramer (Gil Lang); Elspeth Eric (Addie). Written by Roy Winsor.

A young model attempting to murder her wealthy, older husband has her plan thwarted when he takes a brief ride in the Death Coach.

2911. "Tony's Market" (10/11/82; rebroadcast 12/23/82)

Cast: Earl Hammond (Tony); Joan Shay (Amelia); Carol Teitel (Cordelia); Robert Kaliban (Albie); Arnold Moss (Harry). Written by Sam Dann.

Three people, bent on bettering their lives, meet their death when a sudden and unexpected burst of gunfire disturbs the sanctuary of Tony's Market.

2912. "The Romance of Mary Oates" (10/12/82; rebroadcast from 7/5/82)

2913. "Fly Swatter" (10/13/82; rebroadcast 12/24/82)

Cast: Fred Gwynne (Lou Valentine); Bernard Grant (Mr. Mosca); Evelyn Juster (Lil Valentine). Written by Sam Dann.

A pick-pocketing couple become victims of a bizarre scam when they take jobs as domestics for a nouveau rich family.

2914. "Code Word: Caprice" (10/14/82; rebroadcast from 7/7/82)

2915. "The Flash Point" (10/15/82; rebroadcast 12/27/82)

Cast: Paul Hecht (Harvey); Joyce Gordon (Carol); Carol Teitel (Miss Rader); Court Benson (Big Jim). Written by Sam Dann.

An outset engineering executive cannot rest until he seeks revenge against the man who caused his demise.

2916. "Desert Maiden" (10/18/82; rebroadcast 12/28/82)

Cast: Mason Adams (Sonny); Bob Dryden (Mr. Tolliver); Patricia Elliott (Ruth); Joan Shay (Bernice). Written by Sam Dann.

An advertising agency executive travels to the desert to seek out a legend, but discovers the truth about himself instead.

2917. "The Hand of Amnesia" (10/19/82; rebroadcast from 7/12/82)

2918. "Last Days of a Dictator" (10/20/82; rebroadcast 12/29/82)

Cast: Bernard Grant (Mussolini); Louis Turrenne (Adolf Hitler); Earl Hammond (Bottai); Marian Seldes (Clara); William Griffis (Grandi). Written by G. Frederic Lewis, based on actual historical events.

In the final horrifying days of World War II, Benito Mussolini thought his ally Adolf Hitler has rescued him from an unkind end, only to find that Hitler had planned far well in advance for his own "Il Duce."

2919. "Come Back Next Week" (10/21/82; rebroadcast from 7/9/82)

2920. "Three Fireflies in a Bottle" (10/22/82; rebroadcast 12/30/82)

Cast: Russell Horton (Robbie); Evelyn Juster (Buffie); Lloyd Battista (Major); Cynthia Adler (Arl). Written by Nancy Moore.

A small boy alienates his friend from outer space, triggering a series of dramatic events in an attempt to win him back.

2921. "Resident Killer" (10/25/82; rebroadcast 12/31/82)

Cast: Mason Adams (George); Russell Horton (President); Carol Teitel (Ella). Written by Sam Dann.

The timeless traits of aggression and forcefulness overcome a peaceful futuristic society, disrupting the lives of its most humane members.

2922. "The Innocent Murderer" (10/26/82; rebroadcast from 7/14/82)

2923. "The Voice That Wouldn't Die" (10/27/82)

Cast: Norman Rose (Colonel Mortimer); Bernard Grant (Dr. Stewart); Mia Dillion (Rowena); Earl Hammond (Jarvis). Written by G. Frederic Lewis.

An abandoned house on a Scottish moor still houses spirits that hauntingly beckon to the new family in town.

2924. "The Great Catherine" (10/28/82; rebroadcast from 7/16/82)

2925. "I Hate Harold" (10/29/82)

Cast: Larry Haines (George); Bob Dryden (Walter); Paul Hecht (Harold); Diana Kirkwood (Gretchen). Written by Henry Slesar.

A meek and mild-mannered jeweler's assistant, jealous of a brash new sales manager, sets out to catch him in the act of stealing the company's prize collection.

2926. "Formula Z—The Protector" (11/1/82; rebroadcast from 7/20/82)

2927. "The Sensible Thing" (11/2/82)

Cast: Lee Richardson (Curtis); Teri Keane (Helen); Ralph Bell (Damon). Written by Elspeth Eric.

A second marriage, an old pet dog and imaginary late-night conversations all contribute to the awakening of a stalwart yet unfeeling businessman.

2928. "Yearbook" (11/3/82; rebroadcast from 7/22/82)

2929. "The School Mistress" (11/4/82)

Cast: Patricia Elliott (Marya); Earl Hammond (Semyon); Lloyd Battista (Sergei). Adapted by James Agates, Jr., based on the 1897 short story *Home* by Anton Chekov.

The intervention of a cantankerous driver obliterates the dreams of a mild-mannered school mistress.

2930. "Adolf and Eva" (11/5/82; rebroadcast from 7/27/82)

2931. "Mind Over Mind" (11/8/82; rebroadcast from 7/29/82)

2932. "Portrait of the Past" (11/9/82)

Cast: Bill Griffis (Silus); Bernard Grant (Magnus); Robert Kaliban (Jason); Carol Teitel (Maria). Written by G. Frederic Lewis.

A painting of a beautiful young girl and a unique brooch raise a battery of questions for a visiting nephew.

2933. "Redhead" (11/10/82; rebroadcast from 8/3/82)

2934. "The Twelfth Juror" (11/11/82)

Cast: Marian Seldes (Rosalind); Lloyd Battista (Alfred); Mandel Kramer (Edward); Joan Shay (Lieutenant Alice McEller). Written by Sam Dann.

A wealthy businesswoman is forever linked to her lover by a small gold trinket purchased before his death.

2935. "Murder by Decree" (11/12/82; rebroadcast from 8/5/82)

2936. "A Pair of Green Eyes" (11/15/82; rebroadcast from 8/10/82)

2937. "The Magic Dust" (11/16/82)

Cast: Tony Roberts (Ellsworth); Evelyn Juster (Diane); Arnold Moss (Ballard). Written by Sam Dann.

A battle for control revolves around precious—and useful—metals not always used to achieve constructive ends.

2938. "The Man with the X-Ray Eyes" (11/17/82; rebroadcast from 8/12/82)

2939. "Diamond Dotty" (11/18/82)

Cast: Teri Keane (Harriet); Earl Hammond (Joe); Carol Teitel (Mary Lou); Bernard Grant (John). Written by Sam Dann.

They always say members of a western town quickly discover that diamonds are not always a girl's best friend, especially when times change as the years go by.

2940. "Famous Last Words" (11/19/82; rebroadcast from 8/17/82)

2941. "Eleanora" (11/22/82; rebroadcast from 8/19/82)

2942. "The Smile" (11/23/82)

Cast: Tony Roberts (Bill); Marian Seldes (Grace); Fred Gwynne (Uncle William). Written by G. Frederic Lewis.

A gigantic "smile" in the sky reunites an estranged couple but quickly torments them at the same time.

2943. "Funeral Without a Corpse" (11/24/82; rebroadcast from 8/24/82)

2944. "The Reigate Mystery" (11/25/82)

Cast: Gordon Gould (Sherlock Holmes); Ray Owens (Barney); William Griffis (Dr. Watson); Lloyd Battista (Inspector Forester). Adapted by Murray Burnett, based on the 1893 short story *The Reigate Squires* by Sir Arthur Conan Doyle.

Dr. Watson and a very tired Homes visit the small town of Reigate, in Surrey, for a little rest and relaxation. But when the local library is ransacked, and later a coachman is found murdered, a weary Holmes strains himself long enough to advance an invitation to solve the crime.

2945. "Barn Burner" (11/26/82; rebroadcast from 8/26/82)

2946. "How Do You Like Those Apples?" (11/29/82; rebroadcast from 8/31/82)

2947. "The Goddess of Death" (11/30/82)
Cast: Diana Kirkwood (Yvonne); Mandel Kramer (George); Bob Dryden (Pierre). Written by James Agate, Jr.
When a highly acclaimed young artist paints one of his greatest pieces ever, he announces it to be his final work. But no matter how many people question his actions, only the model depicted in the painting knows the reason why.

2948. "The Rim of Eternity" (12/1/82; rebroadcast from 9/2/82)

2949. "The Last Plan" (12/2/82)
Cast: Mia Dillon (The Girl); Paul Hecht (The Boy). Written by Elspeth Eric.
Eros and Thanatos, the gods of love and hate, are the driving forces behind a woman's deadly plot to gain control of her surroundings.

2950. "Scenes from a Murder" (12/3/82; rebroadcast from 9/7/82)

2951. "The Riddle" (12/4/82; rebroadcast from 9/9/82)

2952. "The Boatman and the Devil" (12/7/82)
Cast: Alexander Scourby (Sasha); Earl Hammond (Vassily); Russell Horton (Anton); Marian Seldes (Natasha). Adapted by James Agate, Jr., based on the a short story by Anton Chekhov.
Second thoughts and guilty feelings cloud an attempt to escape a life in exile.
Notes: This was the final original episode of the series. From December 8, 1982, to the end of the series, all episodes were rebroadcasts.

2953. "The Forbidden House" (12/8/82; rebroadcast from 9/14/82)

2954. "Two Sisters" (12/9/82; rebroadcast from 9/16/82)

2955. "The Way Station" (12/10/82; rebroadcast from 9/20/82)

2956. "Pursuit of a Dream" (12/13/82; rebroadcast from 9/22/82)

2957. "The Force of Evil" (12/14/82; rebroadcast from 9/24/82)

2958. "Roll Call of the Dead" (12/15/82; rebroadcast from 9/27/82)

2959. "The Million Dollar Leg" (12/16/82; rebroadcast from 9/29/82)

2960. "Escape from Anzio" (12/17/82; rebroadcast from 10/1/82)

2961. "The Ninth Commandment" (12/20/82; rebroadcast from 10/4/82)

2962. "The Abraham Lincoln Murder Trial" (12/21/82; rebroadcast from 10/6/82)

2963. "The Pale Horse" (12/22/82; rebroadcast from 10/8/82)

2964. "Tony's Market" (12/23/82; rebroadcast from 10/11/82)

2965. "Fly Swatter" (12/24/82; rebroadcast from 10/13/82)

2966. "The Flash Point" (12/27/82; rebroadcast from 10/15/82)

2967. "Desert Maiden" (12/28/82; rebroadcast from 10/18/82)

2968. "Last Days of a Dictator" (12/29/82; rebroadcast from 10/20/82)

2969. "Three Fireflies in a Bottle" (12/30/82; rebroadcast from 10/22/82)

2970. "Resident Killer" (12/31/82; rebroadcast from 10/25/82)

Appendix 1
The CBS/General Mills Radio Adventure Theater

Broadcast on Saturdays and Sundays from February 5, 1977, to July 30, 1977, for 52 episodes, The CBS/General Mills Radio Adventure Theater was a spinoff of The CBS Radio Mystery Theater *and featured stories aimed towards a younger audience. Sponsored by General Mills, this show featured tales of adventure and fantasy. The series was broadcast on most stations that also featured* Mystery Theater. *Himan Brown directed the episodes, and Tom Bosley served as host. Only a few of the episodes were originals; most were adaptations. The series was recommended by the National Education Association (NEA). The second episode, "A Very Special Place," won an ARC of Excellence Median Award, given by the National Association for Retarded Citizens. Instead of the famous creaking door, the opening featured thunder and eerie music.*

1. "Kidnapped" (2/5/77)
Cast: Kris Tabori, Bob Dryden, Ian Martin, Paul Tripp, and Bill Griffis. Based on Robert Louis Stevenson's novel, and adapted for *Adventure* by Paul Tripp.

2. "A Very Special Place" (2/6/77)
Cast: Russell Horton, Earl Hammond, Court Benson, and Bob Dryden. Written for *Adventure* by Allan Sloane.

3. "With Malice Toward None" (2/12/77)
Cast: Skip Hinnet, Mary Flirscham, Ian Martin, and Bill Griffis. Written for *Adventure* by Ian Martin.

4. "Moby Dick" (2/13/77)

Cast: Howard Da Silva, Mason Adams, Court Benson, and Leon Janney. Based on the novel by Herman Melville, and adapted for *Adventure* by Allan Sloane.

5. "The Boy Who Would Be a Sailor" (2/19/77)

Cast: Kevin McCarthy, Jack Grimes, Bill Griffis, and Don Scardino. Based on a story by Rudyard Kipling, and adapted for *Adventure* by Sam Dann.

6. "King Solomon's Mines" (2/20/77)

Cast: Ralph Bell, Court Benson, William Griffis, and Ian Martin. Based on the novel by H. Rider Haggard, and adapted for *Adventure* by Paul Tripp.

7. "The Caliph of Bagdad" (2/26/77)

Cast: Fred Gwynne, Leon Janney, Lloyd Battista, Paul Tripp, Bob Dryden, Ruth Anders. Adapted for *Adventure* by Paul Tripp, from *The Arabian Nights*.

8. "Pinocchio" (2/27/77)

Cast: Evelyn Juster, Bob Dryden, Russell Horton, Joan Shay, and Leon Janney. Written for *Adventure* by Paul Tripp, from the classic children's tale.

9. "The Railway Children" (3/5/77)

Cast: Sarah Parker, Tobi Parker, Ian Martin, Teri Keane, Bill Griffis, and Gilbert Mack. Written for *Adventure* by Robert Newman.

10. "The Other World" (3/6/77)

Cast: Jada Rowland, Russell Horton, Evelyn Juster, and Bob Dryden. Written for *Adventure* by Ian Martin.

11. "Aladdin and His Wonderful Lamp" (3/12/77)

Cast: Roger Baron, Evelyn Juster, Bob Dryden, Norman Rose, and Roger De Koven. Adapted for *Adventure* by Paul Tripp from *The Arabian Nights*.

12. "Black Arrow" (3/13/77)

Cast: Skip Hinnet, Ann Costello, Jackson Beck, William Griffis, Court Benson, and Gilbert Mack. Based on a novel by Robert Louis Stevenson, and adapted for *Adventure* by Robert Newman.

13. "20,000 Leagues Under the Sea" (3/19/77)

Cast: Paul Hecht, William Griffis, Ian Martin, and Jackson Beck. Based on the novel by Jules Verne, and adapted for *Adventure* by Ian Martin.

14. "Robin Hood and His Merry Men" (3/20/77)

Cast: Kevin McCarthy, Frances Sternhagen, Paul Tripp, Court Benson, and Ian Martin. Based on the life of Robin Hood, and written for *Adventure* by Paul Tripp.

15. "Survival Test" (3/26/77)

Cast: Jack Grimes, Russell Horton, Evelyn Juster, and Bob Dryden. Written for *Adventure* by Victoria Dann.

16. "Jason and the Golden Fleece" (3/27/77)

Cast: Kris Tabori, Ian Martin, Leon Janney, Court Benson, Earl Hammond, and Paul Tripp. Written for *Adventure* by Paul Tripp.

17. "Captains Courageous" (4/2/77)

Cast: Skip Hinnet, Fred Gwynne, Russell Horton, Ian Martin, and Bob Dryden. Based on the novel by Rudyard Kipling, and adapted for *Adventure* by Ian Martin.

18. "The Bravest of the Brave" (4/3/77)

Cast: Jada Rowland, Bryna Raeburn, Russell Horton, and Bob Dryden. Written for *Adventure* by Teri Keane.

19. "The Last of the Mohicans" (4/9/77)

Cast: Ian Martin, Court Benson, Morgan Fairchild, Bob Dryden, and Russell Horton. Based on the novel by James Fenimore Cooper, and adapted for *Adventure* by Paul Tripp.

20. "I Remember Alice" (4/10/77)

Cast: Mary Flirscham, Bob Dryden, Evelyn Juster, Hetty Galen, and Earl Hammond. Based on the Lewis Carroll story *Alice in Wonderland*, and adapted for *Adventure* by Gerald Lewis.

21. "Three Swords" (4/16/77)

Cast: Kris Tabori, Bob Dryden, Russell Horton, Evelyn Juster, and Ian Martin. Written for *Adventure* by Elspeth Eric, based on historical documents about King Arthur.

22. "The Clown Who Wasn't" (4/17/77)

Cast: Corrine Orr, Ralph Bell, Leon Janney, William Griffis, and Evelyn Juster. Written for *Adventure* by Ian Martin.

23. "Lewis and Clark" (4/23/77)

Cast: Mason Adams, Bob Kaliban, Teri Keane and William Griffis. Based on the famed expedition, written for *Adventure* by G. Frederic Lewis.

24. "Journey to the Center of the Earth" (4/24/77)

Cast: Ian Martin, Don Scardino and Jada Rowland. Based on the novel by Jules Verne, and adapted for *Adventure* by Ian Martin.

25. "A Different Ghost Town" (4/30/77)

Cast: Corrine Orr, Roger Baron, Court Benson, and Evelyn Juster. Written for *Adventure* by Elizabeth Pennell.

26. "The Red Badge of Courage" (5/1/77)

Cast: Kris Tabori, Bryna Raeburn, Earl Hammond, Court Benson, and Jackson Beck. Based on the novel by Stephen Crane, and adapted for *Adventure* by Fletcher Markle.

27. "Treasure Island" (5/7/77)

Cast: Jim Debis, Paul Tripp, William Griffis, Bob Dryden, and Leon Janney. Based on the novel by Robert Louis Stevenson, and adapted for *Adventure* by Paul Tripp.

28. "The Man Without a Country" (5/8/77)

Cast: Russell Horton, Ian Martin, Earl Hammond, Bob Dryden, and William Griffis. Based on the biography of Nathan Hale by Edward Everett Hale, and adapted for *Adventure* by G. Frederic Lewis.

29. "Three Tales of Hans Anderson" (5/14/77)

Cast: Joan Shay, Heddy Galen, Evelyn Juster, Earl Hammond, Ian Martin, and Kris Tabori. Based on the tales *The Ugly Duckling*, *The Tinderbox*, and *The Swineherd and the Princess* by Hans Christian Anderson, and adapted for *Adventure* by G. Frederic Lewis.

30. "A Coat of Many Colors" (5/15/77)

Cast: Tony Roberts, Bob Dryden, Ralph Bell, William Griffis, and Ian Martin. Based on the story of Joseph, from the Bible, and adapted for *Adventure* by Paul Tripp.

31. "They Called Him Slim" (5/21/77)

Cast: Russell Horton, Ann Pitoniak, Hans Conried, Lloyd Battista, and Earl Hammond. Based on the life of Charles Lindberg, and written for *Adventure* by G. Frederic Lewis.

32. "Then They Called Him Lucky" (5/22/77)

Cast: Russell Horton, Ann Pitoniak, Nat Polen, Court Benson, and Earl Hammond. Based on the life of Charles Lindberg, and written for *Adventure* by G. Frederic Lewis.

33. "The Gold Bug" (5/28/77)

Cast: James Debis, Gordon Heath and Bob Dryden. Based on the novella by Edgar Allan Poe, and adapted for *Adventure* by Elizabeth Pennell.

34. "The Travels of Ulysses" (5/29/77)

Cast: Michael Wager, Ann Williams, Ian Martin, Jackson Beck, and Bob Dryden. Based on Homer's *The Iliad* and *Odyssey*, and adapted for *Adventure* by Paul Tripp.

35. "Cinderella" (6/4/77)

Cast: Catherine Byers, Bob Dryden, Kris Tabori, Evelyn Juster, and Ruth Anders. Based on the children's classic, and adapted for *Adventure* by Paul Tripp.

36. "Remember the Alamo" (6/5/77)

Cast: Paul Hecht, Russell Horton, Jackson Beck, and Ian Martin. Based on the historical event, and written for *Adventure* by G. Frederic Lewis.

37. "The Adventures of Oliver" (6/11/77)

Cast: Evelyn Juster, Court Benson, Robert Kaliban, Earl Hammond, and Gilbert Mack. Based on Charles Dickens' novel *Oliver Twist*, and adapted for *Adventure* by G. Frederic Lewis.

38. "The Boy David" (6/12/77)

Cast: Skip Hinnet, Leon Janney, Bob Dryden, Carol Teitel, and William Griffis. Based on the Biblical event, and adapted for *Adventure* by G. Frederic Lewis.

39. "Three Times Magic" (6/18/77)

Cast: Don Scardino, Court Benson, Mia Dillion, Earl Hammond, and Bryna Raeburn. Based on the fairy tales *Jack and the Beanstalk*, *Rumpelstilskin*, and *Beauty and the Beast*, and adapted for *Adventure* by Paul Tripp.

40. "The Eyes of Vishnu" (6/19/77)

Cast: Jack Grimes, Bryna Raeburn, Mary Flirscham, and William Griffis. Written for *Adventure* by James Lawrence.

41. "Ali Baba and the Forty Thieves" (6/25/77)

Cast: Gordon Heath, Martha Greenhouse, William Griffis, Bob Dryden, and Roberta Maxwell. Based on the *Arabian Nights*, and adapted for *Adventure* by G. Frederic Lewis.

42. "The Valiant Little Tailor" (6/26/77)

Cast: Bob Dryden, Evelyn Juster, Jackson Beck, and Leon Janney. Based on the story by the Brothers Grimm, and adapted for *Adventure* by G. Frederic Lewis.

43. "The Sea Wolf" (7/2/77)

Cast: Kris Tabori, Marian Seldes, Joseph Silver, Ian Martin, and Joe Di Santis. Based on the novel by Jack London, and adapted for *Adventure* by James Agate, Jr.

44. "The Master Thief" (7/3/77)

Cast: Paul Hecht, William Griffis, Bryna Raeburn, and Bob Dryden. Based on the story by the Brothers Grimm.

45. "The Sailor Who Wouldn't Give Up" (7/9/77)

Cast: Russell Horton, Bob Dryden, Earl Hammond, and Ian Martin. Based on the story by Jack London, and adapted for *Adventure* by James Agate, Jr.

46. "Youth" (7/10/77)

Cast: Russell Horton, Arnold Moss, Bob Dryden, and William Griffis. Based on the story by Joseph Conrad, and adapted for *Adventure* by James Agate, Jr.

47. "Mowgli" (7/16/77)

Cast: Fred Gwynne, Marian Seldes, Ian Martin, Bob Dryden, and Don Scardino. Based on Rudyard Kipling's novel *Jungle Book*, and adapted for *Adventure* by James Agate, Jr.

48. "Tiger, Tiger" (7/17/77)

Cast: Don Scardino, Fred Gwynne, Bob Dryden, Marian Seldes, and Ian Martin. Based on Rudyard Kipling's novel *Jungle Book*, and adapted for *Adventure* by James Agate, Jr.

49. "The Man in the Iron Mask" (7/23/77)

Cast: Paul Hecht, William Griffis, Russell Horton, and Court Benson. Based on the novel by Alexander Dumas, and adapted for *Adventure* by G. Frederic Lewis.

50. "Gulliver's Travels" (7/24/77)

Cast: Michael Tolan, Ian Martin, Earl Hammond, and Court Benson. Based on the story by Jonathan Swift, and adapted for *Adventure* by G. Frederic Lewis.

51. "Ivanhoe" (7/30/77)

Cast: Kevin McCarthy, Don Scardino, Arnold Moss, Bob Dryden, Ian Martin, and Elizabeth Lathem. Based on the novel by Sir Walter Scott, and adapted for *Adventure* by Ian Martin.

52. "Daniel, the Oracle" (7/31/77)

Cast: Russell Horton, Norman Rose, Jackson Beck, and Court Benson. Based on the Biblical story, and adapted for *Adventure* by Madeline Ferber.

Appendix 2
Broadcast Log

Included below is the complete broadcast log for the 1998 revival of the CBS Radio Mystery Theater:

June

Wednesday, June 3—"The Ghost Plane," starring Casey Kasem and Richard Crenna

Thursday, June 4—"The Chinaman Button," starring Mason Adams and Paul Hecht

Friday, June 5—"Time and Again," starring Joan Beal and Bryna Raeburn

Monday, June 8—"The Other Life," starring Mercedes McCambridge

Tuesday, June 9—"The Master Computer," starring Robert Dryden and Augusta Dabney

Wednesday, June 10—"A Scaffold for Two," starring Bret Morrison and John Beal

Thursday, June 11—"The Voice of Death," starring Victor Jory

Friday, June 12—"The Bride That Wasn't," starring Janet Waldo and Anne Seymour

Monday, June 15—"The Death Wisher," starring Michael Zaslow and Anne Pitoniak

Tuesday, June 16—"The Angels of Devil's Mountain," starring Warren Stevens and Anne Seymour

Wednesday, June 17—"Trapped," starring Nina Foch and Charles Aidman

Thursday, June 18—"The Grey Ghost," starring Betsy Palmer and Evie Juster

Friday, June 19—"The Root of All Evil," starring Norman Rose and Ann Shepherd

Tuesday, June 23—"The Other Self," starring Howard DaSilva and Joan Lovejoy

Wednesday, June 24—"The Lady is a Jinx," starring Marian Seldes and Larry Haines

Thursday, June 25—"The Spots of the Leopard," starring Ann Shepherd and Russell Horton

Friday, June 26—"The Headless Hessian," starring Lloyd Bochner and Jack Grimes

Monday, June 29—"The Poisoned Pen," starring Roberta Maxwell and Catherine Byers

Tuesday, June 30—"Snake in the Grass," starring Sandy Dennis and Ralph Bell

July

Wednesday, July 1—"Nightmare's Nest," starring Gordon Gould and Ian Martin

Thursday, July 2—"The Thomas Jefferson Defense," starring Paul Hecht and Russell Horton

Friday, July 3—"The Third Person," starring Marian Seldes and Evie Juster

Monday, July 6—"Fateful Reunion," starring Jennifer Harmon and Robert Dryden

Tuesday, July 7—"The Unbearable Reflection," starring Patricia Elliot and Robert Dryden

Wednesday, July 8—"Woman from Hell," starring Joan Lovejoy and Norman Rose

Thursday, July 9—"Appointment in Uganda," starring William Redfield and Arnold Stang

Friday, July 10—"The Stuff of Dreams," starring Marian Seldes and Bryna Raeburn

Monday, July 13—"Carmilla," starring Mercedes McCambridge

Tuesday, July 14—"He Moves in Mysterious Ways," starring Teri Keane and Leon Janney

Wednesday, July 15—"The Man Must Die," starring Kristoffer Tabori and William Prince

Thursday, July 16—"The Velvet Claws," starring Gordon Gould and Evie Juster

Friday, July 17—"The Dark Closet," starring Fred Gwynne and Jada Rowland

Monday, July 20—"The Deadly Double," starring Marian Seldes and Robert Dryden

Tuesday, July 21—"Death is a Dream," starring Mercedes McCambridge and Robert Dryden

Wednesday, July 22—"Killer of the Year," starring Norman Rose and Teri Keane

Thursday, July 23—"It's Murder, Mr. Lincoln," starring Keir Dullea and Paul Hecht

Friday, July 24—"The Doppelganger," starring Howard DaSilva and Rosemary Rice

Monday, July 27—"The Key to Murder," starring Mercedes McCambridge

Tuesday, July 28—"Sleepy Village," starring Martha Greenhouse and Norman Rose

Wednesday, July 29—"When the Death Bell Tolls," starring Mary Jane Higby and Rosemary Rice

Thursday, July 30—"The Precious Killer," starring Arnold Moss and Beatrice Straight

Friday, July 31—"The Man Who Heard Voices," starring Larry Haines and Suzanne Grossman

August

Monday, August 3—"Dead for a Dollar," starring Paul Hecht and Joe Julian

Tuesday, August 4—"And Nothing But the Truth," starring Arnold Moss and Kristoffer Tabori

Wednesday, August 5—"A Death of Kings," starring Mercedes McCambridge and Robert Dryden

Thursday, August 6—"Concerto of Death," starring Ian Martin, Carol Teitel and Marian Seldes

Friday, August 7—"The Girl Who Found Things," starring Norman Rose and Martha Greenhouse

Monday, August 10—"The Wakeful Ghost," starring Paul Hecht

Tuesday, August 11—"A Challenge for the Dead," starring Howard DaSilva and Teri Keane

Wednesday, August 12—"The Transformation," starring Kevin McCarthy and Ian Martin

Thursday, August 13—"My Own Murderer," starring Mandel Kramer and Robert Dryden

Friday, August 14—"Speak of the Devil," starring Bryna Raeburn and Jada Rowland

Monday, August 17—"The Killer Inside," starring Anne Meara and Bryna Raeburn

Tuesday, August 18—"Them," starring Jordan Charney and Alan Hewitt

Wednesday, August 19—"Three Women," starring Ruth Ford and William Redfield

Thursday, August 20—"A Very Old Man," starring Santos Ortega and William Redfield

Friday, August 21—"Deadly Honeymoon," starring Betsy Von Furstenberg and Mason Adams

Monday, August 24—"The Ring of Truth," starring Agnes Moorehead

Tuesday, August 25—"Sting of Death," starring William Prince and Tony Roberts

Wednesday, August 26—"Black Widow" starring Evie Juster and Robert Dryden

Thursday, August 27—"The Imp in the Bottle," starring William Redfield and Joan Loring

Friday, August 28—"The Eye of Death," starring Joan Hackett

Monday, August 31—"The Voices of Death," starring Norman Rose and Mary Jane Higby

Tuesday, Sep 1—"Deadline for Death," starring Michael Tolin and Joseph Julian

September

Wednesday, Sep 2—"The Spectral Bride," starring Joan Loring and Michael Wager

Thursday, Sep 3—"The Garden" starring Jack Grimes

Friday, Sep 4—"Murder to Perfection," starring Mercedes McCambridge and Joseph Campanella

Monday, Sep 7—"Island of the Lost," starring Norman Rose and Marian Seldes

Tuesday, Sep 8—"Deadly Blindman's Bluff" starring Mason Adams

Wednesday, Sep 9—"Double Exposure" starring Kim Hunter

Thursday, Sep 10—"The Hand That Refused to Die," starring Mandel Kramer

Friday, Sep 11—"What Happened to Mrs. Forbush?," starring Patricia Wheel
Monday, Sep 14—"Thicker Than Water," starring Jay Gregory
Tuesday, Sep 15—"The Trouble with Murder," starring Robert Morse
Wednesday, Sep 16—"Masks," starring John Beal
Thursday, Sep 17—"All the Time in the World," starring Ralph Bell
Friday, Sep 18—"The Unseen Watcher," starring Mandel Kramer
Monday, Sep 21—"The Love God," starring Marian Seldes and Court Benson
Tuesday, Sep 22—"Enemy from Space," starring Mandel Kramer and Evie Juster
Wednesday, Sep 23—"Watcher of the Living," starring Tony Roberts
Thursday, Sep 24—"Shadows from the Grave," starring Kristopher Tabori
Friday, Sep 25—"The Fall of Gentryville," starring Michael Tolin
Monday, Sep 28—"The Adventures of the Red-Headed League," starring Kevin McCarthy
Tuesday, Sep 29—"If I Can't Have You," starring Bob Kalaban and Russell Horton
Wednesday, Sep 30—"No Way Out," starring Earl Hammond and Roberta Maxwell

October

Thursday, October 1—"It Has To be True," starring John Beal
Friday, October 2—"The Power of Evil," starring Lloyd Battista and Evie Juster
Monday, October 5—"Don't Die Without Me," starring Robert Dryden and Marian Seldes
Tuesday, October 6—"Let the Buyer Beware," starring Joan Lovejoy and Earl Hammond
Wednesday, October 7—"The Long, Long Sleep" starring Larry Haines and Anne Williams
Thursday, October 8—"The Wandering Wind," starring John Beal and Teri Keane
Friday, October 9—"The Dead House," starring Robert Dryden
Monday, October 12—"Side Effects," starring Robert Dryden and Mandel Kramer
Tuesday, October 13—"The Look," starring Michael Tolin and Earl Hammond
Wednesday, October 14—"Love After Death," starring Ralph Bell and Norman Rose
Thursday, October 15—"The Great Brain," starring Gordon Heath and Russell Horton
Friday, October 16—"The Burning Bough," starring Norman Rose and Grace Matthews
Monday, October 19—"The Shock of His Life," starring Larry Haines and Joan Shea
Tuesday, October 20—"The Dominant Personality," starring Roberta Maxwell and Ralph Bell
Wednesday, October 21—"Assassination in Time," starring Ian Martin
Thursday, October 22—"The Onyx Eye," starring Frances Sternhagen and Michael Wager
Friday, October 23—"The Prison of Glass," starring Lois Nettleton

A Week of Edgar Allan Poe (October 26-30)

Monday, October 26—"The Cask of the Amontillado," starring Richard Kiley

Tuesday, October 27—"The Murders in the Rue Morgue," starring Paul Hecht

Wednesday, October 28—"The Tell-Tale Heart," starring Fred Gwynne

Thursday, October 29—"The Pit and the Pendulum," starring Tony Roberts and Marian Seldes

Friday, October 30—"The Premature Burial," starring Keir Dullea and Paul Hecht

November

Monday, November 2—"The Sinister Shadow," starring Teri Keane

Tuesday, November 3—"Everybody Does It," starring Robert Dryden and Carol Teitel

Wednesday, November 4—"The Missing Day," starring Russell Horton and Court Benson

Thursday, November 5—"Wuthering Heights," starring Paul Hecht and Roberta Maxwell

Friday, November 6—"The Light That Failed," starring Mason Adams and Tony Roberts

Monday, November 9—"Tobin's Palm," starring Robert Dryden and Fred Gwynne

Tuesday, November 10—"Hickory, Dickory, Doom," starring Tony Roberts and Patricia Elliott

Wednesday, November 11—"The Strange Case of Lucas Lauder," starring Robert Lansing

Thursday, November 12—"The Ghostly Rival," starring Will MacKenzie

Friday, November 13—"Must Hope Perish," starring Hugh Marlowe and Marian Seldes

Monday, November 16—"Faith and the Fakir," starring Howard DaSilva and Guy Sobel

Tuesday, November 17—"The Golden Cauldron," starring Paul Hecht and Russell Horton

Wednesday, November 18—"The Widow's Auxiliary," starring Lenka Peterson and Gordon Gould

Thursday, November 19—"That Hamlet was a Good Boy," starring Will MacKenzie

Friday, November 20—"Hung Jury," starring Howard DaSilva

Monday, November 23—"The Triangle," starring Mercedes McCambridge

Tuesday, November 24—"Guilty," starring Jack Grimes and Ann Pitoniak

Wednesday, November 25—"Murder Will Out," starring Mason Adams and Leon Janney

Thursday, November 26—"The Doll," starring Joanne Linville and Karl Swenson

Friday, November 27—"Solid Gold Soldiers," starring Michael Wager and Evie Juster (LAST BROADCAST)

Index

References are to entry numbers